Network+™ Certification Bible

Network+™ Certification Bible

Joseph Byrne, Diane McMichael Gilster, Trevor Kay, NIIT, James Russell, Series Editor Ron Gilster

Hungry Minds™

Best-Selling Books • Digital Downloads • e-Books • Answer Networks • e-Newsletters • Branded Web Sites • e-Learning

New York, NY ✦ Cleveland, OH ✦ Indianapolis, IN

Network+™ Certification Bible

Published by
Hungry Minds, Inc.
909 Third Avenue
New York, NY 10022
www.hungryminds.com

Copyright © 2002 Hungry Minds, Inc. All rights reserved. No part of this book, including interior design, cover design, and icons, may be reproduced or transmitted in any form, by any means (electronic, photocopying, recording, or otherwise) without the prior written permission of the publisher.

Library of Congress Control Number: 2002100343

ISBN: 0-7645-4880-8

Printed in the United States of America

10 9 8 7 6 5 4 3 2 1

1P/SU/QU/QS/IN

Distributed in the United States by Hungry Minds, Inc.

Distributed by CDG Books Canada Inc. for Canada; by Transworld Publishers Limited in the United Kingdom; by IDG Norge Books for Norway; by IDG Sweden Books for Sweden; by IDG Books Australia Publishing Corporation Pty. Ltd. for Australia and New Zealand; by TransQuest Publishers Pte Ltd. for Singapore, Malaysia, Thailand, Indonesia, and Hong Kong; by Gotop Information Inc. for Taiwan; by ICG Muse, Inc. for Japan; by Intersoft for South Africa; by Eyrolles for France; by International Thomson Publishing for Germany, Austria, and Switzerland; by Distribuidora Cuspide for Argentina; by LR International for Brazil; by Galileo Libros for Chile; by Ediciones ZETA S.C.R. Ltda. for Peru; by WS Computer Publishing Corporation, Inc., for the Philippines; by Contemporanea de Ediciones for Venezuela; by Express Computer Distributors for the Caribbean and West Indies; by Micronesia Media Distributor, Inc. for Micronesia; by Chips Computadoras S.A. de C.V. for Mexico; by Editorial Norma de Panama S.A. for Panama; by American Bookshops for Finland.

For general information on Hungry Minds' products and services please contact our Customer Care department within the U.S. at 800-762-2974, outside the U.S. at 317-572-3993 or fax 317-572-4002.

For sales inquiries and reseller information, including discounts, premium and bulk quantity sales, and foreign-language translations, please contact our Customer Care department at 800-434-3422, fax 317-572-4002 or write to Hungry Minds, Inc., Attn: Customer Care Department, 10475 Crosspoint Boulevard, Indianapolis, IN 46256.

For information on licensing foreign or domestic rights, please contact our Sub-Rights Customer Care department at 212-884-5000.

For information on using Hungry Minds' products and services in the classroom or for ordering examination copies, please contact our Educational Sales department at 800-434-2086 or fax 317-572-4005.

For press review copies, author interviews, or other publicity information, please contact our Public Relations department at 317-572-3168 or fax 317-572-4168.

For authorization to photocopy items for corporate, personal, or educational use, please contact Copyright Clearance Center, 222 Rosewood Drive, Danvers, MA 01923, or fax 978-750-4470.

LIMIT OF LIABILITY/DISCLAIMER OF WARRANTY: THE PUBLISHER AND AUTHOR HAVE USED THEIR BEST EFFORTS IN PREPARING THIS BOOK. THE PUBLISHER AND AUTHOR MAKE NO REPRESENTATIONS OR WARRANTIES WITH RESPECT TO THE ACCURACY OR COMPLETENESS OF THE CONTENTS OF THIS BOOK AND SPECIFICALLY DISCLAIM ANY IMPLIED WARRANTIES OF MERCHANTABILITY OR FITNESS FOR A PARTICULAR PURPOSE. THERE ARE NO WARRANTIES WHICH EXTEND BEYOND THE DESCRIPTIONS CONTAINED IN THIS PARAGRAPH. NO WARRANTY MAY BE CREATED OR EXTENDED BY SALES REPRESENTATIVES OR WRITTEN SALES MATERIALS. THE ACCURACY AND COMPLETENESS OF THE INFORMATION PROVIDED HEREIN AND THE OPINIONS STATED HEREIN ARE NOT GUARANTEED OR WARRANTED TO PRODUCE ANY PARTICULAR RESULTS, AND THE ADVICE AND STRATEGIES CONTAINED HEREIN MAY NOT BE SUITABLE FOR EVERY INDIVIDUAL. NEITHER THE PUBLISHER NOR AUTHOR SHALL BE LIABLE FOR ANY LOSS OF PROFIT OR ANY OTHER COMMERCIAL DAMAGES, INCLUDING BUT NOT LIMITED TO SPECIAL, INCIDENTAL, CONSEQUENTIAL, OR OTHER DAMAGES.

Trademarks: All trademarks are the property of their respective owners. Hungry Minds, Inc., is not associated with any product or vendor mentioned in this book.

Hungry Minds™ is a trademark of Hungry Minds, Inc.

About the Authors

Ron Gilster (i-Net+, Network+, A+, MBA, and AAGG), Series Editor, has been operating, programming, and repairing computers for more than 30 years. Ron has extensive experience in training, teaching, and consulting in computer-related areas, having spent more than 10 years as a college-level instructor in A+, CCNA, MCSE, and MOUS programs. His experience includes mainframes, minicomputers, and virtually every type of personal computer and operating system in use. In addition to a wide range of positions that have included systems programming supervisor, customer service manager, data processing manager, management information systems director, and vice president of operations in major corporations, Ron has served as a management consultant with both an international accounting firm and his own consulting firm. He is the author of *A+ Certification For Dummies, Network+ Certification For Dummies, CCNA For Dummies, Cisco Certification For Dummies, i-Net Certification For Dummies,* and *Server+ Certification For Dummies,* plus several books on networking, the Internet, computer and information literacy, and programming.

Diane McMichael Gilster (MCSE 2000, MCSE NT, Network+, and i-Net+) has been active in computing for over 20 years and networking over 10 years. Diane's experience includes stints as a network manager, network consultant, and PC and network technician in both large and small networking environments, including wireless networking applications. Diane presently is active as an IT certification trainer, consultant, and author, with a currently popular book on home networking.

Trevor Kay (A+, Network+, and Server+) is a CompTIA Professional Member and a Subject Matter Expert (SME) for CompTIA, (the Computing Technology Industry Association) for their Server+ and Linux+ exam certification development. Born and raised in London, Ontario, Canada, he started his IT career working at a local museum as a desktop publisher. From there he has held many positions, from IT helpdesk, technical support, and network administrator positions for local companies, to having a key role in the Y2K project of one of the largest financial institutes in Canada. Trevor now is concentrating full-time on technical writing.

Credits

Acquisitions Editor
Katie Feltman

Project Editor
Pat O'Brien

Technical Editor
Jim Kelly

Copy Editors
Barry Childs-Helton
Michelle Milani

Editorial Managers
Kyle Looper
Ami Frank Sullivan

Vice President and Executive Group Publisher
Richard Swadley

Vice President and Executive Publisher
Bob Ipsen

Vice President and Publisher
Joseph B. Wikert

Editorial Director
Mary Bednarek

Project Coordinator
Regina Snyder

Graphics and Production Specialists
Joyce Haughey
Heather Pope
Bette Schulte
Julie Trippetti
Jeremey Unger
Erin Zeltner

Quality Control Technicians
Laura Albert
John Greenough
Andy Hollandbeck

Permissions Editor
Carmen Krikorian

Media Development Specialist
Megan DeCraene

Proofreading and Indexing
TECHBOOKS Production Services

To Connie, who understands and supports me and my writer persona.

RG

Preface

Welcome to the *Network+ Certification Bible!* This book is designed to help you acquire the knowledge, skills, and abilities you need to pass CompTIA's Network+ Certification.

This book deals with all of the objectives stated by CompTIA for the Network+ exam. You will learn the different media and topologies, protocols and standards, including TCP/IP and the OSI model, network implementation, and network support. This book will also teach you how to use TCP/IP troubleshooting utilities including tracert, ping, and NSLOOKUP. You will also learn remote connectivity troubleshooting and client/server network configurations.

My hope is that you'll find this book the most helpful Network+ Certification product reference that you've ever read. I also hope that you'll use it to prepare for CompTIA's Network+ Certification exam, then come back to it again and again as you perform your day-to-day Network Technician tasks.

How This Book Is Organized

This book is organized into four major parts, followed by a robust glossary, an index, and one compact disc.

Here's what you'll find in this book:

Part I: Media and Topologies

Part I presents the information needed to understand the common media used and the different types of topologies used on a network. This part covers the common media standards and the popular network components such as hubs, switches, bridges, routers, and gateways.

Part II: Protocols and Standards

Part II covers the different protocols used on a network. In this part you will learn about MAC addresses, the OSI model, and the common network protocols such as TCP/IP, FTP, SMTP, and TFTP, for example. This part also covers TCP/UDP port functionality, network services such as DHCP, DNS, WINS, and SNMP. IP Addressing is also covered in this part along with understanding public and private networks, WAN technologies, remote access, and security protocols.

Part III: Network Implementation

Part III presents the information needed to implement a successful network installation. In this part you will learn the differences between server- and client-side operating systems, VLANs, and network-attached storage. This part also covers fault tolerance, disaster recovery, configuring remote connectivity, firewalls, proxy servers, and network configuration settings.

Part IV: Operation

Part IV is all about supporting your network. In this part you will learn how to troubleshoot your network using TCP/IP utilities and how to troubleshoot remote connectivity. In this part you will also learn client- and server-side network configurations along with wiring troubleshooting tools and using diagnostic utilities. The end of this part covers network troubleshooting such as the different techniques used to identify and isolate a network problem. You will also learn how to troubleshoot network topology issues, client connectivity problems, and wiring and infrastructure.

CD-ROM

The compact disc included with this book contains some excellent resources and programs. You'll find this entire book in Adobe PDF format and a variety of different programs that I hope you will find useful. To find out more about the CD-ROM, please see Appendix A.

How Each Chapter Is Structured

This book is structured and designed into the specific elements that will provide you with the best possible learning and exam-preparation experience.

Here are the elements you'll find in each chapter:

- ✦ The complete exam objectives that are covered in the chapter
- ✦ A Chapter Pre-Test to test your knowledge before reading the chapter
- ✦ Clear, concise text on each topic
- ✦ Screenshots and graphics that are worth more than a thousand words
- ✦ Summary
- ✦ A comprehensive Study Guide for review

How to Use This Book

This book can be used either by individuals working independently or by groups in a formal classroom setting.

For best results, I recommend the following plan of attack as you use this book: First, take the Chapter Pre-Test, and then read the chapter and the Summary. Use this summary to see if you really understand the key concepts. If you don't, go back and reread the section(s) that you're not clear on. Then do all of the Assessment Questions and Scenarios at the end of the chapter. Remember, the important thing is to master the tasks that are tested by the exams.

If you feel that you already know the chapter contents before reading, try the Assessment Questions and Scenarios at the end of the chapter to test your knowledge. If you find that you are having trouble with certain topics, you should probably read the topics of the chapter you aren't clear on. Remember that even if you feel you know a topic very well, the exam objectives are the most important part of your studying process.

The chapters of this book are designed to be studied sequentially. In other words, it's best if you complete Chapter 1 before you proceed to Chapter 2. However, each chapter's topic can be studied individually, if desired.

After you've completed your study of the chapters and reviewed the Assessment Questions in the book, use the test engine on the compact disc included with this book to get some experience answering practice questions. The practice questions will help you assess how much you've learned from your study and will also familiarize you with the type of exam questions you'll face when you take the real exam. After you identify a weak area, you can restudy the corresponding chapters to improve your knowledge and skills in that area.

Prerequisites

Although this book is a comprehensive study and exam preparation guide, it doesn't start at ground zero. I assume that you have the following knowledge and skills at the outset:

- ✦ Knowledge of basic computer terminology and functions
- ✦ Basic mouse and keyboard skills: being able to left-click, right-click, double-click; use the pointer, type special characters; use the function keys, keypad, and so on
- ✦ Knowledge of basic computer hardware, software applications, and operating systems

If you meet these prerequisites, you're ready to begin this book.

Conventions Used in This Book

Every book has its own set of conventions, so I'll explain the icons I've used in this book to you right up front.

You'll see icons throughout each chapter. Six different types of icons are used in this book. Below are the explanations of each icon:

Caution — This icon warns you that something unfortunate could happen if you're not careful. It also points out information that could save you a lot of grief. It's often easier to prevent a tragedy than to fix it afterwards.

Cross-Reference — This icon points you to another place in this book for more coverage of a particular topic. It may point you back to a previous chapter where important material has already been covered, or it may point you ahead to let you know that a topic will be covered in more detail later on.

Exam Tip — This icon points out important information or advice for those preparing to take the Network+ certification exam.

In the Real World — Sometimes things work differently in the real world than books — or product documentation — say they do. This icon draws your attention to the author's real-world experiences, which will hopefully help you on the job if not on the Network+ certification exam.

Tip — This icon draws your attention to a little piece of friendly advice, a helpful fact, a shortcut, or a bit of personal experience that might be of use to you.

Acknowledgments

I would like to thank the wonderful folks who helped get this book published, especially Katie Feltman, Barry Childs-Helton, Regina Snyder, and Jim Kelly.

RG

Contents at a Glance

Preface. ix
Acknowledgments xiii

Part I: Media and Topologies 1
Chapter 1: Network Topologies and Technologies 3
Chapter 2: Media Standards 27
Chapter 3: Network Components 39

Part II: Protocols and Standards 69
Chapter 4: MAC and IP Addressing 71
Chapter 5: The OSI Model 99
Chapter 6: Network Protocols 123
Chapter 7: TCP/UDP Port Functionality 139
Chapter 8: Network Services 165
Chapter 9: Public and Private Networks 185
Chapter 10: WAN Technologies and Remote Access 199
Chapter 11: Security Protocols 227

Part III: Network Implementation 255
Chapter 12: Network and Client Operating Systems 257
Chapter 13: VLANs 309
Chapter 14: Data Storage 327
Chapter 15: Keeping Your Data Available 357
Chapter 16: Configuring Remote Connectivity 381
Chapter 17: Firewalls, Proxy Servers, and Security 419
Chapter 18: Network Configuration Settings 447

Part IV: Operation 473
Chapter 19: TCP/IP Troubleshooting Utilities 475
Chapter 20: Small/Home Office Network Troubleshooting 499

Chapter 21: Remote Connectivity Troubleshooting 535
Chapter 22: Client/Server Network Configuration 549
Chapter 23: Wiring 577
Chapter 24: Network Troubleshooting 609

Appendix A: What's on the CD-ROM 635
Appendix B: Exam Objectives 639
Appendix C: Practice Exam 647
Appendix D: Glossary 667

Index 677
Hungry Minds, Inc. End-User License Agreement 703

Contents

Preface ix
Acknowledgments xiii

Part I: Media and Topologies — 1

Chapter 1: Network Topologies and Technologies 3
Bus Topology 5
Star Topology 6
Mesh Topology 7
Ring Topology 9
Communication Protocols for Data Transmission 10
    Ethernet 10
    Ethernet 802.2 11
    Ethernet 802.3 12
Basic Ethernet Concepts 12
Token Ring/IEEE 802.5 14
Basic Token-Ring Concepts 15
802.11b (Wireless) 16
FDDI (Fiber Distributed Data Interface) 17
Summary 18
Assessment Questions 20
Scenarios 24
Answers to Chapter Questions 24
    Chapter Pre-Test 24
    Assessment Questions 25
    Scenarios 26

Chapter 2: Media Standards 27
Ethernet in the Beginning 29
    IEEE 802.3 becomes the Ethernet standard 29
    Ethernet access method 29
    Understanding "10Base" identifiers 30
    10Base5 standard 31
    10Base2 standard 31
    10BaseT standard 31
    10BaseF standard 32
    Gigabit Ethernet 33
    802.11b 33
    802.15 33
    Cabling considerations 33

Contents

Cable Connectors 34
    RJ-11 34
    RJ-45 34
    AUI 34
    BNC 35
Summary 35
Assessment Questions 36
Answers to Chapter Questions 38
    Chapter Pre-test 38
    Assessment Questions 38

Chapter 3: Network Components 39

The Network Interface Card (NIC) 41
Hubs 42
Switches 44
    Store-and-forward data transport 45
    Cut-through data transport 46
Bridges 46
Routers 48
    Basic routing concepts 48
    Comparing bridges, switches, and routers 49
Gateways 50
CSU/DSU 50
ISDN Adapters 51
System-Area Network Cards 52
Wireless Access Points 53
Modems 55
    Serial-port connections 55
    USB (Universal Serial Bus) 56
    Basic configuration settings 56
Key Point Summary 57
Assessment Questions 59
Scenarios 63
Answers to Chapter Questions 64
    Chapter Pre-test 64
    Assessment Questions 65
    Scenarios 66

Part II: Protocols and Standards   69

Chapter 4: MAC and IP Addressing 71

Host Addressing 73
    MAC addressing — basics 73
    Hexadecimal notation 73
    Resolving MAC addresses on a network 76
    Composition of a MAC address 78

IP Addressing 80
    Converting decimal to binary 82
    Converting binary to decimal 83
    IP addressing basics 83
    IP addressing and subnetting 84
    Identifying the hosts 87
    Determining when a router is required 90
Summary 91
Assessment Questions 92
Answers to Chapter Questions 95
    Chapter Pre-test 95
    Assessment Questions 96
    Answers to Labs 97

Chapter 5: The OSI Model 99

Networking and the OSI Model 101
Seven Layers of the OSI Model 103
    Application layer 104
    Presentation layer 105
    Session layer 105
    Transport layer 105
    Network layer 109
    Data Link layer 110
    Physical layer 113
Protocols and the OSI model 114
Summary 115
Assessment Questions 116
Scenarios 119
Answers to Chapter Questions 119
    Chapter Pre-Test 119
    Assessment Questions 120
    Scenarios 121

Chapter 6: Network Protocols 123

Internal Network Protocols 125
    TCP/IP internal protocols 125
    Application-Layer protocols 125
    Transport-Layer protocols 131
    Network-Layer protocols 132
    IPX/SPX — Internetwork Packet Exchange/Sequence
        Packet Exchange internal protocols 133
Summary 134
Assessment Questions 135
Answers to Chapter Questions 137
    Chapter Pre-Test 137
    Assessment Questions 137

Chapter 7: TCP/UDP Port Functionality 139
TCP/UDP Ports 141
    TCP/UDP 141
    Server and client ports 142
    Well-known ports 142
Common Ports 151
Securing Ports 152
    Shutting down unused ports 152
    System audit 153
    System security 153
    Service and application updates 154
Summary 154
Assessment Questions 156
Scenarios 159
Lab Exercises 160
Answers to Chapter Questions 161
    Chapter Pre-Test 161
    Assessment Questions 161
    Scenarios 163

Chapter 8: Network Services 165
Network Services 167
    Understanding DHCP 167
    Understanding DNS 168
    Understanding WINS 170
    Understanding NAT/ICS 171
Using SNMP to Monitor Your Network 174
    How SNMP functions 174
    Understanding the SNMP Management Information Base 175
    Understanding SNMP commands 175
    SNMP thresholds 176
Summary 177
Assessment Questions 178
Scenarios 181
Answers to Chapter Questions 182
    Chapter Pre-Test 182
    Assessment Questions 182
    Scenarios 184

Chapter 9: Public and Private Networks 185
Public Networks 187
    Advantages of public networks 188
    Disadvantages of public networks 188
Private Networks 189
    Firewalls 189
    Advantages of private networks 192
    Disadvantages of private networks 193

Differences Between Public and Private Networks 193
Virtual Private Network 194
Summary 195
Assessment Questions 196
Answers to Chapter Questions 197
    Chapter Pre-Test 197
    Assessment Questions 198

Chapter 10: WAN Technologies and Remote Access 199

WANs and Internetworks 201
Remote Networking Basics 201
    Data carrier services 201
    Modulation 203
    Multiplexing 204
    Packet switching and circuit switching 205
Wide Area Network Technologies 208
    ATM 208
    Cable modems 209
    DSL 210
    FDDI 211
    Frame Relay 211
    ISDN 212
    SONET/SDH 213
Remote Access Protocols and Services 214
    ICA 214
    PPP 216
    PPTP and VPNs 217
    RAS 217
    SLIP 218
Summary 218
Assessment Questions 219
Scenarios 223
Answers to Chapter Questions 223
    Chapter Pre-Test 223
    Assessment Questions 224
    Scenarios 225

Chapter 11: Security Protocols 227

Privacy Over Public Networks? 229
Encryption Basics 230
    Ciphers versus codes 230
    Key cryptography 231
    Signed data 234
    Sockets 235
Public-Key Infrastructures 235
    Certificates 236
    Certificate authorities (CAs) 238
    Certificate publishers 238

Common Security Protocols 239
  IPSec 239
  Kerberos 241
  L2TP 244
  SSL 245
Assessment Questions 248
Scenarios 252
Answers to Chapter Questions 252
  Chapter Pre-Test 252
  Assessment Questions 253
  Scenarios 254

Part III: Network Implementation   255

Chapter 12: Network and Client Operating Systems 257

Network Operating Systems 259
  Types of network operating systems 259
  Major network operating systems 261
  Sharing with users and groups 262
  Administrator users 263
  Network operating system protocols 264
  Directory services and X.500 264
NetWare 265
  NetWare features 265
  NetWare versions 265
  NetWare Directory Services 267
  NetWare file system 270
  NetWare protocols 272
  NetWare administration 273
UNIX/Linux 277
  UNIX features 278
  Versions of UNIX 280
  Linux stew 280
  UNIX administration 282
  UNIX file systems 284
  UNIX protocols 284
  UNIX commands and utilities 285
Windows NT/2000 286
  Windows release hierarchy 286
  NTFS 287
  Windows protocols 287
  Windows NT 3.x 289
  Windows NT 4.0 289
  Windows 2000 295
Macintosh 297

Client Operating Systems 298
    Windows clients 298
    UNIX/Linux 300
    Macintosh 300
Summary 300
Assessment Questions 301
Scenarios 305
Answers to Chapter Questions 305
    Chapter Pre-Test 305
    Assessment Questions 306
    Scenarios 307

Chapter 13: VLANs 309

Why Use VLANs? 311
    Problems with multiple LANs 311
    VLANs versus multiple LANs 312
    Benefits of VLANs 312
VLAN Basics 313
    Workgroups 313
    Types of VLANs 314
    Implicit versus explicit VLANs 315
Examples of VLAN Configurations 315
    A simple VLAN structure 316
    A more complex VLAN structure 317
Summary 319
Assessment Questions 320
Lab Exercises 322
Answers to Chapter Questions 324
    Chapter Pre-Test 324
    Assessment Questions 325

Chapter 14: Data Storage 327

Storage Basics 329
    Basic storage requirements 329
    Network storage media 330
    Storage controller interfaces 334
    Parallel processing 341
Direct-Attached Storage 342
    DAS media 342
    Problems with networks and DAS 342
Network-Attached Storage 343
    Benefits of NAS 344
    How NAS works 345
    NAS technologies 346
    NAS management 347
    DNAS 347
Storage Area Networks 347

Contents

Summary 349
Assessment Questions 350
Scenarios 354
Answers to Chapter Questions 354
    Chapter Pre-Test 354
    Assessment Questions 354
    Scenarios 355

Chapter 15: Keeping Your Data Available 357

Backups 359
    Types of backups 359
    Scheduled backups 360
    Restoring from backup 361
    Off-site storage 361
    Backup tips 361
Fault Tolerance 362
    Some important fault-tolerance concepts 363
    Types of fault tolerance 364
"RAID!?!" 366
    Understanding RAID 367
    How RAID works 367
    Types of RAID 370
System-Area Networks 372
Summary 373
Assessment Questions 374
Scenarios 378
Answers to Chapter Questions 378
    Chapter Pre-Test 378
    Assessment Questions 379
    Scenarios 380

Chapter 16: Configuring Remote Connectivity 381

Remote Access Services (RAS) 383
    Features of RAS 384
    RAS connection methods 385
    RAS security 386
    RAS architecture 388
    NetBIOS gateway 388
    IP/IPX router 388
Installing and Configuring RAS 389
    Hardware requirements 389
    Installing RAS 389
    Configuring Dial-up Networking 401
Virtual Private Networking (VPN) 407
    VPN protocols 407
    Types of VPNs 408

Advantages of VPNs 408
Configuring a VPN Solution 409
Summary 412
Assessment Questions 413
Scenario 415
Answers to Chapter Questions 415
Chapter Pre-Test 415
Assessment Questions 416
Scenario 417

Chapter 17: Firewalls, Proxy Servers, and Security 419

Defining a Security Policy 421
Identifying the Purpose, Benefits, and Characteristics of the Firewall . . . 421
Things a firewall can't do 422
Types of firewalls 423
Network address translation 424
Demilitarized Zone 424
Firewall filtering methods 426
Packet filters 426
Application-Layer Gateways 427
Circuit-level firewalls 428
Stateful inspection 429
Comparing firewall technologies 430
Identifying the Purpose, Benefits, and Characteristics of Using a Proxy . . . 430
Bastion server 433
Predicting the Impact of a Particular Security Implementation
on Network Functionality 434
NAT performance overhead 435
Proxy/Application Gateways 435
Preparing for other performance issues 437
Summary 437
Assessment Questions 439
Scenarios 442
Lab Exercises 443
Answers to Chapter Questions 444
Chapter Pre-Test 444
Assessment Questions 444
Scenarios 446

Chapter 18: Network Configuration Settings 447

Network Protocols 449
Nonroutable protocols 449
Routable 450
Network communication 452

Installation and Configuration of Protocols 453
    NetBEUI installation and configuration 454
    IPX/SPX-NWLINK installation and configuration 457
    Installation and configuration of TCP/IP 459
    NetBIOS-to-HOST-name resolution 462
    Windows Internet Naming Service (WINS) Server 463
    Domain Name System 463
    Dynamic Host Configuration Protocol (DHCP) 465
Summary 468
Assessment Questions 469
Answers to Chapter Questions 471
    Chapter Pre-test 471
    Assessment Questions 471

Part IV: Operation   473

Chapter 19: TCP/IP Troubleshooting Utilities 475

Using TCP/IP Utilities 477
    Using the Ping utility 477
    Using the Tracert utility 479
    Using the Arp utility 481
    Using the Netstat utility 483
    Using the Nbtstat utility 484
    Using the Ipconfig/Ifconfig utilities 485
    Using the Winipcfg utility 486
    Using the Nslookup utility 487
Summary 488
Assessment Questions 490
Scenarios 494
Lab Exercises 494
Answers to Chapter Questions 496
    Chapter Pre-Test 496
    Assessment Questions 497
    Scenarios 498

Chapter 20: Small/Home Office Network Troubleshooting 499

Remote-access protocols (line protocols) 503
Characteristics of the Plain Old Telephone System (POTS) 504
    How Modems Communicate 506
    Troubleshooting POTS 508
xDSL and Troubleshooting Connections 511
    Troubleshooting xDSL 514
Digital Cable and Troubleshooting Connection 515
    Troubleshooting cable access 519
    Characteristics and problems of satellite Internet 522
    Troubleshooting satellite access 523

SOHO Wireless 523
    Troubleshooting wireless access 525
Summary 525
Assessment Questions 528
Scenarios 531
Answers to Chapter Questions 532
    Chapter Pre-test 532
    Assessment Questions 533
    Scenarios 534

Chapter 21: Remote Connectivity Troubleshooting 535

Troubleshooting RAS 537
    Common RAS problems 537
Troubleshooting VPNs 540
    Common problems with VPNs 541
    Windows 2000 utilities for diagnosing remote connectivity 543
Summary 544
Assessment Questions 545
Answers to Chapter Questions 547
    Chapter Pre-Test 547
    Assessment Questions 547

Chapter 22: Client/Server Network Configuration 549

Windows NT/2000 551
    Configuring file and print services 551
    Accessing file and print services from NetWare clients 558
    Accessing file and print services from Macintosh clients 558
Linux Server 559
    Network File System 559
    Samba 563
Novell NetWare Server 567
    Networking protocols 567
    Domain Name Service 569
    NetWare FTP services 569
    Accessing NetWare services from Windows 570
MAC OS X Server 571
    Installing and configuring Macintosh services 571
    Accessing Macintosh services from Windows 572
Summary 573
Assessment Questions 574
Answers to Chapter Questions 576
    Chapter Pre-Test 576
    Assessment Questions 576

Chapter 23: Wiring 577

Types and Characteristics of Common Network Cables 579
    Twisted-pair cable 579
    Coax cable 582

Using a Wire Crimper	583
Terminating twisted-pair cables	584
Using a Media Tester/Certifier	587
Using a Punch Down Tool	590
Using a Tone Generator	591
Using Optical Testers	593
Given a Wiring Task, Select the Appropriate Tool	596
Important Definitions	597
Summary	598
Assessment Questions	600
Scenarios	603
Labs	604
Answers to Chapter Questions	606
Chapter Pre-Test	606
Assessment Questions	606
Scenarios	607

Chapter 24: Network Troubleshooting 609

Network Troubleshooting	611
Troubleshooting by Network Topology	613
Ring	613
Star	614
Mesh	614
Bus	614
Wireless	615
Troubleshooting Client Connectivity	615
Troubleshooting basics	616
Diagnostic utilities	616
Hardware problems	616
Software	617
Wiring and Infrastructure Troubleshooting	618
Troubleshooting Resources	620
Previous Documentation	621
Hardware or software manual	621
Software or hardware ReadMe file	621
Hardware or software installation media	621
Manufacturer's Web site	622
Telephone technical support	622
E-mail support	622
Warranty support	623
Summary	624
Assessment Questions	626
Scenarios	630
Answers to Chapter Questions	630
Chapter Pre-Test	630
Assessment Questions	631
Scenarios	633

Appendix A: What's on the CD-ROM 635

Appendix B: Exam Objectives 639

Appendix C: Practice Exam 647

Appendix D: Glossary 667

Index 677

Hungry Minds, Inc. End-User License Agreement 703

Media and Topologies

PART

1

In This Part

Chapter 1
Network Topologies and Technologies

Chapter 2
Media Standards

Chapter 3
Network Components

Network Topologies and Technologies

CHAPTER 1

EXAM OBJECTIVES

- ✦ Recognize the following logical or physical network topologies from a schematic diagram or description:
  - Bus
  - Star/hierarchical
  - Mesh
  - Ring
  - Wireless
- ✦ Specify the main features of 802.2 (LLC), 802.3 (Ethernet), 802.5 (Token Ring), 802.11b (Wireless), and FDDI networking technologies, including:
  - Speed
  - Access method
  - Topology
  - Media

CHAPTER PRE-TEST

1. What are the primary advantages of a Bus network topology?
2. What is the typical cable type used with a Star topology?
3. How does the network react to a cable break with a Bus topology?
4. What is the primary goal of building a Mesh network?
5. What is the most common type of Ring network?
6. What is the connection method used by Ethernet?
7. What are messages sent to all stations on an Ethernet LAN called?
8. Why is it not possible for one station to monopolize a Token Ring LAN?
9. What is the connection method used by Wireless 802.11b LANs?
10. What makes FDDI LANs more reliable than other types?

✦ Answers to these questions can be found at the end of the chapter. ✦

Chapter 1 ✦ **Network Topologies and Technologies**

A *local-area network* (LAN) is basically defined as two or more computers connected by a structured wire system for the purpose of sharing resources and files. In this chapter we will explain the various 'structured wire systems' that the Network Engineer will deal with during the course of their job. Wireless LANs are becoming more and more popular, but even these devices rely on some amount of physical wires in most cases.

Throughout the history of the LAN, various techniques have been deployed to connect the end-user devices together. Overall, the layouts of these cable systems are the *network topologies* that define the shape of a LAN or other communications system. There are four principal topologies used in the modern LAN that we will cover here in more detail.

Bus Topology

One of the earliest methods of connecting PCs together for a LAN was the Bus topology. The Bus method utilizes a single cable (usually coax) terminated at each end. Each network device (computer, printer, or other component addressable on the network) "tap" into the cable between the terminated ends (see Figure 1-1). Both Ethernet and LocalTalk networks can use a Bus topology. Table 1-1 lists the advantages and disadvantages of this method.

Table 1-1
Bus Topologies: Benefit Comparison

Advantages	Disadvantages
Inexpensive: Does not require additional hardware to interconnect the attached devices.	Entire network shuts down if there is a break in the main cable.
Easy to Install: Coax cable is durable and performs well in harsh environments.	Difficult to identify the problem if the entire network shuts down.
Flexible: New devices can be added by simply installing a new 'T' connector.	Performance: Coax technology is usually limited to a maximum of 10mbs.
Uses less cable than other topologies.	Not intended for use as a standalone solution in a large building.

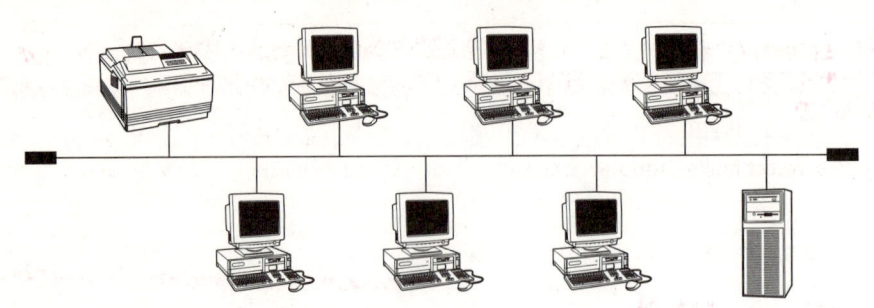

Figure 1-1: Example of a Bus network

> **Cross-Reference:** Refer to Chapter 2 for details of cabling and cable connectors for all these topologies.

Star Topology

Modern networks normally utilize a Star topology; the cables fan outward from a central network hub or concentrator, forming a starlike shape. Data on a Star network passes through the hub or concentrator before continuing to its destination. The hub or concentrator

- Manages and controls all network functions
- Acts as a repeater for the data flow

This type of topology is most common with twisted-pair wires, although coax or fiber-optic cables can also be installed Star-fashion.

Figure 1-2 provides a visual representation of a Star network. Table 1-2 describes the network's benefits and problems.

Table 1-2
Star Topologies: Benefit Comparison

Advantages	Disadvantages
Easy to Install: Each device on the network simply requires a cable run between it and the concentrator device.	Requires more cable than a Bus topology.
Flexible: Devices can be added or removed without affecting the other devices on the network.	If the hub or concentrator fails, attached devices are disabled.

Advantages	Disadvantages
Performance is greater with speeds capable of 10mbps to 100mbps or more.	More expensive than Bus topologies because of the cost of the concentrators.
Easy to detect faults and to remove parts.	Twisted-pair cables typically used in Star topologies are not as immune to interferences as coax.

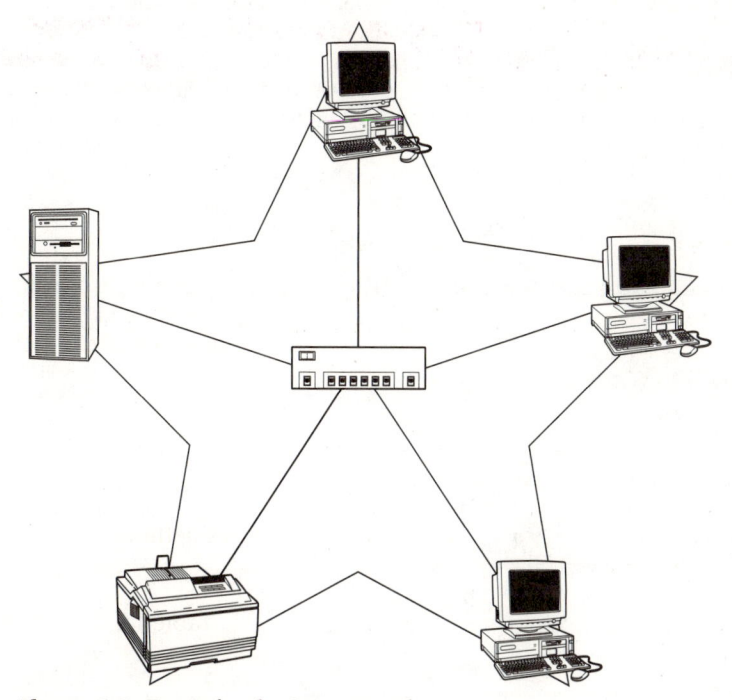

Figure 1-2: Example of a Star network

Mesh Topology

The Mesh topology is used primarily in environments where redundancy and high availability of every device is highly critical. With a Mesh network, each device has at least two separate connections between devices (as shown in Figure 1-3). Many wireless networks are structured in a Mesh topology. All devices on the network are directly connected to all other devices. Another example is a room full of people all talking to each other. There are two types of Mesh topologies, the full Mesh and the partial Mesh.

A full Mesh topology is created when every device on the network has a connection to every other device on the network. Full Mesh is generally expensive to implement but yields the greatest amount of redundancy, so in the event that one of the devices fails, network traffic can be directed to any of the other devices.

A partial Mesh topology is less expensive to implement and, therefore, offers less redundancy than full Mesh topology. With partial Mesh, some devices are organized in a full Mesh scheme but others are only connected to one or two in the network. Partial Mesh topology is commonly found in peripheral networks connected to a full meshed backbone. Table 1-3 describes their benefits and problems.

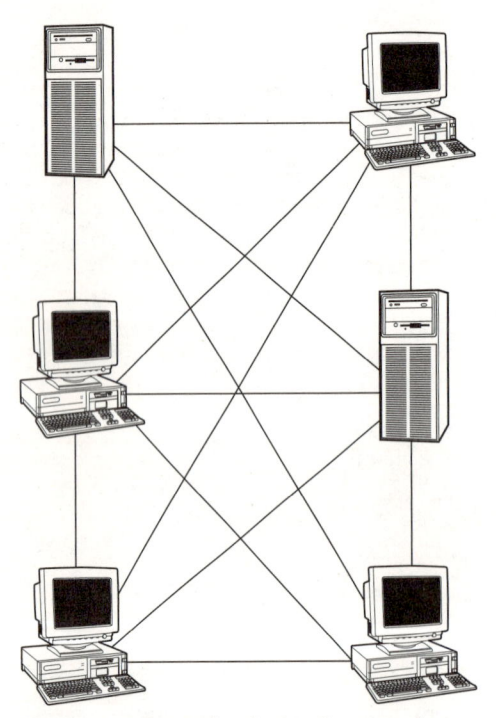

Figure 1-3: Example of a Mesh network

Table 1-3
Mesh Topologies: Benefit Comparison

Advantages	Disadvantages
Provides redundancy and fault tolerance between devices and ensures the best possibility that the network is always available.	Much more costly to install and maintain.
Easier troubleshooting.	Delays and extra processing time as a result of the communication routing through intervening devices.
Guaranteed communication capacity.	

Ring Topology

The Ring architecture connects each device in a closed loop. Data signals travel from one device to the next in a single direction around the loop. A server in a Ring topology is just one of several devices and does not provide routing functions. The most common type of ring topology is *Token Ring*, made popular by, and almost exclusively found with, IBM networks. Within a token-ring LAN, each device in the ring is guaranteed an equal time slice to transmit data. Unlike other network methods like Ethernet, no single device on a Ring network can monopolize the communications of the network. ATM Ring networks have two rings traveling in opposite directions to provide redundancy for the topology. Should one ring fail, data can still be transmitted on the remaining ring. Table 1-4 summarizes their benefits and problems. Figure 1-4 shows an example of a Ring network.

Table 1-4
Ring Topologies Benefit comparison

Advantages	Disadvantages
Easy to install and expand.	More expensive than a Bus topology.
Better performance than the basic Bus at higher levels of traffic, especially rings designed with fiber-optic cabling.	Like the Bus method, a break in the cable causes a complete failure of the network.
Can provide guaranteed transmission time for each device on the LAN.	Network hardware for Ring networks generally cost more than Ethernet components.

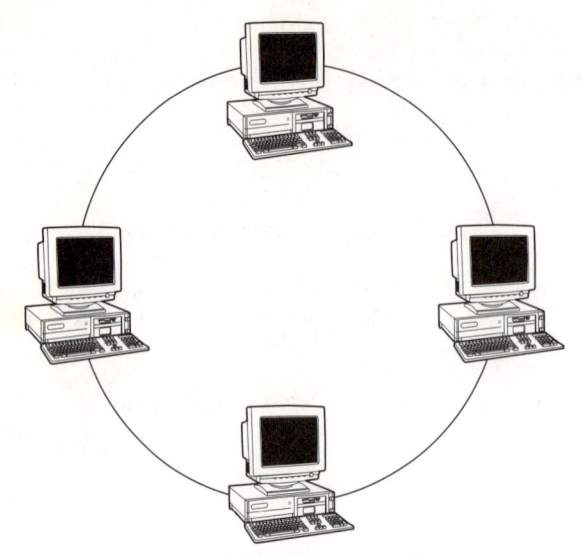

Figure 1-4: Example of a Ring network

Communication Protocols for Data Transmission

As important as the cable design is, without a method of transmitting data across the lines a network is pretty useless. Many transmission methods (called *protocols*) developed over the years — some proprietary, some not — but each is a specific set of directions, or rules, that define the proper sending and receiving of data between network devices. To ensure that hardware and software from multiple vendors could effectively interoperate on the LAN, some form of standard was necessary.

Ethernet

In late 1978, the first experimental network system was created to interconnect the Xerox Altos PCs to one another and to servers and laser printers. This first experimental network was called the Alto Aloha Network. In 1979 the name was changed to "Ethernet," to make it clear that the system could support any computer — not just Altos — and to point out that the new network mechanisms had evolved well beyond the Aloha system. The base word *ether* was chosen as a way of describing an essential feature of the system; the physical medium (a cable) carries bits to all stations, in much the same way that astronomers once thought a "luminiferous aether" propagated electromagnetic waves universally through space.

By several orders of magnitude, Ethernet is the most common — and most popular — network protocol for local-area networks. Ethernet is inexpensive, scalable, flexible, and easy to implement. Because thousands of hardware and software vendors create Ethernet products, the cost per device for connecting to an Ethernet network is typically under U.S.$60.00. Ethernet works equally well on coax, twisted-pair, or fiber cables with transmission speeds over 1GHz (although 10Mb and 100Mb speeds are the most common). Modern connection switching techniques allow an Ethernet LAN to support thousands of user devices with exceptional performance.

As the holder of the trademark, Xerox established and published the original Ethernet standards — and no technology could become a truly international standard for a wide variety of equipment if a single U.S. corporation controlled the protocol's rules. The Institute of Electricians and Electrical Engineers (IEEE) was assigned the task of developing formal international standards for all local-area network technology. It formed the "802" committee to look at Ethernet, Token Ring, Fiber-optic, and other LAN technology. The objective of the project was to

- Standardize each LAN individually
- Establish rules that would be global to all types of LANs so data could easily move from Ethernet to Token Ring or fiber-optic networks

In the process of standardizing the Ethernet protocols, some conflicts with the original Xerox system were inevitable. The IEEE was careful to separate the new and old rules. It recognized that there would be a period when old DIX messages and new IEEE 802 messages would have to coexist on the same LAN. The result was a published set of standards known as 802.2 and 802.3. For Token Ring networks, this committee published the 802.5 standard. In the following section, we'll look at these IEEE standards in detail, and then we'll follow-up with a primer on the basic function of the Ethernet and Token Ring protocols.

Ethernet 802.2

The 802.2 Ethernet standard was designed primarily to be compatible with the Xerox Ethernet format. The frame structure for these data packets defined a 'type' field with a number pre-assigned by Xerox. This Type field identifies the higher-level protocols (such as IP, IPX, or AppleTalk) associated with the data packet. The type field value determines how the data field is interpreted.

Cross-Reference For additional clarification on the routing differences between 802.2 and 802.3, refer to Chapter 5 for details of the OSI model, specifically the Logical Link Control layer.

Ethernet 802.3

The 802.3 relaxed the dependence on Xerox's type definition by replacing the Type field with the data length field. This defines the length, in bytes, of the data portion of the Ethernet packet.

To allow collision detect (see next section for further details), Ethernet requires a minimum packet size of 64 bytes. Any shorter message must be padded with zeros. The requirement to pad messages is unique to Ethernet and does not apply to any other LAN media. For Ethernet to be interchangeable with other types of LANs, it would have to provide a length field to distinguish significant data from padding.

The Xerox standard did not need a length field because the vendor protocols used (XNS, DECNET, IPX, IP) all had their own length fields. However, the 802 committee needed a standard that did not depend on the good behavior of other programs. The 802.3 standard, therefore, replaced the two-byte type field with a two-byte length field.

Xerox had not assigned any important types to have a decimal value following 1500. Because the maximum size of a packet on Ethernet is 1500 bytes, there was no conflict or overlap between the Xerox and 802 standards. Any Ethernet packet with a type/length field less than 1500 is in 802.3 format (with a length) while any packet in which the field value is greater than 1500 must be in Xerox format (with a type).

The 802 committee then created a new field to substitute for the Type field. The 802.2 header follows the 802.3 header (and also follows the comparable fields in Token Ring) The 802.2 header is three bytes long for control packets, the kind of connectionless data sent by old Xerox protocols. A four-byte header is defined for connection-oriented data, which refers primarily to SNA and NetBEUI. The first two bytes are set to 0x0404 for SNA and 0xF0F0 for NetBEUI.

Exam Tip Remember that 802.2 and 802.3 Ethernet can perform at 10Mb, 100Mb, or 1Gb speeds. Both standards support coax, shielded twisted-pair (STP) wire, and fiber-optic cables but coax is limited to 10Mb and STP to 100Mb.

Basic Ethernet Concepts

As stated earlier, Ethernet is by far the most popular networking protocol in use today. Ethernet is fast with speeds from 10Mbps to 1Gbps (gigabits per second). An Ethernet based LAN can be built from hundreds of readily available, inexpensive products. Ethernet is easy to configure and is supported by all the major Network Operating Systems (NOS).

Ethernet transmits data in *frames*, or small *packets*. The first 12 bytes of every frame contain the 6-byte destination address (the recipient) and a 6-byte source address (the sender). Each Ethernet adapter card has a unique factory installed address (the "Media Access Control", or MAC address). Use of this hardware address guarantees a unique identity to each card.

Ethernet uses a transmission protocol method known as Carrier Sense Multiple Access/Collision Detection (CSMA/CD). To best understand this concept, know that Ethernet only allows one device at a time to "talk" on the wire. When a network device wants to transmit data, the Ethernet protocol states that the cable must be without any other traffic. This is the Carrier Sense and Multiple Access portion of the CSMA technology. It is likely that devices will "listen" on the wire at the exact same time and not hear any other traffic. They will then assume that the cable is free and begin transmitting their data. Because only one device is allowed to "talk" on the wire at a time, this situation breaks the rules of the Ethernet protocol. When this happens, the data bits collide with one another and basically make a real mess of things. Examine, too, this situation.

An Ethernet station sends data at a rate of 10 megabits per second, which equates to 100 nanoseconds per bit. Light and electricity travel about one foot in a nanosecond. Therefore, after the electric signal for the first bit has traveled about 100 feet down the wire, the station has begun to send the second bit. However, an Ethernet cable can run for hundreds of feet. If two stations are located 250 feet apart and both begin transmitting at the same time, they will be in the middle of the third bit before the signal from each reaches the other station. The Ethernet protocol then, must be able to detect these collisions and do something about it — hence, the second part of our technology, Collision Detection.

When a collision is detected, the devices are programmed to "back off" and wait a random amount of time before trying the process over again. This back-off algorithm is built into the Ethernet devices to ensure different timing states between attempts to retransmit. (It certainly wouldn't work if each device waited the exact same amount of time and started sending their data again. The collisions would simple reoccur and no data would ever get through!) When a packet is sent out on the wire, the sending device must wait a predetermined time and listen for a collision before beginning to send the next packet of information.

It should be obvious that a number of potential problems exist with this protocol. First of all, an Ethernet backbone would collapse completely if too many devices are trying to share the same cable. In fact, the utilization of any single cable segment should never exceed 30 percent. (Peaks and spikes of utilization over 30 percent are normal and acceptable, but sustained utilization should always remain following the 30 percent mark). The term Collision Domain serves to describe a group of devices that share a single cable segment and, therefore, contend for time on the same wire. When a Collision Domain starts to exceed the 30 percent threshold, you need to do something to break up or *segment* the domain to reduce the total number of devices sharing the cable. Typically this would be done with devices known as *routers*, *bridges*, or *switches*.

Cross-Reference See Chapter 3 for details on bridges, switches, and routers.

Another problem with this access method appears when the length of the cable segment is too long. Because the protocol calls for the transmitting device to listen for collisions for a specific amount of time, a collision could occur too far away from the device before it starts to send more data. In the real world, this is a common mistake and one that often leads to excessive diagnostic time. A number of cable testers available on the market can identify segments that exceed specifications.

Ethernet is considered a *broadcast* form of protocol. Broadcasts are packets sent out on the cable topology with no specific destination address given (the 6-byte source address field is set to all zeros). All devices on the wire will pick up a broadcast packet to determine if it has any reason to respond. A good example of this is a common login sequence. When a PC first comes on line, it performs a broadcast looking for a server to authenticate to. Basically, the PC is telling every device on the cable that it is looking for a server so that it can log in to the network. All devices will see this data packet, but only file servers will respond. It is critically important to understand the implications of the broadcast system. When a broadcast packet is sent out on the LAN, every device connected to that network segment will stop what it's doing and look at the broadcast packet. Because a device does not know whom the specific broadcast message is for, it must stop what it's doing to check the packet even if it does not need to respond. When too many broadcasts are being sent on a LAN, all devices will be too busy checking these messages to do any real work. This is a common Ethernet problem known as a *broadcast storm*. Broadcast storms can be caused deliberately by a potential intruder, or (most likely), from a malfunctioning NIC.

In most real world situations, Ethernet should be given first consideration when designing a new LAN. Faster Ethernet technologies are being developed more than any other protocol, and with a little care to watch your specifications, Ethernet is quite simple to configure and maintain.

Exam Tip Ethernet uses the Carrier Sense Multiple Access/Collision Detection (CSMA/CD) access method.

Token Ring/IEEE 802.5

Token Ring is a protocol primarily developed and maintained by IBM. As its name implies, this type of network is designed in a Ring topology that controls the transmission of data on the network by passing a *token* (a special-purpose frame) from station to station around the ring. Only the station possessing the token may transmit data.

Token Ring and IEEE 802.5 networks are basically compatible, although the specifications differ in minor ways. IBM's Token Ring network specifies a Star topology with all end stations attached to a device called a *multistation access unit* (MAU). In contrast, IEEE 802.5 does not specify a topology, although virtually all IEEE 802.5 implementations are based on a Star. Other differences exist, including media type (IEEE 802.5 does not specify a media type, although IBM Token Ring networks use twisted-pair wire) and the size of the routing-information field.

Basic Token-Ring Concepts

Token Ring and IEEE 802.5 are two principal examples of token-passing networks (FDDI being the other). Token-passing networks move a small frame, called a **token**, around the network. Possession of the token grants the right to transmit. If a device receiving the token doesn't have any information to send, it passes the token on to the next station. Each station can hold the token for a predetermined maximum period of time.

When a station needs to send data, (assuming it has control of the token), it first modifies the token's **start-of-frame** header identifying that this station is circulating data. The data is then put out on the wire. Each station in turn takes a look at the token to see if the data is addressed to them, if not, the token is regenerated on to the next station in the ring. When the proper station sees the token is addressed to it, the message is copied and the token is re-circulated back on the cable. Finally the transmitting station gets the token back where it removes the message from the network and transmits a new token for the next station that needs to transmit data. The protocol uses a process called **token-holding timer** to regulate the maximum time a workstation can transmit data; no single station can monopolize the network.

The biggest drawbacks to Token Ring/IEEE 802.5 have typically been the near-proprietary nature of IBM's influence, the higher price of the basic equipment, and its maximum speed limitation of 16Mbps. The later of these issues may well be dwindling, however, as Fast Token Ring networks (with speeds up to 1Gbps) are beginning to make some headway.

Token Ring has some major advantages over Ethernet:

- The maximum frame size for Token Ring is 4k, which is much more efficient that the small Ethernet maximum.
- Token Ring has long-distance capability.
- Every station in the ring is *guaranteed* access to the token at some point; thus, every station can transmit data.
- Error detection and recovery techniques are also enhanced in a Token Ring environment by using a monitor function normally controlled by a server. For example, if the token is lost or corrupted, the protocol provides a mechanism to generate a new token after a specified time interval has elapsed.

Exam Tip: Remember that 802.5 can transfer data at 4Mb, 16Mb, 100Mb, or 1Gb speeds. The 802.5 standard supports coax and shielded twisted-pair (STP) wire and uses the token-passing access method.

802.11b (Wireless)

In 1997, after seven years of work, the IEEE published 802.11, the first internationally sanctioned standard for wireless LANs. In 1999, they ratified the 802.11b "High Rate" amendment to the standard, which added two higher speeds (5.5 and 11 Mbps).

Like the other IEEE 802 standards, the 802.11 standards focus on the bottom two levels of the OSI model, the Physical layer and Data Link layer. Therefore, any application, NOS, or higher-level protocol (such as TCP/IP IPX) will run on an 802.11-compliant network as easily as over standard Ethernet.

The basic architecture, features, and services of 802.11b are defined by the original 802.11 standard. The 802.11b specification affects only the Physical layer, adding higher data rates and more robust connectivity. IEEE 802.11b data is encoded using DSSS (direct-sequence spread-spectrum) technology, similar to such wireless devices as telephones.

Caution: The most important difference between the wireless LAN and the MAC protocol of most wired networking applications is that *a wireless LAN doesn't detect collisions*. With the receiving and sending antennas immediately next to each other, a station can't see any signal but its own — so it sends a complete packet before an incorrect checksum can reveal that a collision has happened. If you're using a wireless LAN, make sure you limit the number of collisions to the absolute minimum.

This is achieved by a protocol called Carrier Sense Multiple Access with Collision Avoidance (CSMA/CA). The idea is to prevent collisions at the moment they are most likely to occur. All clients are forced to wait for a random number of timeslots and then sense the medium again before starting a transmission. If the medium is sensed to be busy, the client freezes its timer until the medium is free again — which reduces the chance of two clients starting to send simultaneously.

The overhead introduced by the Collision Avoidance delays should be as small as possible. However, the protocol also needs to keep the number of collisions to a minimum, even under the highest possible load. To this end, the range of the random delay, or the contention window, is set to vary with the load. In the case of a collision, the delay doubles progressively (15, 31, up to 1023) until a successful transmission occurs; then the delay resets to its minimal value. The 802.11 standard does not fix minimum and maximum values for the contention window. However, it does advise a minimum of 15 or 31 and a maximum of 1023.

Future 802.11 Developments

There is a flurry of activity in the wireless markets. Work has already begun on specifications to address some of the drawbacks of the 802.11b standard. The 802.11a specification operates in the 5GHz frequency band with a maximum data rate of 54Mbps. A few major manufacturers have already committed to this standard although the technology doesn't yet have a clear path to commercial success. One major obstacle is Europe's HiperLAN/2 standard, which occupies the same 5GHz frequency band but isn't compatible with 802.11a.

The proposed 802.11g standard might also have a chance if European reluctance delays the acceptance of 802.11. The 802.11g standard stays in the crowded 2.4GHz frequency range that 802.11b now uses. It will use a different modulation scheme, however, to achieve raw speeds of over 20Mbps. There are no clear indications whether these standards will ever make it into actual products.

Wireless LANs can be intermixed with standard wired LANs by means of a device called a *wireless access point*, a device that connects to your wired LAN like any other device but acts as a bridge between wired and wireless devices.

Exam Tip Remember that 802.11b wireless LANs transfer data between 1Mb and 11Mb, uses the DSSS (direct-sequence spread-spectrum) technology to transmit data, and the Carrier Sense Multiple Access with Collision Avoidance (CSMA/CA) access method.

FDDI (Fiber Distributed Data Interface)

FDDI (normally pronounced *fid-dee*) has found its niche as a reliable, high-speed backbone for mission-critical and high traffic networks. It can transport data at a rate of 100 megabits per second and can support up to 500 stations on a single network. FDDI was designed to run through fiber cables, transmitting light pulses to convey information between stations, but it can also run on copper using electrical signals.

FDDI is highly reliable because FDDI networks consist of two counter-rotating rings. A secondary ring provides an alternate data path in the event a fault occurs on the primary ring. FDDI stations incorporate this secondary ring into the data path to route traffic around the fault as seen by the diagram in Figure 1-5.

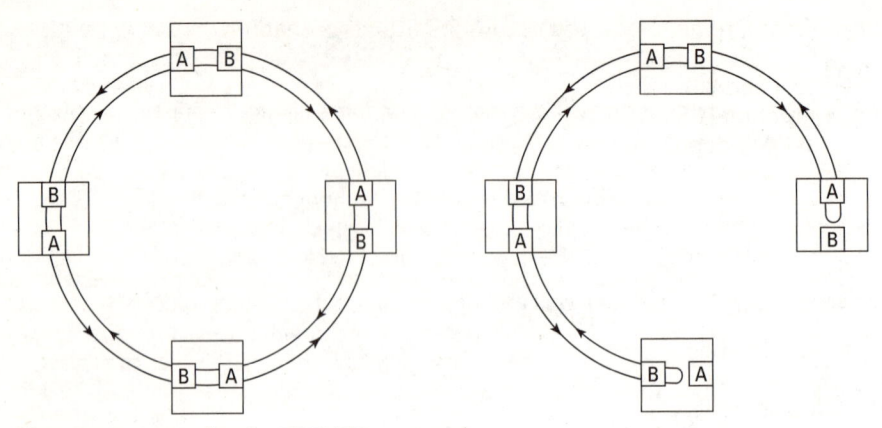

Figure 1-5: Example of a FDDI Ring network

The sequence in which stations gain access to the medium is predetermined. Similar to our previous coverage of Token Ring, stations on FDDI networks generate a special signaling sequence Token that controls the right to transmit. The Token is continually passed around the network from one node to the next. When a station has something to send, it captures the token, sends the information in formatted FDDI frames, and then releases the token. The header of these frames includes the address of the station(s) that will copy the frame. All nodes read the frame as it is passed around the ring to determine if they are the recipients of the frame. If they are, they extract the data, retransmitting the frame to the next station on the ring. When the frame returns to the originating station, the originating station strips the frame. The token-access control scheme thus allows all stations to share the network bandwidth in an orderly and efficient manner.

Exam Tip Remember that FDDI can transfer data up to 100Mb per second over fiber-optic or copper cable and uses the token-passing access method.

Summary

In this chapter we looked at the various methods of designing the physical layout of a LAN. This layout is called the *topology*. The primary topologies are Bus, Star, Ring, and Mesh. After outlining how network devices are physically attached, the chapter examined transport protocols used in communication — 802.2 and 802.3 Ethernet networks, 802.5 Ring networks, 802.11b Wireless, and FDDI networks.

Chapter 1 ✦ **Network Topologies and Technologies** 19

For the exam, remember these key points from this chapter:

✦ 802.2 and 802.3 Ethernet uses a Carrier Sense Multiple Access with Collision Detection (CSMA/CD) access method and can transport data from 10Mb to 1,000Mb depending on cable types. Ethernet can be used on Coax, twisted-pair wire, or fiber-optics.

✦ 802.5 Ring networks use an electronic "token" passed around to each device on the LAN. A device can only send data on the LAN when it has control of the token. Ring networks can use coax cable, but normally use twisted-pair or fiber-optic cable and transmit data from 2Mb to 100Mbps.

✦ 802.11b specification is for spread spectrum wireless technologies. The connection method for this wireless is Carrier Sense Multiple Access with Collision Avoidance (CSMA/CA) since the access antennas make it impossible for the device to see signals other than its own. Under this specification, wireless speeds range from 1Mb to 11Mbps, depending on the distance to the access point and other interfering obstacles.

✦ A FDDI network uses a redundant ring that sends data in a direction opposite to that of the primary ring, which provides redundancy. Should a break in the cable occur, data could still be transported by rerouting the stream across the secondary line. FDDI networks can transfer data up to 1000Mb on fiber-optic cable.

✦ ✦ ✦

STUDY GUIDE

Assessment Questions

1. A section of coax on a Bus network is accidentally kicked, causing it to separate on one side of the file server. Assuming all workstations on the opposite site of the server remain connected to the cable, will they remain connected to the server?

    A. Yes but the performance will be slower.

    B. Yes; performance will be faster because fewer PCs are on the wire.

    C. No, because the segments will be unbalanced.

    D. No, because the cable is not longer terminated on both ends.

2. To repair a bad NIC in a workstation located on a Bus network, the "T" connection is removed from the Network Interface Card so the PC can be moved to the service department. Will the network continue to function with this computer removed?

    A. Yes; this will have no effect on the network at all.

    B. Yes but performance will be slower.

    C. No, because the segments will be unbalanced.

    D. No, because the cable is not longer terminated on both ends.

3. A Cable that was not properly mounted is accidentally pulled out of a hub on a Star network. The PC it is connected to loses connection to the network. Will the other devices still function on the network without interruption?

    A. Yes, if the device has a surge protector.

    B. No; the sudden loss of power will drop the connections.

    C. Yes, as long as they remain connected to the hub.

    D. No, the cables will no longer be terminated properly.

4. An Ethernet Network has a hub with both a coax Bus connection and 8 ports for twisted-pair cable in a Star formation. If a section of the coax portion of the LAN is disconnected, will the remaining 8 PCs in the Star topology remain connected?

    A. Yes, if the devices have surge protectors.

    B. No; the sudden loss of power will drop all connections.

C. Yes, as long as they remain connected to the hub.

D. No, the cables will no longer be terminated properly.

5. Which network topology requires the greatest number of Network Interface Cards per device?

   A. Bus

   B. Mesh

   C. FDDI

   D. Star

6. What is the maximum speed of a coax Bus network?

   A. 2Mb

   B. 4Mb

   C. 10Mb

   D. 100Mb

7. Collisions on an Ethernet segment _____.

   A. Must be avoided at all costs

   B. Should be minimized where possible

   C. Are normal and necessary

   D. Never occur because the token is passed in sequence

8. A Token Ring network ensures equal access to transmit data on a LAN because:

   A. Each device gets equal access to the token.

   B. Collisions are minimized by the MAU so more time is available to talk.

   C. The token can transmit data from more than one device at a time.

   D. The ring design eliminates the collision problem associated with Ethernet.

9. A Star network suffers a lightning strike that burns out the central hub. Although all the computers are unaffected and the cables are in working order, will these devices be able to log in to the network?

   A. No, if the hub fails, attached devices are disabled.

   B. No, a lightning strike of that size would ruin the cables.

   C. Yes, a hub is simply a connecting point for the cables

   D. Yes, if the hub has additional ports available.

10. A cable break occurs between two devices on Ring Network. Will the remaining devices be able to continue normal communications?

    A. Yes, the token detects the break and skips the effected devices.

    B. No, Like the Bus topology, a break in the cable causes a complete failure of the Ring network.

    C. Yes, the MAU is the connection unit of the network and like a Star network allows access to each device independently.

    D. No, a break in the cable would cause a broadcast storm that would prevent the token from moving around the ring.

11. 802.2 and 802.3 Ethernet can operate over which cable types (select all that apply)?

    A. Shielded Twisted-pair

    B. Unshielded Twisted-pair

    C. Coax

    D. Fiber-optic cable

12. An 802.3 Ethernet LAN with Twisted-pair cable is limited in speed to

    A. 2Mb

    B. 16Mb

    C. 100Mb

    D. 10Mb

13. A healthy Ethernet LAN will have a sustained collision rate of

    A. 70% or higher

    B. No more than 65%

    C. 10%

    D. No more than 30%

14. When a collision is detected by the Ethernet protocol, every sending device

    A. Backs-off for a random amount of time before trying to resend the data

    B. Backs-off until the collision rate drops 10%

    C. Backs-off until the token comes back around

    D. Resends whatever data packets were part of the collision

15. The best way to maximize performance of an Ethernet LAN is to:
   A. Eliminate all collisions
   B. Use only 32-bit operating systems like Windows 2000
   C. Make sure NICs are not creating unnecessary broadcasts
   D. Eliminate any broadcast being made on the LAN

16. When a broadcast is made on an Ethernet LAN, which device(s) will examine it?
   A. Only the device that the broadcast is intended for
   B. Only the device(s) that can offer the specified service
   C. Only Servers and Printers
   D. Every device in the broadcast domain

17. On a Ring Network using Token technology, which devices read the data payload from the sending device with the token?
   A. Only the device where the payload is addressed
   B. Only the device(s) that can offer the specified service
   C. Only Servers or printers unless the MAU readdresses the packet
   D. Each device in the ring until the destination station removes the data

18. The practical maximum speed of most standard Token Ring Networks is:
   A. 16Mb
   B. 100Mb
   C. 1Gb
   D. 4Mb

19. One major advantage of Token Ring over Ethernet is:
   A. Requires less cable
   B. Is usually less expensive
   C. The Token Ring Packet size is 4k compared to Ethernets 1k
   D. MAUs are faster than hubs

20. Wireless networks, as defined by the IEEE 802.11b specification provides no method of connecting a wired network to a wireless network.
   A. True
   B. False

Scenarios

1. A company needs to build a network in a new location. Because the building has not been wired for computers before, they are taking advantage of the situation to design a new LAN from scratch. They have identified that high speed is critical to most users although 20% do not need speeds over 10Mb. There will be 30 computers located over 3 floors but the lowest level has all concrete walls making it costly to install cables. What topology and protocol would meet these requirements?

2. A small county sheriff's office needs to network 6 PCs and 2 printers in a single room. The single most important requirement is always being able to access the data. They have a custom application that distributes the primary database among all 6 PCs. What topology would give the sheriff the best protection against inaccessible data?

Answers to Chapter Questions

Chapter Pre-Test

1. Inexpensive; Easy to install; Uses less cable than other topologies.
2. Shielded twisted-pair, commonly Category 5.
3. All devices on the segment stop communicating.
4. Creating redundant connections between stations
5. IBM's Token Ring
6. Carrier Sense Multiple Access/Collision Detection (CSMA/CD)
7. Broadcasts
8. Each station gets the token for a specific amount of time before it must be released for the next station down the line
9. Carrier Sense Multiple Access/Collision Avoidance (CSMA/CA)
10. A secondary ring provides access in the event there is a break in the primary ring.

Assessment Questions

1. D. A break in a Bus topology removes the termination from one end so the signal is never bounced back on the wire causing a total loss of communication on the LAN.

2. A. Because the "T" connector is removed from the NIC, the physical cable connection is not interrupted; therefore, the network will function normally.

3. C. A primary advantage to a Star topology is that each device is independent of the others so removing one from the network doesn't hinder the remaining connected devices.

4. C. Even though the devices on the Bus side will lose network connectivity, the devices in the Star will not. The concentrator is simply a bridge between the two sides but does not change the nature of the topologies.

5. B. In a Meshed network, each device is directly connected to every other device and requires a network card for each connection.

6. C. Coax Bus networks have a maximum capacity of 10mb.

7. C. The standards for Ethernet define a collision detection scheme. Too many collisions indicate a problem, but collisions in general are normal on an Ethernet network.

8. A. A Ring network uses a "token" to dictate which device is allowed to transmit data on the network. Each device is given equal access to the token and not allowed to monopolize it for more than the designated time. If a device has more data to send than it can do once it has the token, it must wait for its next turn before sending the rest of the data.

9. A. The concentrator (hub) is the central connecting point in a Star network. If it fails, no communications can take place.

10. B. The Ring network described by the 802.5 specification does not provide for a redundant path so the cable break would cripple the rest of the network.

11. B, C, and D. Ethernet is flexible and will work on most cable types. However, Shielded twisted-pair wire causes too much interference between the wires for Ethernet to function reliably.

12. C. There are some proprietary twisted-pair products that can reach 1gb transfer rates, but the published maximum is 100mb.

13. D. Although peaks can reach as high as 100%, sustained collision rates should never be more than 30%. If collision rates exceed this, the LAN must be separated into smaller cable segments.

14. A. The collision detection function of the Ethernet protocol states that each device trying to communicate when a collision occurs must stop sending, wait a random number of milliseconds, and then listen for traffic again before trying to retransmit the data.

15. C. For devices to initially communicate with certain servers and other devices on an Ethernet LAN, broadcasts must be performed. However, excessive broadcasts will slow a network down and possibly stop all other communications completely.

16. D. Because broadcasts do not contain a destination address, every device within the range of the broadcast (the broadcast domain) must stop what it's doing and examine the contents of the broadcast packet.

17. D. When a station sends data, each station in turn looks at the token to see if the data is addressed to them; if not, the token is regenerated on to the next station in the ring. When the proper station sees the token is addressed to it, the message is copied and the token is re-circulated back on the cable.

18. A. Although there are 100mb Token Ring products available, the standard protocol provides for a maximum transmission speed of 16mb.

19. C. The Token Ring packet size has a potential maximum of 4508k compared to Ethernet's 1503; therefore, data can be transmitted with fewer packets on Token Ring.

20. B. Wireless LANs can be intermixed with standard wired LANs by means of a device called a wireless Access Point. The wireless access point connects to your wired LAN like any other device and acts as a bridge to the wireless devices

Scenarios

1. Since high speed is a requirement, Ethernet is probably the best choice since the LAN can be configured for speeds up to 1gb if necessary. Because the lower floor is going to be cost prohibitive for running new cable, a wireless solution can be implemented for the users who don't need the higher speeds.

2. Since the primary database is distributed between multiple computers, a central server is not a critical component. Any topology that did not support more than one connection between any two PCs would be unacceptable. The sheriffs department could not afford a design that had a single point of failure such as a Star or Bus. Although a FDDI network would fit the requirements by providing a redundant ring, it wouldn't take advantage of the distributed data as well as a fully meshed network would. Therefore, the full Mesh LAN would probably be the best choice in this situation.

Media Standards

CHAPTER 2

EXAM OBJECTIVES

- Specify the characteristics (e.g., speed, length, topology, cable type, and so on) of the following:
  - 802.3 (Ethernet) standards
  - 10BASE-T
  - 100BASE-TX
  - 10BASE2
  - 10BASE5
  - 100BASE-FX
  - Gigabit Ethernet
- Recognize the following media connectors and/or describe their uses:
  - RJ-11
  - RJ-45
  - AUI
  - BNC
  - ST
  - SC
- Choose the appropriate media type and connectors to add a client to an existing network.

PRE-TEST QUESTIONS

1. What is the common term for the 802.3 standard?
2. What access method does the Ethernet use?
3. What does the "10" in 10BASE2 signify?
4. What are the other common terms for 10Base5?
5. What are the other common terms for 10Base2?
6. What does the "T" in 10BaseT signify?
7. What does the "F" in 10BaseF signify?
8. What topology is used with 10Base5?
9. What topology is used with 10BaseT?
10. Which medium has a maximum individual segment length of 1000 meters?

✦ Answers to these questions can be found at the end of the chapter. ✦

Ethernet in the Beginning

The origins of Ethernet go back thirty years. Late in 1972, Dr. Robert M. Metcalfe and his colleagues developed the first experimental Ethernet to interconnect the Xerox Alto (a personal workstation) with a graphical user interface (GUI). Metcalfe developed the Ethernet LAN protocol at the Xerox Palo Alto Research Center in cooperation with DEC and Intel in 1976. In 1980, a consortium of vendors created the DIX (DEX-Intel-Xerox) standard and published the formal specifications for Ethernet. The standard specifies the physical and lower software layers of a network.

IEEE 802.3 becomes the Ethernet standard

It wasn't until 1985 that the IEEE published the forerunner of the Ethernet standard under the title of "IEEE 802.3 Carrier Sense Multiple Access with Collision Detection (CSMA/CD) Access Method and Physical Layer Specifications." By adopting the IEEE 802.3 specification, the International Organization for Standardization (ISO) made it a worldwide networking standard. Since its 1985 publication, the Ethernet standard has governed how most network equipment is built. Today Ethernet is the most widely implemented LAN standard.

The 802.3 standard is regularly updated to include new technology. Since its creation and adoption, the standard has evolved to include new media systems for 10Mbps Ethernet (including twisted-pair media), as well as the latest set of specifications for 100Mbps Fast Ethernet.

As it now exists, the 802.3 specification — commonly accepted as the Ethernet standard — supports Bus and Star topologies. Using appropriate hardware and media, transfer rates for such networks range from 10Mbps up to 100Mbps. The media used for Ethernet include *Thicknet* (thick coaxial cable), *Thinnet* (thin coaxial cable), twisted-pair wire, and fiber-optic cable. A typical Ethernet network has three basic characteristics:

- **A physical medium:** Whether a cable or some form of wireless transmission, this is where data transfer takes place.
- **Access-control rules:** These rules (which are embedded in the Ethernet interface) govern the use of the transmission medium.
- **Ethernet frames:** These standardized sets of bits serve as virtual "containers" to carry data over the system.

Ethernet access method

Ethernet uses an access method called Carrier Sense Multiple Access with Collision Detection (CSMA/CD) to send and receive data signals and avoid having to handle simultaneous demands from different clients. Each Ethernet interface listens for a signal (called a *carrier*) on the channel. If it does not detect a signal, it may begin transmitting. If the Ethernet interface detects a carrier, it waits before attempting to send a signal. This process of sensing and responding to the presence of carriers is the "Carrier Sense" part of the access method.

In effect, all Ethernet interfaces on a network stand the same chance of sending signals; no one has priority over any other. Of course, signals on a network take a finite amount of time to reach their destination — and are not detected by the other Ethernet interfaces at exactly the same time — so more than one Ethernet interface can send a signal at precisely the same moment as another. When this occurs, the Ethernet system senses the signal *collision* — a conflict cause by simultaneous demands — and halts the transmission. Then the system waits until it detects no signal and resends the frames. This process of detecting and responding to collisions is the "Collision Detect" part of the access method.

After each packet transmission, all interfaces use the same CSMA/CD protocol to determine when the system can next send a transmission. The CSMA/CD protocol provides equal access to the public channel; all interfaces have equal opportunity to access the network.

Understanding "10Base" identifiers

IEEE shorthand identifiers, such as 10Base5, 10Base2, 10BaseT, and 10BaseF include three pieces of information:

+ **The number 10:** At the front of each identifier, *10* denotes the standard data-transfer speed over these media — ten megabits per second (10Mbps).

+ **The word *Base*:** Short for *Baseband,* this part of the identifier signifies a type of network that uses only one carrier frequency for signaling and requires all network stations to share its use.

> **Tip**
> "10Base" always signifies Ethernet — a *10*Mbps transfer speed over *Base*band cabling (which can *only* carry Ethernet signals).

+ **The segment type or segment length:** This part of the identifier can be a digit or a letter:

   • **Digit** — shorthand for how long (in meters) a cable segment may be before attenuation sets in. For example, a 10Base5 segment can be no more than *500* meters long.

   • **Letter** — identifies a specific physical type of cable. For example, the *T* at the end of 10BaseT stands for *twisted-pair.*

10Base5 standard

10Base5 is the IEEE specification for the use of thick coaxial cable, also known as Thicknet, Thickwire, or thick Ethernet, on an Ethernet network. 10Base5 has a maximum individual segment length of 500 meters (approximately 1640 feet). Longer segments will cause signal loss referred to as signal attenuation. This specification is often used as backbone segments for interconnecting Ethernet hubs as it carries signals relatively long distances, has a low cost, and good electrical shielding. 10Base5 only supports the Bus topology.

Thick coaxial cable is approximately 1 cm (.4 inches) in diameter and is fairly inflexible. It has a solid copper core and its outer insulation is made of PVC Belden 9880, which is a yellow color, or it is made of Teflon Belden 89880, which is an orange-brown color. The Teflon covered thick coaxial cable is for situations that require plenum-rated cable — for example, installation in air-handling spaces (also called *plenums*). PVC-coated cable gives off poisonous gases when it burns; plenum does not. Therefore plenum is safer to use where the air is circulated throughout a building.

10Base5 is limited to 10Mbps signals only. The specifications suggests that the segments be created using a single piece of cable from the cable spool or from the same manufacturing lot to avoid buildup of excessive signal reflections caused by any variations in electrical characteristics that can take place between different cable manufacturers or cable lots.

10Base2 standard

Also known as *thin coax* or *Thinnet*, 10Base2 has a maximum individual segment length of 185 meters (roughly 200m; the IEEE identifier for this standard rounds upward).

Thinnet is approximately half a centimeter in diameter (.5cm = 3/16 inch); as such it's more flexible, less expensive, and easier to work with than thick coaxial cable. The 10Base2 standard calls for 50-ohm coaxial cable, it is also known as RG-58 A/U. Like Thicknet, Thinnet is limited to 10Mbps signals.

Thinnet only supports daisy-chain or single-connection topologies. Thinnet cables are connected with BNC connectors. The Network Interface Card (NIC) connects to the cable with a T-connector (which also connects two cables from adjacent computers). Each endpoint on this cable must have a 50-ohm terminator.

10BaseT standard

One of the most widely used media standards for desktop connections, the 10BaseT specification, was first published in 1990. Also known as *twisted-pair* or *twisted-pair*

Ethernet, 10BaseT is made up of two strands of copper wires twisted around each other, one pair to receive data signals and the other pair used to transmit data signal. Twisted-pair has a maximum individual segment length of 100 meters (approximately 328 feet). This standard operates at 10Mbps and uses baseband transmission methods. 10BaseT supports the use of the Star topology.

The 10BaseT standard uses the Star topology with the computers connected to a central hub or concentrator. The cables connect using RJ-45 connectors. 10BaseT cable is thinner and more flexible than the coaxial cable used for the 10Base5 or 10Base2 standards. There are two types of twisted-pair cabling:

Unshielded twisted-pair (UTP)

UTP is specified in the Electronic Industries Association and Telecommunications Industries Association (EIA/TIA) 568 Commercial Building Wiring Standard. It is particularly susceptible to *crosstalk* (signals from one line getting mixed with signals from another line). Shielding reduces crosstalk.

Shielded twisted-pair (STP)

STP has a higher-quality, more protective jacket than UTP. The jacket consists of a woven copper braid. STP also has a foil wrap between and around the wire pairs, and internal twisting of the pairs. STP supports higher transmission rates over long distances than does UTP, and is less susceptible to electrical interference.

10BaseF standard

The 10BaseF specification was defined in the 1980s and is also known as Fiber-optic Ethernet. Fiber-optic Ethernet cable uses modulated light pulses instead of electrical currents to send signals. Optic fiber cabling is known for its high-speed, high-capacity data transmission with a lack of attenuation over great distances at high speeds. It is completely non-conductive to normal indoor electrical hazards and provides protection from more powerful electrical hazards such as lightning strikes and electrical ground currents. This is good for Ethernet segments outside of a building such as those used to link detached buildings together.

Fiber-optic medium has a maximum individual segment length of 1000 meters when between two repeaters. 10BaseF operates at speeds between 10Mbps and 100Mbps. It is a multimode fiber cable (MMF) with a 62.5-micron fiber-optic core and 125-micron outer cladding (62.5/125). The optical fiber core consists of an extremely thin cylinder of glass, surrounded by a concentric layer of glass, known as the cladding. The glass is sometimes substituted for plastic; even though plastic is easier to install, it cannot carry light pulses as far as glass. Each communication link uses two strands of fiber in separate jackets, one to transmit data and one to receive data. Each strand sends signals in only one direction. A layer of reinforcing plastic surrounds each glass strand. Kevlar fibers provide the strength in the fiber-optic connector surrounding the two plastic-encased cables.

Gigabit Ethernet

The first Gigabit Ethernet standard was published by the IEEE 802.3 Committee in 1998, called the 802.3z standard. Gigabit Ethernet supports data transfer rates of 1 Gigabit (1,000 megabits) per second.

802.11b

The 802.11 standard is for Wireless Local Area Networks (WLANS). 802.11b is the more dominant standard concerning WLANS. 802.11b supports data transfers at a rate of 11Mbps through the use of a 2.4-gigahertz (GHz) frequency band. 802.11a supports data transfer rates at a maximum of 54 Mbps through a 5GHz frequency band.

WLANS can function in two different formats. They can be set up to connect to wireless access points that function as bridges between the clients and the existing network backbone to access network resources. WLANS can also be set up temporarily as peer-to-peer (ad-hoc) LANS.

Wireless networks have become quite convenient because of the ability to set up temporary networks, lack of cabling, networking where it wasn't possible before, and their scalability.

802.15

Wireless Personal Area Networks (WPANs) are specified in the 802.15 standard. WPANs are ad-hoc wireless networks used with a personal operating space (POS). A POS is considered a circular area with a 10-meter radius. The two most significant WPAN technologies are Bluetooth and infrared light.

Bluetooth is a WPAN technology that uses radio waves to transmit signals within a 30-foot radius. With Bluetooth technology walls, briefcases, pockets, and windows do not cause any interference. Infrared light must have a clear line of sight to operate. There cannot be any object blocking the signal path from the sending device to the receiving device and vice versa. Infrared light signals have a short range: the device they link to must be no more than 1 meter away.

The Bluetooth Special Interest Group (SIG) published the first Bluetooth specification in 1999. The IEEE has established the 802.15 working group standard for WPANS. Their key goals are ease of use, low power consumption, interoperability between different manufacturers and products, and coexistence with 802.11 networks.

Cabling considerations

When you plan your network's cabling, you have various factors to consider — some primarily physical, some primarily electronic, and some data-related. The following checklist illustrates a typical set of such factors:

- **Installation logistics:** These concerns include the distances the cable must traverse, physical security of the cable, and the characteristics of the area chosen for installation.
- **Shielding:** How much "noise" (electrical interference) is present in the area where the cable will be run?
- **Crosstalk:** Signal mixing caused by unshielded cable.
- **Transmission speed:** Copper cable = 10 > 100 Mbps. Fiber-optic cable = 1Gbps.
- **Cost:** Cable that is easy to work with and install is less expensive (at least immediately) than cable that transmits data securely over long distances. Balancing initial outlay against the potential savings to be realized from greater security can be a challenge.
- **Distance:** Specifications outline maximum individual segment length to avoid *attenuation* (loss of signal due to extreme segment lengths).

Cable Connectors

RJ-11

RJ-11 is the acronym for Registered Jack-11, a four- or six-wire connector primarily used to connect telephone equipment. Some types of local area networks (LANs) use RJ-11 connectors.

RJ-45

The acronym for Registered Jack-45 is RJ-45. The RJ-45 connector is an eight-wire connector that is commonly used to connect computers to a local area network (LAN), particularly Ethernet LANs. Although they are slightly larger than the more commonly used RJ-11 connectors, RJ-45s can be used to connect some types of telephone equipment.

AUI

AUI is the acronym for Attachment Unit Interface. AUI is the part of the Ethernet standard that specifies how a Thicknet cable is to be connected to an Ethernet card. AUI specifies a coaxial cable connected to a transceiver that plugs into a 15-pin socket on the network interface card (NIC).

BNC

BNC is short for British Naval Connector (or Bayonet Nut Connector or Bayonet Neill Concelman), a type of connector used with coaxial cables such as the RG-58 A/U cable used with 10Base2 Ethernet. BNC connectors are used on both Thicknet and Thinnet. The common BNC connector has a male type mounted on each end of the cable. This connector has a pin pointing out of the center and a metal tube connected to the outer cable shield. The cable is then connected to a female connector with a rotating ring outside the tube that locks the cables together.

Summary

There are several types of Ethernet cables and connectors. Know the performance and cost trade-offs for success on the exam.

✦ ✦ ✦

STUDY GUIDE

Assessment Questions

1. Unshielded twisted-pair (UTP) is particularly susceptible to:
    - A. Attenuation
    - B. Packet collision
    - C. Signal detection
    - D. Crosstalk

2. 802.11 transfers data by using:
    - A. Infrared light
    - B. Mental telepathy
    - C. Radio Waves
    - D. Light Pulses

3. Ethernet supports which of the following topologies?
    - A. Bus and Star Topologies
    - B. Ring and Star Topologies
    - C. Ring and Mesh Topologies
    - D. Bus and Mesh Topologies

4. 802.3 uses which of the following access methods?
    - A. Token passing
    - B. Carrier Sense Multiple Access with Collision Avoidance (CSMA/CA)
    - C. Carrier Sense Multiple Access with Collision Detection (CSMA/CD)
    - D. Spread Spectrum Frequency Hopping

5. Thinnet is the common term for:
    - A. 10BaseF
    - B. 10Base5
    - C. 10Base2
    - D. 10BaseT

6. Of the following factors, which should you consider when choosing cabling for your network? (Choose all that apply.)

    A. Temperature

    B. Shielding

    C. Distance

    D. Light

7. The 10Base2 standard specifies which of the following connectors?

    A. RJ-11

    B. RJ-45

    C. AUI

    D. BNC

8. 10BaseF cabling has a center core of:

    A. Glass

    B. Solid copper

    C. Twisted copper strands

    D. Aluminum

9. Bluetooth technology was developed with which of the following considerations in mind? (Choose all that apply.)

    A. Low power consumption

    B. Size of equipment

    C. Interoperability with various manufacturers and products

    D. Coexistence with 802.11 networks

10. Plenum-rated cable was designed for use in:

    A. Areas with high humidity

    B. Areas with severe radio interference

    C. Air ducts

    D. Water pipes

Answers to Chapter Questions

Chapter Pre-test

1. The commonly used term for 802.3 is Ethernet.
2. Ethernet uses the Carrier Sense Multiple Access with Collision Detection (CSMA/CD) as its access method. This allows fair access to all clients without any preference. CSMA/CD also helps to prevent and recover from packet collisions on the network.
3. The *10* in the standard abbreviation *10Base2* signifies that this standard operates at 10Mbps.
4. 10Base5 is commonly referred to as Thicknet, Thick Ethernet, or Thickwire.
5. 10Base2 is commonly referred to as Thinnet, Thin Ethernet, or Thinwire.
6. The *T* in *10BaseT* signifies that this standard uses twisted-pair cabling, also known as Unshielded Twisted-pair (UTP) or Shielded Twisted-pair (STP).
7. The *F* in *10BaseF* signifies that this standard uses fiber-optic cabling.
8. The 10Base5 standard supports the use of the Bus topology.
9. The 10BaseT standard supports the use of the Star topology.
10. The 10BaseF standard has a segment length of 1000 meters.

Assessment Questions

1. D. Unshielded twisted-pair is particularly susceptible to crosstalk because it does not have a mesh copper outer jacket (as does shielded twisted-pair).
2. C. 802.11 transfers data by using radio waves. 802.11 is the IEEE standard for Wireless Local-Area Networks (WLANs).
3. A. Ethernet supports the Bus and Star topologies.
4. C. The access method used by 802.3 is Carrier Sense Multiple Access with Collision Detection.
5. C. Thinnet is the common term for 10Base2.
6. B and C. When choosing network cabling, you should consider shielding and distance.
7. D. The 10Base2 standard specified the BNC connectors be used.
8. A. 10BaseF cabling has a center core of glass.
9. A, C, and D. Bluetooth was developed to address considerations of low power consumption, interoperability with various manufacturers and products, and coexistence with 802.11 networks.
10. C. Plenum-rated cable was designed for use in air ducts.

Network Components

CHAPTER 3

EXAM OBJECTIVES

- Identify the purpose, features, and functions of the following network components
  - Network interface cards
  - Hubs
  - Switches
  - Bridges
  - Routers
  - Gateways
  - CSU/DSU
  - ISDN adapters
  - System-area network cards
  - Wireless access points
  - Modems

CHAPTER PRE-TEST

1. What is the primary purpose of a network interface card?
2. What three settings are normally necessary for a NIC to function properly?
3. What is the difference between an active hub and a passive hub?
4. What does a switch do that is beneficial to a congested Ethernet LAN?
5. What two methods are used by switches to transport data through the device?
6. Which switching method provides the fastest performance?
7. What is the primary function of the bridge?
8. Name one specific difference between a router and a bridge.
9. What is the basic difference between a system-area network card and a normal network card?
10. What two items are critical for trouble-free wireless operations?

✦ Answers to these questions can be found at the end of the chapter. ✦

Chapter 3 ✦ **Network Components**

The previous two chapters discussed the components required to physically build a network. Chapter 3 details the necessary hardware components.

The Network Interface Card (NIC)

In order to communicate on a network, all devices require a *network interface card*, commonly called a NIC. Figure 3-1 shows the basic add-in NIC for a PCI-based PC. As networks began to proliferate, most computer manufacturers began installing NICs as standard equipment. Even the home PC vendors have begun incorporating NICs into their computers due to the increasing number of broadband Internet services available. Most of these services, such as cable and DSL provide the traffic via standard Ethernet.

> **Cross-Reference** Refer to Chapter 21 for more information on broadband technologies.

Basic NICs range in price from under $20.00 to well over $150.00, depending on brand, connection speed, and features. For devices without a built-in NIC, one must be installed and properly configured before it can participate on the network. For most computers, a NIC based on PCI (Peripheral Component Interconnect) is best; modern Plug-and-Play technology usually supports this type of bus, making such a NIC easier to configure. Even so, NICs require some specific computer resources to operate properly — in particular, a dedicated IRQ and (often) an I/O address and a DMA channel. For non-Plug-and-Play devices, these system settings must be configured properly on both the hardware and in the Operating System for the NIC to work. In addition, the NIC must support the cable type used on the network. If the network topology is coax, the NIC must have a BNC connector; for twisted-pair cables, the NIC must have an RJ-45 jack; for fiber optics, the NIC must support the proper media connectors.

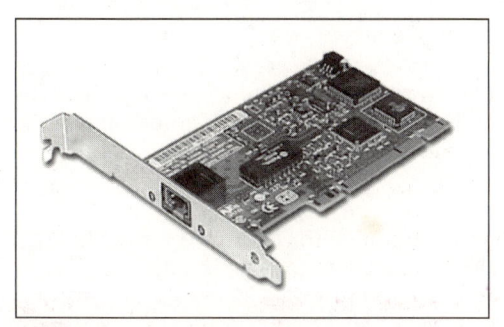

Figure 3-1: Standard add-in network adapter card.

The network card must also match the network's protocol and speed. For example, token-ring cards won't function on an Ethernet LAN. Most modern NICs can auto-sense and auto-adjust to the speed of the network, but older cards may not support faster speeds. If the network is designed to run at 100Mbps, then the network cards must support 100Mbps transfer rates or they may not be able to communicate on the LAN. With Ethernet, it is possible to mix speeds on the same network. For example, if one device is beyond the distance limitations of a 100Mb Cat5 cable segment, it is possible to build a 10Mb coax between the twisted-pair concentrator and the distant device. Any devices attached to the coax segment are reachable by member devices on the twisted-pair side, but the coax devices can only transmit data at a maximum of 10Mb. The NICs for the coax devices must support 10mb transfer rates and a concentrator that supports both twisted-pair and coax must be used.

Although NICs perform the same function, many of the high-end brands offer benefits and features that justify the extra expense. For example, many high-end server class network cards employ proprietary ASIC (*Application Specific Integrated Circuit*) chips to boost overall performance. This chip has a small amount of RAM to buffer the data as it enters the network card. The card is then able to send the data up to the higher lever hardware components on one end while accepting new data off the cable on the other end. Other ASIC designed cards provide additional performance mechanisms as well as specific error checking and correcting. These special features are especially important when selecting cards for critical, high-volume devices such as network servers. Because many client devices are constantly sending data to (and requesting it from) servers, the servers' network cards must handle the flow of data as quickly as possible. Most basic NICs are not designed to handle the number of data packets a normal network server is likely to have, so server-class NICs must be used to avoid unnecessary network bottlenecks.

Hubs

Networks using a Star topology require a central point for the devices to connect. Originally this device was called a concentrator since it consolidated the cable runs from all network devices. The basic form of concentrator is the hub.

As shown in Figure 3-2, the hub is a hardware device that contains multiple, independent ports that match the cable type of the network. Most common hubs interconnect Category 3 or 5 twisted-pair cable with RJ-45 ends, although Coax BNC and Fiber Optic BNC hubs also exist.

The hub is considered the least common denominator in device concentrators. Hubs offer an inexpensive option for transporting data between devices, but hubs don't offer any form of intelligence. Hubs can be *active* or *passive*. An active hub strengthens and regenerates the incoming signals before sending the data on to its destination. Passive hubs do nothing with the signal.

Figure 3-2: Cisco 116c Ethernet Hub.

In an Ethernet environment, hubs do not segment the collision domains. Ethernet is based on the principle of collisions — and on collision detection. As devices are added to a cable segment, an exponential number of collisions occur. Because the hub is a shared device offering no routing or segmenting of the logical LAN, it does nothing to reduce the size of the Ethernet collision domain. For example, referring to Figure 3-3, adding a second hub on an Ethernet LAN does not create two separate LAN segments, but merely extends the LAN to accommodate more devices. In this example, the two separate LANs are connected to form a single LAN with one common collision domain. Any traffic generated by PCs on the top hub will cause collisions with PCs transmitting data through the bottom Hub.

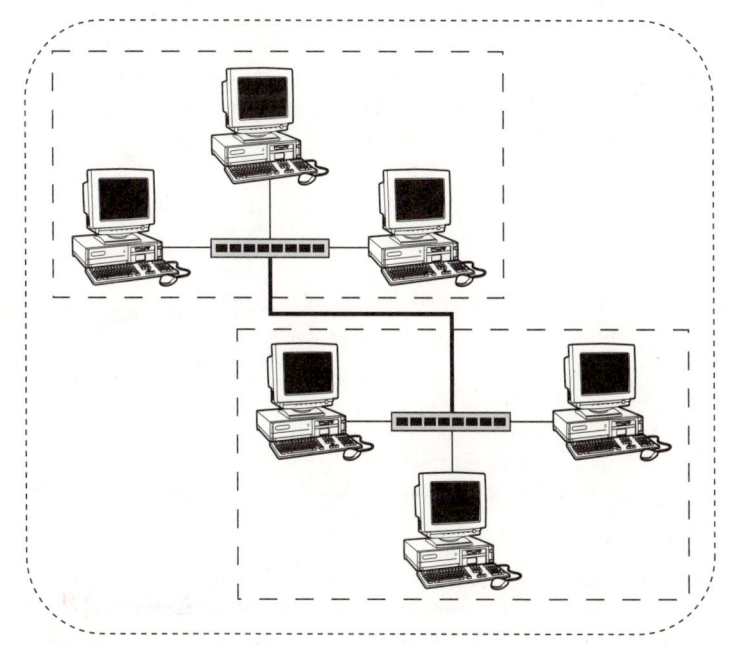

Figure 3-3: Two LANs connected by hubs to create a single LAN with one collision domain.

> **In the Real World**
> When connecting two hubs together, you must use a crossover cable or use a hub with a special 'up-link' port that crosses the transmit and receive lines on one end.

Switches

In most circumstances, the switch has become the predecessor of the hub. A switch (sometimes called a *switching hub*) offers a number of improvements over the basic hub. The switch creates a point-to-point channel between two devices. If you have a workstation and a file server connected to different ports on the same switch, the switch creates a dedicated connection between these two computers without requiring them to share the path with any other device. This process eliminates the Ethernet collision domain completely since the switch creates a path that only these two devices are communicating over. Both devices can take full advantage of the speed capabilities of the media.

Since the function of the switch is to create dedicated connections between devices, it is an excellent solution for segmenting large collision domains on Ethernet LANs. When a single collision domain begins to slow a LANs performance, a switch can be introduced to create multiple, smaller collision domains. As seen in Figure 3-4, a switch placed between two hubs on a large network creates two separate collision domains while allowing complete communications between both segments. The hubs on both sides of the switch are separate collision domains. The devices within each of these segments contend for the wire only among themselves, unaffected by traffic generated on the other segment. The switch, however, can create communication channels between devices on both sides.

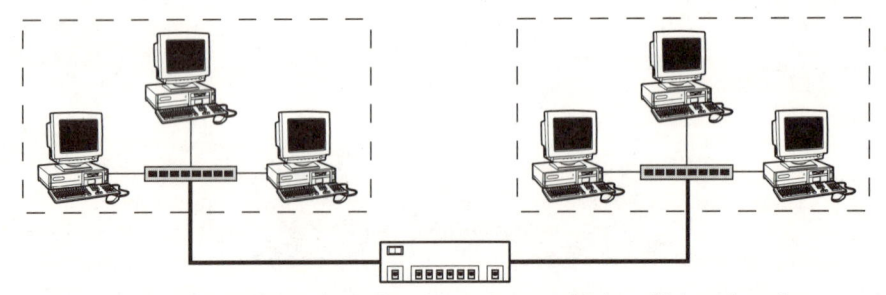

Figure 3-4: Using a switch to segment a LAN into multiple collision domains.

The intelligence built into switching technology offers a number of additional advantages. Among them, the switch offers the ability to create *Virtual LANs*, or *VLANs* within the larger network. The concept is similar to the segmenting of collision domains but does not require additional hubs. The switch can be programmed to group a number of physical ports into separate, private networks. To visualize the benefit of this technology, imagine a LAN that serves several departments. Some of these departments process sensitive data that must be secured, such as payroll information. Although this group could be physically placed on their own network, they would lose the ability to communicate with the rest of the company. Using the intelligence of the switch, the payroll group can be secured by grouping their physical connections into a private VLAN on the switch. Any shared devices within the VLAN group are only visible to other members of the VLAN, allowing these members to communicate privately with each other while still accessing the rest of the network. With proper design and programming, the switch can be used to provide an extremely high level of security within a common network.

Switches also offer a high level of error identification and protection on a LAN. Specific thresholds can be defined so a switch can shut down all communications to a specific port if certain conditions are met. For example, the Ethernet protocols use broadcasts for a wide variety of purposes. Broadcasts are common and necessary. However, a hardware failure, corrupted device driver, or intentional network attack can cause a *broadcast storm* — broadcast packets flood the network, causing every device to stop its normal processing to examine the broadcasts. The switch can be configured to shut down the port that contains the device generating the excessive broadcasts; optionally, the switch can send a warning to a network administrator.

Switches also perform data transport, using either of two methods — store-and-forward or cut-through — each with its own benefits and drawbacks: The following sections examine these methods of transport.

Store-and-forward data transport

This method accepts the incoming data in total before sending it on to its destination. This method provides a high degree of error checking and correction.

For example, the tail end of a data packet contains a CRC code that indicates whether the packet was corrupted someplace in transit. If an error was encountered, the switch can ask the sending device to resend the data reducing unnecessary network traffic. If the switch did not perform this function, the bad data would be sent to the destination device where the error checking would take place. Upon detection, the destination device would send a request to resend the data. A switch in store-and-forward mode would eliminate all traffic between it and the destination device.

When a LAN is properly maintained, errors and packet corruption should be minimal. Therefore, the cut-through mode of a switch (explained next) can greatly increase overall performance on the LAN.

Cut-through data transport

As the name implies, switch configured for cut-through data transport accepts just enough of the data packet to have the source (sending) and destination addresses. It then "cuts into" the packet to retrieve those addresses. The switch then builds the connection between the two devices and passes all remaining data though without any further interference. This process pushes data between two devices at the fastest possible speeds, but since the data-detection components are at the end of the packet, any bad data has already been transmitted before the switch is aware of it. Therefore, the destination device must perform all error detection and correction.

> **Tip:** Certain sophisticated, high-quality switches operate in *both* modes. First the switch performs cut-through processing to maximize efficiency, but tracks the number of error packets transmitted. If a predetermined threshold of errors is reached, the switch automatically changes to store-and-forward mode. When shopping for a switch, know which method (if not both) your chosen device can perform — and whether it automatically adjusts the transfer mode to comply with error-detection thresholds.

Bridges

An older device used to segment networks is the bridge. Although switches normally offer better performance and overall management, the bridge is still useful for this purpose as well. Although bridges create multiple collision domains, all bridged segments are still in one *broadcast domain*. Bridges work at the data-link layer and are protocol independent. Because of this, they are normally faster than routers.

A bridge has two or more access ports of a specific protocol, such as Ethernet or Token-ring. Bridges do not typically route between mixed protocols although they can support different cable types, such as coax and twisted-pair, within a single protocol. Each segment is connected via cable to one port on the bridge. Bridges automatically "learn" the location of devices on each segment and only route traffic between segments when necessary. To visualize this process, refer to Figure 3-5.

Assume that PC (b) must send data to PC (f) and no previous communications have occurred on the LAN.

1. PC (b) first sends a broadcast out on the wire asking PC (f) to reply with its MAC (hardware) address.
2. The bridge senses the broadcast on segment 1 and realizes that PC (f) did not respond on that segment. The bridge then checks its list of known addresses and not finding an entry for PC (f) proceeds to send the broadcast out on all segments.

3. PC (f) receives the broadcast and replies with its MAC address.

4. The bridge records the address for PC (f) for future reference.

5. Communication between PC (b) and PC (f) now begins.

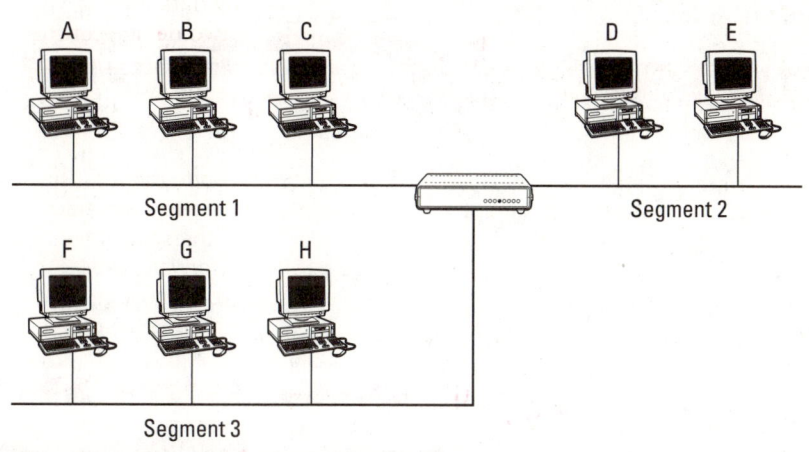

Figure 3-5: Example of a bridged network.

From this point on, the bridge "knows" that PC (f) exists on segment 3, so it routes data for PC (f) to segment 3 directly. If another broadcast is made for PC (f), the bridge intercepts it and responds for PC (f), thereby reducing the number of broadcasts transmitted across the LAN.

This form of bridging is known as *transparent bridging* since the function of data routing is unobtrusive to the end-user. All the communication occurs automatically, without user intervention, regardless of what segment the desired device resides on.

Ring networks use a different bridging process — *source route bridging* — using a protocol different from that of transparent bridging: The bridge itself does not contain the routing table; instead, the devices do. When a device on a Ring network attempts to contact another device for the first time, it sends a *Hello* packet out on the wire. Source route bridges only copy frames that contain source-routing information in the packet header. Because this Hello package does not contain routing information yet, the token is transmitted through the rings until the destination device is located. When the proper station sees that the frame is addressed to it, it places its MAC address into the header and sends it back through the bridge to sending station. The original device then updates its internal routing table so all further communication between these stations can occur directly. When more than one bridge must be crossed, each bridge adds its address to the header so the full route to the destination is known.

Routers

Routers provide specific, intelligent delivery of data between two or more (potentially extended) segments. The segments may or may not be of the same topology or protocol. For example, a router may be used on a LAN to establish a communications path between an Ethernet LAN and a token-ring LAN. Routing information must be contained within the data packet (not all protocols are *routable*). Broadcasts and multicasts are never propagated across a router because the exact destination (routing) information is not contained in these types of packets. Using a postal analogy, the router is like a mail carrier. The mail carrier must know the exact street address on his or her route to deliver the mail. Routers are interested only in local MAC (hardware) addresses; they keep track of the network segments and share this address information with other routers.

As with bridges, routers can be used to segment LANs to balance traffic, but unlike a bridge, routers can be used to filter traffic for security purposes. The router's capability to filter out specific packet types, or packets from unknown locations, makes them useful as security devices. Most routers are specialized devices optimized for communications; however, router functions can also be implemented by the network operating system (NOS) within the file server. For example, the NT and NetWare NOSs can route from one subnetwork to another if each segment is connected to a separate NIC in the file server.

As networks become more complex, a need emerges to extend network services across larger geographic areas — and routing the data becomes critical in network technology. Where bridges connect to network segments, routers typically connect two or more LANs. These LANs can be physically located in the same building, or across countries, continents, or hemispheres. When a router connects to geographically dispersed areas, the network is usually termed a *wide-area network*, or WAN. There are many ways routers on each end can be connected, but the most common way is through dedicated lease lines or packet switching technology such as frame relay or ATM.

Basic routing concepts

Routers use flat lookup tables stored in RAM to make forwarding decisions. These tables are either static or dynamic. Static routing requires a network administrator to physically calculate the routes between segments and enter these addresses into the router's databases. Static routing is only recommended for small networks with only one or two routers.

Dynamic routing uses special routing protocols that enable routers to exchange data with each other. The two most common routing protocols are Routing Information Protocol (RIP) and Open Shortest Path First (OSPF). RIP performs route discovery according to hops, or the number of routers that must be crossed to reach various segments. The newer and preferred protocol, OSPF, bases its routing calculations on the available bandwidth rather than hops.

Using the RIP protocol, all routing tables are sent to the neighboring routers every 30 seconds. RIP sends the entire routing table at each update interval. Using OSPF, a router that obtains a change to a routing table or detects a change in the network, immediately multicasts the information to all other routers in the network so all have the same routing table information. Unlike the RIP, OSPF sends only the parts of the routing table that has changed and only when changes actually occur.

These routing protocols exchange their tables with adjacent routers so each router on the network knows how to get a data packet from any one point to another. According to routing tables, any router on the network should be able to direct a packet either to the desired segment (if that segment is attached to the router) or on to another router that forwards the packet according to its routing tables.

Even with this table exchange, many possibilities can occur to keep a router from knowing which router to send data to. Therefore, a concept called the *default route* is used. Every router should be configured with a default route. Then, if a packet is received with a destination address that the local router does not have in its routing tables, it simply passes the packet on to its default route — and the receiving router deals with the problem. When designing a routed network, pay special attention to the default routes of each router. A data packet typically is passed on by a maximum of 16 routers (each segment of the route is a *hop*), before the packet is considered undeliverable and is discarded. When a client workstation is configured for IP, a default gateway address is usually defined with TCP/IP properties. When the workstation must send data beyond its local network, the data flows to this default gateway (the router); the workstation lets the router handle the process of finding the data's destination location. This approach is typical on a LAN where Internet access is required. Because Internet addresses always exist beyond the boundaries of a private LAN, a router is necessary to pass data to the Internet systems. In the default-gateway scenario, the router has a *local IP address* (a private address for the LAN) and a different *public address* on the Internet.

IP and IPX can be routed because their packets contain segment-address information — but not all protocols are routable. Some protocols, such as NetBEUI (used frequently in Microsoft networking) and SNA (Systems Network Architecture, used on IBM networks) are *nonroutable*. Such a protocol cannot travel across a network; if its data packets are addressed to destinations outside the local LAN, they are discarded.

Comparing bridges, switches, and routers

These three devices are not necessarily competing technologies, but rather complementary ones. The primary difference between the devices is the layer at which they operate. Bridges and switches are Data-Link-layer devices; routers operate at the Network layer. Some operational contrasts illustrate these differences:

✦ Segments connected by bridges all have the same network address; routers, by contrast, create *separate* network addresses for connected segments on the same Network layer.

- Where Data-Link-layer devices are used, packets do not contain addressing information to tell them when the destination device is located. When Network-layer devices are used, destination addresses are provided in the packet header.

- Bridges and switches are designed to connect LAN segments and to break up collision domains to provide more useable bandwidth. Routing information is not available at the bridge level, so routers are the devices that connect multiple networks. Thus routers divide broadcast domains into segments and enhance security because they can filter out packets according to protocol type or address.

Tip: One school of thought is to "Bridge/switch when you can; route when you must."

Gateways

A *gateway* is a device used to connect networks operating under different protocols. Gateways are task-specific — dedicated to performing a specific type of data transfer. For example, an older Novell LAN using just IPX as the network protocol might have a TCP/IP gateway device to provide Internet services. The gateway is directly connected to both networks. Incoming data is disassembled then encapsulated using the target network's protocol to allow transmission. Gateways are often required (or preferred) to bridge PC-based LANs with legacy mainframe equipment. Other common uses for gateways include fax services, Internet e-mail, and network management.

CSU/DSU

The CSU/DSU, or Channel Service Unit/Data Service Unit, is a hardware device about the size of an external modem. This unit merely provides a "translation" between the telephone company's equipment and the router. The router actually delivers information to the CSU/DSU over a serial connection, much like your computer uses with a modem, only at a much higher speed.

The CSU/DSU performs line encoding and conditioning functions and often has a loopback function for testing. Although CSU/DSUs look similar to modems, they are not modems since they don't modulate or demodulate between analog and digital signals. All they really do is provide an interface between a 56K, T1, or T3 line and serial interface (typically a V.35 connector) that connects to the router. Many newer routers have a 56K or T1 CSU/DSU built in. These interfaces are not interchangeable as a general rule.

A T1 line is actually a group of 24 different channels passing data in 64K chunks (time slots). Often, the cost of a full T1 can be justified if some of these 64k lines can be used to transport voice. In situations like this, the CSU/DSU serves to split the data channels from the voice channels. The voice lines can be routed to the telephone equipment while the data lines are transferred to the router.

ISDN Adapters

Integrated Services Digital Network, or ISDN, is an all-digital transmission service that has been around for over a decade. ISDN was designed not only to be a low-cost alternative to traditional T-carrier services, but also to provide acceptable speeds for video broadcasting. Although ISDN is becoming less popular as newer technologies (such as DSL) gain in popularity, many small businesses use ISDN because of its wide availability and better performance than analog alternatives. ISDN is an end-to-end network that allows simultaneous transmission of voice, data, and video information. With two full-duplex digital channels, Basic Rate Interface (BRI) ISDN provides high-speed connections for Internet access and other data applications. 128kbps is typical; up to 512kbps can be achieved with data compression. BRI is the version most residences and small businesses use. Primary Rate Interface (PRI) bundles twenty-three channels together, to provide speeds of up to 1,544 kbps. PRI is used mostly by larger businesses to connect their geographically dispersed sites together at costs generally less than T-line carrier services.

ISDN uses *bearer channels* (B channels) to carry voice and data. B channels occupy a bandwidth of 64 Kbps, although some providers limit B channels to a capacity of 56 Kbps. A *data channel* (D channel) handles signaling at 16 Kbps or 64 Kbps, depending on the service type. The signaling provides the process of setting up, maintaining, and tearing down communication connections.

To access ISDN service, it is necessary to subscribe to an ISDN phone line. You must also be within 18,000 feet (about 3.5 miles or 5.5 km) of the telephone company central office; beyond this distance, signal strength falls off and expensive repeater devices are required (or ISDN service may not be available at all).

In order to use ISDN services, special equipment is required to communicate with the phone company switch and with other ISDN devices. The most common of these devices is the *ISDN terminal adapter* (sometimes incorrectly called an "ISDN modem"). The Terminal Adapter performs the basic functions of creating the communication session and maintaining the routing of the data during transmission.

> **Note** The term *modem* really doesn't apply to what a terminal adapter does. No analog signals are present, so there is nothing to modulate/demodulate. Some people may have created the misnomer "ISDN modem" simply because *modem* was a familiar-sounding term and *terminal adapter* was not as familiar.

In a BRI configuration, the ISDN terminal adapter usually connects directly to a network-terminating device (normally provided by the service provider). The network-terminating device converts the signals between the ISDN device on the LAN and the signaling standards used by the local telephone company's switch. Additionally, this device takes care of ISDN line electrical requirements, powering the line and shielding ISDN equipment from power surges. The ISDN adapter can be arranged in one of two configurations: a short-passive bus to support up to 8 ISDN devices, or an extended passive bus to support a maximum of 4 devices at greater distances. In addition, a dedicated, internal ISDN adapter can be used to provide service to a single device. To reduce costs, some vendors have integrated the network-terminating device into their ISDN BRI adapters. Although suitable for the simplest of ISDN environments, this strategy is limiting since it usually prevents multiple devices from sharing a single ISDN line, a clear disadvantage for small office environments.

System-Area Network Cards

Much of a computer's communication performance is determined by how well it interacts with the network. Such interaction is critical for latency-sensitive applications, such as parallel programs that send frequent, short messages. Fortunately, networks have improved dramatically, especially system-area networks (SANs). System-area networks deliver high bandwidth (more than 1GB/second) with low latency. SANs are switched, with a typical hub supporting 4 to 8 nodes (although larger networks can be built by cascading multiple hubs).

A *system-area network* is usually a point-to-point, packet-switched collection of high-performance servers working together to achieve maximum performance and scalability. This concept, sometimes called *clustering*, has helped shape many advances in enterprise-wide distributed computing. These connected servers rely on new generation Network cards to maintain both performance and fault tolerance.

The new *system-area network cards* (SAN NICs) differ from existing high-performance NICs in several ways. SAN network adapters implement reliable transport service, similar to TCP, directly in the hardware. The network adapters use individual endpoints for transportation between cards. Each endpoint is usually represented by a set of memory-based queues and registers shared by the processor and the network adapter controller. By mapping the data requests directly to memory, processes can be performed directly by the hardware with no system calls and no intermediate data copying. SAN network cards provide bulk data transfer through a Remote Direct Memory Access (RDMA) mechanism. The initiator specifies a buffer on the local system and a buffer on the remote system. Data is then transferred directly between the two locations by the network adapters without CPU involvement at either end. Both read and write transfers can be supported. The remote address is prearranged through a message exchange making this a connection orientated, reliable transport. Figure 3-6 shows a universal SAN/PCI interface.

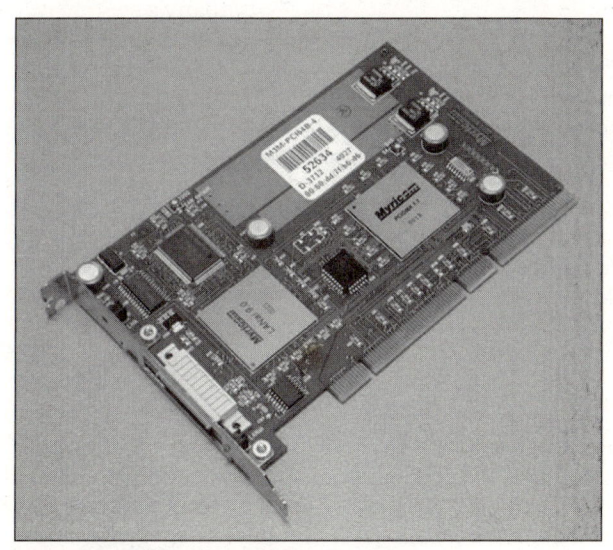

Figure 3-6: Universal SAN/PCI interface.

Wireless Access Points

As discussed in Chapter 1, the 802.11 specifications for wireless networking provides a special device called the Wireless Access Point, or WAP, that performs two basic functions.

As depicted in Figure 3-7, a WAP can be used as a bridge between a wireless and wired LAN. Because the two protocols are different (802.2 uses collision detection instead of collision avoidance), a standard hub or switch is not sufficient to bridge these two technologies.

> **Note** In Figure 3-7, the wireless clients are on the same subnet (that is, `192.168.1.x`) as the Ethernet clients. This is because the Wireless Access Point acts as a bridge and therefore does not create another subnet.

WAP devices can contain connections for just about any wired LAN topology to interconnect wireless and wired devices. Most vendors, however, only manufacture Ethernet products due to market demand.

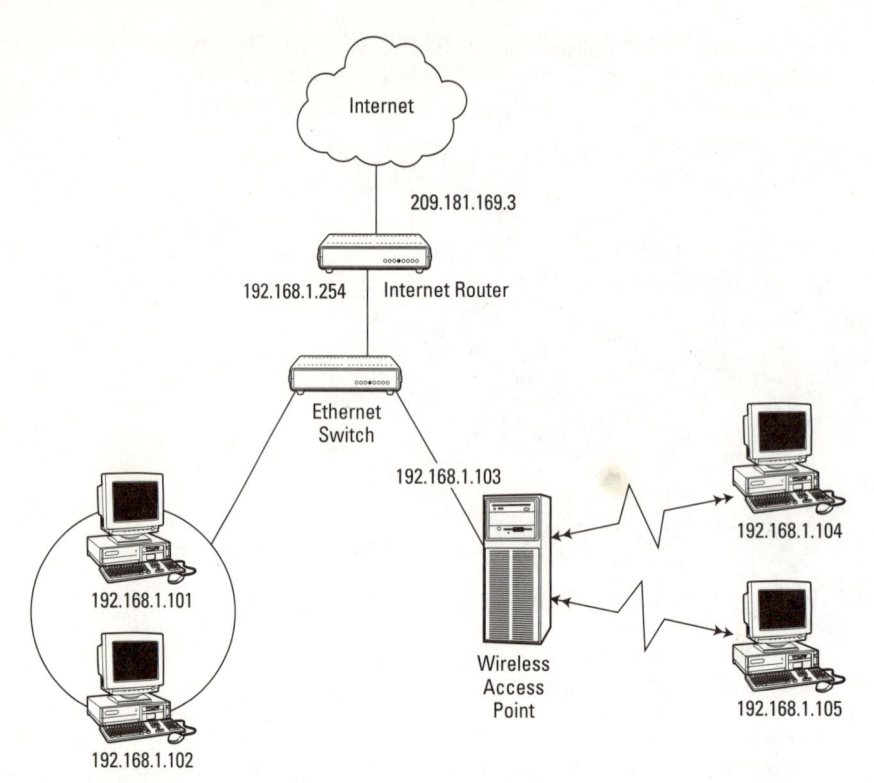

Figure 3-7: Example TCP/IP network with both wired and wireless clients.

The other use of wireless access points is to extend the overall reach of the wireless network. This process provides a *roaming* feature allowing mobile devices to move throughout a building without losing the connection to the network. The process is much like the cellular telephone technology; as mobile devices leave the coverage area of one WAP, the next access point picks up the signal to continue the connection.

> **Note** WAPs do not communicate with each other via wireless technology. WAPs can only communicating with wireless *clients*. Therefore, in a large, wireless LAN that uses multiple access points to extend the overall coverage area, standard cables must connect the WAPs themselves. Methods used to interconnect WAPs are often proprietary; just as often, an original 802.11b wireless NIC can't operate properly in such an environment.

Antenna placement and distance between wireless network nodes is critical to performance. Table 3-1 provides a rough guide to give you some idea of what to expect.

> **Note:** Most manufacturers' published specs are optimistic compared to the actual effective data rate you'll see. It's not uncommon to have an indoor range of less than 50 feet (in a typically constructed building) and to see speed begin to drop if you have a few walls between stations.

Table 3-1
Typical Distance Ranges Between Wireless Access Points

Range	Maximum Speed
Up to 100 feet	11 Mbps
Up to 150 feet	5.5 Mbps
Up to 300 feet	2 Mbps

Modems

Probably the oldest (and easiest) remote-connection device is the standard analog modem. Almost everyone who has connected to the Internet has done so with a dial-up modem. One of the most compelling reasons to use dial-up technology is its wide availability. In nearly any location in the world, a plain old telephone system (POTS) connection is available. Because remote communication by analog modem is still commonplace, you should be familiar with the basic configuration and troubleshooting techniques for these devices. Great strides have been made in the Plug and Play technology of modems, but many real world problems still require manually configuring the hardware and their associated devices.

Serial-port connections

Most modems utilize a serial port for communication. External modems are typically connected to the serial ports on the back of the computer. These ports are usually 9 or 25-pin connectors. DOS and Windows natively recognize the serial ports as COM (communication ports) 1 through 4. To avoid conflict with other serial devices, configure your modems to use either the COM1 or COM2 port. Internal modems typically create a new COM port when they are installed into the computer. If the system board already has COM1 and COM2 enabled as external connections, the modem must be set to COM3 or COM4. Unless both external COM ports are in use, it is wise to disable one of these ports to enable the internal modem to be configured as one of the first two COM ports. With Plug and Play devices in a Plug and Play operating system (such as Windows 9x /2000/ME/XP) internal modems automatically are configured for the next available COM port.

On non-Plug and Play systems like Windows NT, the COM port of an internal modem is typically configured with jumpers on the card, or by a software utility provided by the manufacturer.

Regardless of how you configure your modem's COM port, it is necessary to identify which serial ports are already in use before installing the new modem. Assuming that your COM ports are integrated in your motherboard, the safest method is to check the serial port configuration in the computer BIOS or CMOS setup screen. The method used to view and configure the serial devices varies from PC to PC, so you may have to refer to the motherboard's documentation.

In order to avoid conflict with other serial devices, make sure that the desired COM port is available for use by the modem. If you are installing an external modem, just make sure the physical port is unused and is defined as COM1 or COM2 in the BIOS setup. You should also set the speed of the port to the maximum permissible in your BIOS configuration.

USB (Universal Serial Bus)

Why an "up-to-date" serial bus? The answer is practical: Most serial-port technologies you are likely to encounter in legacy systems have a number of drawbacks, including difficult configuration, line interrupt-request (IRQ) conflicts, and performance issues. To address these, a number of new serial designs have been introduced. Rising to the top of the available options is the Universal Serial Bus, or USB. Almost all PCs and many network devices are being manufactured with USB capabilities. The USB specification (now at version 2.0) makes the promise of Plug-and-Play a reality. USB devices can be *hot-swapped* (added to and removed from the computer without powering-down the PC). In addition, a single USB port on a computer can be used to connect a USB hub, which in turn can support up to 127 devices. Clearly, for new external modems, a USB model should be seriously considered.

Basic configuration settings

Regardless of the type and connection chosen, all modems require some basic settings to operate efficiently. Before making any adjustments to your modem's setting, you should become familiar with install and configuration utilities provided by your operating system. Even within the Windows family, the tools and location of the modem settings vary significantly. This is true also with different versions of Linux.

After you have determined where to make modem changes in your operating system, several primary settings must still be configured correctly before you have a properly functioning modem connection. These are signal-timing and error-detection settings for the serial transfers; unless you have specific needs that require you to change these settings, use the defaults, which are as follows:

- 8 data bits
- No parity bit (here you would specify none)
- 1 stop bit

The last item to consider is the maximum speed of the modem itself. Analog modems all have the same maximum speed — 56 Kbps — although this speed can't actually be achieved in the United States (and rarely achieved anywhere in the world). In the U.S., the Federal Communications Commission (FCC) has limited the maximum data-transfer rate over standard voice-grade telephone lines to 53 Kbps. To achieve any speed over 33.6 Kbps, one of the modems in the communicating pair must be digital, which saves a step by eliminating voice-to-digital signal modulation. If both ends are converting analog signals to digital and back again, they can achieve a true through-put rate of no more than 33.6 Kbps.

Key Point Summary

This chapter looked at the hardware components that connect devices to networks — and networks to other networks. The primary device is the network interface card. Hubs and switches connect multiple devices in two distinct ways: Hubs serve as basic concentrators, unable to perform any "smart" operations on the data they transfer; switches can do basic routing by establishing direct connections between two previously unconnected devices. Accordingly, switching nearly eliminates collisions between data packets on Ethernet segments, greatly increasing LAN performance.

The bridge is a useful device for breaking up overpopulated collision domains on Ethernet networks and shortening the ring lengths of Ring networks. Routers are intelligent devices that combine two or more networks (such as private LANs and the Internet). To divide a connection line (such as a T-carrier line) into channels, a CSU/DSU is required.

ISDN is a lower-cost alternative for transmitting digital data between two points. Special ISDN terminal adapters are required to utilize ISDN. System-area networks are fast, clustered LANs that use special SAN interface cards and can perform all data transmission at the card level.

Wireless access points (WAPs) extend the overall coverage of wireless LANs, acting as bridges between wireless and wired networks. (WAPs themselves cannot communicate with each other via wireless protocols; they use traditional cables for that purpose.)

Although an age-old technology (by computer standards), the analog modem remains a perennial standby. Because the POTS system is available in nearly every location, analog modems are likely to be a mainstay in data communications for a long time to come. Modems are serial devices that can be installed on existing serial ports of the computer, or use more modern USB connectors.

For the exam, remember the following key points from this chapter:

- **Hubs and switches are the primary concentrators used on Ethernet LANs to centralize the network cables.** Hubs do not provide any routing (whether intelligent or not). Switches provide segmentation of collision domains.

- **Bridges learn where devices are located and prevent needless broadcasts from crossing LAN segments.** Although bridges are useful when a LAN must be segmented (whether to reduce collision rates or to meet the requirements of security or administration), switches are usually more efficient in this task.

- **Gateways interconnect dissimilar networks and network protocols.** For example, a gateway device with both an Ethernet connection and an SNA connection can provide mainframe access to a PC-based LAN. Common gateway products are used for Internet access and for fax services.

- **Routers are intelligent devices that interconnect multiple LANs.** When these LANs traverse distances beyond a single building, the resulting network is normally referred to as a *Wide-area network* or WAN. Routers "talk" to each other to determine what networks are reachable by processes called the *Router Internet Protocol* (RIP) or *Open Shortest Path First* (OSPF).

- **System-area networks are a point-to-point, packet-switched collection of high-performance servers.** As with clustering, these servers work together; as part of a single network, they can achieve maximum performance and scalability.

- **Integrated Services Digital Network, or ISDN, is a low-cost, copper-based telephone service that provides reasonably fast, all digital connections.** ISDN requires special adapter cards on each end for proper communications.

- **Wireless Access Points extend the overall reach of the wireless LAN.** Access Points do not communicate with each other over wireless protocols but rather they are physically connected together with cable.

- **For the foreseeable future, analog dial-up modems will play a continuing role in remote communications.** Modems are serial devices that use computer resources — serial (COM) ports — and although USB connections have eased the crunch on limited resources, analog modern equipment retains a foothold because it's widely available and less expensive.

✦   ✦   ✦

STUDY GUIDE

Assessment Questions

1. A small company has 5 PCs but never needed the benefits of connecting them together. They have decided to invest in a broadband Internet solution to share among the 5 computers rather than use separate modems. What hardware is necessary to complete this installation?

    A. USB modems using USB 2.0 specification

    B. Network interface cards in each PC, cables, and either a switch or hub

    C. A T1 router and a switch

    D. DSL Network cards in each PC

2. A business has recently expanded by adding a large warehouse to process new orders. The shipping office is located at the farthest end of the building, beyond the distance limits of its existing 100Mbps Ethernet LAN. Wireless is not an option, since machinery used in this facility would severely disrupt the service. Is it possible to connect this office to the primary LAN and if so, how?

    A. No. The distance prevents these locations from being connected.

    B. Yes. A T1 connection with routers and CSU/DSUs on each end.

    C. Yes. Wireless is ok because it is not susceptible to outside interference.

    D. Yes. Use a coax run between the hubs.

3. A growing company is experiencing increasingly sluggish performance on their shared hub Ethernet LAN. What benefit would this LAN receive by replacing the hubs with switches?

    A. None, neither device has a direct effect on LAN performance.

    B. The switches would nearly eliminate the number of collisions on the LAN making the network more efficient.

    C. The switch processes data at 100Mbps where hubs only operate at 10Mbps.

    D. Switches eliminate broadcasts that slow Ethernet networks down.

4. A company has determined that network security for the payroll department must be improved. They do not want any non-administrative access to the shared folders on the payroll computers — yet, removing these PCs from the LAN is not an option since they need access to corporate e-mail, printers, and other network services. What device can be used to accomplish this goal and how?

   A. A hub directly connected to the file server

   B. System-area network Cards that support VLANs

   C. A switch that supports VLANs

   D. Routers that support Virtual Private Networks (VPNs)

5. When researching switches, your company wants to ensure that data transfers happen as fast as possible — but they are concerned that overall performance may decrease if a network card goes bad. What switch features would you require to avoid this potential problem?

   A. Cut-through mode with automatic conversion to store-and-forward mode if a predefined threshold of errors occurs

   B. VLANs

   C. VPNs

   D. Automatic failover to a standby switch is a predefined threshold of errors occurs

6. When a bridge is added to a Token-Ring network to shorten the overall length of the ring, where is the routing information of devices on the non-local rings stored?

   A. In the DHCP server

   B. In the Bridge

   C. In each PC

   D. In the network card

7. A growing company needs high-speed Internet access but the lower-cost DSL and cable options are not available in their area. Therefore, they have elected to install a T1 line. To help offset the cost, they can strip 6 channels off to provide dedicated voice lines to their satellite office 100 miles away. What device(s) must they install to provide both services?

   A. A router a and CSU/DSU

   B. A switch and a CSU/DSU

   C. A bridge and a switch

   D. A router and a switch

8. What additional advantages will the company described in question 7 receive by installing this equipment?

   A. Reduced collisions on the primary LAN.

   B. The router can be programmed to provide basic security to the LAN by disallowing un-requested inbound data.

   C. Better security because the CSU/DSU will only pass analog data.

   D. Better performance because the CSU/DSU creates separate broadcast domains.

9. What is the primary difference between RIP and OSPF?

   A. The time-to-live and the cost to route a packet using RIP is determined by the actual number of routers between the source and destination. OSPF on the other hand calculates these values according to available bandwidth.

   B. The time-to-live and the cost to route a packet using RIP is determined by the available bandwidth between the source and destination. OSPF on the other hand calculates these values according to actual number of routers.

   C. OSPF is an older technology not standards-based.

   D. RIP is an older technology not standards-based.

10. A Network Engineer has been hired to find methods to increase performance of the WAN. Among the recommendations, he has suggested upgrading the routers to newer versions that use OSPF instead of RIP. Why would this increase overall performance over a private wide-area network?

    A. OSPF allows more hops between routers.

    B. The newer OSPF protocol works better with TCP/IP than RIP does.

    C. OSPF supports a mix of Ethernet and SNA mainframe protocols so LANs on both sides can talk to each other without an intermediate gateway.

    D. The OSPF protocol only sends changes to the routing table when an actual change has been detected.

11. You have been hired to assist your client in connecting their PC-based Ethernet LAN to their legacy mainframe computer. What device would be the best choice for connecting these two systems?

    A. A gateway

    B. A system-area network adapter

    C. An ISDN terminal adapter

    D. A router

12. Your boss has asked you to recommend a high-speed digital connection for a new work-at-home employee. The employee's home is 3 miles from the telephone company's central office. It is not reasonable to run new lines into the residential area; existing lines will have to be used. What technology can meet these requirements, and what special equipment must be purchased?

    A. Digital Subscriber Line (DSL) and a special DSL router

    B. A T1 and a router (since DSL doesn't reach 3 miles out)

    C. ISDN and a special ISDN terminal adapter

    D. Analog modem and a USB 2 port

13. Doctors in a hospital setting are feeling constrained by the current wired network. Each doctor has a laptop computer that they carry with them but are finding it too difficult to use because they have to plug and unplug the network cable each time they change rooms. It is not possible to eliminate the existing wired LAN however. What device can be used to introduce wireless technology into the hospital's network?

    A. The Wireless Access Point

    B. The Wireless Access Router

    C. The Wireless Access Terminal Adapter

    D. The Wireless Access Network Card

14. Each hospital corridor is 400 feet long. To maintain a minimum access speed of 5Mbps from any point in the hall, how many access points would be needed?

    A. 100

    B. 400

    C. 3

    D. 80

15. The hospital management wants to eliminate all network cables and convert to a 100% wireless LAN. Is this a practical solution?

    A. No

    B. Yes

16. What is the maximum number of routers that a data packet can cross before it is discarded?

    A. 3

    B. 6

    C. 16

    D. 32

17. In source-route bridging, what name is given to the discovery packet sent out to locate a new device?

    A. A Seeker

    B. A Ping

    C. An Echo

    D. A Hello

18. When a switch is in cut-through mode, why is it unable to intercept a corrupted packet and ask the sending device to resend the information?

    A. Switches cannot "see" the actual data.

    B. Switches provide only point-to-point communications.

    C. A Switch would need a firewall to perform error checking.

    D. The error information is located at the end of the data packet.

19. How many collision domains are created on a LAN with 3 hubs and 1 bridge?

    A. 2

    B. 4

    C. 3

    D. 1

20. What is the fastest speed possible between two devices using dial-up modems connected to USB ports?

    A. 56kbps

    B. 53kbps

    C. 48kbps

    D. 33.6kbps

Scenarios

1. Your company's primary line of business software is being upgraded and will require a significant upgrade in hardware. The company is taking advantage of this situation to overhaul the entire infrastructure. After performing an inventory of existing PCs and analyzing the amount of traffic anticipated during normal hours, management worries that performance may still be an issue after the PCs are replaced. Individual departments can share data locally, so the new software uses a large percentage of peer-to-peer communications.

The network cable system connects three floors, all wired with Category 5 (shielded twisted-pair) cable. All cables terminate to central hubs — one on each floor, interconnected with coax cable to the server room. What other hardware upgrade would significantly improve the performance of this network, and what would be the best way to configure its use?

2. A large company is expanding by opening a branch office in another city 100 miles away. Plans for the new office require 8 inside salespeople to spend a combined average of 4 hours a day on the telephone with the main office. In addition, the network engineers have designed a terminal-server process that does all data processing at the home office. Estimated monthly costs for telephone time total $1,800.00 using traditional, in-state dial-up connections. What communications solution might be more cost-effective and what would its hardware requirements be?

Answers to Chapter Questions

Chapter Pre-test

1. A network interface card (NIC) serves to physically connect a device to the network for data to be passed between other devices on the network.
2. IRQ, DMA address, and I/O address.
3. An active hub strengthens and regenerates the incoming signals before sending the data on to its destination. The passive hubs do nothing with the signal.
4. A switch can be introduced to create multiple, smaller collision domains which increases overall Ethernet performance.
5. Switches perform data transport using two methods, cut-through and store-and-forward.
6. Cut-through. This method only holds the incoming data packets until it has the full destination address then directly passes all remaining data on.
7. A bridge serves to break up collision domains on Ethernet LANs and shorten ring lengths on Ring LANs.
8. Broadcasts and multicasts are never propagated across a router because the exact destination (routing) information is not contained within these types of packets. Also, while bridges and routers can both be used to segment LANs to balance traffic, only the router can be used to filter traffic for security purposes.
9. SAN NICs operate on a peer basis at the hardware level requiring no CPU cycles, which provides low latency and submicrosecond data transfer speeds.
10. Antenna placement and distance between wireless network nodes is critical to wireless performance.

Assessment Questions

1. B. A network interface card must be installed in each PC with cables that connect to either a switch or hub. A Ring would be inappropriate in this situation because most broadband services are provided over Ethernet.

2. D. The easiest method would be to run a coax line between the LANs primary HUB and a new hub located in the shipping office. The coax line running at 10Mbps would be compatible with the existing 100Mbps LAN providing that proper hubs or switches are deployed that support a BNC connection.

3. B. The switches would nearly eliminate the number of collisions on the LAN making the network more efficient.

4. C. A switch can be used that supports VLANs. A VLAN is a specific group of computers that the switch treats as an "island". Only traffic originally requested from inside the VLAN is allowed to enter in (other than predetermined Administrative users). The VLAN still allows all outbound connections to be performed.

5. A. The switch should operate under normal conditions in a cut-through mode but be able to convert to store-and-forward mode if a predefined threshold of errors occurs. In addition, the switch should be programmable so it can shut down specific ports when too many packets are corrupt.

6. C. Unlike the transparent bridging used on Ethernet LANs, bridged Ring networks use source route bridging. With this method, each device maintains its own address list of all destination devices instead of relying on the bridge to do so.

7. A. A router is necessary to route the traffic outside the local LAN. A CSU/DSU can be used to channelize (separate the use) of the individual channels on the T1 line.

8. B. The router can be programmed to provide basic security to the LAN by disallowing un-requested inbound data

9. A. The time-to-live is determined by the actual number of routers between source and destination; that number also determines the cost of using RIP to route a packet. OSPF, on the other hand, calculates these values according to available bandwidth.

10. D. RIP sends routing tables to each neighboring router every 30 seconds and sends the complete table at each update interval. The OSPF protocol only sends changes to the routing table and then only sends them when a change has been detected. Because this is a private WAN, there are few changes in the routing (therefore OSPF generates much less routing-information traffic).

11. A. A gateway.

12. C. Although Digital Subscriber Line (DSL) service might be an option, ISDN is likely to be the better choice according to the 3-mile distance. Assuming ISDN is available, a special ISDN terminal adapter is needed. Because ISDN is a copper-based technology and can carry voice on the same line, this solution would not require new wiring in the home.

13. A. The Wireless Access Point, or WAP.

14. C. Properly placed, each corridor would need 3 WAPs since each one can cover roughly 150 feet at 5.5Mbps.

15. A. WAPs cannot "see" each other using wireless technologies; therefore the WAPs must be connected via cable. In addition, the 802.11b specification only supports 11Mb maximum throughput; a 100% wireless solution is unlikely to offer acceptable overall network performance.

16. C. 16

17. D. A "hello" packet.

18. D. The error checksum information is located at the end of the data packet. In cut-through mode, the switch looks at the actual data only long enough to identify the source and target destinations. Then it passes the rest of the data through without interruption. By the time the switch realizes that the data was corrupt, the entire packet has been passed through.

19. A. 2. Only the bridge can segment the possible collision domains.

20. D. 33.6. A 56K modem can achieve a speed higher than 33.6K if one of the modems in the communicating pair is all-digital. This eliminates the analog-to-digital conversion that slows down the overall transfer rate.

Scenarios

1. A company considering a hardware upgrade should pay careful attention to its existing hubs. If the hubs are still in use, they should be replaced with switches whenever possible. By simply replacing the switch for a hub and doing nothing more with the switch, the network will generally achieve better overall performance by reducing the number of collisions on Ethernet LANs and minimizing the number of devices per ring segment on Ring networks. However, the best option is to purchase switches that perform in both cut-through and store-and-forward modes. In addition, the switch should be configurable to start in cut-through mode and automatically switch to store-and-forward if an unacceptable number of bad packets are transmitted through a given port. Some of the better existing hubs can be stored away as emergency backup devices in the event that one or more switches would fail.

2. Depending on regional costs and how long a company is willing to commit to a given technology, T-line carrier service (or E-line carrier in European countries) could cost significantly less and provide dedicated point-to-point private lines between the two offices. With a router and CSU/DSU on both ends, part of the T1/E1 lines could be stripped off to provide high-quality voice-grade connections. The remaining channels can be dedicated to data transfer. Using terminal services, this should provide ample data bandwidth for acceptable performance. This scenario also offers the benefit of fixing the cost of data and voice transfer month by month (normally preferable from a budgeting standpoint).

Protocols and Standards

PART II

In This Part

Chapter 4
MAC and IP Addressing

Chapter 5
The OSI Model

Chapter 6
Network Protocols

Chapter 7
TCP/UDP Port Functionality

Chapter 8
Network Services

Chapter 9
Public and Private Networks

Chapter 10
WAN Technologies and Remote Access

Chapter 11
Security Protocols

MAC and IP Addressing

CHAPTER 4

EXAM OBJECTIVES

- Given an example, identify a MAC address
- Identify IP addresses (IP v4, IPv6) and their default subnet masks.
- Identify the purposes of subnetting and default gateways.

PRE-TEST QUESTIONS

1. What is a host's MAC address based on?
2. What are the two ways of resolving IP addresses to MAC addresses?
3. What is communication on a TCP/IP network based on?
4. How many classes of IP addresses are there and what are they called?
5. What does the subnet mask of a network identify?
6. When is a router required on a network?
7. What is the base of the hexadecimal number system?
8. What is the base of the binary number system?
9. What is the address range of a Class C network?
10. To make a network more manageable, what must happen?

✦ Answers to these questions can be found at the end of the chapter. ✦

Host Addressing

On every network, each host can be referenced and accessed in many ways — through name, Media Access Control (MAC) address or Internet Protocol (IP) address. This chapter focuses on referencing hosts by their MAC and IP addresses. Recall from previous discussions that a *host* is any device that accesses the network through a Network Interface Card (NIC). A host can be a client computer, router, printer, switch, or other device.

MAC addressing — basics

A host's MAC address is based on a 12-digit hexadecimal address. Usually, but not always, the MAC address is burned in the NIC through the use of a *Programmable Read Only Memory* (PROM) module, or the address can be burned into a special chip called an *electronic PROM* (EPROM). The MAC address is identified in the second layer of the seven-layer OSI model, the Data Link Layer.

Of the seven OSI layers, the Data Link layer is the only one that has 2 sublayers: the MAC Layer, and the Logical Link Control (LLC).

Although the MAC address is always used in networking, it cannot be routed. The MAC address is not routable for two reasons:

- It does not pass through routers (because of its position in the OSI model).
- It has no network address.

Hexadecimal notation

Hexadecimal (or *hex*) notation uses base-16 numbers — along with a simple alphanumeric numbering system — to efficiently represent up to 16 numerical places. (The term *places* is used because the numbering system starts at 0 instead of 1; including all the places from 0 to 15 results in 16 places.)

Converting hex and decimal

The process of converting hex to decimal and decimal to hex is simple. Hex uses the letters A – F to represent the decimal equivalents of 10 – 15, respectively. Table 4-1 summarizes the hex numbering system.

Table 4-1
Decimal and Hexadecimal Number Equivalents

Decimal	Hexadecimal	Decimal	Hexadecimal	Decimal	Hexadecimal
0	0	16	10	32	20
1	1	17	11	33	21
2	2	18	12	34	22
3	3	19	13	35	23
4	4	20	14	36	24
5	5	21	15	37	25
6	6	22	16	38	26
7	7	23	17	39	27
8	8	24	18	40	28
9	9	25	19	41	29
10	A	26	1A	42	2A
11	B	27	1B	43	2B
12	C	28	1C	44	2C
13	D	29	1D	45	2D
14	E	30	1E	46	2E
15	F	31	1F	47	2F

Once 15 has been reached, the next digit must be used — in this case, the number 16, which is written as 10 and read as *one-zero*, not as *ten*.

Table 4-2 shows the multipliers of 16 and their conversion to decimal values.

Table 4-2
Hexadecimal Multiplier Values

Hex	Decimal
10	16
20	32
30	48
40	64

Hex	Decimal
50	80
60	96
70	112
80	128
90	144
A0	160
B0	176
C0	192
D0	208
E0	224
F0	240
FF	255

In the hex number FF, both digits have the highest value possible. To go beyond 255, an additional digit must be used to represent a multiplier of the decimal value 256. Here are a few examples of three-position hex numbers:

```
100h(hex)= 256 decimal
200h = 512 decimal
300h = 768 decimal
400h = 1024 decimal
500h = 1280 decimal
```

Often hexadecimal numbers must be converted to decimal values. Here is a formula that helps to convert a hex number (with up to 3 digits, in this case) to its equivalent decimal value:

```
(256 * first digit) + (16 * second digit) + last digit
```

The following example converts the hex value 4A7 to decimal:

```
4A7 = (256 * 4) + (16 * 10) + 7 = 1191
```

Why convert from hex to decimal and decimal to hex? The answer is simple — configuration. While setting up a network configuration, an administrator may have to do such conversions several times to set values on network devices. For example, sometimes the MAC address on a NIC can (or must) be manually entered.

Resolving MAC addresses on a network

Addressing on a network can take one of three forms:

- **Computer names:** On a typical network, most users prefer to use computer names to communicate; computer names are far easier to remember than IP addresses. A computer name is the logical equivalent of an IP or MAC address.
- **IP (Internet Protocol) addresses:** Although users can (technically, at least) use IP addresses, customarily IP addresses are used primarily by applications to communicate with locations on or outside the network.
- **MAC (Media Access Control) address**: MAC addresses are the physical addresses of network devices and if users use computer names and applications use IP addresses, then computers and other networked devices use MAC addresses to access other devices on the network.

With three ways to address elements on a network, there must be ways to resolve each type of address to its equivalent(s). (This section is concerned primarily with resolving IP addresses to MAC addresses.)

Cross-Reference: For more about the methodology of resolving computer names to IP addresses, see Chapter 22.

Once a computer name has been resolved to an IP address, that IP address must be resolved to a MAC address. The two usual ways to resolve an IP address to its equivalent MAC address are via the Address Resolution Protocol (ARP) and the Reverse Address Resolution Protocol (RARP).

ARP and RARP

ARP is a broadcast-based resolution method — and because it uses broadcasts, ARP traffic cannot pass through routers. RARP requires a server for IP-MAC resolution and is most commonly used in Unix environments. Microsoft networks (on the other hand) use ARP exclusively to resolve IP addresses.

As an example of how the ARP process works, consider the following: When a user wishes to access a resource on the network using its computer name, the name is resolved to its IP address equivalent using WINS or NetBIOS. When the IP address of the destination device is known, the client then sends out an ARP request to obtain the device's (or the computer's) MAC address. When this process (which occurs solely through broadcasts) is complete, the client that initially sent the ARP request updates its ARP cache.

The following scenario details the ARP process for two clients on a single network segment.

Client 1 has the following configuration:

IP address 131.107.40.16

MAC address 00-3B-1E-34-B6-73

Client 2 has the following configuration:

IP address 131.107.40.19

MAC address 00-2E-6B-81-1D-4A

Client 1 wants to establish a connection with Client 2. Client 1 has used a name-resolution method to obtain the IP address of Client 2.

Cross-Reference Name-resolution methods are covered in Chapter 18.

Client 1 ARPs (sends out an ARP broadcast message) for the MAC address of Client 2. The ARP request is sent as a network broadcast and every client on the network receives the request; however, only the client that exactly matches the IP address responds.

When Client 1 sent the ARP request, the MAC address of Client 1 was included in the packet. When Client 2 receives the ARP request, the ARP table or ARP cache is updated with Client 1's information.

The ARP table/cache is a listing of IP addresses to the corresponding MAC address. By default, most Microsoft operating systems use a cache life of 2 minutes. During the 2 minutes, the ARP cache is checked to try to avoid sending out a network broadcast to obtain resolution. When 2 minutes have elapsed, the entry is flushed from the cache.

Client 2 responds to the request from Client 1 by sending its MAC address back, which results in both clients now having the MAC address of the other.

The ARP process is different when clients are on different network segments. Because the ARP process uses broadcasts, routers will not forward the broadcasts. Client 1 is located on Segment 1 and Client 2 is located on Segment 2. Router A connects the two segments. The following details the process between Client 1 and Client 2 in this situation.

Client 1 sends an ARP packet to Router A. Router A connects to Client 2 with an ARP request. Client 2 updates its ARP cache with the MAC address of Router A and Router A is updated with the MAC address of Client 2. Router A then updates Client 1 with the MAC address of Router A. Thus Client 1 and Client 2 have received the MAC address of Router A — and Router A has received the MAC addresses of Client 1 and Client 2.

Maintaining the ARP cache

You can update the ARP cache either dynamically or statically. The process described in the preceding section is an example of the dynamic method of updating the ARP cache. However, clients can create static entries in the ARP cache using the ARP –s command, which places an entry in the ARP cache with an indefinite expiration not subject to the 2-minute drill. This is useful when servers on the network that all clients access frequently (such as file servers or login servers).

Here are the more commonly used ARP commands:

- `ARP -a` displays the ARP cache.
- `ARP -s` creates a static entry in the ARP cache.
- `ARP -d` deletes a static entry from the ARP cache.
- `ARP -IP address` displays the MAC address of the entered IP address.

Composition of a MAC address

A MAC address is defined on the MAC sublayer of the OSI model's Data Link layer (Layer 2) and is only able to pass through network devices that operate on Layer 2 or Layer 1 (Physical layer). Data Link devices (such as switches, bridges, hubs, and repeaters) are designed to natively process a MAC address.

Cross-Reference: See Chapter 5 for more information on the OSI Reference Model and its seven layers.

A MAC address is a 48-bit number divided into 6 two-digit hex numbers. Each segment of a MAC address represents a specific identifier. The first three segments, or the first 6 digits of the MAC address identify the manufacturer.

Table 4-3 lists a few manufacturer codes issued by the IEEE (hundreds of MAC manufacturer codes exist).

Table 4-3
IEEE MAC Address Manufacturer Codes

Company	MAC ID
3COM	00 00 2E
Cisco	00 00 0C
Datapoint	00 00 15
IBM	10 00 5A

Company	MAC ID
Intel	00 00 4A
Madge	00 00 F6
SMC	00 00 03

Tip — Don't assume that the code listed in Table 4-3 is the only code assigned to a particular manufacturer. It's fairly common for a single manufacturer to have several such codes assigned.

The second part of the MAC address (the remaining 6 two-digit segments) contains a universally unique identity number assigned to each device by the manufacturer. Each manufacturer can assign 16,777,216 unique addresses. In effect, the device ID portion of the MAC address is like a serial number. Here is an example of a complete MAC address:

```
00-A0-CC-34-0A-3E
```

This MAC address, when decoded, identifies a network interface card from Linksys.

Note — Although duplicate MAC addresses should (supposedly) never occur, sometimes they do. On such rare occasions, troubleshooting duplicate MAC addresses can be tedious, taxing, and time-consuming.

If you wish to display the MAC address on your own computer, use the steps listed in Labs 4-1 (Windows 98) and 4-2 (Windows 2000).

Lab 4-1 Displaying the IP Configuration on a Windows 98 System

1. Access the Run box from the Start menu.
2. Enter WINIPCFG in the Run box and click OK.
3. A display box appears (see Figure 4-1) that contains, in addition to other IP configuration information, the MAC address on your network adapter.

Lab 4-2 Displaying the IP Configuration on a Windows 2000 system

1. Access the Run box from the Start menu.
2. Enter `cmd` to open a command prompt window.
3. Enter `ipconfig/all` at the command prompt to display the IP configuration of the workstation (see Figure 4-2).

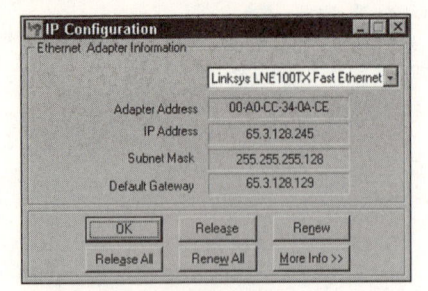

Figure 4-1: The WINIPCFG command displays the IP configuration on a Windows 98 system.

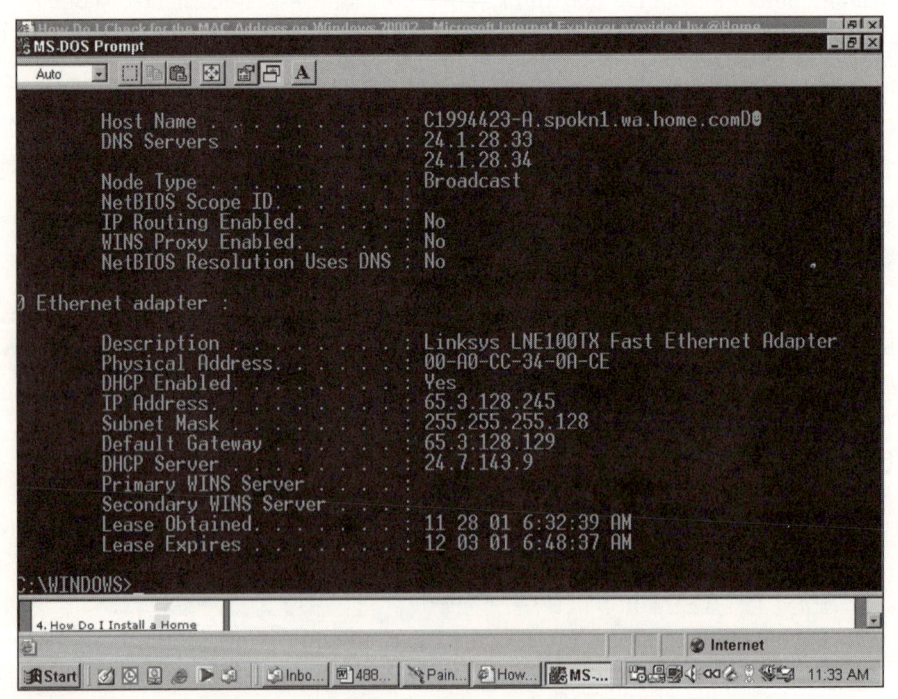

Figure 4-2: IPCONFIG displays the IP configuration of a Windows 2000 system.

IP Addressing

The native addressing scheme on a TCP/IP network is a 32-bit binary-based address (commonly called an *IP address*) divided into 4 eight-bit sections called *octets*. Octets are usually represented in decimal notation (for easier use by humans), and can represent a value range from 0 to 255. If you ever see an IP address with a number higher than 255, you are either in the middle of a test, or you are watching *The Net*.

Understanding IP addressing requires a solid knowledge of the binary system. many books that detail IP addressing and subnetting; at first glance, IP addressing and subnetting can be intimidating. Remember that all IP addressing and subnetting centers around two numbers, one and zero. When a numbering system only has two numbers, how hard can it possibly be?

Binary notation is a base-2 numbering system. In effect, every number used in an IP address can be calculated by using some combination of the powers of 2. The first step in learning IP addressing and subnetting is to understand the powers of 2; a chart is an efficient way to represent them (see Table 4-4). Exponent notation is nothing more than taking a number and multiplying it by itself a number of times equal to the exponent (for example, $2^5=2*2*2*2*2=32$). Table 4-4 lists the values of 2 raised to the power of x for the values 0 to 10.

Table 4-4
Powers of 2

Value of X	2^x
0	1
1	2
2	4
3	8
4	16
5	32
6	64
7	128
8	256
9	512
10	1024

Generally, knowing the powers of 2 through 2^{10} is sufficient for just about anything you'll do with IP addresses. In an IP address, the highest power of 2 that can be represented is 2^7. 8 bits per octet in an IP address: $2^7\ 2^6\ 2^5\ 2^4\ 2^3\ 2^2\ 2^1\ 2^0$. Placing a one in one of the eight value positions, effectively turns on (or adds into the value being represented) the power of two for that position. If the value of the bit is needed to make an IP address, that bit is considered turned on. Each of the eight positions in an octet represents a different value — ascending from 2^0 to 2^7, left to right, as follows:

2^7	2^6	2^5	2^4	2^3	2^2	2^1	2^0
128	64	32	16	7	4	2	1

Converting decimal to binary

Given that computers depend on binary notation to do their work, knowing how to convert values from other notations (in particular, decimal) to binary is useful. Fortunately, the computer itself provides a helpful hint: 1 means on, 0 means off. To convert from decimal to binary in the range of 0 – 255, you can use this hint (along with Table 4-4) to repeating a two-step operation: Find the highest bit value used in the number, and then "turn on" that bit value by placing a one in its place. Continue this process until you get a remainder of 0.

The decimal number 27, for example, can be converted to binary in the following manner:

1. Because the highest bit used in 27 is 16 (which is 2^4), place a 1 in the 2^4 position.
2. Because the value of 2^4 is 16, that 16 has to be subtracted from 27. This leaves a remainder of 11.
3. Apply the process of finding the highest bit value in 11. That value is 2^3, which is 8.
4. Subtract 8 from 11, which gives you a remainder of 3.
5. Find the highest bit value in 3. That value is 2^1, which is 2.
6. Subtract 2 from 3 and (again) apply the process to the remainder of 1. The only bit value that can have the value of 1 is 2^0. When you reach a remainder of 0, binary conversion is complete.

A compact summary of these steps:

27	The highest bit value used is 2^4, which is 16.
16	Subtract 16 from 27. Remainder =11
11	The highest bit value used is 2^3, which is 8.
8	Subtract 8 from 11. Remainder = 3.
3	The highest bit value used is 2^1, which is 2.
2	Subtract 2 from 3. Remainder =1
1	The only bit value that can be used with 1 is 2^0.
	Remainder = 0. Conversion complete.

Once the conversion is complete, the bit values that were used are turned on. When a bit is turned on, the bit becomes 1.

Thus the binary equivalent of 27 = 00011011.

When a bit is not turned on, the bit value is 0, and must be present in the binary number. The binary equivalent of 0, using 8 bits, is 00000000.

The binary equivalent of 255, using 8 bits, is 11111111 (128 + 64 + 32 + 16 + 8 + 4 + 2 + 1 = 255).

Converting binary to decimal

The process of converting binary to decimal requires only adding up the values represented by the bits in the binary number. For example, in the binary number 01011011, the bits represent the values of 64, 16, 8, 2, and 1, right to left. Adding these values should yield a decimal value of 91.

IP addressing basics

IP addresses have two parts: a network ID and a host (or node) ID. The length of the network ID (meaning the number of octets or bits used to represent) depends on the address class of the IP address.

The five classes of IP addresses are Class A, Class B, Class C, Class D, and Class E. Of these, only three can be assigned to hosts on a network: Class A, Class B, and Class C. Class D addresses are used for multicasting (a process that transmits a message to a fixed set of IP addresses simultaneously); Class E is reserved for experimental and future uses.

As explained earlier, each IP address has 4 octets. The first octet of each IP address identifies the class to which it belongs:

```
Class A networks have a range of 1-126 in the first octet.
Class B networks have a range of 128-191 in the first octet.
Class C networks have a range of 192-223 in the first octet.
Class D networks have a range of 224-239 in the first octet
Class E networks have a range of 240-255 in the first octet.
```

Yes, 127 is missing from the list just given — that's because addresses with 127 in the first octet are used for *loopback* addressing (a process that tests the internal configuration of the TCP/IP software and allows a host to reference its own resources). Packets addressed to a 127 address are treated as part of a loopback operation and are not placed on the network.

Once the network class has been identified, the network *address* must be identified. The following rules simplify the identification of the network address.

- ✦ A is the first letter of the alphabet. A Class A network uses the first octet of the IP address as the network identifier.

- ✦ B is the second letter of the alphabet. A Class B network uses the first two octets of the IP address as the network identifier.

✦ C is the third letter of the alphabet. A Class C network uses the first three octets of the IP address as the network identifier.

What these apparently simplistic rules mean is that Class A addresses use 8 bits (1 octet) to represent the network ID. Class B addresses use 16 bits (2 octets) for the network ID — and Class C addresses use 24 bits (3 octets) to represent the network ID. The remaining bits in the IP address — those not used in the network ID — are used for the *host ID*.

Regardless of the IP address, using the three simple rules just given should help you to identify the network address to be easily identified. To convert the network ID into its IP address, the remaining octet values (those not used in the network ID) are set to 0. For example, for the IP address 16.165.234.98, the network ID is 16.0.0.0. The IP address 16.165.234.98 is a Class A address because the first octet is in the range of 1 – 126, which means that only the first octet is used for the network ID.

Here are a couple of other examples.

The IP address 131.107.54.198 is a Class B address because the first octet is in the range of 128 – 191. Class B networks use the first two octets to identify the network address. The network address is 131.107; once the remaining octets are set to 0, the complete network address is 131.107.0.0.

The IP address 206.192.150.27 is a Class C address because the first octet is in the range of 192 – 223. Class C networks use the first three octets to identify the network address. The network address is 206.192.150; once the remaining octets are set to 0, the complete network address is 206.192.150.0.

IP addressing and subnetting

By applying a binary mask (called a *network mask*) and using Boolean algebra operations, you can extract the network ID from an IP address. Each address class has its own default network mask:

✦ **Class A:** 255.0.0.0
✦ **Class B:** 255.255.0.0
✦ **Class C:** 255.255.255.0

As explained later in this section, the value 255 — which represents the highest binary value (11111111) that can be represented in a single octet — is used as a filter to mask the network ID from the IP address. In a nutshell, anywhere a 1-bit occurs, the corresponding bit in the original IP address is used; anywhere a zero occurs, the corresponding bit is discarded and replaced with 0.

When converted to binary the default network masks are represented like this:

```
Class A    11111111 00000000 00000000 00000000
Class B    11111111 11111111 00000000 00000000
Class C    11111111 11111111 11111111 00000000
```

Subnetting and subnet masks

Subnetting is a way of organizing a network that is much like managing a large apartment complex floor by floor, instead of as one whole building. When you subnet a network, it is easier to manage each segment/subnet individually, instead of manipulating the whole network at once to meet the needs of a single part.

The trick to understanding IP addressing and subnetting is to understand the subnet mask. The subnet mask associated with an IP address does the following:

- Identifies the number of subnets/segments on a network.
- Identifies the number of hosts per subnet/segment.
- Identifies the subnet/segment address.
- Identifies the start and stop point for each subnet/segment.

A subnet is a portion of the entire network. The subnet is synonymous with segment. Without the ability to break large networks into more manageable sections, network administration would be an overwhelming task.

Each IP address class has a predefined number of hosts it can represent:

- **Class A**: 16,777,214 hosts
- **Class B**: 65,534 hosts
- **Class C**: 254 hosts

Can you imagine the difficulty in managing a network with 16.7 million hosts? A network that size would be unmanageable. To make the network more manageable, the network must be separated into subnets/segments.

Before a network can be segmented, the default subnet mask must be identified. The default subnet mask details how many hosts are allowed on the network. The first rule of subnet masking is that all bits used to represent the network ID in the mask must be contiguous. A contiguous subnet mask places all the 1s together and all 0s together. There can be no 1s between 0s and no 0s between 1s when the subnet mask is converted to binary. When the rule is applied, the following will be valid subnet masks.

```
255.0.0.0           255.255.0.0         255.255.255.0
255.128.0.0         255.255.128.0       255.255.255.128
255.192.0.0         255.255.192.0       255.255.255.192
255.224.0.0         255.255.224.0       255.255.255.224
```

```
255.240.0.0        255.255.240        255.255.255.240
255.248.0.0        255.255.248.0      255.255.255.248
255.252.0.0        255.255.252.0      255.255.255.252
255.254.0.0        255.255.254.0
```

A subnet mask written in decimal notation, such as `255.255.224.0` is called *standard notation*. Another way of representing both the number of bits used to identify the network ID and the number of 1-bits in the subnet mask is using the *Classless Interdomain Routing* or *CIDR* (pronounced as either "cedar" or "cider" depending on who you ask) *notation*. CIDR notation adds the number ones in the subnet mask to the end of the IP address notation, such as `255.255.0.0/16`, where the /16 indicates that 16 1-bits (the first 16 positions left to right) are used to extract the network ID.

For example, the following shows the CIDR notation for the default masks for each IP address class:

- **Class A:** `255.0.0.0=\8`
- **Class B:** `255.255.0.0=\16`
- **Class C:** `255.255.255.0=\24`

Converting Standard Notation to CIDR

To convert from standard notation to CIDR notation, convert the octets in the subnet mask to their binary values, count the number of contiguous ones starting from the leftmost bit; add that number with a slash to the end of the mask.

For example, the subnet mask `255.255.240.0` contains two octets that have eight 1-bits apiece. The third octet's binary value is 11110000. Thus the number of contiguous ones is 20 and the mask is represented as `255.255.240.0/20`.

Converting CIDR to Standard Notation

To convert from CIDR notation to standard notation, divide the CIDR value by 8 (setting aside any remainder for now), which yields the number of 255's (octets made up of all ones) in the subnet mask. The remainder (which indicates the number of ones not yet accounted for) then serves to calculate the value of the next octet.

Table 4-5
Value for Remainder Bits During CIDR to Standard Conversion

Remainder	Binary Value	Octet Value
1	10000000	128
2	11000000	192
3	11100000	224
4	11110000	240

Remainder	Binary Value	Octet Value
5	11111000	248
6	11111100	252
7	11111110	254

Here's an example of how this works when converting a CIDR notation of /26 to standard notation:

1. Divide the CIDR notation by 8. In this case, 26/8 = 3 with a remainder of 2.

   The number 3 represents the number of 255's in the subnet mask. So far, the standard notation subnet mask is `255.255.255.`

2. Using the information in Table 4-5, a remainder of 2 represents an octet value of 192. Thus the standard notation for the CIDR /26 notation is `255.255.255.192`.

Identifying the hosts

The second rule of subnetting is that 0s = hosts. To calculate the number of hosts per subnet, follow these steps.

1. Convert the subnet mask to binary
2. Count the number of contiguous zeroes in the subnet mask.
3. Raise 2 to the power of the result in step 2 and then subtract 2.

   Subtracting 2 sets aside the network (subnet) and broadcast addresses for the subnet, which cannot be used as host addresses. When all host bits are equal to 0, the result is the network address. When all host bits are equal to 1, the result is the broadcast for the network.

Table 4-6 shows the maximum number of hosts available when the default subnet masks are used.

Table 4-6
Maximum Number of Hosts by Address Class

Address Class	Number of Zeroes	Maximum Number of Hosts
A	24	16,777,214
B	16	65,534
C	8	254

> **Tip** The calculation of the number of hosts is the same regardless of the subnet mask.

Calculating the number of subnets

Another part of subnetting a network is to calculate the number of subnets available. The third rule of subnetting is that 1s indicate the presence of subnetting. To calculate the number of subnets for a given subnet address, follow these steps:

1. Convert the subnet mask to binary.
2. Identify the number of ones bits in the default mask.
3. Count the number of remaining 1s.
4. 2^X = the number of subnets, where X is the number of remaining 1-bits.

Take the Class A network address `16.0.0.0` that has a subnet mask of `255.252.0.0`. The subnet mask could also be written as a CIDR notation of /14, indicating 14 contiguous 1s at the start of the subnet mask.

If you apply the rules just given, the steps look like this:

1. The subnet mask `255.252.0.0` converts to
   `11111111.11111100.00000000.00000000`
   in binary values.
2. The number of 1-bits used in the default mask for a Class A network is 8.
3. The number of remaining bits in the subnet mask is 6.
4. Two to the sixth power is 64. (2^6 = 64.), which means that 64. subnets can be identified with this subnet mask.

Calculating the number of hosts

You can calculate the number of hosts available on a subnet by taking the number of 0s from the subnet mask after the subnet mask is converted to binary. If the CIDR notation is given, the number of hosts is easily found by subtracting the CIDR value from 32. The difference will be the number of 0s in the subnet mask. 32 indicates the total number of bits in the subnet mask; the CIDR is the number of 1s used in the subnet mask.

However, the same issue exists with hosts that you have with networks: you must set aside the network address (all 1s) and the broadcast address (all 0s) of the subnet — which means that you must reduce the number of host addresses by two.

The number of host bits available in the subnet mask `255.252.0.0` is 18 (32 – 14 = 18) and using the formula of $2^{18} - 2$ yields 262,142 ($2^{18} - 2$ = 262,142) hosts on each subnet of this network.

To take these calculations one step further: The total number of hosts available on the entire network is equal to the number of subnets times the number of hosts per subnet or 262,142 * 64 = 16,777,088, which is close to the maximum for a Class A network. The same process and calculations used to determine the number of subnets and hosts on a Class A network can do likewise for Class B or Class C networks.

Identifying subnet addresses

After a network is subnetted, each subnet takes on the characteristics (especially the addressability), of a mini-network. Therefore, for any given subnet mask, you must also identify the subnet address for each available subnet on the network.

The first step in identifying the address of a subnet is to identify the *subnet multiplier* — the incremental value of the network's subnets. Using the steps outlined earlier (see "Calculating the number of subnets"), you can determine that network 56.0.0.0/13 has 32 subnets available.

The subnet multiplier (also called the *increment*) determines the amount of increment between subnet addresses. To find the subnet multiplier for network 56.0.0.0/13, follow these steps:

1. Identify the last non-zero octet after the default mask bits.

    For network 56.0.0.0/13, the subnet mask is 255.248.0.0 and the last non-zero octet has a value of 248.

2. Subtract the last non-zero octet value from 256. In this case, this is 256 – 248 = 8. The multiplier is 8, which is the increment between subnet addresses on this network.

The last non-zero octet after the default octets is where the subnet addresses are located in the network address and where the increments for the subnet addresses take place. Here are the subnet addresses for network 56.0.0.0/13:

```
56.0.0.0      56.8.0.0      56.16.0.0     56.24.0.0     56.32.0.0
56.40.0.0     56.48.0.0     56.56.0.0     56.64.0.0     56.72.0.0
56.80.0.0     56.88.0.0     56.96.0.0     56.104.0.0    56.112.0.0
56.120.0.0    56.128.0.0    56.136.0.0    56.144.0.0    56.152.0.0
56.160.0.0    56.168.0.0    56.176.0.0    56.184.0.0    56.192.0.0
56.200.0.0    56.208.0.0    56.216.0.0    56.224.0.0    56.232.0.0
56.248.0.0
```

The rules for identifying subnet addresses are the same regardless of which class of address you're identifying. What does the subnet address reveal about the subnet? Most importantly, it specifies where the subnet starts and where it ends.

The address of the third subnet on 56.0.0.0/13 is 56.16.0.0. The next subnet starts at 56.24.0.0. Because each subnet has the characteristics of a network, each subnet must also set aside a broadcast address, which is one less than the next subnet address.

One less than 56.24.0.0 is 56.23.255.255 (and 56.23.255.255.0 is the broadcast for the subnet 56.16.0.0). The subnet ID and the broadcast address must be subtracted when calculating the number of hosts on the subnet — which is the reason for the minus 2 in the formula ($2^{subnet\ bits} - 2$) that determines how many available hosts a subnet has.

The IP addresses between the subnet ID and the broadcast address is a valid host address, even if addresses end with 0 or 255. The valid host addresses for the subnet ID 56.16.0.0 are as follows:

56.16.0.255	56.16.1.0	56.16.1.255	56.16.2.0	56.16.2.255
56.16.3.0	56.16.3.255	56.16.4.0	56.16.4.255	56.16.5.0
56.16.5.255	56.16.6.0	56.18.0.0	56.19.0.0	56.20.0.0
56.21.0.0	56.22.0.0	56.23.0.0	56.18.255.255	56.19.255.255
56.20.255.255	56.21.255.255	56.23.255.254		

Determining when a router is required

A router is required for communication for hosts on different subnets. To determine if hosts have the same subnet ID, follow these steps.

1. Convert both addresses to binary.
2. Identify the CIDR bits used in the addresses for both hosts.
3. Compare the CIDR bits in the addresses for both hosts. If the CIDR bits are the same, no router is required. If the CIDR bits are different, a router is required.

On network 56.0.0.0/11, Host 1 has an IP address of 56.41.26.10 and Host 2 has an IP address of 56.65.104.2. Do the hosts require a router for communication? Applying the rules yields the following sequence of steps:

1. Host 1 IP address in binary = 00111000 00101001 00011010 00001010

    and

    Host 2 IP address in binary = 00111000 01000001 01101000 00000010

2. Host 1 CIDR bits = 00111000 001

    and

    Host 2 CIDR bits = 00111000 010

3. The CIDR bits do not match, therefore a router is required for Host 1 and Host 2 to communicate.

Exam Tip This chapter offers enough details of IP addressing to provide more than adequate knowledge to be successful on the Network + exam. More advanced topics, such as supernetting and routing, are covered in detail in the *TCP/IP Bible*.

Summary

This chapter covered the fundamentals of addressing for hosts. Hosts are identified by two unique addresses, a MAC address and an IP address.

MAC addresses are 12-digit hexadecimal addresses used to identify a client's hardware address. The MAC address is typically factory set and cannot be changed. MAC addresses are not routable. MAC addresses are resolved by using a network broadcast called ARP or by using a server-based ARP called RARP.

IP addresses are unique 32-bit binary addresses assigned to each client for communication on a TCP/IP network. IP addresses are manually configured on each client or dynamically through a DHCP server. Each IP address has an associated subnet mask that details the segment/subnet of the network on which the host is located. The subnet mask determines the number of subnets and the number of hosts per subnet. In addition, the subnet mask determines the address of each subnet/segment.

✦ ✦ ✦

STUDY GUIDE

Assessment Questions

1. What is the decimal representation for the hexadecimal value 2E1?

    A. 325

    B. 988

    C. 123

    D. 737

2. What is the hexadecimal representation for the decimal value 432?

    A. 110

    B. 1B0

    C. 210

    D. 2B0

3. What is the decimal representation for the binary value 10101010?

    A. 170

    B. 248

    C. 84

    D. 4

4. What is the binary representation for the decimal value 120?

    A. 10001100

    B. 01111000

    C. 01010101

    D. 00110011

5. What is the IP range for a Class C network?

    A. 192 – 223

    B. 191 – 234

    C. 128 – 191

    D. 127 – 193

6. What is the network address for a host at 131.70.212.10?

    A. 131.70.212.0

    B. 131.70.0.0

    C. 131.0.0.0

    D. 131.70.212.256

7. How many subnets and hosts are available on the subnet mask 27.110.240.16/18?

    A. S = 512; H = 32,766

    B. S = 1024; H = 16,382

    C. S = 2048; H = 8190

    D. S = 4096; H = 4096

8. What is the binary representation for the CIDR notation of 16?

    A. 11111111 00000000 00000000 00000000

    B. 11111111 10000000 00000000 00000000

    C. 11111111 11111111 00000000 00000000

    D. 00000000 00000000 00000000 00010000

9. What is the standard notation for the CIDR notation of 12?

    A. 255.255.240.0

    B. 255.255.255.240.0

    C. 255.0.0.0

    D. 255.240.0.0

10. Which client will exist on the same subnet with 162.68.70.5/21?

    A. 162.68.86.5

    B. 162.68.90.4

    C. 162.68.71.160

    D. 162.68.112.5

Labs

1. Convert the following numbers from hexadecimal to decimal.

   44
   A4
   8A
   CA
   3CF
   6BE
   F5D

2. Convert the following decimal numbers to binary.

   17
   29
   38
   56
   65
   127
   160
   199
   208
   239

3. Convert the following binary numbers to decimal.

   00010001
   00011101
   00100110
   00111000
   01000001
   01111111
   10100000
   11000111
   11010000
   11101111

4. Convert the CIDR notation /18 to a subnet mask in standard notation.

5. Calculate the number of subnets available on the Class B network 131.107.0.0/26.

6. Calculate the number of subnets and the number of hosts per subnet for the network address 206.184.21.0/28

7. A network with an address of 131.170.0.0 has been assigned a CIDR of 21.

    Host 1 has been assigned an IP address of 131.170.201.63.

    Host 2 has been assigned an IP address of 131.170.207.10.

    Do the hosts require a router for communication?

Answers to Chapter Questions

Chapter Pre-test

1. A host's Media Access Control (MAC) address is based on a 12-digit hexadecimal address. The MAC address is burned into the Network Interface Card (NIC) through the use of a Programmable Read Only Memory (PROM) module, or the address can be burned into an Electronic PROM (EPROM).

2. The two ways of resolving IP addresses to MAC addresses: Address Resolution Protocol (ARP) and Reverse Address Resolution Protocol (RARP).

3. Communication on a TCP/IP network uses a 32-bit binary-based address.

4. The 5 classes of IP addresses: Class A, Class B, Class C, Class D, and Class E.

5. The subnet mask of a network identifies the number of subnets/segments on a network, the number of hosts per subnet/segment, the subnet/segment address, and the start and stop point for each subnet/segment.

6. A router is required on a network when the network has been subnetted or segmented.

7. The hexadecimal numbering system is a base 16 numbering system.

8. The binary numbering system is a base 2 numbering system.

9. The address range of a Class C network is 192 – 223 in the first octet of the 32-bit network IP address.

10. To make the network more manageable, the network must be separated into subnets/segments.

Assessment Questions

1. D. The decimal representation for the hexadecimal value 2E1 is 737. (2*256) + (14 * 16) + (1 * 1) = 737.

2. B. The hexadecimal representation for the decimal value 432 is 1B0. 432-(1*256)-(11*16)=0

3. A. The decimal representation for the binary value 10101010 is 170. 128+32+8+2=170.

4. B. The binary representation for the decimal value 120 is 01111000. 64+32+16+8=120.

5. A. The IP range for Class C network addresses is 192 – 223.

6. B. The network address for a host at 131.70.212.10 is 131.70.0.0. Because it is on a Class B network, the first two octets remain constant and the following two octets become 0s.

7. B. A network with an IP address of 27.110.240.16/18 has 1024 subnets and 16,382 hosts. This is a Class A network so the default 1-bits in the binary representation of the subnet mask will be 8. That leaves 10 bits (all 1s), which are the subnet bits. Subnets = $2^{subnet\ bits}$ = 2^{10}. Of the 32 bits in the binary representation of the subnet mask, 18 are 1s and the rest (32-18=14), are 0s. These 14 bits that are 1s are the host bits. Hosts=$2^{host\ bits}$ – 2=2^{14}-2=16,382.

8. C. The binary representation for the CIDR 16 is

   11111111 11111111 00000000 00000000

   All bits in the first octet are turned on, and are 1s; all bits in the second octet are also turned on, and are 1s.

9. D. The standard notation for the CIDR 12 is 255.240.0.0. All bits in the first octet are turned on, and are 1s; the first four bits of the second octet of bits are turned on, and are 1s. You must first convert these to the binary value of

   11111111 11110000 00000000 00000000

   and then convert the binary value to decimal as 255.240.0.0.

10. C. The client that exists on the same network with 162.68.70.5/21 is 162.68.71.160. They both share in common the first 21 bits of the binary representation of their subnet mask. Convert the standard notation of the IP's to the following:

    10100010 01000100 01000110 00000101
    10100010 01000100 01000111 10100000

    The first 21 bits are identical. Therefore they are on the same network.

Answers to Labs

1. The formula used to convert hex numbers to decimal values is as follows:

    `(256 * first digit) + (16 * second digit) + last digit`

    You should have converted the hex values to the following decimal equivalents:

    44 = 68

    A4 = 164

    8A = 138

    CA = 202

    3CF = 975

    6BE = 1726

    F5D = 3933

2. The binary values you should have yielded are as follows:

    17 = 00010001

    29 = 00011101

    38 = 00100110

    56 = 00111000

    65 = 01000001

    127 = 01111111

    160 = 10100000

    199 = 11000111

    208 = 11010000

    239 = 11101111

3. The decimal values yielded should be as follows:

   00010001 = 17

   00011101 = 29

   00100110 = 38

   00111000 = 56

   01000001 = 65

   01111111 = 127

   10100000 = 160

   11000111 = 199

   11010000 = 208

   11101111 = 239

4. The steps used to convert a CIDR /18 into a standard subnet mask notation are as follows:

   - 18/8=2 with a remainder of 2. The subnet mask is, at this point, `255.255.0.0`.
   - A remainder of 2 yields 192 (11000000).
   - The standard notation for a CIDR /18 is `255.255.192.0`.

5. The number of subnets available on network `131.107.0.0/26` is 1024.

6. For network `206.184.21.0/28`, 16 subnets are available — with 14 hosts available on each subnet.

7. Using the rules in "Determining when a router is required," you should get the following results:

   A. Host 1 IP address in binary= 10000011 10101010 11001001 00111111

   and

   Host 2 IP address in binary= 10000011 10101010 11001111 00001010

   B. Host 1 CIDR bits = 10000011 10101010 11001

   and

   Host 2 CIDR bits = 10000011 10101010 11001

   C. The CIDR bits do match; therefore a router is not required for Host 1 and Host 2 to communicate.

The OSI Model

CHAPTER 5

EXAM OBJECTIVES

- Identify the seven layers of the OSI model and their functions
- Identify the OSI layers at which the following network components operate:
  - Hubs
  - Switches
  - Bridges
  - Routers
  - Network Interface Cards

CHAPTER PRE-TEST

1. How many layers does the OSI model use to describe the concept of networking?
2. What is the Data Link layer responsible for?
3. What is the most popular form of error checking?
4. What is sequencing information used for?
5. Which layer is typically responsible for error checking?
6. On which layer(s) do routers operate?
7. Which layer is responsible for opening a connection with a target host?
8. Which device can, but doesn't always, run on the Network layer of the OSI model?
9. Which layer is defined by the IEEE 802 standards?
10. What type of addresses do routers use with transmissions on the Network layer?

✦ Answers to these questions can be found at the end of the chapter. ✦

Networking computers can be a complex undertaking; this fact is not new. Back in the 1960s, networking was a nightmare of gargantuan mainframes and huge bundles of cables running everywhere. With the onset of the PC revolution in the early 1980s, hardware got much smaller, and new standards sprouted up all over, proposed by companies like IBM, Commodore, Hewlett-Packard, and Sun Microsystems (to name just a few). A growing and bewildering variety of PC hardware began to appear, further complicating networking standards.

To try to make some sense of networking in general, in the early 1980s the International Standards Organization (ISO) released the Open System Interconnection Reference Model (or *OSI model*), which deftly categorizes all the pieces of a network into a reference model that employs a system of layers. The intent (and the achieved result) of the OSI model as designed by the ISO was as follows:

✦ To help network administrators determine which hardware and software to use for their chosen network implementation.

✦ To create a standard for hardware manufacturers and software developers that encourages the creation of networking products that can communicate with one another over a network.

This chapter discusses the seven layers of the OSI model and how they work together, as well as how the basic networking hardware fits into the model.

Networking and the OSI Model

The OSI model views networking from a modular perspective, making it easy to replace technologies within one layer as long as the replacement technology can properly communicate with the other layers. For example, most of the world can ignore the fact that NetBEUI exists and just go with TCP/IP, because both perform the same function on the same layer, only TCP/IP is better. The other layers don't care one way or another which protocol is used, as long as it works.

The OSI model refers to the packets of data passed between layers of the OSI networking model as *protocol data units,* or PDUs. (PDU is simply another term for *packet;* other references might call these *datagrams* or even *frames*.)

No matter what you call them, packets include not only the files being transported over the network but also a consistent body of information tacked onto the packet at each successive layer. This information, called a *header,* includes instructions on how to restore the file to its original state when it gets to the target system. As a packet travels down the layers toward the Physical layer, it is broken down further and further until it winds up in bit format, streaming across the network toward its destination.

As a packet passes through each of the six lower layers of the OSI model, a header is added to the packet with information to the peer layer on the destination system for reconstructing the data on its way back up through the layers of the destination network.

The following list shows you how the OSI model works, step by step. To visualize the example, match the steps given here with their corresponding numbers in Figure 5-1.

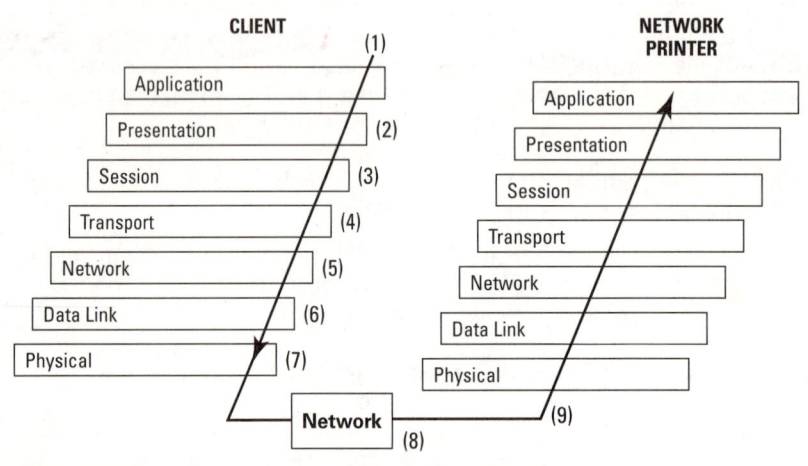

Figure 5-1: A packet on its way through the network.

1. An application requests a service, which itself invokes the Application layer.

   An example of this invocation is when a user clicks the Print button in an application such as Netscape Navigator, which then makes a request of a networked printer.

2. The Application layer makes a request in the form of a data packet to the Presentation layer, which packages the data in the proper format to be passed on to the Session layer.

3. The Session layer picks up a data packet from the Presentation layer and opens a communication session with the target network resource.

   Any security issues (such as a required password) are dealt with on this layer; then the packet is passed to the Transport layer.

4. After a communication session has been established, the Transport layer checks to see which media and protocols the packet will use to travel down to reach its destination, breaks the request data into pieces as necessary based on that information, and transfers those pieces onto the Network layer.

5. The Network layer receives data from the Transport layer, analyzes its IP address (also called a *network address*) to determine where it has to go, and then sends the data along the proper route to the desired destination.

   This layer also translates IP addresses into MAC addresses so the MAC sublayer of the Data Link layer knows where to send the packet after the packet makes it onto the host network.

6. The Data Link layer reformats the data packets as bits for the Physical layer and ensures that the data remains uncorrupted along its way.

7. The Physical layer picks up the bits of data from the Data Link layer and transmits these actual data bits over the network.

8. The packet is transferred over the network to the destination system's Physical layer, which transfers the data to the Data Link layer of the destination system.

9. The packet travels back up through the OSI layers on the destination system in reverse order, shedding header information until eventually it makes its way to the upper layers (where the file is printed, in this example).

See the following section for more info on the seven layers of the OSI model.

Seven Layers of the OSI Model

The OSI model (OSI stands for Open System Interconnect) breaks the concept of networking into seven main layers. As a packet passes from layer to layer, each layer adds a header to the packet with instructions for reformatting the file to the peer layer on the target network (the *peer layer* of a host system's Transport layer would be the target system's Transport layer). Table 5-1 shows the seven OSI layers from top to bottom.

> **Tip** The Application layer is the "top" of the hierarchical OSI model; Level 7; the Physical layer (the "bottom" OSI layer) is at Level 1. It may help you to keep the layer numbers straight if you envision the OSI model as a seven-story building with the seventh floor on top.

Table 5-1
The Seven Layers of the OSI Model

Layer Number	Layer Name	What It Does
7	Application	Requests and receives network resources or services from the Presentation layer.
6	Presentation	Reformats data for transmission to and from the network.
5	Session	Configures and opens the connection with the remote network resource.
4	Transport	Breaks data into pieces when transmitting data and reassembles the pieces when receiving at the destination.
3	Network	Routes data beyond a LAN by converting IP addresses to physical addresses.
2	Data Link	Packages data for transmission to and from the Physical layer.
1	Physical	Comprises the hardware, cabling, and other tangible accessories that are the physical attributes of a network; transmits, receives, and processes data as bits.

The following sections discuss each of the seven layers of the OSI model in more depth.

Exam Tip Of the seven layers described in the following sections, only the last four are covered directly on the exam. Although you should also know the basics of the "upper" three layers (the Application, Presentation, and Session layers), focus on the details of the last four layers (Physical, Data Link, Network, and Transport layers) for the test.

Application layer

At the top layer of the OSI model, the Application layer, the end user sends messages, saves files, retrieves data, prints documents, and performs any other actions within a network setting. In a perfect world, this layer is the only one the users would see. Instant messaging clients, e-mail, and print services are all examples of software that commonly requests network services at the Application layer.

> **Note:** The *applications* referred to in the name of this layer are actually *network services* such as FTP, HTTP, SMTP, and Telnet — not commercial software applications such as Netscape Navigator or StarOffice. Netscape Navigator, for example, frequently requests that network services make available the resources needed to provide Web pages, file downloads, and e-mail access.

Presentation layer

The Presentation layer reformats data for network transmission, in accordance with the direction the data is coming from. When receiving data from the Application layer, the Presentation layer formats the data into a smaller format with compression (if possible) and encrypts or decrypts the data as required. When receiving data from the Session layer, the Presentation layer reformats the requested data so that it can be forwarded on to the Application layer and then viewed and manipulated by the user.

Session layer

The Session layer does what it sounds like it does: manages sessions with remote computers. The Session layer also communicates with the upper layers in the event that there is a problem with network resources. When a user tries to print a Web page from Netscape Navigator and gets an error telling them that the printer is not available, for example, this complaint comes from the Session layer.

The protocols typically used on the Session layer are NetBIOS and remote procedure calls (RPCs). NetBIOS (not to be confused with NetBEUI) is an application-programming interface (API) that can run atop several protocols, including NetBEUI, TCP/IP, and IPX. RPCs, used widely by Microsoft in its Outlook e-mail client, allow remote processes to seem local to the user.

Transport layer

The Transport layer is responsible for organizing data according to the protocols and network media that lie between the data's source and its destination. The Transport layer performs critical functions in a transmission — including error checking, sequencing, synchronization, multiplexing, and name resolution. The following sections describe each of these concepts within the context of the OSI model.

Error checking

Three major types of error checking are used in modern networking: cyclic redundancy checks (CRCs), parity bits, and checksum calculations. The following sections describe these methods.

CRC

Many protocols perform error-checking operations at the Transport layer, although some protocols perform these operations at other layers, such as the Data Link layer where *cyclic redundancy checks* (CRC) on the data are performed. A CRC is a mathematical calculation performed on the data separately by both the LLC sublayer of the source system and its peer sublayer on the destination system. This calculation results in a unique profile of the data.

The following steps show how a CRC works:

1. The protocol on the source system performs the calculation first and attaches its results to the packet with a header. When the LLC sublayer of the destination system receives the data, it, too, performs the same calculation.
2. If the calculation matches, all is well and the header information including the calculation results of the source LLC sublayer is removed, and the packet goes on its merry way.

   If the calculation results don't match the results recorded in the packet by the source system's LLC sublayer, then the destination system's LLC sublayer cries foul and forces a resend of the file(s), which it assumes to be corrupted.

Parity bits

This method of error checking goes into effect after the systems have connected and the request has been made: The two hosts agree whether to use an odd or even number of parity bits. If (for example) the remote host detects an even number of parity bits in a frame but was expecting an odd number, the data is considered corrupt and is thrown out.

For example, if two packets are missing out of a total 353, that's 351 packets — still an odd number, so the parity-bit method assumes that the data is okay. Because this method can't do much to ensure the continued health of data packets, that burden shifts to the protocols that operate on the Transport layer. These protocols use more sophisticated methods to guarantee data integrity during transmission.

> **Caution** The "guarantee" that the parity bit provides in asynchronous transmission is hardly a guarantee at all: There's a whopping 50 percent chance that if any packets are in fact missing, the parity bit method won't catch it. This is because if an even number of packets is missing, the parity-bit *total* will still be even or odd, just as expected by the remote host — and the host will assume that the data is fine, even though it's actually corrupted.

Checksum

In this simple method of error checking, the source system counts the number of bits in a given packet and adds the result of this calculation to the packet as header information. When the destination system verifies the file, it counts the number of bits and matches that number against the checksum results recorded in the packet by the source system. If the number of bits matches, the header information is removed and the packet is sent to the upper layers of the destination system. If the number of bits does not match, the destination system forces a resend of the data, assuming it to be corrupt.

Flow control

When two computers talk to one another, often one computer will be capable of a much faster transmission than the other computer is able to handle. The Transport layer uses *flow control* to allow communication between two computers.

> **In the Real World**
>
> When you surf the Internet and download a file, your computer is usually operating at lower speeds than the server you're downloading the file from. Especially with 56 Kbps and (shudder) slower dial-up connections, your computer's modem is typically capable of downloading at only 56 Kbps *at best*. (The server could give the file to you in an instant if your computer were using a cable modem or some other broadband solution.) To avoid slamming your modem with more than it can handle, your computer negotiates with the server you're downloading from; both agree on a rate that your system can handle (again, with dial-up not much more than 53 Kbps) and the download proceeds at that slower speed. If your computer uses a cable modem, it can download at up to 50 times that speed; case, flow control would allow the transfer at that higher speed.

Flow control can be implemented in either hardware or software. The hardware method, RTC/CTS (Ready To Send/Clear To Send), involves two wires on a modem: the RTS and the CTS. The receiving system simply uses its CTS wire to indicate to the sending server when it's ready to receive data and when it's not. The software solution, XON/XOFF (which means *transmit ON, transmit OFF*) sends a control signal to the sending host letting it know when to start and stop sending data.

The following two major types of flow control are used in modern networking:

- ✦ Guaranteed flow control — In this type of flow control, computers agree on the time span that the transfer will take place.

- ✦ Window flow control — In this type of flow control, the receiving host uses a buffer to store data in until it has time to process it. You can set the size of the buffer in one of two ways:

    - **Manually:** This type of setting is called a *static window*.
    - **Dynamically:** A dynamic setting that depends on network load is called a *dynamic window*.

        Devices that use dynamic windows respond to sudden surges in workload by sending *choke packets* to the sending server to tell it to stop sending data until the receiving server can catch up.

Multiplexing

Multiplexing allows multiple applications to use the same data stream to transfer data using ports.

> **Cross-Reference**: See Chapter 7 for more information on ports and protocols.

Name resolution

Name resolution — associating network locations with their assigned names — is a big responsibility of the Transport layer.

> **Cross-Reference**: See Chapter 8 for more information on DNS, the most commonly used name-resolution protocol.

Sequencing

As packets pass from the initiating system's upper layers to that system's Transport layer, services on this Transport layer break the data into smaller pieces and add sequencing information to the packet with instructions for the destination system's Transport layer on how to put the packet back together in the proper sequence. The destination system's Transport layer removes the sequencing header from the packet after properly reassembling it and then sends the packet on to the upper layers of the destination system.

Figure 5-2 shows a simple example of how sequencing works as a packet passes through the destination system's Transport layer and is restored to its proper sequential order. Note that the Transport layer also removes the sequencing information from the packet as it passes through the Transport layer.

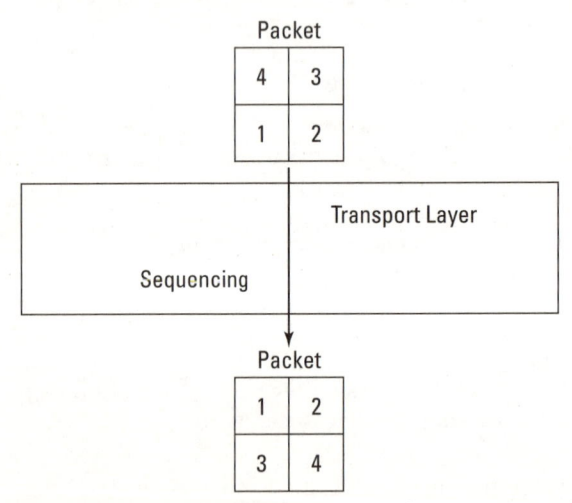

```
        Packet
       ┌─────┬─────┐
       │  4  │  3  │
       ├─────┼─────┤
       │  1  │  2  │
       └─────┴─────┘
              │
              ▼
┌────────────────────────────────────┐
│              Transport Layer       │
│   Sequencing                       │
└────────────────────────────────────┘
              │
              ▼
        Packet
       ┌─────┬─────┐
       │  1  │  2  │
       ├─────┼─────┤
       │  3  │  4  │
       └─────┴─────┘
```

Figure 5-2: A packet being sequenced into proper order by the Transport layer.

Synchronization

Synchronization of two computers is the process of getting two computers timed to operate accurately with each other before opening a transmission session between them. The following types of synchronization happen at the Data Link layer:

+ **Asynchronous transmission:** Similar to bit synchronization (described in the "The Physical layer" section later in this chapter), asynchronous transmission uses a start bit and a stop bit to set up a transmission session with a remote host. Asynchronous transmission goes one step further than bit synchronization, though, by adding an extra bit called a *parity bit* (described earlier in this chapter) to help guarantee (sort of) the integrity of the data after transfer.

+ **Isochronous transmission:** This type of transmission uses a third-party device to process data. One host fills in an available time slot in the third-party device, which distributes the data itself to the destination.

+ **Synchronous transmission:** This type of transmission includes time information with the data packet as a way of forcing both source and destination hosts to use the same clock. Synchronous transmissions use cyclic redundancy checks, or CRCs (CRCs are discussed in the "Error checking with CRC" section earlier in this chapter) to ensure the continued health of a given data packet. Although using this method can be a complex undertaking, it offers the following advantages over the other two types of transmission:

  • Greater security over asynchronous transmission by using CRCs.

  • More reliability than isochronous transmission. With isochronous transmission, you put all your proverbial eggs in one basket (or device). If that device fails, you've got no network because your Data Link layer is set up to talk to that particular device, not the destination system itself, as is the case with the other two types of transmission.

  • Less overhead than asynchronous transmission. Adding parity bits to data packets can increase file size, slowing down the network.

Network layer

Routing is the process of moving data from one network segment to another, and this is the main function of the Network layer. When two or more independent networks are successfully linked, the result is called an *internetwork* — a bunch of routers that point to each other using IP addresses — and internetworks are the domain of the Network layer.

Cross-Reference: See Chapter 3 for more information on the major networking hardware components, including routers and bridges.

The process involved in creating an internetwork is similar to the process in which bridges (which are part of the Data Link layer) handle LAN traffic, only on a much wider scale. Although a typical medium-sized LAN is made up of at least two network segments, an entire LAN is itself considered a network segment on an internetwork. Figure 5-3 shows an example of an internetwork made up of two LANs connected by routers into a small internetwork.

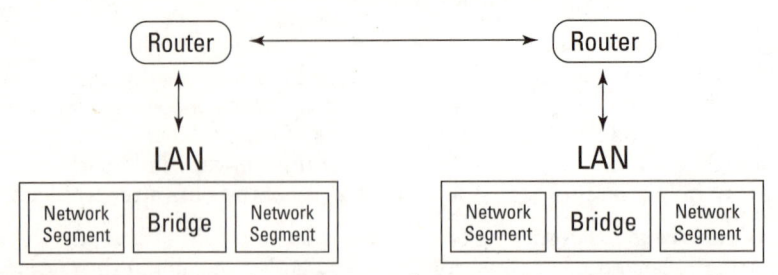

Figure 5-3: Two LANs become network segments in an internetwork.

In the Real World

The most visible example of an internetwork is the Internet, which uses thousands upon thousands of routers and IP addresses to allow the internetworking of computers worldwide.

Data Link layer

The Data Link layer is responsible for transferring information between network segments of a LAN. The Data Link layer must defer to the Network layer to go beyond the LAN; when going out to the Internet, for example. In the context of a local area network (LAN), the Data Link layer can handle all the communications that would be handled by the Network layer in the context of a wide area network, or WAN (WANs are discussed in Chapter 11).

The main duties of the Data Link layer include the following:

✦ Formatting data into bits for sending over the Physical layer.

✦ Sending the data over the Physical layer.

✦ Ensuring the integrity of the data before and after transmission of the data (although this duty is often handled by the Transport layer).

The Data Link layer is made up of two independent sublayers: the LLC (logical link sublayer) and the MAC (media access control) sublayers. Figure 5-4 shows how the LLC and MAC sublayers fit into the overall OSI model.

As you can see from the figure, the MAC sublayer sits closest to the Physical layer and the LLC sublayer sits on top of that, directly underneath the Network layer. When the Data Link layer receives packets for the Physical layer, it formats that data into binary digit, or *bit,* form for transmission over the network; as it sends the bits off over the Physical layer, it attaches instructions to the Data Link layer on the destination system so that the destination Data Link layer can properly reconstruct the data.

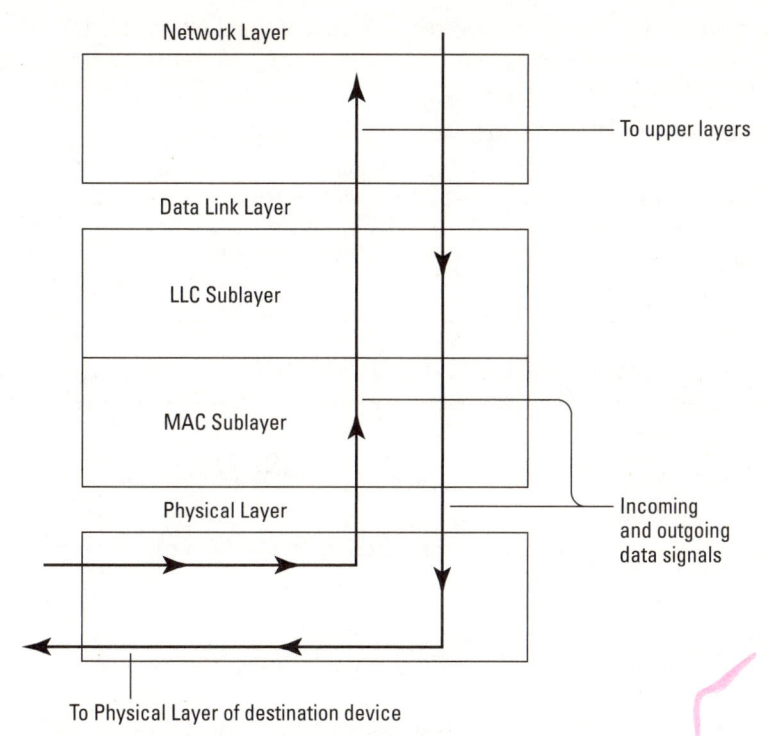

```
                    Network Layer
                ┌─────────────────────┐
                │                     │
                │                     │────── To upper layers
                │                     │
                └─────────────────────┘
                    Data Link Layer
                ┌─────────────────────┐
                │    LLC Sublayer     │
                │                     │
                └─────────────────────┘
                ┌─────────────────────┐
                │    MAC Sublayer     │
                │                     │
                └─────────────────────┘
                    Physical Layer
                ┌─────────────────────┐
                │                     │────── Incoming
                │                     │       and outgoing
                │                     │       data signals
                └─────────────────────┘
              To Physical Layer of destination device
```

Figure 5-4: The LLC and MAC sublayers of the Data Link layer.

LLC (Logical Link Control) sublayer

The LLC sublayer is defined in the IEEE 802.1 and 802.2 standard (which is discussed in the preceding section) and is not dependent on any one topology. The LLC layer provides the following services:

✦ Transmitting data using both connectionless and connection-oriented services.

> **In the Real World**
> Connectionless services allow faster networks because they don't involve the extended error checking that connection-oriented services do. Connectionless services are often used at the LLC layer because the Transport layer does its own, better error-checking anyway, and so any error-checking at the LLC sublayer is redundant, in any case.

✦ Acknowledging, sequencing, and controlling data traffic.

✦ Flow control of data between network devices running at different speeds.

✦ Establishing, maintaining, and terminating links to remote resources.

✦ Connecting Network layer protocols to MAC sublayer protocols.

✦ Checking for corrupted data and forcing the data to be resent in case corruption is found.

Note: See Chapter 1 for more information on the IEEE 802.2 standard and the LLC.

MAC (media access control) sublayer

Each NIC card is assigned a MAC (media access control) address, and the MAC sublayer of the Data Link layer uses these addresses to route the data to its destination. The MAC sublayer sits just above the Physical layer and works directly with the NICs (Network Interface Cards) on the Physical layer.

The following list describes how the MAC sublayer works:

1. When receiving packets from the LLC sublayer, the MAC sublayer determines the media, electronic signals, and MAC addresses that will be required to get the packet to its destination.
2. The MAC sublayer reformats the data based on what it found out in step 1.
3. The MAC sublayer then listens in on the network to make sure that all's quiet, and when it's sure the coast is clear it sends the packet over the network via the Physical layer.

Cross-Reference: MAC addresses are discussed at length in Chapter 4.

Sometimes, even if the MAC sublayer thinks the network is quiet, another device on the network may have thought the network was quiet, too, and in these cases both devices can sometimes send their signals simultaneously, resulting in a *collision*. The MAC sublayer responds to a collision by using CSMA/CD (Carrier Sense Multiple Access with Collision Detection), which is defined in the IEEE 802.3 specification. CSMA/CD uses what is commonly called a *backoff algorithm* to calculate a random amount of time for each device and then instructs both devices to try sending their data again at these randomly generated future times.

IEEE and the Data Link layer

The Data Link layer is itself further defined by the IEEE (Institute of Electronics and Electrical Engineers) 802 standards. The 802 project (so named for the date the standard was created: February 1980) was designed to assist hardware manufacturers in making hardware that could communicate across networks regardless of brand. Not all networking hardware is made in strict compliance to the 802 standards, but most modern hardware is fully compliant. Table 5-2 shows the major IEEE 802 specifications.

Exam Tip: The 802.6, 802.7, 802.8, 802.9, 802.10, and 802.11 standards are *outside* the Data Link layer.

Cross-Reference: See Chapter 1 for more information on the IEEE standards that you must know about for the exam: 802.2, 802.3, and 80.5.

Table 5-2
The 802 Specifications

Number	Description
802.1	Specifications for the Physical and Data Link layers, as well as standards for the internetworking on LANs and WANs.
802.2	The Logical Link Control (LLC) sublayer of the Data Link layer.
802.3	The main Ethernet standard, which runs at 10 Mbps.
802.3u	This substandard defines Fast Ethernet, which runs at 100 Mbps.
802.4	Interfaces, media, and topology for token bus networks.
802.5	Interfaces, media, and topology for token ring networks.
802.6	Metropolitan Area Network (MAN)
802.7	Broadband technologies
802.8	Fiber Optics
802.9	Integrated Voice/Data networks
802.10	LAN Security
802.11	Wireless networking
802.12	High-speed networks (such as 100VG and 100VG-AnyLAN)

Physical layer

When a packet of data is transferred over a network, at some point that data must physically be transferred from one location to another. The Physical layer encompasses all networking hardware involved in this process of physically moving data, including (but by no means limited to) cabling, connectors, terminators, hubs, and network interface cards (NICs), along which information passes en route from the source computer to the destination computer.

> **Cross-Reference**
> Some hardware resides on layers above the Physical layer; bridges reside on the Data Link layer and routers are part of the Network layer. See the next section for more information on how the major networking components fit into the OSI model; see Part I for more info on the basic networking hardware.

For the exam, you need to identify which of the major components of the Physical layer of the OSI model are associated with the major types of networking components. The following list shows where the major network components fit within the OSI model:

- **Bridges:** Bridges (and brouters, which are bridges that can also act as routers) connect network segments of a LAN by using MAC addresses to determine where to send data packets. Bridges are incapable of transmitting beyond a LAN, however, and as such these devices only operate on the Physical and Data Link layers of the OSI model. Bridges are discussed in detail in Chapter 3.

- **Hubs and repeaters:** Hubs and repeaters operate at the Physical layer of the OSI model; all they do is collect and redistribute data in its current form. They do no repackaging, sniffing, error protection, or other higher-level procedures. In effect, hubs and repeaters are just glorified wire connectors for all the upper layers of the OSI model.

- **Network Interface Cards:** The NIC operates at the Physical layer of the OSI model. Bridges, which connect network segments within a LAN, take information from NICs — namely their MAC address — and use this information to route packets to their appropriate destinations.

- **Routers:** Routers direct traffic over internetworks, and for this reason routers are considered part of the Network layer of the OSI model.

- **Switches:** Switches are really nothing more than one-way bridges with multiple ports; as such, switches work on the same two layers as bridges: the Physical and Data Link layers.

Cross-Reference: See Chapter 3 for more information on the major networking components.

Protocols and the OSI model

The OSI model puts many of the assorted protocols into a logical structure that helps you keep the various protocols, and particularly which talk to whom and why, straight in your mind. Figure 5-5 shows you where the most common protocols reside on the various OSI layers.

As you can see from the figure, three major groups of protocols exist: application, transport, and network protocols.

Cross-Reference: See Chapter 6 and later chapters in this part for more information on protocols.

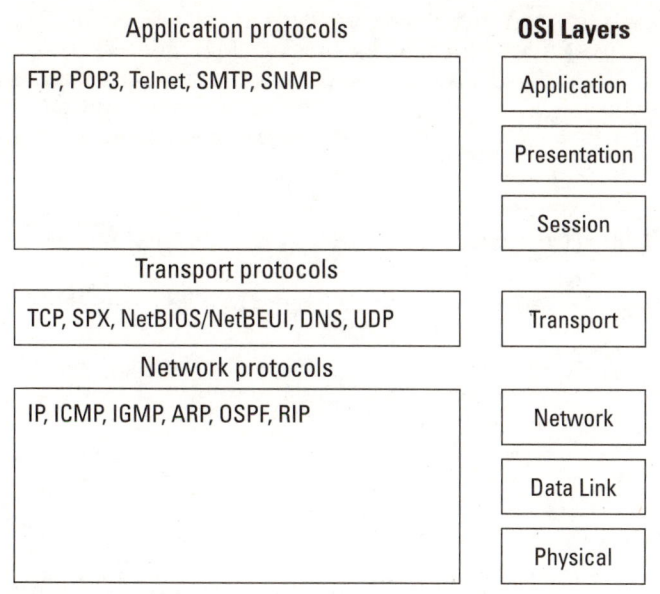

Application protocols	OSI Layers
FTP, POP3, Telnet, SMTP, SNMP	Application
	Presentation
	Session
Transport protocols	
TCP, SPX, NetBIOS/NetBEUI, DNS, UDP	Transport
Network protocols	
IP, ICMP, IGMP, ARP, OSPF, RIP	Network
	Data Link
	Physical

Figure 5-5: The major protocols and their contexts within the OSI layers.

Summary

This chapter has described the OSI model and shown you how to identify the following:

- The seven layers of the OSI model and their functions
- How the IEEE standards relate to the OSI model
- Which hardware resides on which layer of the OSI model
- Which protocols reside on which layer of the OSI model

✦ ✦ ✦

STUDY GUIDE

Assessment Questions

1. Which of the following layers does not add a header to a data packet?

    A. Application

    B. Transport

    C. Session

    D. Physical

2. Which of the following layers accepts data from the Presentation layer?

    A. Application

    B. Transport

    C. Session

    D. A and C

3. Which of the following is not one of the seven OSI layers?

    A. The Logical Link Control layer

    B. The Session layer

    C. The Transport layer

    D. The Data Link layer

4. True or False: Most error checking goes on in the LLC sublayer of the Data Link layer.

5. Which of the following layers is the last layer that a packet sees when leaving the source system?

    A. Network

    B. Session

    C. Data Link

    D. Physical

6. Which of the following is a sublayer of the Data Link layer?

    A. Network

    B. Transport

    C. Logical Link Control

    D. Session

7. Which of the following layers is designated as Layer 7 of the OSI model?

    A. Application

    B. Transport

    C. Session

    D. Data Link

8. The SMTP protocol operates on which of the following layers of the OSI model? *(Simple Mail Transfer Protocol)*

    A. Application

    B. Transport

    C. Data Link

    D. Physical

9. Which of the following types of error checking is wrong 50 percent of the time if packets are lost in the process of transmission?

    A. CRC

    B. Parity bit

    C. Checksum

    D. Telnet

10. What kind of flow control specifies the amount of data for the sending system to send before stopping for the receiving host to catch up?

    A. Window

    B. Guaranteed

    C. Parity bit

    D. CRC

11. True or False? Synchronization describes the process of putting received data packets back into their proper order.

12. Which of the following IEEE 802 standards defines Fast Ethernet?

    A. 802.2

    B. 802.3u

    C. 802.11

    D. 802.12

13. Which of the following IEEE 802 standards is not part of the Data Link layer?

    A. 802.2 — Ether Physical

    B. 802.4 } Token Ring

    C. 802.5

    D. 802.8 — ?

14. Which of the following IEEE 802 standards defines the LLC sublayer of the Data Link layer?

    A. 802.1

    B. 802.2

    C. 802.3

    D. 802.12

15. Which of the following protocols is not an application protocol according to the OSI model?

    A. SMTP

    B. SNMP

    C. POP3

    D. IGMP

16. Which of the following types of hardware operates on the Network layer of the OSI model?

    A. Routers

    B. Switches

    C. Bridges

    D. NICs

17. Which of the following layers of the OSI model do brouters operate on?

    A. Physical

    B. Data Link

    C. A and B

    D. Transport

18. A LAN is considered what part of an internetwork?

    A. A router

    B. A network node

    C. A network bridge

    D. A network segment

19. True or False: Bridges operate on the Network layer of the OSI model.

20. Which of the following layers do NICs operate on?

    A. Application

    B. Transport

    C. Data Link

    D. Physical

Scenarios

1. You are a network administrator in a medium-sized company. A user complains that their network access is down, but the user notes that all the users in her surrounding area are not having the same problems. Which OSI layer is the problem likely under?

2. You are a consultant for a firm that has given high priority to security on its system. Should you recommend dynamic or static routers for this firm's implementation?

Answers to Chapter Questions

Chapter Pre-Test

1. The OSI model subdivides the concept of networking into seven layers.

2. The Data Link layer is responsible for formatting a data packet and then sending it over the network as bits.

3. CRC (cyclic redundancy check) is the most popular form of error checking.

4. Sequencing information serves to put packets back into their proper order on the destination system.

5. The Transport layer is typically held responsible for error checking.

6. Routers operate on the Network layer.

7. The Session layer is responsible for starting a connection with a target host.

8. Brouters can run on the Network layer only when they're being used as routers, not when they're being used as bridges.

9. The Data Link layer is defined by the IEEE 802 standards.

10. Routers use IP addresses in communications on the Network layer.

Assessment Questions

1. A. The Application layer does not add a header to the packet. For more information, see the "Networking and the OSI Model" section in this chapter.

2. D. Both the Application and Session layers accept information from the Presentation layer. For more information, see the "Networking and the OSI Model" section in this chapter.

3. A. The Logical Link Control "layer" is actually the Logical Link Control (LLC) sublayer of the Data Link layer. For more information, see the "Data Link layer" section in this chapter.

4. False. Most error checking happens at the Transport layer. For more information, see the "Transport layer" section earlier in this chapter.

5. D. The Physical layer is the last layer to send off a packet across a network. For more information, see the "Networking and the OSI Model" section in this chapter.

6. C. The Logical Link Control (LLC) is a sublayer of the Data Link layer. For more information, see the "Data Link layer" section earlier in this chapter.

7. A. The Application layer is designated as Layer 7 of the OSI model. For more information, see the "Networking and the OSI Model" section in this chapter.

8. A. The SMTP protocol operates on the Application layer of the OSI model. For more information, see the "Protocols and the OSI Model" section in this chapter.

9. B. The parity-bit method of error control can be fooled if an even number of bits is missing from a packet. Because the number of bits missing from a data packet is equally likely be odd or even, this method has a 50 percent rate of failure in detecting corrupt data. For more information, see the "Transport layer" section in this chapter.

10. A. Window flow control specifies an amount of data for the sending system to send before stopping for the receiving host to catch up. For more information, see the "Transport layer" section in this chapter.

11. False. The process of organizing received data packets back into their proper order is called sequencing. For more information, see the "Transport layer" section in this chapter.

12. B. The 802.3u substandard defines Fast Ethernet. For more information, see the "IEEE and the Data Link layer" section in this chapter.

13. D. The IEEE 802.8 standard is not part of the Data Link layer. For more information, see the "IEEE and the Data Link layer" section in this chapter.

14. B. The IEEE 802.2 standard defines the LLC sublayer of the Data Link layer. For more information, see the "IEEE and the Data Link layer" section in this chapter.

15. D. IGMP is not an application protocol, according to the OSI model. For more information, see the "Protocols and the OSI Model" section in this chapter.

16. A. Routers operate on the Network layer of the OSI model. For more information, see the "Physical layer" section in this chapter.

17. C. Brouters can act as either bridges or routers, and so can operate on both the Physical and Data Link layers. For more information, see the "Physical layer" section in this chapter.

18. D. A LAN is a network segment of an internetwork. For more information, see the "Network layer" section in this chapter.

19. False. Bridges operate on the Physical and Data Link layers of the OSI model. Even brouters (which are a combination of bridges and routers) follow this guideline; if they were operating on the Network layer, they'd be operating as routers, not as bridges. For more information, see the "Physical layer" section in this chapter.

20. D. NICs operate on the Physical layer of the OSI model. For more information, see the "Physical layer" section in this chapter.

Scenarios

1. If other users on the same network segment are not having the same problem as the complaining user, the problem is likely to reside in the physical media between the user's client and the network — which is a Physical layer problem.

2. Because a static router allows the greatest security, you should recommend static routers to the firm.

Network Protocols

CHAPTER 6

EXAM OBJECTIVES

+ Differentiate the following network protocols in terms of routing, addressing schemes, interoperability, and naming conventions:
  - TCP/IP
  - IPX/SPX
  - NetBEUI
  - AppleTalk
+ Define the purpose, function, and/or use of the following protocols within TCP/IP:
  - IP
  - TCP
  - UDP
  - FTP
  - TFTP
  - SMTP
  - HTTP
  - HTTPS
  - POP3/IMAP4
  - TELNET
  - ICMP
  - ARP
  - NTP

PRE-TEST QUESTIONS

1. What is needed for DHCP broadcasts to pass through routers?
2. FTP is used primarily for what purpose?
3. What service does WINS supply for clients on a Microsoft network?
4. What does the acronym POP3 stand for?
5. What is the protocol used for sending mail?
6. Telnet uses which protocol to connect to remote servers?
7. What does the acronym SNMP stand for and what is it?
8. Is TCP a connectionless or connection-oriented communication exchange?
9. Is UDP a connectionless or connection-oriented communication delivery service?
10. On which operating system is IPX/SPX the primary protocol?

✦ Answers to these questions can be found at the end of the chapter. ✦

Internal Network Protocols

In previous chapters, network protocols were introduced as the language spoken by hosts on a network. Internal to each transport protocol is a set of upper-layer protocols (also called *application protocols*). These protocols require data packets to have a specific format that the destination services on the receiving host can understand and use. All transport protocols use upper-layer protocols; this chapter focuses on four upper-layer protocols: TCP/IP, IPX/SPX, NetBEUI, and AppleTalk.

TCP/IP internal protocols

One of the most common misconceptions in networking is that TCP/IP is a single protocol. Nothing could be farther from the truth. TCP/IP is a suite of protocols. Internal to TCP/IP are groups of protocols used for communication; which protocols are used depends on the requested service type.

TCP/IP is based on a four-layer model — similar to an abbreviated version of the OSI networking model — in which each layer has its own tasks:

- **Application Layer:** As the uppermost TCP/IP layer, the Application Layer governs selecting the correct protocol for a specific user request.
- **Transport Layer:** Underneath the Application Layer, the Transport Layer governs selecting the type of transport protocol that places the request on the network.
- **Internet Layer:** Underneath the Transport Layer, the Internet Layer governs addressing, routing functions, and packet fragmentation.
- **Network Layer:** As the bottommost TCP/IP layer, the Network Layer governs the basic preparation, sending, and receiving of data packets — formatting them according to network topology, actually placing them on the network, and receiving incoming packets from the network.

> **Tip** In effect, the Network Layer of TCP/IP combines the Data Link and Physical Layers of the OSI model.

Application-Layer protocols

Application-Layer protocols, also called *upper-layer protocols*, have another functional nickname — *user-request protocols* — because they govern the formatting of data packets according to user requests. The following sections identify these protocols.

DNS — Domain Naming Service

As an upper-layer protocol, DNS governs the passing of user requests (in particular, those for hostname and domain-name resolution) to a DNS server on the network. Requests for resolution are sent whenever a user browses the network, requests a Web site, or uses name-lookup utilities. DNS attempts communication by sending two User Datagram Packets (UDPs); if the requests are not successful, DNS tries again, sending one Transmission Control Protocol (TCP). If neither UDP nor TCP requests are successful, the user is notified with a communication error message. DNS operates via port 53.

> **Cross-Reference**: TCP and UDP are discussed in more detail later in this chapter.

DHCP — Dynamic Host Configuration Protocol

When used on the host side of an online transaction, DHCP governs requests for IP addresses; on the server side, DHCP governs how IP addresses can be provided to requesting hosts. DHCP initially uses network broadcasts (therefore it is not routable without additional configuration). Before hosts can access a DHCP server through a router, the router must be configured to comply with the industry standards specified in the *requests for comments* (RFCs) maintained online by the Internet Engineering Task Force — specifically, RFC 1542.

RFC 1542 allows the bootpass protocol to propagate through the router. If an RFC-1542-compliant router is not available (or wanted), each network segment that has DHCP clients (but has no DHCP server) must have a DHCP Relay Agent to reduce the amount of broadcast traffic that the router must handle. Configured with the address of the DHCP server, the DHCP Relay Agent operates via ports 67 and 68, forwarding DHCP clients' requests directly to the DHCP server.

FTP — File Transfer Protocol

FTP allows clients to download and upload files from a server running the FTP service. FTP is a service not based on a particular operating system. Because FTP is not dependent on a particular operating system, any client can download or upload files from any server running the FTP service. FTP uses TCP for communication from client to server and server to client, and uses acknowledgment packets during file transfer. TCP is covered later in this section. Every TCP/IP stack (the software that loads the TCP/IP protocol suite) loads the FTP utility. Generally, without additional software, FTP is a command-line-based utility. FTP is used heavily in heterogeneous client environments. FTP is an easy way to share information between clients using different operating systems. FTP uses port 20 for FTP server operations, and port 21 is for client operations.

TFTP — Trivial File Transfer Protocol

TFTP is used when a file transfer does not require an acknowledgment packet during file transfer. TFTP is used often in router configuration. TFTP is similar in operation to FTP. TFTP is also a command-line-based utility. One of the two primary differences between TFTP and FTP is speed and authentication. Because TFTP is used without acknowledgment packets, it is usually faster than FTP. TFTP does not provide user authentication like FTP and therefore the user must be logged on to the client and the files on the remote computer must be writable. TFTP supports only unidirectional data transfer (unlike FTP, which supports bi-directional transfer). TFTP is operated over port 69.

WINS — Windows Internet Naming Service

WINS resolves NetBIOS names on a Microsoft network. WINS reduces network broadcasts by using a Dynamic NetBIOS Name resolution service. NetBIOS clients are configured with the address of a WINS server. When clients boot, names are announced and stored in the WINS database. Clients contact the WINS server when requesting resolution for a NetBIOS name instead of using network broadcasts. Although WINS improves network utilization by reducing broadcast traffic, WINS also poses a great security risk when placed on a server directly connected to the Internet. WINS operates via ports 137, 138, and 139 — all of which are available (by default) on all Microsoft servers. WINS uses both TCP and UDP for network communication.

Caution: The ports left open by default on Microsoft servers can sometimes provide hackers with a way to gain unauthorized access. Take this potential security problem into account if you use the WINS protocol on your network.

HTTP — HyperText Transfer Protocol

HTTP is often called the protocol of the Internet. HTTP received this designation because most Internet traffic is based on HTTP. When a user requests a Web resource, it is requested using HTTP. The following is a Web request:

```
http://www.nexusww.com
```

When a client enters this address into a Web browser, DNS is called to resolve the Fully Qualified Domain Name (FQDN) to an IP address. When the address is resolved, an HTTP get request is sent to the Web server. The Web server responds with an HTTP send response. Such communication is done several times throughout a single session to a Web site. HTTP uses TCP for communication between clients and servers. HTTP operates on port 80.

HTTPS — HyperText Transfer Protocol Secure

HTTP is for Web sites using additional security features such as certificates. HTTPS is used when Web transactions are required to be secure. HTTPS uses a certificate-based technology such as VeriSign. Certificate-based transactions offer a mutual authentication between the client and the server. Mutual authentication ensures the server of the client identity, and ensures the client of the server identity. HTTPS, in addition to using certificate-based authentication, encrypts all data packets sent during a session. Because of the encryption, confidential user information cannot be compromised. To use HTTPS, a Web site must purchase a certificate from a third-party vendor such as VeriSign, CertCo, United States Postal Service, or other certificate providers. When the certificate is issued to a Web site from a third-party vendor, the Web site is using trusted communication with the client. The communication is trusted because the third party is not biased toward either the Web site or the client. To view a certificate during a HTTPS session, simply double-click the lock icon in the lower-right area of the Web browser. HTTPS operates on port 443 and uses TCP for communication.

POP3 — Post Office Protocol version 3

POP3 is a mail-drop service, used heavily for Internet mail systems such as Hotmail, providing user access only to the Inbox. POP3 governs contacting the mail server (which the user specifies during mail setup) and requesting a mail drop. POP3 is for mail delivery only; it does not handle sending mail. The biggest disadvantage of POP3 is that clients are only able to access an Inbox. Additional mail folders (such as sent items, deleted items, and contacts) are not available when using a POP3 client. Outlook Express version 3 is an example of a POP3 client. POP3 operates on port 110 and uses TCP for communication.

Secure POP3

Secure POP3 also allows users to access an Inbox over a secure connection. As with HTTPS, the security provided by Secure POP3, is certificate-based and encrypts all mail traffic during a session. One difference between HTTPS and Secure POP3 is in the provider of the certificate used for communication. Secure POP3 can use an internally provided certificate because communication to the Secure POP3 server is from internal users connecting remotely. Thus, a trusted third-party certificate provider is optional. Secure POP3 operates on port 993 and uses TCP for communication.

IMAP4 — Internet Message Access Protocol Version 4

When a client needs to access more than just the Inbox, a different messaging protocol is required. IMAP4 allows a client to access other boxes such as: deleted items, sent items, drafts, contacts, and public folders. Most of the newest Internet Mail clients are IMAP4 compliant. Although IMAP4 offers access to more mail folders, both POP3 and IMAP4 are mail-drop services; neither one can send mail.

IMAP4 operates on port 143 and uses TCP for communication.

Secure IMAP4

Similar in operation to Secure POP3, Secure IMAP4 provides encryption during each user session, and uses either internal or trusted certificates. All communication during a Secure IMAP4 session is secure. Secure IMAP4 operates on port 995 and uses TCP for communication.

SMTP — Simple Mail Transport Protocol

As mail-drop services, POP3, Secure POP3, IMAP4, and Secure IMAP4 cannot send mail; they can only receive mail. Other protocols, such as SMTP, are used for sending mail. SMTP is a standard electronic-mail protocol that handles the sending of mail from one SMTP to another SMTP server. To accomplish the transport, the SMTP server has its own MX (mail exchanger) record in the DNS database that corresponds to the domain for which it is configured to receive mail.

When equipped for two-way communication, mail clients are configured with the address of a POP3 server to receive mail and the address of an SMTP server to send mail. The clients can configure server parameters in the properties sheets of the mail client, basing the choices on an FQDN or an IP address. SMTP uses TCP for communication and operates on port 25.

TELNET — terminal emulation

Another of the popular misconceptions in the world of networking is the operation of Telnet. First, two different entities are known as Telnet — *TELNET* the protocol, and *Telnet* the application. Although many people think Telnet and TELNET are the same, they are not interchangeable. The Telnet application uses the TELNET protocol to connect to remote servers.

> **Note:** As used here, the term *server* is not specific to any operating system; it refers to *any* TCP/IP host running a service that allows the host to respond to client requests.

The TELNET protocol provides two-way communication that allows telnet clients and telnet servers to communicate with each other. One of the main uses of TELNET is to provide a communication facility between heterogeneous environments. TELNET allows Microsoft clients to communicate with Unix clients as well as other networking clients.

The TELNET protocol is mainly used for remote administration. Clients attached to a TELNET server can execute character-based applications remotely. TELNET is commonly used to verify service operations — and to open remote ports, such as

- SMTP
- POP3
- IMAP4

TELNET uses TCP for communication over the default port of 23.

NNTP — Network News Transfer Protocol

NNTP is, in effect, the modern-day Bulletin Board System (BBS). NNTP operates much the same way as the old BBSs did. NNTP allows clients to share information with each other by accessing *newsgroups*. Newsgroups are managed databases of information pertaining to specific topics. NNTP allows many configurations. NNTP can allow newsgroups to receive unmoderated postings from clients. Clients are allowed to post any information they want on unmoderated newsgroups. Moderated newsgroups have the content of the postings checked prior to posting the data to the newsgroup. Microsoft Outlook Express is an example of an NNTP client. NNTP uses TCP for communication over port 119.

> **Tip** One of the most common uses of NNTP is for technical downloads. One benefit of being a certified trainer is that you receive access to restricted newsgroups that provide product information, course guides, and mentoring to all members. NNTP requires that a client be able to access newsgroups.

SNMP — Simple Network Management Protocol

SNMP is a two-way network management protocol. SNMP consists of two components, the SNMP Agent, and the SNMP Management Console. The SNMP Management Console is the server side for SNMP. The management console sends requests to the SNMP Agents as `get` commands that call for information about the client such as

- Network configuration
- Resource allocation
- DHCP configuration
- DNS configuration
- WINS configuration
- Device configuration
- Device error and event messages

The SNMP Agent responds to the Management Console's `get` request with a `trap` message. The `trap` message has the requested information for the Management Console to evaluate. Security can be provided in many ways with SNMP; however, the most common form of security for SNMP is the use of *community names,* associations that link SNMP Agents to their Management Consoles:

- Agents, by default, respond only to Management Consoles that are part of the same community name.
- If an SNMP Agent receives a request from a Management Console that is not part of the same community name, then the request for information is denied.

Because SNMP is an industry-standard protocol, heterogeneous environments are common. Many vendors provide versions of SNMP Management Consoles. Hewlett Packard, for example provides HP Open View (one of the most popular Management Consoles on the market); Microsoft provides SNMP Server with the Windows NT and 2000 Resource Kits and Systems Management Server.

SNMP Management Consoles request information according to a Management Information Base (MIB) format. An MIB is a numeric value that specifies the type of request, and to which layer of the OSI model the request is being sent.

SNMP uses UDP to request information and operates on ports 161 and 162.

Transport-Layer protocols

The Transport Layer provides the transport protocol for the data packets. The Transport Layer specifies whether the data is to be sent with or without acknowledgment. The Transport Layer uses the Transmission Control Protocol (TCP) and the User Datagram Protocol (UDP) to send data packets.

TCP — Transmission Control Protocol

TCP provides a connection-oriented communication exchange. Because TCP establishes a connection before hosts can exchange data, the data exchange is considered to be reliable. TCP uses sequence numbers and acknowledgment numbers to provide the reliable communication exchange. The *connection* is based on a *three-way handshake* that synchronizes the sequence numbers and acknowledgment numbers. TCP breaks data packets into segments and assigns each packet a sequence number. The source host must acknowledge each segment, and if no acknowledgment packet is received, the data is retransmitted. To protect the validity of the data, a checksum is added to each segment sent. The checksum servers act as a parity check for the data, and if the checksum calculation performed by the client does not match the checksum sent by the server, the data is considered corrupt and the packet is discarded.

TCP uses a parameter called the *window size* to specify the amount of data that can be buffered on a single connection. The *window size* is an operating system independent parameter, and therefore a default value on a Microsoft operating system does not apply to a Unix operating system; however, the *window size* is negotiated between client and server during the three-way handshake.

Because TCP uses the three-way handshake, the time to transmit the data is longer than when using UDP, and therefore, is considered to be slower in network data transfer.

UDP — User Datagram Protocol

UDP provides a connectionless communication delivery service. UDP uses datagrams to send network communication. A datagram requires an IP address and a UDP port for communication to be successful. A port is an entrance point to an IP address. Each IP address can have 65,536 ports. A port is a way to multiplex communication to a single IP address. Each network service uses a unique port. Because UDP does not establish a connection for data transfer, the transmission of data is considered unreliable. Packets are numbered in the same manner as TCP segments; however, no sequence packet specifies how to arrange the packets. If a client does not receive a data packet, no retransmission of the data packet is done because the client does not send acknowledgment packets during a UDP session.

Network-Layer protocols

Network-Layer protocols provide network addressing and routing functions. The core protocols of the Internet Layer are the Internet Protocol (IP), Address Resolution Protocol (ARP), Internet Control Message Protocol (ICMP), and the Internet Group Management Protocol (IGMP).

IP — Internet Protocol

IP governs placing IP addressing and routing information on data packets. IP also uses a mathematical calculation called *ANDing* to determine whether a packet needs to be sent to a router. IP provides *packet fragmentation,* also called *segmenting*. When IP receives a packet that is too large to transmit, IP breaks the packet into smaller sections and number each packet, so the packet can be reassembled on the receiving client. In addition, IP on a router governs decrementing a packets Time-To-Live (TTL) as it passes through the router. Each packet on a network has a default TTL, and when the TTL reaches 0, the packet is discarded, or what is sometimes called, stored in the bit bucket. To avoid network congestion, it is recommended that an administrator periodically empty the *bit bucket*.

ARP — Address Resolution Protocol

ARP governs the resolution of an IP address into a MAC address. ARP is not a routable protocol, and therefore is restricted to local segment communication. ARP is discussed in more detail in later chapters.

ICMP — Internet Control Message Protocol

ICMP provides network diagnostic functions and error reporting. One of the most used IP commands is the Packet Internet Grouper (PING) command. When a host PINGS another client, it sends an ICMP ECHO request, and the receiving host responds with an ICMP ECHO REPLY. PING checks network connectivity on clients and routers.

ICMP also provides a little network help for routers. When a router is being overloaded with route requests, the router sends a *source quench* message to all clients on the network, instructing them to slow their data requests to the router.

IGMP — Internet Group Management Protocol

Hosts communicate in one of three ways: unicast, multicast, and broadcasts. A *unicast* is a communication packet between two hosts. A *broadcast* is a communication packet addressed to all hosts on a network. A *multicast* is a data packet addressed to a group of clients on a network. to use multicasts for communication, IGMP must be used.

IGMP is one of the hidden protocols of the Internet. Hosts use IGMP; often the user is unaware that his or her workstation is included in a multicast group. If a person has been in a chat room, or used a network collaboration application like net meeting, then that person has used IGMP.

IPX/SPX — Internetwork Packet Exchange/Sequence Packet Exchange internal protocols

IPX/SPX is the primary protocol of Novell NetWare (in particular, versions 4.0 and earlier, though it can be used on all versions). IPX/SPX provides many of the same features as TCP/IP, and is a routable transport protocol that allows networks to be segmented. However, network segmentation with IPX/SPX is done with network numbers and not with subnet masks. IPX/SPX is also similar to TCP/IP because IPX/SPX relies on internal protocols for network communication.

IPX

IPX is similar to the operation of UDP of TCP/IP. IPX is a connectionless datagram transfer service. Because it is connectionless, like UDP, it does not require any preliminary connection setup to transmit the data packets. A disadvantage to connectionless communication is that flow control and error correction are not provided during network communication. In addition, packet delivery is not guaranteed. IPX also provides addressing and routing of packets within and between network segments.

SPX

SPX is similar to the operation of TCP of TCP/IP. SPX is connection-oriented data transfer over IPX. Because SPX is connection oriented, flow control and error correction are provided along with packet delivery acknowledgments. SPX allows a single packet to remain unacknowledged at one time. If a packet is unacknowledged, the packet is retransmitted a total of 8 times. If there's no acknowledgment, SPX considers the connection failed.

SPXII

SPXII is an enhancement to SPX. SPXII has several improvements over SPX. SPXII allows more than one packet to remain unacknowledged. SPXII also allows for a larger packet size, which improves network performance by reducing the number of acknowledgment packets placed on the network.

NCP — NetWare Core Protocol

The internal NetWare protocol that allows clients to access shared network resources on a NetWare network is the NetWare Core Protocol. NCP is the protocol that governs communication between clients and servers about resource sharing.

SAP — Service Advertising Protocol

The Service Advertising Protocol is the protocol that provides name resolution to clients requesting network services. SAP collects information from file servers, print servers, and application servers and stores the information in a database called the SAP table. The SAP table is stored on IPX routers and NetWare servers.

AppleTalk

The AppleTalk routing protocol is, amazing as it may sound, used by Macintosh networks. There are two important factors to understand about the AppleTalk protocol: *zones* and *network numbers*.

AppleTalk *network numbers* assign AppleTalk networks unique numerical values that identify them as segments. Clients and servers can be part of only one network number. Because AppleTalk is routable, clients can access servers from any network number.

AppleTalk also uses *zones* to aid clients in browsing an AppleTalk network. Zones allow servers, printers, and clients to be grouped logically for the purpose of resource access. Unlike network numbers, servers, printers, and clients can be part of more than one zone. Having membership in more than one zone allows clients easier access to network resources. Clients need not use the Chooser to view the resources of multiple zones.

Summary

The TCP/IP protocol suite includes protocols that operate on virtually every layer of the OSI model. The Network+ examination focuses on those TCP/IP protocols that operate on the lower layers (Physical, Data Link, Network, and Transport), but you should also be familiar with the protocols of the upper layers as well.

Other protocols, such as IPX/SPX (native to NetWare) and AppleTalk (native to the Macintosh operating system), are also included in the objectives of the Network+ exam; you should be familiar with their structure, functions, and features as well.

For the exam, your best bet is to know what each protocol acronym stands for — as well as the application and OSI layer of each protocol.

✦ ✦ ✦

STUDY GUIDE

Assessment Questions

1. Which protocol can resolve the FQDN to an IP address when HTTP is being used?

    A. WINS

    B. POP3

    C. FTP

    D. DNS

2. What boxes does POP3 allow a client to access? (Choose all that apply)

    A. Sent Items

    B. Deleted Items

    C. Inbox

    D. Contacts

3. ARP governs the resolution of an IP address into what type of address?

    A. MAC address

    B. Web address

    C. Host address

    D. POP3 server address

4. When using DHCP, what is required for each segment of a network?

    A. WINS Server

    B. DHCP request agent

    C. RFC 1542 router

    D. DHCP relay agent

5. What does a datagram require for communication to be successful?

    A. IP address

    B. UDP port

    C. Web address

    D. SMTP

6. When a Web transaction is required to be secure, what protocol would be necessary to use?

    A. HTTP

    B. TFTP

    C. HTTPS

    D. Secure POP

7. A user can receive mail but cannot send mail. What is missing?

    A. POP3

    B. SMTP

    C. FTP

    D. UDP

8. A user can send mail but cannot receive mail. What is missing?

    A. POP3

    B. SMTP

    C. FTP

    D. UDP

9. WINS uses which two protocols for network communications?

    A. HTTP

    B. FTP

    C. TCP

    D. UDP

10. PING checks for what on clients and routers?

    A. Network connectivity

    B. Window size

    C. Secure connections

    D. Telnet connections

Answers to Chapter Questions

Chapter Pre-Test

1. For hosts to access a DHCP server through a router, the router must be configured as an RFC (Request For Comment) 1542 compliant router or each network segment must have a DHCP relay agent.
2. FTP primarily downloads and uploads files from a server running the FTP service.
3. WINS resolves NetBIOS names on a Microsoft network.
4. POP3 is an acronym for Post Office Protocol version 3. POP3 is a mail-drop service. It does not send mail.
5. SMTP is the acronym for Simple Mail Transport Protocol. SMTP is a standard electronic-mail protocol that handles the sending of mail from one SMTP to another SMTP server.
6. Telnet uses the TELNET protocol to connect to remote servers.
7. SNMP is the acronym for Simple Network Management Protocol. SNMP is a two-way network management protocol.
8. TCP is a connection oriented communication exchange. TCP uses sequence numbers and acknowledgment numbers to provide the reliable communication exchange.
9. UDP is a connectionless communication delivery service. UDP uses datagrams to send network communications.
10. IPX/SPX is the primary protocol of Novell's NetWare. IPX/SPX is a routable transport protocol that provides many of the same features as TCP/IP.

Assessment Questions

1. D. DNS resolves Fully Qualified Domain Names (FQDNs) to IP addresses when a client enters an address into a Web browser.
2. C. POP3 is a mail-drop service. POP3 only allows users access to the Inbox.
3. A. ARP governs the resolution of an IP address into a MAC address.
4. C and D. RFC 1542 allows the bootpass protocol to be propagated thru the router. If an RFC 1542 router is not available or wanted, DHCP clients on segments without the DHCP server must have a DHCP relay agent.
5. A and B. A datagram requires an IP address and a UDP port. A port is an entrance point to an IP address.

6. C. HTTPS is used when Web transactions are required to be secure. HTTPS uses a certificate-based technology. Certificate-based transactions offer a mutual authentication between the client and the server.

7. A. POP3 is a mail-drop service. POP3 does not send mail.

8. B. SMTP is used when sending mail from one SMTP to another SMTP server.

9. C and D. WINS uses both TCP and UDP for network communications.

10. A. PING is one of the most used IP commands. PING checks for network connectivity on clients and routers.

TCP/UDP Port Functionality

CHAPTER 7

EXAM OBJECTIVES

- Define the function of TCP/UDP ports. Identify well-known ports.

CHAPTER PRE-TEST

1. Which protocol is considered a connectionless protocol?
2. Why should unused services be disabled?
3. What is the common port used for HTTP Web connections?
4. Which protocol is considered a reliable protocol?
5. What are well-known ports?
6. What is the difference between a server and a client port?
7. What is the purpose of a port scanner?
8. How can a firewall protect your service ports?
9. What is the common port used for SMTP mail traffic?
10. Explain the importance of keeping your applications and services up to date?

✦ Answers to these questions can be found at the end of the chapter. ✦

In order for TCP and UDP services and applications to run, they must use a port to enable connection to and from the server they are located on. These ports are needed because when clients connect to a server, the server does not know which application or service they are trying to use, unless the request contains a specific port number that it wants to use. Hundreds of assigned ports exist, but only a subset of those is used frequently. This chapter explains the functions of these ports and covers some of the more popular ports that are used every day in TCP/IP communications. It also covers the importance of securing unused ports to prevent unauthorized access.

TCP/UDP Ports

In order for computers on a network to see each other, they need to speak a common network protocol to transfer information back and forth. As the networking part of the TCP/IP protocol, each network device needs its own address, so each computer on a network has an IP address. In the transport layer of the TCP/IP protocol, we have protocols that direct network packets to specific applications named TCP and UDP.

TCP/UDP

The Transmission Control Protocol (TCP) and the User Datagram Protocol (UDP) are used to transmit network data to and from server and client applications. The main difference between the two protocols is that TCP uses a connection-oriented transport, while UDP uses a connectionless type of communication.

When the TCP protocol is used, a special connection is opened up between two network devices, and the channel remains open to transmit data until it is closed. On the other hand, a UDP transmission does not make a proper connection and merely broadcasts its data to the specified network address without any verification of receipt. For certain types of applications and services, a TCP connection makes more sense, while other types are more efficiently provided by UDP communication. The advantage of TCP is that the transmission is much more reliable because it uses acknowledgement packets to ensure delivery. The advantage of UDP is that there is no connection, so it is much faster without all the checks and acknowledgements going on, but is also less reliable. In Table 7-1, some common TCP/IP applications are shown with the type of protocol they use.

Table 7-1
TCP/IP Applications and Their Protocols

TCP	UDP
FTP	TFTP
SMTP	SNMP
Telnet	DNS

Just as the IP protocol needs a source and destination address to communicate network data, these transport protocols need a source and destination port.

Exam Tip For the exam, know the differences between a TCP and a UDP connection.

Server and client ports

Two different types of network ports exist: server and client. A server port is one that is "listening" for incoming requests. The server does not have to be an actual "server," it can be any machine or device running an application or service that is waiting for requests. The service waits until a client tries to connect to it on that port. At that time, the application replies and begins to process the request. For example, an FTP server sits and waits for incoming FTP requests. When one is received, it starts up an FTP session and provides the client computer with a logon. When the FTP session is finished, the program closes, and the server waits for the next connection. Most heavily used servers handle many connections simultaneously.

On the client side, it the one that usually initiates the connection with a server. Depending on the type of application, the client may use random port numbers and not any one specific port. This is different from the server, as for certain applications, the ports are standardized for different services. These common, or "well-known," ports encompass most of the widely used network services such as FTP, HTTP, and DNS.

Well-known ports

A total of 65,535 ports exist on a computer system. These ports are separated into three main categories, well-known ports, Registered ports, and Private/Dynamic ports.

The Internet Assigned Number Authority (IANA—www.iana.org) assigns these ports. The well-known ports are numbered 0-1023 and are typically base system services for UNIX, Windows, and the TCP/IP protocol. They can usually be used by root, administrator users, or system services.

Chapter 7 ✦ **TCP/UDP Port Functionality** 143

Registered ports are numbered 1024-49151. These are general ports that can be used by anyone, although they can be registered for specific applications. Examples of applications that use these port numbers include instant messaging programs and peer-to-peer file-sharing services.

Dynamic/Private ports are numbered 49152-65535 and are ports that anyone can use freely on a private basis.

Here is a list of the first 150 well-known ports from the Internet Assigned Number Authority, which consists of the most popular and often-used protocols and their allocated ports. The Keyword column lists the common name of the protocol's port, and the Port column shows the number of the port and indicates whether it uses TCP or UDP communications. The Description and Reference columns give a description of the port's usage and a contact name and address for the creator.

```
Keyword             Port        Description                         References
-------             ----        -----------                         ----------
                    0/tcp       Reserved
                    0/udp       Reserved
#                               Jon Postel <postel@isi.edu>
tcpmux              1/tcp       TCP Port Service Multiplexer
tcpmux              1/udp       TCP Port Service Multiplexer
#                               Mark Lottor <MKL@nisc.sri.com>
compressnet         2/tcp       Management Utility
compressnet         2/udp       Management Utility
compressnet         3/tcp       Compression Process
compressnet         3/udp       Compression Process
#                               Bernie Volz <VOLZ@PROCESS.COM>
#                   4/tcp       Unassigned
#                   4/udp       Unassigned
rje                 5/tcp       Remote Job Entry
rje                 5/udp       Remote Job Entry
#                               Jon Postel <postel@isi.edu>
#                   6/tcp       Unassigned
#                   6/udp       Unassigned
echo                7/tcp       Echo
echo                7/udp       Echo
#                               Jon Postel <postel@isi.edu>
#                   8/tcp       Unassigned
#                   8/udp       Unassigned
discard             9/tcp       Discard
discard             9/udp       Discard
#                               Jon Postel <postel@isi.edu>
#                   10/tcp      Unassigned
#                   10/udp      Unassigned
systat              11/tcp      Active Users
systat              11/udp      Active Users
#                               Jon Postel <postel@isi.edu>
#                   12/tcp      Unassigned
#                   12/udp      Unassigned
daytime             13/tcp      Daytime (RFC 867)
```

```
daytime         13/udp      Daytime (RFC 867)
#                           Jon Postel <postel@isi.edu>
#               14/tcp      Unassigned
#               14/udp      Unassigned
#               15/tcp      Unassigned [was netstat]
#               15/udp      Unassigned
#               16/tcp      Unassigned
#               16/udp      Unassigned
qotd            17/tcp      Quote of the Day
qotd            17/udp      Quote of the Day
#                           Jon Postel <postel@isi.edu>
msp             18/tcp      Message Send Protocol
msp             18/udp      Message Send Protocol
#                           Rina Nethaniel <---none--->
chargen         19/tcp      Character Generator
chargen         19/udp      Character Generator
ftp-data        20/tcp      File Transfer [Default Data]
ftp-data        20/udp      File Transfer [Default Data]
ftp             21/tcp      File Transfer [Control]
ftp             21/udp      File Transfer [Control]
#                           Jon Postel <postel@isi.edu>
ssh             22/tcp      SSH Remote Login Protocol
ssh             22/udp      SSH Remote Login Protocol
#                           Tatu Ylonen <ylo@cs.hut.fi>
telnet          23/tcp      Telnet
telnet          23/udp      Telnet
#                           Jon Postel <postel@isi.edu>
                24/tcp      any private mail system
                24/udp      any private mail system
#                           Rick Adams <rick@UUNET.UU.NET>
smtp            25/tcp      Simple Mail Transfer
smtp            25/udp      Simple Mail Transfer
#                           Jon Postel <postel@isi.edu>
#               26/tcp      Unassigned
#               26/udp      Unassigned
nsw-fe          27/tcp      NSW User System FE
nsw-fe          27/udp      NSW User System FE
#                           Robert Thomas <BThomas@F.BBN.COM>
#               28/tcp      Unassigned
#               28/udp      Unassigned
msg-icp         29/tcp      MSG ICP
msg-icp         29/udp      MSG ICP
#                           Robert Thomas <BThomas@F.BBN.COM>
#               30/tcp      Unassigned
#               30/udp      Unassigned
msg-auth        31/tcp      MSG Authentication
msg-auth        31/udp      MSG Authentication
#                           Robert Thomas <BThomas@F.BBN.COM>
#               32/tcp      Unassigned
#               32/udp      Unassigned
dsp             33/tcp      Display Support Protocol
dsp             33/udp      Display Support Protocol
#                           Ed Cain <cain@edn-unix.dca.mil>
```

```
#               34/tcp      Unassigned
#               34/udp      Unassigned
                35/tcp      any private printer server
                35/udp      any private printer server
#                           Jon Postel <postel@isi.edu>
#               36/tcp      Unassigned
#               36/udp      Unassigned
time            37/tcp      Time
time            37/udp      Time
#                           Jon Postel <postel@isi.edu>
rap             38/tcp      Route Access Protocol
rap             38/udp      Route Access Protocol
#                           Robert Ullmann <ariel@world.std.com>
rlp             39/tcp      Resource Location Protocol
rlp             39/udp      Resource Location Protocol
#                           Mike Accetta <MIKE.ACCETTA@CMU-CS-A.EDU>
#               40/tcp      Unassigned
#               40/udp      Unassigned
graphics        41/tcp      Graphics
graphics        41/udp      Graphics
name            42/tcp      Host Name Server
name            42/udp      Host Name Server
nameserver      42/tcp      Host Name Server
nameserver      42/udp      Host Name Server
nicname         43/tcp      Who Is
nicname         43/udp      Who Is
mpm-flags       44/tcp      MPM FLAGS Protocol
mpm-flags       44/udp      MPM FLAGS Protocol
mpm             45/tcp      Message Processing Module [recv]
mpm             45/udp      Message Processing Module [recv]
mpm-snd         46/tcp      MPM [default send]
mpm-snd         46/udp      MPM [default send]
#                           Jon Postel <postel@isi.edu>
ni-ftp          47/tcp      NI FTP
ni-ftp          47/udp      NI FTP
#                           Steve Kille <S.Kille@isode.com>
auditd          48/tcp      Digital Audit Daemon
auditd          48/udp      Digital Audit Daemon
#                           Larry Scott <scott@zk3.dec.com>
tacacs          49/tcp      Login Host Protocol (TACACS)
tacacs          49/udp      Login Host Protocol (TACACS)
#                           Pieter Ditmars <pditmars@BBN.COM>
re-mail-ck      50/tcp      Remote Mail Checking Protocol
re-mail-ck      50/udp      Remote Mail Checking Protocol
#                           Steve Dorner <s-dorner@UIUC.EDU>
la-maint        51/tcp      IMP Logical Address Maintenance
la-maint        51/udp      IMP Logical Address Maintenance
#                           Andy Malis <malis_a@timeplex.com>
xns-time        52/tcp      XNS Time Protocol
xns-time        52/udp      XNS Time Protocol
#                           Susie Armstrong <Armstrong.wbst128@XEROX>
domain          53/tcp      Domain Name Server
domain          53/udp      Domain Name Server
```

```
#                          Paul Mockapetris <PVM@ISI.EDU>
xns-ch         54/tcp      XNS Clearinghouse
xns-ch         54/udp      XNS Clearinghouse
#                          Susie Armstrong <Armstrong.wbst128@XEROX>
isi-gl         55/tcp      ISI Graphics Language
isi-gl         55/udp      ISI Graphics Language
xns-auth       56/tcp      XNS Authentication
xns-auth       56/udp      XNS Authentication
#                          Susie Armstrong <Armstrong.wbst128@XEROX>
               57/tcp      any private terminal access
               57/udp      any private terminal access
#                          Jon Postel <postel@isi.edu>
xns-mail       58/tcp      XNS Mail
xns-mail       58/udp      XNS Mail
#                          Susie Armstrong <Armstrong.wbst128@XEROX>
               59/tcp      any private file service
               59/udp      any private file service
#                          Jon Postel <postel@isi.edu>
               60/tcp      Unassigned
               60/udp      Unassigned
ni-mail        61/tcp      NI MAIL
ni-mail        61/udp      NI MAIL
#                          Steve Kille <S.Kille@isode.com>
acas           62/tcp      ACA Services
acas           62/udp      ACA Services
#                          E. Wald <ewald@via.enet.dec.com>
whois++        63/tcp      whois++
whois++        63/udp      whois++
#                          Rickard Schoultz <schoultz@sunet.se>
covia          64/tcp      Communications Integrator (CI)
covia          64/udp      Communications Integrator (CI)
#                          Dan Smith <dan.smith@den.galileo.com>
tacacs-ds      65/tcp      TACACS-Database Service
tacacs-ds      65/udp      TACACS-Database Service
#                          Kathy Huber <khuber@bbn.com>
sql*net        66/tcp      Oracle SQL*NET
sql*net        66/udp      Oracle SQL*NET
#                          Jack Haverty <jhaverty@ORACLE.COM>
bootps         67/tcp      Bootstrap Protocol Server
bootps         67/udp      Bootstrap Protocol Server
bootpc         68/tcp      Bootstrap Protocol Client
bootpc         68/udp      Bootstrap Protocol Client
#                          Bill Croft <Croft@SUMEX-AIM.STANFORD.EDU>
tftp           69/tcp      Trivial File Transfer
tftp           69/udp      Trivial File Transfer
#                          David Clark <ddc@LCS.MIT.EDU>
gopher         70/tcp      Gopher
gopher         70/udp      Gopher
#                          Mark McCahill <mpm@boombox.micro.umn.edu>
netrjs-1       71/tcp      Remote Job Service
netrjs-1       71/udp      Remote Job Service
netrjs-2       72/tcp      Remote Job Service
netrjs-2       72/udp      Remote Job Service
```

```
netrjs-3         73/tcp     Remote Job Service
netrjs-3         73/udp     Remote Job Service
netrjs-4         74/tcp     Remote Job Service
netrjs-4         74/udp     Remote Job Service
#                           Bob Braden <Braden@ISI.EDU>
                 75/tcp     any private dial out service
                 75/udp     any private dial out service
#                           Jon Postel <postel@isi.edu>
deos             76/tcp     Distributed External Object Store
deos             76/udp     Distributed External Object Store
#                           Robert Ullmann <ariel@world.std.com>
                 77/tcp     any private RJE service
                 77/udp     any private RJE service
#                           Jon Postel <postel@isi.edu>
vettcp           78/tcp     vettcp
vettcp           78/udp     vettcp
#                           Christopher Leong <leong@kolmod.mlo.dec.com>
finger           79/tcp     Finger
finger           79/udp     Finger
#                           David Zimmerman <dpz@RUTGERS.EDU>
http             80/tcp     World Wide Web HTTP
http             80/udp     World Wide Web HTTP
www              80/tcp     World Wide Web HTTP
www              80/udp     World Wide Web HTTP
www-http         80/tcp     World Wide Web HTTP
www-http         80/udp     World Wide Web HTTP
#                           Tim Berners-Lee <timbl@W3.org>
hosts2-ns        81/tcp     HOSTS2 Name Server
hosts2-ns        81/udp     HOSTS2 Name Server
#                           Earl Killian <EAK@MORDOR.S1.GOV>
xfer             82/tcp     XFER Utility
xfer             82/udp     XFER Utility
#                           Thomas M. Smith <Thomas.M.Smith@lmco.com>
mit-ml-dev       83/tcp     MIT ML Device
mit-ml-dev       83/udp     MIT ML Device
#                           David Reed <--none--->
ctf              84/tcp     Common Trace Facility
ctf              84/udp     Common Trace Facility
#                           Hugh Thomas <thomas@oils.enet.dec.com>
mit-ml-dev       85/tcp     MIT ML Device
mit-ml-dev       85/udp     MIT ML Device
#                           David Reed <--none--->
mfcobol          86/tcp     Micro Focus Cobol
mfcobol          86/udp     Micro Focus Cobol
#                           Simon Edwards <--none--->
                 87/tcp     any private terminal link
                 87/udp     any private terminal link
#                           Jon Postel <postel@isi.edu>
kerberos         88/tcp     Kerberos
kerberos         88/udp     Kerberos
#                           B. Clifford Neuman <bcn@isi.edu>
su-mit-tg        89/tcp     SU/MIT Telnet Gateway
su-mit-tg        89/udp     SU/MIT Telnet Gateway
```

```
#                           Mark Crispin <MRC@PANDA.COM>
##########  PORT 90 also being used unofficially by Pointcast #########
dnsix           90/tcp      DNSIX Securit Attribute Token Map
dnsix           90/udp      DNSIX Securit Attribute Token Map
#                           Charles Watt <watt@sware.com>
mit-dov         91/tcp      MIT Dover Spooler
mit-dov         91/udp      MIT Dover Spooler
#                           Eliot Moss <EBM@XX.LCS.MIT.EDU>
npp             92/tcp      Network Printing Protocol
npp             92/udp      Network Printing Protocol
#                           Louis Mamakos <louie@sayshell.umd.edu>
dcp             93/tcp      Device Control Protocol
dcp             93/udp      Device Control Protocol
#                           Daniel Tappan <Tappan@BBN.COM>
objcall         94/tcp      Tivoli Object Dispatcher
objcall         94/udp      Tivoli Object Dispatcher
#                           Tom Bereiter <--none--->
supdup          95/tcp      SUPDUP
supdup          95/udp      SUPDUP
#                           Mark Crispin <MRC@PANDA.COM>
dixie           96/tcp      DIXIE Protocol Specification
dixie           96/udp      DIXIE Protocol Specification
#               Tim Howes <Tim.Howes@terminator.cc.umich.edu>
swift-rvf       97/tcp      Swift Remote Virtual File Protocol
swift-rvf       97/udp      Swift Remote Virtual File Protocol
#                           Maurice R. Turcotte
#               <mailrus!uflorida!rm1!dnmrt%rmatl@uunet.UU.NET>
tacnews         98/tcp      TAC News
tacnews         98/udp      TAC News
#                           Jon Postel <postel@isi.edu>
metagram        99/tcp      Metagram Relay
metagram        99/udp      Metagram Relay
#                           Geoff Goodfellow <Geoff@FERNWOOD.MPK.CA.US>
newacct         100/tcp     [unauthorized use]
hostname        101/tcp     NIC Host Name Server
hostname        101/udp     NIC Host Name Server
#                           Jon Postel <postel@isi.edu>
iso-tsap        102/tcp     ISO-TSAP Class 0
iso-tsap        102/udp     ISO-TSAP Class 0
#                           Marshall Rose <mrose@dbc.mtview.ca.us>
gppitnp         103/tcp     Genesis Point-to-Point Trans Net
gppitnp         103/udp     Genesis Point-to-Point Trans Net
acr-nema        104/tcp     ACR-NEMA Digital Imag. & Comm. 300
acr-nema        104/udp     ACR-NEMA Digital Imag. & Comm. 300
#                           Patrick McNamee <--none--->
cso             105/tcp     CCSO name server protocol
cso             105/udp     CCSO name server protocol
#                           Martin Hamilton <martin@mrrl.lut.as.uk>
csnet-ns        105/tcp     Mailbox Name Nameserver
csnet-ns        105/udp     Mailbox Name Nameserver
#                           Marvin Solomon <solomon@CS.WISC.EDU>
3com-tsmux      106/tcp     3COM-TSMUX
3com-tsmux      106/udp     3COM-TSMUX
```

```
#                             Jeremy Siegel <jzs@NSD.3Com.COM>
#########     106             Unauthorized use by insecure poppassd protocol
rtelnet       107/tcp         Remote Telnet Service
rtelnet       107/udp         Remote Telnet Service
#                             Jon Postel <postel@isi.edu>
snagas        108/tcp         SNA Gateway Access Server
snagas        108/udp         SNA Gateway Access Server
#                             Kevin Murphy <murphy@sevens.lkg.dec.com>
pop2          109/tcp         Post Office Protocol - Version 2
pop2          109/udp         Post Office Protocol - Version 2
#                             Joyce K. Reynolds <jkrey@isi.edu>
pop3          110/tcp         Post Office Protocol - Version 3
pop3          110/udp         Post Office Protocol - Version 3
#                             Marshall Rose <mrose@dbc.mtview.ca.us>
sunrpc        111/tcp         SUN Remote Procedure Call
sunrpc        111/udp         SUN Remote Procedure Call
#                             Chuck McManis <cmcmanis@freegate.net>
mcidas        112/tcp         McIDAS Data Transmission Protocol
mcidas        112/udp         McIDAS Data Transmission Protocol
#                             Glenn Davis <support@unidata.ucar.edu>
ident         113/tcp
auth          113/tcp         Authentication Service
auth          113/udp         Authentication Service
#                             Mike St. Johns <stjohns@arpa.mil>
audionews     114/tcp         Audio News Multicast
audionews     114/udp         Audio News Multicast
#                             Martin Forssen <maf@dtek.chalmers.se>
sftp          115/tcp         Simple File Transfer Protocol
sftp          115/udp         Simple File Transfer Protocol
#                             Mark Lottor <MKL@nisc.sri.com>
ansanotify    116/tcp         ANSA REX Notify
ansanotify    116/udp         ANSA REX Notify
#                             Nicola J. Howarth <njh@ansa.co.uk>
uucp-path     117/tcp         UUCP Path Service
uucp-path     117/udp         UUCP Path Service
sqlserv       118/tcp         SQL Services
sqlserv       118/udp         SQL Services
#                             Larry Barnes <barnes@broke.enet.dec.com>
nntp          119/tcp         Network News Transfer Protocol
nntp          119/udp         Network News Transfer Protocol
#                             Phil Lapsley <phil@UCBARPA.BERKELEY.EDU>
cfdptkt       120/tcp         CFDPTKT
cfdptkt       120/udp         CFDPTKT
#                             John Ioannidis <ji@close.cs.columbia.ed>
erpc          121/tcp         Encore Expedited Remote Pro.Call
erpc          121/udp         Encore Expedited Remote Pro.Call
#                             Jack O'Neil <---none--->
smakynet      122/tcp         SMAKYNET
smakynet      122/udp         SMAKYNET
#                             Pierre Arnaud <pierre.arnaud@iname.com>
ntp           123/tcp         Network Time Protocol
ntp           123/udp         Network Time Protocol
#                             Dave Mills <Mills@HUEY.UDEL.EDU>
```

```
ansatrader       124/tcp    ANSA REX Trader
ansatrader       124/udp    ANSA REX Trader
#                           Nicola J. Howarth <njh@ansa.co.uk>
locus-map        125/tcp    Locus PC-Interface Net Map Ser
locus-map        125/udp    Locus PC-Interface Net Map Ser
#                           Eric Peterson <lcc.eric@SEAS.UCLA.EDU>
nxedit126/tcp    NXEdit
nxedit126/udp    NXEdit
#   Don Payette <Don.Payette@unisys.com>
###########Port 126 Previously assigned to application below#######
#unitary         126/tcp    Unisys Unitary Login
#unitary         126/udp    Unisys Unitary Login
#                           <feil@kronos.nisd.cam.unisys.com>
###########Port 126 Previously assigned to application above#######
locus-con        127/tcp    Locus PC-Interface Conn Server
locus-con        127/udp    Locus PC-Interface Conn Server
#                           Eric Peterson <lcc.eric@SEAS.UCLA.EDU>
gss-xlicen       128/tcp    GSS X License Verification
gss-xlicen       128/udp    GSS X License Verification
#                           John Light <johnl@gssc.gss.com>
pwdgen           129/tcp    Password Generator Protocol
pwdgen           129/udp    Password Generator Protocol
#                           Frank J. Wacho <WANCHO@WSMR-SIMTEL20.ARMY.MIL>
cisco-fna        130/tcp    cisco FNATIVE
cisco-fna        130/udp    cisco FNATIVE
cisco-tna        131/tcp    cisco TNATIVE
cisco-tna        131/udp    cisco TNATIVE
cisco-sys        132/tcp    cisco SYSMAINT
cisco-sys        132/udp    cisco SYSMAINT
statsrv          133/tcp    Statistics Service
statsrv          133/udp    Statistics Service
#                           Dave Mills <Mills@HUEY.UDEL.EDU>
ingres-net       134/tcp    INGRES-NET Service
ingres-net       134/udp    INGRES-NET Service
#                           Mike Berrow <---none--->
epmap            135/tcp    DCE endpoint resolution
epmap            135/udp    DCE endpoint resolution
#                           Joe Pato <pato@apollo.hp.com>
profile          136/tcp    PROFILE Naming System
profile          136/udp    PROFILE Naming System
#                           Larry Peterson <llp@ARIZONA.EDU>
netbios-ns       137/tcp    NETBIOS Name Service
netbios-ns       137/udp    NETBIOS Name Service
netbios-dgm      138/tcp    NETBIOS Datagram Service
netbios-dgm      138/udp    NETBIOS Datagram Service
netbios-ssn      139/tcp    NETBIOS Session Service
netbios-ssn      139/udp    NETBIOS Session Service
#                           Jon Postel <postel@isi.edu>
emfis-data       140/tcp    EMFIS Data Service
emfis-data       140/udp    EMFIS Data Service
emfis-cntl       141/tcp    EMFIS Control Service
emfis-cntl       141/udp    EMFIS Control Service
#                           Gerd Beling <GBELING@ISI.EDU>
```

```
bl-idm          142/tcp     Britton-Lee IDM
bl-idm          142/udp     Britton-Lee IDM
#                           Susie Snitzer <---none--->
imap            143/tcp     Internet Message Access Protocol
imap            143/udp     Internet Message Access Protocol
#                           Mark Crispin <MRC@CAC.Washington.EDU>
uma 144/tcp     Universal Management Architecture
uma144/udp      Universal Management Architecture
#   Jay Whitney <jw@powercenter.com>
uaac            145/tcp     UAAC Protocol
uaac            145/udp     UAAC Protocol
#                           David A. Gomberg <gomberg@GATEWAY.MITRE.ORG>
iso-tp0         146/tcp     ISO-IP0
iso-tp0         146/udp     ISO-IP0
iso-ip          147/tcp     ISO-IP
iso-ip          147/udp     ISO-IP
#                           Marshall Rose <mrose@dbc.mtview.ca.us>
jargon          148/tcp     Jargon
jargon          148/udp     Jargon
#   Bill Weinman <wew@bearnet.com>
aed-512         149/tcp     AED 512 Emulation Service
aed-512         149/udp     AED 512 Emulation Service
#                           Albert G. Broscius <broscius@DSL.CIS.UPENN.EDU>
sql-net         150/tcp     SQL-NET
sql-net         150/udp     SQL-NET
```

Common Ports

Exam Tip: For the exam, know the port numbers of some of the popular Internet services, such as FTP, Telnet, and HTTP.

Here are some of the most common or well-known ports that are used by popular applications and services:

- **HTTP (Port 80):** This is the port that is used by most Web browsers and Web servers to access and service World Wide Web HTTP content.

- **FTP (Ports 20, 21):** These ports are used for FTP (File Transfer Protocol) sessions. FTP enables a system to upload or downloads files to and from another system. Port 21 is used for actual connection and communication, while port 20 is used for data transfer.

- **DNS (Port 53):** The Domain Name Service (DNS) provides domain name resolution for client computers. The DNS server returns an IP address for a requested domain name such as www.hungryminds.com.

- **Telnet (Port 23):** Telnet is a terminal emulation program that enables you to connect to another computer and create a console session there. You can also use the telnet command to connect to another service's "listening" ports. For example, to connect to a Web server on port 80, you can telnet to port 80, the HTTP port, and establish a session with the Web server.

- **POP/IMAP (Ports 110, 143):** For mail services, the Post Office Protocol (POP) and Internet Message Access Protocol (IMAP) are used to retrieve mail from mail servers. POP uses port 110 and IMAP uses port 143.
- **SMTP (Port 25):** Popular mail transfer agents use the Simple Mail Transfer Protocol (SMTP) to relay e-mail from one host to another. Port 25 is commonly used for outgoing mail.
- **LDAP (Port 389):** Lightweight Directory Access Protocol (LDAP) is used for locating and accessing information directories such as company mailing and address lists.
- **NTP (Port 123):** The Network Time Protocol (NTP) is used to synchronize computer clocks with a central Internet clock. These communications use port 123.
- **Windows Ports:** Microsoft Windows has a number of special ports for their system services:
  - **WINS (Port 137):** The Windows Internet Naming Service (WINS) is used to map NetBIOS computer names to IP addresses. It communicates information using port 137.
  - **NetBIOS Datagrams (Port 138):** Used for Windows network broadcasts, such as the Windows network browser.
  - **NetBIOS Session (Port 139):** Another port used for establishing NetBIOS communications.

Securing Ports

Many initial installations of operating systems install some of the major services and applications by default. These default installations create a security risk, because many of these services do not need to be running on certain servers, and this opens the server up to attack from unauthorized users trying to connect on these service ports.

Shutting down unused ports

To increase security on your system, you should shut down any unused ports and services. For example, if you have just installed a file/print server on your local LAN, you may find that you have many Internet services installed by default by the operating system. On top of general file sharing, you may also have a Web server and an FTP server installed. These servers create points of entry for unauthorized users. Web servers and FTPs are the most commonly attacked servers by hackers, and many exploits exist to use security weaknesses in those points to gain entry to a system through them.

The first step after installing an operating system is to examine what services are currently running; if any services are not needed, shut them down. If they are services that are needed, you must not shut them down or you will cause operating system and network disruption. For example, some services such as DHCP and DNS may be needed by your system and network to run properly.

System audit

To fully understand what services your system should and should not be running, you should perform a service audit of your system. Many utilities are available that can scan your system for open ports and services and report them to you. The simplest of these programs is called a port scanner. This program scans your system for all open TCP/UDP ports, starting from the first port, and then every port from then on upwards. This scan can take some time, because hundreds of ports must be checked. When the program is finished, it can give you a list of ports that it found it could connect to. If any are there that you are not using, and it is not a special system or network function, then stop that service.

A good idea is to run a port scanner on your system on a regular basis to scan for any new ports that might have been opened after the installation of a software package. It may also discover certain ports that are used by many "back door" or Trojan programs that are special programs that enable unauthorized users to gain access to a system.

> **In the Real World**
> Hackers also use port scanners to find weaknesses in servers and computers that are connected to the Internet. A good firewall solution can stop these unauthorized users from accessing your systems.

System security

In order to fully secure your network and servers, you may wish to install a firewall. A firewall is a special hardware device or software program that can block certain incoming and outgoing network traffic. A firewall is used most often as a barrier between a public and a private network, but it can also be used to regulate the type of network traffic going to a specific server or device. By using a series of rules and tables, a firewall can analyze incoming traffic, and, depending on the rule that applies towards that particular type of network communication, the firewall may let it through, or it may block the network packets.

For example, you can tell a firewall to block any network traffic destined for port 80 (HTTP) for a specific server. This is typically a Web server request, but certain requests can contain malicious code or data that can compromise or disable the server. If you are running a Web server, but you do not want Web requests from an outside network to reach the server, you can set up a rule on the firewall to do this. Most firewalls can also block traffic from specific networks and IP addresses.

You should set up your firewall so that by default it blocks all network traffic, except for the specific ports and networks that you have allowed access. This setup is much safer and more efficient than letting all traffic through and trying to block the ones that you think may harm your system or network. By using the first method, you are immediately securing your network from all access, and then slowly adding rules to allow access to only the servers and services that are needed.

> **In the Real World**
>
> Many home users who use DSL or cable Internet connections make use of personal software firewalls, which protect them from unauthorized users accessing their PC, because they are connected to the Internet all the time.

Service and application updates

To increase service and port security, you should ensure that all your applications are up to date and contain the most recent security patches. For example, you may be running a very old version of an FTP server, which contains a number of bugs or security holes. Even if you allowed only FTP ports access to the server, that port can be exploited to enable unauthorized access to the system. Even a firewall cannot block this sort of attack on the weakness of a service.

> **In the Real World**
>
> Many Internet Web and FTP servers have been compromised because the administrator has not patched the applications for security holes. The software vendors have secured most of these application weaknesses very quickly after discovery, but many administrators are slow to patch their servers.

Summary

This chapter detailed the use and function of TCP and UDP ports. Some of the most popular service ports were discussed, and finally, the importance of securing unused ports was stressed. For the exam, keep these key points in mind:

✦ Know the popular ports:
- HTTP (Port 80)
- FTP (Ports 20, 21)
- DNS (Port 53)
- Telnet (Port 23)
- SMTP (Port 25)
- POP / IMAP (Ports 110, 143)
- Microsoft Windows NetBIOS ports (137-139)

- Use firewalls to protect against unauthorized port access, and disable ports not in use.
- Use a port scanner to discover open ports.
- Keep applications and service software up to date and patched to remove security issues.

✦ ✦ ✦

STUDY GUIDE

The Study Guide section provides you with the opportunity to test your knowledge about the Network+ exam objectives that are covered in this chapter. The Assessment Questions provide practice for the real exam and the Scenarios provide practice with real situations. If you get any questions wrong, use the answers to determine the part of the chapter that you should review before continuing.

Assessment Questions

1. Which of the following protocols is connectionless?

    A. UDP

    B. TCP

    C. DHCP

    D. ICMP

2. Which of the following protocols opens a special connection between two network devices and leaves the channel open until all the data has been transmitted?

    A. UDP

    B. TCP

    C. SMTP

    D. SNMP

3. Which of the following protocols, when transmitted, does not make a proper connection, and merely broadcasts its data to the specific network device without any verification of the receipt?

    A. UDP

    B. TCP

    C. SNMP

    D. SMTP

4. Which of the following protocols is considered most reliable?

   A. TCP

   B. SMTP

   C. UDP

   D. IP

5. Which of the following protocols uses acknowledgement packets to ensure delivery?

   A. DHCP

   B. UDP

   C. FTP

   D. TCP

6. Which of the following TCP/IP applications uses the UDP protocol?

   A. SNMP

   B. SMTP

   C. Telnet

   D. FTP

7. Which of the following TCP/IP applications uses the TCP protocol?

   A. FTP

   B. TFTP

   C. SNMP

   D. DNS

8. How many types of network ports are there?

   A. 1

   B. 2

   C. 3

   D. 4

9. Which two of the following are network ports?

   A. Client ports

   B. Server ports

   C. User ports

   D. Admin ports

10. What is the total number of ports on a computer system?

    A. 175

    B. 36,764

    C. 10,000

    D. 65,535

11. What is the numbered range of registered ports?

    A. 24-51

    B. 1228-6924

    C. 1024-49151

    D. 1352-7654

12. What is a default port number for FTP?

    A. 21

    B. 25

    C. 80

    D. 23

13. What is the default port number for Telnet?

    A. 110

    B. 23

    C. 53

    D. 21

14. What utility would you use to scan your system for open ports and services?

    A. IP scanner

    B. Netstat

    C. Loopback adapter

    D. Port scanner

15. What can you install to increase system security?

    A. DHCP

    B. Password protection

    C. Firewall

    D. Port Scanner

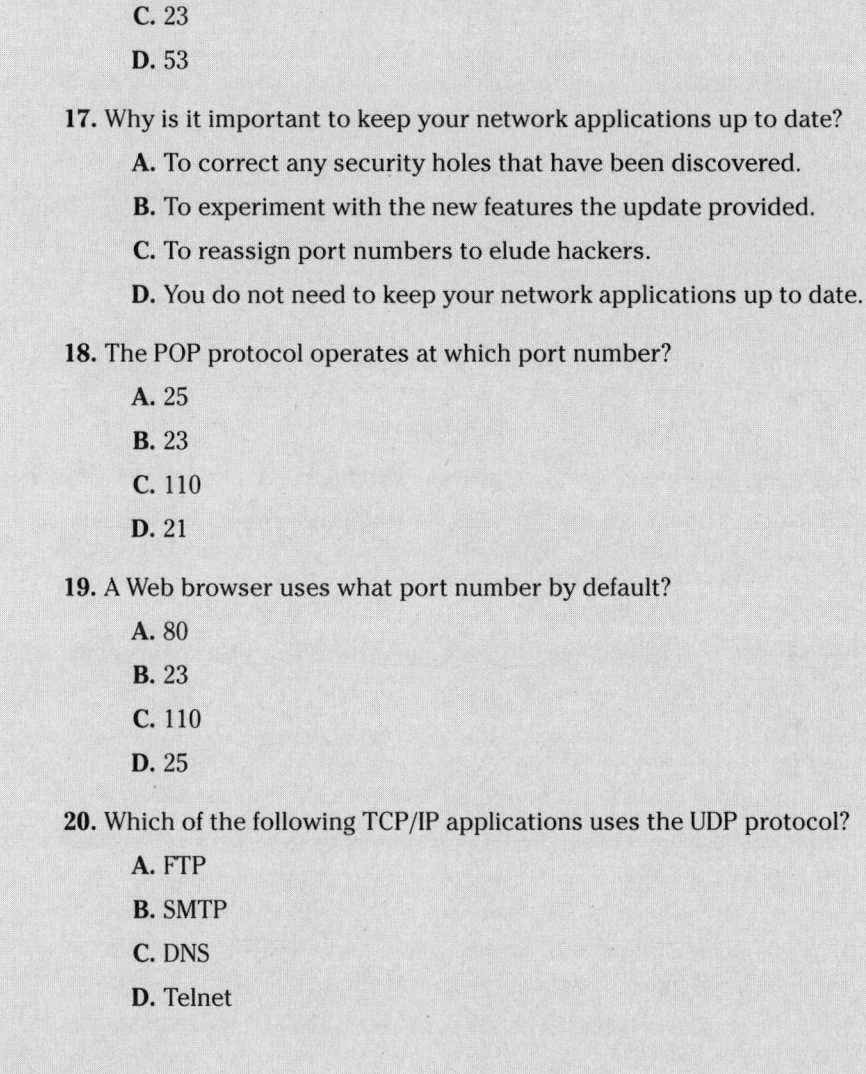

16. What is the default port number for DNS?

   A. 80

   B. 20

   C. 23

   D. 53

17. Why is it important to keep your network applications up to date?

   A. To correct any security holes that have been discovered.

   B. To experiment with the new features the update provided.

   C. To reassign port numbers to elude hackers.

   D. You do not need to keep your network applications up to date.

18. The POP protocol operates at which port number?

   A. 25

   B. 23

   C. 110

   D. 21

19. A Web browser uses what port number by default?

   A. 80

   B. 23

   C. 110

   D. 25

20. Which of the following TCP/IP applications uses the UDP protocol?

   A. FTP

   B. SMTP

   C. DNS

   D. Telnet

Scenarios

1. Hackers recently compromised an FTP server. You find that they gained access through an exploit through the HTTP Web server that was running at the same time on the same server. This Web server was not being used. What can you do to prevent future security problems with this server?

2. After running a port scanner to examine open ports on your DNS server, you find that you have the following services open and running: DNS, HTTP, FTP, and SMTP. What does this indicate, and what should you do to fix any potential problems?

Lab Exercises

Lab 7-1 Using Telnet to Connect to Ports

The objective of this hands-on lab exercise is to gain familiarity with some of the most common network ports using the `telnet` command. You should be able to use any networked computer and operating system for this exercise.

1. From a command-line prompt, use the `telnet` command to connect to specific open ports on a system. For example, if you know the address of a Web server on your network, you can enter this command:

   ```
   telnet webserver 80
   ```

   This command opens a terminal session with the HTTP port of that Web server.

2. Try using `telnet` to connect to a server that is not running a Web service using the same command. What is the message you receive? You should get a "Connection refused" or similar message. This is because that port is not open to accept connections.

3. Use `telnet` to try to connect to your mail server using this command:

   ```
   telnet mailserver 110
   ```

   Port 110 is the POP3 protocol and is used by mail programs to retrieve e-mail from the server. If the POP3 protocol is running, you should receive some type of login prompt, which is required for authentication to the server.

4. If your mail server is using the IMAP protocol for mail retrieval, try connecting to it using its port number of 143:

   ```
   telnet mailserver 143
   ```

   If the service is running, you receive a login prompt similar to the POP3 protocol. If not, you get a connection refused.

5. Try accessing other well-known ports on some of your servers, such as SMTP (25) or FTP (21).

Answers to Chapter Questions

Chapter Pre-Test

1. UDP is a connectionless protocol, because it does not establish a session when communicating.

2. Unused services leave certain ports open and waiting for requests. Unauthorized users can compromise these ports, enabling them access to the system.

3. HTTP communications, which are used by Web browsers and Web servers to communicate, use port 80.

4. TCP is a reliable protocol, because it establishes a direct channel between two systems, with constant acknowledgments of received communications.

5. Well-known ports are the first 1024 ports assigned by the IANA to common TCP/IP network services and applications such as FTP, HTTP, and Telnet.

6. Server ports constantly listen to a specific port waiting for requests to a service or application. A client can use any port to connect to a server.

7. A port scanner is used to scan all ports on a system to see which ones are available and listening for requests.

8. A firewall program can be set to allow only certain network traffic to a specified port on a system. This setup helps security by blocking any other types of communications on other ports that can be compromised.

9. SMTP mail traffic uses port 25.

10. Older applications and services are security risks, because they may contain known bugs and security holes that can be compromised by unauthorized users. By keeping them up to date, you have all the latest security patches.

Assessment Questions

1. A. UDP is a connectionless protocol. TCP is a connection-oriented protocol. For review see the "TCP/UDP" section.

2. B. The TCP protocol creates a special connection between two network devices and leaves the channel open until all the data has been transmitted. For review see the "TCP/UDP" section.

3. A. The UDP protocol is faster than the TCP protocol, because when the UDP protocol is transmitted it does not make a proper connection and basically broadcasts its data to the specific network device. No verification of the receipt is needed. For review see the "TCP/UDP" section.

4. A. The TCP protocol is more reliable than UDP, because when TCP is used, a special connection is opened up between the two network devices, and the channel remains open to transmit data until it is closed and receives verification that the data has been received. For review see the "TCP/UDP" section.

5. D. The TCP protocol uses acknowledgement packets to ensure delivery. For review see the "TCP/UDP" section.

6. B. SMTP uses the UDP protocol. SNMP, Telnet, and FTP all use the TCP protocol. For review see the "TCP/UDP" section.

7. A. FTP uses the TCP protocol. TFTP, SNMP, and DNS all use the UDP protocol. For review see the "TCP/UDP" section.

8. B. Two types of network ports exist: client and server ports. For review see the "Server and client ports" section.

9. A and B. Client and server ports are the only two real network ports. User ports and Admin ports do not exist. For review see the "Server and client ports" section.

10. D. A total number of 65,535 ports exist on a computer system. For review see the "Well-known ports" section.

11. C. The range of registered ports is from 1024–49151. These are general ports that can be used by anyone, although they can be registered for specific applications. For review see the "Well-known ports" section.

12. A. The default port number for FTP is 21. For review see the "Common Ports" section.

13. B. The default port number for Telnet is 23. For review see the "Common Ports" section.

14. D. A port scanner can detect open ports and services and report them to you. A port scanner is good to use to discover any unauthorized open ports. For review see the "System audit" section.

15. C. A firewall can be used to block certain incoming and outgoing network traffic. You would use a firewall to create a secure barrier between a public and private network. For review see the "System security" section.

16. D. The default port number for DNS is 53. For review see the "Well-known ports" section.

17. A. Keeping your network applications up to date is one of the best ways to correct any security holes or program bugs that have been discovered. For review see the "Service and application updates" section.

18. C. The POP protocol uses port 110 by default. For review see the "Common Ports" section.

19. A. Port 80 is the default port for a Web browser. For review see the "Common Ports" section.

20. C. DNS uses the UDP protocol. SMTP, FTP, and Telnet all use the TCP protocol. For review see the "TCP/UDP" section.

Scenarios

1. Because the Web server application is not being used, it should be disabled so that the server is not listening for requests on the HTTP port 80. Any other services that are not needed on the server, with the exception of FTP, should be disabled. A firewall can also be installed so that it can permit only FTP traffic on ports 20 and 21 and prevent any other types of access.

2. The port scanner shows any open or "listening" ports on your system. If any unused services are running, you should disable them to prevent any unauthorized access on these ports. In this example, HTTP (port 80), FTP (ports 20, 21), and SMTP (port 25) should be disabled. DNS is the main function of this machine, so that service and its related ports should remain enabled.

Network Services

CHAPTER 8

EXAM OBJECTIVES

- Identify the purpose of the following network services: DHCP/bootp, DNS, NAT/ICS, WINS, and SNMP.

CHAPTER PRE-TEST

1. What type of server automatically assigns IP addresses to client workstations at boot up?
2. What other TCP/IP properties can a DHCP server assign automatically?
3. What network service makes it easier to identify a host by a domain name?
4. What is the difference between a DNS server and a WINS server?
5. What type of server translates NetBIOS names to IP addresses?
6. What does SNMP stand for?
7. What are two main components SNMP relies on to function properly?
8. What types of devices can an SNMP agent reside on?
9. What is a community string?
10. What is the default name of a community string?

✦ Answers to these questions can be found at the end of the chapter. ✦

Network Services

Network services are additional components that you can use on your network that can help automate certain functions, such as assigning IP addresses to other devices on the network, translating host names and domain names to IP addresses, mapping NetBIOS names to IP addresses, translating network addresses, and monitoring networks.

This chapter addresses the most popular network services:

- DHCP
- DNS
- WINS
- NAT/ICS
- SNMP

Understanding DHCP

DHCP stands for Dynamic Host Configuration Protocol. This protocol assigns network IP addresses to clients on the network at startup. With DHCP, each client workstation does not need to be set up with a static IP address.

DHCP is recommended on large networks. It would be very time consuming to manually assign a static IP address to every workstation on your network. With static IP addressing, the IP address that you assign to a device never changes. A DHCP server contains a pool of IP addresses that it can draw from to assign to devices that are connecting to the network. Other TCP/IP properties, such as default gateways, DNS servers, and subnet masks can also be assigned automatically.

How DHCP works

When a client workstation boots, it sends a request to the DHCP server, which offers an IP address lease to the client. The client sends back a message accepting the lease, and the DHCP replies with an acknowledgement. The client then configures its TCP/IP stack with the information provided by the DHCP server.

The IP address is offered for a period of time called a *lease*. The length of the lease is specified at the server level and sets a period of time in which the client can use that address. This time period is usually set to between three and seven days, but can be any period of time. When the lease is almost over, the client contacts the DHCP server to renew the lease. The client continues to use the same IP address when the lease is renewed. If the client is removed from the network for a period of time greater than the lease, the IP address it was using is put back into the pool of IP addresses and may be assigned to new computers joining the network.

The DHCP server is configured with a range of IP addresses that it can assign, which corresponds to the particulars of your current network. Other information can also be provided to DHCP clients, such as the default gateway or router address, and DNS and WINS servers. If any of your network equipment changes addresses (for example, with the introduction of a new DNS server), you need to update only the DHCP server settings, which propagate automatically to the clients. You don't need to change the settings of each and every client machine.

> **Exam Tip** DHCP stands for Dynamic Host Configuration Protocol and assigns network IP addresses to clients on the network. DHCP can also assign other TCP/IP properties, such as default gateways, DNS servers, and subnet masks.

BOOTP

An older but similar protocol to DHCP is BOOTP (Bootstrap Protocol). BOOTP is most often used by diskless client workstations to obtain an IP address to communicate with the network. BOOTP is also used in conjunction with the capability to boot the operating system of the client. Most DHCP servers can receive these BOOTP requests and configure the client the same way as it does with proper DHCP clients.

Understanding DNS

TCP/IP networks communicate with hosts using their IP addresses. It would be very difficult for someone to have to memorize the different IP addresses for the hosts they want to connect to on the network. A Domain Name Service (DNS) makes it easier to identify a host by a domain name. A domain name uses words rather than numbers to identify Internet hosts.

Suppose you want to connect to the CompTIA Web site by using your Web browser. You would enter `http://www.comptia.org` in the address bar to go to the CompTIA Web page. `www.comptia.org` would be a common name used for a numerical IP address. You could use 216.119.103.72 instead, but `www.comptia.org` is easier to remember. A DNS server translates these addresses. Your Web browser asks the TCP/IP protocol to ask the DNS server for the IP address of `www.comptia.org`. When the browser receives the address, it connects to the Web site.

> **Exam Tip** Remember that DNS stands for Domain Name System (or Domain Name Service) and that a DNS server translates domain names into their IP addresses.

Internet names are split into various domains depending on their function. The most popular root level domains today are as follows:

- .com (commercial)
- .org (organization)
- .net (network)
- .gov (government)
- .edu. (education)

In the Real World

The number of names registered under the .com domain is enormous. At this point, most of the common names available are already registered. To help further subdivide Internet domain names, new top-level domains have been recently added including .biz and .info.

The full address is referred to as a fully qualified domain name (FQDN). For `www.comptia.org`, the address represents a host, www, within the comptia.org domain. A DNS server keeps a table of hosts and domains and their corresponding IP addresses. The Internet has several root DNS servers that store the database of domain names and corresponding IP addresses for all Internet sites. For local area networks, a DNS server aids you in naming common machines in your environment.

DNS tables

A sample DNS table or zone file, which is a list of domain names and their corresponding IP addresses in a linear record format, typically looks something like this:

```
;       Nameservers
;
                IN      NS      ns1.nameserver.com.     ; x.x.x.x (IP)
                IN      NS      ns2.nameserver.com.     ; x.x.x.x (IP)
;
;       Domain Mail Handlers
;
mynetwork.com.          IN      MX      0       mail
mynetwork.com.          IN      MX      10      mail
;
;
; hosts in order
;
mynetwork.              IN      A       192.168.10.0
www                     IN      A       192.168.10.5
smtp                    IN      CNAME   www
pop                     IN      CNAME   www
ftp                     IN      CNAME   www
mail                    IN      A       192.168.10.10
;
; end
```

In this example, the first lines of the DNS zone file indicate the location of the name servers that are authoritative for your particular domain. For the purpose of mail transfer, a special record called an *MX record* indicates where to send mail that is coming in to your domain. This record points to your mail server.

Most typical DNS record entries contain the name of the system and its corresponding IP address. This is called an *"A" record*.

Other types of records include "CNAME," which stands for canonical name. CNAME represents another name or alias for a certain server on your network. In this case, the SMTP, POP, and FTP services are provided by "www," which is set to 192.168.10.5.

Most DNS servers keep these zone files as simple text files on the server itself. Because of the enormous task in keeping DNS servers up to date with each other, these files are replicated automatically and are dynamically updated.

Understanding WINS

NetBIOS is a way of communicating with other machines on the network. Windows networks must know the name of the machines with which they are communicating. NetBIOS was not designed to work in a routed environment, so routers are not an option with this method. Microsoft developed a solution to this problem by wrapping a shell around the NetBIOS packet with an IP address. This way the NetBIOS packet is able to cross a router only if it obtains the IP address of the workstation.

To solve this problem, a WINS (Windows Internet Naming Service) server was developed. For Windows networks, WINS performs a function similar to DNS. For networks that are running NetBIOS over a TCP/IP network, a WINS server translates NetBIOS names to IP addresses. WINS services can also be combined with Windows DNS services, to enable WINS queries to be resolved by DNS servers. The DNS tables are dynamically updated from the WINS server database.

The WINS service has both a server and a client component. The WINS server performs the major backbone communications and publishes and retrieves WINS data. A WINS server performs these functions:

- ✦ Handles the name registration and release requests from Windows clients, and also registers or releases their names and IP addresses
- ✦ Responds to name queries from WINS clients by returning an IP address for the name queried
- ✦ Replicates the WINS database to other WINS servers on the network

A WINS server dynamically builds its own reference table. When a workstation attached to the network is booted, it uses the WINS address setting, as shown in Figure 8-1 in the TCP/IP configuration to communicate with the WINS server.

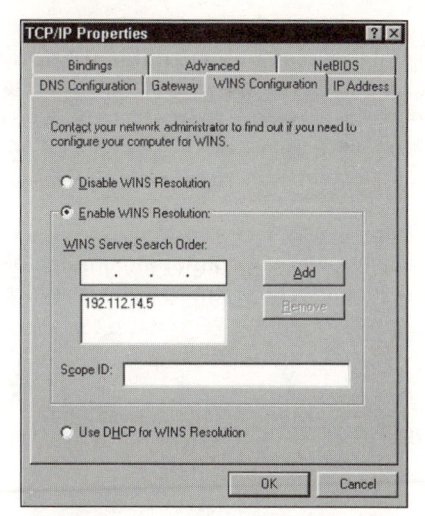

Figure 8-1: Windows WINS address setting tab

Multiple WINS servers are used to replicate WINS data and provide for greater availability and load balancing for larger networks.

The WINS client can be any Windows-based PC or server and performs these functions:

- Registers and releases its name with the WINS server when it enters or leaves the network
- Queries the WINS server for name and IP address resolution of other clients on the network

Understanding NAT/ICS

NAT (network address translation) connects multiple computers to other IP networks (including the Internet) using one IP address. A NAT box has two main purposes:

- To act as a firewall by hiding internal IP addresses
- To enable the combination of multiple internal IP addresses into a single Internet connection

Because of the shortage of IP addresses, not that many high-level address blocks can be assigned. By utilizing NAT, a single external IP address can represent an entire network of computers for external communications, while internally, a number of private IP addresses can facilitate communications between systems. You need to perform NAT translations only on systems that you need exposed on the external network.

NAT is also useful when you want to have the workstations on your network access the Internet but want the actual IP addresses of the workstations hidden. NAT hides the IP address of each workstation on the internal network. It does this by exchanging its IP address for the address of any requesting station. The reason you would want to exchange these IP addresses is to enhance network security and to hide from others (hackers for example) your real IP address that is specific to your internal network.

Because only one IP address is sent out on the Internet, all communications look as if they originate from the one device. Web servers also hide the specific IP address from which a request is being sent.

How NAT works

When you have an external packet coming into your network, your NAT service or device performs the following functions:

- Examines the packets destination address
- Compares the address with mapping table
- Converts the destination address to the private internal IP address and forwards the packet
- If destination address does not match any known address, drops or rejects the packet

The same also happens for communications in the opposite direction, except this time the source address is modified:

- Examines packet source address
- Compares the address to mapping table
- Converts source address to the NAT external IP address and forwards packet

ICS

ICS (Internet Connection Sharing) is a built-in feature of Windows 98 Second Edition, Windows 2000, and Windows Me. ICS provides networked computers with the capability to share a single connection to the Internet. Multiple users can use ICS to gain access to the Internet through a single connection by using Dial-Up Networking or local networking.

An ICS network is a type of local area network that relies on a single computer through which all other computers and TCP/IP-capable devices connect to the Internet, as shown in Figure 8-2. The hardware and software needed to set up a home network include the following:

- ✦ A primary computer (identified as a gateway)
- ✦ Windows 98 Second Edition, Windows 2000, or Windows Me with Internet Connection Sharing enabled
- ✦ One or more computers running TCP/IP enabled client software, such as:
  - Windows 95
  - Windows 98/Me
  - Windows NT 4.0
  - Windows 2000
- ✦ Devices that can connect to the Internet
- ✦ A network connection device for each computer
- ✦ Network media (cabling, hubs)
- ✦ A single modem (or an ISDN or ADSL line) for the entire network
- ✦ Internet browser software and TCP/IP drivers installed on each device that shares the connection

To enable Internet Connection Sharing for Windows 98 and Windows Me, follow these steps:

1. Choose Start ➪ Settings ➪ Control Panel.
2. Double-Click Add/Remove Programs.
3. On the Windows Setup tab, double-click Internet Tools.
4. Click to select the Internet Connection Sharing check box, and then click OK.
5. Click OK, and then follow the instructions on the screen to run the Internet Connection Sharing wizard.

To enable Internet Connection Sharing for Windows 2000 follow these steps

1. Open network dial-up connections
2. Right-click the dial-up, VPN, or incoming connection you want to share, and then click properties.
3. On the Sharing tab, select the Enable Internet connection sharing for this connection check box.

Tip: If you want this connection to dial automatically when another computer on your home network attempts to access external resources, select the Enable on-demand dialing check box.

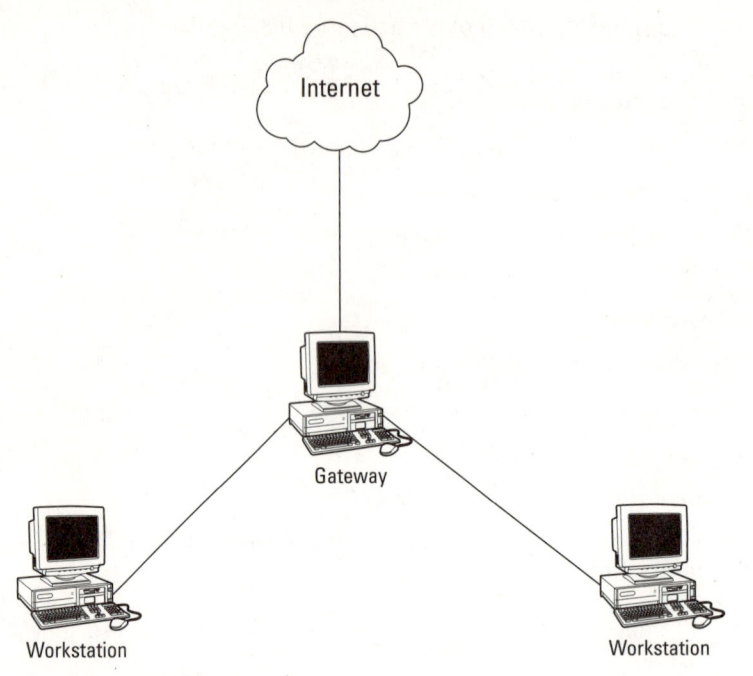

Figure 8-2: An ICS network

Using SNMP to Monitor Your Network

SNMP (Simple Network Management Protocol) is a network protocol that enables you to collect and exchange information between devices on your network. SNMP is part of the TCP/IP protocol that enables you to do the following:

- Simplify network management.
- Monitor network performance.
- Diagnose and troubleshoot network problems.
- Aid in capacity planning.

How SNMP functions

SNMP relies on two main components to function properly:

- An SNMP agent
- A network management system (NMS)

An SNMP agent's main function is to collect and store management information about a specific device and to make that information about that device available to the NMS. An SNMP agent can reside on all types of network devices, including routers, switches, hubs, servers, workstations, and printers.

You can run the NMS on a single system. The NMS runs an application that monitors and collects information about the managed devices. Figure 8-3 shows the relationship between various components that make up a functioning SNMP system.

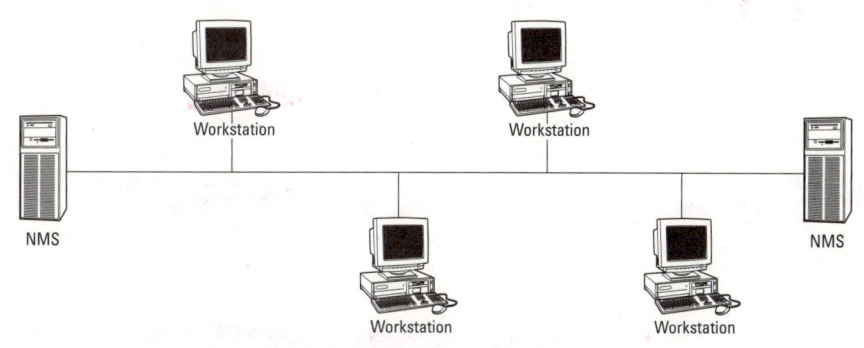

Figure 8-3: The SNMP system with the NMS collecting information from the managed devices.

Understanding the SNMP Management Information Base

The Management Information Base (MIB) consists of a database of information about a managed device. The database consists of objects, which describe various functions that can be measured and monitored within that device. You can gather many different kinds of information from a network device, such as memory, disk and CPU usage, network information, and user and application information for example. The CompTIA Network+ exam does not go into full detail about every command available with SNMP. This section describes the basic SNMP commands that appear on the exam.

Understanding SNMP commands

SNMP has four basic SNMP operations:

- Read
- Write
- Trap
- Traversal

The NMS uses the read operation to monitor devices and to examine the MIB object information hierarchy. `Get` is an example of a read operation command, which reads SNMP value from a device.

The NMS uses the write operation to control devices by changing the object's variables of the managed device. `Set` is an example of a write operation command.

Managed devices use the trap operation to relay information and events to the NMS. An alert or event causes a trap to be sent to the NMS. The actual SNMP command is `trap`.

The NMS uses traversal operations to scan devices for SNMP compatibility and to support and gather that information sequentially. The `GetNext` command is an example of a traversal operation.

SNMP uses a community string as a security measure. A community string is a type of identification or password that is set for all SNMP operations. When the SNMP management system receives SNMP information, it compares the community string to the incoming SNMP data with its own community string. The strings have to be the same to be accepted. If the strings are different, the SNMP management system discards the request. The default name of a community string is called *public*. Community strings can be set for different types of SNMP information:

- Read Only: The Read Only community string enables a device to only read SNMP information from another device.

- Read-Write: The Read-Write community string enables a device to both read and write information to and from another device.

- Trap: The Trap community string is used whenever SNMP trap messages are sent from one device to another.

Tip You should change the default public community string to prevent unauthorized SNMP access to your monitored devices.

SNMP thresholds

You can set SNMP thresholds on MIB objects with all SNMP management programs, which can also respond with an alert notification when these thresholds are reached. Thresholds provide a way to measure your network against certain baselines, which helps you to set your thresholds according to what you perceive to be a performance issue.

Don't set your thresholds too high or too low for the SNMP traps to be effective. If these thresholds are set too high, you might be ignoring conditions that are harming your server and network. If the thresholds are set too low, you will continually be notified with false alarms when no real performance issue exists.

Summary

This chapter covered the common network services that you can use on your network to automate certain functions. Remember these key points:

- ✦ A DHCP server assigns IP addresses to client workstations automatically at boot up.
- ✦ A DNS server keeps a database of tables that translates fully qualified Internet domain names to their respective IP addresses.
- ✦ A WINS server translates NetBIOS names to IP addresses.
- ✦ NAT stands for network address translation and connects multiple computers to other IP networks.
- ✦ ICS stands for Internet Connection Sharing and is a built-in feature of Windows 98 Second Edition, Windows 2000, and Windows Me. ICS provides networked computers with the capability to share a single connection to the Internet.
- ✦ SNMP stands for Simple Network Management Protocol, which is a network protocol that enables you to collect and exchange information between devices on your network.

✦ ✦ ✦

STUDY GUIDE

The Study Guide section provides you with the opportunity to test your knowledge about the Network+ exam objectives that are covered in this chapter. The Assessment Questions provide practice for the real exam, and the Scenarios provide practice with real situations. If you get any questions wrong, use the answers to determine the part of the chapter that you should review before continuing.

Assessment Questions

1. You need to install a server that will automatically assign IP addresses to devices when they connect to the network. What type of server would you use?

    A. WINS server

    B. DHCP server

    C. DNS server

    D. NetBIOS server

2. Why would you use a DHCP server on a large network?

    A. To help cut down on network congestion

    B. To assign a static IP address to a client workstation

    C. To assign a dynamic IP address to a client workstation

    D. To translate host names into domain names

3. Which of the following is a network service?

    A. Ping

    B. WINS

    C. Event Log

    D. NetBEUI

4. What is the function of a DNS server?

    A. To translate domain names to their respective IP addresses

    B. To enable users to dial in to the server using a modem

    C. To assign network IP addresses to clients on a network

    D. To forward network requests on behalf of another client or server

5. Which of the following is a recognized domain name?

   A. .edu

   B. .top

   C. .int

   D. .htm

6. What does FQDN stand for?

   A. Fast quick domain naming

   B. Full queued domain name

   C. Fully qualified domain name

   D. Fully queued domain name

7. Which type of server found on a Windows network functions similarly to a DNS server?

   A. DHCP

   B. NAT

   C. WINS

   D. SNMP

8. SNMP enables you to do which three things?

   A. Simplify network management

   B. Diagnose and troubleshoot network problems

   C. Monitor network performance

   D. Assign IP addresses to workstations

9. Which service resolves NetBIOS names to IP addresses?

   A. DNS

   B. SNMP

   C. WINS

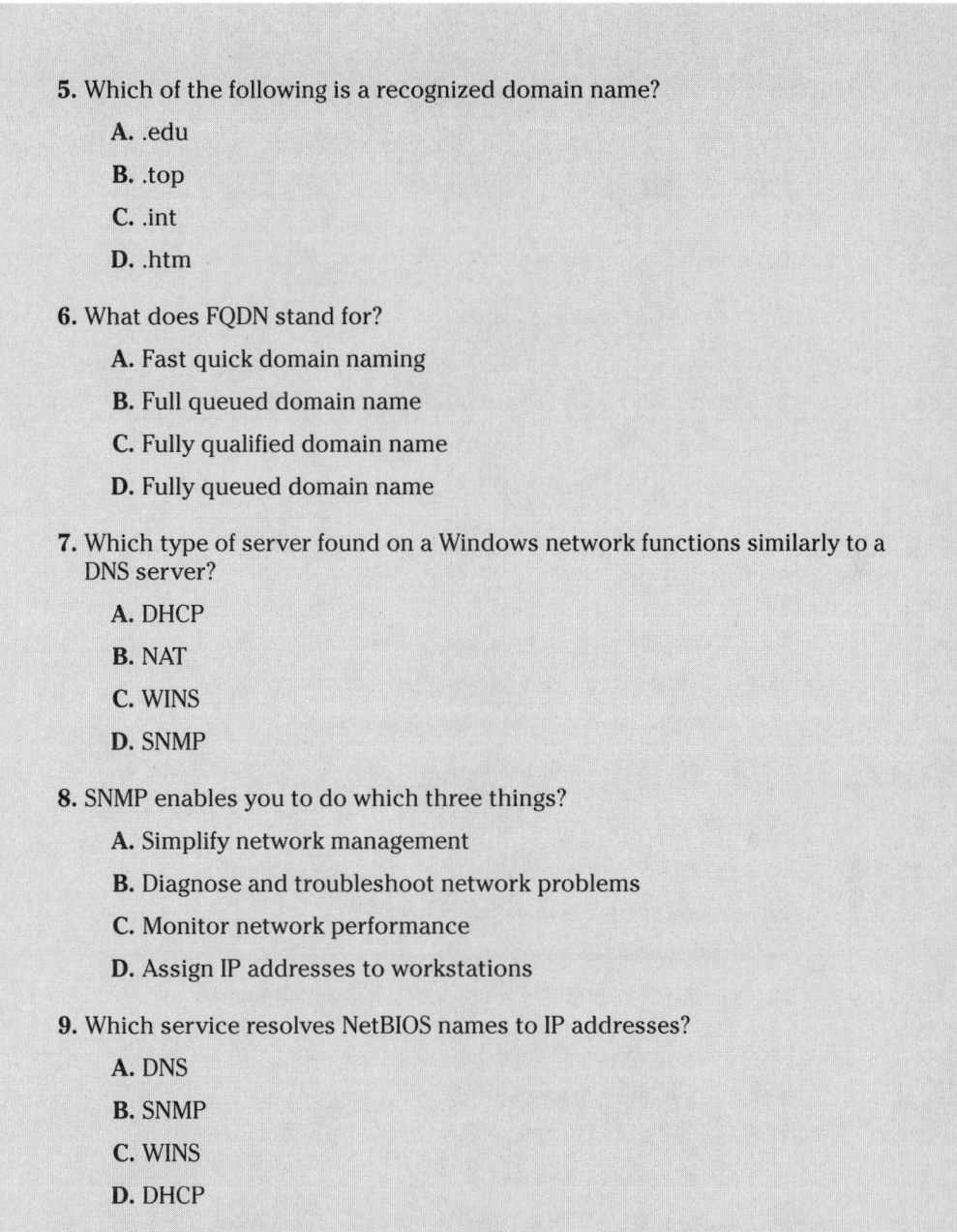

   D. DHCP

10. What is the function of an SNMP agent?

   A. To collect and store management information about a specific device

   B. To monitor information about a specific device

   C. To resolve IP addresses to host names

   D. To act as a Web server

11. What kind of network devices can an SNMP agent reside on?

    A. Routers

    B. Switches

    C. Hubs

    D. Servers

12. What does a MIB database consist of?

    A. Information about managed devices

    B. Objects, which describe various functions

    C. Information about DNS entries

    D. Objects, which hold NetBIOS names

13. You can't connect to a server when you use its domain name, but you can connect to it if you use its IP address. What is the most likely cause of the problem?

    A. The WINS server isn't working correctly.

    B. The DHCP server isn't working correctly.

    C. The SNMP agent isn't running on the server.

    D. The DNS server isn't working correctly.

14. What is the purpose of a NAT?

    A. To assign IP addresses to workstations dynamically

    B. To monitor the network for bottlenecks

    C. To run the SNMP agent

    D. To connect multiple computers to other IP networks

15. What feature does a NAT support to help with network security?

    A. It can act like a firewall.

    B. It can act like a DHCP server.

    C. It can act like a DNS server.

    D. It can act like a WINS server.

16. By hiding your real IP address on the Internet, you are protecting your Internal network from what?

    A. Hackers

    B. Viruses

C. Trojans

D. Unsolicited e-mail

17. What service provides networked computers with the capability to share a single connection to the Internet?

    A. Domain Name Service

    B. Internet Connection Sharing

    C. Dynamic Host Configuration Protocol

    D. Simple Network Management Protocol

18. What service consists of a primary computer identified as a gateway?

    A. Domain Name Service

    B. Windows Internet Naming Service

    C. Dynamic Host Configuration Protocol

    D. Internet Connecting Sharing

19. What type of server keeps a database of tables that translates fully qualified Internet domain names into their respective IP addresses?

    A. DNS server

    B. DHCP server

    C. WINS server

    D. NAT server

20. Which of the following is needed to set up an ICS network?

    A. A DHCP server

    B. A network connection device for each computer

    C. A firewall

    D. A SNMP agent

Scenarios

1. You are a network administrator in an office that has only five computer systems that run the Windows 98 Second Edition (SE) operating system. One of the computer systems has a modem that it uses to connect to the Internet. What type of Windows service can you install on every computer system to enable all five computer systems to access the Internet?

2. You are a new network administrator for a large company and your WINS and DNS servers need to be assigned new IP addresses. The previous network administrator used static IP addresses for these servers. What would be the most effective way of assigning these two servers new IP addresses?

Answers to Chapter Questions

Chapter Pre-Test

1. A DHCP (Dynamic Host Configuration Protocol) server automatically assigns IP addresses to client workstations at boot up.

2. Besides automatically assigning IP addresses, a DHCP server can also assign the default gateway and subnet mask.

3. A DNS (Domain Name Service) identifies a host by a domain name. Words are used instead of numbers to identify Internet hosts. A DNS server resolves these names to their respective IP addresses.

4. The difference between a DNS server and WINS server is that a DNS server resolves host names into IP addresses and a WINS server resolves NetBIOS names into IP addresses.

5. A Windows Internet Naming Service (WINS) translates NetBIOS names to IP addresses.

6. SNMP stands for Simple Network Management Protocol. SNMP enables you to collect and exchange information between devices on your network.

7. The two main components of SNMP are an SNMP agent and a network management system.

8. An SNMP agent can reside on network devices such as routers, switches, hubs, servers, workstations, and printers.

9. SNMP uses a community string as a security measure. SNMP is a type of identification or password that is set for all SNMP operations.

10. *Public* is the default name of a community string. You should rename the default public community string to help prevent unauthorized SNMP access to the monitored devices.

Assessment Questions

1. B. A DHCP server automatically assigns addresses to devices connecting to the network. For review see the "Understanding DHCP" section.

2. C. You would use a DHCP server to assign dynamic IP addresses to the client workstations. On a large network you should use a DHCP server. If you do not use a DHCP server on a large network, you have to assign the IP addresses to

the client workstations manually, which is very time consuming. For review see the "Understanding DHCP" section.

3. B. WINS is the only network service in the list. WINS stands for Windows Internet Naming Service. This service translates NetBIOS names to IP addresses. For review see the "Understanding WINS" section.

4. A. A DNS server translates domain names to their respective IP addresses. For review see the "Understanding DNS" section.

5. A. .edu is the domain for education. Other popular domain names are .com for commercial, .gov for government, .org for organization, and .net for network. For review see the "Understanding DNS" section.

6. C. FQDN stands for fully qualified domain name. For example, `www.hungryminds.com` is a fully qualified domain name: www is the host, hungryminds is the second-level domain, and .com is the top-level domain. For review see the "Understanding DNS" section.

7. C. A WINS server is used on networks that are running NetBIOS over a TCP/IP network. A WINS server translates NetBIOS names to IP addresses. For review see the "Understanding WINS" section.

8. A, B, and C. SNMP stands for Simple Network Management Protocol. This service enables you to collect and exchange information between devices on your network. Monitoring network performance and diagnosing network problems are some of the features with SNMP. For review see the "Using SNMP to Monitor Your Network" section.

9. C. A Windows Internet Naming Service (WINS) server performs the function of translating NetBIOS names to IP addresses. A WINS server builds its own reference table dynamically of all NetBIOS names on the network by collecting the date when each workstation is booted up. For review see the "Understanding WINS" section.

10. B. The main function of an SNMP agent is to collect and store management information about specific devices and make that information about that device available to the NMS. For review see the "Using SNMP to Monitor Your Network" section.

11. A, B, C, and D. An SNMP agent can reside on routers, switches, hubs and servers. An SNMP agent can also run on workstations and printers. For review see the "Using SNMP to Monitor Your Network" section.

12. A and B. A MIB database consists of information about managed devices and it also consists of objects, which describe various functions that can be measured and monitored. For review see the "Using SNMP to Monitor Your Network" section.

13. D. The DNS server isn't working. If you can connect to the server by its IP address but not its domain name, the DNS server is down or isn't working correctly. If the DNS server were working correctly, you would have no problem connecting to the server by its domain name. For review see the "Understanding DNS" section.

14. D. The purpose of a NAT is to connect multiple computers to other IP networks. A NAT acts like a firewall and enables the combination of multiple internal IP addresses into a single Internet connection. For review see the "Understanding NAT/ICS" section.

15. A. A NAT acts like a firewall by hiding internal network IP addresses. Only one IP address is sent out on to the Internet, which makes all communications look as if they originate from one device. For review see the "Understanding NAT/ICS" section.

16. A. To gain access to your internal network, a hacker needs an internal IP address. Because a NAT, for example, does not enable your real IP address to leave the internal network, you are increasing your network security from hackers. For review see the "Understanding NAT/ICS" section.

17. B. Internet Connection Sharing (ICS) provides networked computers with the capability to share a single connection to the Internet. For review see the "Understanding NAT/ICS" section.

18. D. When using the Internet Connection Sharing service, one primary computer is used as the central point through which all other workstations connect to the Internet. This primary computer is called the gateway. For review see the "Understanding NAT/ICS" section.

19. A. A DNS (Domain Name Service) server translates fully qualified Internet domain names to their respective IP addresses; this information is kept in a database on the DNS server. For review see the "Understanding DNS section.

20. B. Each computer needs a network connection device, such as a network card or modem. Each computer must use one of these devices to connect to the primary computer to access the Internet. For review see the "Understanding NAT/ICS" section.

Scenarios

1. The service that can connect all systems to the Internet is Internet Connection Sharing (ICS). ICS is a built-in feature of Windows 98 Second Edition, Windows 2000, and Windows Me. ICS provides networked computers with the capability to share a single connection to the Internet.

2. Using the DHCP (Dynamic Host Configuration Protocol) service, you eliminate the tedious manual configuring of TCP/IP configurations when a server needs to be assigned a new IP address. DHCP is capable of automatically assigning IP addresses when a specific device boots up on the network. With DHCP, static IP addresses can be eliminated.

Public and Private Networks

CHAPTER 9

EXAM OBJECTIVES

* Identify the differences between public and private networks.

CHAPTER PRE-TEST

1. The most common example of a public network is the _____.
2. _____ is a major area of concern for public networks.
3. Data transmission over public networks can be secured by _____.
4. Private networks use _____ to protect computers from unauthorized access.
5. Data is transmitted over the Internet as _____.
6. A _____ uses a combination of existing dedicated internal networks and the Internet to securely communicate information.

✦ Answers to these questions can be found at the end of the chapter. ✦

Networks provide the core of many businesses today. The key issue for businesses is to have a network that addresses their needs adequately. Deciding on the type of network needed depends on issues such as scale, location, growth, security requirements, and cost. All these issues must be measured and balanced to find an appropriate network solution for the work in hand. This chapter looks at a basic categorization of networks: public and private networks. We also look at a network solution that combines the advantages of both these networks.

Public Networks

The simplest definition of a *public network* is a network accessible to everyone. In effect, any network shared between multiple administrative domains can be referred to as a public network. The most cited example of a public network is the Internet. The Internet is a classical public network because access is unrestricted. Anyone who has the appropriate hardware and software can access the Internet. Another example of a public network could be a long distance telephone network that serves many customers.

Public networks provide lucrative business opportunities. Internet commerce, online banking, online stock exchange are just some examples of the great avenues that public networks open up. But due to the architecture of public networks, there are ways for people to intercept and replace data in transit. Anyone can intercept and eavesdrop on your private conversations or credit card exchanges. People might also replace your information with their own and send it back on its way.

Most public networks do not require users to have special permissions or passwords to access the shared information. Therefore, the information available on public networks is not inherently secure. However, data transmission over public networks can be secured by using encryption. Encryption is the process of using a mathematical algorithm to transform information into a format that can't be read, called the cipher text format. Decryption is the process of using another algorithm to transform encrypted information back into a readable format, called the plain text format. The process of encryption and decryption of data is also commonly called cryptography. Traditionally, cryptography means that the sender uses a secret key (or code) to encrypt the data and the receiver uses a secret key to decrypt the information. Some popular cryptography methods include public-key cryptography and private-key cryptography.

In addition to encryption, you can also authenticate data transmission over a public network. Authentication is digital verification of who you are, much in the same way your driver's license proves your identity. Normally, over a public network, it is easy to send spoofed mail. You can pretend to be somebody else while sending mail. With unencrypted e-mail facilities, you have no way to verify who the sender is. With digital verification that uses digital signatures and certificates, you can digitally encode verifiable proof of your identity (or that of any other legitimate user) into the mail message itself.

A *digital signature* is a method (based on cryptography) of authenticating transactions taking place over the Internet. Organizations called *Certificate Authorities* (CAs) issue digital certificates. These electronic documents attach to e-mail messages and contain the secret keys (public and private keys) that enable you to create digital signatures.

A digital signature is made with a cryptographic algorithm. The algorithm is based on the keys provided by the CA, and cannot be forged without access to the keys. Usually, you use your private key to sign documents. When you send such signed documents, the receiver uses the public key to decrypt the documents.

Advantages of public networks

The most obvious advantage of a public network is that it costs much less to set up than a secure private network. Often you can add computers to a public network without much additional cost and with minimum effort or complexity. The mechanisms that make networks secure are often complex and costly, partly because they require knowledge and expertise in security and networking to run properly. Also, the time taken to set up computers on a public network is normally much less than that for setting up computers on a secured private network. Public networks provide means of communicating with people across the world. Education, businesses, entertainment, and various other industries benefit greatly from public networks.

Disadvantages of public networks

As mentioned earlier, the biggest disadvantage of a public network is its lack of security. The information available on a public network can be accessed by almost anybody. For this reason, such networks cannot be used for communicating or transferring confidential information, unless special security measures (such as encryption or authentication) are in place.

If an organization's computers share a public network, intruders might get in and tamper with the information, creating major problems. By virtue of their wide-open accessibility, public networks are prone to virus attacks; no network-wide mechanism exists to filter all the data that passes through a public network. Configuring computers with antivirus software (and other such protection) is not an adequate solution; intruders are always finding new and more devastating ways to break into networks.

As we now understand, public networks are not appropriate for sharing critical information. To overcome their shortcomings, private networks are used in areas that must provide greater security for the information that travels over them.

Private Networks

Private networks are usually organization specific or are restricted to a group of users. Such networks are dedicated and designed to satisfy the needs of a specific organization. Common examples of private networks include LAN and PABX.

Consider some typical real-world implementations of private networks. Some companies, for example, allow only their employees to access their corporate networks. In the banking industry, access to the private ATM network is available only to customers who have appropriate PIN numbers and/or passwords. Many private networks are set up as *intranets* — secured networks that are internal to the organization (although they function in exactly the same way as the Internet does). Normally the data found on an intranet is protected from Internet users.

In a private network, computers have IP addresses that are not part of the Internet's addressing scheme; thus, the computers on the private network can access the Internet, but computers on the Internet cannot access the computers on the private network.

A *router* connects the private network to the Internet; this device must mediate between the privately addressed computers and their IP-addressed counterparts — a task called *network address translation* (NAT) — to achieve communication with external networks such as the Internet. The router must have a valid Internet IP address because it interacts with other computers on the Internet. However, the computers on the private network can have any IP addresses since they are not connected to the Internet directly.

If a computer on the private network wants to interact with a computer on the Internet, data packets with Internet requests are sent to the router. The router then forwards them on to the requested server on the Internet. Responses from the Internet servers are directed to the router. The router automatically finds what packets are for which computer on the private network. The router is also often capable of deciding which packets to forward and which to discard due to security reasons.

Firewalls

When computers within a private network communicate with the Internet, it is extremely important that precautions are taken so that unauthorized people cannot access the private network with malicious intent. This is commonly done by installing and configuring *firewalls* — systems whose role is to protect sensitive information by ensuring that all communication between an organization's network and the Internet — in both directions — conforms to the organization's security policies.

A typical firewall consists of a computer system (or group of computer systems) configured to reinforce information security and placed between a private network and an outside network. The most important aspect of a firewall is that it is at the entry point of the networked system it protects. All information passing between external and internal networks must go through the firewall. Therefore, the firewall is the ideal point at which to implement filtering, monitoring, and logging of any sessions that link one network and another.

The firewall protects your information system from attacks originating outside your network, but can also protect external systems against attacks originating from *within* your network. Both types of protection are necessary.

Two main types of firewalls exist:

- Packet-filtering firewalls
- Application-based firewalls

Packet-filtering firewalls

All Internet traffic travels as *packets*. A packet is a quantity of data of limited size, kept small for easy handling. When larger amounts of continuous data must be sent, it is broken up into numbered packets for transmission and reassembled at the receiving end.

A packet generally contains information regarding:

- The data, acknowledgment, request, or command from the originating system
- The source IP address and port
- The destination IP address and port
- The protocol by which the packet is to be handled
- Error handling
- The type and status of the data being sent

In a packet-filtering firewall, the protocol and the address information of each packet is examined. Its contents and context are ignored. The firewall does not consider the applications on the host or local network. The source of the incoming data is also ignored. This is the original and most basic type of firewall.

The packets are allowed or disallowed to pass into the system based on the protocol and address information matching the security policies set for the internal network.

Packet-filtering policies may be based upon any of the following:

- Source IP address
- Destination port
- Protocol

Advantages of packet-filtering firewalls

The main advantages of a packet-filtering firewall are as follows:

- It is transparent, which means that applications don't have to be reworked to take advantage of them
- It is cost-effective
- It can filter any service built around the network protocols supported by the firewall.

Disadvantages of packet-filtering firewalls

The disadvantages of this firewall system are as follows:

- To make effective use of this system, the network administrator must be thoroughly familiar with the network and with the protocols used on this network.
- There is no user authentication. The filtering is based on the hardware system's network address.
- Packet filtering doesn't conceal the network's internal architecture.
- With DHCP, IP addresses aren't fixed. The hardware system can have a different IP address each time it's started up.

Application-based firewalls

In this type of firewall, clients do not connect directly to the outside network. All communication is directed through the firewall. The firewall establishes a connection with the outside network for the client, sends requests, receives responses, analizes them, and then relays them to the client within the internal network. This makes the internal system invisible to the external network.

An application-based firewall can allow or disallow traffic according to specific rules, such as allowing only specific commands to a server, limiting file access to certain types, and varying rules according to authenticated users. This type of firewall may also perform detailed logging of traffic and monitoring of events on the host system, and can often be instructed to sound alarms or notify an operator under defined conditions.

Such a firewall provides good security, because monitoring takes place at application level. This makes the system more flexible and powerful.

If an external network attacks the internal network, only the connection between the attacker and the firewall is affected. The other computers on the internal network remain safe.

> **Tip**
>
> You may also see application-based firewalls called *application proxies*.

Advantages of application-based firewalls
The advantages of an application-based firewall are as follows:

- Security rules are easy to define
- User authentication is implemented
- The internal architecture of the network can be concealed, because all connections to the outside network pass through the firewall
- All transactions are logged

Disadvantages of application-based firewalls
Application-based firewalls have some characteristic disadvantages as well:

- Both the hardware and software for such systems are costly
- This system is not cost-effective for small networks
- Special client software is needed to take advantage of the firewall
- System administration is more demanding than with this system

Advantages of private networks

Setting up a private network has a number of advantages, including security and simpler management. However, the single most common reason for setting up a private network is to use a single IP address to connect to the Internet.

There are also advantages to a private network if you have some type of dedicated connection. In this case, if you set up your computers as a private network, you won't have to pay for IP addresses for every computer on your network. Also, for larger networks, private IP addresses are easier to manage; they need not use a particular assigned address range, and you never have to request additional addresses.

A private network is also much more secure. Computers on the private network are not directly connected to the Internet, so it is extremely difficult for unauthorized users to access computers on the private network. However, a private network is complex to set up, if its servers or other computers are to be made safely accessible from outside.

If your bandwidth requirements are high but availability is low, setting up a private network solves a lot of problems. The thing to note here is that when you set up a private network, ownership costs increase but bandwidth costs come down. You'll have to estimate the costs before deciding on the best option.

Private networks offer flexibility in terms of the number of machines you can set up and the functions those computers can perform on the network. Private networks also offer a stable, reliable, and more secure platform for those functions.

Private networks are cost-effective for connecting buildings physically close or for organizations that have multiple buildings in a small geographical location.

Disadvantages of private networks

Private networks are restricted to specific users. Therefore, such networks cannot be used for providing services to many customers. These networks are suitable for performing only specific tasks applicable to the group of authorized users.

Sometimes, the costs of acquiring and setting up private network infrastructures are high. This is because devices such as routers, switches, and special cables are necessary to set up a private network with access to the Internet.

Differences Between Public and Private Networks

Public and private networks differ not only in structure but also in function — both have characteristic advantages and disadvantages. Table 9-1 summarizes the differences between the two types of networks and compares them in terms of some common networking parameters.

Table 9-1
Differences Between Public and Private Networks

Parameter	Public Networks	Private Networks
Security	Not secure unless special methods such as encryption or authentication are employed.	Very secure. Only authorized users have access to such networks.
Cost	Low cost to join a public network and use the facilities.	High infrastructure cost to set up and maintain private networks.
Reach	Global reach. Everyone has access to public networks. No geographical restrictions.	Limited to a group of people with specific needs. Restricted to small geographical locations.
Complexity	Easy to set up. Anyone with the appropriate hardware and software can access public networks.	Complex set up required for computers within the network to interact with the Internet.
Usability	Can be used for online banking, trading, education, entertainment, and many other activities involving people across the world.	Can be used for specific business purposes serving a defined set of customer base.

Virtual Private Network

To combine the advantages of public and private networks, *virtual private networks* (VPNs) were developed. A VPN uses a combination of existing dedicated internal networks and Internet connections to provide secure communication and transport of information. In effect, a VPN carries private data over a public network — and keeps it private.

Increasingly, businesses are going global and basing employees around the world. The remote-site employees constantly need access to the corporate network and its business-critical applications (such as group messaging, file sharing, and databases). Private networks are too expensive to deploy in such a situation; public networks are too insecure. Virtual private networking provides a secure solution — communication over the Internet that allows remote employees and business partners to access their private corporate network with minimal risk.

VPNs provide data privacy, access control, data integrity, and authentication services at a low level in the network and are independent of the applications using the network. When connected by VPN links, two networks can act as one secure network.

VPN technology works to provide a dedicated secure communication channel between networked computers. VPNs use advanced encryption technologies to establish secure, end-to-end, private network connections over public networks, such as the Internet. VPNs employ various tunneling and authentication protocols, such as L2TP (Layer 2 Tunneling Protocol), PPTP (Point-to-Point Tunneling Protocol), IPSec (IP Security), and CHAP (Challenge Handshake Authentication Protocol) to provide secure communication. Authentication techniques such as digital certificates are also often used.

The private corporate networks have a router or gateway that communicates with the Internet. The gateways at each point of entry into the corporate networks are configured as VPN gateways that secure the connections.

When a connection is established between two entities, both entities (whether departments or organizations) can consistently ensure the security of their data if they negotiate a security policy to be used in their subsequent communications. During this negotiation, issues such as the form of authentication, the key lengths and whether encryption is used, are decided. When the two entities communicate, they reference the established security policy to authenticate and secure the information.

Summary

This chapter examined public and private networks, the differences between them, and their respective advantages and disadvantages. Next, the chapter explained the use of cryptography and firewalls to enhance network security, and looked at virtual private networks (VPNs) as a way to combine the advantages of public and private networks.

✦ ✦ ✦

STUDY GUIDE

This study guide presents assessment questions to test your knowledge of the exam topic area.

Assessment Questions

1. Your server stores sensitive data regarding employee salaries. You have to share this data with the HR department at a location in a different city across the company WAN. How can you best ensure that the data remains confidential during transmission?

    A. Encrypt the data before transmission

    B. Encode the data before transmission

    C. Reformat the data to include unnecessary accounting information to confuse unauthorized users

    D. Set share-level security on the data store before transmission

2. What is the most important security function of a firewall?

    A. Allows people on the Internet to see just one IP address

    B. Does not allow any connections to the server

    C. Restricts unauthorized users from accessing sensitive data

    D. Manages password functions

3. A packet-filtering firewall uses which parts of a packet? (Select all that apply)

    A. The destination port Number

    B. Source IP address

    C. WINS server name

    D. DNS lookup order

4. You want to set up a secured communication connection (a VPN) between your offices in New York and London over the Internet. Which of the following communication protocols should you use?

    A. UDP

    B. TCP/IP

    C. SLIP

    D. PPTP

5. How does a server on the Internet know where to deliver data packets?

   A. Data IP number

   B. Destination IP address and port number

   C. Packet ID number

   D. IP protocol

6. You want to set up a system so the structure of your corporate network is hidden from unauthorized Internet users. What should you do?

   A. Set up a packet-filtering firewall

   B. Encrypt all communication

   C. Set up an application-based firewall

   D. It cannot be done

7. Which network device may provide public-to-private network security?

   A. Hub

   B. Switch

   C. Bridge

   D. Router

8. Digital signatures involve which of the following? (Select all that apply)

   A. Complete data encryption

   B. Public- and private-key cryptography

   C. Encrypted API

   D. Certificate Authorities

Answers to Chapter Questions

Chapter Pre-Test

1. The most common example of a public network is the *Internet*.

2. *Security* is a major area of concern for public networks.

3. Data transmission over public networks can be secured by *encryption*.

4. Private networks use *firewalls* to protect computers from unauthorized access.

5. Data is transmitted over the Internet as *packets*.

6. A *VPN* uses a combination of existing dedicated internal networks and the Internet to securely communicate information.

Assessment Questions

1. A. Encryption of data ensures that it cannot be read or tampered with in transit. For more information, refer to the section titled "Public Networks."

2. C. Firewalls prevent unauthorized access to private networks, thus protecting confidential data from unauthorized access. For more information, refer to the section titled "Firewalls."

3. A, B. A packet-filtering firewall authenticates data according to information contained in the packet: specifically, the source and destination IP addresses and the port number. For more information, refer to the section titled "Packet-Filtering Firewalls."

4. D. A VPN normally uses PPTP to establish secure communication, though it may also use other protocols (such as L2TP and IPSec) for that purpose. For more information, refer to the section titled "Virtual Private Networks."

5. B. Data packets contain a lot of identifying information, including the destination IP address and port number. This information guides data packets to their correct destinations. For more information, refer to the section titled "Packet-Filtering Firewalls."

6. C. Application-based firewalls encapsulate the network structure, limiting accessibility from external networks. For more information, refer to the section titled "Application-Based Firewalls."

7. D. Routers are often used to establish a firewall or a gateway between public and private networks. For more information, refer to the section titled "Private Networks."

8. B, D. Authentication by digital signature encrypts the data by using a private key — and decrypts it by using a public key. The Certificate Authority provides the private and public keys. For more information, refer to the section titled "Public Networks."

CHAPTER 10

WAN Technologies and Remote Access

EXAM OBJECTIVES

- ✦ Identify the basic characteristics (for example, speed, capacity, media) of the following WAN technologies:
  - Packet switching vs. circuit switching
  - ISDN
  - FDDI
  - ATM
  - Frame Relay
  - SONET/SDH
  - T1/E1
  - T3/E3
  - OCX*

- ✦ Define the function of the following remote access protocols and services:
  - RAS
  - PPP
  - PPTP
  - ICA

CHAPTER PRE-TEST

1. What is a WAN?
2. What is packet switching?
3. What is circuit switching?
4. How does a modem transmit digital signals over analog lines?
5. What is multiplexing?
6. What are the three major carrier signal standards?
7. Which two protocols are most used for point-to-point connections?
8. What is a tunneling protocol used for?
9. What is a Virtual Private Network?
10. What is a thin client?

✦ Answers to these questions can be found at the end of the chapter. ✦

As explained in earlier chapters of this book, LANs use certain technologies and protocols to talk to one another over what is called a *wide area network,* or *WAN.*

This chapter covers the basic concepts behind WANs, and the commonly used WAN technologies that you should know for the Network+ exam, such as

- Packet switching
- Circuit switching
- Analog and digital carrier signals

WANs and Internetworks

The most common example of a WAN is the Internet, which takes its name from the word internetwork (an alternate term for WAN). The Internet is the most complex possible example of an internetwork. At its simplest, a WAN is a combination of at least two *local area networks,* or LANs.

Tip You can think of a WAN as a larger LAN with at least two LANs acting as network segments on the WAN.

Just as LANs require their own types of hardware to function (for example, WANs use routers instead of bridges), WANs also use their own protocols and technologies.

Remote Networking Basics

Before we dive into the technologies themselves, you must be familiar with certain concepts, including packet switching and circuit switching, or the functions of the protocols and technologies don't make much sense. WAN technologies are all either packet switching or circuit switching.

Data carrier services

A *carrier service* is a provider (such as an ISP) of data transmission over a physical medium. Two main types of carrier services exist today:

- Analog
- Digital

The following sections describe each of these types of carrier services, and the main technologies behind each.

Analog carrier services

Analog carrier services carry analog signals over the POTS, which is a rather funky-looking acronym for *plain old telephone system* (which is also called the *Public Switched Telephone Network,* or PSTN). POTS refers to pretty much exactly what it sounds like: the analog wiring used by good ol' Ma Bell and her descendents, the Baby Bells. POTS uses twisted-pair wires to connect homes to the central office. After about four miles, a repeater must be installed to overcome the wire's attenuation limitations.

The most popular method of connecting to the Internet is over dial-up modems, which

+ Modulate digital computer data into analog data for transmission over phone lines
+ Demodulate analog data into digital data on the receiving end of a transmission

Digital carrier services

Digital lines transmit data digitally (in binary format) from source to destination, eliminating the level of abstraction — and speed reduction — that analog carrier services add to a network. Three major standards for digital carrier signals exist, including the digital signal (DS) standard and the T and E carrier standards. The following list shows the major carrier signal standards, and Table 10-1 shows the major levels of each standard along with their speeds and relationship to one another.

+ **DS levels:** The ANSI DS standard (DS stands for digital signal) defines digital signal rates based on multiples of 64 Kbps, which is the typical speed of a POTS line (see the "Analog signals" section earlier in this chapter). Table 10-1 shows the DS signals, their multiples and data rates, and where the E- and T-carrier signals match up to those signals.

> **Note:** In Table 10-1, the T-1, T-2, and T-3 standards align comfortably with the DS1, DS2, and DS3 standards, but the E-carrier standards never seem to coincide with DS designations at all.

+ **T-carrier levels:** The T-carrier system, introduced in the U.S. in the 1960s by Ma Bell, was the first system to support digitized voice transmission. The T system uses twisted pair wires, but can also run on coax, fiber-optic cable, and others. In the United States, Canada, and Japan, the T-carrier system is the standard used for digital transmissions. T signals use a 24-pulse code modulation (PCM) signal with time-division multiplexing (TDM, explained in the "Multiplexing" section later in this chapter) at a rate of 1.544 million bits per second (Mbps). T1 lines transport their signal over copper wire and are typically used for distances between or within major metropolitan areas.

In the Real World

Internet service providers (ISPs) commonly use the T-1 and T-3 transmission rates, and they typically connect their own equipment to the Internet by renting a T-1, T-3, or fractional T-1 network line from a major telephone company.

+ **E-carrier levels:** The E-carrier system was created by the ITU-TS and is used in Europe in place of the T-carrier system (which is used mostly in North America and Japan). The E-1 signal format is the rough equivalent to the T-1 format in the United States. The E-2 through E-5 signal formats are multiples of the E-1 standard, which explains why they have no relation whatsoever to the T-2 through T-2 or T-3 standards.

Exam Tip

Remember the data rates and multiples for the four levels of the T-carrier system, and that an E-1 is roughly equivalent to a T-1.

Table 10-1
DS Signals

DS Designation	Data Rate	Multiple	T-Carrier Signal	E-Carrier Signal
DS0	64 Kbps	0	-	-
DS1	1.544 Mbps	24	T-1	-
-	2.048 Mbps	32	-	E-1
DS2	6.312 Mbps	96	T-2	-
-	8.448 Mbps	128	-	E-2
-	34.368 Mbps	512	-	E-3
DS3	44.736 Mbps	672	T-3	-
-	139.264 Mbps	2,048	-	E-4
DS4	274.176 Mbps	4,032	-	-
-	565.148 Mbps	8,192 (or four E-4 channels)	-	E-5

Modulation

The process of transferring data to a signal carrier, or the actual pushing of data over a network, is called *modulation*. Modulation in a networking environment typically involves a modem, which translates digital signals into analog signals for transmission over an analog network and then back to digital after the data makes it to the receiving end. Modems modulate data by changing the 1s and 0s of the bit data into high (for 1s) and low (for 0s) tones that are then reinterpreted on the receiving end as 1s and 0s. Modems perform this function so quickly that the resulting sound is like screeching; if you have ever had a dial-up Internet connection, chances are that you know this noise.

How a T-1 gets its speed

Although you really don't need to know information this detailed for the Network+ exam, if you're wondering how the speed of a given signal carrier is determined, a good example is the most popular example: the T-1 carrier system.

In a T-1 system, voice data is sampled at a rate of 8,000 times a second, with each sample being digitized into an 8-bit package called a *word*. The T-1 has 24 channels being digitized simultaneously, which means that a 192-bit frame (that includes 24 channels each with one 8-bit word) is transmitted 8,000 times in every second. During transmission, each frame is separated from the next by a single bit. Multiplied by the number of these frames sent per second (8,000), including the single bits (193 times 8000), the result is the per-second rate of a T-1: 1.544 Mbps. The following figure illustrates this concept.

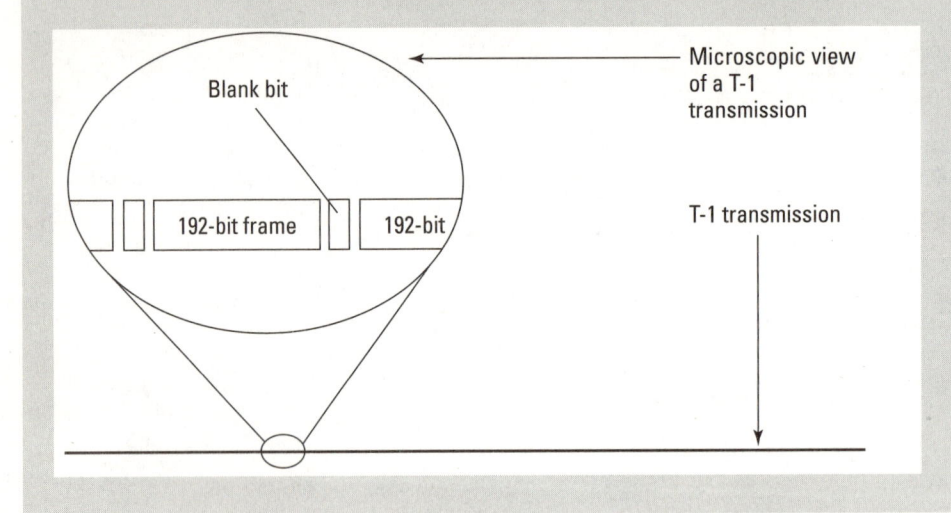

Multiplexing

Multiplexing is the transmission of data in multiple pieces simultaneously along the same channel. Multiplexing uses the same kind of hardware on either end of a high-bandwidth, long-distance cable:

- At the sending end, it's called the *multiplexer*
- At the receiving end, it's called the *demultiplexer*.

The same devices can be used as multiplexer and demultiplexer, depending on which end is sending and which is receiving.

The two main methods of multiplexing are as follows:

- **Time Division Multiplexing (TDM):** Used for digital communication, TDM utilizes time slots to divide a transmission. In this model, the multiplexer on the sending end of the network spits out data in short, timed bursts, dynamically adjusting the time sequences depending on available bandwidth. TDM is best used in situations where the bandwidth required by users varies.

- **Frequency Division Multiplexing (FDM):** Used for analog communication, FDM uses multiple channels, called *subchannels,* of a single channel.

  Each subchannel uses a different frequency for each input, enabling data from multiple users to be sent along the same channel at the same time. FDM is best used when the bandwidth required by each user can be easily predicted.

Packet switching and circuit switching

Packet switching enables multiplexing, a networking feature that enables users to share the same data stream. Packet switching is an important concept to understand (not to mention that it's on the test) because it's so widely used in modern WANs, including the Internet. Also, packet switching helps you to understand the difference between connectionless and connection-oriented modes of transporting data over a network.

Circuit switching

Circuit switching, by contrast with packet switching, utilizes one consistent circuit, be that circuit virtual (a dedicated route from source to destination) or physical (an actual dedicated circuit).

Here's how a typical circuit-switching session works:

1. A user requests a circuit-switching service (for example, by picking up a phone and dialing the number of a person he or she wants to call).

2. The server sets up a dedicated communication circuit (or path) for a communication session (such as a phone call). Until the session (or call) is broken, that circuit is dedicated solely to that service (in this case, the phone call).

> **Exam Tip:** A circuit can be either a physical circuit or a virtual circuit. Some software technologies, such as ISDN, use virtual circuits to set up "lines" that are dedicated to one customer. With classic circuit switching, such as with the telephone companies, actual circuits are used. The general concepts involved in both processes are the same, even if the implementation is different. The concepts are all you really need to know for the exam.

3. When the session (or call) ends, the circuits are free to be dedicated to another session.

Figure 10-1 shows a visual representation of how circuit switching works. The step numbers in the list above correspond to the numbers in the figure.

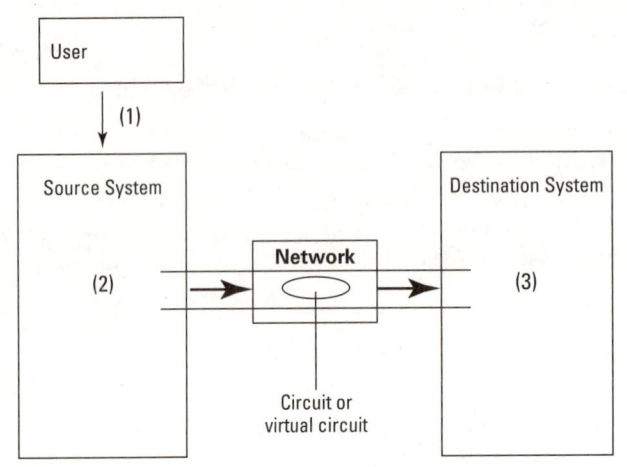

Figure 10-1: A visual representation of circuit switching

The problem with the circuit-switching model in a typical networking environment is that when one user is transmitting over a given line, no one else can do so. Therefore, implementing a circuit-switching environment requires a great deal of overhead, including

- Constant monitoring of the ongoing service
- Dedication to ensuring the continued quality of the service
- Lots of server storage space and bandwidth

Packet switching

Packet switching involves sending packets in bursts over a network *asynchronously* (which just means they're not sent in order) and then reassembling those packets into the requested data on the receiving end of the transmission.

Here's how a typical packet-switching session works:

1. A user requests a service (for example, by sending a file over the Internet).
2. The TCP/IP protocol stack on the source system starts a connection with the remote host, attaches the destination IP address in the form of header information to each of the new packets, and does a CRC calculation (see Chapter 5 for more info on CRC) on the data and records that information with each individual packet.
3. TCP/IP breaks the packet into asynchronous chunks.

4. TCP/IP sends packet chunks over the network individually.

5. The TCP/IP stack on the destination system receives the packets in no particular order (certainly not the proper order) and then performs sequencing on the packets (using header information) to put them back into their proper sequence. The TCP/IP stack on the destination system then does a CRC (see Chapter 5 for more info on CRC) on the data to ensure that it's all there and then delivers the data to its destination.

Figure 10-2 shows a visual representation of how packet switching works. The step numbers in the list above correspond to the numbers in the figure.

Packet switching vs. circuit switching

Packet switching has one major advantage over circuit switching: Using packet switching, the data from literally hundreds of users can all be traveling on the same line simultaneously and, most importantly, *no one has to wait*. However, packet switching isn't entirely without disadvantages. Here are the two biggest disadvantages of packet switching as opposed to circuit switching:

✦ Data has a higher chance of being corrupted en route to its destination when using packet switching.

✦ The quality of service (QoS) isn't often as high as it is with circuit switching.

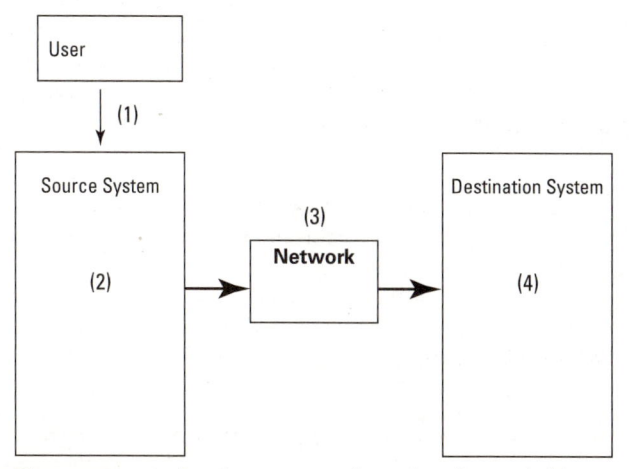

Figure 10-2: A visual representation of packet switching

In the Real World

If you have ever used a Webcam to talk to a friend over the Internet and have seen the terrible quality of the picture, you know what a QoS "issue" feels like. That choppy video you see when talking to grandma using Microsoft NetMeeting is a result of dropped packets.

Still, despite the failings of packet switching, the benefits of the feature in enabling users to share service space is so great that this model is used almost exclusively on the Internet and in typical network settings. Also, advanced forms of packet switching (such as ATM, which is explained later in this chapter) are appearing now that enable more flexibility than circuit switching while maintaining the quality of service that packet switching typically can't guarantee.

Wide Area Network Technologies

As with LANs and the protocols they require, certain technologies are required to make wide area networks (WANs) a reality. This section explains the major WAN technologies that you need to know for the Network+ exam.

ATM

ATM (which stands in this case for *Asynchronous Transfer Mode*, not to be confused with ATM bank machines) uses dedicated hardware-switching technology to perform the following tasks:

- Organize digital data into 53-byte fixed-length packets called *cells*
- Transmit those cells asynchronously in digital signals over a network

Because ATM uses packets to transfer data, ATM is considered a packet-switching protocol (and is even called *fast packet switching* by some), even though it allows for high-quality multimedia transmissions without a physical, dedicated circuit. With ATM, packets are transmitted asynchronously on a network and carry error-checking information.

ATM is designed to accommodate (and even prioritize) multiple types of transmissions, especially where multimedia is concerned (remote conferencing and collaboration, for example), and is often commonly used by customers who require a high quality of service in these types of multimedia transmission. Granted, not many administrators deal with networks that require multimegabit video streams, but ATM's popularity is growing at a rapid rate all the same, because the protocol gives administrators enormous flexibility in customizing data-transfer systems.

The following list describes a few of the major advantages that ATM offers:

- Although ATM is a connection-oriented protocol, it can act in a connectionless mode if necessary (to emulate TCP/IP functionality, for example).
- Administrators can use ATM to define the route for communications to travel over a network without physical circuits.
- ATM can prioritize data on a network, depending on the data's origin. For example, an IT administrator could give the transmissions of the upper brass of a company (such as the CEO and the chairman of the board) priority over everyone else in the company.

Chapter 10 ✦ WAN Technologies and Remote Access

- ATM isn't compatible with Ethernet packet sniffers. Using a less-commonly implemented protocol is actually a benefit in this case if security is an issue.
- ATM was designed to be able to switch between many different types of traffic with ease.

ATM operates at the Data Link Layer of the OSI model (Chapter 5 covers the OSI model) and rides on top of SONET and SDH (which are explained later in this chapter), which operate on the Physical Layer of the OSI model. Like SONET, ATM is a key technology of broadband ISDN (both technologies are explained elsewhere in this chapter).

ATM works much like frame relay, but it uses a virtual circuit that defines the source, destination, and route, but does not dedicate bandwidth to the connection. Virtual circuits can be dedicated into permanent virtual circuits or can be controlled dynamically using switching. And ATM can achieve higher switch speeds than frame relay because ATM implements much of its process via hardware, rather than software. ATM networks can run at speeds up to a staggering 10 Gbps. Note that ATM makes use of some of the carrier levels, OC3, OC12, and OC192.

In the Real World: ATM may be much faster than frame relay, but as a result, it's also much more expensive to implement than a frame relay solution is. If you or a client is looking for an inexpensive solution to connecting LAN networks, ATM isn't that solution. However, ATM is still known as the most efficient solution, aside from its cost. If performance is important to you or a client, ATM may well be the best choice.

Cable modems

Cable modems aren't really modems at all; they don't modulate or demodulate anything. Cable modems send data over coaxial cable that's normally used for cable television services. Cable modems typically use Ethernet to connect the cable modem itself to a computer, usually via either

- Network interface card
- USB network adapter

Home consumers typically use cable modems, and the technology competes directly with DSL. Cable modem ISPs can offer anywhere from 512 Kbps to 52 Mbps on a given line, although most PCs can handle only up to 10 Mbps each. Cable modem providers subdivide users on the same 52 Mbps cable, so speed achieved by each PC on a given line is dependent on how many users are online at one time. Unlike with DSL, the distance from the central office does not have any effect on the speed of the connection.

Caution: Cable modems have been derided in the press for their lack of security. Security concerns include the fact that, although cable modems use dynamically assigned IP addresses, many cable providers leave the same address assigned for days or weeks, making it easier for IP-address hunters to find and break into the computer. Also, coaxial cable can be tapped into, potentially enabling someone to monitor your Internet usage and private information.

DSL

DSL (which stands for Digital Subscriber Line) is one of the most popular technologies today for bringing high-bandwidth Internet to homes and small businesses that want continuous access to the Internet, and competes directly with ISDN in the market for small businesses and with cable modems in the market for home-user Internet services. DSL runs over ordinary copper telephone lines, but requires a certain geographic proximity to the telephone company's central office. DSL offers connections that enable download speeds ranging from 1.544 Mbps to 512 Kbps to 6.1 Mbps (although getting above 1.544 Mbps isn't typical) and a 128 Kbps upload rate.

DSL is extremely popular due to its capability to use the same phone line for simultaneous voice and data transmissions; with DSL, you can call someone over the telephone and download a large file over the same phone line.

Analog transmissions use only a small amount of the available bandwidth of typical copper wires. This unused bandwidth makes DSL possible. The following list describes the key features of DSL:

- DSL doesn't require modulation from digital to analog signal and back, like ISDN does. Instead, DSL uses the entire bandwidth for a digital transmission, carving out some of the bandwidth for analog signals (such as phone calls).

- The maximum attenuation distance for DSL without using a repeater is 5.5 km (18,000 feet). The closer you are to the telephone company's central office, the faster your connection is. Fiber-optic cable can provide DSL to users outside of the 5.5 km loop, but fiber-optic cable isn't as widespread as it needs to be to offer DSL to everyone.

- DSL requires the use of a *Digital Subscriber Line Access Multiplexer* (or DSLAM) on either end of the network; as with standard multiplexers, the sending multiplexer multiplexes the signal and the receiving multiplexer (called the *demultiplexer*) demultiplexes the signal. DSL can run using TCP/IP or ATM.

In the Real World

Although high-speed IP is a cornerstone of DSL's reason for existence, many DSL providers actually utilize ATM instead of IP, because ATM uses *ATM adaption layers* (or AALs), each of which is designed for a specific type of application. These layers enable administrators to prioritize certain types of communication over others, a feature not offered with TCP/IP. See the "ATM" section earlier in this chapter for more information.

The most common type of DSL is ADSL. ADSL (*Asymmetric Digital Subscriber Line*) travels over regular telephone wiring, using the unused frequency spectrum in the POTS. See the "DSL" section later in this chapter for more info on ADSL. ADSL is called *asymmetric* because the download speeds are far higher than the upload speeds. This is intentional: the POTS only has so much available bandwidth and, typically, Web users rarely upload large requests. ADSL offers up to 6.1 Mbps download speeds and up to 640 Kbps upstream speeds. Having ADSL is like having a constantly on, dedicated line; unlike with cable modems, you don't compete for bandwidth.

FDDI

When networking across long distances, 10BaseT cabling just doesn't cut it — the attenuation point of 10BaseT and similar cables is simply not long enough. FDDI (which stands for Fiber Distributed Data Interface) is a standard that utilizes fiber-optic lines to transmit data between LANs. Maximum geographic spread for these networks range up to 200 km (124 miles) if using one ring only, or up to 100 km (62 miles) if using two rings, and can support thousands of users.

FDDI is based on the token ring networking model and uses the following two token rings:

- **Primary ring:** This ring carries data, offering capacity up to 100 Mbps.
- **Secondary ring:** This ring is optional, and when used cuts the possible geographical breadth of the network in half (to 100 km). This ring exists in case the primary ring goes down, and it also has a capacity of 100 Mbps. When the primary ring is up, this ring carries data and can increase the total capacity of the FDDI network to 200 Mbps. If the primary ring goes down, the secondary ring routes around the problem as necessary to restore connection to at least most of the network while the bad segment of the primary ring is examined and fixed, cutting the total capacity of the network to 100 Mbps.

FDDI-II is a newer version of the FDDI standard that is made to be compatible with the OSI model of network layering (refer to Chapter 5 for more information on the OSI model). FDDI-II is a circuit-switched technology that enables voice signals to be handled by FDDI.

Frame Relay

Frame relay distributes data on the Data Link Layer of the OSI model and generally uses a T-1 or a fractional T-1 carrier (a *fractional T-1 carrier* is just part of the bandwidth of a T-1 line). Available from large phone companies such as AT&T, the frame relay service is a packet-switching service designed for low-cost transmission of data traffic either between LANs or between end points in a WAN. Most frame relay implementations act as either a *private virtual circuit* (or *PVC* — which isn't in reference to the material often used to make plastic pipes), or a dedicated network path between two locations.

In the Real World — Frame relay is roughly equivalent to ISDN in performance (ISDN is explained elsewhere in this chapter), and is often used as a cheaper alternative to ATM, which supports much higher speeds.

Frame relay is based on the older X.25 technology (X.25 is a packet-switching technology that was designed for transmitting analog data), but unlike X.25, frame relay is a connectionless service that leaves the responsibility of error checking to other network layers. Frame relays package data in units called frames and send them in variable-length packets over the network. Frame relay is a connectionless service, leaving the error checking to other layers of the OSI model. Frames can incorporate information from different protocols, including X.25 and Ethernet.

Note: The ATM protocol works in a similar fashion to frame relay, but at much faster speeds. See the "ATM" section earlier in this chapter for details.

A disadvantage to frame relay is that it requires a dedicated connection while transmitting. For this reason, frame relay networks aren't ideal for networks that use services requiring lots of transmission of streaming data, such as voice or video conferencing.

ISDN

ISDN (which stands for Integrated Services Digital Network) is a digital circuit-switching technology that was designed to replace the old telephone network. ISDN requires that the phone company (most, if not all major phone companies offer ISDN) to install an ISDN line at the location that will use ISDN. One ISDN adapter on each side of the connection is required; both the customer and the ISP must have an ISDN adapter. Whereas modems translate data from digital to analog form before transferring data over a network, ISDN connects digitally to a remote computer over the digital ISDN line.

ISDN never really took off, and it probably never will. With the onslaught of DSL and cable modems taking over the broadband market, and taking into account the ease, low cost, and generally higher connection speeds of those solutions, ISDN is quickly becoming a rarely seen white elephant in the market for high-speed network connections.

Exam Tip: Even though ISDN isn't particularly popular, you find questions mentioning ISDN on the Network+ test, so at least familiarize yourself with the basics of the technology, even if you wouldn't be caught dead using it.

Types of ISDN channels

Each ISDN connection includes a certain number of dedicated channels. The following two types of channels are used with ISDN:

- **B-channels:** (The B stands for *bearer*.) Carry data such as Web pages, streaming media, voice transmissions, video, so on. B-channels can be distributed piecemeal among individual workstations (distributed in individual 64 Kbps connections), or combined to achieve higher speeds using what's known as inverse multiplexing.

- **D-channels:** (The D stands for *data*.) Carry control and signal information.

Levels of service

ISDN has three major levels of service, each targeted at different levels of markets: Basic ISDN, Primary ISDN, and Broadband ISDN. The following list explains these three levels:

- **Basic Rate Interface (BRI):** Targeted at home and small business users, BRI is designed to operate over standard telephone lines. The BRI interface includes one 16 Kbps D-channel and two 64 Kbps B-channels, which can provide two 64

Kbps connections or one 128 Kbps connection. For BRI, the telephone company installs an NT1 (network terminator) device on the consumer's end of the network. Note that when an incoming voice call makes itself known to the ISDN line, the second channel stops being used for data and is then dedicated solely to the voice call. While no voice calls are going on over the phone lines, both phone lines are then used to transfer data.

> **Note:** Another way of achieving a 128 Kbps connection is to use the V.90 modem standard to "strap" two modems together (called *multisession*), although this technique isn't often used.

- **Primary Rate Interface (PRI):** Targeted at large corporate customers who need fast access between remote locations, PRI allows for a connection up to 1.544 Mbps, the speed of a T1. PRI includes twenty-three 64 Kbps B-channels and one 64 Kbps D-channel. With a PRI, the telephone company installs an NT2 network terminator device on the consumer's end of the network.

> **Exam Tip:** Remember that the primary rate ISDN runs at roughly the equivalent speed of a T-1.

- **Broadband ISDN (B-ISDN):** B-ISDN is a new technology based on the ISDN concept of integrating analog and voice data with digital data on the same network, but using fiber-optic cable and radio media. B-ISDN uses a similar implementation to regular ISDN, using the same key protocols, including frame relay, ATM, FDDI, and SONET/SDH (all of which are explained in this chapter). When implemented, B-ISDN supports transmissions from 2 Mbps and higher.

SONET/SDH

SONET and SDH are two technology standards for transmitting data across optical media such as fiber-optic cable. SONET is a U.S. standard defined by the American National Standards Institute (ANSI), and SDH is its international equivalent. Together, SONET and SDH enable digital networks to connect across international borders. The following sections explain SONET, SDH, and OCx (the carrier standards on which SONET and SDH are modeled).

SONET has a maximum line rate of 9.953 Gbps, with actual line rates sometimes even approaching 20 Gbps. SONET runs on the Physical Layer of the OSI model (refer to Chapter 5 for more information on the OSI model), and is considered the base technology for broadband ISDN (or B-ISDN). ATM runs as a layer on top of SONET.

SONET standardizes the transmission of digital signals over optical fiber by using multiples of 51.84, which is considered the standard's base rate. Table 10-3 lists the more commonly used optical carrier levels.

SDH (synchronous digital hierarchy) standard defines a way of transmitting data across optical media, such as fiber-optic cable. SDH is the international equivalent of SONET. SDH uses *Synchronous Transport Modules,* which correspond to four of the OC levels, as shown in Table 10-2.

Table 10-2
Optical Carrier Levels

OC Level	Rate	Equivalent STM Module
OC-1	51.84 Mbps	—
OC-3	155.52 Mbps	STM-1
OC-12	622.08 Mbps	STM-4
OC-24	1.244 Gbps	—
OC-48	2.488 Gbps	STM-16
OC-192	10 Gbps	STM-64
OC-256	13.271 Gbps	—
OC-768	40 Gbps	—

Remote Access Protocols and Services

When connecting to remote resources, certain protocols and services are required, depending on what resource is requested. The following sections explain the most used remote protocols.

ICA

The Citrix *Independent Computing Architecture* (ICA) enables *thin clients*. Thin clients don't run their own software. They connect to servers that

- Start the application
- Execute the application
- Transfer only the application's interface to the user's client

From that point on, the only data that travels between server and client are such user interfaces as mouse actions and keyboard actions.

Features of ICA

The ICA protocol offers the following benefits:

- **Low resource consumption:** Using the ICA protocol, applications use as little as one-tenth their normal network bandwidth.
- **Clients can be made with dirt-cheap hardware:** ICA enables clients to use hardware as old as an Intel 286 chipset with 640 KB of RAM and still run

applications that typically require massive system resources, such as Microsoft Office. Granted, at first gasp it doesn't seem particularly thrilling that you can do this, but take into account that PDAs typically use less powerful hardware than PCs, for example, and you get the idea.

✦ **Clients use low bandwidth:** Because the ICA protocol requires less than 20 Kb of bandwidth, this enables it to operate consistently even with slow connections, regardless of the application being executed. This also enables the use of thin, inexpensive wires (such as twisted-pair cable) in a network. ICA is capable of running efficiently over even a paltry 14.4 Kbps connection.

✦ **Support for multiple platforms:** Applications for Linux, Unix, Java, and Windows can all be run using the ICA protocol, allowing for a network environment that actually enables Linux and Mac users on that network to make use of Windows applications. Further, ICA was designed to be platform independent, and has been ported to Java, Linux, and Windows.

✦ **A simplified protocol solution:** ICA controls the application from source to destination (including a server client and network protocol) and enables transmissions from server to client and back over standard connections (including NetBEUI, IP, ADSL, dial-up, ISDN, frame relay, and ATM).

✦ **Open licensing:** ICA enables original equipment manufacturers (OEMs) to supply applications to any type of thin client (even fat clients) with an open license. ICA has already been adopted by many big companies for inclusion within new hardware and software products, including companies such as Microsoft, IBM, Sun Microsystems, Sharp, Compaq, HP, Psion, Nokia, Casio, and others.

How ICA works

The following list shows how the ICA process works with an ultra-creative application called "App". Note that the steps in the following list correspond to the numbers in Figure 10-3.

1. A user requests an application from her client. This client can be just about anything, from a cell phone to a high-end server system.

2. The request travels over the network to the application server.

3. The server executes the application and separates the interface from the application's processes.

4. The application server sends the application's interface over the network back to the client. Screen updates, mouse clicks, and keystrokes are then the only things sent over the network from the user to the application server.

As you can see from the figure, App is being served by the application server to all sorts of different clients, and the user actions are transported back across the network to the application server. In this way, for example, Microsoft Word could be served to either a PC or a cellphone without either device requiring a hard drive large enough to actually house Word.

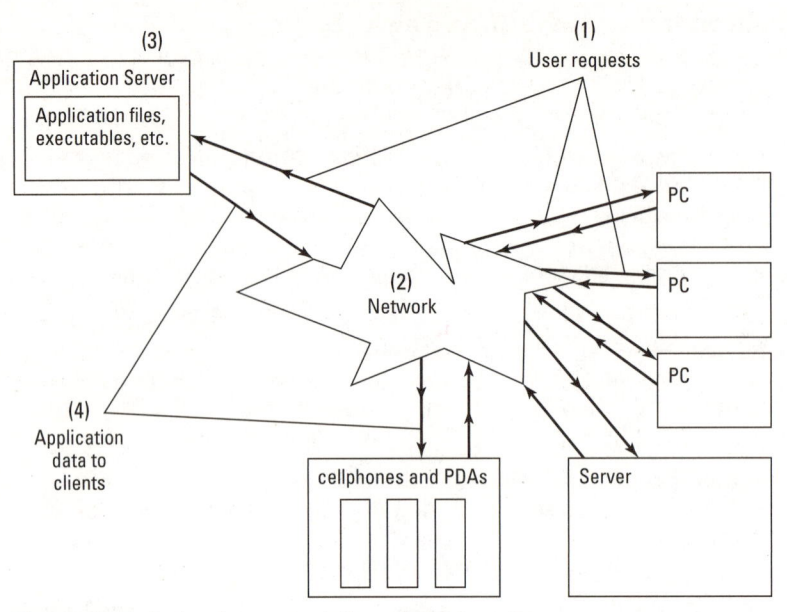

Figure 10-3: A visual representation of ICA in action

PPP

PPP (Point-to-Point Protocol) is an easy-to-configure service that enables a connection between two computers via a serial interface, usually over a phone line between a personal computer and a remote server. The dynamics of a PPP connection are similar to that of Ethernet, except PPP uses a serial connection, which is slower than Ethernet.

> **In the Real World**
>
> PPP is typically used by Internet Service Providers to enable paying users to connect to the Internet from home over a dial-up modem, enabling you to access services such as e-mail, the Internet, and instant messaging.

PPP can operate on either the Data Link Layer or the Physical Layer of the OSI model (refer to Chapter 5 for more information on the OSI model) and uses a variation of the High Speed Data Link Control standard to encapsulate TCP/IP packets and send them over the Internet. PPP can run on any type of connection, although it is mostly used for dial-up connections.

Advantages of PPP over SLIP

PPP was designed to replace SLIP and offers the following features that SLIP does not:

✦ An interface that's easy to configure, especially compared to SLIP. With PPP, a user needs to provide only his login name, password, and the phone number that he's dialing to connect to the remote server.

- PPP has error detection (SLIP does not).
- PPP can handle synchronous and asynchronous communications (SLIP can handle only asynchronous communications).
- Unlike SLIP, PPP establishes its configuration parameters automatically when it starts, making PPP far easier to use than SLIP.
- PPP can handle protocols other than IP – such as IPX (SLIP supports only IP).
- PPP can run over any major physical media, including but not limited to twisted-pair cable, fiber-optic lines, or satellite relay (SLIP is able to run only over serial lines).
- PPP typically runs on IP and is sometimes considered part of the TCP/IP protocol suite. But PPP can handle other protocols, too, including AppleTalk, IPX, and NetBEUI.

Configuring PPP

For information on configuring PPP, see Chapter 17.

PPTP and VPNs

PPTP is an extension of the PPP protocol that enables companies to use an ISP to connect securely to a server somewhere else in the user's company, basically using a WAN that actually acts like a single LAN; this practice results in what is typically called a *Virtual Private Network* (or *VPN*). Virtual Private Networks can be used as a cheaper alternative to leasing private lines, because PPTP enables them to use public lines through what's called a *tunnel* through the public networks.

PPTP and VPNs include the following features:

- They enable remote users to log in to a secure server over the public Internet using a local dial-up connection, which is far cheaper than having users log in to the Internet via the corporate network.
- They hide the Internet routing and switching process from users so that the network seems to be accessed by local means (when in fact it is remote).
- They provide security for file transfer via encryption.

RAS

RAS (Remote Access Service) is the service for Windows NT/2000 that enables network traffic to travel over a WAN. RAS handles the same tasks that are handled by Dial-Up Networking in Windows 9x, although RAS can also enable a Windows computer to act as a dial-up server in addition to a client. Using RAS, a user can log into a Windows NT/2000 system using a dial-up modem. In Windows NT, RAS was a separate module, but Windows 2000 installs RAS by default, integrating RAS tightly with networking functions.

SLIP

PPP has overwhelmingly replaced SLIP in the market for encapsulation protocols, although SLIP is still used by some cell phone companies and in some other limited circumstances. SLIP often requires a Herculean effort to configure, especially compared to PPP.

Exam Tip Remember how to configure PPP, but don't worry about how to configure SLIP. Because SLIP is so little used and because it's not on the Network+ exam, it's not explained in detail here.

Like PPP, which was designed to replace it, SLIP (which stands for Serial Line Internet Protocol) encapsulates TCP/IP packets for transmission over asynchronous lines, such as that of the public telephone network. SLIP was used in the early days of the Internet when there was no standard for encapsulation protocols. SLIP is nowhere near as easy to configure as PPP; most SLIP connections require users to manually configure IP addresses and other cryptic parameters.

SLIP made it possible for users to transmit and receive files directly from the originating server to their computer over standard telephone lines using modems. Back then you couldn't even download a file directly to your computer – you had to log in to a remote server, download the file to your local server, and then use another protocol altogether to download the file from the local server to your system.

Summary

Remote access is more and more important in the modern technology market every day, and the protocols and technologies involved are various and sundry. This chapter explained the following major points:

- ✦ Wide area networks (or WANs) typically involve connecting at least two LANs.
- ✦ Remote access technologies are all based on either analog or digital transmissions, and often (as with modems) a combination of both.
- ✦ Various technologies are becoming quite popular for high-bandwidth Internet, including, most notably, DSL and cable modems.
- ✦ Dial-up remote access is made possible by technologies such as SLIP and PPP that encapsulate one type of data into another and then back.
- ✦ Virtual Private Networks (VPNs) enable secure access to a network by using tunneling protocols such as PPTP.
- ✦ Thin network clients are made possible by application server protocols such as ICA.

✦ ✦ ✦

STUDY GUIDE

Assessment Questions

1. Which of the following best defines a WAN?

    A. A LAN with more than ten network segments is called a WAN.

    B. A WAN is two LANs or more in a network.

    C. A WAN is a collection of at least 100 LANs.

    D. A WAN is at least three LANs that are more than 50 miles distant from one another.

2. Which of the following uses a system of high and low audio tones to translate binary data into analog data?

    A. A router

    B. A multiplexer

    C. A modem

    D. A terminator

3. Which of the following is the term for the process of sending multiple data streams along the same data stream simultaneously?

    A. Multiplexing

    B. Modulation

    C. Packet switching

    D. Circuit switching

4. Which of the following protocols resembles frame relay in functionality but is faster?

    A. ICA

    B. PPP

    C. ATM

    D. PPTP

5. Which of the following protocols enable prioritization of certain data types over others?

    A. ATM

    B. TCP/IP

    C. IPX/SPX

    D. PPP

6. Which of the following is equivalent to the OC3 standard for digital optical transmissions?

    A. T-1

    B. STM-1

    C. E-1

    D. OC4

7. Which of the following standards isn't a standard for optical data transmissions?

    A. FDDI

    B. OC-*x*

    C. SONET

    D. SDH

8. Which of the following services enables a Windows NT 4.0 machine to act as a dial-up server?

    A. Kerberos

    B. WINS

    C. PPTP

    D. RAS

9. Which of the following is the term for the process of translating data from digital into analog form and back into digital?

    A. Multiplexing

    B. Modulation

    C. Packet switching

    D. Circuit switching

10. Which of the following protocols was replaced by the PPP standard?

    A. ICA

    B. PPTP

    C. ATM

    D. SLIP

11. Which of the following technologies enables a download data stream of up to 128 Kbps and is being replaced by technologies such as cable modems and DSL?

    A. ATM

    B. Frame relay

    C. ISDN

    D. FDDI

12. Which of the following protocols creates a virtual private network over the public Internet?

    A. PPP

    B. PPTP

    C. FDDI

    D. ICA

13. Which of the following WAN technologies is based on the token ring standard?

    A. Frame relay

    B. ATM

    C. ICA

    D. FDDI

14. Which of the following types of broadband technologies requires the user to be within 18,000 feet of the phone company's central office?

    A. DSL

    B. Cable modems

    C. Dial-up modems

    D. VPNs

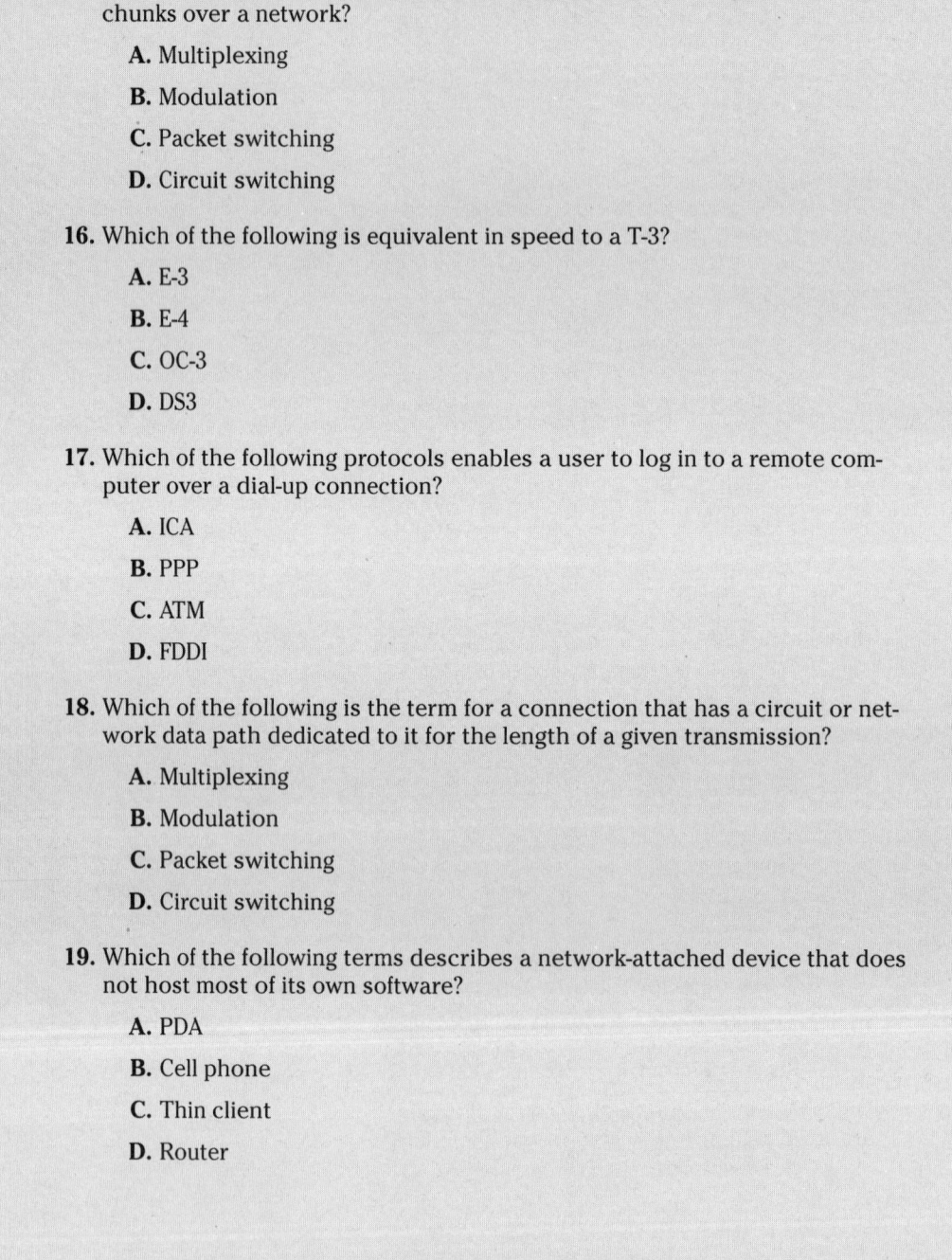

15. Which of the following is the term for the process of sending data in small chunks over a network?

   A. Multiplexing

   B. Modulation

   C. Packet switching

   D. Circuit switching

16. Which of the following is equivalent in speed to a T-3?

   A. E-3

   B. E-4

   C. OC-3

   D. DS3

17. Which of the following protocols enables a user to log in to a remote computer over a dial-up connection?

   A. ICA

   B. PPP

   C. ATM

   D. FDDI

18. Which of the following is the term for a connection that has a circuit or network data path dedicated to it for the length of a given transmission?

   A. Multiplexing

   B. Modulation

   C. Packet switching

   D. Circuit switching

19. Which of the following terms describes a network-attached device that does not host most of its own software?

   A. PDA

   B. Cell phone

   C. Thin client

   D. Router

20. Which of the following protocols serves an application's interface to a client over a network?

   A. ICA
   B. PPP
   C. ATM
   D. PPTP

Scenarios

1. You're consulting for a company that uses a lot of video-conferencing. They want to be able to prioritize certain types of data over others and cost isn't a concern. What type of WAN solution should you recommend to the client?

2. You're an administrator of a company that uses exclusively Windows clients and wants to enable workers to log in and work from home, but they don't want to lease dedicated lines or maintain a modem pool at the corporate headquarters. What type of solution should you recommend implementing?

Answers to Chapter Questions

Chapter Pre-Test

1. A WAN, or wide area network, is a network made up of at least two LANs. See the "WANs and Internetworks" section for more information.

2. Packet switching is the method used by network protocols to send data in packets that are then reassembled on the target machine. In this way, many users can utilize the same bandwidth simultaneously. Packet switching contrasts with circuit switching. See the "Packet switching" section in this chapter for details on packet switching.

3. Circuit switching is the method used by phone companies for telephone calls; one circuit is dedicated to each session, and while the session lasts, that circuit cannot be used for any other transmission. See the "Circuit switching" section in this chapter for more information.

4. Modems transmit data via modulation, where digital signals are translated into analog signals and back to digital by devices called modems. See the "Modulation" section in this chapter for more information about modems and modulation.

5. Multiplexing is the transmission of multiple signals simultaneously over the same medium. See the "Multiplexing" section in this chapter for more information.

6. The major carrier signal standards are the DS, OC, T, and E standards. See the "Data carrier services" section in this chapter for more information on these standards.

7. SLIP and PPP are used for point-to-point connections, where one host is logging in to a remote host. See the "SLIP" and "PPP" sections in this chapter for more information on point-to-point connections and protocols.

8. A tunneling protocol such as PPTP can create a secure tunnel through the public Internet. See the "PPTP and VPNs" section in this chapter for more information on PPTP and tunneling.

9. A virtual private network (or VPN) can create a secure tunnel though the public Internet. See the "PPTP and VPNs" section in this chapter for more information on VPNs and the PPTP tunneling protocol.

10. A thin client is a machine that does not run all of its own software; it instead has applications served to it by application servers. See the "ICA" section in this chapter for more information.

Assessment Questions

1. B. A WAN is a collection of at least two or more LANs.
2. C. Modems modulate binary data into audio frequencies using high and low tones to represent binary 1s and 0s.
3. A. Multiplexing is the process of sending multiple data streams along the same data stream.
4. C. The ATM protocol resembles frame relay in functionality, but at much faster speeds.
5. A. The ATM protocol can prioritize types of data.
6. B. STM-1 is the equivalent to the OC-3 standard for optical signal carriers.
7. A. FDDI isn't a standard for optical data transmissions, it's a WAN technology based on the token ring standard.
8. D. The RAS service enables Windows NT 4.0 to act as a dial-up server.
9. B. Modulation is the term for the process of translating data from digital into analog form and back again.
10. D. SLIP was replaced by the PPP protocol.
11. C. ISDN enables a download data stream of up to 128 Kbps and is currently being replaced by technologies such as cable modems and DSL.

12. B. PPTP is the protocol most often used to create a virtual private network over the public Internet.

13. D. FDDI is based on the token ring standard.

14. A. DSL requires that a user be located within 18,000 feet of the telephone company's central office, although a repeater can carry the signal farther.

15. C. Packet switching is the term for sending multiple packets of data over a network.

16. D. The DS3 standard is equivalent in speed to a T-3 connection.

17. B. PPP enables access to a remote computer over a dial-up connection.

18. D. Circuit switching is the term describing a connection where one circuit or network data path is dedicated to one circuit.

19. C. A network-attached device that does not host most of its own software is called a thin client.

20. A. The ICA protocol serves an application over a network.

Scenarios

1. If data prioritization is a desire of the company and cost isn't a concern, an ATM network is probably the best solution.

2. If a company wants to enable remote logins without having to pay the high cost for a dedicated line, you should probably recommend a Virtual Private Network solution using PPTP

Security Protocols

CHAPTER 11

EXAM OBJECTIVES

- Identify the following security protocols and describe their purpose and function:
  - IPSec
  - L2TP
  - SSL
  - Kerberos

CHAPTER PRE-TEST

1. Encryption is the opposite of _____.
2. Public-key cryptography involves the use of _____ key(s).
3. Which type of key cryptography does SSL use?
4. What is the main security issue in secret-key encryption?
5. What is the main advantage of public-key encryption?
6. The set of guidelines that define a public-key encryption system is called a _____.
7. The _____ protocol uses a ticket-granting server (or TGS).
8. The _____ protocol can only be used with IP.
9. The _____ protocol tunnels a PPP connection to a remote location.
10. The _____ protocol uses an encrypted socket to transfer data securely over a network.

✦ Answers to these questions can be found at the end of the chapter. ✦

When a network is only as big as one office or a household, it's usually easy enough to ensure that no one hacks into those cables and intercepts the data flowing through them: you lock the door. If you're really worried about security, you consider getting onsite security, an alarm system, or whatever. By contrast, a network as big as the Internet — which involves thousands of miles of cabling, stretching all over the world, — has no way to ensure that a given data stream will avoid interception. When users go to Amazon.com to buy a book, for example, how do they know that they haven't been redirected to an Amazon.com lookalike site scamming for their credit card information? Or how does Amazon.com *know* that customer John Doe is not some malicious hacker posing as John Doe?

As has become increasingly evident in the past few decades, computer networks are not inherently secure. Weaknesses in networking software or physical taps into network cabling can result in compromised data. Wireless networks — which use radio frequencies that don't even require physical taps into cabling to intercept — are by nature almost horrifically insecure.

To ensure all humanity doesn't shun the Internet as a sordid public bulletin board of everyone's private information, security protocols have been developed to help ensure security over the Internet. After all, if people don't feel that convenient Internet features such as online banking, auctions, and shopping offered secure environments for transactions, those features won't be used — no matter how useful they are.

This chapter discusses the basic concepts behind security protocols, explains why they're necessary and how they work, and examines the security protocols know for the Network+ exam.

Privacy Over Public Networks?

The basic meaning of the word *privacy* involves being able to keep what's yours to yourself. Over a public network, however, privacy is a multifaceted concept. In networking, the following concerns are most prevalent in offering secure services:

- **Authentication:** E-commerce has concerns that are no different from those of any market in which funds or important information are exchanged: To ensure a successful transaction, you have to know whom you're dealing with. In e-commerce, users and online merchants (as well as other handlers of secure online transactions) exchange data or information that's considered private, such as credit card information. Due to the sensitive nature of credit-card data, both parties in such a transaction must necessarily be able to verify who is sending and receiving data. This process of verifying identification information over a network is called *authentication*.

- **Non-repudiation:** This concept is sometimes overlooked as a concern in e-commerce, but it's an important one. Just as with a real signature, digital signatures need to be secure enough to be binding. You can't be able to go back later and claim "I didn't sign that" when, in fact, you did sign it. Non-repudiation is handled by *digital signatures*, which are discussed in the "Digital signatures" section later in this chapter.

- **Secure data:** Probably the most obvious of privacy concerns is the integrity of sensitive data. E-commerce simply isn't a possibility if no one feels that their data is safe when in transit over the Internet.

Just because the Internet is insecure by definition doesn't mean that people who use it for secure purposes are bonkers; the answer to an insecure Internet is actually quite simple: If you can't stop hackers from retrieving sensitive data, encrypt that data so well that it is useless to the hacker when intercepted.

The following section discusses the technologies used in the major security protocols. For more information on the specific protocols covered on the Network+ exam, see the "Common Security Protocols" section later in this chapter.

Encryption Basics

Encryption is the process of changing the form of data in such a drastic way that that data can only be understood by authorized parties. The name for the reverse process of encryption, in which data is translated from encrypted form back into readable form, is called *decryption*. Using encryption and decryption, online merchants can be more confident that sensitive customer data such as credit card information) is not being stolen by unauthorized third parties (such as hackers or unscrupulous competitors) while in transit over the Internet.

Several key concepts underlie the process of encryption — in particular, ciphers, keys, and certificates. The following sections discuss the basic workings of encryption as well as the technologies involved.

Ciphers versus codes

The process of encrypting data involves the use of mathematical algorithms to translate readable data into seemingly meaningless nonsense called *ciphertext* (some call this nonsense a *hash*). Only authorized parties (those who hold the proper decryption key) can reassemble ciphertext into properly readable text.

Some people confuse the concept of a *code* with the concept of *ciphertext*, but the two are distinct. *Codes* actually have nothing to do with encryption; a code is merely a way of saying one thing using a different language. For example, computer systems use binary codes of 1s and 0s to represent data; Morse code uses a series of long and short tones to indicate letters. In effect, a code is a communication tool; *ciphers*, on the other hand, are arrangements of symbols specifically designed to hide the contents of a message, obscuring its meaning to everyone except those by whom the data was meant to be read.

The typical use of keys is simple — like the replacement keys used in Crypt-a-Quote cartoons that you see in newspapers, only on a much larger scale. When you eventually work out the right combination — say, replacing all the *A*s with *I*s, all the *J*s with *D*s, and so on — you can decipher the message. Only the lack of a key makes this method relatively secure. Of course, ciphertext uses far more complicated algorithms than a Crypt-a-Quote, but you get the idea.

Key cryptography

The algorithms used for sophisticated encryption and decryption are known as *keys*. PKI-capable applications use keys that are 40- or 128-bit binary numbers merged with readable data; the result reads like nonsense until the data is decrypted using the correct key. Two main types of key cryptography exist: *secure-key cryptography* and *public-key cryptography*. The following sections describe each of these types, as well as the most popular specific methods of key cryptography used in modern networks such as the Internet. For an example of what cryptography looks like, see Listing 11-1 later in this chapter, which shows a certificate before and after being encrypted..

Secure-key cryptography

The concept of passwords is similar to that of secure-key cryptography, which involves the use of one secret key that both the sending and receiving parties have access to. The problem with this method is that any key transmitted over the Internet can be intercepted along the way and compromised. Further, just as with passwords, access to your secret key remains with whomever you give it to — until you change it.

Secure-key cryptography is not commonly used on the Internet today, and certainly not as much as public-key cryptography is used. The main technology on the market that still uses secure-key cryptography is the fantastically complex Kerberos protocol. (See the "Kerberos" section later in this chapter to see how Kerberos works.)

Public-key cryptography

By contrast with secure-key cryptography, which uses a single key transmitted back and forth over the Internet, public-key cryptography uses two keys for each transaction, as follows:

- ✦ **Public key:** This key encrypts messages meant for use with the corresponding private key. Easily available to the public (but useless without its corresponding private key), this key is the only one ever sent over the network at any time.

- ✦ **Private key:** The private key resides on only one computer; it decrypts data that was encrypted using the corresponding public key. The private key is held only on the client computer; it's never sent over the Internet.

The two main benefits to public-key cryptography are readily apparent:

+ **Each key is useless without its partner:** Neither the public nor the private key can be used to reveal the workings of the other; both keys are required to translate data.

+ **High security for the private key:** Although public keys are easily accessible, private keys are never transmitted over the Internet. Thus, only the most local of security breaches can compromise a private key — someone must physically access your workstation to get your private key.

Figure 11-1 shows how public and private keys are used to secure Internet transactions.

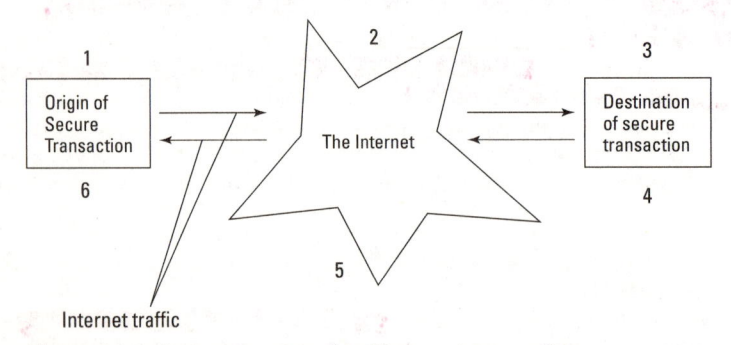

Figure 11-1: A generic example of Internet encryption.

Figure 11-1 illustrates the following aspects of key cryptography (the numbers in the steps correspond to those you see in the figure):

1. A user clicks a button on a Web page or activates a secure transaction by some other means.

2. The encryption software on the user's computer obtains the public key of the desired resource and encrypts the data using that key.

3. The data leaves the user's client and travels over the network between source and destination in encrypted form.

4. The data arrives at its destination in encrypted form.

5. The private key of the destination resource, known only by that resource, serves to decrypt the data.

6. The destination partner in the transaction does what it needs to with the data, obtains the user's public key from the network, and then encrypts any information that needs to be sent back to the user using that key.

7. Any data that needs to be sent back over the network leaves the destination partner's machine and travels over the network in encrypted form to the user.

8. The data arrives on the user's machine and is decrypted with that user's private key, which only the user themselves hold.

9. The data is received by the user in unencrytpted form.

Because this is an important concept to grasp, Figure 11-2 shows a more specific example of how key encryption can secure an online transaction.

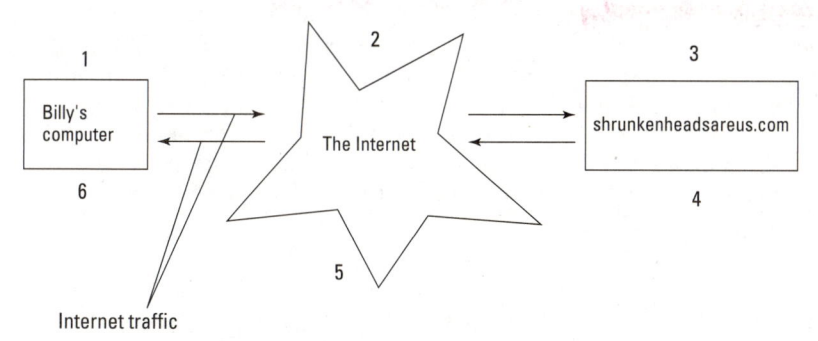

Figure 11-2: A specific example of a secure transaction.

You can see the following from Figure 11-2 (the numbers in the stepscorrespond to those you see in the figure):

1. Bob wants to purchase a rare shrunken head from shrunkenheadsareus.com. Bob puts the desired shrunken head in his online "cart", fills in his credit card information, and clicks the Submit button.

    The encryption software on Bob's Mac encrypts the credit card information using the public key that's been assigned to shrunkenheadsareus.com by a certificate server.

2. The data leaves Bob's Mac and travels over the Internet in encrypted form.

3. The data arrives at its destination in encrypted form — and the private key of shrunkenheadsareus.com is used to decrypt the data.

4. The shrunkenheadsareus.com server verifies that Bob's credit card is good, verifies that Bob is really Bob (at least according to the key used to encrypt the data), and approves the purchase.

    The shrunkenheadsareus.com server encrypts Bob's receipt and shipping information, using the public key assigned to Bob by his copy of Netscape Navigator.

5. The encrypted transaction results are sent over the network from the shrunkenheadsareus.com server to Bob.

6. The encrypted data from shrunkenheadsareus.com arrives on Bob's computer and is decrypted with the private key assigned to him by Netscape Navigator.

When used with companion security technologies such as firewalls, *good* passwords, and proxies, a carefully planned public-key infrastructure like that used on the Internet today locks out all but the most determined hackers.

Key escrows

A *key escrow* is a repository of all keys in existence for use by the United States federal government and other governments in preventing terrorists from using online encryption to thwart the law. Essentially, every time a certificate server creates an encryption algorithm, the government is automatically sent a copy of the algorithm. Critics of a government-stored key escrow argue that hackers could compromise these escrows and wreak absolute havoc on consumers, organizations, the government, or everyone with the information they steal. After the mind-numbingly brutal terrorist attacks on the U.S. — and the subsequent surge of interest in security — key escrows are becoming a topic of fresh interest in the United States Congress. Secure or not, they are likely to become reality soon.

Commonly used key encryption methods

The two most commonly used methods of key encryption are as follows:

- **DES encryption:** DES uses single-key cryptography to scramble data into unintelligible 64-bit blocks of code, which are then encrypted individually using the Data Encryption Algorithm (DEA; not to be confused with the Drug Enforcement Agency). 56 bits of each code block are used for data; the other 8 bits are used for error detection.

- **Diffie-Hellman:** Diffie-Hellman is an often-used single-key encryption protocol that involves both server and client agreeing on an encryption algorithm for only the pending session. The server and client then use this *session key* to encrypt the data.

- **RSA encryption:** RSA encryption (which stands for Rivest-Shamir-Adleman, the names of the men who designed the technology) uses the public-key cryptography method and is used in the SSL protocol as well as its descendant TSL (which are discussed later in this chapter).

Exam Tip For the exam, know that DES and RSA encryption use secret-key cryptography and public-key cryptography, respectively.

Signed data

This method of authentication uses public and private keys, as discussed in the "Public and private keys" section earlier in this chapter. Digital signatures also verify the integrity of the data itself, using a method similar to that of cyclic redundancy checks used in error correction with protocols such as TCP/IP (CRCs are discussed in Chapter 5). If you use a digital signature to "sign" a contract over the Internet, that signature is just as binding as if you had actually put pen to paper.

Sockets

Sockets are defined as a connection from a client to an *endpoint* (typically the remote resource). For example, SSL operates above TCP/IP on the Network Layer of the OSI model, managing the TCP/IP functions for the Application Layer above it (for example, the HTTP protocol used with Web pages).

> **Cross-Reference**
> Network Layers are discussed at length in Chapter 5.

The concept behind sockets is similar to that of ports (discussed in Chapter 7) — and is even analogous to the concept behind virtual private networks. (VPNs use secure protocols such as PPTP to tunnel a secure connection through the public — that is, unsecured — Internet). A socket secures the connection when an application requests a remote secure service; the socket disappears after the user is finished with that service.

> **Cross-Reference**
> SSL, the main protocol that uses sockets; is discussed in the "SSL" section later in this chapter.

Tunnels are like really big sockets stretched out over greater distances. That is, tunnels are private, encrypted connections over public networks. Tunnels are often called *virtual private networks,* or VPNs.

Public-Key Infrastructures

A *public key infrastructure* (or PKI) is a set of guidelines for offering privacy over a public network such as the Internet. A public key infrastructure performs the following services:

- ✦ **Key administration:** A PKI needs to enable the creation of new keys, the revoking of existing keys, and be able to change the trust level associated with a given key, no matter who the key's issuer was.

- ✦ **Key publishing:** A PKI needs to offer a method of publishing keys, as well as providing access to information about the validity of those keys. That is, if someone can't look up a public key to see if it's valid, the key is altogether useless.

- ✦ **Key utilization:** , keys aren't useful if they can't easily be used. A PKI must offer intuitive methods of using keys to authenticate e-mail, signatures on data, and so on.

PKIs typically include *certificate authorities* (or CAs), certificate publishers, and software tools for administration and use of PKI-enabled applications. The following sections discuss each of these elements.

Certificates

A *certificate* (or *digital certificate* as it's formally called) is a digital document containing enough information to positively identify an individual an organization beyond a reasonable doubt. Certificates are issued by an appropriate authority called a *certificate authority* (or *CA*), as discussed in the next section. Digital certificates can be purchased from CAs (such as VeriSign) to enable secure transactions over the Internet. Users who purchase digital certificates can have their public keys stored in online registries so other users can look up their public key and use that key to send them encrypted information.

Certificates can include all sorts of information, such as (but not limited to) the following:

- Name of the person or organization
- The serial number of the certificate, different depending on which CA issued it
- The public key of the person or organization
- The e-mail address of the person or organization
- The certificate's serial number (which is unique among the certificates issued by that CA)
- Information about the user (it's usually this information that requires encryption from a CA and authentication from an RA)
- Certificate extensions, which are optional, to tell servers or clients what type of certificate they're looking at
- The name of the algorithm used to encrypt the certificate
- Time the certificate was issued
- Time the certificate expires

Listing 11-1 shows a sample certificate before encryption. Listing 11-2 shows the same certificate in encrypted form:

Listing 11-1: A plaintext certificate

```
Certificate:
    Data:
        Version: v3 (0x2)
        Serial Number: 3 (0x3)
        Signature Algorithm: PKCS #1 MD5 With RSA Encryption
        Issuer: OU=Ace Certificate Authority, O=Ace Industry, C=US
        Validity:
            Not Before: Fri Oct 17 18:36:25 1997
            Not  After: Sun Oct 17 18:36:25 1999
        Subject: CN=Jane Doe, OU=Finance, O=Ace Industry, C=US
        Subject Public Key Info:
```

```
            Algorithm: PKCS #1 RSA Encryption
            Public Key:
                Modulus:
                    00:ca:fa:79:98:8f:19:f8:d7:de:e4:49:80:48:e6:2a:2a:86:
                    ed:27:40:4d:86:b3:05:c0:01:bb:50:15:c9:de:dc:85:19:22:
                    43:7d:45:6d:71:4e:17:3d:f0:36:4b:5b:7f:a8:51:a3:a1:00:
                    98:ce:7f:47:50:2c:93:36:7c:01:6e:cb:89:06:41:72:b5:e9:
                    73:49:38:76:ef:b6:8f:ac:49:bb:63:0f:9b:ff:16:2a:e3:0e:
                    9d:3b:af:ce:9a:3e:48:65:de:96:61:d5:0a:11:2a:a2:80:b0:
                    7d:d8:99:cb:0c:99:34:c9:ab:25:06:a8:31:ad:8c:4b:aa:54:
                    91:f4:15
                Public Exponent: 65537 (0x10001)
        Extensions:
            Identifier: Certificate Type
                Critical: no
                Certified Usage:
                    SSL Client
            Identifier: Authority Key Identifier
                Critical: no
                Key Identifier:
                    f2:f2:06:59:90:18:47:51:f5:89:33:5a:31:7a:e6:5c:fb:36:
                    26:c9
    Signature:
        Algorithm: PKCS #1 MD5 With RSA Encryption
        Signature:
            6d:23:af:f3:d3:b6:7a:df:90:df:cd:7e:18:6c:01:69:8e:54:65:fc:06:
            30:43:34:d1:63:1f:06:7d:c3:40:a8:2a:82:c1:a4:83:2a:fb:2e:8f:fb:
            f0:6d:ff:75:a3:78:f7:52:47:46:62:97:1d:d9:c6:11:0a:02:a2:e0:cc:
            2a:75:6c:8b:b6:9b:87:00:7d:7c:84:76:79:ba:f8:b4:d2:62:58:c3:c5:
            b6:c1:43:ac:63:44:42:fd:af:c8:0f:2f:38:85:6d:d6:59:e8:41:42:a5:
            4a:e5:26:38:ff:32:78:a1:38:f1:ed:dc:0d:31:d1:b0:6d:67:e9:46:a8:
            dd:c4
```

Listing 11-2: **An encrypted certificate**

```
-----BEGIN CERTIFICATE-----
MIICKzCCAZSgAwIBAgIBAzANBgkqhkiG9w0BAQQFADA3MQswCQYDVQQGEwJVUzER
MA8GA1UEChMITmV0c2NhcGUxFTATBgNVBAsTDFN1cHJpeWEncyBDQTAeFw05NzEw
MTgwMTM2MjVaFw05OTEwMTgwMTM2MjVaMEgxCzAJBgNVBAYTAlVTMREwDwYDVQQK
EwhOZXRzY2FwZTENMAsGA1UECxMEUHViczEXMBUGA1UEAxMOU3Vwcml5YSBTaGV0
dHkwgZ8wDQYJKoZIhvcNAQEFBQADgYOAMIGJAoGBAMr6eZiPGfjX3uRJgEjmKiqG
7SdATYazBcABu1AVyd7chRkiQ31FbXFOGD3wNktbf6hRo6EAmM5/R1AskzZ8AW7L
iQZBcrXpcOk4du+2Q6xJu2MPm/8WKuMOnTuvzpo+SGXelmHVChEqooCwfdiZywyZ
NMmrJgaoMa2MS6pUkfQVAgMBAAGjNjAOMBEGCWCGSAGG+EIBAQQEAwIAgDAfBgNV
HSMEGDAWgBTy8gZZkBhHUfWJM1oxeuZc+zYmyTANBgkqhkiG9w0BAQQFAAOBgQBt
I6/z07Z635DfzX4XbAFpjlRl/AYwQzTSYx8GfcNAqCqCwaSDKvsuj/vwbf91o3j3
UkdGYpcd2cYRCgKi4MwqdWyLtpuHAH18hHZ5uvi0OmJYw8W2wUOsYORC/a/IDy84
hW3WWehBUqVK5SY4/zJ4oTjx7dwNMdGwbWfpRqjd1A==
-----END CERTIFICATE-----
```

As you can see, the text from the original certificate isn't even vaguely visible with the encrypted certificate.

> **Exam Tip**: You do not have to know encryption algorithms or the details of certificate syntax for the Network+ exam; the preceding listings simply illustrate how encryption works in general — which you *do* have to know for the exam.

Certificate authorities (CAs)

The certificate issued by a certificate authority is trusted because the certificate is encoded with the signature of the CA, which itself is trusted. CAs differ depending on the network. In a LAN for a medium-sized corporation, for example, the CA might be the IT department, which could grant certificates to help authenticate interoffice purchase orders via e-mail, for example. On the Internet, huge companies like VeriSign offer certificates for a fee. In either case, both sides of a given transaction need to have a valid certificate before a secure transaction (with a protocol such as SSL) can take place.

Certificate publishers

For a PKI to work, all public decryption keys in use on a given network must be published so PKI-enabled software has a place to look to find — and verify — public keys. These repositories are posted on ultra-secure servers with mirror sites all over the world. Figure 11-3 shows how certificate publishers fit into a basic, certificate-based transaction.

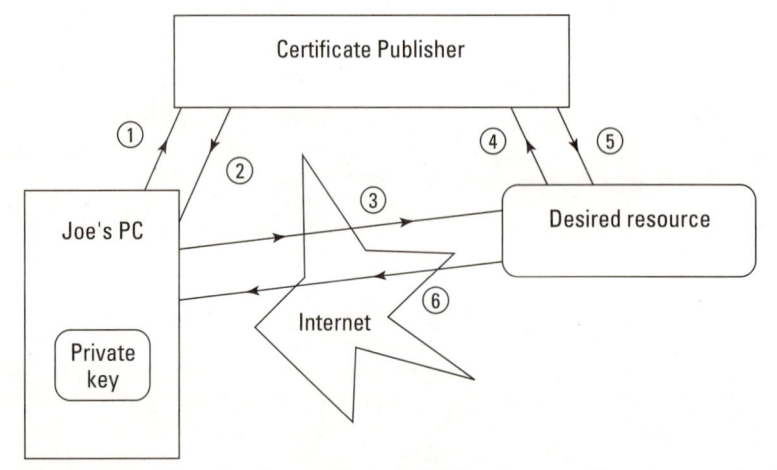

Figure 11-3: The role of a certificate publisher in a certificate transaction.

Here's what's going on in Figure 11-3:

1. Joe's computer finds the certificate information from the desired resource and then checks a certificate publisher to verify the authenticity of the certificate.
2. The certificate publisher checks the certificate information submitted by Joe's computer and sends back verification that the certificate is authentic. Joe's computer now trusts the desired resource's certificate.
3. Joe's computer encrypts data and sends it to the desired resource over the Internet.
4. The desired resource checks Joe's certificate information with the certificate publisher.
5. The certificate publisher confirms to the desired resource that Joe's certificate is authentic.
6. The desired resource grants Joe's request and sends the requested data over the Internet to Joe.

Note: Again, a user's private key is never transmitted over the Internet, and so private keys are not held in public certificate registries.

Certificate publishers also publish certificate revocation lists (or CRLs) that include records of all revoked certificates so SSL-enabled software can check against to make sure someone isn't trying to use a revoked certificate.

Common Security Protocols

Although a wide variety of security protocols are in use in the networking world, the Network+ exam focuses on four of them in particular — IPSec, IKE, Kerberos, and L2TP — which are (not coincidentally) by far the most-used protocols in their class. Earlier sections of this chapter discuss the basics of how security protocols in general function; the following sections focus on the features that distinguish each technology.

IPSec

IPSec (which stands for IP Security) is a standard security protocol that's implemented at the Network Layer of the OSI networking model (as discussed in Chapter 5). IPSec operates at the Network Layer of the OSI model (Layer 3) — not the Data Link Layer as L2TP does — and was written to be the single solution for virtual private networks operating over the TCP/IP protocol stack. IPSec basically consists of a set of extensions to TCP/IP itself and as a result can only be used with the IP protocol.

Note: The abbreviation for *IP Security* is often given as *IPsec* — sometimes even *ipsec* or *IPSEC*. Although the IETF standard was and is *IPsec*, you're likelier to see it as given here (*IPSec*).

IPSec can tunnel connections between two hosts, between a host and a network, or between networks, and is a key player in virtual private network technologies, much like PPTP (which is discussed in Chapter 10) before it. But unlike PPTP, IPSec was written by the IETF (Internet Engineering Task Force) as a TCP/IP-centric protocol.

IPSec is similar in features to SSL and L2TP, but IPSec does not require applications to be IPSec-aware. If applications that have no notion of IPSec request secure data via TCP/IP, they can still get it because IPSec uses TCP/IP on their behalf and establishes the proper security. Although many applications can be made to recognize and use IPSec themselves, they don't have to. SSL, by contrast, requires SSL-enabled applications to help it ensure security.

IPSec subprotocols

IPSec offers the following security protocols internally:

- **Authentication Header (AH):** The protocol that encrypts and authenticates the header of an IP packet.
- **Encapsulating Security Payload (ESP):** Encrypts the payload (that is, everything after the header) of an IP packet and encrypts the data.

Exam Tip: You don't need to know IPSec subprotocols for the exam.

Using both AH and ESP encrypts everything except for the packet's IP header, required to get the packet from one place to the other. The AH encrypts the all header information except IP header information; ESP encrypts the data itself. AH and ESP can be used together or one can be used alone. Using AH and ESP together is called *tunneling mode*; using AH alone is called *transport mode*.

IPSec keys can be handled either manually or via an automated key-management system (the preferred system in larger networks) called IKE, described in the next section.

The Internet key-exchange system (IKE)

To authenticate clients and servers on the network, IPSec uses the *Internet key exchange* (IKE), a key-management system that works with the *ISAKMP/Oakley* protocol (a hybrid of the Diffie-Hellman key-exchange system). IKE is almost disgustingly flexible: It can use RSA encryption (and, accordingly, certificate authorities), or single-key cryptography (methods such as Diffie-Hellman).

IKE offers the following features:

- Auto-configuration of IPSec security parameters.
- Extremely high-encryption (168-bit encryption) with Triple DES (DES is 56-bit, so three times 56 is 168).
- Up to 65,534 different security policies can be defined and used on a given IKA network, and those policies can be prioritized (with 1 being the highest).
- Enables you to specify a limited "lifespan" for an IPSec security association.

Kerberos

Kerberos is an authentication method based on the secret-key encryption method that was developed at the Massachusetts Institute of Technology (MIT) as part of the Athena project (the same project that birthed the X Window System). Yes, Kerberos uses secret-key encryption — the same method mentioned earlier as not particularly secure — but gives that method an unusual twist.

Kerberos is not just any secret-key encryption method, it's a complex, secret-key encryption method built to withstand the inherent insecurity of networks that use a single secret key and have to send it over the Internet. The construction of Kerberos actually goes to great pains to avoid the common pitfalls of secret-key cryptography, and is considered a best-of-breed security protocol (along with SSL, TSL, and others).

Exam Tip Kerberos is the name of the three-headed dog in Greek mythology that guarded the gates of Hades (*Cerberus* is the Latin spelling, pronounced with a hard *C*.) The Kerberos you need to know for the exam is the protocol; unless the origin of the name helps you remember the protocol, never mind the dog.

The following sections discuss the basics of Kerberos, how it operates, and the major technologies behind the protocol.

How Kerberos works

Kerberos operations are similar to SSL and the use of certificates, although with Kerberos the process is even more complex because the use of one key requires the building of a lot more checks into the system to ensure the integrity of user information. Kerberos also uses secret-key cryptography (with one key) where SSL uses public-key cryptography (two keys).

Figure 11-4 illustrates how Kerberos works.

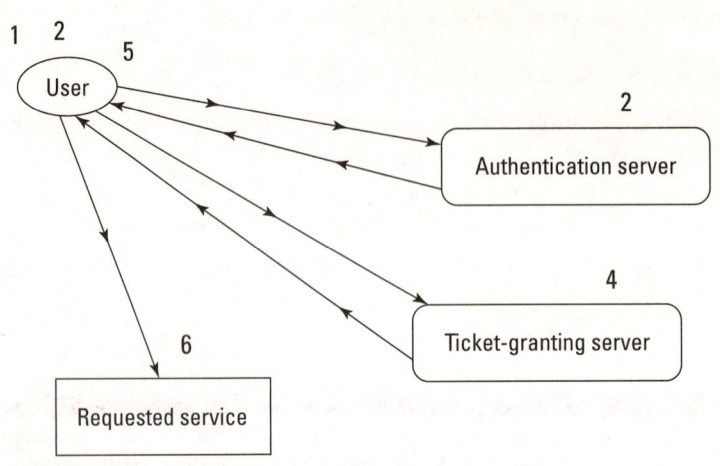

Figure 11-4: A basic Kerberos authentication session.

You can see the following from Figure 11-4 (the numbers of the steps following correspond to those you see in the figure):

1. A user requests a service that requires authentication, such as sending a request via Telnet. The request leaves the client and travels over the network to the authentication server (AS), which creates a session key based on the user's password.

2. The authentication server sends the *session key* over the network back to the user's client. This session key is also called a *ticket-granting ticket*, because its only use is to enable the user's client to request and acquire a ticket.

> **In the Real World**
> As an example of how a ticket-granting ticket works, consider the process analogous to the process with which airlines handle tickets and boarding passes. First you purchase the ticket itself from the airline, and then you take that ticket to the airport and check in, at which point you're handed a boarding pass. That is, you're essentially trading one ticket for another.

3. The user's client submits the ticket-granting ticket to the *ticket-granting server* (TGS).

> **Note**
> The TGS can be the same server as that of the AS, but if so it is performing a completely different function and using different tools than the AS when it acts as the TGS.

4. The TGS sends a ticket back to the user's client (which can then be used to request a service, such as printing or accessing resources from a remote computer).

5. The client sets up a session with the service.

6. The service and client authenticate one another successfully.

7. As long as the ticket is still good, the service that was requested is performed for the user.

> **Note** This entire process is completely transparent to users: the user simply requests a service, enters his or her password (provided the software hasn't saved it — a popular feature in modern e-mail clients and other clients that use authentication), and receives the service within a few seconds.

Tickets

Tickets in Kerberos are similar in concept to certificates (as discussed in the "Certificates" section later in this chapter). Tickets include information about the user, as well as a unique ID for that user, the user's network address, and the code of the Kerberos server that authorized the ticket. Tickets are reusable in Kerberos for as long as the ticket is not expired, as determined by the time stamp on each ticket.

Authentication sessions

Kerberos solves the problem of how to make tickets reusable without compromising security by requiring the use of one-time only authentication sessions that accompany the ticket along each stage of its journey through the network. The catch is that, although these sessions can (theoretically) be used only once, a five-minute window is allowed for the use of each authentication session. This does represent a security hole in Kerberos, although version 5 of the Kerberos protocol solves this by requiring each TGS to store a copy of every authentication session it sees. This way, even if an authentication session is stolen and used within the five-minute window during which it is good, the TGS can reject the stolen session as one it has already seen.

Kerberos for Windows 2000

Kerberos is an open source protocol that uses a less stringent license than that of software like Linux that requires a company that changes the software at all must publish those changes. FreeBSD is also used under this license, and this is probably why Apple chose FreeBSD over Linux when choosing an open source version of Unix to base Mac OS X on.

In a process called *embrace and extend*, Microsoft adopted Kerberos for its Windows 2000 system — but not until the company had "modified" the protocol until it would work only with the Windows versions of Kerberos. For this reason, ordinary Kerberos clients based on the Unix version of the protocol (created at MIT) don't work with the Windows version of Kerberos. Additionally, in its present form, the Windows version of Kerberos won't work on any operating system other than the higher-end Windows products (NT, 2000 or XP). So pay close attention to compatibility issues if you seek to implement Kerberos on multiplatform systems.

Caution: The Windows implementation of Kerberos works only with networks that use all Windows 2000-based networks. This Windows-only version of the originally platform-independent Kerberos doesn't work well with anything but the Windows 2000 version of Kerberos. Thus, Kerberos is best used only on networks that run Windows 2000 exclusively.

L2TP

L2TP (which stands for Layer 2 Tunneling Protocol) combines the best features of the PPTP protocol from Microsoft and the L2F protocol from Cisco Systems. As the predominant protocol of virtual private networks, L2TP creates a powerful virtual private network (VPN) solution. The following sections discuss when L2TP is useful, as well as how it works.

Why L2TP?

L2TP is most useful for a medium-to-large corporation who want to enable employees to log in to an intranet or to the Internet from anywhere. L2TP works with a number of technologies — including Frame Relay, ATM, and others — such that users can log in even while surfing over PPP (or over dial-up, DSL, or other connections). One kludgy solution is to allow all these users to log in remotely via PPP connection — but the long-distance charges can become daunting if large numbers of users log in remotely. L2TP enables these users to log in to the remote central servers via a *tunneled* PPP connection, bypassing long-distance charges because the connection is (technically) terminated locally.

L2TP subprotocols

The L2TP protocol has the following two subprotocols:

- **L2TP Access Concentrator (LAC):** The LAC is a locally accessible connection terminator. The LAC terminates the local connection and tunnels PPP packets to the LNS.

- **L2TP Network Server (LNS):** The LNS sits on the remote end of the connection and terminates the logical PPP connection created by the LAC.

How L2TP works

L2TP works by divorcing the function of processing data packets from any particular point of connection termination. In a typical PPP environment, a user logs in to a local network access server (NAS) that contains the endpoint to that user's PPP connection. For example, if you log in to an ISP that has servers in your city (or near enough where your dial-up connection is a local call) with a dial-up modem, the PPP connection starts at your computer and ends at the ISP's server — locally. In such a situation, PPP is typically used alone. Figure 11-5 illustrates this concept.

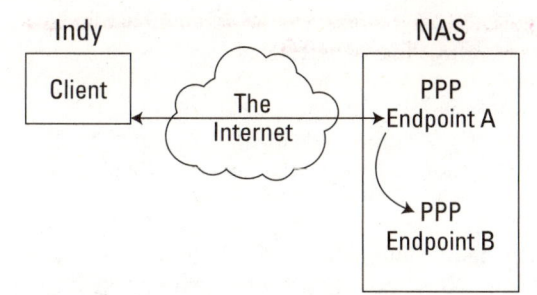

Figure 11-5: A PPP session with two remote endpoints.

Problems with PPP arise if the NAS is *not* local — in which case, long-distance charges apply to the connection. For example, say a user logs in to the to a network in San Diego from her remote location in Indianapolis, using her home desktop workstation. The user's dial-up Internet connection is actually local, but L2TP tunnels the PPP packets to the remote NAS, which itself contains both PPP endpoints, as shown in Figure 11-6.

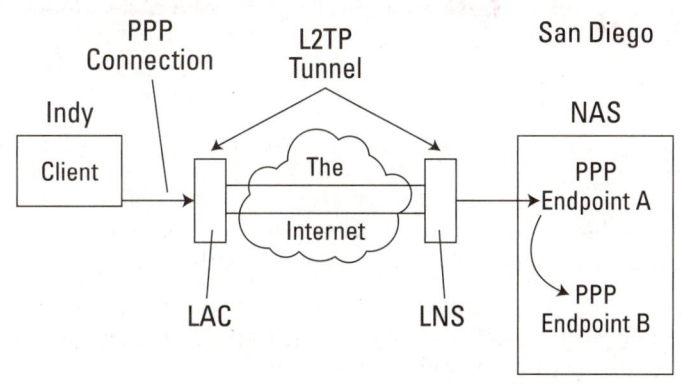

Figure 11-6: An L2TP tunnel makes the PPP endpoints appear to be on the same NAS.

SSL

Originally developed by the venerable Netscape Communications (now a subsidiary of AOL-Time Warner), SSL is a protocol typically used to manage the security of messages as they're being transmitted over the Internet (or any other network that calls for its degree of security). Support for SSL is built into all major Web browsers — including Netscape Navigator and Microsoft Internet Explorer — as well as most Web-server products (such as the open source Apache Web server).

SSL uses sockets (discussed in the "Sockets" section earlier in this chapter) to pass data back and forth from client to server computers, or between different networking layers within the same computer. SSL runs at the Network Layer of the OSI model, handling security transactions for the Application Layer.

SSL uses both public-key cryptography and secret-key cryptography, resulting in an extremely secure environment — one secure enough that the U.S. government restricts the distribution of high-encryption software such as Netscape Navigator to the United States only.

In the Real World

The U.S. government dropped the ban on international distribution of high-encryption (128-bit) software in the year 2000, but after the terrorist attacks on New York's twin towers, the restriction was at least partially resurrected (to exclude Afghanistan and other Taliban-controlled regions). It's unclear how the restrictions will be handled in the future, but a key-escrow solution is possible (see the "Key escrows" section earlier in this chapter for more information).

SSL subprotocols

SSL actually is made up the following two subprotocols:

- **The SSL record protocol:** Establishes which algorithms will be used for a given session
- **The SSL handshake protocol:** uses the SSL record protocol to set up a session with a remote source

How SSL works

The following list gives you a generic example of an SSL session from beginning to end:

1. The client initiates the connection by sending the server the client's SSL version number, the cipher algorithms it supports, and any other information that the server needs to establish an SSL connection with the client.

2. The server replies with its own SSL version number, cipher information, and its certificate, along with any other information needed to establish an SSL connection. If the server needs to authenticate the client, it requests a certificate in return.

3. The client authenticates the server and, if it can't, warns the user of the problem and aborts the process.

4. Using the as-far exchanged data, the client encrypts this data with the server's public key (called a *premaster secret*.).

5. If the client must be authenticated, it sends its authentication information along with the premaster secret.

6. If the server requires client authentication, the server uses the data sent with the premaster secret to authenticate the client. If the attempted authentication fails, the server aborts the session. Otherwise the process continues.

7. After authentication is out of the way, both client and server perform a series of actions on the premaster secret to create the master secret.

8. Client and server use the master secret to create the session key for that particular session. Note that the session key also serves to verify the integrity of the data — if so much as a binary digit changes in the data along the way, the SSL transaction forces a resend of the information.

> **Note** This is where symmetric encryption enters SSL. Until this step, public-key encryption has been used exclusively.

9. The client and server send a message back and forth, agreeing on the session key.
10. The session is established and the client and server both use the session key to encrypt and decrypt the data they exchange.

TSL

TSL is the successor to Netscape's SSL 3.0. Although TSL is not interoperable with SSL, the technology can default back to an SSL-3.0-compatible mode when it comes up against a client that doesn't support TSL.

TSL is composed of its own two subprotocols:

+ **The TSL Record Protocol:** Provides connection security using an encryption method such as DES, an alternative to the RAS protocol that is restricted from export beyond the U.S due to its strength.
+ **The TSL Handshake Protocol:** Similar to the SSL handshake, the TSL Handshake protocol uses an encryption algorithm to assign the keys used to secure the transaction.

> **Exam Tip** Because SSL is still used far more commonly than TSL, the Network+ exam doesn't cover TSL, which is why TSL is not discussed in great detail here. Remember (primarily) that TSL is the successor to SSL.

Summary

Without security protocols, few would consider using the Internet (or any network) for anything, much less for e-commerce, where sensitive information is required. This chapter covered the following key points:

+ Security protocols are used to protect sensitive data in transit over the Internet from being easily acquired and compromised.
+ Most security protocols in use on the Internet today use either public-key cryptography or secret-key cryptography to encrypt data, or some combination of both.
+ Encryption is often used to create secure tunnels over the insecure Internet.
+ The four most-used security protocols are IPSec, Kerberos, L2TP, and SSL.

STUDY GUIDE

Assessment Questions

1. What is the process of verifying the authenticity of the identity of a company or person over the Internet called?

    A. Authentication

    B. Encryption

    C. Decryption

    D. Public-key cryptography

2. Which of the following is not a major encryption method?

    A. DES

    B. RSA

    C. Diffie-Hellman

    D. SSL

3. Which of the following technologies does SSL use to set up a secure connection?

    A. Ports

    B. Sockets

    C. Tunnels

    D. Virtual private networks (VPNs)

4. Which of the following security protocols does Microsoft use in Windows 2000?

    A. IPSec

    B. Kerberos

    C. L2TP

    D. SSL

5. Which of the following protocols is basically a set of extensions to TCP/IP?

   A. IPSec

   B. Kerberos

   C. L2TP

   D. SSL

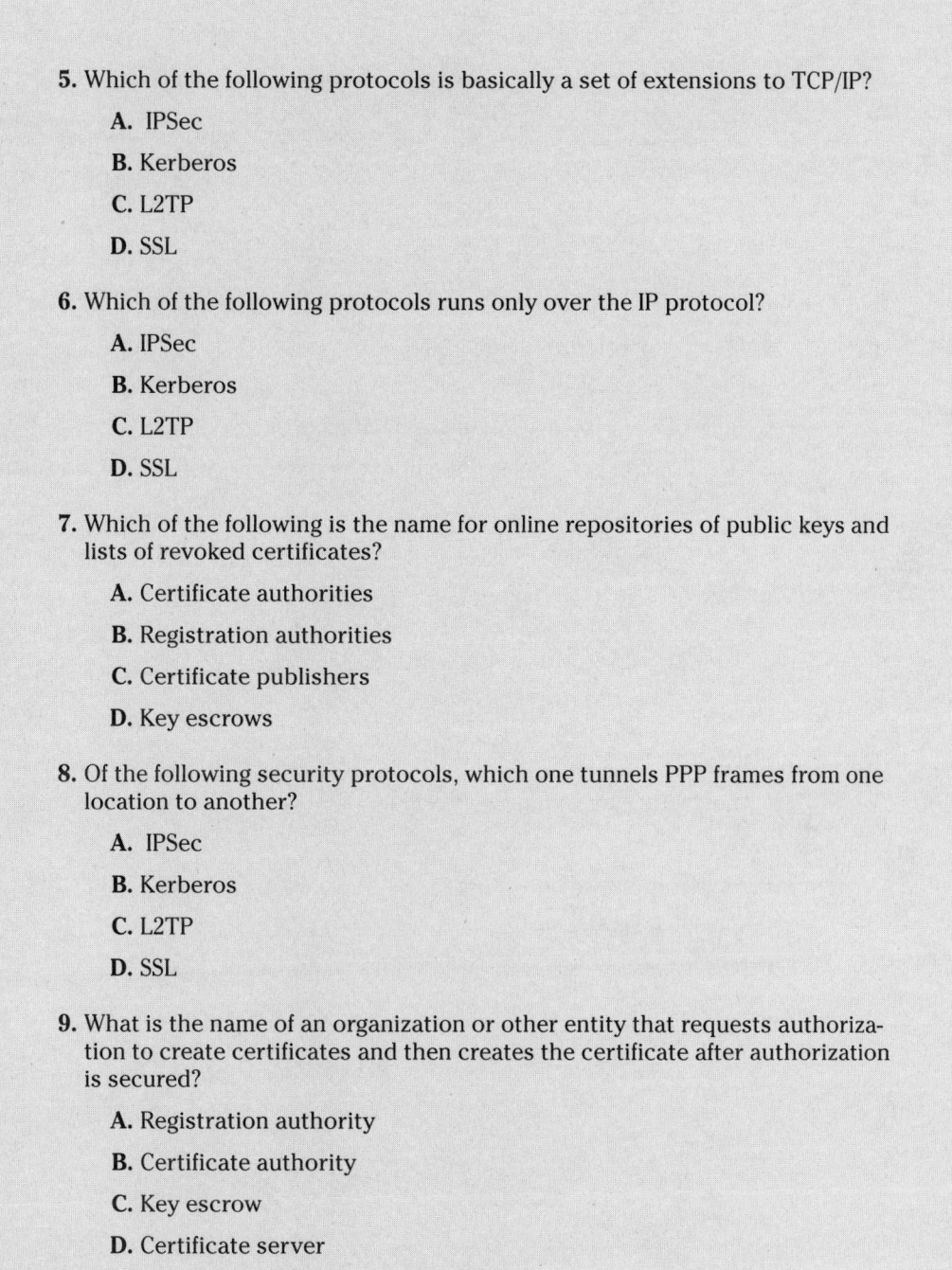

6. Which of the following protocols runs only over the IP protocol?

   A. IPSec

   B. Kerberos

   C. L2TP

   D. SSL

7. Which of the following is the name for online repositories of public keys and lists of revoked certificates?

   A. Certificate authorities

   B. Registration authorities

   C. Certificate publishers

   D. Key escrows

8. Of the following security protocols, which one tunnels PPP frames from one location to another?

   A. IPSec

   B. Kerberos

   C. L2TP

   D. SSL

9. What is the name of an organization or other entity that requests authorization to create certificates and then creates the certificate after authorization is secured?

   A. Registration authority

   B. Certificate authority

   C. Key escrow

   D. Certificate server

10. Which of the following protocols uses secret-key encryption exclusively?

    A. IPSec

    B. Kerberos

    C. L2TP

    D. SSL

11. Which of the following key encryption method(s) does SSL employ?

    A. Public-key encryption

    B. Secret-key encryption

    C. Both public-key encryption and secret-key encryption

    D. Neither public-key encryption nor secret-key encryption (SSL doesn't use keys for encryption)

12. Which of the following protocols runs over a PPP connection?

    A. IPSec

    B. Kerberos

    C. L2TP

    D. SSL

13. Which of the following is the name for a government-managed repository of copies of every encryption key created?

    A. Certificate

    B. Registration authority

    C. Certificate authority

    D. Key escrow

14. What is the name for the process involved in setting up a secure SSL connection?

    A. TSL

    B. The Sockets Layer

    C. Encryption

    D. The handshake

15. Which of the following protocols uses tickets instead of certificates?

    A. IPSec

    B. Kerberos

C. L2TP

D. SSL

16. Which of the following protocols includes the best features of both PPTP and L2F?

   A. IPSec

   B. Kerberos

   C. L2TP

   D. SSL

17. What is an organization or other entity that authorizes the creation of a certificate called?

   A. Registration authority (RA)

   B. Certificate authority (CA)

   C. Key escrow

   D. Certificate server

18. Which of the following protocols uses the IKE key management system?

   A. IPSec

   B. Kerberos

   C. L2TP

   D. SSL

19. The Local Network Server (LNS) is a subprotocol of which of the following protocols?

   A. IPSec

   B. Kerberos

   C. L2TP

   D. SSL

20. Which of the following is the protocol that L2TP was designed to replace?

   A. SSL

   B. PPTP

   C. IKE

   D. PKI

Scenarios

1. You are a consultant for a client that has just finished a transition from an all-Windows 95 to a Windows XP/Linux hybrid network. Which security protocol should you definitely *not* recommend the client use?

2. Your firm is spread all over the United States, with hordes of sales teams logging in via laptop from all over the country. You are an IT manager and are setting up a new network infrastructure to help reduce the costs of remote access. Which security protocol should you choose?

Answers to Chapter Questions

Chapter Pre-Test

1. Encryption is the opposite of decryption. See the "Encryption Basics" section in this chapter for details.

2. Public-key cryptography involves the use of two keys. See the "Encryption Basics" section in this chapter for details.

3. SSL uses both public-key cryptography and secret-key cryptography. See the "Key cryptography" section in this chapter for details.

4. The main security issue in secret-key encryption is the use of a sole key that must be transmitted over the Internet and is thus subject to being intercepted and potentially compromised. See the "Key encryption" section in this chapter for details.

5. The main advantage to public-key encryption is that, unlike with secret-key encryption, two keys are used, and one of them never travels over the network. See the "Key cryptography" section in this chapter for details.

6. The set of guidelines that define a public-key encryption system is called a public-key infrastructure, or PKI. See the "Public-Key Infrastructures" section in this chapter for details.

7. The Kerberos protocol uses a ticket-granting server (TGS). See the "Kerberos" section in this chapter for details.

8. The IPSec protocol can only be used with IP. See the "IPSec" section in this chapter for details.

9. The L2TP protocol tunnels a PPP connection to a remote location. See the "L2TP" section in this chapter for details.

10. The SSL protocol uses an encrypted socket to transfer data securely over a network. See the "SSL" section in this chapter for details.

Assessment Questions

1. A. Authentication is the name of the process by which parties in a given network transaction verify the identity of one another.
2. D. SSL is a security protocol, not an encryption method.
3. B. SSL uses sockets to set up a secure connection over a network.
4. B. Microsoft includes a Windows 2000/XP-only version of the open source Kerberos protocol in Windows 2000/XP.
5. A. IPSec is basically a set of extensions to the TCP/IP protocol stack.
6. A. IPSec can only be used with the IP protocol.
7. C. A certificate publisher is the name for the online repositories of public keys and revoked certificates.
8. C. L2TP tunnels PPP frames from one location to another.
9. B. Certificate authorities request authorization to create certificates from registration authorities (RAs) and then creates the certificate after authenticating the requestor of the certificate.
10. B. Kerberos uses secret-key encryption exclusively.
11. C. SSL uses both public-key encryption and secret-key encryption.
12. C. L2TP runs over a PPP connection.
13. D. A key escrow is a government-managed repository of copies of every encryption key created.
14. D. The SSL handshake is the name for the process at the beginning of an SSL transaction when SSL sets up the socket between the two parties.
15. B. Kerberos uses tickets instead of certificates, although the concept behind the two is the basically the same.
16. C. L2TP includes the best features of both PPTP and L2F.
17. A. A registration authority (RA) is an organization or other entity that authorizes the creation of a certificate).
18. A. IPSec uses the IKE key management system.
19. C. The LNS is a subprotocol of the L2TP protocol.
20. B. L2TP was designed to replace the PPTP protocol.

Scenarios

1. For a hybrid Linux/Windows network, Kerberos is a no-no, because Kerberos can only be properly used on pure Windows-2000/XP networks.

2. In the case of a firm with lots of users logging in remotely from all over the United States, using the L2TP protocol — and its ability to tunnel PPP connections across long distances — can save considerably on the cost of long-distance charges.

Network Implementation

P A R T

III

In This Part

Chapter 12
Network and Client Operating Systems

Chapter 13
VLANs

Chapter 14
Data Storage

Chapter 15
Keeping Your Data Available

Chapter 16
Configuring Remote Connectivity

Chapter 17
Firewalls, Proxy Servers, and Security

Chapter 18
Network Configuration Settings

Network and Client Operating Systems

CHAPTER 12

✦ ✦ ✦ ✦

EXAM OBJECTIVES

✦ Identify the basic capabilities (that is, client support, interoperability, authentication, file and print services, application support, and security) of the following server operating systems:
- UNIX/Linux
- NetWare
- Windows
- Macintosh

CHAPTER PRE-TEST

1. What is a network operating system?
2. What is a client operating system?
3. What is a multipurpose operating system?
4. What are the major network operating systems?
5. What are the major client operating systems?
6. How does a network administrator make sure only those who need certain sensitive files can access them?
7. How do major network operating systems ensure that they can communicate with each other?
8. What is the name of the standard by which all major directory services abide?
9. What dominant protocol do all major operating systems use?
10. What is the role of an administrator user?

✦ Answers to these questions can be found at the end of the chapter. ✦

Chapter 12 ✦ **Network and Client Operating Systems** 259

The operating system is a crucial component in any networking model. It is equally crucial to the interface that the user of the operating system utilizes to perform the basic function calls to a computer device's hardware. For the Network+ exam, you must:

✦ Distinguish which operating systems are used in which environments in the context of modern networking

✦ Know their basic functions

This chapter explains the most common networking and client operating systems and their major features and functions. If you need a quick primer on how operating systems work in general, see the following sidebar.

Network Operating Systems

A *network operating system (NOS)* provides services to clients over a network. Both the client/server and peer-to-peer networking models use network operating systems, and as such, NOSes must be able to handle typical network duties such as the following:

✦ Providing access to remote printers, managing which users are using which printers when, managing how print jobs are queued, and recognizing when devices aren't available to the network

✦ Enabling and managing access to files on remote systems, and determining who can access what — and who can't

✦ Granting access to remote applications and resources, such as the Internet, and making those resources seem like local resources to the user (the network is ideally transparent to the user)

✦ Providing routing services, including support for major networking protocols, so that the operating system knows what data to send where

✦ Monitoring the system and security, so as to provide proper security against viruses, hackers, and data corruption.

✦ Providing basic network administration utilities (such as SNMP, or Simple Network Management Protocol), enabling an administrator to perform tasks involving managing network resources and users.

Types of network operating systems

Two major types of network operating systems exist:

✦ Client/server

✦ Peer-to-peer

Operating Systems: A Primer

Although the test does not directly cover operating system basics, it's important to understand operating systems in general before you start trying to comprehend the differences between network and client operating systems. Briefly, an operating system manages the following services for applications:

- Memory (and virtual memory) for applications to work within
- Data input and output (or I/O) between hardware devices such as hard drives, printers, and modems
- The interface between the user and the operating system, which can be either a shell interface (text-only) or a graphical user interface (GUI)
- Message routing about system status (for example, error messages) between applications and users
- Multitasking multiple open applications and enabling them to interrupt each other when necessary

The following figure shows the basic relationship between user applications, APIs, and the OS to a computer's hardware.

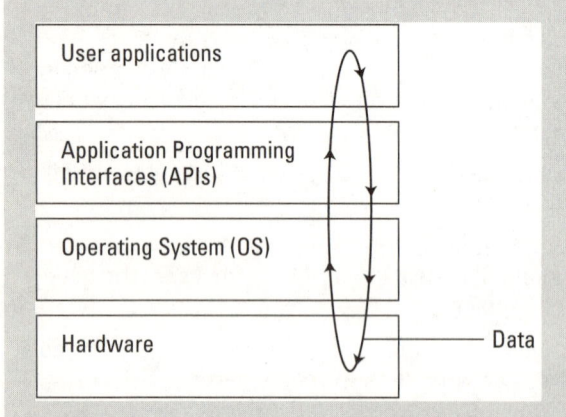

```
┌─────────────────────────────┐
│ User applications           │
├─────────────────────────────┤
│ Application Programming     │
│ Interfaces (APIs)           │
├─────────────────────────────┤
│ Operating System (OS)       │
├─────────────────────────────┤
│ Hardware              ──── Data
└─────────────────────────────┘
```

Users communicate with applications using either a shell (command-line) or graphical user interface (GUI). For their part, the applications communicate with the operating system using an *application programming interface* (or *API*); an API is basically a set of utilities for software developers that enables them to create applications that call certain necessary functions, such as saving or printing, from the operating system.

Some operating systems can cross over and perform as either type (Windows and UNIX); other network operating systems can be only one or the other (NetWare). The following sections explain each of these types of network operating systems.

Client/server operating systems are dedicated to being the server in a client/server network. Clients can be practically any type of device, from cellular phones to servers to cable boxes. Even applications can act as servers and clients; the same application can even act as both in different cases. Figure 12-1 shows the most basic implementation of a client/server model.

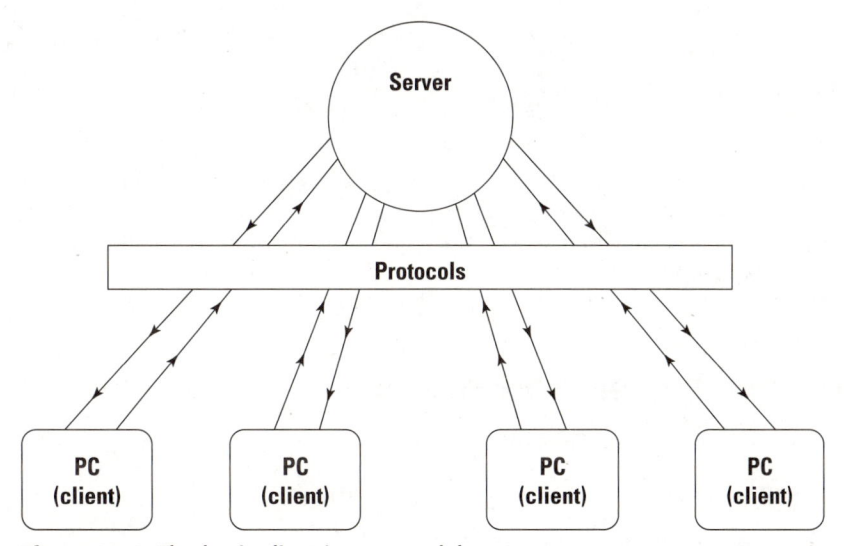

Figure 12-1: The basic client/server model

As shown in the figure, data is transmitted between clients and the server using transport protocols. Whichever protocols are used (almost overwhelmingly TCP/IP these days), must be implemented on both client and server.

Peer-to-peer network operating systems can be used in networks where

- All of a network's workstations are chained together with cabling.
- No one workstation is in charge of the others.

> **Exam Tip:** Windows and UNIX/Linux can act as peer-to-peer client operating systems, but NetWare cannot, because no client version of NetWare exists. (See the "What? No NetWare Client?" sidebar later in this chapter for more information on NetWare's lack of a client version).

Major network operating systems

Many network operating systems abound in the networking world of today; even Macintosh is considered a network operating system (especially Mac OS X; see the

"Mac OS X: Not on the Test—Yet" sidebar later in this chapter). However, the vast majority of network operating systems in use today (those covered on the test) include the following:

- **UNIX/Linux:** Although UNIX is the oldest of the major network operating systems, a great many users still consider it the most powerful and versatile of the lot. Linux in particular is gaining more and more market share from other major network operating systems every day. See the UNIX/Linux section later in this chapter for more information on UNIX and Linux.

- **Novell NetWare:** Still one of the most-used network operating systems around, but it's losing ground steadily to both Windows NT/2000 and Linux.

- **Windows NT/2000:** A multipurpose operating system targeted mostly at corporate users. Windows also has client versions of its operating systems, including Windows 95 and later releases of the same system under different names (Windows 98, Me, etc.). See the "Windows NT/2000" and "Client Operating Systems" sections later in this chapter for more details on Windows.

Sharing with users and groups

On a network, users must have some way to

- Store their information, such as files and settings
- Control access to their information

Most network operating systems use the concept of *users* and *groups* to protect resources from those who shouldn't be able to access them. Typically, users all have individual user accounts with unique passwords to prevent unauthorized access. To simplify resource access, you can then organize users into groups depending on what resources they need. Similarly, you can strip resources from a user by removing the user from an existing group. This capability enables administrators to assign certain access for groups only, not individual users. Figure 12-2 shows an example.

You can see the following from the figure:

- User `maryg` belongs to the `produce` group and does not belong to the `accounting` group, so she will be denied access to the Accounting server.
- User `johnd` is a member of the `accounting` group but not the `produce` group, so he will be denied access to the Produce department's server should he attempt to access it.
- Both users are members of the `global` group, so both have access to the global server.

Note: This figure shows a typical overview of how user and group relationships work. Please refer to the appropriate section for each operating system later in this chapter for the specifics of how each operating system handles users and groups.

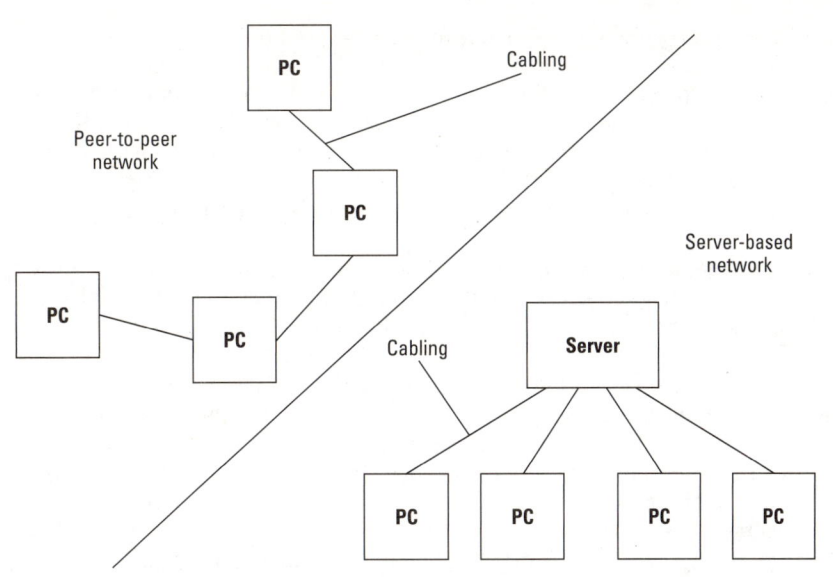

Figure 12-2: An example of a user/group permission structure

Administrator users

All three of the major network operating systems delegate administration of the machine to one all-powerful user account that can do pretty much anything it wants with the system, from managing user information to editing system initialization and configuration files. In a network setting where security is an issue, the administrator should use the administrator-level account only when necessary, so that the administrator doesn't accidentally and irrevocably screw something up (like delete all files from a system).

Administrator users typically perform the following duties:

- **User maintenance:** Deleting users, adding users, changing user passwords, and so on
- **Systems maintenance:** Maintaining server and client software and hardware
- **Network configuration maintenance:** Enabling communication between servers and clients on the network by editing configuration and initialization files

Exam Tip In Windows NT/2000, UNIX/Linux, and NetWare, these accounts are called Administrator, root (or superuser), and ADMIN or SUPERVISOR (for NetWare 4.x and above and NetWare 3.x, respectively). These accounts are explained in more detail in later sections of this chapter.

Network operating system protocols

One of the common threads to the major network operating systems is that all of them use protocols to talk to one another and to clients on the network. Historically, each operating system has used proprietary protocols as their native protocols (NetWare, for example, used to push IPX/SPX instead of TCP/IP), which made communications between different types of networks a complicated undertaking.

> **Cross-Reference** The coverage of protocols in this chapter is focused on helping you associate the various proprietary protocols with their respective network operating systems. See Chapter 6 for more information on the protocols and how they work.

Most modern network operating system vendors have switched to using TCP/IP as the default protocol (or at least having TCP/IP installed by default alongside proprietary protocols, as is the case with Apple and Macintosh). Why? The reason is simple: If they don't, people won't buy the operating system. TCP/IP is the protocol that is by far the most-used protocol on the Internet, and in the past five years the Internet has become an absolutely required resource for many, many people in this world. Anymore, proprietary protocols (like IPX/SPX and AppleTalk) only add an unnecessary level of abstraction to networking; why should you use a dozen protocols to network between Macs, Windows PCs, NetWare systems, and UNIX systems when you can just use TCP/IP? People don't want to haggle with all of those protocols if they can avoid it; it just doesn't make sense, so most networks use TCP/IP where possible.

> **Exam Tip** Unfortunately, the Borg-like assimilation of TCP/IP isn't yet complete in today's networking world, and alternative protocols are still used. So, for the foreseeable future at least, you're expected to know the alternative protocols that are associated with each network operating system, even if you only ever use TCP/IP yourself. The network operating system protocols associated with each network operating system are described in the appropriate sections for each operating system later in this chapter.

Directory services and X.500

The X.500 Directory Service standard, also called a *global white pages database*, is used as the basis for many directory services, including Novell's NDS, Microsoft's Active Directory, and LDAP. The standard defines a basic directory service using a common root directory in a tree hierarchy of country, organization, organizational unit, and person. Collectively, this is called a directory *schema*, and works in a way that makes sense for the geographical organization of a company. See the "NetWare Directory Services," "Active Directory," and "UNIX protocols" sections later in this chapter for a good look at the three major X.500-based directory services.

NetWare

NetWare has been a great LAN operating system for years, but only recently (with NetWare 5.x, to be specific) has NetWare moved beyond the LAN to where it can easily be a part of larger networks. Until quite recently, Novell NetWare used to be the single most-used network operating system (NOS). However, first Windows NT, and more recently Windows 2000 and Linux, have steadily eaten into the NetWare market share for network operating systems. Currently, all three operating systems have a roughly equal share of the network operating system market, which means that NetWare is still used in at least one-third of all server systems.

Exam Tip NetWare is the one major network operating system that is used as a network operating system only; no client version of NetWare exists. Both Windows and UNIX/Linux have client and server versions available. See the "What? No NetWare Client?" sidebar later in this chapter for more information on why NetWare doesn't use clients. For the exam, remember that NetWare doesn't have a client version.

NetWare features

NetWare offers the following features (other features are explained in later sections):

- **Multiprocessor kernel:** This feature enables one NetWare operating system to utilize multiple processors. This process is called *symmetric multiprocessing* (SMP). SMP enables processors to share memory and bus paths, even coordinating the processing of a single application in parallel.

- **NLMs:** Where UNIX uses daemons and Windows uses services, NetWare uses *NetWare Loadable Modules* (or NLMs) to provide services from the server. NLMs are programs that run in the background on the server to provide consistent services to the network.

- **PCI Hot Plug:** This feature enables administrators to dynamically configure PCI network components while the system is running. You can replace, upgrade, or add new cards with the Hot replace, Hot upgrade, and Hot expansion features, respectively.

- **Dozens of administration tools:** See the "NetWare utilities" section later in this chapter for more information on NetWare utilities.

NetWare versions

In its first incarnations (NetWare 3.x and 4.x), NetWare was primarily a LAN operating system. Newer versions of NetWare (such as 5.x and 6.x) have taken NetWare to another level, where the operating system is now capable of participating in larger network configurations, such as WANs. The following sections explain the major version cycles of the NetWare operating system and some of the important features that were introduced within those version cycles.

NetWare 3.x

NetWare 3.x, unlike later releases, was largely a LAN-only operating system. The most notable difference between NetWare 3.x and later versions is the bindery, a database that resides on each NetWare (3.x) server and includes user, group, and security information.

NetWare 3.x was not a very flexible network operating system, particularly when compared with more recent versions of the system. With the bindery, users must have a separate login account for each server that they need to access on the network. As you can imagine, these requirements create an environment that gets exponentially more nightmarish the larger the network you're dealing with. Luckily, the bindery was dropped in NetWare 4.x in favor of the far superior directory service NetWare Directory Services (NDS). See the "NetWare Directory Services" section later in this chapter.

Exam Tip NetWare 3.x coverage is limited on the exam, but you should remember the bindery and its limitations.

NetWare 4.x

NetWare version 4.x brought Novell Directory Services (NDS) to the NetWare platform, giving the operating system an edge against Windows NT until Windows 2000 introduced Active Directory to compete with NDS. NDS replaced the bindery in NetWare 3.x. For more information on NDS, see the "NetWare Directory Services" section later in this chapter. Unlike the bindery, NDS enables users to log in from anywhere on the network, not just from the particular server that provides their services.

NetWare 4.x and above includes the NetWare Storage Services (NSS) service to provide compatibility with the NetWare File System (NWFS) that was used in NetWare 3.x.

IntranetWare

IntranetWare is a suite of utilities that simplifies intranetworking in NetWare and was released as part of NetWare 4.11. The utilities that are a part of IntranetWare are as follows:

- **FTP Services for NetWare:** Enables users to log in to an FTP server and download files
- **NetWare IPX/IP Gateway:** Acts as a gateway between IP and the proprietary IPX protocol from Novell
- **NetWare Multiprotocol Router with WAN Extensions:** A router that interfaces between NetWare LANs and WANs, provides support for TCP/IP, IPX, AppleTalk, NetBIOS, and SNA/LLC2 protocols, and enables transmission over WAN technologies such as ISDN, frame relay, or ATM

> **Cross-Reference:** See Chapter 11 for more information about WAN technologies.

- **NetWare Web Server:** Enables NetWare to offer Web services such as Web sites, e-mail, and Internet service

NetWare 5.x

NetWare 5.x was functionally quite similar to NetWare 4.x, at least in terms of its core feature set (the two systems can coexist peacefully in the same NDS tree), but NetWare 5.x was actually a pretty big step for NetWare in terms of new features. The goal with NetWare 5.x was to rework the NetWare operating system so that it could support heterogeneous networks, such as the Internet, instead of being tied to proprietary protocols that often function only to complicate networking.

Following are some of the more notable features that NetWare 5.x brought to the NetWare party:

- **Pure TCP/IP networking:** In NetWare 5.x, Novell finally threw in the towel and made TCP/IP the default protocol stack for NetWare (rather than IPX/SPX, which previous NetWare versions had used). In previous versions, the only way for NetWare to communicate with TCP/IP was by using a tunnel through IPX/SPX. As of NetWare 5.x, IPX/SPX doesn't even need to be installed on NetWare.

- **ConsoleOne:** A Java-based utility, it runs over the server console, enabling administrators to manage the server via a graphical interface.

- **Integration with Internet services:** In NetWare 5.x, the following TCP/IP tasks were integrated with NDS:
    - DNS
    - DHCP
    - Netscape FastWeb server

- **Zero Effort Networks (or Z.E.N.works):** A suite of utilities, Z.E.N.works enables administrators to manage workstations from a single location.

NetWare Directory Services

First implemented in NetWare 4.x, *Novell Directory Services (NDS)* is a central database that stores information for all users, network resources, and other objects. Where the NetWare 3 bindery service forced users to create new accounts for each server, NDS enables users to log in from any point along the network without having to know the location of their own resources in relation to the NDS tree.

NetWare 6.x

Although NetWare 6 will probably be out by the time this book is published (the beta is out as of this writing), the exam does not yet cover NetWare 6 at all. Still, NetWare 6 is the newest flagship in the NetWare line, and knowing what additional features NetWare 6 includes can help give you a better understanding of what NetWare 5.x lacks (at least in the eyes of Novell).

Perhaps not surprisingly, the focus of NetWare 6 is the Internet. Following are several of the new features offered with NetWare 6:

+ **iFolder:** This useful feature enables users to keep constant access to the most updated versions of their files no matter where they log in to the network. Using browser plug-ins, LDAP authentication, and iFolder clients, users can work on files from their client and have them backed up and synchronized with the network transparently. This functionality is necessary in high-availability networks (such as those primarily using laptops or Tablet PCs) where files need to be server-stored, constantly accessible, and always up to date.

+ **Novell Internet Printing:** This feature enables management of print jobs through Web browsers and allows for full automation of workstation print drivers.

+ **Data shredding:** NetWare 6 now includes the capability to completely erase files so that they can never be recovered (Microsoft would have benefited from this before their antitrust trial; the company was positively slaughtered in court by their own e-mail records).

Following are some of the more notable features of NDS:

+ **Advanced file attributes:** NetWare enables customization of file attributes like no other network operating system. See Table 12-1 later in this chapter for more information on these attributes.

+ **Replicas:** NDS can reside on multiple servers; in some cases, NDS is redundantly installed on multiple servers. These redundant copies of NDS are called replicas, and they help increase the fault tolerance of the overall network (see Chapter 16 for more information on fault tolerance).

+ **Single seat of administration:** This concept is simple: An administrator can manage the network from one location.

NetWare Administrator: This ultrahandy tool for managing a NetWare network from a client was introduced alongside NDS in NetWare 4.x.

NDS has a standard concept behind its typical directory structure based on objects called the *schema*. An object in an NDS schema can be a server, a user, a printer, or any other network client or resource. Conceptually, NDS arranges objects in a reverse tree structure: At one end of a tree is the [root] container that contains all other objects within the network, and at the other end are the leaves. The three main types of objects in an NDS network tree model are as follows:

- **[root]:** This object owns all the others; every piece of the network falls under [root].
- **Container objects:** Container objects do exactly what their name implies: They contain other objects. Containers are themselves contained within [root].
- **Leaf objects:** These objects are named after their location in a typical NDS tree.

Figure 12-3 shows a typical NDS tree.

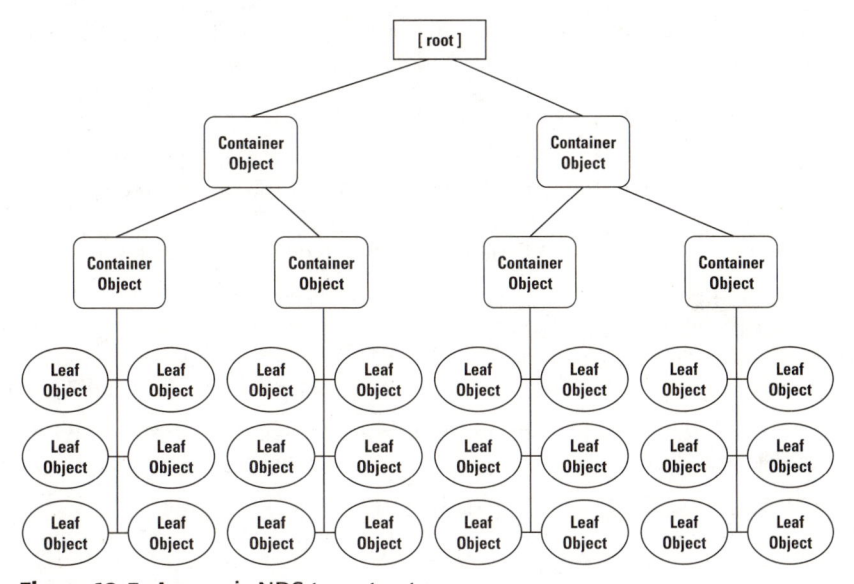

Figure 12-3: A generic NDS tree structure

You can see the following from Figure 12-3:

- The [root] container contains two container objects.
- The two container objects directly under [root] contain two container objects each.
- The four containers in the second level of the figure contain six leaf objects each.

Of course, Figure 12-3 shows only a theoretical representation of how an NDS tree structure is set up. Figure 12-4 shows an example tree of a hypothetical small publisher called PublisherA.

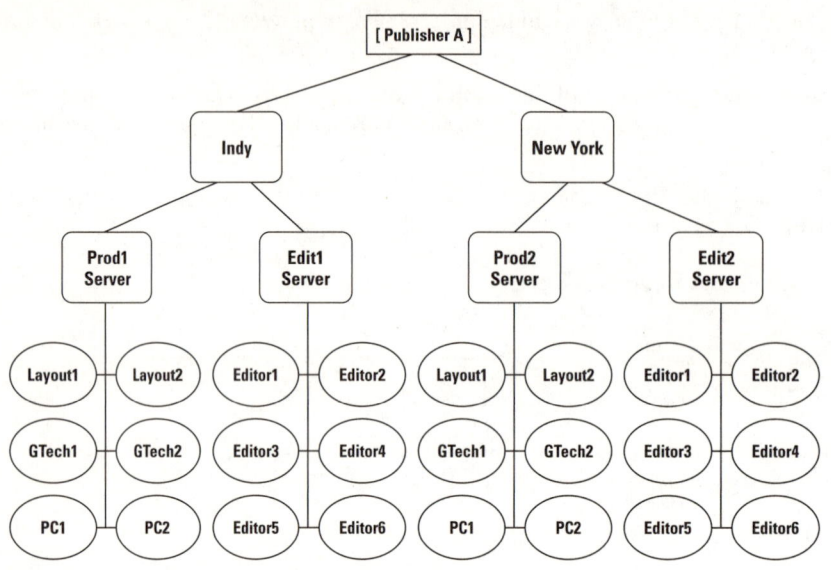

Figure 12-4: An example NDS tree structure for Publisher A

You can see the following from Figure 12-4:

- The root object, [PublisherA], contains two major servers: Indy and New York.
- The Indy container object includes two container objects (Prod1 and Edit1) and the New York container object includes two container objects (Prod2 and Edit2).
- The leaves of each of the Prod and Edit containers correspond to individual workstations.
- The workstations under the Edit containers are for six editors each (Editor1–Editor6).
- The workstations under the Prod containers contain workstations for two production coordinators, two layout technicians, and two graphics technicians.

This configuration enables PublisherA to split up editorial services (where editors edit text for books like this one) and production services (where production coordinators run the book through layout and graphics services).

NetWare file system

NetWare's file system isn't dissimilar from other popular file systems, such as NTFS or NFS, at least in terms of security and functionality. Basically, one root directory houses a number of volumes, which NetWare uses to break up its file system architecture. The first volume in a NetWare environment is called the *SYS volume,* which NetWare uses for operating system files.

> **Note:** The SYS volume is created during the installation of NetWare.

Volumes act much like letter designators do in MS-DOS; for example, a directory on the SYS directory would be designated as SYS:*DIRECTORY*. NetWare uses the following two types of volumes:

- **Physical volumes:** Physical volumes are made up of up to 32 volume segments. Up to eight volume segments can be stored per hard drive (or other type of disk). Figure 12-5 shows an example of this concept, which isn't terribly easy to visualize.

- **Logical volumes:** NetWare manages physical volumes by sectoring off portions of physical volumes into *logical volumes*.

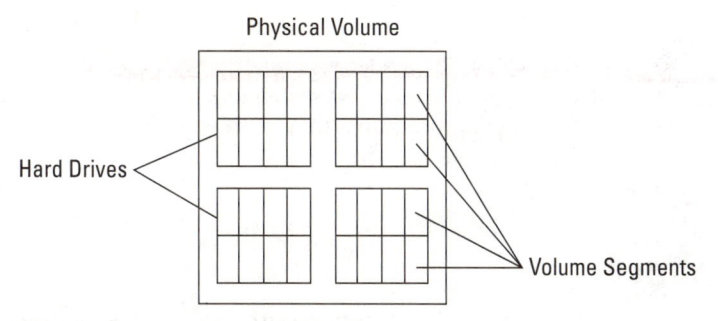

Figure 12-5: A NetWare physical volume

Volumes can be up to 32TB (TB stands for terabytes) in size, and in larger networks, administrators can use as many physical and logical volumes as make sense given the network's NDS schema and hardware configuration. For example, say that one logical volume is to be shared by ten users. If those users are in different departments, it may make sense to keep the workspace for these users separate, so the network administrator may decide to carve up a physical volume segment into multiple logical volumes, say one for each user. Or, if the users are in the same department and even in the same group, the administrator may instead share one volume among all ten users so that the users all see the same directories and files (see the "Sharing with users and groups" section earlier in this chapter for more information on users and groups).

Typically, a hard drive is a physical volume that acts as one volume segment. This physical volume is then cut into logical volumes when the operating system is installed. The SYS volume, for example, is usually a logical volume on a hard drive, although in larger settings, SYS could even be on its own physical volume. Other volumes on the same hard drive could be for user files, applications, and so on.

In larger networks, a physical volume can be made up of various physical parts, as long as it has no more than 32 volume segments per physical volume. Having four hard drives with eight volume segments each works (as shown in Figure 12-5, but so does 32 hard drives with one volume segment each. The possibilities are various and sundry; the available hardware, the resources required by the network, and the level of fault tolerance the network is willing to handle determine the volume structure of a given network.

> **Cross-Reference:** Please refer to Chapter 16 for coverage of fault tolerance.

NetWare uses *namespaces* as a way of supporting different file systems within the same network. For example, the DOS namespace saves files in 8.3 (8.3 means that the filename can be no more than eight characters long with an extension no more than three characters long). Namespaces are provided with NetWare using special modules with the .NAM file extension.

NetWare protocols

One major learning curve for a new NetWare administrator is the NetWare proprietary protocols that were used before NetWare 5.x instead of that system's native TCP/IP model. The two NetWare protocols that you should know about for the Network+ exam are:

- **IPX (Internetwork Packet Exchange):** IPX provides the same connectionless service as IP.
- **SPX (Sequenced Packet Exchange):** SPX provides the same connection-oriented service that TCP does.

IPX and SPX are two parts of a replacement protocol stack for TCP/IP based on proprietary Novell protocols. NetWare supports TCP/IP by default in 5.x and later versions, although you can still use IPX should you need to for legacy reasons.

> **Cross-Reference:** Please refer to Chapter 6 for coverage of protocols.

NetWare administration

You can manage a NetWare network on two levels:

- Client systems
- NetWare server

Other network operating systems enable this level of management, but in Windows, for example, administration utilities don't ship with client versions of the operating system because Microsoft wants to sell those utilities as part of its enterprise-level operating system, not its client operating system. NetWare has no client version, and you cannot use NetWare as a client system with any real success, so most of the utilities made for NetWare are client-based.

The following sections cover the basics of NetWare administration, including

- File permissions
- Administrator accounts
- NetWare utilities

ADMIN and SUPERVISOR accounts

As is typical among network operating systems, with NetWare, one user is assigned authority over all other users. In Linux, this user is the root user; in Windows, this user is the Administrator; and in NetWare, this user is the SUPERVISOR (NetWare 3.x) and ADMIN (NetWare 4.x and higher) accounts.

- The SUPERVISOR and ADMIN accounts are all-powerful in NetWare.

    They can do anything they need, such as

    - Deleting users and adding new ones.
    - Changing the permissions for files or directories based on personnel changes.

- The SUPERVISOR and ADMIN accounts are also the only users that can run system administration utilities.

Access permissions

On any network with files that are sensitive in one way or another, there must be some method of keeping files stored on the network from being viewed by unauthorized eyes. The most common way of implementing NetWare enables administrators to restrict access to files on two levels:

✦ Access permissions

✦ File attributes

Access permissions instruct NetWare as to which users can access which files. Lower directories and files automatically inherit the permissions of a directory unless an *inherited rights filter* tells NetWare that it should stop certain rights from being inherited down a given avenue of the directory tree. For example, say that the example `adir` directory contains `bdir` and `cdir`. Ordinarily, `bdir` and `cdir` have the same rights as `adir` by inheritance of their rights from `adir`. An inherited rights filter in the `adir` directory could stop this inheritance from trickling down to either or both of the `bdir` and `cdir` directories.

File attributes determine what users can actually do to a file after they have accessed it. The file attributes used in NetWare are listed in Table 12-1.

Exam Tip For the exam, you don't have to memorize all the NetWare file attributes. Familiarize yourself with those that have asterisks next to their attribute names in Table 12-1. By name, the attributes you should know for the exam are Archive (A), Execute Only (X), Hidden (H), Read-Only (RO), Read-Write (RW), and Shareable (SH).

Table 12-1
NetWare Extended File Attributes

Attribute Name	Designator	Function
Archive*	A	Indicates that a directory or file has been changed since the last backup and needs to be archived (or backed up)
Copy Inhibit	Ci	Disenables a user from copying Macintosh files
Can't Compress	Cc	Set automatically if no significant amount of space will be gained by compressing a file
Don't Compress	Dc	Disenables NetWare from compressing a file or directory
Delete Inhibit	Di	Disenables users from deleting a file or directory
Don't Migrate	Dm	Disenables a file or directory from being migrated to a high-capacity storage unit

Attribute Name	Designator	Function
Don't Suballocate	Ds	Instructs NetWare to store a file on only whole blocks, rather than on suballocated blocks, of the server's hard drive
Execute Only	X	Disenables users from modifying, erasing, or copying a file. This attribute cannot be removed after it has been set.
Hidden	H	Indicates that the file is not shown when using list commands in the directory where they reside
Immediate Compress	Ic	Compresses a file immediately
Indexed	I	Turns on Turbo FAT indexing for a file
Migrated	M	Set automatically after a file is migrated
Purge	P	Removes a file irrevocably
Read-Only	RO	Indicates that a file can be accessed but not changed (and saved)
Read-Write	RW	Indicates that a file can be accessed and changed (and saved)
Rename Inhibit	Ri	Disenables users from renaming a file or directory
Shareable	SH	Indicates that multiple users can access the file simultaneously
System	SY	Indicates a system file that is required for NetWare to function
Transactional	T	NetWare Transaction Tracking System files

NetWare utilities

Two major types of NetWare utilities exist:

- ✦ Server-console utilities
- ✦ Client utilities

NetWare is unique as a network operating system in that many of the administrative utilities for the system were designed to be run from a client operating system, such as Windows. Indeed, several utilities made by Novell for NetWare run only on Windows or MS-DOS.

The main NetWare utilities are shown in Table 12-2. Included in the table is information on what NetWare version each utility works with and whether the utility is server- or client-based.

Table 12-2
Major NetWare Utilities

Utility	Function	NetWare Version	Client or Server-Based?
CONFIG	Used to display current network adapters and their configurations	All versions	Server-based
ConsoleOne	Designed to enable remote Web administration of a NetWare network; a Java-based application that displays limited NDS tree information	NetWare 5.x	Server-based
FLAG	Command-line utility that changes file attributes	All versions	Client-based
INETCFG	Displays current protocols, networks adapters, and configurations	NetWare 4.x and 5.x	Server-based
INSTALL or NWCONFIG	Used to configure hard drives, volumes, startup configuration files, and NLM applications	All versions	Server-based
MONITOR	Displays performance statistics	All versions	Server-based
NDPS Manager	Displays NDPS printers and their status and statistics	NetWare 5.x	Server-based
NDS Manager	A Windows application that enables management of NDS data replication on a NetWare network	NetWare 4.x and up	Client-based
NetWare Administrator	A Windows application that enables centralized administration of a NetWare network; NetWare administrator shows a tree similar to what is used in Windows Explorer that corresponds directly to the structure of the NDS tree. An administrator can drill down to the appropriate leaf object and modify it from NetWare Administrator.	NetWare 4.x and up	Client-based

Utility	Function	NetWare Version	Client or Server-Based?
PCONSOLE	Displays printers and their status and statistics	All versions	Server-based
RIGHTS	Enables the administrator to manage file permissions	All versions	Client-based
SET	A command-line tool that enables an administrator to set configuration parameters for NetWare	All versions	Server-based
SERVMAN	In NetWare 4.x, SERVMAN helps configure SET parameters; in NetWare 5.x, SERVMAN ismerged with MONITOR.	NetWare 4.x	Server-based
Workstation Manager	A Windows application that manages user accounts for both Windows NT users and groups and the NetWare network by storing NT user and group information within NDS		Client-based

UNIX/Linux

UNIX, created originally by Bell Labs (under AT&T), is a powerful server operating system that can be used in peer-to-peer or client/server networks. UNIX was the first operating system written in the C programming language. Due to an antitrust ruling forbidding AT&T from releasing operating systems commercially, AT&T released UNIX upon its completion in 1974 to universities, mostly, enabling people to go in and actually view the source code to the system, which enabled coders to reconstruct the basic functions of the original UNIX operating system. From this practice, called *reverse engineering*, came Linux, which was first developed in the late 1980s by a young student at the University of Helsinki in Finland named Linus Torvalds.

> **Note** Because UNIX and Linux are so similar in functionality, in this chapter both are described as "UNIX/Linux" or just "UNIX" for the most part.

In its original incarnations, UNIX was developed for larger computers than the PCs that typically use it these days; initially the system was intended for mid-range servers (sometimes called mini-computers), which are meant for solutions that don't require mainframes but do require more computing muscle than the typical PC of the time could provide (in the 1970s, when UNIX became popular, the concept of PCs hardly existed).

UNIX is a multipurpose operating system. Although UNIX itself used to have a reputation for including only a shell-based interface, in the past decade this has changed dramatically. Indeed, Apple based its new operating system [Mac OS X] on the FreeBSD version of UNIX — a testament to the graphics capabilities of the UNIX system. As a result, UNIX (and especially Linux) is considered both a client and network operating system (often called a *multipurpose operating system*).

UNIX features

UNIX (and Linux by extension) systems offer the following features:

- **Fully protected multitasking:** This means that UNIX can easily switch between tasks without the operating system crashing, because all UNIX processes are separate from those of the operating system. Even if an application crashes, unless it somehow manages to take down the X Windows system with it (which does happen), the operating system just keeps right on humming.

- **High performance and stability:** Many servers running UNIX or Linux have run for years without crashing once. The multitasking capabilities of UNIX, along with the rapid rate at which the operating system matures (especially with Linux, which is free and can be changed by anyone), make UNIX or Linux a powerful solution, especially for server systems.

- **Multiuser capabilities:** True multiuser systems enable different users to be logged in to the same system simultaneously. In UNIX and Linux, not only can a user log in to the same system at the same time as other users, that user can log in multiple times on the same system as the same user without the operating system batting an eyelash (such things are often necessary when administrating a network, particularly when managing users).

- **Tons of high-quality software:** From Apache Server (a Web server that's used on a whopping 6 in 10 major Web servers on the Internet) to the long-awaited Mozilla.org Mozilla 1.0 open source Web browser/e-mail software (Mozilla is an open source version of the venerated Netscape Communicator) to the powerful free Gimp graphics manipulation software, Linux is packed with tons of free, high-quality software. The trick is that, with UNIX/Linux, you give up compatibility with commercial software that's available only for Windows and/or Macintosh, currently.

- **Easy customization:** While other operating systems seem to offer less and less choice to the user about which applications to install with the operating system (Windows XP is this way), UNIX and especially Linux are the exact counterpoint to that model. With UNIX or Linux, you can actually customize your operating system kernel, stripping it down to just drivers and networking or installing everything possible.

- **Modular architecture:** The modular architecture of UNIX (and especially Linux) is directly responsible for how customizable UNIX is. Modular really means just what it sounds like: The operating system is built with a kernel that attaches modules to itself based on what the user needs.

✦ **POSIX compliance:** With a free operating system like UNIX, the different distributions (or flavors) of UNIX quickly became difficult to manage. Currently, hundreds of different implementations of UNIX are available. To enable programmers to have some idea of how to code their software such that it would run on any version of UNIX, the Institute of Electrical and Electronics Engineers, Inc. (IEEE) defined the Portable Operating System Interface (POSIX).

> **Note** Windows NT is actually considered POSIX compliant, although that compliance isn't to the level of UNIX and Linux.

✦ **Use of TCP/IP as the standard protocol stack:** UNIX overwhelmingly uses TCP/IP as the protocol stack of choice. If you consider that the vast majority of the servers that help make up the Internet are UNIX computers of one form or another, you start to get the idea why TCP/IP is so popular.

✦ **A shell interface:** All versions of UNIX (at least those you care about for the exam) include a shell interface of some sort. If you have ever seen your computer use a completely black screen with white words written on it, that's a shell interface. You simply type in commands at the prompt and hit Enter to execute those commands. The hard part in using these interfaces is simply the effort it takes to learn all of those rather cryptic commands. Making life even more difficult, UNIX is ultimately customizable and can use different shells. The bash shell (likely the most popular shell in use today) and the tcsh shell, for example, have different commands for the same action.

✦ **A graphical user interface:** Although most versions of UNIX (such as Red Hat Linux) include a graphical user interface (GUI) these days, this has not always been the case. Historically, UNIX has been derided for its cryptic interface, and the advent of the GUI into popular UNIX systems was a direct result of this. Popular UNIX GUIs include KDE and GNOME. KDE is mostly used with Linux, but GNOME has versions for the Sun Solaris operating system, and therefore crosses the border from Linux into UNIX proper.

✦ **Support for dumb terminals:** Traditionally, UNIX was used for dumb terminals, and just about all versions of UNIX still include this capability. The traditional dumb terminal model involves one central UNIX server that is used by remote terminals to execute applications. Basically, a user logs in to a UNIX system via Telnet or some other remote connectivity application and uses UNIX commands to tell the remote system what functions to perform. In this way, users can download and check e-mail via a text-based e-mail client such as Pine. The dumb terminal in this form isn't used much anymore; Web browsers are definitely more than just dumb terminals — and Web browsers are now the clients most often seen by UNIX servers (at least those that make up the Internet). However, wireless devices such as cell phones and mobile Internet e-mail clients such as AOL's Mobile Communicator device are good examples of modern dumb terminals. The devices have nearly no storage at all, and don't carry large e-mail clients on the device; the message is simply transferred as text from one end to the other.

Versions of UNIX

Many versions of UNIX exist in the operating system market today, and all of them are at least slightly different. However, all forms of UNIX operate similarly, and most of them (other than FreeBSD or Linux systems, which are free) cost a lot of money.

Exam Tip Many, many versions of UNIX are available in today's market. For the Network+ exam, you don't need to be familiar with all the different versions of UNIX, but you should probably be aware of the major distributions of UNIX and their features for background information.

The following list summarizes a few of the most popular versions of UNIX.

+ **HP-UX:** A version of UNIX created for the Hewlett Packard HP-9000 series of enterprise servers, which includes incarnations from midrange servers (more powerful than a PC but less-so than a mainframe computer) all the way up to computers that are practically mainframes, such as the Superdome computer, which uses up to 64 processors in parallel to create a server powerhouse.

+ **AIX:** Made for the IBM RS/6000 series of computers, which offers low-range workstations up to high-end cluster servers based on the RISC processor. IBM focuses on scalability with its UNIX implementation, making it simple to create networks of any size or configuration.

+ **Solaris:** Based on the BSD version of UNIX, Solaris is available on Intel *x*86 processors and on the Sun SPARC processors. Solaris has 32- and 64-bit implementations, with the 64-bit performance being about ten times as efficient as the 32-bit implementation. Solaris is fully compatible with TCP/IP and other open standards, and even has a version of GNOME for it.

+ **IRIX:** Made by Silicon Graphics, Inc. (SGI), IRIX was the first UNIX system to support symmetric multiprocessing (SMP) and was the first to support both 32-bit and 64-bit applications.

Linux stew

Linux has many distributions — almost as many as UNIX. The following list summarizes the most popular versions of Linux.

+ **Caldera OpenLinux:** One of the most POSIX-compliant versions of Linux around. Where Red Hat targets the server market and Debian targets purist developers, OpenLinux by Caldera targets corporate users, who mostly use Windows.

+ **Corel Linux:** Targeted at business professionals and home users, unlike most versions of Linux. Corel Linux has a one- or two-click operating system installation process, for example, which is reminiscent of Macintosh operating systems.

Corel has recently announced a major partnership with the Microsoft .Net initiative and has distanced itself from Corel Linux, so the future of this distribution is uncertain.

- **Debian GNU/Linux:** Almost the polar opposite of Red Hat Linux: Red Hat is commercial and defined by one company; Debian, by contrast, is ferociously open, even so far as including "GNU" in the distribution's name. Debian runs on Alpha, ARM, Intel x86, PowerPC, and SPARC processors.
- **Mandrake Linux:** Originally based on Red Hat Linux (and Mandrake utilizes the RPM package system from Red Hat), but Mandrake has made a name for itself for its enhancements to usability, such as the DrakX graphical installer.
- **Red Hat Linux:** By far the most popular distribution of Linux, at least as far as retail numbers show. At last count, Red Hat Linux accounted for about 60 percent of all versions of Linux purchased through retail channels: That's a big percentage. Red Hat Linux is most famous for the Red Hat Package Manager (RPM), which enables one-step installation of applications from both the command-line and graphical environments. Some distributions of Linux, including, most notably, Mandrake Linux, use Red Hat Linux as a base.

Note: Red Hat is probably the closest you can find to a company that "supports" Linux like Microsoft "supports" Windows, but you have to use Red Hat Linux to get support, and you have to pay for it.

- **Slackware:** Supports Alpha, Intel x86, and SPARC processors, and has made its very existence based on keeping Linux as UNIX-compliant as possible. Like UNIX, Slackware encourages shell-based interfaces, and because of its UNIX leaning, the Slackware initialization files are implemented differently from most other distributions of Linux.
- **SuSE:** Prides itself on being absolutely packed with software and has seen amazing growth in the market for Linux distributions in recent years. SuSE also supports more processors than most distributions, including Alpha, Intel x86, PowerPC, and SPARC.
- **TurboLinux:** Newer versions run only on Intel x86 hardware; is most known for its Cluster Web Server clustering software. TurboLinux was based originally on Red Hat Linux and thus supports the RPM system for packages.
- **Yellow Dog Linux and LinuxPPC:** Made specifically for the PowerPC (PPC) processor. Because Mac uses PPC hardware, LinuxPPC and Yellow Dog Linux are popular as solutions for dual booting between Mac OS and Linux on a PPC.

In the Real World: Linux is currently eating the overall UNIX share of the server market alive, and the mind share of the UNIX community. Go to any of the Web sites for versions of Linux in the preceding list and you see some sort of "Linux-compatible" claim somewhere. The fact is that Linux is as good, if not better, than many versions of UNIX, and it's free. When faced with a choice between a version of UNIX you have to pay for and Linux, more and more companies are choosing the cheap, high-quality Linux.

UNIX administration

UNIX administration can be summed up as

- Knowing which files to edit
- Knowing where those files are within the structure of the UNIX system

For example, to change your configuration for the X Window System on a UNIX system you need to edit the XF86Config file. Changing a system's screen resolution is accomplished by tweaking a few numbers in this file with a text editor (such as emacs or vi).

Exam Tip The Network+ exam does not test you on UNIX specifics. For example, you don't need to know how to edit your X Windows System configuration, as is described in the example in the following paragraph. But you should know certain methodologies for UNIX administration. The following sections cover these UNIX networking basics.

UNIX users and groups

UNIX uses user and group accounts, and the access permissions of each, to determine who can access what on a UNIX system (see the next section). User information in UNIX is stored in the /etc/passwd file (or /etc/shadow file if using shadow passwords), and group information is located in the /etc/group file. You can add new users and delete old users by merely modifying these files on a Linux system.

Note With shadow passwords, only the root user can access the /etc/shadow file.

In UNIX, you typically give a new user his or her own directory on the server in the /home/username directory. As soon as you add a new user to a UNIX system, UNIX creates a new group with the same name as the username and adds the new user to his or her own group.

Root user

The root user (or *superuser,* as it's also commonly called) is responsible for administration duties on a UNIX system. Because UNIX is a multiuser operating system, the root user (or other superuser) can log in from literally any terminal on the network and perform the same duties that he or she could on their home system.

Caution The root user has the power to do anything and everything on a UNIX system, including removing the entire contents of a hard drive. For this reason, UNIX administrators are wise not to use the root account except when absolutely necessary.

UNIX security

UNIX handles file-sharing security by assigning permissions to files or directories based on their owner, group, and user. Each file has a permission setting that defines four sets of three letters, in the following order:

- **u:** The user who owns the file
- **g:** The users in the group that the owner user belongs to
- **o:** Other normal users not in the group that the owner user belongs to
- **a:** All other users, including guest users without normal permissions

UNIX permission settings use combinations of the following three letters:

- **r:** *read access*

    Users can open the file and read it.

- **w:** *write access*

    Users can modify, save, or delete a file.

- **x:** execution permission

    Users can execute a file.

The following example permission grants permissions to do everything possible to the file for every single user who can access the file's location on the network:

```
rwx rwx rwx rwx
```

In the preceding example, the letters and their sequence determine permissions as follows:

- r is the permission for read, w is the permission for write, and x is the permission that enables a user to execute an executable file.
- The first set of letters is for the owner, the second set is for the owner's group, the third set is for other users on the system not in the owner's group, and the fourth set is for all other users.

Printing in UNIX

In UNIX, printing is handled by the lpd (Line Print Daemon), and all configuration for printing in UNIX is performed in the /etc/printcap file, which contains information about all network printers, local or remote. The lpd puts print requests into a file on the hard drive to free up system memory, usually to the /var/spool directory.

The lpq and lpr commands are the most used print commands in UNIX.

- lpq enables an administrator to monitor the print queue and the print jobs within it.
- You can use lprm to remove print jobs from the queue using their job ID (for example, if a job is bogging the printer down).

UNIX file systems

UNIX has many, many different file systems, and the Network+ exam is cognizant of this. Linux, for example, uses the ext2 file system, while many versions of UNIX use the Network File System (NFS), and so on. However, most UNIX file systems operate at least similarly, and they use the same basic structure as follows:

- All directories are considered files by the operating system.
- File types aren't determined by extension, as they are in Windows, although they can and often are used this way.
- Remote file systems are usually mounted manually to the system with the `mount` command.
- All UNIX systems follow the same basic file system structure, with the root directory at the top (designated by a /).

UNIX protocols

UNIX really uses one protocol stack for just about everything: TCP/IP, at least when possible. When participating in a heterogeneous network with clients other than UNIX (such as Windows or NetWare), other protocols are sometimes necessary.

The following list summarizes the major protocols in UNIX.

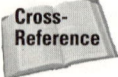

Cross-Reference: See Chapter 6 for more information on protocols.

- **UDP (User Datagram Protocol):** A connectionless alternative to TCP, which works with IP in place of TCP. UDP is faster than TCP, because it doesn't require verification for packets received.
- **ICMP:** Receives and transmits error messages that are meant for TCP/IP. ICMP runs over IP, so it is connectionless. Because ICMP does not perform error control, it is faster than TCP.
- **NIS (Network Information System):** Provides UNIX directory services. NIS enables users to mount remote file systems as if they were local drives.
- **LDAP:** The most used directory service in UNIX. LDAP directories can be shared across multiple servers; the more redundancy, the higher the system's fault tolerance is (see Chapter 16 for more information on fault tolerance). Both NDS and Active Directory are LDAP-compliant, so LDAP can browse both of those directory services.

UNIX commands and utilities

UNIX and Linux collectively have literally thousands of utilities, and the Network+ exam doesn't expect you to know even most of them. In UNIX, most utilities are built into the main shell interface, although a few of them are either solely graphical utilities or have interfaces in both shell and graphical environments (the Emacs text editor is a good example of this).

Some of these UNIX utilities are critical to UNIX administration and you should know them. Table 12-3 shows some of the most used UNIX administration utilities.

Table 12-3
Command UNIX/Linux Commands/Utilities

Command/Utility	Function
cat	Combine the content of two or more files or the output of two or more commands.
chmod	Change permissions of a file or directory.
kernelcfg	Configure the Linux kernel.
kill	Kill a process.
ps	Monitor system processes and find process IDs (PIDs) of programs you need to kill.
Linuxconf	Configure just about everything in Linux.
lpc and lpr	Manage print jobs.
ls	Display the contents of a directory.
fsck	This vaguely obscene-looking command means "file system check."
man	Get help on a command (for example, man cat gives information on the cat command).
mount	Mount file systems.
passwd	Manage user accounts and passwords.
RPM	When using Red Hat Linux or any other version of Linux that supports RPM, this utility enables you to add and remove software in a manner similar to how a Windows .exe file executes. Other package managers exist, but RPM is by far the most widely supported package manager for Linux.
tar	The most used compression utility for Linux.

Windows NT/2000

Windows NT (NT is rumored to stand for "new technology") was originally designed as a more stable alternative to the Microsoft Windows 95 operating system. Windows NT was a departure from Microsoft from MS-DOS for their first multipurpose client network operating system. Windows 2000 was based on Windows NT, so understanding one helps understand the other. The following sections explain the basics of Windows NT and then show you what effect Windows 2000 had on the NT line.

Windows release hierarchy

Although the Network+ exam doesn't include much version-specific information for operating systems, Windows has had a rather complex history, and it's not a bad idea to know the basic Windows operating system release hierarchy — to know your Windows from your Windows. Figure 12-6 shows the Windows operating system hierarchy, beginning with Windows 3.x in the early 1990s and ending with Windows XP, the newest version of Windows at the time of this writing. If you want a bit more information on Windows XP, which isn't covered on the Network+ exam (yet), see the nearby sidebar.

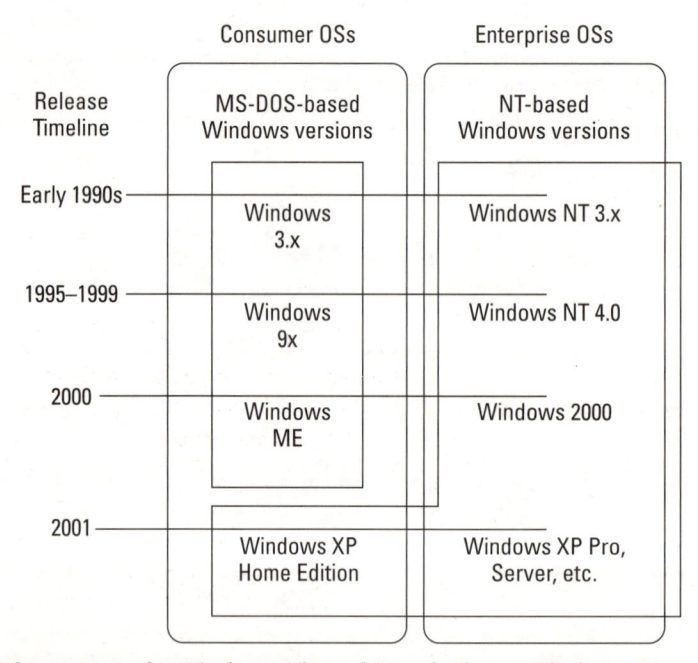

Figure 12-6: The Windows release hierarchy favors Windows NT

> ### Windows XP: It's an NT After All . . .
>
> Windows XP isn't covered on the Network+ exam quite yet, but it can't hurt to know that Windows XP (XP stands for *experience*) is based on Windows 2000, which is based on Windows NT 4.0. Windows XP is especially noteworthy in that the Windows environment now uses the same basic operating systems for all client (Windows XP Home) and enterprise operating system releases (Windows XP Professional, and so on), allowing for software compatibility that could only be forced between Windows NT and MS-DOS-based (Windows 9*x*/Me) versions of Windows.
>
> The release of Windows XP Home edition brings an end to the MS-DOS-based operating system line altogether, at least in terms of new Microsoft releases. Because Windows XP Home Edition is just a version of Windows XP Professional without all the networking administration capabilities, compatibility between the client and networking versions of the Microsoft operating systems has never been greater; Windows XP Home is the same operating system as Windows XP Professional, there's just less of it. Future releases of Windows XP will include embedded versions and equivalents to Windows 2000 Advanced Server and Windows 2000 Datacenter Server, but again, they will all be just variegated versions of the late-model Windows NT: Windows XP.

NTFS

The Windows NT file system, typically called NTFS, is a software driver that loads when Windows NT/2000 boots up and handles the file management for Windows NT systems. Windows NT 4.0 uses the 4.0 release of NTFS; Windows 2000 uses the 5.0 release of NTFS.

NTFS drives are cut into partitions; and at least one primary partition must exist to run Windows. The drive can then be cut up into further extended partitions, which can themselves be cut up into 23 logical partitions.

NTFS is an alternative to FAT and FAT32 file systems that are used by other versions of Windows. NTFS is a much more efficient and secure file system than FAT, but FAT is generally easier to deal with, and while other operating systems (such as UNIX) can access FAT systems, they can't typically access NTFS systems.

> **Tip** In a typical Windows homogenous network, workstations often use FAT file systems and servers typically use NTFS.

Windows protocols

Like all major network operating systems, recent versions of Windows have given over trying to invent new protocols to further complicate networking and have just jumped onto the TCP/IP bandwagon. However, that doesn't mean that Microsoft doesn't support its older products — it does. While a Windows 2000 network can run on TCP/IP alone, earlier versions of Windows used NetBIOS to communicate, so Windows still supports NetBIOS functionality for networks where it's necessary.

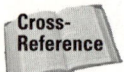

> **Cross-Reference**
>
> See Chapter 6 for more information on the protocols listed in this chapter.

Windows supports three major types of protocols. The three types are explained in the following list, as are the protocols themselves:

✦ **CIFS:** The Common Internet File System (or CIFS) is a Windows protocol that facilitates the transfer of requests for files and services between remote locations on an internetwork. Based on the client/server networking model, CIFS is an open form of Microsoft's Server Message Block (SMB) protocol.

> **Note**
>
> The UNIX version of SMB is the Samba Protocol, which allows UNIX computers to share files with Windows computers.

✦ **Windows legacy protocols:** Protocols such as NetBEUI (which is actually an API more than a bona fide protocol) and WINS were used in older versions of Windows and are supported only for this reason.

- **NetBEUI (NetBIOS Enhanced User Interface):** A LAN-only (non-routable) protocol used in early Windows networks based on the NetBIOS API, NetBEUI is a Windows protocol that even Microsoft doesn't recommend for any but the most isolated networks. NetBEUI isn't required for NetBIOS functionality.

- **WINS:** Another Microsoft-proprietary protocol that is designed to replace NetBIOS, although Microsoft now encourages the use of pure DNS networks.

- **RIP:** Performs routing services for an NT network.

✦ **Other vendors' network operating system protocols:** The best way to take on a competitor in the market for operating systems is to first offer compatibility with your system and theirs. Hence, protocols such as Services for Macintosh and NWLink.

- **NWLink (NetWare Link IPX/SPX compatible protocol):** A reverse-engineered version of NetWare IPX/SPX. Used to communicate with NetWare networks.

- **Services for Macintosh:** A Windows AppleTalk implementation, this networking component enables Windows networks to talk to networks using the AppleTalk protocol.

✦ **Standard protocols:** Grudgingly, Microsoft has moved to full support for standard protocols, and in particular that one made popular by the UNIX environment: TCP/IP.

- **ARP (Address Resolution Protocol):** DHCP uses ARP to assign IP addresses to clients.
- **DLC (Data Link Control):** Used to connect to mainframe computers.
- **NetBIOS:** An API for Windows naming and referencing functions, NetBIOS is included in every version of Windows but shouldn't be used outside of small networks.
- **TCP/IP:** TCP/IP is now used as the major protocol on all new operating system releases from any vendor, and Windows has come along with it.

Windows NT 3.x

Windows NT 3.5 was the first version of Windows NT to make any real dent in the market for network operating systems. Windows NT 3.x isn't covered on the exam, so it isn't covered in detail here. Although the operating system isn't used much anymore in the networking world, it was noteworthy as the first version of Windows that was not built on MS-DOS. Windows NT 3.x had an interface like that of Windows 3.1 and Windows 3.11 for Workgroups (for those who remember back that far in the annals of IBM-compatible PC history).

Windows NT 4.0

With the release of Windows NT 4.0, Microsoft really started to gain market share from Novell NetWare. The following sections explain the major features of Windows NT 4.0, and basic administration tools and concepts.

Windows NT features

Windows NT 4.0 offers a great many networking features that are just not present (or even possible) with the MS-DOS-based versions of Windows (Windows 9x/Me; also known as the *client versions* of Windows). In terms of previous versions of Windows NT (namely 3.51), the main benefit of Windows NT 4.0 is that its interface is comfortably similar to Windows 95, making networks using Windows NT and Windows 95 attractive, at least from a perspective of consistent usability.

Windows NT offers many features, including the following:

- **Fully protected multitasking:** Windows 9x is often disparaged for its lack of this feature, which enables the operating system to continue running unhindered when a renegade process crashes an application.
- **A multiuser operating system:** One of the major obstacles to using Windows 9x/ME as a serious networking operating system is that, although the operating system can be tricked into supporting multiple users, the operating system itself only ever recognizes one user. Windows NT and Windows 2000 are multiuser operating systems, so multiple users can be logged in to the same system at the same time.

- **A graphical user interface exactly like that of Windows clients:** Windows NT/2000 systems are almost the polar opposite of UNIX in terms of administration interfaces; with Windows, almost all administrative tasks can be performed with one graphical utility or another; with UNIX, graphics utilities are extremely secondary to the shell-based tools, and often you can't even find a graphical version of the more common utilities.

- **Compatibility with most Windows applications:** Windows NT can run both 32-bit and 16-bit Windows applications, although not all of them work properly (and some don't work at all). While network operating systems don't have to be able to run big applications, some organizations find comfort in using the same interface to perform both administration and client tasks from the same system.

- **Support for standard protocols:** Windows NT/2000 supports major protocols such as TCP/IP, DHCP, and DNS, and proprietary protocols from earlier Microsoft operating systems such as NetBEUI and NetBIOS, and proprietary protocols from other vendors, such as Novell and Apple. (See the Windows protocols section later in this chapter for more information.)

- **Integration with other Microsoft technologies:** While Microsoft technologies aren't always considered the most secure (search at www.news.com for *Nimda worm*), they are usually cost-effective and easy to use and manage. Technologies that integrate with Windows NT include IIS (a Windows-only Web server), and Microsoft Transaction Server and Microsoft Message Queue Server.

Windows NT 4.0 versions

Windows NT 4.0 comes in two main forms, with different versions for clients (workstations) and servers:

- **Windows NT Workstation:** The term *workstation* typically describes one desktop within a network, and that's what this version of Windows is for. Windows NT Workstation is basically a stripped version of Windows NT Server that includes protocols that enable the system to connect to either Windows computers or NetWare computers. Windows NT Workstation is explained in more detail in the Client Operating Systems section later in this chapter.

- **Windows NT Server:** Windows NT Server includes more advanced networking technologies than Windows NT Workstation, enabling Windows to provide file, print, and other services over a network.

Windows NT administration

Administration duties on a Windows NT network are performed by the Administrator user account, which is a global account (stored in the SAM on the PDC) that can perform any function necessary to manage the network. You can also rename this account to increase security.

Domains and domain controllers

Windows NT 4.0 uses an organizational concept called *domains* to separate members of a network, including users, printers (and other network peripherals), and servers. Domain organization is logical; the physical location of the elements doesn't matter — the domain address defines a member of a network.

Windows NT domains require one primary computer to house the database that contains network information about users and computers that are on the domain. This computer is called a *primary domain controller,* or *PDC.* Backup controllers can also be added to increase the fault-tolerance of a network (as explained in Chapter 16). These backup controllers, called *backup domain controllers,* or *BDCs,* can provide duplicates of the PDC that can do the following:

✦ Take over in case of PDC failure

✦ Alternate incoming requests between PDC and BDCs.

   Alternating requests reduces the load on the server by half with one PDC, two-thirds with two BDCs, and so on

The PDC stores the Security Accounts Manager (SAM) database and the user profiles for each network. Windows NT profiles contain information about user preferences (such as desktop settings) and user favorites (such as IE favorites and Start menu favorites). Because each Windows NT PDC contains its own SAM database, for a user of one domain to access the resources of another requires a trust relationship (as well as the proper access permissions).

Figure 12-7 shows how a PDC works with one BDC when the PDC is up and running; Figure 12-8 shows a BDC handling network traffic when the PDC is down (hopefully a rare actuality).

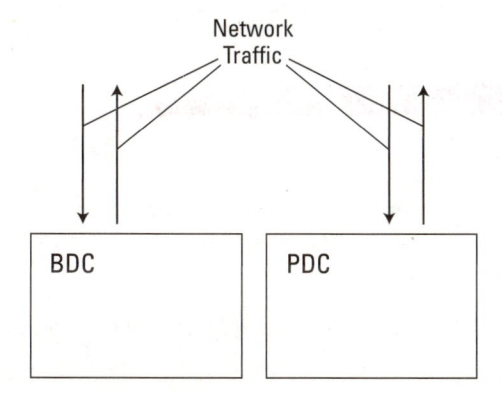

Figure 12-7: Network traffic being handled by a PDC and a sole BDC

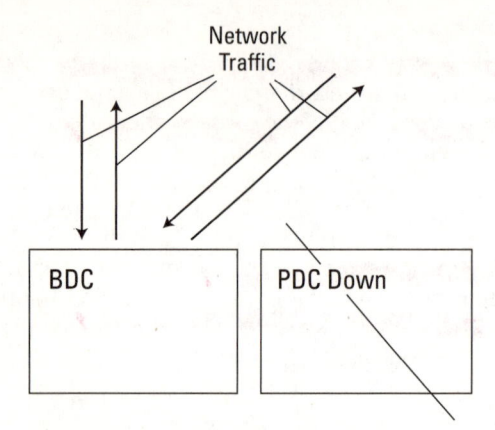

Figure 12-8: Network traffic being handled by a BDC when the PDC is down

NT trust relationships

Trust relationships come into play when a user on one domain on an internetwork wants to access resources on another domain in an internetwork. Trust relationships originate from one domain and reach to one other domain, but they don't go both ways on Windows NT. A resource domain trusts a master domain, but that doesn't mean that the master domain trusts the resource domain. The thing is, it doesn't have to. As long as the resource domain trusts the master domain, where the user account information and permissions are stored, then users on the network can access the resource domain.

Trusts can be set up both ways, and this type of trust is called *complete trust* between two or more domains. These trust relationships are difficult to set up and aren't used very often, because they are usually redundant and unnecessary.

Security

Windows NT security is based on users and two kinds of groups:

- **Local groups**

    Local groups or user accounts are stored locally (on the server and/or workstation) and involve only the security on one server.

- **Domain groups**

    Domain user accounts or groups are stored in the SAM on the PDC, and apply to the whole network.

The Microsoft-recommended group/user model for a Windows NT network is shown in Figure 12-9.

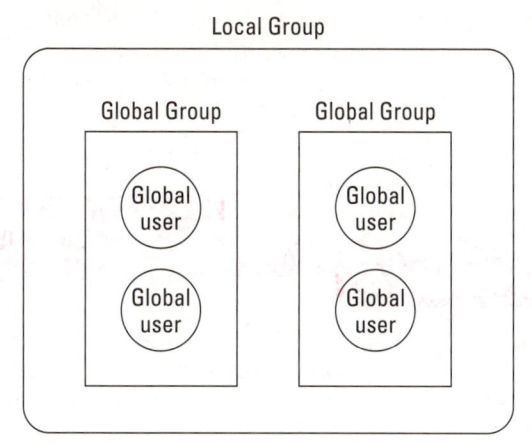

Figure 12-9: Global groups within a local group

As you can see from the figure, in a typical scenario, domain users should be added to domain groups, and then those groups should be made part of local groups depending on resource requirements for each user. Following this method (which is recommended by Microsoft) results in a simple-to-maintain security environment in which resources accessible by a user can be added or maintained by merely assigning that user to be a member of certain groups.

Windows utilities

Because Windows is based on a graphical environment, the vast majority of the utilities for Windows servers are graphically based. The following list summarizes the most used Windows networking utilities.

- **Administrative Wizard:** This utility contains a bunch of helper utilities, or wizards, that assist administrators in performing some of the more common administration tasks. The wizards that make up the Administrative Wizard are as follows:
    - **Add User Accounts Wizard:** Add new users.
    - **Group Management Wizard:** Create and manage groups.
    - **Managing File and Folder Access Wizard:** Manage access to files and directories.
    - **Add Printer Wizard:** Add a network printer.
    - **Add/Remove Programs Wizard:** Add or remove programs.
    - **Install New Modem Wizard:** Install a modem.
    - **Network Client Administrator Wizard:** Configure or reconfigure client workstations.
    - **License Wizard:** Manage software licenses.

- **Disk administrator:** The Windows Disk Administrator enables management of hard drives, volumes, and partitions via a graphical interface. You can use Disk Administrator to create and modify Windows partitions and to change drive letter designations.

- **Event Viewer:** Event Viewer shows all system events using logs, which are basically text recordings of the origin, execution, and result of all system events. Depending on how much you want to monitor, you can enable or disable the logging of certain types of events, and monitor those events, with Event Viewer. This custom policy is called an *audit policy* (probably because that's what logs do: They audit the network).

- **Server Manager:** Similar to the User Manager for Domains utility (explained later in this list), Server Manager enables you to manage servers, domains, and workstations, and individual resources (such as users, directories, and so on) within those workstations.

- **Network Neighborhood:** Network Neighborhood is a user-level navigational utility that, when opened, enables a user to click to the desired network location. Network Neighborhood offers a view of the network starting from the client and working up through the network.

- **Performance Monitor:** Monitor the performance of a system using a dynamically refreshing graph.

- **RAS:** Remote Access Services (RAS) is a suite of utilities that enables remote administration of a Windows NT network. RAS is explained in detail in Chapter 11.

- **System Policy Editor:** The System Policy Editor enables administrators to manage system.

- **User Manager for Domains:** This tool creates, modifies, deletes, and otherwise manages users and groups on a Windows NT server using domains. In a peer-to-peer environment, User Manager replaces the User Manager for Domains, which performs largely the same function but on a smaller scale.

    You can install and run User Manager for Domains from either

    - A client workstation
    - A server

- **Windows Explorer:** Windows Explorer is used in all versions of Windows starting with Windows 95 and Windows NT/2000 to provide directory services. Windows Explorer enables users to navigate their system by clicking on folder icons in a tree format. Users access remote file systems through Windows Explorer by the use of *mapped drives,* which are basically just shortcuts to network locations to make them as easily accessible as if they were local.

Windows 2000

Windows 2000 was named Windows NT 5.0 until the last year or so of development, when Microsoft dropped the "NT" moniker altogether, and this dropped name truly puts Windows 2000 in its place: Windows 2000 is simply the update to Windows NT 4.0, not an entirely new operating system. However, the time gap between the release of NT 4.0 and Windows 2000 (about five years) enabled Microsoft to completely redesign Windows NT around a fully functional directory service: Active Directory.

The following sections describe the major features that Windows 2000 brought to the NT party, and some of the key differences between how Windows 2000 and Windows NT work.

Windows 2000 features

Some of the features introduced with Windows 2000 include the following:

- **Active Directory:** Targeting Novell's NDS, the Microsoft Active Directory service stores information about all system resources in a hierarchy within which security is assured. See the "Active Directory" section later in this chapter.

- **Kerberos authentication:** Capitalizing on the same open source initiatives it so often derides publicly, Microsoft integrated the open source Kerberos authentication service into Windows 2000.

- **Native LDAP integration:** LDAP is the protocol for X.500 standard directory services. The Microsoft Active Directory is X.500-compliant, and therefore can access LDAP, NDS, and X.500 directory services.

- **Native ATM support:** Windows 2000 improved its WAN technologies from Windows NT 4.0, including native support for ATM (see Chapter 11 for more information on ATM).

- **Support for Plug and Play:** Plug and Play enables administrators to plug in hardware and have the device instantly recognized and configured by the operating system. Plug and Play has been supported in Windows 9*x* for years, but Windows 2000 is the first version of Windows NT to support Plug and Play (NT 4.0 did not support Plug and Play).

- **Support for DHCP:** Windows 2000 supports the Dynamic Host Configuration Protocol natively; Windows NT 4.0 did not (see Chapter 6 for more information on DHCP).

- **A distributed file system:** NTFS (NT File System) is a distributed file system. A distributed file system can contain single directories across multiple storage devices.

- **Dynamic Domain Name Server (DDNS):** When a client is reconfigured, DDNS uses Active Directory, DHCP, and WINS to reconfigure the network according to the changes.

Windows 2000 versions

Windows 2000 offers four major versions, including versions for clients (workstations), servers, big servers, and *really* big servers. The following list describes the four major releases of Windows 2000.

Exam Tip You only need to worry about Windows 2000 Server and Windows 2000 Professional for the exam, and you don't need to know much in the way of operating system specifics. Focus on how network operating systems work alike.

- **Windows 2000 Server:** Basically just the upgrade from Windows NT 4.0 Server.
- **Windows 2000 Professional:** The new name for Windows NT Workstation.
- **Windows 2000 Advanced Server:** Includes clustering and load-balancing software for network operating system functions and application servers. Advanced Server can handle up to 8-way symmetric multiprocessing (SMP).
- **Windows 2000 Datacenter Server:** Designed for massive data servers, including those that power the Internet (for example, the Yahoo.com search database), this version of Windows supports up to 16-way symmetric multiprocessing (SMP) and up to 64GB of RAM.

Active Directory

Active Directory is the Microsoft directory service for Windows 2000; it was first introduced with Windows 2000. Active Directory has a broader scope than the Windows NT concept of domains; due to new features such as DNS and fully qualified domain names (FQDN), Active Directory can handle parent/child domain relationships.

Unlike with Windows NT domain services, Active Directory enables different parts of the same domain to have different administrative rights. For example, the parent domain `hungryminds.com` could have a child domain of `bibles.hungryminds.com`, one for `frommers.hungryminds.com`, and one for `dummies.hungryminds.com`. Each of these domains can be entirely different organizations in different parts of the world, but still unified under the same `hungryminds.com` Active Directory forest.

Active Directory implements a type of organization similar to other directory services such as NDS using different terminology. Active Directory organizational units are called *domains*, for example. Domains with parent or child domains are called *trees*, and when multiple trees are part of the same network that network is called a *forest*. A forest must have one domain name at its root. In the preceding example with `hungryminds.com`, `hungryminds.com` is the root domain in any child domain (such as `dummies.hungryminds.com`).

Active Directory is based on the X.500 standard for directory services, as are both NDS and LDAP (for NetWare and UNIX, respectively). Being X.500-compatible means that Active Directory follows the same basic organizational structure as NDS; see the NetWare Directory Services" section earlier in this chapter to get an idea of how an Active Directory structure looks.

Windows 2000 trust relationships

Active Directory uses trust relationships just like Windows NT, but the trust relationships of Active Directory differ from NT trust relationships in the following two critical ways:

- Active Directory sets up trust relationships automatically, where in NT, they had to be manually configured.
- Active Directory trusts are transitive, whereas NT trusts are one-way only. Transitive trusts extend beyond the initial trust relationship in such a way that if `Domain1` trusts `Domain2` and `Domain2` trusts `Domain3`, `Domain1` trusts `Domain3` by implication.

Windows 2000 domain controllers

Windows 2000 does not use the concept of primary domain controllers or backup domain controllers. All Windows 2000 domain controllers are considered peers, or equals, and can all perform the same functions. In Windows NT 4.0, the primary domain controller updated the backup domain controllers on a regular basis, but to users the backup domain controllers were read-only.

Macintosh

Macintosh networks are kind of like unicorns — you don't see one very often. As a result, the details of Macintosh as a network operating system aren't covered in detail on the Network+ exam. However, you should know about two protocols used to connect older Macintosh networks:

- **AppleTalk:** An Ethernet standard for connecting networks using primarily Macintosh computers. After Mac OS 8, Apple abandoned AppleTalk in favor of TCP/IP as the default networking protocol for new Macintosh systems. However, Apple supports AppleTalk in all new versions of the Mac OS for legacy purposes.
- **TokenTalk:** The Token Ring version of AppleTalk (which is an Ethernet standard).

Cross-Reference: Chapter 6 includes a detailed coverage of protocols.

Mac OS X: Not on the Test — Yet

For the Network+ exam, you really don't need to know much, if anything, about Mac OS X. If you know that Mac OS X is based on FreeBSD, you know enough about Mac OS X for the exam. FreeBSD is a free version of UNIX that is similar to, but distinct from, Linux). Apple calls their FreeBSD OS core *Darwin*. To the UNIX aficionado, Darwin is just a modified version of FreeBSD UNIX made for the PowerPC processor (as are Yellow Dog Linux and LinuxPPC).

The main differences between Mac OS X and other versions of UNIX are mostly cosmetic; for example, Mac OS X restricts the user to one GUI theme, where Linux, for example, has hundreds of interface themes available. But Mac OS X has one advantage over competing versions of UNIX (Red Hat Linux or the Sun Solaris system, for example) — Mac OS X has already enlisted support from huge vendors such as Microsoft (which ships a version of Office for Mac OS X) and Adobe (for Photoshop, Illustrator, Acrobat, etc.) for its UNIX system, which no other UNIX distribution has ever been able to do.

Client Operating Systems

Many, many client operating systems are available in today's modern operating systems market; however, the Network+ exam doesn't ask you about all the possibilities — simply too many exist. You won't find a question about your old Commodore Amiga 1200, for example, or BeOS. The major client operating systems used in modern networks are typically Windows, UNIX/Linux, or Macintosh clients. The following sections summarize these major client operating systems.

Cross-Reference: See Chapter 23 for more information on configuring clients.

Windows clients

The vast majority of workstations in this world use one version of Windows or another as their desktop operating system. Windows simply has the lion's share of the software market for major applications, and the numbers are undeniably stacked behind Windows as the single most-used client operating system. Windows clients can participate within all-Windows networks with Windows-only protocols such as NetBEUI and WINS, or as part of homogeneous networks using TCP/IP.

The vast majority of Windows clients are Windows 95 clients or their late-model derivatives. The various versions of Windows that are used as clients in modern networks are

- **Windows 95:** Still used in many networks. As a client operating system, it wasn't too bad for its time. Early versions of Windows 95 used the original FAT16 file system, which couldn't support very large hard drives, and had a less-customizable desktop environment than later versions of Windows. The first few releases of Windows 95 were also not hard-coded to Internet Explorer as are Windows 98 and later versions of Windows, so Windows 95 isn't only smaller than Windows 98 as far as operating systems go, it's typically faster and more secure as well.

- **Windows 98:** The first major bug-fix release of Windows 95, and also the first version of Windows 9*x* to really integrate the Web browser with the operating system. Windows 98 Second Edition was a 1999-era bug fix to Windows 98 that included IE 5.0 instead of IE 4.0.

- **Windows Me (Millennium Edition):** The 2000-era release of Windows 98; sports IE 5.5, Windows Media Player, and a desktop environment that looks similar to that of Windows 2000. The resemblance to Windows 2000 ends there, however: Windows Me is still an MS-DOS-based operating system, just like Windows 98.

Windows 9*x*/Me operating systems don't allow the user concept; as far as MS-DOS or versions of Windows based on it are concerned, only one user exists for the operating system. Although these systems can be tweaked to seem to support multiple users, a network operating system must be a multiuser operating system to be considered for serious use in a network of more than a few people (such as a peer-to-peer network).

Windows NT has always been released with a stripped-down client version alongside it, as well, although these client versions of Windows are more expensive than client versions of Windows 9*x* has historically been, so Windows NT-based clients historically are less-used than Windows 9*x*-based clients. The Windows NT 4.0 client release is Windows NT 4.0 Workstation, and Windows 2000 Professional is the Windows 2000 equivalent. Both operating systems are far more stable and efficient as clients than the MS-DOS-based versions of Windows are.

What? No NetWare Client?

If you're new to NetWare, you're likely to be surprised at how many of its utilities are actually made to run on either MS-DOS (for NetWare 3.*x*, which was released around the same time as Windows 3.1) or Windows NT/2000 clients (for NetWare 4.*x* plus, which was released roughly the same time as Windows 95). No NetWare clients exist: That animal simply doesn't walk the earth. NetWare is the only major network operating system that does not have a companion client version, and this is the reason that many of its utilities, indeed, all its graphical utilities, are Windows applications.

The assumption on the part of Novell in this design is that a network operating system shouldn't be used as a client, because this both taxes the server that hosts the network operating system and opens a potential for security risks. In Linux books, you're likely to come across warnings practically every other page about how the root administrator account shouldn't be used as much as a regular user account because malevolent users on the Internet can potentially hack into the root account and do whatever they want to your system. With NetWare, these warnings aren't necessary because you simply cannot use NetWare as a client system.

UNIX/Linux

UNIX itself isn't used terribly often in a client environment, at least not within heterogeneous networks. UNIX clients are typically used in situations of software development, where high-end clients are necessary, or in other environments where typical software applications aren't necessary. Linux, however, is becoming an increasingly used alternative to Windows in the desktop workstation operating system market, although not in the consumer sector, where the application lacks software support for applications that consumers typically require, such as AOL.

Macintosh

Macintosh computers took over the graphics computing market after Commodore exited stage bankrupt in the early 1990s. Image-oriented professions still use Macintosh networks a lot, as do some schools and universities. As an example, the crew who laid out the pages of this book and created the illustrations that you see within its pages use an all-Macintosh network that's nested within a larger Windows network within Hungry Minds. And this is the most typical implementation of Macintosh computers — not as servers, but as clients within larger, homogeneous networks.

Summary

The operating system is a critical piece to the networking puzzle. This chapter's key points are as follows:

- ✦ A network operating system (NOS) performs duties in a network such as providing file, print, and communications services.
- ✦ A client operating system does not need all the networking features of a network operating system, but it needs to be able to connect to network operating systems via protocols.
- ✦ The three major network operating systems are UNIX/Linux, NetWare, and Windows NT/2000.
- ✦ All major directory services follow the X.500 standard to ensure interoperability between them, including the NetWare NDS service, the Microsoft Active Directory, and LDAP.
- ✦ The modern versions of all major network operating systems encourage the use of pure TCP/IP networks.
- ✦ All network operating systems have similar concepts of functionality, even if the actual implementation in each network operating system is a bit different.

✦ ✦ ✦

STUDY GUIDE

Assessment Questions

1. Which is by far the most-used client operating system?
    A. UNIX/Linux
    B. Windows
    C. Mac OS
    D. NetWare

2. What is the common, smaller-scale alternative to the client/server model?
    A. Host-based networks
    B. Peer-based networks
    C. NetBEUI-based networks
    D. Server-based networks

3. Which of the following isn't a major network operating system?
    A. UNIX/Linux
    B. Windows
    C. Mac OS
    D. NetWare

4. What is the protocol used by Windows NT systems to talk to NetWare networks?
    A. NetBIOS
    B. NetBEUI
    C. RIP (IPX)
    D. NWLink

5. Which of the following network operating systems uses the Line Print Daemon to handle printing?

   A. UNIX/Linux

   B. Windows

   C. Mac OS

   D. NetWare

6. Which of the following operating systems uses NFS?

   A. UNIX/Linux

   B. Windows

   C. Mac OS

   D. NetWare

7. What is the name for the NetWare administrator user?

   A. root

   B. superuser

   C. ADMIN

   D. Administrator

8. What is the name of the Microsoft LDAP-compliant directory service?

   A. Active Directory

   B. Windows NT

   C. SAM

   D. Dynamic DNS

9. What open-source authentication software does Microsoft use in Windows 2000?

   A. Active Directory

   B. RIP

   C. IPX

   D. Kerberos

10. Which of the following does Windows NT use to talk to Macintosh networks?

    A. NWLink

    B. Services for Macintosh

    C. Netatalk

    D. NetBEUI

11. Which of the following operating systems uses the root administrator account?

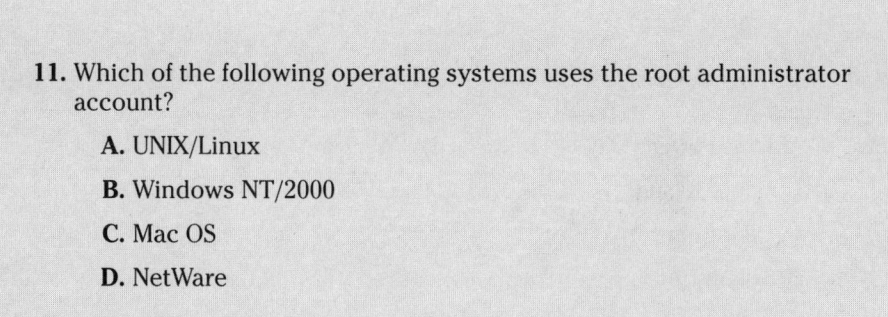

　　A. UNIX/Linux

　　B. Windows NT/2000

　　C. Mac OS

　　D. NetWare

12. Which of the following is a Windows-only protocol?

　　A. WINS

　　B. IPX/SPX

　　C. UDP

　　D. TCP/IP

13. In all major network operating systems, what organizational unit are users typically organized in?

　　A. Volumes

　　B. Modules

　　C. File systems

　　D. Groups

14. Which of the following protocols do all major operating systems now encourage the sole use of?

　　A. IPX/SPX

　　B. UDP/IP

　　C. TCP/IP

　　D. NetBIOS

15. Which Windows utility would you use to monitor logs in Windows NT?

　　A. User Manager for Domains

　　B. Event Viewer

　　C. Server Manager

　　D. Log Manager

16. What is the common name for the networking model in which a server provides services to clients?

    A. Peer-to-peer

    B. Client-based

    C. Client/server

    D. Token ring

17. What is the main domain controller in the Windows NT network called?

    A. The primary domain controller

    B. The main domain controller

    C. The domain controller

    D. DC1

18. Multiple trees in an Active Directory schema are called what when part of the same network?

    A. Cousins

    B. A forest

    C. MultiTrees

    D. Domains

19. What is the Windows NT equivalent to the NetWare NDS service?

    A. Windows NT Server

    B. Active Directory

    C. Kerberos

    D. Network Neighborhood

20. Which of the following operating systems enjoys the least support in terms of consumer-level software applications?

    A. UNIX/Linux

    B. Windows

    C. Mac OS

    D. NetWare

Scenarios

1. You're a consultant for a firm that has only six computers and wants to use Microsoft Outlook to manage e-mail and other electronic communications. What network operating system and protocol would you recommend to this firm?

2. You're a consultant for a non-profit organization that wants as cheap a server solution as possible, but wants mission-critical stability and security. The client specifies that they want to use one operating system for both server and client, for simplicity, and that they don't require a system with major commercial software. Which network operating system would you recommend to this client?

Answers to Chapter Questions

Chapter Pre-Test

1. A network operating system is an operating system capable of delivering services to clients, such as print services, file services, and access to other remote network resources. See the "Network Operating Systems" section.

2. A client operating system runs on a client and typically must support at least TCP/IP to be part of a major network. See the "Client Operating Systems" section.

3. A multipurpose operating system can be used as either a client or a network operating system. Windows and UNIX/Linux are multipurpose operating systems, but NetWare is *only* a network operating system. See the "Network Operating Systems" section.

4. The major network operating systems are Windows NT/2000, NetWare, and UNIX/Linux. See the "Network Operating Systems" section.

5. The major client operating systems are Windows, NetWare, and UNIX/Linux. See the "Network Operating Systems" section.

6. Network administrators use file access restrictions and permissions to restrict access to sensitive files. See the "Network Operating Systems" section.

7. Major network operating systems communicate with one another via protocols. See the "Network Operating Systems" section.

8. All major directory services abide by the X.500 standard for directory services. See the "X.500" section.

9. TCP/IP is the dominant protocol that's used by all major operating systems, whether network or client. See the "Network Operating Systems" section.

10. An administrator user typically has power to set up, manage, and maintain network elements. As such, the administrative user is typically imbued with the power to do anything from erasing the server's hard drive to deleting users from the network. See the "Administrator users" section.

Assessment Questions

1. B. Windows is by far the most-used client operating system in today's market for personal computers.
2. B. The peer-based network, where no computer is in charge of providing services, is the common, smaller-scale alternative to the client/server model.
3. C. Mac OS isn't a major network operating system, and it isn't covered as a major network operating system on the Network+ exam.
4. D. NWLink is the Microsoft version of the NetWare IPX/SPX protocol.
5. A. UNIX/Linux uses the Line Print Daemon (lpd) to handle printing.
6. A. UNIX/Linux uses the network file system (NFS).
7. C. ADMIN is the name of the NetWare administrator user.
8. A. Active Directory is the name of the Microsoft LDAP-compliant directory service.
9. D. Microsoft uses the open source Kerberos authentication software in Windows 2000.
10. B. The Service for Macintosh module is used for communicating between Windows and Macintosh AppleTalk networks.
11. A. UNIX/Linux uses the root administrator account.
12. A. WINS is a Windows-only protocol.
13. D. Users are typically organized into groups.
14. C. All major network operating systems encourage the use of TCP/IP as the sole protocol, although this solution is often impractical without migrating entire networks.
15. B. Use the Windows Event Viewer to monitor logs in Windows.
16. C. The networking model in which a server provides services to clients is called the client/server model.
17. A. The main domain controller in a Windows NT network is called a primary domain controller.
18. B. Multiple trees in an Active Directory schema are called a forest.
19. B. The Windows 2000 equivalent to the NetWare NDS service is called Active Directory.
20. D. NetWare does not have a client version of its operating system, so it doesn't have any client software support at all.

Scenarios

1. If a firm has only six computers and wants to network between those computers and the Internet (for e-mail), and specifies that they want to use Outlook, you should probably recommend Windows. Which version of Windows you choose to recommend depends on more specific client needs.

2. If a firm wants to use the same operating system for both client and server and wants as low-cost a solution as possible with a high-quality product, you should probably recommend Linux. Linux is free, extremely stable, and has enough software support for a full office-productivity environment. The one major weakness of Linux is its commercial software support, which is almost nil, but this firm specified that commercial software was not a concern.

VLANs

CHAPTER 13

EXAM OBJECTIVES

♦ Identify the main characteristics of VLANs

CHAPTER PRE-TEST

1. VLANs act as multiple, logical _____ within a LAN.
2. _____ VLAN technologies explicitly state the VLAN owner information of a given packet by adding header information to that packet.
3. _____ VLAN technologies imply VLAN ownership of a packet by using MAC addresses instead of adding header information to a packet.
4. Using VLANs typically results in _____ routers than using multiple physical LANs.
5. VLANs reduce _____ traffic on a network.
6. Protocol-based VLANs operate on the _____ layer of the OSI model.
7. _____-based VLANs define VLAN ownership on the different ports of a switch.
8. VLANs can _____ one another so that a member of one VLAN can be a member of more than one VLAN.
9. VLAN technologies are either _____ or _____ in the way that they assign VLAN ownership.
10. The IEEE _____ standard defines VLANs.

✦ Answers to these questions can be found at the end of the chapter. ✦

Often, one LAN within an organization isn't enough to properly divide the network bandwidth and resources. The more people that are on a physical LAN, the more broadcasts are being shouted all over the network at any one time. Further, everyone on the same LAN can potentially intercept traffic from someone else on the same LAN.

Thus, it makes sense to have multiple LANs, one for each department, say, and perhaps one that all departments can be part of. However, multiple LANs can quickly become a nightmare to deal with. That's where VLANs come in.

Why Use VLANs?

Local area networks (LANs) offer a great deal of flexibility in ensuring the security and continued integrity of sensitive network resources. For example, Figure 13-1 shows a small LAN with only two network segments. This network is perfect for a LAN, because it is small and has only a few dozen users.

However, large, monolithic (meaning "one piece") networks also become increasingly challenging to manage and maintain, especially as the number of departments with differing job duties increase and the need for security increases.

The following sections compare the use of VLANs with the major alternative to VLANs, multiple LANs, and explain the benefits of VLANs in general.

Problems with multiple LANs

Many companies use multiple LANs in their networks, particularly when separated by long distances, as segments of a WAN (a WAN is a connection of two or more LANs by a router — WANs are explained in detail in Chapter 10). But the use of multiple LANs when unnecessary can create unnecessary network bottlenecks that increase with each router that is added to the WAN. The following factors can cause bottlenecks:

- **Higher network traffic:** With VLANs, all network traffic within a given VLAN only travels down network infrastructure dedicated to that VLAN using *broadcasts*. Without using VLANs, the traffic of the entire network is all traveling down the same wires, potentially causing lower overall network transmission speeds.

- **Added packet complexity:** Each router must add routing information to a given packet, increasing the size of the packet to a limited extent and adding a level of complexity to packet structures.

- **Router overhead:** Each router takes time to process a given packet, although the amount of time depends on the quality of the router in question. Regardless of the amount of time it takes, that time builds with each router between LANs.

✦ **Wiring nightmares:** Every network segment in a LAN is made up of at least one switch and one (usually more) network node, such as a PC, printer, or whatever. If your network has 100 switches with 10 ports filled on each, that's 1000 network nodes that potentially need to be rewired when the network changes, not to mention the wiring from the switches to the routers. Imagine a large company merger (like that of AOL-Time Warner, for example), and then imagine having to reorganize the post-merged company wiring involved to get everybody communicating with the proper servers.

VLANs versus multiple LANs

VLANs make changing a network potentially much less complex than using multiple physical LANs (that is, using routers). For example, imagine that you are the IT administrator for a company that wants to perform a complete reorganization from ten departments to forty, all of which want to have their own LAN. Using multiple physical LANs, this task would involve buying 30 more routers, not to mention having to potentially rewire every network node on the network. Worse, the addition of all those routers would result in slower network performance, which you would have to compensate for with other potentially expensive purchases.

Now, imagine the same scenario using VLANs. Using VLAN technology, a network reorganization of this magnitude involves a reworking of the network's workgroups and switches, and the adjustment of at least some of the existing VLANs.

Benefits of VLANs

VLAN implementations offer the following benefits:

✦ **You don't have to rewire the entire network when you make a change to the network.** Instead, you need to merely reconfigure the switches around the new workgroup structure.

✦ **Fewer switches are necessary.** Again, you just need to reconfigure the switches in the network to accommodate the new structure. If you are reorganizing 10 departments into 40, the likely result is that for every four ports that you previously assigned to one VLAN, you assign one instead. Same number of switches, four times as many VLANs.

✦ **Network traffic is isolated by workgroup.** Where possible, broadcast traffic of a VLAN travels only within the network infrastructure of that VLAN, which helps alleviate the potential for broadcast storms. This feature also helps IT administrators keep track of network bandwidth issues. If the janitorial department of a software company uses less bandwidth than the software engineering department, as is likely, more servers can be dedicated to the VLAN for the engineering department.

✦ **VLANs can overlap one another.** One of the more powerful features of explicit VLANs (implicit VLANs aren't typically capable of overlapping) is that users can be members of more than one VLAN at a time, enabling administrators a great deal of flexibility in how different users can be given access to different resources. For a simple example of overlapping VLANs, see the "A simple VLAN structure" section later in this chapter.

VLAN Basics

Much like a hard drive is carved up into logical partitions (every hard drive must have at least one partition), a VLAN is essentially a LAN carved into smaller, logical LANs. VLANs can span global networks and still offer the privacy of a LAN. The following sections explain the basic features of VLANs. Figure 13-1 shows a basic conceptual diagram of how a VLAN works.

Caution Some vendors do not include VLAN capabilities in their hardware. Before implementing VLANs, stock should be taken of how much network hardware will need replacing to accommodate a VLAN solution.

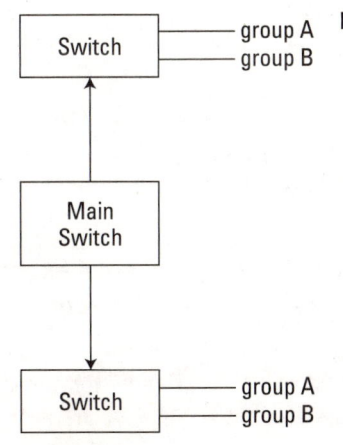

Figure 13-1: The basic concept of a VLAN

Workgroups

Put simply, you implement VLANs by dedicating certain network paths to particular workgroups. A workgroup is just what it sounds like: a group of workers. Members of a given workgroup tend to do the same types of work; for example, everyone in the Accounting department of a company could be on the same workgroup, or if the company is large enough, you could even cut the Accounting department itself into multiple workgroups. The possible configurations for workgroups are limited only by the imagination of the IT administrator and the needs of the network.

Types of VLANs

Three major models for VLANs exist: port-based, MAC address–based, and protocol-based, as explained in the following sections.

Port-based VLANs

Port-based VLANs are based on assigning the ports on a network's switches to certain VLANs. For example, you might assign ports 1 through 4 to the Human Resources VLAN, ports 5 and 6 to the Engineering VLAN, and ports 7 through 9 to the Executive VLAN. This example is illustrated in Figure 13-2.

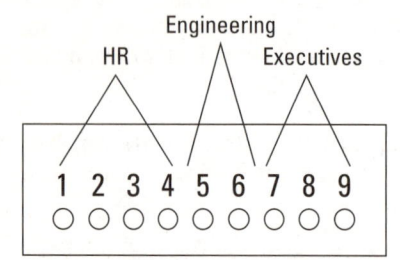

Figure 13-2: An example VLAN port configuration

Switches determine which VLAN owns which packet by monitoring the ports on which the packets arrive. If the port from which a given packet arrives belongs to the Sales VLAN, for example, the switch sends the data along the remaining ports assigned to that VLAN.

Port-based VLANs are flexible; if a user changes offices for some reason, for example, the port on the switch that the user's workstation is plugged in to can be simply reassigned to the user's VLAN.

The one major drawback to this model is that if a repeater is installed on any port, all users connected to that repeater must be members of the VLAN assigned to that port.

Mac-address-based VLANs

In this model, packets are routed to the proper VLANs over a network by their MAC address. The switches on the network maintain a table of MAC addresses along with their assigned VLANs. One strength of this model is that if a user moves ports, the switch that the user's workstation is plugged into doesn't need to be updated.

A major weakness with this model, though, is that assigning one MAC address to multiple VLANs can cause serious confusion with bridge and switch forwarding tables. As a result, this model isn't recommended if users need to be on more than one VLAN.

Protocol-based VLANs

Also called Layer 3–based VLANs, protocol-based VLANs are by far the most flexible, and the most logical. This type of VLAN operates at the Network Layer of the OSI model, using the same addresses that protocols such as IP, IPX, and NetBIOS use to transfer data over a network. VLANs can be assigned to IP subnets, for example.

The IEEE group chose the protocol-based VLAN technology when they defined the standard for VLANs, IEEE 802.1q, and future VLAN technologies are likely to be almost exclusively protocol-based due to its incredible flexibility.

Implicit versus explicit VLANs

All types of LANs fall under one of two classifications:

+ Implicit

    Implicit VLANs use MAC addressing; therefore, the MAC-addressing model of VLAN technology is an implicit VLAN model.

+ Explicit

    Explicit VLANs add information to packets that includes the user's VLAN information as the packet travels from the user and through the local switch (the switch closest to the user in the network).

    Explicit VLAN models include:

    • Port-based VLANs

    • Protocol-based VLANs

    The IEEE 802.1q standard defines its VLAN standard using explicit VLAN technology.

The terms *explicit* and *implicit* may not seem logical in this context, but if you take the following into account, you can see that this terminology actually makes sense:

+ Explicit VLAN technologies use packet header information to *explicitly specify* the VLAN that owns a given packet.

+ Implicit VLAN technologies enable the user's MAC address to *imply* the VLAN that owns a packet. The packet itself doesn't specify VLAN ownership; the MAC address implies that ownership.

Examples of VLAN Configurations

After you have the basics of VLANs down (as explained in the preceding section), it helps to fully understand the power, flexibility, and potential complexity of VLANs by actually looking at some examples of VLANs. The following sections give you a look at three different example VLAN setups of increasing complexity, from the simplest type of VLAN to the most complex.

A simple VLAN structure

For this scenario, imagine a small publishing company with two departments: Editorial and Production. Figure 13-3 illustrates this example.

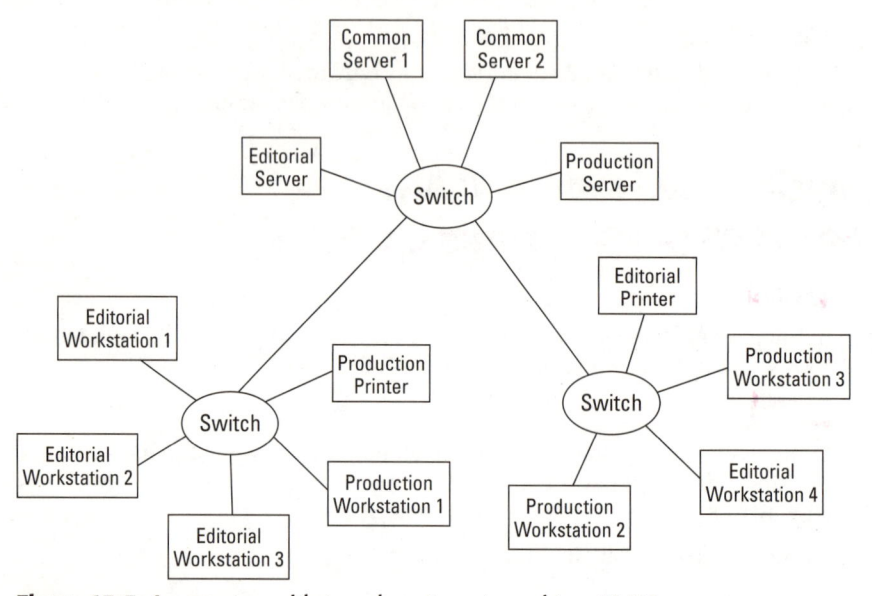

Figure 13-3: A company with two departments and two VLANs

In the figure, notice the following:

- One editor is on the switch that mostly delivers resources for the Production department.
- One member of the Production department is actually on the switch that mostly delivers network resources to the Editorial department.
- The Production printer is on the switch that mostly services the Editorial department.
- The Editorial printer is on the switch that mostly services the Production department.

Why would a network be set up this way? Remember that with VLANs it doesn't matter which switches a user is plugged into. The port that you give to a certain resource is assigned to a particular VLAN, so all VLANs are secure no matter which switches its members are on. For this example, the following circumstances could easily cause a network to be set up this way:

- The publishing house in this example is in a really small building.
- The Production printer can fit in only one particular room because of its size and noisiness, which happens to be closer to the switch nearest the Editorial department.
- There is no room for the Editorial printer near the editors, but there is room for it in with the Production folk near the production switch.
- There is only enough room for six cubes in the main room of the building, and two cubes (one editor and one member of the production staff) are in odd locations.

As you can see, the environment that houses the network defines its structure, illogical or no. If it didn't work this way, the Production printer would be on the street.

Luckily, VLANs are flexible enough that it doesn't matter if the network is fashioned in such a wacky way. In Figure 13-3, then, even though some of the members of each VLAN reside on different switches, the following lists define the logical VLANs.

The Editorial VLAN is made up as follows:

- Editors 1 through 4
- Editorial server
- Editorial printer

Similarly, the Production VLAN is defined as follows:

- Production members 1 through 4
- Production server
- Production printer

Figure 13-4 is just like Figure 13-3, but is shaded to show the preceding VLAN structure. Notice that the switches and common servers are members of both VLANs. This is only possible with explicit VLAN technologies.

If you're wondering how the VLANs talk to one another, some server operating systems can be on multiple VLANs, so as you can see from Figure 13-3, the common servers in this sample configuration are members of both VLANs.

A more complex VLAN structure

Not all VLANs are as simple as that shown in the previous section; indeed, most aren't. The reality of networking is that it's never as simple as you might hope it will be. Often, planning a VLAN structure isn't as easy as figuring out which group of users to put on which VLAN; many times, users need access to multiple VLANs, which adds a level of complexity to the VLAN implementation in question.

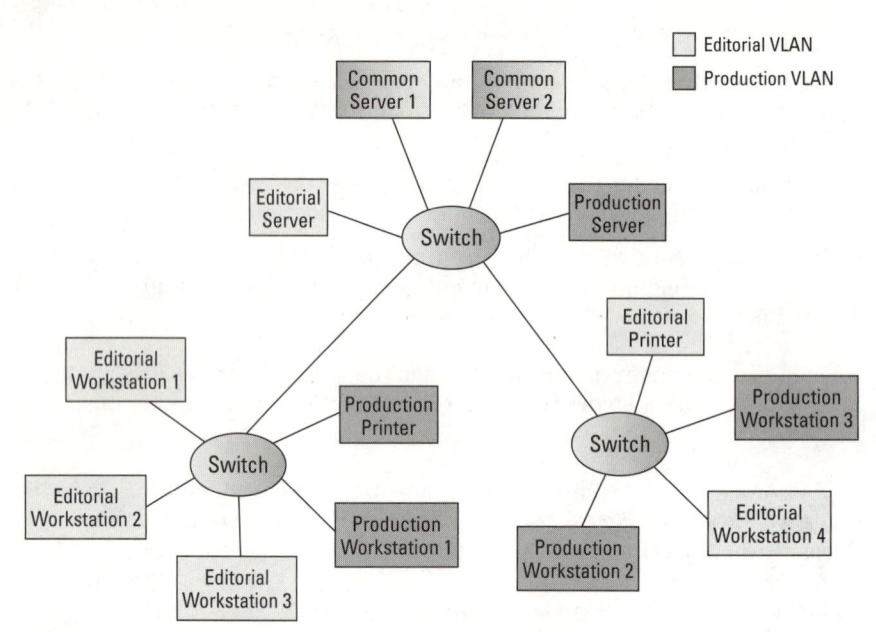

Figure 13-4: The VLAN structure of a publishing house

To illustrate a more complex VLAN structure, imagine a fictional software company, call it Chewie4Ever Inc., which has the following eight departments, each of which have their own floor in an eight-story building. The departments are as follows: Sales, Human Resources, Engineering, IT, Executives, Payroll, R & D, and Customer Support. (Most software companies likely have more departments than this, but these eight departments are good enough to illustrate this example.)

Chances are, all these departments need access to some of the same network resources, such as company e-mail, announcements, employee classifieds, and human resources documentation. Figure 13-5 shows an example of a logical LAN structure.

> **Note** Figure 13-5 is from a higher-level view than that of Figures 13-3 and 13-4 in the previous section, largely because looking at a figure with that detail in a company this size would be more daunting than it would be useful. Just note that the resources within each of the eight main VLANs can be on any of the network's switches, as long as the port they're plugged into is dedicated to the VLAN they belong to.

As you can see from the figure, this simple network is set up with nine VLANs, eight of which are assigned to one each of the eight departments. Members of these eight VLANs are all also members of the ninth VLAN. In this way, each department has control of its own resources and access to resources common to both departments.

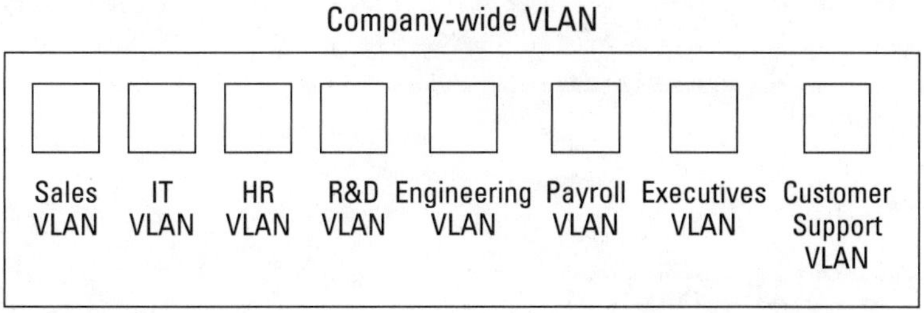

Figure 13-5: A VLAN structure with nine VLANs and eight departments

Summary

VLANs are extremely useful for maximizing the efficiency and security of any given network. The following key points about VLANs were covered in this chapter:

- VLANs are logical LANs within a physical LAN.
- VLANs are implemented by configuring a network's server and switches with information about which network resources and users belong to which VLAN.
- VLANs are implemented via network protocols, through port configuration, or with MAC addresses.
- VLANs often overlap such that members of one VLAN can be members of other VLANs, too.
- VLANs are either implicit or explicit.

✦ ✦ ✦

STUDY GUIDE

Assessment Questions

1. Which of the following types of network would you use if you wanted to use multiple LANs within a LAN?

    A. Multiple LANs

    B. A VPN

    C. A WAN

    D. A VLAN

2. Which of the following IEEE standards defines explicit VLAN technologies?

    A. IEEE 802.p

    B. IEEE 802.q

    C. IEEE 802.r

    D. IEEE 802.w

3. Which of the following VLAN technologies cannot be easily used to make members of VLANs members of multiple VLANs?

    A. Port-based VLANs

    B. Protocol-based VLANs

    C. MAC address-based VLANs

    D. Explicit VLANs

4. Which of the following types of hardware do VLANs use to add VLAN information to packets?

    A. Routers

    B. Hubs

    C. Bridges

    D. Switches

5. Which of the following types of hardware, when installed on a port with VLAN ownership, requires that all members of the network be members of the VLAN that owns the port?

   A. Hubs

   B. Routers

   C. Switches

   D. Repeaters

6. What do VLANs use to isolate users into VLANs?

   A. Additional user passwords

   B. Encryption

   C. Router tables

   D. Workgroups

7. Which of the following is a potential disadvantage of VLANs?

   A. A more complex maintenance solution

   B. Slowdowns due to the number of routers required in typical VLANs

   C. Higher broadcast traffic on the entire network

   D. Security holes in VLAN software

8. Which of the following types of VLAN technologies is an implicit technology?

   A. Port-based VLANs

   B. Protocol-based VLANs

   C. MAC address–based VLANs

   D. Explicit VLANs

9. Which of the following types of VLAN technologies use the address of a user's or resource's NIC adapter to determine VLAN ownership of a given packet on a network?

   A. Port-based VLANs

   B. Protocol-based VLANs

   C. MAC address–based VLANs

   D. Explicit VLANs

10. Which of the following types of VLAN technologies operates on the Network Layer (Layer 3) of the OSI model?

    A. Port-based VLANs

    B. Protocol-based VLANs

    C. MAC address–based VLANs

    D. Implicit VLANs

11. Which of the following isn't a benefit of VLANs?

    A. Easy configuration

    B. High flexibility

    C. Greater efficiency

    D. Easier reconfiguration than using multiple LANs

12. Which of the following types of VLAN technologies requires that with a repeater on a VLAN-owned port, all members of the network beyond that repeater must be a member of that VLAN?

    A. Port-based VLANs

    B. Protocol-based VLANs

    C. MAC address–based VLANs

    D. Implicit VLANs

13. Where is the VLAN owner information stored on a network?

    A. Router routing tables

    B. Bridge routing tables

    C. Switch routing tables

    D. Server routing tables

Lab Exercises

VLANs can be straightforward to implement, as long as they're planned for carefully. The following lab shows you how to plan for a simple VLAN.

Lab 1: Planning a simple VLAN

To plan for a simple VLAN for this company, you must answer the following questions:

- How many users are there?
- How many VLANs do you need?
- What kind of equipment do you have? For example, how many switches and servers do you have?
- What environmental concerns does the network have?

As an example, say you're hired on as a consultant for a company that makes evil-looking pet rocks called Lazarus Stones. The company, Lazarus Stones, Inc., is a small one. You accept the job and do a survey of network resources and needs, and eventually you come up with the following results:

- The company has four major departments: Accounting, Graphic Design, Painting (as in rock painting), and Sales.
- The company has 15 people that need workstations with access to the network, including two in Accounting, seven in graphic design, two in Painting, and four in Sales.
- The network has four servers, one for e-mail, one for shared server access, one for accounting, and one for backup storage.
- The company has one printer for each department except for IT.
- The company currently has three switches with nine ports each.
- The company's building is small and kind of cramped, although luckily a nice closet exists to house the four servers.

Note See the following list for an example of how environmental factors can dictate how networks are set up.

The following plan would work well in this situation:

1. Create four VLANs: one for everybody, which includes the e-mail and shared storage servers, so that everyone can access those services, and then three additional VLANs, one for each department and its printer. In the case of the Accounting server, that should be only part of the Accounting VLAN.

2. With 15 workstations, four printers, and four servers, and four ports necessary for connecting the switches, the three switches of nine ports just accommodate all switch-to-switch and resource- or user-to-switch wiring for the network resources.

3. Use four ports of the switch closest to the servers — call it Switch 1, for all four servers.

4. Wire the switches together, which takes four ports.

5. Because the server farm closet is closest to three cubes just outside the closet and one of the four printers, use one of the ports on Switch 1 for each of those cubes and one for the printer.

6. Switch 2 is closest to the Graphics department, which has seven members, so use Switch 2 for these users. The printer for the Graphics department is already on Switch 1, but the printer for the Sales department is within a few feet of Switch 2, so it's a good candidate for plugging in to the last open port of Switch 2.

7. Switch 3 is closest to two members of the Sales department (of which five exist, three of which sit outside the server closet and are plugged into Switch 1), both members of Accounting, and both members of the Painting department. Plug all of those users into Switch 3.

8. Configure the switches to place the users into their proper VLANs (remember; four VLANs exist, as described in Step 1).

9. The Accounting printer isn't close to anything else, so plug the port into Switch 3. Similarly, the Painting printer is off in the boonies, so plug it into the remaining port on Switch 3.

The resulting network is illustrated in Figure 13-6.

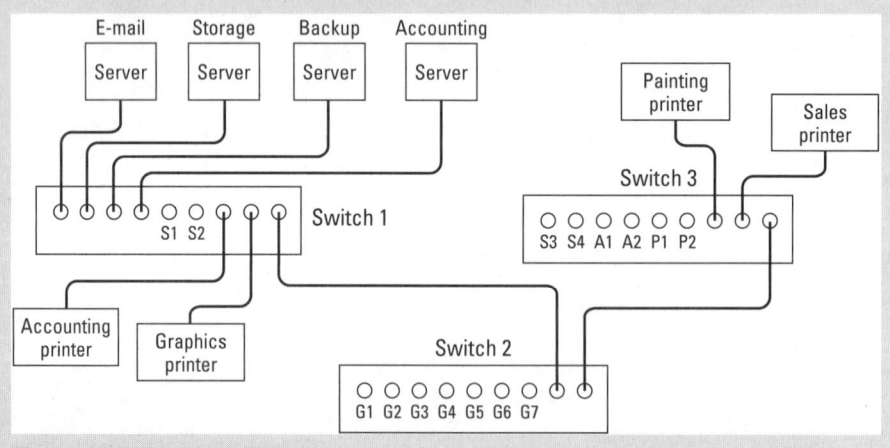

Figure 13-6: A new VLAN setup

Answers to Chapter Questions

Chapter Pre-Test

1. LANs. VLANs act as multiple, logical LANs within a LAN. See the "Why Use VLANs?" section.

2. Explicit. Explicit VLANs explicitly state the VLAN owner information of a given packet by adding header information to that packet. See the "Implicit versus explicit VLANs" section.

3. Implicit. Implicit VLANs imply VLAN ownership of a packet by using MAC addresses instead of adding header information to a packet. See the "Implicit versus explicit VLANs" section.

4. Fewer. Using VLANs typically results in fewer routers than using multiple physical LANs. See the "Why Use VLANs?" section.

5. Broadcast. VLANs reduce broadcast traffic on a network. See the "Why Use VLANs?" section.

6. Protocol-based. Protocol-based VLANs operate on the Network Layer of the OSI model. See the "Protocol-based VLANs" section.

7. Port-based. Port-based VLANs define the owner of VLAN packets by assigning certain ports on the network's switches to certain VLANs. See the "Port-based VLANs" section.

8. Overlap. VLANs can overlap one another so that a member of one VLAN can be a member of more than one VLAN. See the "Benefits of VLANs" section.

9. Explicit or implicit. VLANs use either explicit or implicit methods to assign VLAN ownership. See the "Implicit versus explicit VLANs" section.

10. 802.q. The IEEE 802.q standard defines VLANs. See the "Protocol-based VLANs" section.

Assessment Questions

1. D. You would use a VLAN if you want to use multiple LANs within a LAN.

2. B. The IEEE 802.q standard defines explicit VLAN technologies.

3. C. You cannot easily use MAC address-based VLANs to make members of VLANs members of multiple VLANs.

4. D. You configure VLANs by using information stored in switches.

5. D. Repeaters, when installed on a port with VLAN ownership, requires that all members of the network past the repeater be members of the VLAN that owns the port.

6. D. VLANs use workgroups to isolate users into VLANs.

7. A. VLANs are definitely more complex maintenance-wise than some technologies.

8. C. MAC address–based VLANs use an implicit VLAN technology.

9. C. Mac address–based VLANs use the address of a user's or resource's NIC adapter to determine VLAN ownership of a given packet on a network.

10. B. Protocol-based VLANs operate on the Network layer of the OSI model.

11. A. VLANs aren't exactly easy to configure.

12. A. Port-based VLANs requires that, with a repeater on a given port, every member of the network beyond the repeater must be a member of the VLAN that owns the port.

13. C. VLAN owner information is stored on switch routing tables on a network.

Data Storage

CHAPTER 14

EXAM OBJECTIVES

- Identify the main characteristics of network-attached storage

CHAPTER PRE-TEST

1. When a network is down and cannot be used, it is considered to be _____.
2. The DVD formats most suitable for standard storage are _____ and _____.
3. _____-attached storage connects directly to a computer.
4. _____-attached storage connects directly to a server.
5. _____-attached storage attaches to a network as one node no matter how many devices are attached.
6. The most used storage device is the ____ ____.
7. The least commonly used storage device, which is, despite that fact, still typically installed on most PCs, is the _____.
8. _____ is currently the most used high-speed controller interface.
9. _____ technologies are not standardized yet, so implementing these technologies may result in incompatibility later.
10. Technologies based on _____ standards tend to be cheaper and more compatible with one another than _____ technologies.

✦ Answers to these questions can be found at the end of the chapter. ✦

Chapter 14 ✦ **Data Storage**   329

These days, storage is as important on a network as electricity (which is pretty important), but throwing more hard drives, faster CPUs, and more RAM at servers goes only so far. Likely, by the time you have used a computer for the fifth time, you have discovered for yourself why storage is necessary. Probably you closed a file without saving it, despite the warning, maybe trashed an entire letter to mom before you printed it out. Without storage — and, hence, being able to save your work — there would be little point in doing any serious work electronically.

As you can imagine, for a network of any size, network storage is more important than ever. Network storage is typically a mishmash of different standards, from SCSI and Fiber Channel to the DVD-rewritables. This chapter covers the basics of network storage, and network-attached storage, which you need to know about for the Network+ exam.

Storage Basics

Before you start diving into the different storage configurations that are common in today's enterprises, such as DAS, NAS, and SANs, it's a good idea to know the basics of network storage. For the Network+ exam you need to know about network-attached storage (NAS) in particular, but to really know how NAS fits into the overall scheme of network storage, you need to know something about the alternatives to NAS, as well.

The following sections explain the requirements of network storage, common storage components and how they work together, and the major technologies that are involved in network storage. And, oh yeah, SCSI.

Basic storage requirements

When implementing any storage scheme, no matter how simple or complex, the following requirements must at least be taken into account:

- ✦ **Affordability:** For some networks, affordability is a key necessity, and for others, it becomes a tradeoff for performance. A company that makes one billion dollars in profit every month, for example, is not likely to care much about affordability, at least not as much as a small company that fights for every dollar.

- ✦ **Availability:** For most networks, high availability is a must. If a network is online and people can access data over it, it is available. When a network is down for maintenance, it is unavailable.

- ✦ **Manageability:** To avoid having an IT staff larger than you need, your network should be easy to manage, and thus, so should your storage. If a network drive goes down and all you need to do is swap it out without having to reboot the server, that's manageable storage.

✦ **Performance:** When you double-click a file that's residing on a network drive and it appears as quickly as it would if it were on your hard drive (or faster, even), that's a good example of high network performance. If you double-click a file and you can say "One one-thousand, two one-thousand, three one-thousand" before the file appears, that's a sign of bad network performance, or a storage bottleneck.

✦ **Reliability:** Reliability is related to availability, but it's not the same exactly. For example, if everyone in the company has gone home for the night and no one is there except the IT administrator, if the administrator takes that network down for the night, it can be unavailable but still be a reliable network. Reliability just means that you can expect to be able to access network storage at reasonable performance at any given time. The more this is true, the higher an availability your network storage has.

✦ **Scalability:** Any storage solution worth its salt needs to be implemented with an eye toward what the network in question may need in the future. Implementing an interim solution can often be an excuse to simply spend money, solve the problem temporarily, and then have to spend a ton more money later fixing the problems you created when you spent all the money on the interim solution.

Network storage media

Many types of storage are in use in today's networks, but not all of them are typically used in network storage. The following sections explain the major network storage media used in modern networking, as well as what situations each medium is most useful in.

Floppy disks

Remember back in the 1980s when computers used floppy disks almost exclusively for almost everything, and hard drives were almost completely unheard of? Then, as graphics started becoming important in programs, programs started getting bigger and taking up an inordinate number of floppy disks to install (sometimes you even needed to swap disks while using the program).

In the Real World

One of the more extreme examples of floppy overkill is the early version of Windows 95, which actually came on 25 floppy disks (not counting the initial startup disk) as an alternative to the CD-ROM version.

The floppy's status as a serious distribution media ended in the mid-to-late 1990s (back when AOL could actually fit on a floppy). Increasingly since 1995 or so, nearly all software has been released on CD-ROM. CD-rewritables, or DVD-writables, will soon come down in price and likely replace the floppy altogether. Still, the floppy is often used in today's software market to distribute small files, including, most notably, hardware drivers for new hardware.

Hard drives

In the early 1990s, the hard drive started hitting hard on the storage scene in the PC market. The concept was a new one, at least to early PC users (for example, Commodore 64 users): a central location to store all your files and applications without having to haggle with so many darned floppy disks every time you wanted to use that software.

Initially, hard drives were 100MB, 200MB, and other figures equally as pathetic by today's standards. Today, hard drives that contain anywhere from 40GB up to 100GB of space *per drive* are common.

CDs

The CD-ROM has been the preferred distribution method for software since the early-to-mid 1990s. The 650MB capacity per CD-ROM, compared to the paltry 1.44MB that a typical floppy disk is capable of, simply made moving to CD-ROM the obvious choice.

In 2002, CD-writable and CD-rewritable drives are finally affordable (in the $100-$300 range, depending on what you get) and are popular. However, DVD-rewritables are coming down in price and are more flexible than straight CD-writable drives. For example, Hewlett-Packard ships a drive (the HP DVD-writer dvd100i) that writes in DVD-RW, CD-R, and CD-RW formats.

Eventually, the DVD will likely replace the CD altogether. However, currently the vast majority of software is distributed on CD-ROM, and it will be 2004 at least before DVD software starts really making a splash, because it will take that long to get to a point where most PCs have DVD drives to read DVD software.

DVDs

The high capacity and performance of the DVD format makes for a fantastic storage medium. While DVD rewritable drives still cost just a bit much to be included in the common PC (they're priced at about $600 right now, although within a year they will probably cost half that), DVD looks on track to eventually replace CD-ROM as the preferred format for software distribution.

> **In the Real World**
> Certain software that comes now on something like 4 plus CDs (take Red Hat Linux 7.2, for example) is driving software to DVD format just like Windows 95 on 25 floppies drove software from floppy to CD-ROM in the mid-1990s. Expect to see larger software offered on DVD as soon as DVD players can be assumed by software manufacturers to be in the majority of home and business PCs.

Benefits of DVD

The main benefits of the DVD format over CD-ROM are as follows:

- **High-speed reading of DVDs:** DVD read speed is quite high these days. Together with high-bandwidth controller interfaces such as SCSI or Fiber Channel, high-speed DVD drives allow for lightning fast storage access.

Just for comparison, 1x on a DVD player is equivalent to 9x on a CD drive. So, a 3x DVD player reads at about the same speed as a 27x CD drive would. Today, DVD read speed is up at about 8x, meaning that a DVD is read at about the equivalent to a 72x CD drive (that beast doesn't exist, CD drives go up to about 40x). DVD write speed is at about 2.4x right now, which is the equivalent to a 21.6x CD write speed.

In the Real World Most CD and DVD drives do not come with information such as this on the box, or in reviews of the drives. So, you have to know the above information for yourself and do the math in your head when you're considering purchasing one or more disc drives.

- **Higher storage capacity:** DVD capacity ranges from 4.7GB up to 9.4GB (for a double-sided DVD).
- **Backwards compatibility with CD formats:** In today's market, where most PCs don't have DVD drives, software is still distributed on CD. Therefore, just about all DVD drives can also read (and some can also write to) CD.
- **Flexibility:** Many DVD writable drives can read and write either CD or DVD. So, if you have that last 2GB of data to archive but run out of blank DVDs, but have some old CD-R discs on hand, you can slap those in and finish out your archive on CD. Or, say that you need to archive some small files and other large files, but need each on a separate disc, you can use CD-R when the files are small and use DVDs only for large data.

DVD formats

Major DVD formats are DVD-RW and DVD+RW, although DVD-RAM is also in use. DVD-RW and DVD+RW are actually not similar — DVD-RW does not enable the addition of material to a previously recorded DVD, but it does enable you to erase a previously recorded DVD and then record on it again. DVD+RW enables you to use a DVD just like a giant floppy disk and add new files to previously recorded DVDs.

A drawback to the DVD+RW and DVD-RAM formats for consumers is that the majority of DVD players in the world, including home DVD players and DVD-ROM players, supports neither format. However, for network storage this support is typically not an issue, because the drives are meant to act as file servers, not for consumer use (to record home movies on a DVD for use in a home DVD player, for example).

Tip Coupled with the fact that DVD-RAM looks to be bowing to DVD+RW as the common DVD-rewritable standard, DVD+RW is usually the preferred format for DVD storage.

Tape media

Tape was used early in the computing era for backing up the vast amounts of information on mainframes. Tape uses reels and celluloid-like tape similar to what's used in VHS tapes to store data in electromagnetic encoding on the tape, which can be erased and recorded over at will.

Tape media is probably the weakest of modern hardware storage in terms of degradability. Tapes typically must be replaced after 100 recordings, because the recording surface of the tape gets slightly thinner after each recording, eventually wearing to the point where stored data can be easily corrupted.

The biggest drawback to tape media is that you have to rewind or fast-forward the tape to get to a certain location, which takes seemingly eons and is generally a huge pain. With a CD or DVD, by contrast, you can almost instantly access data anywhere on the disc. Tape media also is typically mounted and unmounted manually on reels, which can be a chore, although automated tape systems are available.

> **In the Real World**
>
> Despite its drawbacks, for larger enterprises that need to archive huge amounts of data that may or may not ever need to be accessed, tape can be and has proved to be a good solution. In cases where data is likely to be needed instantly, however, tape is not the way to go.

Following are the more popular tape formats:

- **Travan drives:** Travan drives, a form of IDE technology, which can plug into a PC or laptop via all sorts of connection methods, including floppy, parallel, ATAPI, or SCSI. Travan drives allow for storage up to 8GB.

- **Digital Audio Tape (DAT) drives:** DAT tape is the latest in tape technologies, using a very high-density recording on a slow-moving tape for the highest data storage yet possible on a tape format. DAT tape uses the Helical Scan recording method, which is the same method used by VCRs.

> **Note**
>
> DAT tapes can play DDS, although DDS players cannot play DAT tapes.

- **Digital Data Storage (DDS):** DDS is a standard that includes what is called *Read-After-Write error detection*, which means that the tape is read after writing is performed to ensure that the data was recorded properly. If it was not, the data is rerecorded. If sectors of tape are found to be bad, the data is moved below the bad tape and recorded there (where it's reread again). The major DDS standards, along with their specifics, are shown in Table 14-1.

Table 14-1
DDS Standards

DDS Version	Max Capacity Per Tape	Max Recording Time Per Tape
DDS-1	1.3GB	60
DDS-2	4GB	90
DDS-3	8GB	120
DDS-4	40GB	125

✦ **Digital Linear Tape (DLT):** DLT is a high-performance, high-cost storage solution that offers storage capabilities of 40GB up to 70GB on a single cartridge and can achieve data transfer speeds up to 10 Mbps. Like DDS, DLT offers Read-After-Write error detection.

Mainframes

Believe it or not, that moldering mainframe you have sitting in your storage shed (yes, that was sarcasm) can make a fantastic storage solution. Mainframes typically offer anywhere from 250GB of information up to 2TB (a terabyte is 1000GB) of information or higher. Think about it: All you need to do is connect a mainframe to your network, implement an NFS-compatible file system so that the network can access the mainframe's storage, and you have potentially thousands upon thousands of GB of storage space!

Using a mainframe for storage isn't actually always a laughable solution, however, given the right circumstances. For example, imagine a scientific research project where all brain scans made in the world are stored in one database for comparison, manipulation, and so on. While just a few servers could probably handle the tasks for processing the data and managing it, you need something big to store all that data and have room to manipulate it. In this scenario, a mainframe would be by far an acceptable solution. Room would probably be left over on the mainframe (storage-wise) for other projects, even.

Other media

Many, many types of media are on the market for personal computers that could, in theory, be used for network storage. However, none of these media are used widely for network storage, and this is largely due to the huge popularity of CDs, and now DVDs, which are increasingly putting companies like Iomega, makers of Zip and Jaz drives, on the ropes. When DVD-rewritable drives come down to a price of $100 or so, the game will likely be over in favor of DVD.

Storage controller interfaces

A great deal of how fast a storage device responds to requests has to do with the controller interface used for the drive. The following sections describe the major controller interfaces, giving special attention in particular to SCSI, which is by far the most-used storage interface in mid-to-large networks.

IDE

Integrated Data Environment (IDE) is the most used controller type for workstation PCs and home PCs. IDE gets its name because the controller is built into the drive's logic circuits. IDE operates on a simple master/slave relationship; one drive acts as the master and the rest of the drives on the same controller are considered slaves. Each controller typically has either three or four connectors, the first of which plugs directly into the motherboard. The remaining two or three connectors can be connected to drives. Figure 14-1 illustrates this concept.

HD-ROM: The future of storage?

HD-ROM (which stands for high-density, read-only-memory) is a format being developed through a joint project with Norsam Technologies and IBM's research team that uses a super-thin beam to increase the amount of data that can be recorded per square inch of storage media. HD-ROM isn't mentioned on the Network+ exam and probably won't be for many years, but if you're curious about the future of storage formats, HD-ROM has a good shot at unseating DVD altogether, if it's ever mass produced, much as DVD is doing to the CD-ROM format now.

An HD-ROM beam is only 50 nanometers wide (as compared to DVD-ROM, which uses a 350 nanometer-wide beam, and CD-ROM, which uses an 800 nanometer-wide beam). A beam this thin is possible because the data writing is performed within a vacuum much like the vacuum of outer space. The vacuum reduces the vibrations that the laser would ordinarily be exposed to outside a vacuum, such as air and sound waves, enabling the beam to be thinner than that of DVD. And of course, the thinner the beam, the more data that fits on a given disc surface.

Some of the more amazing features of HD-ROM include the following:

- On a disc the same size as that of CD and DVD, HD-ROM can hold up to a mind-numbing 165GB per disc *per side* (that's 330 GB for a double-sided disc).
- HD-ROM can write on any type of material that is sturdy enough to handle the laser, including jewelry, a steel pin, anything.
- Data can be encoded in any form, even human-readable form. Data in this form could then be retrieved with what is basically a large microscope.
- Data can be encoded in multiple forms on the same disc. For example, binary data and human-readable data can reside on the same disc.
- HD-ROM discs are impervious to damage from magnetic fields or the normal ravages of time, and tout a life span of at least 5,000 years.
- HD-ROM technology is cheaper than CD-ROM technology; HD-ROM technology is estimated to cost about .5 cents to every one dollar that CD-ROM technology costs.

HD-ROM has not been implemented in any mass form yet, and likely won't be for years. And again, it's not on the Network+ exam. Still, the power and flexibility of HD-ROM technology makes it one to keep an eye on.

EIDE (enhanced IDE), which is faster than IDE, is better for storage purposes than IDE because storage devices can be a bottleneck if they aren't fast, and compared to SCSI, IDE drives simply aren't fast. EIDE at its finest offers a transfer rate of 16.7 Mbps, which pales to Ultra-Wide SCSI's potential for up to 80 Mbps and soon 160 Mbps.

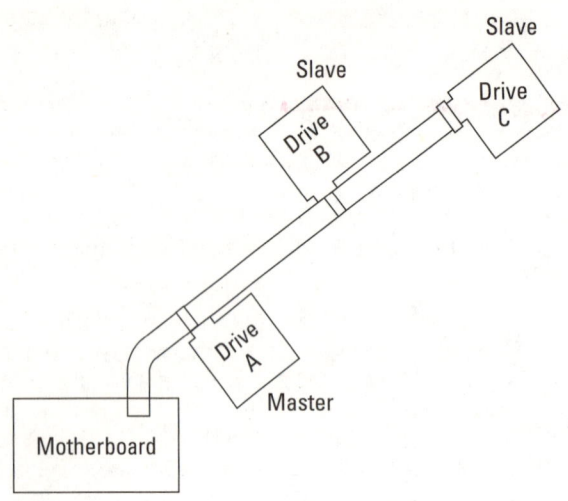

Figure 14-1: IDE uses a simple master/slave relationship between drives.

> **In the Real World**
> In networks that require fast response times, SCSI (explained in the next section) is by far the standard for high-speed data access. In networks where instant network responsiveness is not as large an issue, EIDE may be an acceptable solution.

SCSI

If you have ever dealt with SCSI on any level, you probably remember the occasion. Perhaps you had a word or two for your SCSI drive as the configuration drove you nuts, or perhaps you first scoffed at having to pay such ridiculous prices for drives and cabling. SCSI is a high-speed, high-cost controller interface for storage media. SCSI (which stands for *Small Computer System Interface*) is an extremely diverse standard that was only made a bona fide standard years after companies like Apple were already using it. SCSI supports much higher data transfer rates than the IDE interface, so it has been the controller of choice for servers on a network since the late 1980s.

SCSI: From Proprietary to Open Standard

Interestingly, SCSI sprung up as a standard from the industry itself (from companies such as Apple), not from the standards committees. Later, ANSI looked around at all the different SCSI standards in the market and defined a standard based on the existing equipment. For this reason, SCSI-1 was hurriedly thrown together by ANSI and deliberately named with a 1 in its name to indicate that a SCSI-2 standard was to follow. Indeed, as the SCSI-1 was being drafted, plans for SCSI-2 were already in the preliminary stages.

SCSI buses

SCSI comes in two major bus sizes:

- **8-bit SCSI:** Also called *narrow SCSI* because the actual cables are much smaller than that of wide SCSI, the 8-bit SCSI interface enables up to 10 Mpbs transfer rate.

- **16-bit SCSI:** Also called *wide SCSI* because the cables and connectors are twice as large as those of narrow SCSI, the 16-bit SCSI interface enables up to 20 Mbps transfer rate in SCSI-2 or later.

SCSI cabling

All SCSI cables fall under one of the following designations:

- **Narrow SCSI:** The name for the 8-bit SCSI controller interface, narrow SCSI is so named because 8-bit plugs and wires are much narrower than those of wide SCSI.

- **Ultra-wide SCSI:** Fast-20 SCSI over a 16-bit path is known as Ultra-wide SCSI.

SCSI cables currently can be no longer than 12 meters, although many SCSI technologies enable cables to be only six or even three meters. This limitation is considered a disadvantage in SCSI.

SCSI terminators

SCSI controllers require terminators on either end of a controller cable to prevent the electric signals from reaching the end of the cable and bouncing back onto the wire, causing echoes and potentially botching up data transfers. A terminator can be placed on a plug that is not on the end of the wire, but anything between the terminator and the end of the cable is ignored by the system.

Two types of terminators exist, as follows:

- **Passive terminators:** These types of terminators rely on the electrical power of the entire controller, which tends to vary. If the electrical power is too low or too high, the terminator might not offer enough resistance for electrical signals, or it might offer too much, forcing the signal to bounce back onto the cable and cause echoes.

- **Active terminators:** Active terminators include a voltage regulator to monitor and adjust the amount of power that is received by the terminator, keeping its resistance to the proper settings to prevent echoes. Active terminators are overall more effective at what they do than passive terminators.

Many modern SCSI devices are self-terminating, meaning that the drive includes its own terminator and doesn't need you to install one. These devices typically use jumpers to configure whether the drive self-terminates or not.

Tip: If you ever find that adding a drive on a SCSI controller cable disables those drives that are past it on the controller cable (that is, further from the controller), check to make sure its jumpers haven't been set to terminate the line at the drive you added.

SCSI IDs

Each SCSI on a given system has a unique ID that is set using driver jumpers. Different adapters do things differently, but many cards use a system that uses one of 16 different IDs, 0-15, giving one to each SCSI device (a terminator is also considered a SCSI device). No two devices can share the same SCSI ID. Also, many SCSI devices default to SCSI ID 0, but this ID should be used only for the device the system boots from.

The device from which a system boots is typically designated as SCSI device 0. The controller itself takes up one of the SCSI IDs, typically 7, which is given the highest priority. The remaining devices are given IDs of either 0-6 or 8-15, with the second highest priorities going to devices 6 and 8, and the third layer of priorities going to devices 5 and 9, and so on. In this fashion, devices 0 and 15 have the lowest priorities of all. Figure 14-2 illustrates this concept.

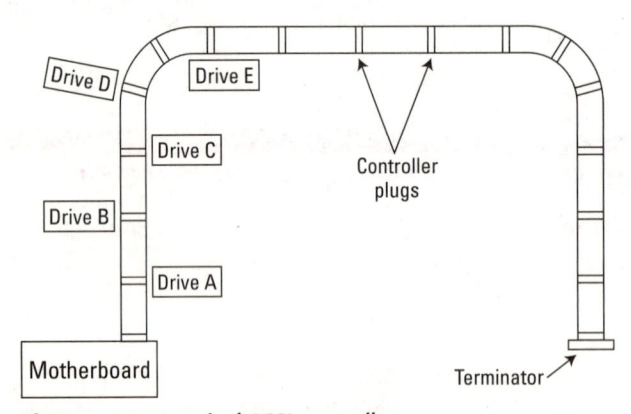

Figure 14-2: A typical SCSI controller

SCSI transfer rates

You can determine the overall transfer rate (formally called the MegaTransfer/second rate) of a given SCSI interface by multiplying the transfer rate, typically at least 10 Kbps for SCSI-2 and later, by the number of bytes the SCSI interface in question is wide. Because 8 bits are in a byte, 8-bit SCSI is 1 byte wide and 16-bit SCSI is 2 bytes wide. Therefore, the MegaTransfer transfer rates for SCSI interfaces can be figured as shown in Table 14-2.

Table-14-2
Determining SCSI Transfer Rates

Interface	How Wide?	Transfer Rate	Calculation	Overall Transfer Rate (or MegaTransfer Rate)
8-bit SCSI (aka *narrow SCSI*)	1 byte	10 Mbps	1 byte times 10 Mbps	10 Mbps
16-bit SCSI (aka *SCSI wide*)	2 bytes	10 Mbps	2 bytes times 10 Mbps	20 Mbps

SCSI standards

Although you can differentiate SCSI technologies many ways, three major standards exist, as follows:

- **SCSI-1:** This first standard allowed for seven devices per system, and a maximum transfer rate of 5 Mbps. SCSI-1 is not typically used anymore.

- **SCSI-2:** SCSI-2, also called plain SCSI because it was the most used SCSI standard for years, added a potential for up to 15 different SCSI devices per SCSI controller, as well as a higher data transfer rate (see Table 14-3). SCSI-2 includes the Fast SCSI standards (see the following section).

- **SCSI-3:** As a rewrite of the standard, overall SCSI-3 was more of a rewrite of the SCSI-2 documentation and was also called Ultra SCSI-3. Various forms of Ultra SCSI exist, as Table 14-3 shows.

Table 14-3 shows an overview of the SCSI standards and how they compare with one another.

Table 14-3
Comparing SCSI Technologies

Technology Name	Max Speed (in Mbps)	Max Number of Devices Per Controller	Max Cable Length (in Meters)
SCSI-1	5	7	6
SCSI-2	5-10	7 or 15	6
Fast SCSI-2	10-20	7	3
Wide SCSI-2	20	15	3
Fast Wide SCSI-2	20	15	3

Continued

Table 14-3 *(continued)*

Technology Name	Max Speed (in Mbps)	Max Number of Devices Per Controller	Max Cable Length (in Meters)
Ultra SCSI-3 8-bit	20	7	1.5
Ultra SCSI-3 16-bit	40	15	1.5
Ultra-2 SCSI	40	7	12
Wide Ultra-2 SCSI	80	15	12
Ultra-3 (or Ultra 160/m) SCSI	160	15	12

Fast SCSI and Ultra SCSI

The terms Fast SCSI and Ultra SCSI refer to later versions of the SCSI standard, but each of these designations has various forms, as follows:

- **Fast SCSI:** The term for 8-bit SCSI running at a rate of 10 Mbps. The derivatives of Fast SCSI are as follows:
    - Fast-20 is the term for 8-bit SCSI running at a rate of 20 Mbps.
    - Fast-40 SCSI is the term for 8-bit SCSI running at a rate of 40 Mbps.
- **Ultra SCSI:** The term for SCSI standards later than the Fast-SCSI standards (including Fast-20 and Fast-40 SCSI), part of the ANSI SCSI-3 standard. Ultra SCSI-3 gave way to Ultra-2 SCSI, which eventually gave way to Ultra-3 SCSI (see Table 14-3), which enables the controller to operate at the full clock rate, unlike Ultra-2 SCSI.

Fiber Channel

Fiber Channel, which humbles even SCSI with data transfer rates of up to 4Gbps, is becoming more and more attractive as a storage controller interface for networks where data transfer access speeds must be at the absolute highest they can be. Fiber Channel is used a great deal in SANs, is an ANSI standard for gigabit-speed communications, and, because of its high speeds, is currently making inroads into enterprise that demand high performance from their storage solutions. Fiber Channel standards for 2Gbps operation are supposed to start surfacing in 2002, and a 10Gbps standard is expected to be released by 2003. Table 14-4 shows how Fiber Channel stacks up against ATM and gigabit Ethernet.

iSCSI

iSCSI is an upgrade to the SCSI standard that will allow for data transfer rates of up to 10 Gbps, far more than what SCSI is capable of today. iSCSI also lowers costs and simplifies networking by using the IP protocol to facilitate transmissions, but implementing iSCSI requires that the IP protocol itself be sped up.

iSCSI is considered a competitor to Fiber Channel, which is used in SAN implementations (SANs are explained later in this chapter), although iSCSI is seen as a technology for networks small enough not to involve SANs, and iSCSI devices are not expected in great numbers until 2003 at the earliest, whereas Fiber Channel is around now. Whether it will take the market from Fiber Channel or not remains to be seen, but iSCSI will definitely offer an attractive upgrade from older SCSI standards.

Table 14-4
Fiber Channel Compared to Other High-Speed Technologies

Technology	Fiber Channel	ATM	Gigabit Ethernet
Technology application	Storage, network, video, clusters	Network, video	Network
Topologies	Point-to-point loop hub, switched	Switched	Point-to-point hub, switched
Baud rate	1.06 Gbps	622 Mbps	1.25 Gbps
Scalability to higher data rates	2.12 Gbps, 4.24 Gbps	1.24 Gbps	Undefined
Guaranteed delivery	Yes	No	No
Congestion data loss	None	Yes	Yes
Frame size	Variable, 0-2K	Fixed, 53B	Variable, 0-1.5KB
Flow control	Credit-based	Rate-based	Rate-based
Physical media	Copper, fiber	Copper, fiber	Copper, fiber
Protocols supported	Network, SCSI, video	Network	Network

Parallel processing

Parallel processing is the term for systems that have more than one processor running in parallel. Those CPUs can be set to collaborate on tasks, alternate in accepting tasks from a given source, or be used for separate tasks altogether. Following are the two major methods of parallel processing:

- A network node (be it server, workstation, NAS, or whatever) that has more than one CPU to share the burden for resource-intensive tasks, such as file serving in large enterprises.

- One or more network nodes that are made to act as one and collaborate on resource-intensive tasks.

With some network operating systems, such as UNIX/Linux (the Sun Solaris system and TurboLinux are good examples) and Windows NT/2000/XP, up to 32 processors (and sometimes 64 or more) can be used together as processing powerhouses. This process, called *clustering,* is basically just parallel processing on a large scale. In some cases, such as with some custom-made Intel CPUs, parallel processing is implemented in the CPUs themselves, rather than by the operating system, which typically allows for greater performance.

Direct-Attached Storage

Direct-attached storage (DAS) originated in the server industry, where server vendors typically sold storage as an add-on component. DAS is easily recognizable in concept to anyone who's ever used a modern PC: Most PCs come with several types of DAS, most notably hard drives.

DAS media

The following commonplace media are all forms of DAS (these media are explained in the "Major storage media" section earlier in this chapter):

- Hard drives
- Zip drives
- Floppy drives
- CD-writable and rewritable drives
- Jaz drives
- DVD-writable and rewritable drives (they're out there, but they're pricey)

Problems with networks and DAS

In many networks, servers store files and serve them to users. This practice, often called *server-attached storage,* can result in bottlenecks as the size of the network grows. The two main most-likely causes for network bottlenecks using server-attached storage are as follows:

- The server's hard drive can run out of room to store files. You can add more hard drives to the server, true, but the more hard drives one server has to keep track of, the more files the server needs to keep track of, and the more files it has to be able to send or receive to and from users. As you can imagine, this can tax the system (see the following bullet).
- Servers that double as file servers can be overtaxed by the sheer CPU cycles of having to deal with the I/O of file transferring in addition to its own server-ly duties, such as (but not limited to) logging, network monitoring, and application serving.

As a result of its problems, DAS is good enough for very low-end or very high-end solutions, but doesn't make much sense for mid-to-large (large as opposed to huge) solutions. Most non-business needs, such as home PCs, result in so few files that need to be backed up that doing so manually is not really a chore. On the other side of the spectrum, huge computers (such as mainframes) that use so much storage space that they really, really need their own storage solutions can benefit from a larger DAS solution.

But what of those true medium-sized networks that are too big for DAS but too small to consider Fiber Channel or SAN technologies (SAN technologies are explained later in this chapter)? Arising from the need for a scalable, affordable storage solution for consumers with mid-to-large storage requirements came NAS. NAS is explained at length in the following section.

Network-Attached Storage

Every network needs storage space. For small networks (like ten or fewer people), shared folders on personal hard drives is a perfectly acceptable solution. On medium-sized networks, something more is required: Usually, file servers carry additional storage space. But for large networks, the solution may be entire hard drives (in whatever physical context) devoted exclusively to file storage, which is where network-attached storage (NAS) comes in.

NAS was designed on the premise that, at some point, a server that doubles as a file server becomes unable to handle all the requests it's receiving and still be able to perform its server application functions at top performance levels. A server so burdened can quickly become a network bottleneck. Adding storage space to your network servers may work for a while when your network starts its growing pains. After awhile, though, the added storage won't mean a thing to the overwhelmed server, which is struggling to keep up with the amount of requests coming in from all over the network, serve those files, and back up files it receives.

The problems with DAS and server-attached storage (as explained in the previous section) are solved by NAS, which removes the file transfer I/O load from application servers. Quite simply, servers perform better when relieved of their file distribution duties, and in the end a network enjoys greater performance for the time when they're not bogged down with file transfer requests.

NAS itself is well suited to file serving because its operating system can be a small, embedded one that doesn't have any distractions from doing anything but following the server's orders and storing or sending files when user requests come in.

> **In the Real World**
> NAS, which is used in some 50 percent of all enterprises today, is by far the most-used storage method in modern networks. By comparison, DAS isn't practical in a mid-sized network and neither is a SAN, which isn't even a real standard yet.

The following sections explain the benefits of NAS as well as the basics of how NAS works.

Benefits of NAS

NAS offers the following benefits to networks:

+ **Cost efficiency:** NAS typically costs a few thousand dollars to purchase, but the servers instantly gain the benefit of reduced I/O, helping your network maximize the use of the equipment it has so that you don't have to keep throwing new servers at it.

> **Tip**
> If data storage is important enough to a network, it can be cheaper to implement NAS early than it would be to spend money over the long haul on such hardware improvements as upgrading server storage and adding more servers to lighten the load on existing servers.

+ **Cross-platform file sharing:** NAS devices can appear to any client as a native file system. This feature is useful in networks where Linux, Mac, and Windows clients are all used on the same network, for example.

+ **Ease of configuration:** NAS devices are about as easy to configure as a typical *simple-to-configure* VCR (not one of those horrific nightmares you always seem to get as wedding presents). If you have ever used a USB device on your PC and had it properly configure itself, then you know how easy NAS solutions are to implement.

+ **Ease of use:** NAS is as easy to use as a second hard drive would be to a local system. In Windows or Mac, for example, you can simply create a shortcut folder or map a network drive (the latter is just a stuffy version of the former) to a NAS location and can put that shortcut anywhere in their PC interface that it's easy to access. After that point, they can always simply click that folder to access that resource, just as if it were a floppy or a CD-ROM.

+ **Easy backups:** Using RAID technologies and multiple hard drives in a NAS solution, disk striping can provide redundancy within one NAS solution.

+ **Extra features various and sundry:** Some NAS solutions come with built-in authentication servers, automatic e-mail error reporting, and other features.

+ **Increased network efficiency:** By alleviating the I/O pressure on the server, NAS helps you to get the maximum potential and performance out of your servers.

✦ **Low cost compared to server-attached storage:** For every NAS device that you implement where you would have implemented a full-fledged server with server-attached storage, you save the following costs:

- **The cost of any server operating system license:** NAS servers don't typically have more than a bare-bones (usually embedded) operating system that includes a networking file system, support for necessary protocols (such as TCP/IP), and hardware drivers.

- **The cost of unnecessary hardware:** NAS setups are designed with as few hardware and software components as necessary to store and transfer files, and no more. NAS servers need not include a monitor, keyboard, or a mouse because NAS servers don't require the use of these things.

✦ **RAID support:** Nearly all forms of NAS support RAID 0, 1, and 5, and virtually all major NAS implementations support at least RAID 5.

> **Cross-Reference:** See Chapter 15 for more information on RAID.

✦ **Vast network storage potential:** Many NAS solutions offer up to 8TB or more of storage, depending on the types of storage media used.

> **Note:** For those who haven't seen TB bandied about much yet, don't feel alone: 1TB is equal to 1000GB. Being that big, terabytes aren't used in storage measure except in the biggest of enterprises — yet.

How NAS works

NAS operates on the same client/server premise that regular servers do, although NAS is a storage-only server. NAS solutions aren't designed like typical servers, even though they are technically servers. NAS differs from the tradition file server by dedicating its hardware specifically to data storage and the transfer of that data over a network.

The effect of adding NAS to a network with overtaxed servers is the same as when you got your first hard drive. Just as you no longer needed to waste time with floppy disks, with NAS a server no longer has to waste time sending files back and forth, it can instead just point the incoming request to the NAS device and let that device serve the file. In this way, a network server is freed of the CPU cycles of serving the actual files itself, and instead simply instructs the NAS device to deliver the files to the user in its stead. Figure 14-3 illustrates this concept.

Clients always access a NAS device via the NAS head, not the device itself. Access to a NAS is usually granted via Ethernet, using a standard NIC card and address. A NAS appears as a single node on the network using the IP address of the NIC, no matter how many physical devices are attached to the NAS itself.

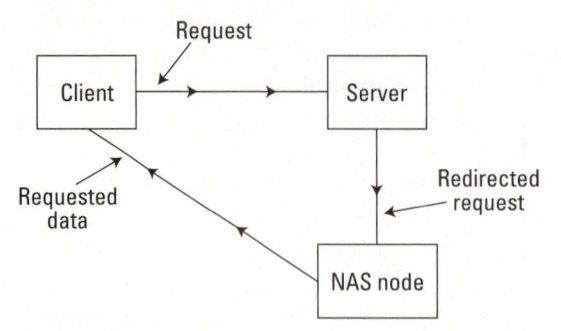

Figure 14-3: The basic network-attached storage model

NAS technologies

NAS devices are typically used in a LAN environment and can be made up of multiple networked NAS devices. NAS devices require only the use of hardware that it needs to serve files. Typically, this hardware is:

- ✦ A bunch of hard drives
- ✦ Controllers to connect the hard drives
- ✦ A NAS head

    The *NAS head* (or NAS box) is the interface between the NAS storage devices and network clients. NAS devices are connected through the NAS head.

NAS devices are usually hard disks using SCSI or other fast controllers, typically including multi-disk RAID systems and software for mapping file locations to the NAS device. NAS can store any types of data files that could be stored on a PC hard drive. Multiple disks (and even tape drives) can be attached to a NAS system to increase capacity.

NAS requires only a network file system, not a full network-operating system, because it does not need to function as a full-fledged server, and so all hardware resources can be devoted exclusively to file transfer. The two network file systems that are most associated with NAS are NFS and CIFS.

Cross-Reference: Both NFS and CIFS are explained in Chapter 13.

Communication with clients to a NAS head can occur via TCP/IP or IPX, and uses industry-standard file sharing protocols (SMB/CIFS, NFS, or HTTP). NAS can also use non-routing protocols, such as the Microsoft NetBEUI protocol.

NAS management

NAS is almost disgustingly simple to manage. Typically, NAS can be managed and configured via a network-attached workstation by using a Web browser such as Netscape Navigator using custom Java or JavaScript applets. Further, nearly all NAS solutions today come such that when you open the box, they fairly leap out of the box and plug themselves in. NAS enables the addition of more storage to a system without having to take the server offline.

DNAS

DNAS can be thought of as a more paranoid implementation of NAS. DNAS operates on the assumption that every single component on the network will fail at some point. Thus, DNAS plans for redundancy of each component on the NAS device. DNAS can be hot-swapped into the network right out of the box by simply plugging it into the network hub, and hard drives and power supplies are mounted in hot-swap ports so that they can be dynamically replaced (replaced without a reboot) when they go bad. DNAS systems are also typically pre-configured for RAID 5.

> **Cross-Reference** Chapter 15 covers RAID at greater length.

Storage Area Networks

Conceptually, a *Storage Area Network (SAN)* is a large network within a larger network (such as a LAN or WAN) that is specifically designed to handle storage. A SAN is a subnetwork connecting various types of storage within a subnetwork of the main network. Clients access the SAN via servers, which themselves access the SAN. Figure 14-4 illustrates this concept.

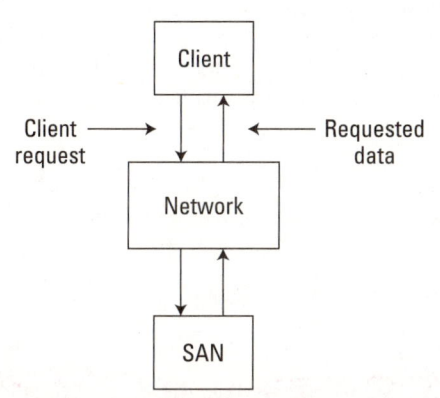

Figure 14-4: A simple illustration of a SAN

> ### Open Standards or Bust
>
> As an example of how proprietary technologies can be bad, consider how IBM nearly killed its vaunted position in the PC market by releasing hardware incompatible with its own, earlier, open PC standards (which IBM itself created, hence the term *IBM-compatible*). In the late 1980s IBM released technology standards that were incompatible with the hardware architecture that IBM itself made popular. This architecture, called Micro-Channel architecture by IBM and *true-blue IBM* by some cynical folk, was actually a very efficient technology that was heralded as ahead of its time. But the higher cost of Micro-Channel architecture and its incompatibility with IBM's own earlier designs, cost Micro-Channel any real chances for broad adoption. After getting burned by Micro-Channel, IBM eventually became "IBM-compatible" again.
>
> SAN technologies have no open standards, only proprietary technologies from companies such as Compaq, ESN, and Auspex. Worse, if a SAN standard is adopted by the industry at some point, it will likely be incompatible with current, proprietary SAN solutions.
>
> Hardware solutions based on open standards are usually cheaper and better to use, because they ensure the purchaser of future compatibility, at least to some degree. No company is going to come out with a PC motherboard that's not ATX-compatible anytime soon, for example. As a result, you can be fairly sure that if you buy an ATX case now, that you will be able to put an ATX form factor motherboard into it later.

The chief benefit of a SAN is its capability to connect storage systems (such as RAID, tape backup, and CD backup devices) into a single storage subnetwork. SAN technologies are estimated to be used in only five percent of enterprise networks. This low use is largely because of the lack of standardization in SAN technologies. As history has shown, proprietary technologies cost more to implement than technologies based on open standards (see the nearby sidebar if you're curious why open standards are better).

Caution: SAN technologies are not typically interoperable with other SAN technologies, and this is a danger in implementing SANs: You're likely to get locked into one company's solution. So, if you broadly implement SAN technologies, you had better be happy with that company's solution, or you may have to spend yourself silly trying to replace those technologies later.

SAN is useful only in narrow circumstances, such as when well-known security risks with SCSI and FC can be contained and performance bottlenecks resulting from Fiber Channel node and link congestion can be avoided.

Note: SANs add a bit of overhead in a network because it adds another layer of abstraction to the network (the communication layer between the server and the SAN).

Note that SAN switches tend to not work with switches from other companies due to the lack of standard SAN technologies. For this reason, the dangers in adopting these technologies are as follows:

- ✦ Purchasing new and updated technologies released by the company you originally purchased your SAN technologies from (again, proprietary solutions are expensive and limit your choices due to non-interoperability), whether you're happy with them or not, just to avoid the mass expenditures of replacing your existing SAN implementation.
- ✦ Scrapping your old equipment altogether and getting an entirely new SAN solution. This option is likely to be expensive.

If you're considering a SAN solution, you may want to look harder at NAS solutions, which are based on open standards and can do pretty much anything important that SANs can do.

Summary

Networks simply wouldn't be useful without storage. For the Network+ exam, you should take the following key points from this chapter:

- ✦ Direct-attached storage (DAS) is adequate for smaller networks and for single-workstation PCs, but for network storage, NAS is usually a far more efficient network solution.
- ✦ Network-attached storage (NAS) is used in one of two networks in today's networks because it is currently by far the best solution for mid-to-large-sized networks.
- ✦ Server-attached storage, the name for storage devices that are attached to a server.
- ✦ Storage area networks are a new technology that, due to lack of standards, tend to be incompatible from one company's SAN solution to another.

✦ ✦ ✦

STUDY GUIDE

Assessment Questions

1. When resources on a network are instantly accessible to a user, that network is said to have a high level of which of the following features?

    A. Availability

    B. Scalability

    C. Performance

    D. Manageability

2. Which of the following controller types is not a preferred media for network storage where performance is a big requirement?

    A. SCSI

    B. IDE

    C. FireWire

    D. Fiber Channel

3. Which of the following media is not typically used for large storage solutions?

    A. DVD rewritables

    B. CD rewritables

    C. Hard drives

    D. Floppy disks

4. Which of the following types of media is installed in almost every modern PC and is used in most storage solutions?

    A. DVD+RW

    B. CD-RW

    C. Hard drives

    D. CD-ROM

5. Which of the following types of media is currently the most popular to distribute software?

   A. Floppy disk

   B. DVD-ROM

   C. CD-ROM

   D. Zip

6. Which of the following DVD formats is typically the best choice for storage?

   A. DVD-RW

   B. DVD+RW

   C. DVD-RAM

   D. DVD-R

7. Which of the following is the weakest media in terms of degradability?

   A. Disk media (such as floppy disks or hard drives)

   B. Tape media

   C. Disc media (such as CDs or DVDs)

   D. Zip disks

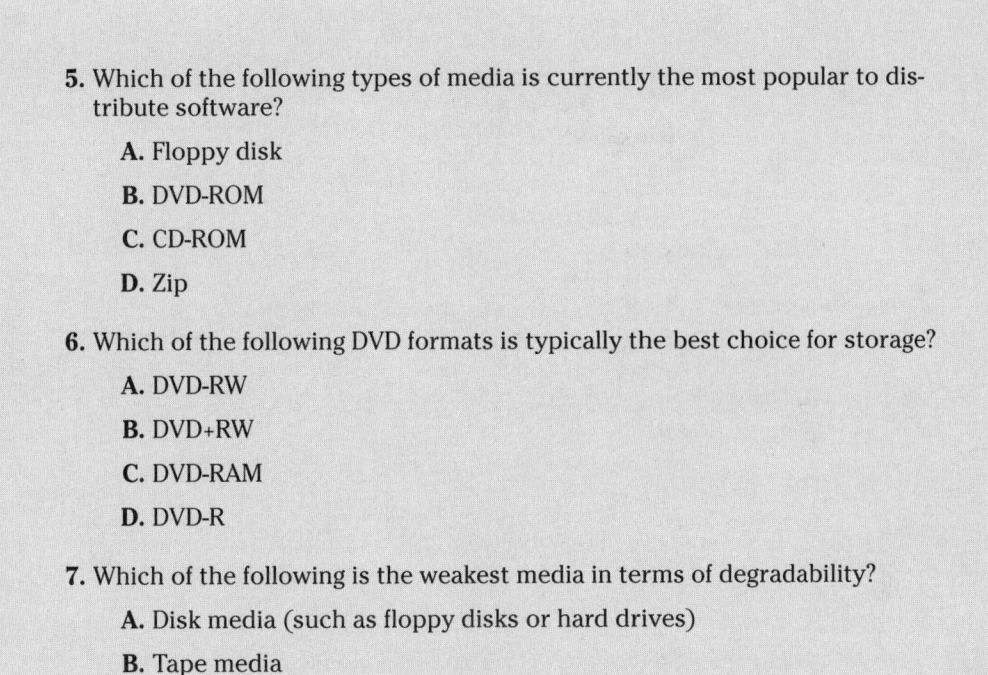

8. What is the name for error-detection that checks a record on a tape after recording to verify that the recorded data is not corrupt?

   A. Write/Read

   B. CRC

   C. Dynamic error correction

   D. Read-after-write

9. Which of the following controller interfaces is generally considered too slow for storage solutions that require fast access speeds?

   A. SCSI

   B. IDE

   C. FireWire

   D. Fiber Channel

10. Which of the following technologies offers the greatest data transfer rates?

    A. SCSI

    B. IDE

    C. USB

    D. Fiber Channel

11. Which of the following terms describes an 8-bit SCSI controller?

    A. Wide SCSI

    B. Fast SCSI

    C. Narrow SCSI

    D. Ultra SCSI

12. What is the size of the bus of a wide SCSI controller?

    A. 8-bit

    B. 16-bit

    C. 24-bit

    D. 32-bit

13. Which of the following ANSI standards includes Fast SCSI?

    A. SCSI-1

    B. SCSI-2

    C. SCSI-3

    D. SCSI-f

14. Which of the following standards is a serious competitor to SCSI, especially in the market for SANs?

    A. Fiber Channel

    B. FireWire

    C. USB

    D. EIDE

15. What is the process of combining a large group (at least 32) CPUs running as one virtual processor called?

    A. Virtual processing

    B. Dual processing

    C. Parallel processing

    D. Consolidation

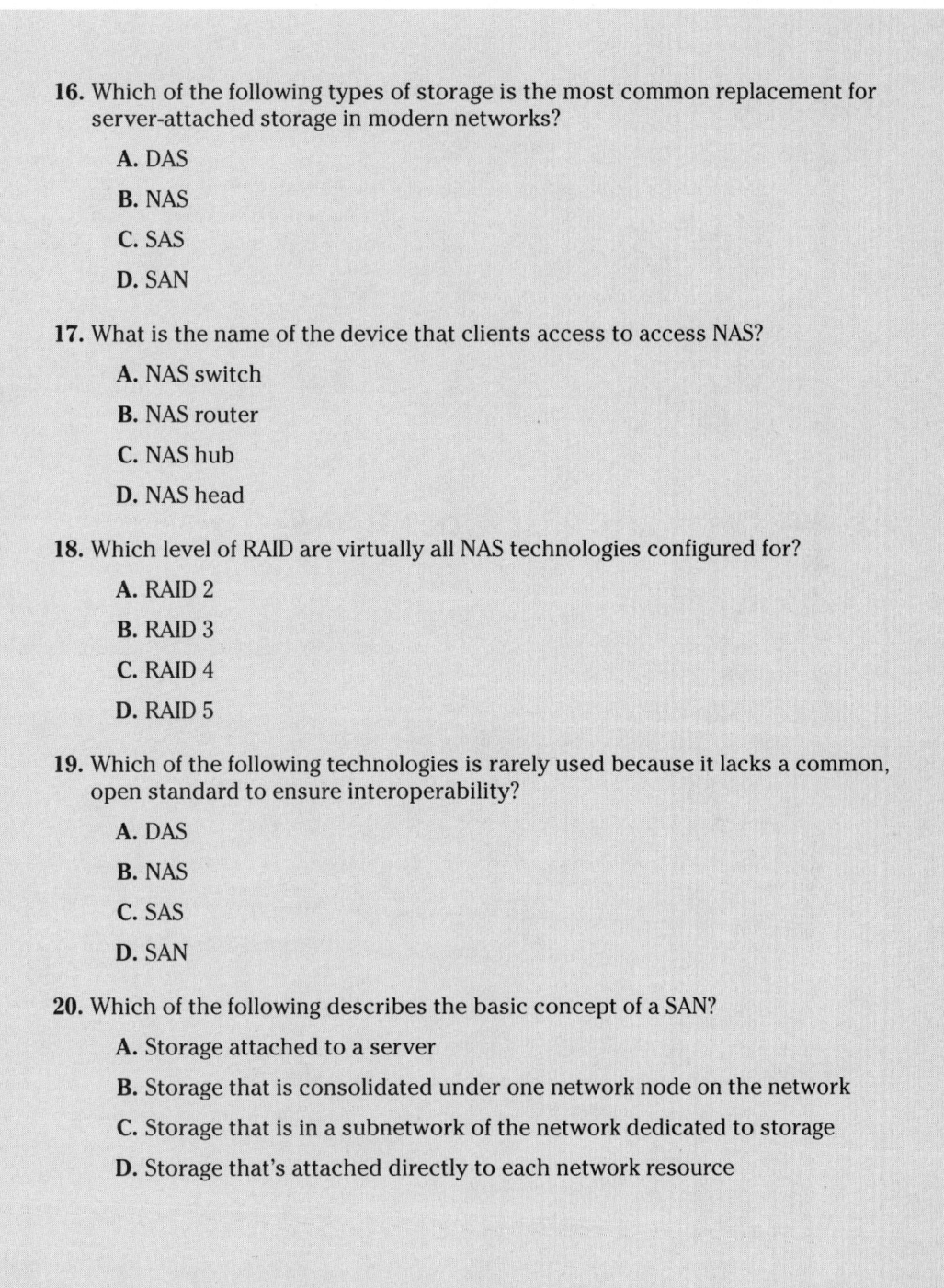

16. Which of the following types of storage is the most common replacement for server-attached storage in modern networks?

    A. DAS

    B. NAS

    C. SAS

    D. SAN

17. What is the name of the device that clients access to access NAS?

    A. NAS switch

    B. NAS router

    C. NAS hub

    D. NAS head

18. Which level of RAID are virtually all NAS technologies configured for?

    A. RAID 2

    B. RAID 3

    C. RAID 4

    D. RAID 5

19. Which of the following technologies is rarely used because it lacks a common, open standard to ensure interoperability?

    A. DAS

    B. NAS

    C. SAS

    D. SAN

20. Which of the following describes the basic concept of a SAN?

    A. Storage attached to a server

    B. Storage that is consolidated under one network node on the network

    C. Storage that is in a subnetwork of the network dedicated to storage

    D. Storage that's attached directly to each network resource

Scenarios

1. You are a consultant for a large (but not monstrous) company whose network servers are constantly overwhelmed with file transfer requests. Users are complaining that they can't get their files fast enough, and other server duties are taking eons to complete as well. You do a little digging and find that the network uses server-attached storage almost exclusively. What technologies should you recommend that the company adopt?

2. You are an IT administrator for a company that must continually archive hordes of large files. Currently, the company uses CD-RW for storage, but this gets old because CDs can hold up to only 650MB of storage. What technology would probably make the most sense for an upgrade in this situation?

Answers to Chapter Questions

Chapter Pre-Test

1. Unavailable. When a network is down and can't be used, it's considered to be unavailable. See the "Basic storage requirements" section for details.
2. DVD+RW and DVD-RAM are the two DVD formats most suitable for storage. See the "DVD formats" section for details.
3. Direct-attached storage connects directly to a computer.
4. Server-attached storage connects directly to a server.
5. Network-attached storage attaches to a network as one node.
6. The most used storage device is the hard drive.
7. The least commonly used storage device is the floppy disk, which is used only for small files.
8. SCSI is currently the most used high-speed interface.
9. SAN technologies are not standardized yet, and implementing these technologies may result in incompatibility later.
10. Technologies based on open standards are usually cheaper and more compatible with one another than proprietary technologies are.

Assessment Questions

1. A. When resources on a network are almost always accessible to users when they need it, regardless of performance, that network is said to have high availability.
2. B. IDE is not a preferred media for high-performance networks, due to its slower transfer rates.

3. D. Floppy disks are not typically used for large storage solutions.
4. C. Hard drives are installed in almost every modern PC, and are used in most major storage solutions.
5. C. CD-ROM is by far the most popular media for software distribution.
6. B. DVD+RW is typically the best choice for storage.
7. B. Tape media is generally the weakest of all major media types in degradability.
8. D. Read-after-write error correction involves checking each sector of a tape after it has been recorded to verify the data's integrity.
9. B. IDE controllers are generally considered too slow for storage solutions that require fast access speeds.
10. D. Fiber Channel, which can offer up to 1 Gbps data transfer rate, offers the fastest data transfer rates.
11. C. Narrow SCSI describes an 8-bit SCSI controller.
12. B. A wide SCSI controller is 16 bits wide.
13. B. Fast SCSI is part of the SCSI-2 standard.
14. A. Fiber Channel is considered a serious competitor to SCSI, especially in the market for SANs.
15. C. The process of combining a large group (at least 32) of CPUs running as one virtual processor is called parallel processing.
16. B. NAS is the most common replacement for server-attached storage in modern networks.
17. D. Clients attach to a NAS head to access NAS.
18. D. Virtually all NAS solutions support at least RAID 5.
19. D. SAN is rarely used (compared to NAS) because SAN technologies lack a common, open standard.
20. C. The basic concept of a SAN is storage that is in a subnetwork of the network dedicated solely to storage.

Scenarios

1. In this scenario, NAS would make a perfect solution. Freed of their file transfer duties, the servers would no longer be overtaxed and storage access speeds would also be increased.
2. If the only real problem with the company's storage solution is the fact that CD-ROMs don't hold enough, DVD+RW would make the most sense as an upgrade path, because DVDs can hold nearly 10GB per DVD.

Keeping Your Data Available

CHAPTER 15

EXAM OBJECTIVES

- Identify the purpose and characteristics of fault tolerance
- Identify the purpose and characteristics of disaster recovery

CHAPTER PRE-TEST

1. Fault tolerance is a measure of how _____ data is at all times.
2. _____ _____ is the process of restoring data after failure of primary storage.
3. To keep data accessible, a network should have at least one _____ of critical data available in case the original data should become corrupt or otherwise unavailable.
4. _____ refers to the model of having one component ready to replace a similar component if it should go bad.
5. MTBF is the mean time between _____.
6. Backup data that's stored in a separate geographical location from the original data is called _____ storage.
7. _____ _____ uses clusters of computers to help balance server load.
8. RAID stands for _____ _____ _____ _____.
9. RAID 1 uses _____ _____ to increase fault tolerance.
10. RAID 5 uses _____ _____ _____ _____ to increase fault tolerance.

✦ Answers to these questions can be found at the end of the chapter. ✦

The information on any network is only as secure as its disaster recovery solution. If an employee has no backup for the files on their hard drive, for example, and their hard drive dies, those files probably can't be recovered. The following causes are the most common reasons a disaster recovery solution is necessary:

- **User error:** The most common type of "disaster" on a network is when a user deletes a file that they shouldn't. If permissions on a network are set up properly, ordinary users typically can't brutalize an entire network, but typically permissions are not this simple. Users generally need at least some permissions before they can do productive work, and sometimes a user can botch a procedure.

- **Natural disasters:** Hurricanes, tornadoes, earthquakes, you name it: no matter where you live, mother nature's got something to throw at your network locations.

- **Malicious hackers:** If a hacker with ill intentions accesses your network, there's literally no end to the damage they can do. If this happens to you, your network stands or falls based on whether you can recover from the damage, and how quickly.

This chapter discusses how to keep your network's data highly available in the face of adversity.

Backups

A network is only as good as its backup solution: the first line of defense in both fault tolerance and disaster recovery. For example, if an employee's hard drive becomes corrupt and the files on it aren't backed up elsewhere, that employee will not have access to their files unless by some miracle those files can be recovered. Even if they can be recovered, recovering files from a corrupted hard drive can be a slow and expensive process, if it's even possible.

Types of backups

The following major types of backups exist:

- **Full:** A full backup is a backup of every possible file on a network, or at least every possible file typically backed up. For example, if your IT department only ever backs up one given set of drives, a backup of everything on those drives would be considered a full backup.

- **Incremental:** Backs up all files that have changed since a certain length of time. . For example, if your network is backed up daily and you need to restore from backup on Wednesday, you'd need to restore the last full backup from the weekend, then restore the Monday backup, then restore the Tuesday backup, and finally restore any Wednesday backups you may have to restore your files to their last-good state.

> **Exam Tip**
>
> The main difference between differential and incremental backups is that incremental backups clear the archive bits to each file as they're restored. Differential backups do not clear archive bits at all.

- **Differential:** Backs up only the information that has changed since the last full backup.
- **Copy:** A copy backup is just that: a complete copy of all files in a backup. For ultra-secure storage, more than one backup can be used. For every backup other than the primary backup, which need be used only in the event that both the original data and the primary backup become corrupted, tape can be used to provide additional fault tolerance to a network without having to pay for more expensive hard drive space.

Backup software uses what's called an *archive bit* to determine which files to back up in a differential or incremental backup. When a file is backed up, its archive bit is cleared. When a file that has no archive bit changes in any way, the archive bit is once again set. In a day when the incremental backup kicks in, it looks at each file and backs up those files with an archive bit set and ignores those files without one.

Note that backing up is more difficult when files are being used at the time of backup. Usually, if a file is open when backups are being performed, the file is skipped and a note is added to the backup log files.

Scheduled backups

Scheduled backups are typical for most large networks. Backups can be done on any major storage media (see Chapter 14), although currently the most popular backup medium is tape because tape devices and media are fairly inexpensive. Cost is a factor because most effective backup policies schedule either a partial or complete backup at regular intervals — usually daily, weekly, or both.

The backup scheme most widely used today is called *grandfather-father-son* because its terminology is reminiscent of genealogy:

- Daily backups are called *sons*.
- The last full backup each week is called a *father*.
- The last full backup of the month is called a *grandfather*.

Completed backup tapes remain in storage until a full cycle of that type of backup is done — then the tapes can be reused For example, daily tapes can be reused after four days (for a five-day schedule) or every six days (for a seven-day schedule). Weekly tapes are reused every fifth week. Monthly tapes, however, are not typically reused, unless the information on them is so time-sensitive that it's literally useless after a year. In that case, monthly backup tapes could be reused every thirteenth month if you wanted to keep a year's worth of backups on hand.

Restoring from backup

Restoring from these backup types must be done in chronological order, starting with the most recent full backup. After restoring this, each incremental backup or differential backup must be applied to the restored full backup.

Suppose, for example, that File A changed on Monday, and that both File A and File B changed on Tuesday. After the full backup is applied, the incremental backup for Monday is applied — changing File A. Then the incremental backup for Tuesday is applied — which updates File A again and changes File B to its most recent state. If File C and File D didn't change at all since the last full backup, then the versions of those files on the full backup are the latest versions.

Off-site storage

The most extreme example of network redundancy is storing a copy of data so far away from the original that it can't likely suffer the same failure as the original data. For example, say your network has two locations — one in New York and one in Los Angeles. In this example, a truly redundant setup would store a complete copy of the data from L.A. *and* New York in both locations. If the network goes down in either location for some reason, you still have copies of the data from both locations on hand.

Taking the concept of off-site storage one step further, data storage can be stored on a non-company site in case both locations (L.A. and New York, in this example) are targeted. For example, if two volcanoes erupt underneath the two main offices of Credit Company A in L.A. and New York, Credit Company A had better hope it has backups of its credit data at a third location. Credit-lending organizations obviously require this type of fault tolerance, as do organizations (such as the U.S. Internal Revenue Service) that deal in large sums of money and also require a high level of data-fault tolerance.

Backup tips

Following are some importantfactors to consider when creating your backup solution:

- ✦ **Test your backups:** The programmer's proverb — "garbage in, garbage out" — is relevant here. If you don't ensure the integrity of your backup, then you may be in for a nasty shock when you have to use that backup: it may be just as corrupt as your original files.

- ✦ **Consider disk clustering:** Disk clustering can nullify the need to have to restore a backup at all. See the "System-area networks" section later in this chapter.

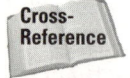

> **Cross-Reference**
> See the "'RAID!?!'" section in this chapter for more information on RAID (a technique similar to clustering), and see the "System-area networks" section in this chapter and Chapter 14 for more information on clustering.

- ✦ **Consider the restore speeds.** When you decide what type of backup media to use for your network, consider how quickly you'll need access to your data should restore from backup. Just because your data is backed up doesn't mean that your backed up data is instantly accessible. If you have to back up from analog tape, for example, it could be quite some time before you're able to access your backed up data. If you back up from DVD, on the other hand, your restore speeds can be quite fast.

- ✦ **Decide what you can afford to spend.** If you can afford the cost, a completely bulletproof network is the way to go, but this is not always an affordable solution. Only a network's budget and the requirements of that network can define what your network's storage solution should be.

- ✦ **Evaluate your processes.** Few networks are set up to the most efficient possible configuration; this fact is a result of the fact that often, networks change quite a bit over time based on company reorganizations, employees leaving and being hired on, and company acquisitions and mergers. Because of this, it never hurts to re-evaluate the efficiency of your network disaster recovery systems from time to time. For example, are your storage systems in need of reorganization so similar data is closer together?

- ✦ **Consider a storage service provider (SSP).** You don't have to provide your own storage, you can choose to find a company to provide storage for you over a VPN or other remote but secure solution.

Fault Tolerance

Fault tolerance is a measure of how much fault a network can tolerate and still remain operable. Networks with high fault tolerance are most readily available at all times. The amount of fault tolerance that a given network requires depends heavily on the mission of the network itself. For example, government organizations such as the IRS, whose data absolutely must be available, implement extremely high fault tolerance. Many networks don't depend that heavily upon their data to be available, but all networks need at least some form of fault tolerance.

Some important fault-tolerance concepts

The following sections describe some more important concepts that go along with understanding fault tolerance.

Load balancing

Load balancing, a feature used quite often for Web servers that get a lot of traffic, divides the work of one computer among multiple computers to increase network response times. As a simple example, if two computers of equal power do the work of one, that work is performed in (roughly) half the time. If four identical computers do the duty of one, that process can be completed in one-quarter of the usual time, and so on.

Server clustering is usually implemented on a network for the load balancing alone, but clustering also provides fault tolerance at the same time. (Note that when two servers are used for load balancing, a third server is usually required to distribute work between those servers.) By and large, however, two approaches exist for the implementation of clustering:

- **Route each request to a different, identical server host address in a DNS table.** Usually do so in *round-robin* fashion, that is, the first request goes to the first server, the second request goes to the second server, and so on until all servers have had a request, at which point the cycle starts again.

- **Route each request to the closest location geographically.** The closer a server is to a user geographically, the fewer routers a given packet of data must travel through to reach its destination — resulting in faster file-access times. For example, if you're in the U.S., all environment variables being equal a Seattle download link is going to offer faster access times than (say) a Timbuktu download link.

> **Tip** Both types of clustering can be used in tandem to create a high level of fault tolerance and network responsiveness.

Latency

The delay between a user's action and its desired result is called *latency*. High latency is when a user clicks to access a network resource, waits a good few seconds for his or her workstation to recognize the resource, double-clicks the resource, and waits a good few seconds more for the resource contents to appear, and so on. Low latency is when a user clicks a resource and it appears as quickly as if it resided on the user's own workstation.

A good deal of latency comes from hardware. For example, the more routers a given packet has to travel through, the higher the latency of that connection will be. If a network is inundated with requests, that increases latency. If CPU resources are overtaxed, then maybe the servers don't have enough RAM — or server-attached storage is hogging server CPU cycles, either of which can result in high latency. Now and then, it's good practice to re-evaluate network connections with the goal in mind of reducing latency.

Mean Time Between Failures (MTBF)

This simple concept is fairly easy to understand: MTBF is the measure of the time between failures of your network. A network failure is defined not as the failure of a single device, or even multiple devices. MTBF is measured in hours, and this number increases as your network's fault tolerance increases.

Failover

Failover goes along with fault tolerance. Failover is a networking model that ensures that if a given component of a network resource, PC, or data path fails, a suitable replacement is already in place to act in its stead without an interruption in services. For example, Microsoft.com does is not highly available because Microsoft's servers never crash, of course they crash. But Microsoft has hundreds if not thousands of servers behind Microsoft.com resulting in a lot of failover and thus a highly available site.

Types of fault tolerance

Appropriate fault tolerance is a goal you can approach from various directions. The following sections discuss the major types of fault tolerance.

Software fault tolerance

Software goes bad, crashes, or is otherwise corrupted or unavailable. Software fault tolerance is typically provided by a real-time embedded operating system such as Compaq's NonStop operating system (formerly Tandem) that sets up checkpoints along transmission paths at which it checks the integrity of critical data. Operating systems like Unix/Linux and Windows NT/2000 also offer fault tolerance features, such as clustering and striping, but hardware fault tolerance, while more expensive, is typically more reliable than that provided by operating systems.

Hardware fault tolerance

Be it power supply, hard drive, or controller, at some point hardware components will go bad. Having redundant hardware in place to automatically take the place of corrupt hardware goes a long way towards increasing a network's fault tolerance.

Hardware fault tolerance is usually achieved by having redundant components for each mission-critical hardware component on a network. If a given component goes bad, another immediately takes its place until the faulty component is fixed or replaced. Some examples of hardware fault tolerance follow:

- ✦ Disks can be mirrored, with the mirrors on separate controllers from one another. This technique is often called *disk duplexing*.
- ✦ Data can be striped across multiple disks with RAID solutions.
- ✦ Processors can be made to run together by *lock-stepping* them — synchronizing the two processors with each other, and then comparing their data output for errors. Often, entire servers are redundant to one another, providing load-balancing and fault-tolerance capabilities at the same time. For example, if a high-traffic Web site is using ten servers that each contain the same data sharing the traffic load, if one of those servers go down, nine servers are still there to serve the page.

Network fault tolerance

Any-to-any connectivity services connect computers on a network redundantly so any computer can access any other computer on the network in the event that one computer or network path fails. Figure 15-1 shows an example of network tolerance in a simple network.

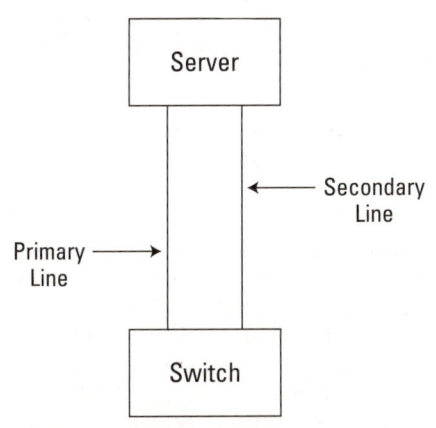

```
         ┌─────────┐
         │ Server  │
         └────┬────┘
              │
              │ ←──── Secondary
              │        Line
Primary ───→  │
  Line        │
              │
         ┌────┴────┐
         │ Switch  │
         └─────────┘
```

Figure 15-1: Fault tolerance in a simple network environment.

Network paths can be duplicated on any level from individual cabling and redundant routers and switches to entire redundant LANs. The Internet, for example, is a network with literally thousands of different possible paths.

Adapter teaming involves a completely redundant link from a given server to the network. If the primary network link goes down, the server will switch over to the secondary network link. Some server systems come with two different adapters on each server, one for a high-speed 1Gbps adapter and one for a standard 100Mbps adapter for a backup line. This would result in slower performance from the server if its main line went down, but at least that server would still be accessible.

Power fault tolerance

Sometimes, power is so important that it must be backed up. For example, say you're working on your laptop and you forget to plug your computer's AC adapter in. If the battery runs out of power, you could lose all your work if you don't save and shut down in time. On the other hand, a fully charged battery serves as a backup power supply for the laptop in the event of an AC power failure — as such, it's a basic example of *power fault tolerance*.

Currently all major laptop vendors include an uninterruptible power supply (UPS) to prevent a total loss of power (typically, the UPS for a laptop is in the form of a battery).

Three major types of device provide power fault tolerance:

- **Power conditioners:** Line noise, voltage spikes, and static can cause power fluctuations or even power failures. Power conditioners suppress spikes and fill in valleys in the power signal, as well as reducing noise.

- **Surge suppressors:** Although these devices resemble common power strips with multiple sockets for power cords, they also have the capacity to block power surges that would otherwise damage your computer's delicate electronics.

> **Caution**
> Don't be fooled by the glorified power strips you see in large retail stores. A true surge suppressor has its own fuses (or even circuit breakers), and typically cost at least $40 or so.

- **Uninterruptible power supply (UPS)**: For desktop (and larger) systems, a UPS is a separate unit that holds sufficient charge to keep the computer running long enough to let the user save documents and shut down in the event of a power failure. When a standard power source is depleted or disrupted, a UPS takes over automatically to prevent loss of data. Most mobile PC equipment (especially current laptops), come with a built-in equivalent to a UPS: If you run out of power, the laptop goes into *hibernate mode* (which consumes almost no power at all) to preserve your information until you can connect the computer to a stable power source.

"RAID!?!"

If you've seen much television in the U.S., you may be familiar with Raid pest-control sprays. In networking, however, RAID has nothing at all to do with roaches — it's a technique for preserving and protecting your data The following sections discuss the basics of RAID, its benefits, and the basics of how RAID works.

Understanding RAID

RAID stands for Redundant Array of Inexpensive Disks (or, more recently, Redundant Array of Independent Disks) — a set of separate drives that store the same data, serving as backups for each other. Operating systems (on network workstations and servers, for example) see a given RAID as a single logical entity, represented as a single hard disk.

RAID enables for increased fault tolerance in a network. For example, if one hard drive becomes corrupt, the data that's on that hard drive can be recovered from a copy of the same data that's stored on another drive. RAID also has the added benefit of I/O overlapping. *I/O overlapping* enables for increased network response times.

For example, when only one disk is for storage, only one source can write to that disk at the same time. However, when data is striped across multiple disks, parts of that data can written to or read from simultaneously by multiple sources. Further, data that's on multiple disks can be read by multiple clients simultaneously.

See the following list for an explanation of each word in this term.

- **Redundant:** In English class, you may have been told that redundancy is usually bad. In networking, redundancy is absolutely critical. A backup is by definition redundant. In RAID, data is duplicated using parity data (see the "Parity" section in this chapter for details on parity).

- **Array:** An array is a multiple of something. In RAID, an *array* is the term for more than one disk.

- Inexpensive/Independent — Although the original paper on RAID used the term inexpensive, the term independent has replaced it in modern usage and definitions. Independent in the original usage just points out that the disks in RAID are actually independent physical disks, not logical drives of some larger physical disk, the benefit being higher fault tolerance.

- **Disks:** This term simply indicates that hard disks are typically used for RAID solutions, as opposed to tape devices.

How RAID works

Understanding how RAID works requires that you understand several key concepts used in RAID technologies. The following sections discuss these concepts.

Parity

Parity data is not actually the data itself, but is rather a bit that is used to perform a calculation on data to determine whether it's corrupt. Parity data is much smaller than the original data, and can be duplicated and stored in much smaller form than the original data. It is in this way that major banks, credit card companies, and government agencies ensure beyond a doubt that your data is always available.

> **Note** Parity is similar to error correction used in the transmission of packets over a network.

Therefore, the best parity solution ensures that the parity data for a given set of data is not kept on the same disk as the original data. Thus, if the drive containing Data A becomes corrupt, but the parity data for Data A is on another disk, the parity data for Data A can be used to reconstruct Data A later.

Striping

RAID uses a method called striping to provide data redundancy. A stripe is basically a way of partitioning RAID disks into what appears to the operating system as one logical drive. Instead of storing data on only one disk, parts of the data are striped across multiple disks. RAID stripes range in size blocks of from 512KB up to several megabytes of information.

Striped data is written in order, not randomly dropped; therefore, when a file is written to a disk, the file is written across disk 1, disk 2, and so on,; order. When the file is read from the same disks, the source then knows how to read that data from multiple disks and then reassemble that data into a single file later.

Stripes on multi-user systems are typically large, stripes on single-user systems tend to be smaller. The more disks a given data block is striped across, the more quickly that data can be accessed. This is because more parts of that data can be accessed simultaneously when more disks are used. For example, a file that's 500MB striped across five disks can be accessed at a speed equivalent to if the file were 100MB in size. By contrast, if the same file were striped across 10 disks, you could access the file at a rate equivalent to if the file were 50MB in size. Figure 15-2 demonstrates this idea.

Disk striping with parity offers double the fault tolerance of typical disk striping, including parity information and data striping. See the "Parity" section earlier in the chapter for more information on parity. Figure 15-3 shows a simple example of disk striping with parity.

Note from the figure that the parity data for a given data set (say "Data A") is never stored on the same disk as part of the data itself. Therefore, if either part of Data A bites it, for example, the parity data for Data A is stored on another disk altogether.

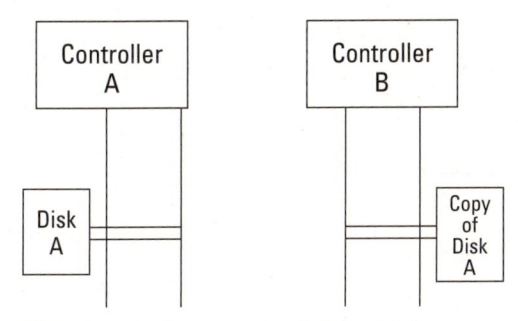

Figure 15-2: An example of data striping.

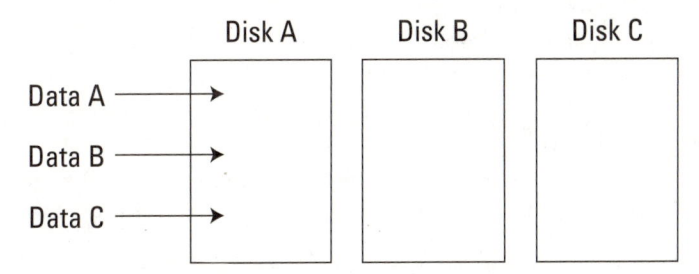

Figure 15-3: An example of data striping with parity.

Disk duplexing

Disk duplexing, also known as RAID 1, involves storing redundant data on not just two different disks but also two entirely different controllers. This way, if the controller of one data source is at fault for its unavailability, the redundant data is still accessible because it's not attached to the faulty controller. Figure 15-4 shows a simple example of disk duplexing.

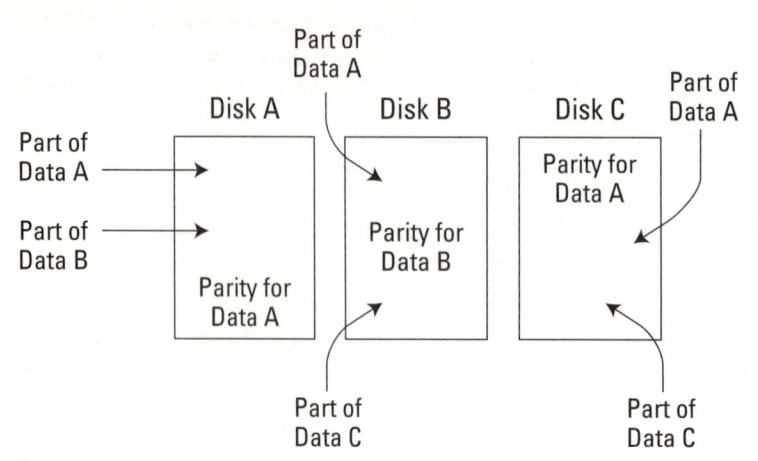

Figure 15-4: A simple example of disk duplexing.

Disk mirroring

Disk mirroring is simply a term for duplication of an entire disk, the simplest possible form of backup. See the definition for RAID 1 later in this chapter for information on how disk mirroring works.

Hardware vs. Software RAID

RAID can be implemented in one of two ways: via hardware or software. Software RAID is provided by the operating system. The disadvantages in such a configuration are as follows:

- ✦ The RAID solution is not available until the operating system responsible for implementing it is booted.
- ✦ Software RAID is slower than hardware RAID (anything implemented in hardware is usually faster than the same feature implemented via software).
- ✦ Because you cannot boot from a stripe set, a software RAID solution requires a separate boot partition.

The preferred method of RAID, and the most reliable, is hardware RAID. Hardware RAID is available without an operating system, and therefore an operating system partition is not required with hardware RAID.

Types of RAID

RAID technologies were first documented in 1987 in a paper entitled "A Case for Redundant Arrays of Inexpensive Disks" that was published by the University of Berkeley. That paper defined RAID levels 1–9 but did not define RAID 0 at all. Thus, although technically a RAID-0 would not be a true RAID at all, the RAID 0 designation has become as common a designation as the official RAID classifications.

Exam Tip

For the Network+ exam, concentrate on RAID 0, 1, and 5. Know their names as well as the minimum number of drives required for each level. RAID levels 6–9 aren't covered on the Network+ exam, and aren't used in modern networking often, and so aren't discussed here.

Table 15-1 sums up the facts about RAID that you should know for the exam:

Table 15-1
Network+ RAID Cheat Sheet

RAID Level	Function	Minimum Disks Required
0	Disk striping without data redundancy or parity	2
1	Disk mirroring	2
5	Disk striping with parity	3

The following list describes the major types of RAID:

- **RAID 0:** Also known as disk striping, RAID 0 isn't technically a RAID at all, because RAID by definition assumes redundancy of data and RAID 0 offers no redundancy of data whatsoever. Therefore, if you lose a drive in a RAID 0 solution, you will lose all the information on that drive if you don't have all the data backed up somewhere else. That is, a loss of one disk invalidates the data on all other disks.

In the Real World

Because RAID 0 offers higher performance than any of the legitimate RAID classifications, it is often used in networks that don't require a lot of fault tolerance

- **RAID 1:** Also known as disk mirroring, RAID 1 does not involve disk striping. Multiple hard drives (at least two) are used, but each drive contains a complete copy of the data on each of the other disks. RAID 1 does offer better read performance than versions of RAID that involve striping because both drives can be accessed for data at the same time. Write performance is identical to that of having a single drive.

Tip

RAID 1 offers the best performance and fault tolerance in a multi-user system, although with larger storage solutions the cost of RAID 1 can be prohibitive.

- **RAID 2:** Similar to RAID 1, RAID 2 adds error-checking and correction (ECC) information to some or all the disks (at least two) in the RAID. RAID 2 is rarely, if ever, used in modern enterprises.

- **RAID 3:** This RAID classification uses striping and ECC information, as with RAID 2, but RAID 3 stores all ECC information on one drive dedicated to that purpose. Because of the extra drive that's required for RAID 3, at least three disks are required for a RAID 3 implementation. RAID 3 is not typically used.

> **Exam Tip** When trying to remember which how many disks minimum each version of RAID requires for RAID 0-5, just remember that RAID 3 is the first RAID classification that requires three disks. All RAID versions above RAID 3 (up to and including RAID 5) also require a minimum of three disks. RAID 0, 1, and 2 all require a minimum of at least two disks.

- **RAID 4:** Nearly identical to the RAID 3 classification, RAID 4 uses larger stripes than RAID 3 so records can be read from any single drive. Due to the increased processing required to change parity information for large blocks of data, RAID 4 is slower than RAID 3.

- **RAID 5:** Also called disk striping with parity, RAID 5 stripes parity information across multiple disks instead of entirely redundant copies of data. Because data can be reconstructed from parity information, the effect of redundancy is still achieved. Striping the parity information across multiple disks enables data to be written by multiple sources simultaneously, unlike with RAID 4. A loss of two or more disks invalidates the remaining data on any surviving disks.

System-Area Networks

SANs connect multiple smaller computers to function as part of a larger computer system, allowing programs to use some — or all — of any workstation, server, or other network resource that's part of the SAN. A SAN doesn't have to use all the resources available to it at a given time, but it has the option to do so. This enables maximum flexibility, because the SAN can dynamically designate resource according to tasks, and then reassign those resources as needed when old tasks are finished or new ones are introduced. SANs are typically connected using high-speed network adapters, special adapter cards, and parallel-messaging software.

> **Note** Storage-area networks also use the acronym SAN. In this section, though, SAN refers to system-area network.

Some schools of thought define storage-area networks as a subset of the system-area network designation, and actually this definition does make sense; a storage-area network is really a system-area network devoted specifically to storage.

The main applications for system-area networks is for critical applications, Web servers, or databases that must be highly available at all times. Clustering can also ensure that not only do these resources continue to be available, but also that they perform better when they are available.

Summary

A network is not worth the silicon it's made from if critical network data is not properly safeguarded against the failure of network components. The following list sums up the key points discussed in this chapter:

- Backups are the first line of defense against data corruption.
- Fault tolerance is a measure of how tolerant your network is to component failure.
- RAID uses multiple disks to provide fault tolerance.
- System-area networks use clustering to provide maximum flexibility in scaling network resources.

✦ ✦ ✦

STUDY GUIDE

Assessment Questions

1. Which type of backup method is most commonly used in modern networks?

    A. Grandfather-father

    B. Father-son

    C. Grandmother-mother

    D. Grandfather-father-son

2. Which type of backup must be applied first when restoring from backup?

    A. The last copy of an incremental backup

    B. The last incremental backup

    C. The last differential backup

    D. The last full backup

3. What does incremental backup software do to a given file when it backs up that file?

    A. Sets the archive bit

    B. Clears the archive bit

    C. The subnet mask

    D. The sticky bit

4. Which of the following terms describes the process of evening out the load for a given server by clustering multiple machines together?

    A. Adapter teaming

    B. Failover

    C. Clustering

    D. Load-balancing

5. Which of the following acronyms stands for the mean time between failures of a given network or network component?

   A. ATBF

   B. MTBF

   C. MTF

   D. ATF

6. Which of the following types of storage by definition would protect data if an entire location became corrupt?

   A. Grandfather-father-son backups

   B. Off-site storage

   C. Disk duplexing

   D. Disk mirroring

7. Which of the following terms refers to the networking model in which one network component has a duplicate ready to take over in case the primary component fails?

   A. MTBF

   B. Disk striping

   C. Disk mirroring

   D. Failover

8. Which of the following terms describes the duplication of entire disks to increase fault tolerance and/or network performance?

   A. Disk striping

   B. Disk duplexing

   C. Disk mirroring

   D. Disk striping with parity

9. Which of the following terms describes the writing of data across multiple disks in an array?

   A. Disk striping

   B. Disk duplexing

   C. Disk mirroring

   D. Disk striping with parity

10. Which of the following terms describes disk mirroring on separate controllers?

    A. Disk striping

    B. Disk duplexing

    C. Disk mirroring

    D. Disk striping with parity

11. Which of the following terms also defines RAID 5?

    A. Disk striping

    B. Disk duplexing

    C. Disk mirroring

    D. Disk striping with parity

12. Which of the following types of RAID is not defined in the original RAID specification?

    A. RAID 0

    B. RAID 1

    C. RAID 3

    D. RAID 5

13. Which of the following types of RAID uses simple disk mirroring?

    A. RAID 0

    B. RAID 1

    C. RAID 3

    D. RAID 5

14. Which of the following types of RAID uses disk striping with no redundancy of data whatsoever?

    A. RAID 0

    B. RAID 1

    C. RAID 3

    D. RAID 5

15. Which of the following types of RAID uses disk striping with parity without error correction?

    A. RAID 0
    B. RAID 1
    C. RAID 3
    D. RAID 5

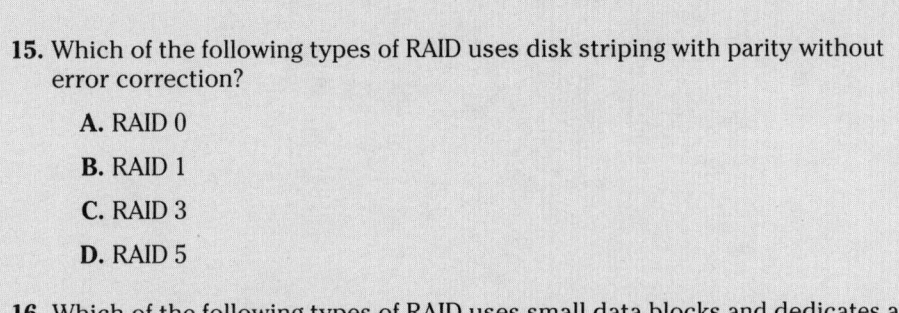

16. Which of the following types of RAID uses small data blocks and dedicates a single drive to parity?

    A. RAID 1
    B. RAID 2
    C. RAID 3
    D. RAID 4

17. Which of the following types of RAID uses large data blocks and dedicates a single drive to parity?

    A. RAID 1
    B. RAID 2
    C. RAID 3
    D. RAID 4

18. Which of the following networking concepts is considered a superset of storage-area networks?

    A. System-area networks
    B. Local-area networks
    C. Wide-area networks
    D. Super storage-area networks

19. Which of the following networking models clusters computers together in such a way that the resources of the resulting network can dynamically change depending on the tasks at hand?

    A. Adapter teaming
    B. System-area network
    C. Load balancing
    D. Network-attached storage

20. Which of the following terms describes the process of servers that use redundant lines in case the primary line goes down?

  A. Disk striping with parity

  B. System-area networks

  C. Disk duplexing

  D. Adapter teaming

Scenarios

1. You're an IT administrator for a company who has just lost access to a major location. The location used a grandfather-father-son backup scheme based on a five-day schedule. Today is Thursday, and the backup for Wednesday was the last successful incremental backup. The last full backup was the previous Friday. What do you do to restore the data from the lost location?

2. You're a consultant for a company who is deciding on what type of storage solution to use to best ensure the integrity of their data. The company doesn't want to break the bank, but they do want at least two levels of fault tolerance. What type of storage solution should you recommend?

Answers to Chapter Questions

Chapter Pre-Test

1. Available. Fault tolerance is a measure of how available network data is at all times. See the "Fault tolerance" section for more details.

2. Disaster recovery. Disaster recovery is the process of restoring data after failure of primary storage. See the "Backups" section for more information.

3. Backup. To keep data accessible, a network should have at least one backup of critical data available in case the original data should become corrupt or otherwise unavailable. See the "Backups" section for more information.

4. Failover. Failover refers to the model of having one component ready to replace a similar component if it should go bad. See the "Fault Tolerance" section for more information.

5. Failure. MTBF is the mean time between failures on a network. See the "Mean Time Between Failures (MTBF)" section for more information.

6. Off-site. Backup data that's stored in a separate geographical location from the original data is called off-site storage. See the "Backups" section for more information.

7. Load-balancing. Load balancing uses clusters of computers to help balance server load. See the "Load balancing" section for more information.

8. Redundant Array of Independent Disks. RAID stands for *Redundant Array of Independent Disks* — though if you said *inexpensive* instead of *independent*, you're still right: both terms are used for the "I" in RAID. See the "RAID!?!" section for more information.

9. Disk mirroring. RAID 1 uses disk mirroring to increase fault tolerance. See the "RAID!?!" section for more information.

10. Disk striping with parity. RAID 5 uses disk striping with parity to increase fault tolerance. See the "RAID!?!" section for more information.

Assessment Questions

1. D. Grandfather-father-son backups are most common in modern networks.
2. D. The last full backup must be applied first when restoring from backup.
3. A. Backup software sets or clears the archive bit of a file when it backs up that file.
4. D. The term *load balancing* describes the process of evening out the load for a given server by clustering multiple computers together.
5. B. The acronym for the mean time between failures is MTBF.
6. B. Off-site storage is the only given term that protects data if an entire network location becomes corrupt; by definition, it's at a different location.
7. D. Failover is the term for the networking model in which one network component has a duplicate ready to take over in case the primary component fails.
8. C. Disk mirroring is the duplication of entire disks to increase fault tolerance and/or network performance.
9. A. Disk striping describes the writing of data across multiple disks in an array.
10. B. Disk duplexing describes disk mirroring where the disks are actually on separate controllers.
11. D. Disk striping with parity also defines RAID 5.
12. A. RAID 0 is not defined in the original RAID specification.
13. B. RAID 1 users simple disk mirroring.
14. A. RAID 0 uses disk striping with no redundancy of data whatsoever.
15. D. RAID 5 uses disk striping with parity without error correction.
16. C. RAID 3 uses small data blocks and dedicates a single drive to parity.
17. D. RAID 4 uses large data blocks and dedicates a single drive to parity.

18. A. System-area networks are considered a superset of storage-area networks.

19. C. Load balancing is a technique that clusters computers in such a way that the resulting network's resources can be allocated dynamically in response to the tasks at hand.

20. D. *Adapter teaming* is the process of servers that use redundant lines in case the primary line goes down.

Scenarios

1. In this scenario, you should restore the last full backup (from Friday) and then apply the incremental backups from Monday, Tuesday, and Wednesday — in that order — to restore the files to their most recent state.

2. In this scenario, the company would probably do well with a RAID 5 solution, which offers two levels of fault tolerance.

CHAPTER 16

Configuring Remote Connectivity

EXAM OBJECTIVES

- Given a remote-connectivity scenario (for example, IP, IPX, dial-up, PPPoE, authentication, physical connectivity, and so on), configure the connection.

CHAPTER PRE-TEST

1. Two popular remote-connectivity solutions for corporate employees are _____ and _____.
2. Clients can connect to a RAS server using _____ and _____.
3. _____ enables encryption of IP data packets to protect the data being transmitted.
4. _____ offers a much faster communication speed than a standard telephone line.
5. _____ is a standard packet-switching communication protocol designed for WAN connectivity.
6. _____ is a challenge-response authentication protocol that uses the industry-standard Message Digest 5 (MD5) one-way encryption scheme to hash the response to a challenge issued by the remote-access server.
7. Name some tunneling and authentication protocols employed by VPNs.
8. _____ encapsulates data packets inside IP tunnels and creates a virtual point-to-point link with routers at remote locations across an IP network.
9. _____ enables secure data transfer over IP-based networks and supports multiprotocol, virtual private networking over public networks such as the Internet.
10. Three types of VPNs are _____, _____, and _____.
11. For secure VPN connections using PPTP, non-Microsoft VPN clients must support _____.

✦ Answers to these questions can be found at the end of this chapter. ✦

Organizations today operate across locations spread all over the world. Employees are constantly on the move. In this scenario, employees want access to their information at any time, from any place. Whether on the move, with customers, or working from home, there is a critical need for employees to access the corporate network. *Remote access* — a capability that enables employees to access their private networks securely from remote locations — has given new life to businesses by answering this need.

Specialized *remote-access servers* provide connectivity to private networks for authorized users, however far-flung. This transparent connection enables clients at remote locations to access network resources, sometimes almost as efficiently as local in-house users with a direct, physical connection to the network.

This chapter presents some remote-connectivity technologies and shows how to configure remote-access connections.

Remote Access Services (RAS)

Windows NT/2000 offers an in-built service called Remote Access Service (RAS) that enables users to log on to an NT/2000-based network remotely. Using RAS, users can log in to a remote network using a dial-up modem, an X.25 connection, or a WAN link. Remote clients can dial in from remote locations and access resources as if they were physically attached to a network. Using RAS, remote clients can establish a transparent connection to a remote-access server. such a connection is called a point-to-point remote-access connection. Clients can also transparently connect to a network to which the remote-access server is connected. This is called point-to-LAN remote-access connection.

Clients can connect to the RAS server using telephone lines and a modem. Faster links are possible using Integrated Services Digital Network (ISDN). RAS clients can also connect using X.25 or the Point-to-Point Tunneling Protocol (PPTP).

RAS is available with Windows 9x as well. In Windows 9x, RAS is installed by default. Dial-up networking starts automatically when any application attempts to connect to a remote machine. On NT/2000, however, RAS is not installed until you add a modem device to the system configuration. Under Windows NT/2000, dial-up networking does not start automatically. The user must explicitly dial a remote machine using RAS. With Dial-Up Networking installed, users can use the phonebook feature of Windows to record telephone numbers that they need to connect and disconnect from remote networks.

RAS is both a dial-in and a dial-out utility. As a dial-in utility, RAS can be configured to support modems up to 256 serial ports that can be configured into a modem pool. Dial-out capability enables the user of RAS computer to dial-out to remote RAS hosts.

RAS is compatible with most major networking protocols, including TCP/IP, IPX, and NetBEUI.

The Windows 2000 server supports five new protocols for remote network access. These are as follows:

- **Extensible Authentication Protocol (EAP):** EAP is an open standard and a source for support for Windows 2000 that enables authentication methods to be written for technologies including token cards and biometrics.

- **Remote Authentication Dial-In User Service (RADIUS):** RADIUS acts as an Internet Authentication Server (IAS) that provides user authentication, maintains audit logs, and performs accounting of call statistics.

- **Layer 2 Tunneling Protocol (L2TP):** L2TP supports a variety of routed protocols, such as IP, IPX, and AppleTalk. It also supports a variety of backbone technologies, such as Frame Relay and X.25.

- **Internet Protocol Security (IPSec):** IPSec enables encryption of IP data packets to protect the data being transmitted. It provides encryption security services to ensure integrity and authenticity of data packets.

- **Bandwidth Allocation Protocol (BAP):** BAP enables you to get additional bandwidth when you require it due to extensive traffic on ISDN lines.

During the course of this chapter, we discuss the features of RAS, connection methods, security issues, as well as installation and configuration of RAS.

Features of RAS

Important features of RAS include the following:

- **RAS supports multi-protocol routing.** The RAS architecture enables clients to run any combination of the network protocols NetBEUI, TCP/IP, or IPX during a RAS session.

- **RAS supports a variety of remote clients.** These include Windows 9*x*, Windows NT/2000, MS DOS, and LAN Manager. Clients can also be non-Microsoft PPP clients.

- **RAS supports a high level of security.** Dial-in users are authenticated by Windows NT/2000 Server standard security. Additional security is available through the callback facility, which can check if the number of the calling client computer is authentic.

- **RAS supports WAN connectivity.** Clients can connect to a RAS server using PSTN and modems, ISDN, X.25, and PPTP.

WAN Connectivity

Remote clients can access a RAS server using various methods including dial-up modems and WAN links. These methods are as follows:

- **PSTN and modems:** RAS uses standard modem connections over Public Switched Telephone Networks (PSTNs). Most modems can interoperate with other modems. Windows NT/2000 can automatically detect modems. It is also possible to install a modem manually through the Phone and Modem options in the Control Panel.

- **ISDN:** ISDN offers a much faster communication speed than a standard telephone line. An ISDN line must be installed at both the server and at the remote site. In addition, an ISDN card must also be installed in place of a modem in both the server and remote clients.

- **X.25:** This standard packet-switching communication protocol is designed for WAN connectivity. RAS supports connections that conform to the X.25 standard by using Packet Assembler/Disassembler (PADs) and X.25 smart cards.

- **PPTP:** RAS also enables access to remote users through the Internet by using PPTP.

When PSTN, ISDN or X.25 is used, remote clients establish PPP connections with a RAS server over a switched network. In contrast, when PPTP is used, instead of using a switching connection to send packets over a WAN, a transport protocol such as TCP/IP sends the PPP packets to the RAS server over a virtual WAN.

RAS connection methods

RAS connections can be established using the Point-to-Point Protocol (PPP), the Serial Line Internet Protocol (SLIP), or a Microsoft RAS DOS client.

PPP

RAS supports Point-to-Point Protocol (PPP). PPP is a set of industry-standard protocols that enables RAS clients and servers to interoperate in a multi-vendor network. PPP support enables computers running Windows NT/2000 to dial in to remote networks through any server that complies with the PPP standard. The PPP architecture also enables clients to load any combination of protocols, such as IPX, TCP/IP, and NetBEUI. PPP also supports dynamic IP address assignment.

SLIP

Serial Line Internet Protocol (SLIP) is a basic protocol developed mainly for the UNIX environment. SLIP has several limitations in comparison to PPP. SLIP requires a static IP address. It supports TCP/IP, but it does not support IPX/SPX or NetBEUI. Windows NT, therefore, does not have SLIP built-in and cannot be used as a SLIP server.

Microsoft RAS Protocol

Microsoft RAS Protocol, also known as *Asynchronous NetBEUI* or *AsyBEUI*, is a remote-access protocol for various Microsoft operating systems.

RAS security

Windows NT/2000 user accounts and domains provide security by using encrypted authentication. RAS provides additional security features, such as callback and data encryption. Third-party security hosts can also be installed to prevent unauthorized access to the network through a Remote Access Server. Let us now discuss some security features of RAS.

Authentication

Windows NT/2000 can authenticate RAS users. If no third-party authentication mechanisms are employed, user credentials are verified by the default Windows NT/2000 authentication mechanism. Either Windows NT/2000 or RADIUS (Remote Authentication Dial-In User Service) can be used as the authentication provider.

Encrypted authentication

Remote users must be authenticated by a remote-access server before they can access resources or generate traffic on the network. User passwords and the authentication procedures are encrypted when transmitted over telephone lines.

RAS uses the Challenge Handshake Authentication Protocol (CHAP) to provide an appropriate response to a server's challenge. The goal is to negotiate the most secure form of encrypted authentication that both the server and client can support.

When a remote-access server issues a challenge, the Challenge Handshake Authentication Protocol (CHAP) uses Message Digest 5 (MD5) — the industry-standard one-way encryption scheme — to hash the response. (CHAP can also use different types of encryption algorithms.)

CHAP authentication involves exchange of three messages:

1. The remote-access server sends a CHAP Challenge message containing a session ID and an arbitrary challenge string.

2. The remote-access client returns a CHAP Response message that contains the username in cleartext and a hash of the challenge string, session ID, and the client's password using the MD5 one-way hashing algorithm.

3. The remote-access server duplicates the hash and compares it to the hash in the CHAP Response.

    If the hashes are the same, the remote-access server sends back a CHAP Success message. If the hashes are different, a CHAP Failure message is sent.

Encrypted exchange of user credentials can also happen via Microsoft Challenge Handshake Authentication Protocol versions 1 and 2 (MS-CHAPv1 and MS-CHAPv2). MS-CHAPv1 is a non-reversible, encrypted, password-authentication protocol. MS-CHAPv2, on the other hand, offers more security for remote-access connections. MS-CHAPv2 is a mutual authentication process that uses a one-way, encrypted password.

When connecting to third-party remote-access servers or client software, RAS can negotiate to the Shiva Password Authentication Protocol (SPAP) or cleartext authentication if the third-party product does not support encrypted authentication. The Shiva Password Authentication Protocol (SPAP) is a two-way, reversible encryption mechanism. SPAP does not offer security against remote server impersonation.

The Password Authentication Protocol (PAP) uses clear-text passwords and is the least sophisticated authentication protocol. The username and password are requested by the remote-access server and returned by the remote-access client in cleartext. PAP, however, is not a secure authentication protocol.

Callback

RAS offers a callback feature, which ensures that only users from specific locations can access the RAS server. When using callback, the user initiates a call and connects with the RAS server, and disconnects. The server then calls the client back at a preset phone number or at a number that was provided during the initial call.

Intermediary security hosts

RAS supports various kinds of intermediary devices between the remote-access client and the remote-access server. These devices include modem pools, security hosts, and X.25 networks.

A *security host* is a third-party authentication device that verifies whether a caller from a remote client is authorized to connect to the remote-access server. This verification supplements the security provided by RAS and the Windows NT/2000 server itself.

The security host is normally placed between the remote user and the RAS server. The security host prompts the remote user to type a username and a password before the connection is established.

Auditing

With auditing, RAS generates audit information on all remote connections. The audit information is logged and can be viewed by using the Event Viewer.

PPTP filtering

PPTP filtering allows only PPTP packets to enter the network; network adapters for all other protocols are disabled. Clients outside the network can use PPTP to connect to the computer through the Internet and gain secure access to a remote network.

RAS architecture

RAS architecture is based on various components, including drivers, libraries, and interfaces. The major components serve the following functions:

- ✦ RAS uses protocols such as TCP/IP, IPX, NetBEUI, and AppleTalk. The communication between the remote networks is established using NetBIOS gateways and IP and IPX routers.

- ✦ RAS consists of packet-level interfaces to protocols, such as TCP/IP, IPX, NetBEUI, and AppleTalk. The NDIS (Network Driver Interface Specification) wrapper, Ndis.sys, provides these interfaces.

- ✦ An intermediate NDIS driver enables communication between the protocol and *miniport drivers* — 32-bit, protected-mode device drivers that Windows uses to control devices.

    The intermediate driver is called the NDISWAN driver, `Ndiswan.sys`. This provides encryption and compression services to remote connections.

- ✦ A series of libraries provide the RAS programming interface for applications, link controls, network-control protocols, and remote-access protocols.

NetBIOS gateway

Windows NT supports the NetBIOS gateway. Remote users can connect to the RAS server by using NetBEUI, and the RAS server translates packets to IPX or TCP/IP. The NetBIOS gateway is the default gateway when remote clients use NetBEUI. This enables users to share network resources in a multi-protocol LAN, but prevents them from running applications that rely on IPX or TCP/IP on the client.

IP/IPX router

Routing Information Protocol (RIP) facilitates the exchange of routing information. It enables a router to exchange information with neighboring routers. Installing RIP for IP provides dynamic routing. When RIP for IP is installed, the RIP routing service is automatically enabled. To enable IPX routing, the IPX protocol and RIP for IPX must be installed. Service Advertising Protocol (SAP) agent is automatically installed. This is similar to the Windows Browser Service. When it is configured, the RAS servers enable remote clients to access NetWare files and print services, and to take advantage of Windows Sockets applications.

The RAS communication process using NetBIOS gateway and IP/IPX routing is illustrated in Figure 16-1.

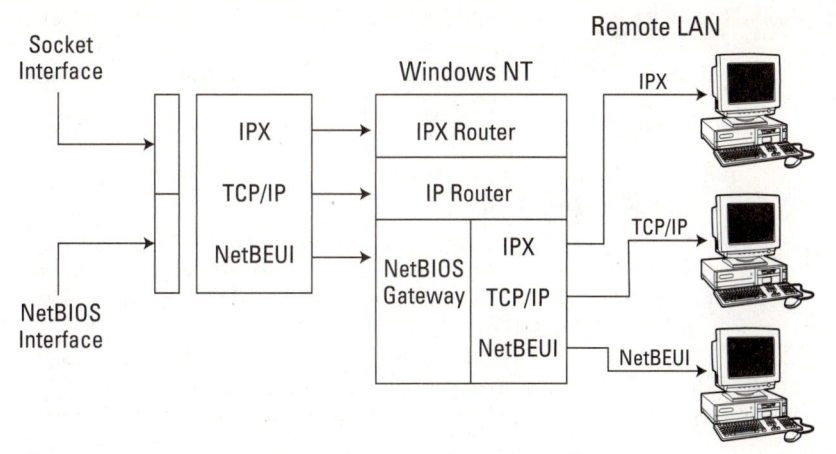

Figure 16-1: RAS — NetBIOS gateway and IP/IPX routing.

Installing and Configuring RAS

In this section we will learn how to install RAS in a Windows 2000 environment. We will also learn to configure the network settings, protocols, and communication ports.

Hardware requirements

Before you begin installing RAS on your system, verify if you have all the required hardware. To install RAS, you'll need the following:

✦ A network adapter card with an NDIS driver

✦ A compatible modem and an available COM port

✦ If you use X.25 network, an X.25 smart card

✦ An ISDN card if you use an ISDN line

Installing RAS

When you install a Windows 2000 server, RAS is automatically installed — but it is disabled (by default). To use the service, you have to start the service — which is called Routing and Remote Access (RRAS).

If your computer is a part of an Active Directory domain, add your computer to the RAS and IAS servers security group. You, as an administrator, can do so by using Active Directory Users and Computers option, or with the following command:

```
netsh ras add registeredserver
```

Installing remote-client protocols

You can configure your server to provide access to remote clients that use TCP/IP, IPX, or NetBEUI. To do so, however, you must install all these protocols on your server. You can install protocols by using the Network and Dial-up Connections option in the Control Panel. To add protocols, follow these steps:

1. Open the Control Panel and double-click Network and Dial-up Connections to open the Network and Dial-up Connections window as shown in Figure 16-2.

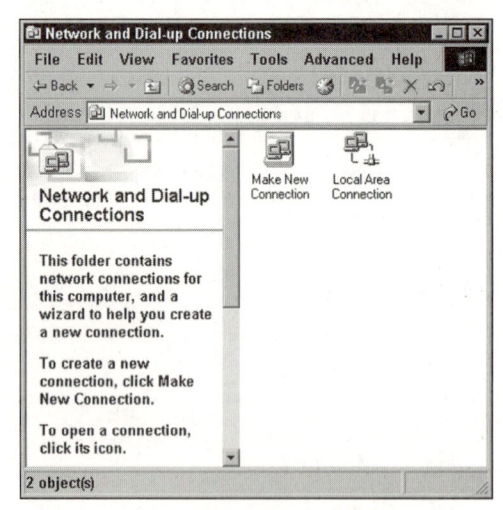

Figure 16-2: The Network and Dial-up Connections window.

2. Right-click Local Area Connection and select Properties to open the Local Area Connections Properties window shown in Figure 16-3.

3. Select Install.

4. In the Select Network Component Type dialog box, select Protocol and select Add.

5. From the Select Network Protocol dialog box, select the appropriate protocol and then select OK. Then close the Local Area Connections dialog box.

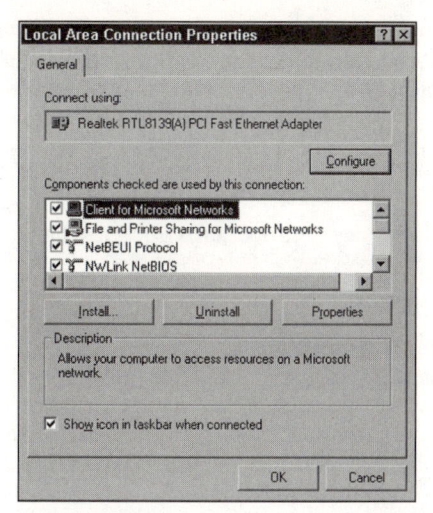

Figure 16-3: The Local Area Connections Properties window.

Enabling and configuring RRAS

To enable RRAS and configure the settings, follow these steps:

1. From the Control Panel, double-click Administrative Tools, and then double-click Routing and Remote Access to open the Routing and Remote Access window, as shown in Figure 16-4.

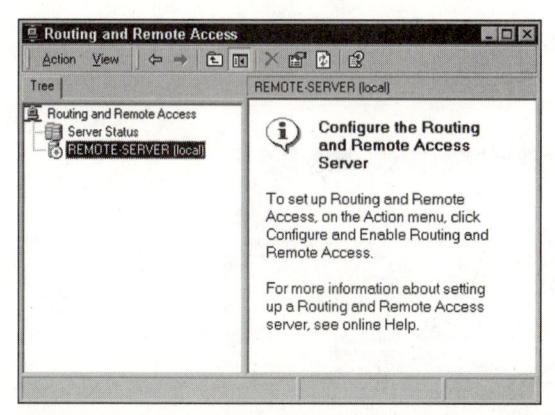

Figure 16-4: The Routing and Remote Access window.

Note Alternatively, you can get to this window by selecting Start ➪ Programs ➪ Administrative Tools ➪ Routing and Remote Access.

2. You can see that the local computer is listed by default as a RAS server. To add another server, select Action ➪ Add Server. From the Add Server dialog box, select the appropriate option and select OK. The Server name appears in the Tree.

3. To enable RRAS, right-click the appropriate server in the Tree and select Configure and Enable Routing and Remote Access.

4. The Routing and Remote Access Server Setup Wizard appears, as shown in Figure 16-5. Select Next.

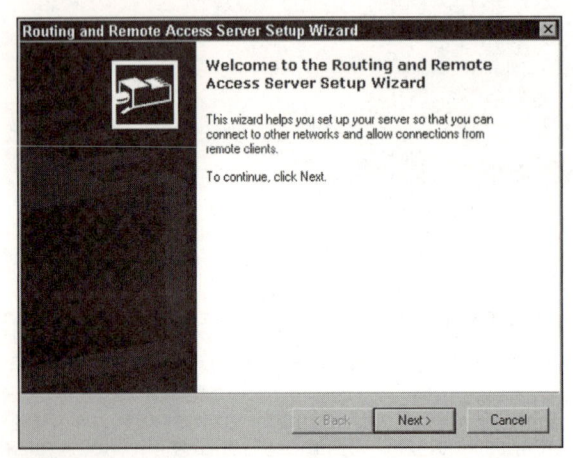

Figure 16-5: The Routing and Remote Access Server Setup Wizard.

5. From the list of configuration options, as shown in Figure 16-6, choose Remote access server and then select Next.

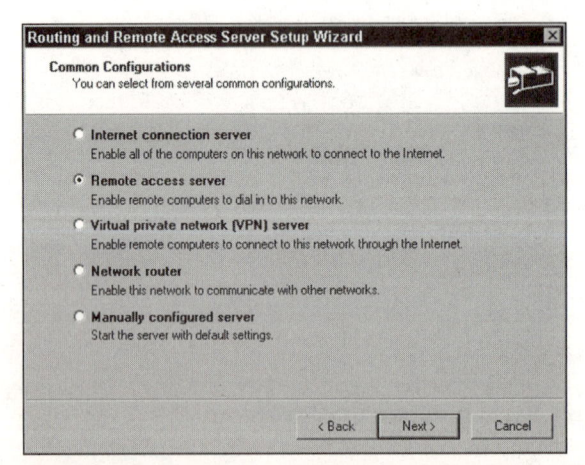

Figure 16-6: Common configuration options in the wizard.

6. Verify that the remote-client protocols you need are listed, as shown in Figure 16-7. If not, add the protocols you want to use on the server for remote access and then select Next.

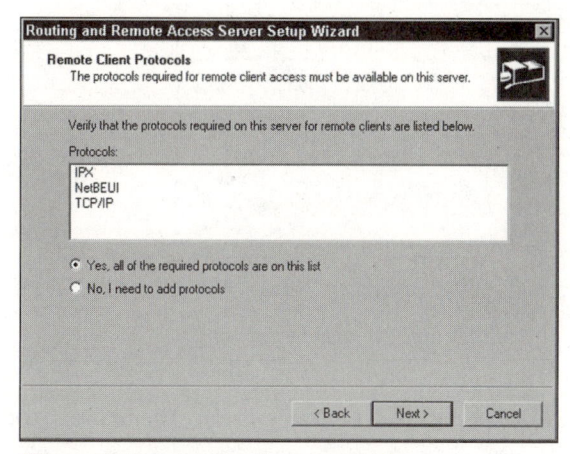

Figure 16-7: Remote-client protocols.

7. Assign the IP addresses to remote clients, as shown in Figure 16-8. You can either use DHCP (Dynamic Host Configuration Protocol) to automatically assign the IP addresses or you can specify a range of addresses to be used for the remote clients. Select Next after you have specified the IP addresses.

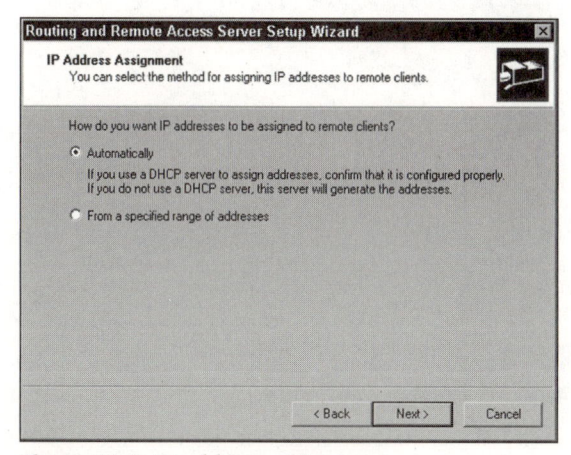

Figure 16-8: IP address assignment.

8. Select if you want to use RADIUS for remote user authentication, as shown in Figure 16-9. Windows 2000 provides a RADIUS solution called the Internet Authentication Service (IAS) as an optional component that you can install through Add/Remove Programs.

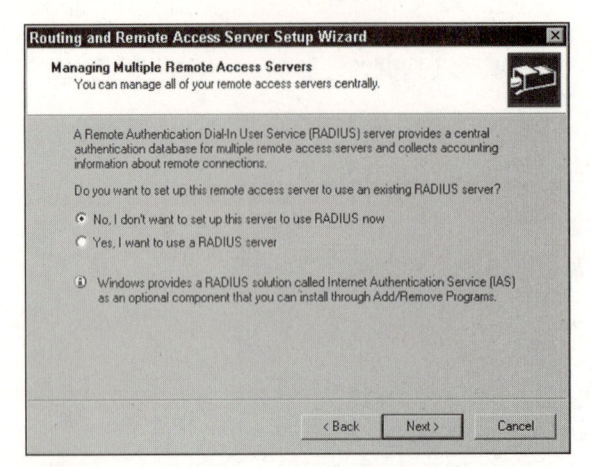

Figure 16-9: Managing multiple remote-access servers.

If you want to use RADIUS for authentication, specify the name of the RADIUS server.

After specifying the authentication method, select Next.

9. Select Finish to enable Routing and Remote Access on your computer, as shown in Figure 16-10. The server components appear in the Routing and Remote Access Microsoft Management Console (RRAS MMC).

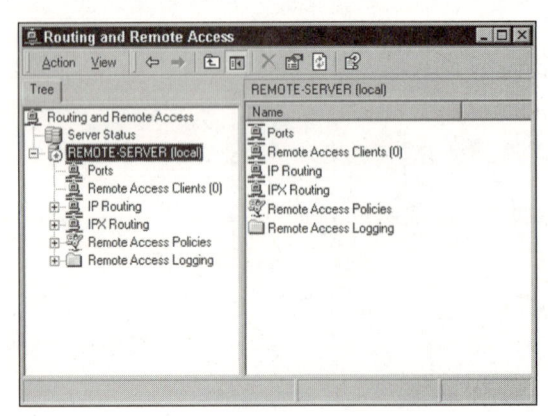

Figure 16-10: Remote Server Components in the RRAS MMC.

10. Right-click the server in the RRAS MMC and select Properties, as shown in Figure 16-11.

   Use the Properties dialog box to configure your server as a remote-access server.

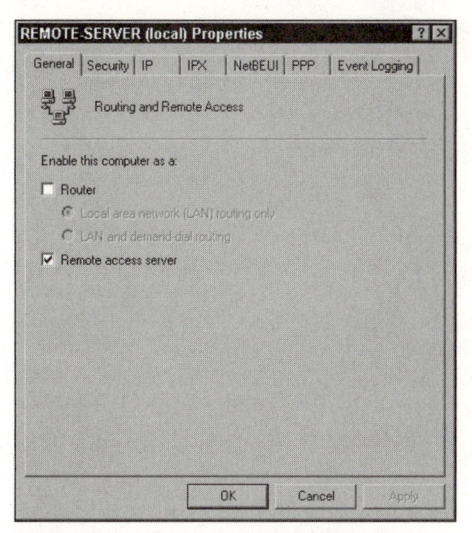

Figure 16-11: Remote Server Properties — the General tab.

11. Select the Security tab, as shown in Figure 16-12. Here you can specify the authentication and accounting providers to be used.

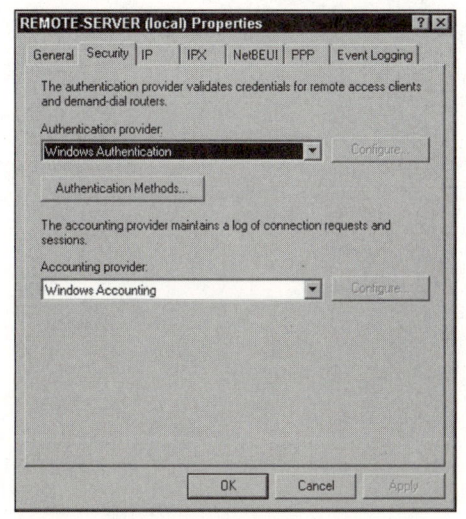

Figure 16-12: Remote Server Properties — the Security tab.

12. Select the Authentication Methods button and then choose the authentication method you want to use for your remote clients, as shown in Figure 16-13.

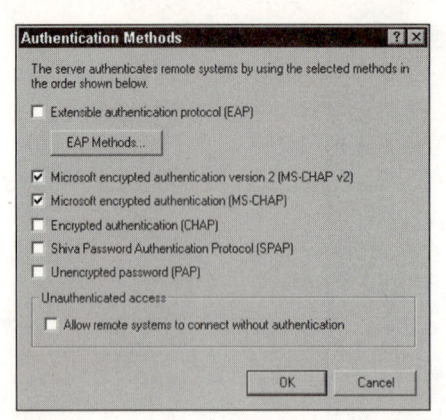

Figure 16-13: Authentication Methods.

13. Select the IP tab, as shown in Figure 16-14. You can specify the range of addresses to be used for your remote clients by selecting Static address pool and then selecting Add. If you need a range of more than 254 addresses, span the address range across more than one subnet.

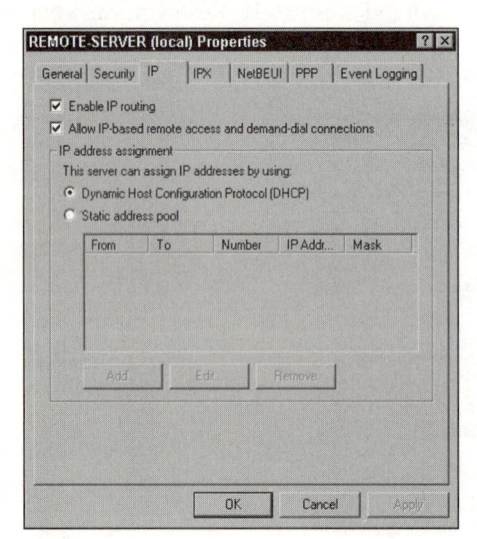

Figure 16-14: Remote Server Properties — the IP tab.

14. Select the IPX tab, as shown in Figure 16-15. You can specify if demand-dial connection should be enabled. You can also assign IPX network numbers for the clients, or you can let the server assign the network numbers automatically.

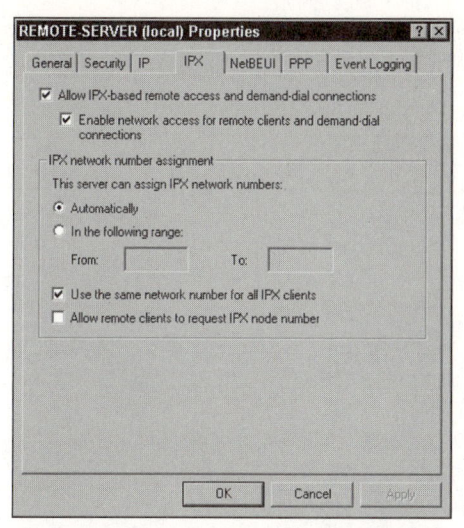

Figure 16-15: Remote Server Properties — the IPX tab.

15. Select the NetBEUI tab, as shown in Figure 16-16. Select *Entire network* to enable clients to access all resources on the network.

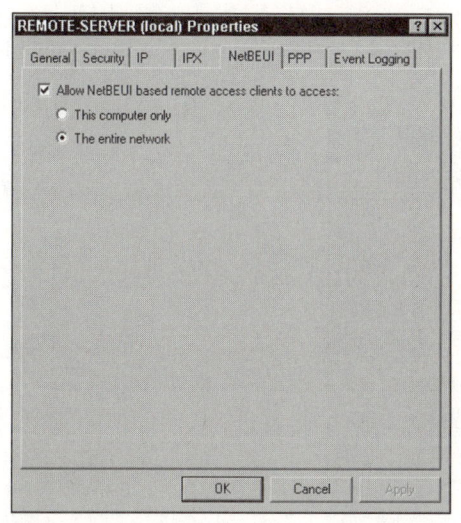

Figure 16-16: Remote Server Properties — the NetBEUI tab.

16. Select the PPP tab, as shown in Figure 16-17. You can enable multilink connections here.

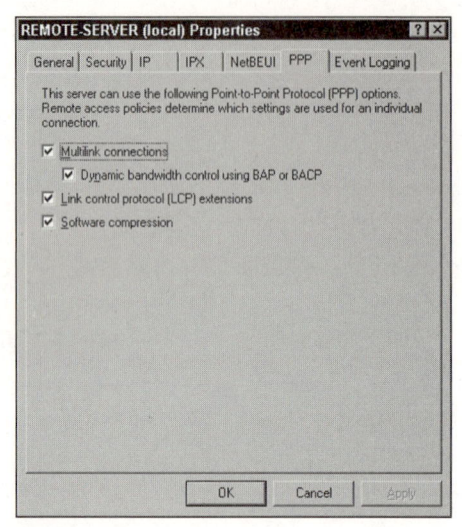

Figure 16-17: Remote Server Properties — the PPP tab.

17. Select the Event Logging tab, as shown in Figure 16-18. Select Log the maximum amount of information for help in troubleshooting connectivity problems.

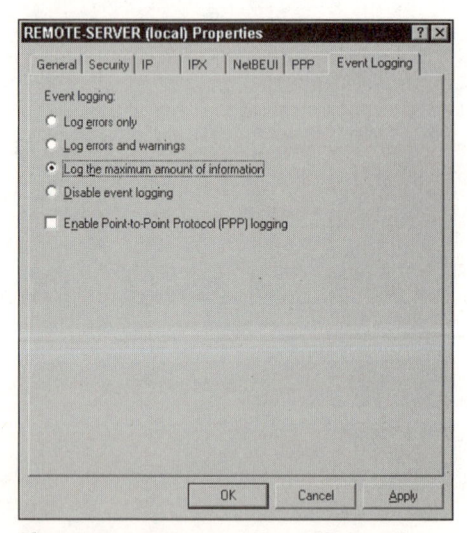

Figure 16-18: Remote Server Properties — the Event Logging tab.

Chapter 16 ✦ Configuring Remote Connectivity 399

18. Click OK to close the Remote Server — Properties dialog box.
19. Right-click Ports in the RRAS MMC and select Properties, as shown in Figure 16-19.

    In the Port Properties dialog box, you can configure your ports to use PPTP or L2TP. Use L2TP if you want to use IPSec.

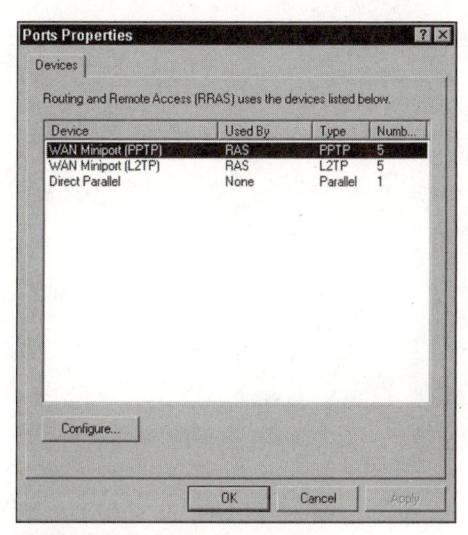

Figure 16-19: Port Properties.

20. Select WAN Miniport (PPTP) and then select Configure, as shown in Figure 16-20. Under PPTP Port Configuration, select *Remote access connections (inbound only)*. Select the number of ports you want (you can configure up to 16,384 ports). Click OK.

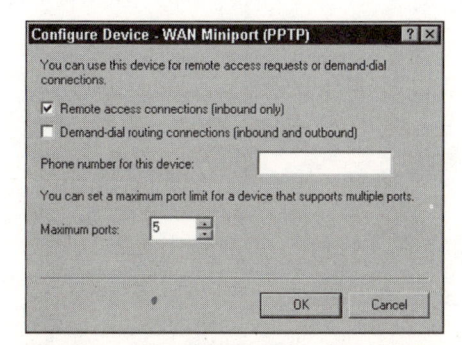

Figure 16-20: PPTP Port Configuration.

21. Click OK in the Ports Properties dialog box.
22. You can see the ports that you defined in the RRAS MMC, as shown in Figure 16-21.

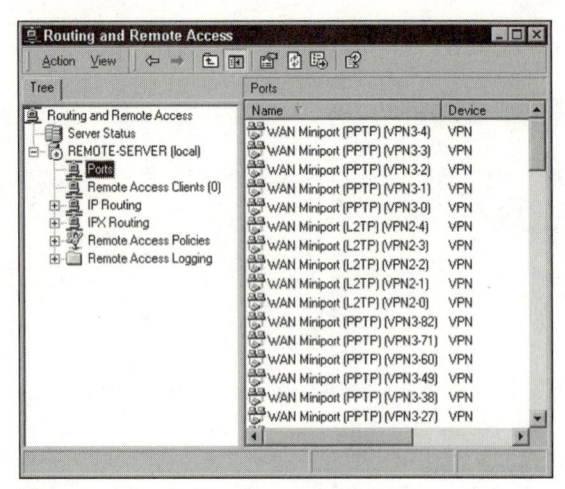

Figure 16-21: Defined ports for RAS.

23. From the RRAS MMC, select Remote Access Logging, as shown in Figure 16-22.

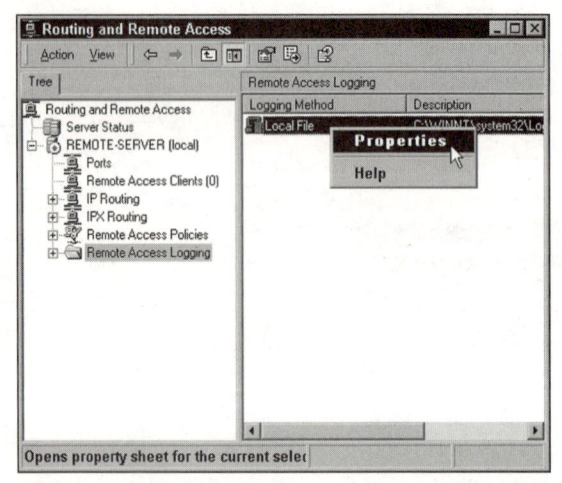

Figure 16-22: Remote Access Logging — Local File in the RRAS MMC.

24. In the right pane, right-click Local File and select Properties, as shown in Figure 16-23.

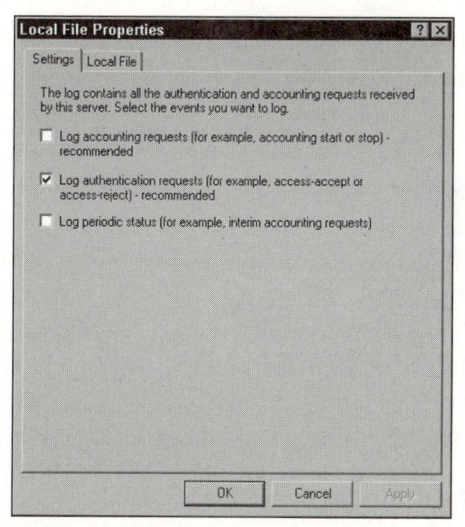

Figure 16-23: Local File Properties.

25. Select Log authentication requests and select OK.

    This procedure tells the system to log all attempts to connect to the server.

This completes the configuration of your RAS server, the network settings, RAS protocols, and the ports.

Configuring Dial-up Networking

To access services provided by a RAS server, enable dial-up connections on the client machine. Create a new connection using the Network and Dial-up Connections option in the Control Panel.

Creating a dial-up connection

To create a new dial-up connection:

1. Open the Control Panel and double-click Network and Dial-up Connections.
2. Double-click Make New Connection to start the Network Connection Wizard and select Next.
3. Select Dial-up to private network and select Next, as shown in Figure 16-24.

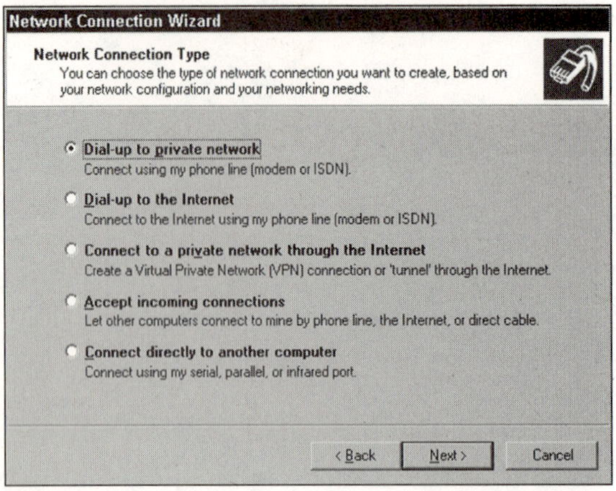
Network Connection Wizard
Network Connection Type
You can choose the type of network connection you want to create, based on your network configuration and your networking needs.
Dial-up to private network
Connect using my phone line (modem or ISDN).
Dial-up to the Internet
Connect to the Internet using my phone line (modem or ISDN).
Connect to a private network through the Internet
Create a Virtual Private Network (VPN) connection or 'tunnel' through the Internet.
Accept incoming connections
Let other computers connect to mine by phone line, the Internet, or direct cable.
Connect directly to another computer
Connect using my serial, parallel, or infrared port.
< Back
Next >
Cancel

Figure 16-24: Selecting network connection type.

4. Specify the phone number you want to dial to as shown in Figure 16-25. If you want to specify the area code and the country you want to dial to, select Use dialing rules. Select Next to specify the connection availability.

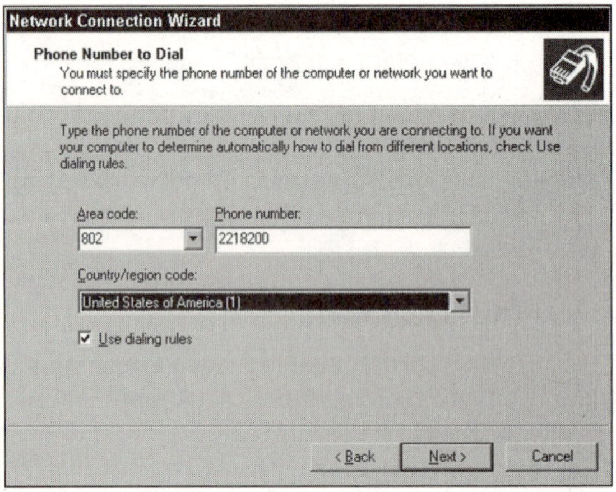
Network Connection Wizard
Phone Number to Dial
You must specify the phone number of the computer or network you want to connect to.
Type the phone number of the computer or network you are connecting to. If you want your computer to determine automatically how to dial from different locations, check Use dialing rules.
Area code:
Phone number:
802
2218200
Country/region code:
United States of America (1)
Use dialing rules
< Back
Next >
Cancel

Figure 16-25: Specifying the phone number to dial.

5. Select *For all users* if you want to make this connection available to all users, and then select Next as shown in Figure 16-26.

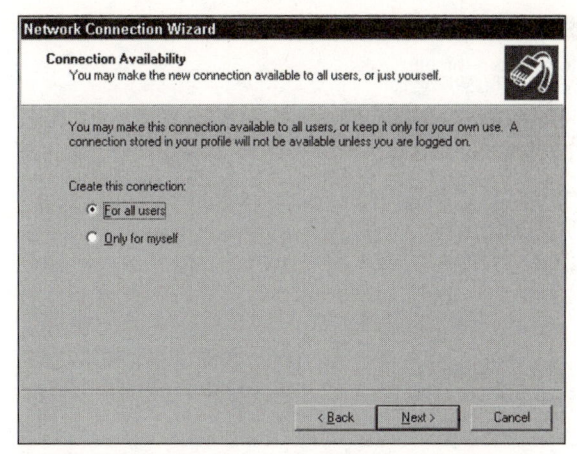

Figure 16-26: Specifying connection availability.

6. Specify whether you want to enable Internet connection sharing and then select Next as shown in Figure 16-27.

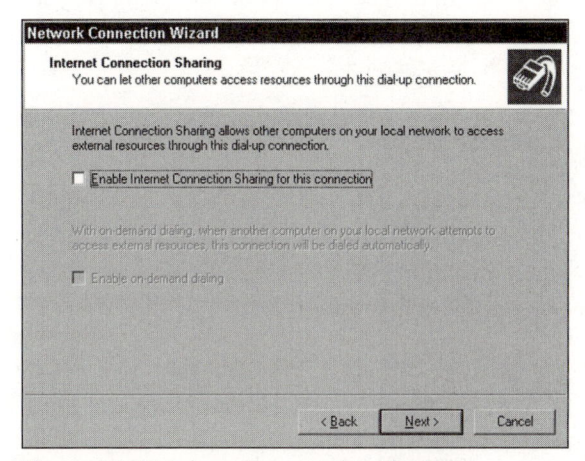

Figure 16-27: Internet connection sharing.

7. Specify a name for the connection and then select Finish as shown in Figure 16-28.

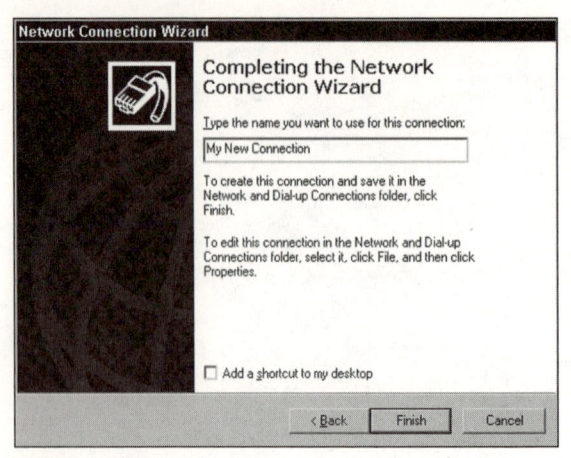

Figure 16-28: Naming the connection.

Configuring a dial-up connection

To configure a new dial-up connection, follow these steps:

1. Right-click the new connection and select Properties. In the General tab you can configure the modem as shown in Figure 16-29. You can also change the connection information.

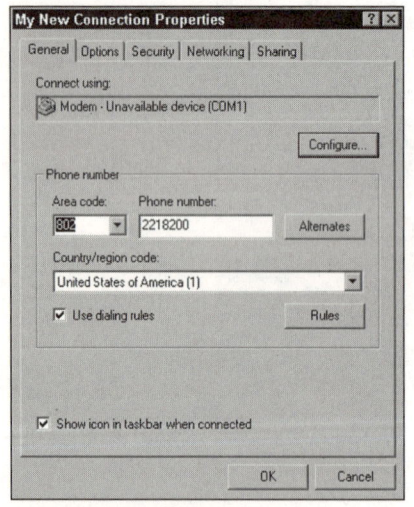

Figure 16-29: New Connection Properties — General Tab.

2. Select the Options tab. Here you can specify the dialing and redialing options as shown in Figure 16-30. If you have an X.25 connection, you can configure it by selecting the X.25 button.

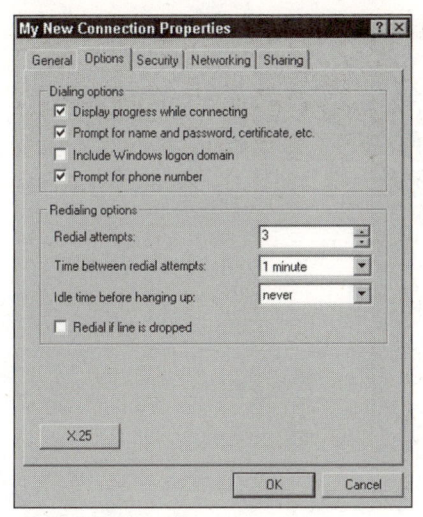

Figure 16-30: New Connection Properties — Options tab.

3. Select the Security tab as shown in Figure 16-31. Select Advanced (custom settings). Select the Settings button. You can specify the authentication protocols to be used for this connection.

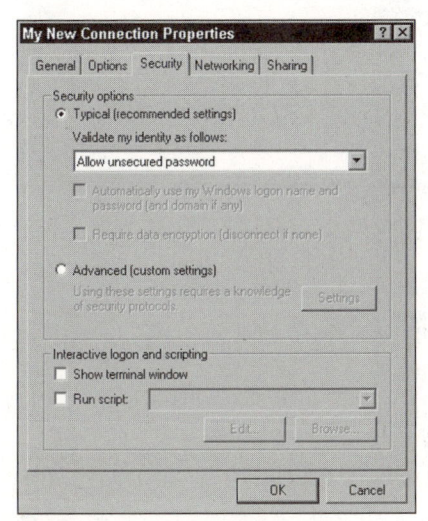

Figure 16-31: New Connection Properties — Security tab.

4. Select the Networking tab as shown in Figure 16-32. You can specify the protocols and services available for this connection.

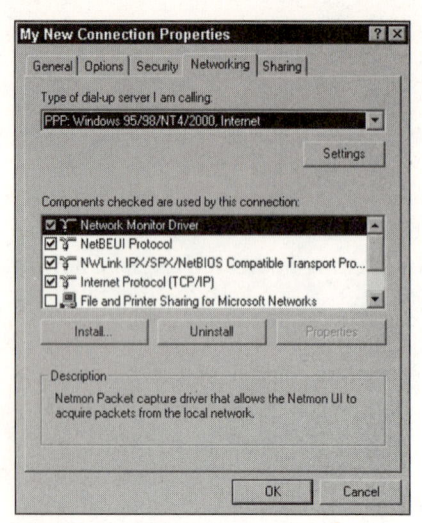

Figure 16-32: New Connection Properties — Networking tab.

5. Select the Sharing tab as shown in Figure 16-33. You can enable Internet connection sharing for this connection.

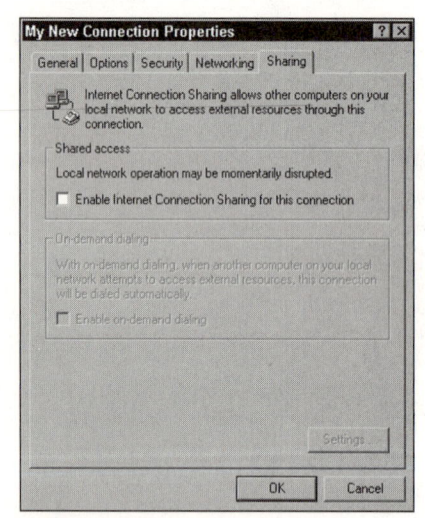

Figure 16-33: New Connection Properties — Sharing tab.

6. Select OK to configure your dial-up connection.

This procedure completes the process of setting up a RAS server and configuring dial-up access to it.

Virtual Private Networking (VPN)

An increasingly popular remote-connectivity option is *virtual private networking*, or VPN — a network solution that uses existing dedicated internal networks and Internet connections to share sensitive information with greater safety. Virtual private networking provides a secure communication over the Internet that enables remote employees and business partners to securely access their private corporate network. VPNs provide data privacy, access control, data integrity, and authentication services at a low level in the network and are independent of the applications using the network. VPN links connect two networks in such a way that they act as one secure network — and are perceived that way by the operating system.

VPN technology works to provide a dedicated secure communication channel between networked computers. VPNs use advanced encryption technologies to establish secure, end-to-end, private network connections over public networks, such as the Internet. VPNs employ tunneling and authentication protocols, such as L2TP (Layer 2 Tunneling Protocol), PPTP (Point-to-Point Tunneling Protocol), IPSec (IP Security), and CHAP (Challenge Handshake Authentication Protocol) to provide secure communication. Authentication techniques such as digital certificates are also often used.

VPN protocols

Many protocols support VPN implementation. Most VPN protocols use tunneling to enable VPN features. Tunneling is a mechanism to encapsulate data within protocols. A tunneling protocol is a standard that manages tunnels and encapsulates data. A tunnel is that part of the network connection that contains the encapsulated data packets. These encapsulated data packets are then transferred from one network to another by using dedicated tunnels.

The most common tunneling protocols used for VPN implementation are as follows:

✦ **Generic Routing Encapsulation (GRE):** This is probably one of the most common tunneling protocols. GRE encapsulates data packets inside IP tunnels and creates a virtual point-to-point link with routers at remote locations across an IP network.

✦ **Layer 2 Forwarding (L2F):** L2F encapsulates data packets into Point-to-Point Protocol (PPP) before transmitting them to an L2F server. The L2F server then de-encapsulates these packets before forwarding them to the destination. It supports multiple tunnel connections from the same Virtual Private Dialup Network (VPDN) client.

- **Point-to-Point Tunneling Protocol (PPTP):** is an extension of PPP. PPTP enables secure data transfer over IP-based networks. PPTP supports multiprotocol, virtual private networking over public networks, such as the Internet.
- **Layer 2 Tunneling Protocol (L2TP):** L2TP supports a variety of routed protocols, such as IP, IPX, and AppleTalk. It also supports a variety of backbone technologies, such as Frame Relay and X.25. L2TP enables VPDN and combines the best features of L2F and PPTP.
- **Microsoft Point-to-Point Encryption (MPPE):** MPPE enables VPN over dial-up networks. MPPE encrypts PPP packets to provide data integrity.
- **Internet Protocol Security (IPSec):** IPSec enables encryption of IP data packets to protect the data being transmitted. It provides encryption security services to ensure integrity and authenticity of data packets.

Types of VPNs

VPNs fall into three general categories that each have a characteristic scope, implementation, and usability. The categories are

- **Remote-access VPN:** Remote-access VPNs connect mobile users, telecommuters, and remote offices to the enterprise network over a shared public network. Remote-access VPNs help reduce communication expenses by using the dial-up infrastructures of an ISP for establishing connections.
- **Intranet VPNs:** Intranet VPNs connect branch offices and corporate departments within an enterprise WAN. As sensitive information is transmitted between different departments, intranet VPNs provide strong encryption services.
- **Extranet VPNs:** Extranet VPNs enable access to an enterprise's shared resources for business partners, customers, and suppliers. These VPNs are based on open, standard-based solutions to ensure interoperability with different networks at business partners and customer ends.

Advantages of VPNs

VPNs offer many advantages. The most important advantage is that VPNs enable businesses to operate globally by allowing users to connect to enterprise networks from remote locations. VPNs provide a fast, secure, and reliable method of sharing information. Other advantages that VPNs provide to organizations include:

- **VPNs are flexible and scalable networks.** Organizations can conveniently extend their networks to provide connectivity to remote offices, business partners, and clients, based on their business requirements.
- **VPNs utilize the IP backbone for connectivity.** This helps in considerable simplification of network topologies. This ultimately leads to reduction in

management burden because an Internet Service Provider (ISP) or Application Service Provider (ASP) owns the IP backbone and they are responsible for its administration.

✦ **VPNs are cost-effective as compared to private networks.** This is because VPNs do not require dedicated leased lines. The total cost of operation for VPNs is also less because they use low-cost transport bandwidth and backbone devices.

Configuring a VPN Solution

Configuring a VPN on a Windows 2000 server is a common scenario. Before you start such configuration, however, make sure your system has the necessary hardware.

Windows 2000 VPN hardware requirements

A VPN server on a Windows 2000 server requires a *multihomed* Windows 2000 server. If the server is not multihomed, you can't install the VPN services. A multi-homed server can support multiple domains. It enables a single machine to serve Web content for multiple host names.

The minimum hardware requirements for your server are as follows:

✦ Pentium 133 or higher processor

✦ 128MB RAM (256 recommended)

✦ 4GB HD

When you configure a VPN server, you should disable services that you don't need. Doing so provides two advantages:

✦ It frees resources and returns them to the server for use by other components.

✦ It helps secure your back-end network by turning off services that could be potential entry points for hackers.

The following services are among those you might decide to shut down:

✦ Distributed File System

✦ Distributed Transaction Coordinator

✦ Fax Services

✦ File Replication

✦ Indexing Service

✦ Internet Connection Sharing

✦ Intersite Messaging

✦ Kerberos Key Distribution Center

- License Logging Service
- Print Spooler
- Task Scheduler
- Telnet
- Windows Installer

> **Caution:** Do not disable the remote Registry service. This service is required for the VPN server to function properly.

Configuring a VPN Server

To configure a VPN server on a Windows 2000 server, follow these steps:

1. Open the Routing and Remote Access window.

   You have two possible ways to open the window:
   - Select Start ➪ Programs ➪ Administrative Tools ➪ Routing and Remote Access.
   - Open the Control Panel and double-click Administrative Tools, and then double-click Routing and Remote Access to open the Routing and Remote Access window.

2. Right click the server and select Configure and Enable Routing and Remote access. The Routing and Remote Access Server Setup Wizard appears.

3. Select Next.

   A list of common configuration options appears. You can take one of two actions:
   - Select Virtual Private Networking and follow the setup wizard instructions
   - Manually configured server

4. Select Manually configured server.

5. Select Finish. You can now set the configuration options in the Routing and Remote Access window.

6. After the service is installed, the wizard prompts you to state if you want to start the service. Select Yes. RRAS is initialized. You can expand the server components in the RRAS Microsoft Management Console (MMC).

7. In the Routing and Remote Access window, right-click the server name and select Properties.

   The information in the general tab shows that you are configuring the server as a Remote-access server and also as a router for LAN and demand-dial routing.

Chapter 16 ✦ **Configuring Remote Connectivity** 411

8. Select the Security tab. You can choose the Authentication provider and the Accounting provider to be either Windows authentication or RADIUS authentication. You can select the Authentication Methods button to select the type of authentication you require.

9. In the Properties dialog box, select the IP tab.

10. Select Static address pool and select Add. Enter a range of IP addresses that the RRAS server should assign to remote clients.

Note If you must assign more than 254 addresses, you'll have to span across subnets.

11. Select the Event Logging tab and select Log the maximum amount of information. This helps you troubleshoot connection problems. This completes configuring the properties of the VPN server. Click OK.

12. Now you'll need to configure the PPTP and L2TP ports. In the RRAS MMC interface, expand the server components and select Ports. A list of tunnel ports appears.

13. Right-click Ports and select Properties.

14. To configure the PPTP ports, select WAN Miniport (PPTP) and select Configure. Deselect Demand-dial routing connections (inbound and outbound) if you do not want to create server-to-server tunnels with this server. Select the number of ports you want. You can configure up to 16,384 ports. Click OK.

15. If you want to use IPSec, configure the L2TP ports by selecting Wan Miniport (L2TP).

16. If you receive a message stating that the current connections might be disconnected, select Yes to continue.

17. Click OK in the Ports Properties dialog box.

    You can see the ports that you defined in the RRAS MMC.

18. From the RRAS MMC, select Remote Access Logging.

19. In the right pane, right-click Local File and select Properties.

20. Select Log authentication requests and select OK. This logs all attempts to connect to the server.

That completes the configuration of your VPN server.

Clients that want to connect to a host using a VPN can do so by specifying the host IP address. Non-Microsoft virtual private network clients that use PPTP or L2TP with Internet Protocol Security (IPSec), can also access a remote-access server running Windows 2000. However, if you want secure VPN connections, you must make sure that the non-Microsoft VPN clients support the proper encryption. For PPTP, Microsoft Point-to-Point Encryption (MPPE) must be supported.

Summary

In this chapter, you learned how clients can remotely access a private network using dial-up techniques or using a public network such as the Internet. You learned about Remote Access Services (RAS), the protocols used, security mechanisms, and RAS architecture. You also learned how to configure a RAS server, network settings, ports, and protocols and how clients can access a RAS server using dial-up networking.

Then you learned about another remote-access solution called VPN. You learned what VPNs are, types of VPNs, and VPN tunneling and authentication protocols. You finally learned to configure a VPN solution.

✦ ✦ ✦

STUDY GUIDE

This study guide presents assessment questions to test your knowledge of the exam topic area.

Assessment Questions

1. Which of the following are secure authentication protocols? (Select all that apply.)

    A. CHAP

    B. MS-CHAPv2

    C. SPAP

    D. PAP

2. Which of the following RAS connection mechanisms uses a transport protocol instead of a switching connection?

    A. PSTN

    B. ISDN

    C. PPTP

    D. X.25

3. RAS supports which of the following communication protocols? (Select all that apply.)

    A. TCP/IP

    B. IPX

    C. NetBEUI

    D. DLC

    E. AppleTalk

4. Which of the following commands adds your computer to the RAS and IAS servers security group in a Windows 2000 Active Directory domain?

    A. `netsh add domainserver`

    B. `netsh ras add domainserver`

    C. `netsh add registeredserver`

    D. `netsh ras add registeredserver`

5. How many IP addresses can you assign to remote clients without spanning more than one subnet?

    A. 16

    B. 254

    C. 255

    D. 16,384

6. What is the maximum number of ports that you can configure for your remote server?

    A. 16

    B. 254

    C. 255

    D. 16,384

7. Which of the following services can you not disable while configuring a VPN server?

    A. Internet Connection Sharing

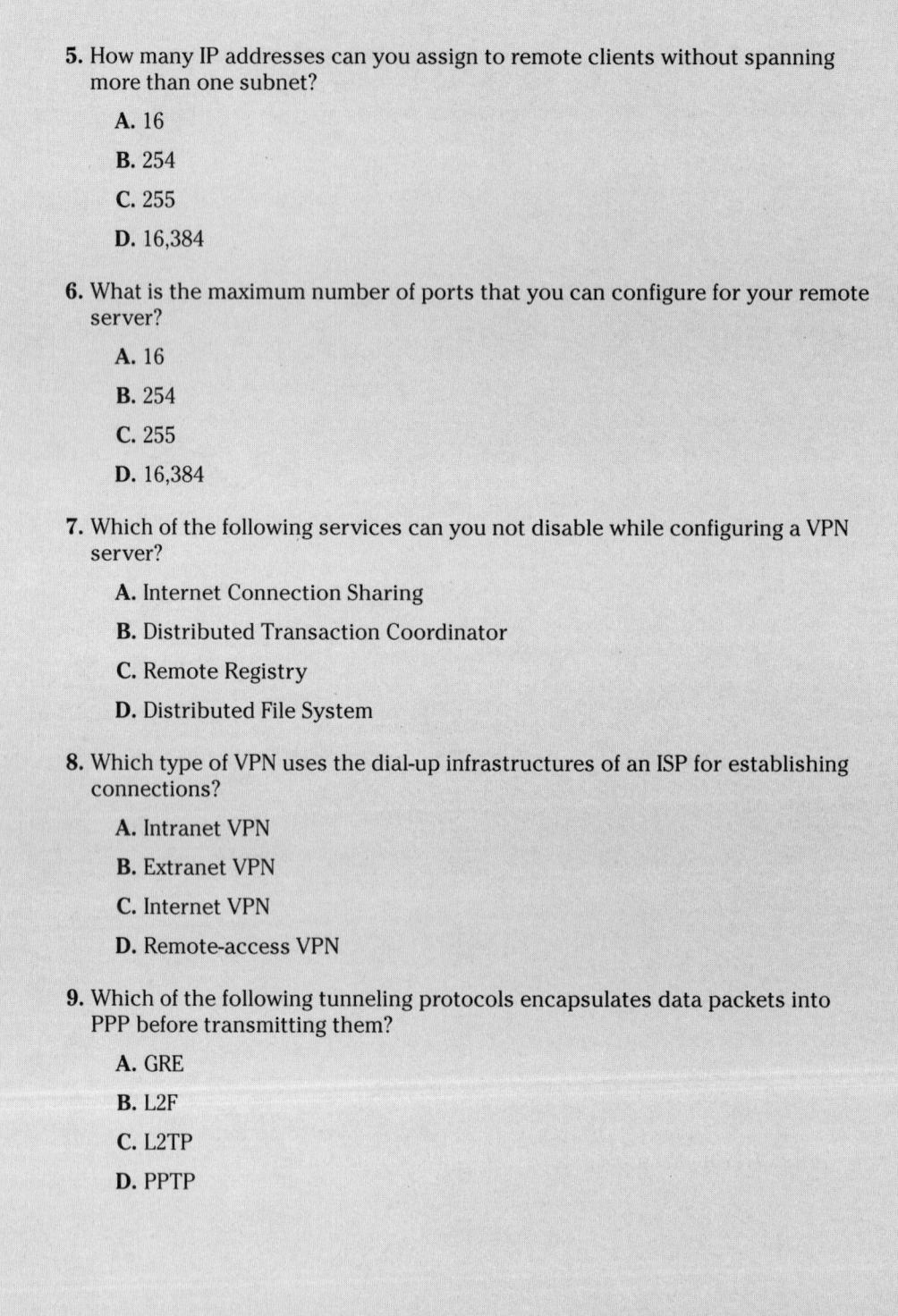

    B. Distributed Transaction Coordinator

    C. Remote Registry

    D. Distributed File System

8. Which type of VPN uses the dial-up infrastructures of an ISP for establishing connections?

    A. Intranet VPN

    B. Extranet VPN

    C. Internet VPN

    D. Remote-access VPN

9. Which of the following tunneling protocols encapsulates data packets into PPP before transmitting them?

    A. GRE

    B. L2F

    C. L2TP

    D. PPTP

10. Which of the following tunneling protocols would be the best choice if you want to establish a remote connection over an X.25 switched network.

    A. PPTP

    B. L2F

    C. L2TP

    D. IPSec

11. Which of the following statements are true with respect to PPP and SLIP? (Select all that apply.)

    A. PPP supports multiple protocols

    B. PPP requires static IP address assignment

    C. SLIP does not support IPX/SPX or NetBEUI

    D. SLIP requires static IP address assignment

Scenario

Two companies, NetAnswers Inc. and NetQuestions Inc., are business partners. James, an employee of NetAnswers Inc., visits NetQuestions Inc. for a presentation. During the presentation, James needs to connect to his company's (NetAnswers Inc.) intranet. How can it be done?

Answers to Chapter Questions

Chapter Pre-Test

1. Two popular remote-connectivity solutions for corporate employees are RAS and VPN.

2. Clients can connect to a RAS server using a telephone line and a modem.

3. IPSec enables encryption of IP data packets to protect the data being transmitted.

4. ISDN offers a much faster communication speed than a standard telephone line.

5. X.25 is a standard packet-switching communication protocol designed for WAN connectivity.

6. Challenge Handshake Authentication Protocol (CHAP) is a challenge-response authentication protocol that uses the industry-standard Message Digest 5 (MD5) one-way encryption scheme to hash the response to a challenge issued by the remote-access server.

7. Some tunneling and authentication protocols employed by VPNs include Generic Routing Encapsulation (GRE), Layer 2 Forwarding (L2F), Layer 2 Tunneling Protocol (L2TP), Point-to-Point Tunneling Protocol (PPTP), Microsoft Point-to-Point Encryption (MPPE), and Internet Protocol Security (IPSec).

8. Generic Routing Encapsulation (GRE) encapsulates data packets inside IP tunnels and creates a virtual point-to-point link with routers at remote locations across an IP network.

9. Point-to-Point Tunneling Protocol (PPTP) enables secure data transfer over IP-based networks and supports multiprotocol, virtual private networking over public networks, such as the Internet.

10. Three types of VPNs are remote-access, intranet, and extranet.

11. For secure VPN connections using PPTP, non-Microsoft VPN clients must support Microsoft Point-to-Point Encryption (MPPE).

Assessment Questions

1. A, B, C. CHAP, MS-CHAPv2, SPAP are all secure authentication protocols. PAP is not a secure authentication protocol as it authenticates clients using a cleartext password. For more information, refer to the section titled "RAS Security."

2. C. When PSTN, ISDN or X.25 is used, remote clients establish PPP connections with a RAS server over a switched network. In contrast, when PPTP is used, instead of using a switching connection to send packets over a WAN, a transport protocol such as TCP/IP sends the PPP packets to the RAS server over a virtual WAN. For more information, refer to the section titled "Features of RAS."

3. A, B, C. The RAS architecture enables clients to run any combination of the network protocols NetBEUI, TCP/IP, or IPX during a RAS session. For more information, refer to the section titled "Features of RAS."

4. D. If your computer is a part of an Active Directory domain, add your computer to the RAS and IAS servers security group. You, as an administrator, can do this by using Active Directory Users and Computers option, or with the following command:

```
netsh ras add registeredserver
```

For more information, refer to the section titled "Installing and Configuring RAS."

5. B. If you assign more than 254 addresses, you'll need to span across subnets. For more information, refer to the section titled "Configuring a VPN Solution."

6. D. You can configure up to 16,384 ports. For more information, refer to the section titled "Configuring a VPN Solution."

7. C. Remote Registry service is required for the VPN server to function properly. For more information, refer to the section titled "Configuring a VPN Solution."

8. D. Remote-access VPNs help reduce communication expenses by using the dial-up infrastructures of an ISP for establishing connections. For more information, refer to the section titled "Types of VPNs."

9. B. L2F encapsulates data packets into Point-to-Point Protocol (PPP) before transmitting them to an L2F server. For more information, refer to the section titled "VPN Protocols."

10. C. L2TP supports a variety of routed protocols, such as IP, IPX, and AppleTalk. It also supports a variety of backbone technologies, such as Frame Relay and X.25. L2TP enables VPDN and combines the best features of L2F and PPTP. For more information, refer to the section titled "VPN Protocols."

11. A, C, D. The PPP architecture also enables clients to load any combination of protocols, such as IPX, TCP/IP, and NetBEUI. PPP also supports dynamic IP address assignment. SLIP requires a static IP address. It supports TCP/IP, but it does not support IPX/SPX or NetBEUI. For more information, refer to the section titled "RAS Connection Methods."

Scenario

James can connect to his company's intranet in two ways:

    A. First, James can directly dial a Remote Access Server at NetAnswers Inc. to make a dial-up connection to the company's intranet. He can do this by using a phone line in the conference room. For this, a RAS server must be configured at NetAnswers Inc. that enables remote clients to dial-up the server.

    B. The second option is that if a VPN server is configured at NetAnswers Inc., James can dial a local ISP and make a VPN connection to the company's intranet by specifying the IP address of the VPN server. For this, James must be an authenticated user of his company's VPN server.

CHAPTER 17

Firewalls, Proxy Servers, and Security

EXAM OBJECTIVES

- Identify the purpose, benefits, and characteristics of using a firewall.
- Identify the purpose, benefits, and characteristics of using a proxy.
- Given a scenario, predict the impact of a particular security implementation on network functionality.

CHAPTER PRE-TEST

1. What is the primary purpose of a firewall?
2. What are the three types of firewalls?
3. Name two security issues a firewall can't protect against.
4. What is the purpose of a security policy?
5. What function of a firewall is useful to an administrator in identifying potential security problems?
6. What is the main purpose of a proxy server?
7. What are two main benefits of network address translation?
8. Under what circumstances is a personal firewall a good solution?
9. What is the primary purpose of the Application Gateway/Proxy?
10. What is a good measuring tool for calculating the performance overhead that a particular security solution may impose?

✦ Answers to these questions can be found at the end of this chapter. ✦

Before entering into network security, especially when the Internet is concerned, you must accept the simple fact that no such thing as a secured network exists. The moment more than one person is allowed to access a shared resource, a potential for undesirable results exists. With that understanding safely tucked in the back of our minds, a number of devices and technologies make breaking into the network more effort than it's worth, and that is the primary objective.

Defining a Security Policy

Before building the physical components of the network security system, you must define your goals and develop a security policy. Each company (or individual) has different security needs. Many trains of thought exist when it comes to creating a security policy and many books have been devoted to just this one topic. In the real world, however, a security policy can be simple. Taking into account the following items can help you in developing a well-designed document:

- Describe the nature of the data contained on the network.
- Identify what groups of people require access to the Internet.
- Describe what service(s) each group needs access to (Web, e-mail, and so on).
- For each service group, describe how the service should be kept secure.
- Write a statement making all other forms of access a violation.

This last item is extremely important. Many managers insist on a technology-based approach to keeping people from accessing non-business services of the Internet. The very nature of the Internet, however, makes this type of policing a difficult task and often leads to a weakened security system. It is easy to get sidetracked by focusing on micromanaging user access and lose sight of the main objective of keeping the bad guys out of the LAN.

Identifying the Purpose, Benefits, and Characteristics of the Firewall

Security is the number one responsibility of the network administrator. You must implement numerous security measures within the network operating system, including securing physical access to the servers and hardware and instituting acceptable use policies. Most of these items are geared toward preventing abuses from the inside of the network and are extremely important. Just as important, however, is keeping the bad guys outside the network at bay. This is especially true when the "outside" is the Internet.

The most common device for securing a network from outside attacks is the *firewall*. In its original implementation, the firewall is a physical boundary between rooms that prevents a fire on one side from penetrating into the room on the other side. Typically, these are bank vaults, chemical storage rooms, and other areas where fire prevention is critical. Building on that concept, the network firewall is intended to be a secure border between the outside world and the LAN.

A firewall is a system or group of systems that enforces an access control policy between two networks. How this is accomplished varies widely, but in principle, the firewall can be thought of as a pair of mechanisms to either block or permit traffic. Some firewalls place a greater emphasis on blocking traffic, while others emphasize permitting traffic. Probably the most important thing to recognize about a firewall is that it implements an access control policy. If you don't have a good idea of what kind of access you want to allow or to deny, a firewall really won't help. It's also important to recognize that the firewall's configuration, because it is a mechanism for enforcing policy, imposes that policy on everything behind it.

Some firewalls permit traffic for only a specific type of service, such as e-mail, thereby protecting the network against any attacks other than attacks against the e-mail service. Other firewalls provide less strict protections and block services that are known to be problems.

Generally, firewalls are configured to protect against unauthenticated logins from the Internet. This protection, more than anything, helps prevent hackers from logging in to machines on the local network. More elaborate firewalls block traffic from the outside to the inside, but permit users on the inside to communicate freely with the outside.

Firewalls provide a single access point where security and auditing can be imposed. Firewalls provide an important logging and auditing function and often provide summary reports so the administrator can quickly see what kinds and amount of traffic have passed through the firewall, and, more importantly, how many attempts were made to break in to it.

Things a firewall can't do

Firewalls can't protect against attacks that don't pass through it. That may seem like an obvious statement, but amazingly, that simple fact is often ignored. Many corporations with Internet connects are very concerned about proprietary data being stolen through that route. Unfortunately, these same corporations often overlook how effectively a magnetic tape can export data. At the management level, many organizations are terrified of Internet access yet have no coherent policy for securing dial-in access or physical access to their servers. A surprisingly large number of organizations implement expensive firewalls while neglecting the numerous back doors into their network.

For a firewall to work, it must be a part of a consistent overall organizational security architecture. Firewall policies must be realistic and reflect the level of security in the entire network. For example, a site with top-secret or classified data doesn't need a firewall at all; these networks shouldn't be connected to the Internet in the first place, or at least they should be isolated from the rest of the corporate network.

A firewall can't really protect against internal threats. Although an industrial spy might export information through a firewall, sensitive data is just as likely to be exported through a telephone, FAX machine, or floppy disk. The firewall also cannot protect the network from human error or sloppiness. Users who reveal sensitive information over the telephone are good targets for social engineering; an attacker may be able to break into your network by completely bypassing your firewall by finding a "helpful" employee who can be fooled into giving revealing passwords or granting access to a modem pool.

Types of firewalls

The term firewall is rather broad, because the features and effectiveness of any particular firewall vary greatly. However, firewalls in general can be classified into three basic forms, as outlined here:

1. A dedicated hardware device
2. A router with traffic filtering/firewall capabilities built in
3. A software based system normally running on a server, PC, or MAC

Dedicated firewall appliances

In recent years, a growing number of dedicated hardware firewalls have often been described as firewall appliances. These appliances are designed to perform only one function: to secure the LAN. A large number of very good firewall appliances are on the market with prices ranging from a few hundred dollars to more than ten thousand dollars. For the small office or home office using cable or DSL connections, the SonicWall SOHO by Sonic Systems (www.sonicwall.com) is a fine example of a secure firewall appliance for under $500.00. For the enterprise, Products by 3Com, Watch Guard Technologies, and Cisco offer better performance and a higher level of safety. These devices, however, cost thousands of dollars and are intended to protect hundreds of users.

Routers with firewall capabilities

Most routers provide basic packet-filtering capabilities (see the "Firewall filtering methods" section later in this chapter) although advanced firewall features are usually available as an additional add-on. Many system engineers prefer to use the Internet router as the firewall. Because all traffic is passing through this device anyway, it makes sense to allow or deny data at this point. However, on the other side is the argument that security is important enough that a specific device should be dedicated to perform this function. You must understand what the filtering capabilities of a router are before selecting one to be the primary line of defense.

Software-based firewalls

The third option, the software-based solution, usually offers a high degree of security and ample flexibility to fit almost any network need. These products can be dedicated to firewall services only, or can be part of a larger suite of other services such as the proxy, which is explained momentarily. Software solutions normally run on a standard computer under a Windows, Linux, UNIX, or MAC operating system. A major advantage to the software-based firewall solution is the fact that it can be easily upgraded, oftentimes automatically.

A new breed of software firewalls for the home user are beginning to proliferate as more people subscribe to broadband Internet services such as cable, DSL, and wireless. These *personal firewalls* run as system services and normally do a very good job of protecting a single PC from outside hackers. Three of the more popular personal firewall products are BlackICE (www.networkice.com), Symantec Desktop Firewall (www.symantec.com), and ZoneAlarm (www.zonealarm.com). All three of these products, licensed per computer, retails for about $50.00. The ZoneAlarm product is one of the few personal firewalls that warn you when a program on your computer attempts to connect to the Internet without your knowing. Because this activity is closely associated with viruses, this level of notification can be a big advantage.

Network address translation

One feature often used by firewalls to add an additional level of security is NAT, or *network address translation*. When NAT is employed, all the IP addresses on the local network are hidden from the outside world. The firewall translates all outbound connections to a single public IP address. People on the outside of the firewall see only this single IP address coming from the LAN, regardless of how many devices are actually inside the firewall. In order to perform this translation, the firewall must create a table to track the route of every internal request so that returning traffic is passed back to the appropriate device. Herein lies one of the basic vulnerabilities of any firewall: If a hacker is able to construct a data packet to look like a response to a valid request from inside the LAN, the firewall allows this packet in, thus compromising security. This attack is typically known as *IP spoofing* and is a fundamental process used by hackers to gain access to a protected system. Because NAT hides the internal IP addressing scheme, and because it tracks and matches requests and replies, IP spoofing to a system using NAT is more difficult than to a system using firewalls that do not perform NAT services. NAT also has the added benefit of eliminating the requirement for many (usually expensive) public IP addresses. NAT is not a service normally found with personal firewalls but is available on most other firewall products.

Demilitarized Zone

The job of a firewall is to keep unrequested traffic outside the LAN. If the LAN happens to run a Web, e-mail, chat, or other server, however, the firewall would also prevent access to these servers. Therefore, the firewall must allow exceptions to its rules in order to enable outside access to inside servers. A fundamental rule when configuring a firewall is to keep closed as many inbound holes as possible. It would be easy enough to program the firewall to allow all inbound HTTP traffic, or all traffic on port 80, in order to provide access to a public Web server, but doing so opens a hole that could be exploited by a hacker. Rather than exposing a complete protocol or port to the outside world, many firewalls offer a special Demilitarized Zone, or DMZ. The DMZ is a separate IP network where public servers can be placed and isolated from the LAN, so as not to compromise security on the internal network. As shown in Figure 17-1, the DMZ is on a separate IP network using public IP addresses while protecting the private LAN. Although this example shows each of the public servers with routable, public IP addresses, the firewall could be configured with NAT on the DMZ side to allow access to each server service through a single public IP address.

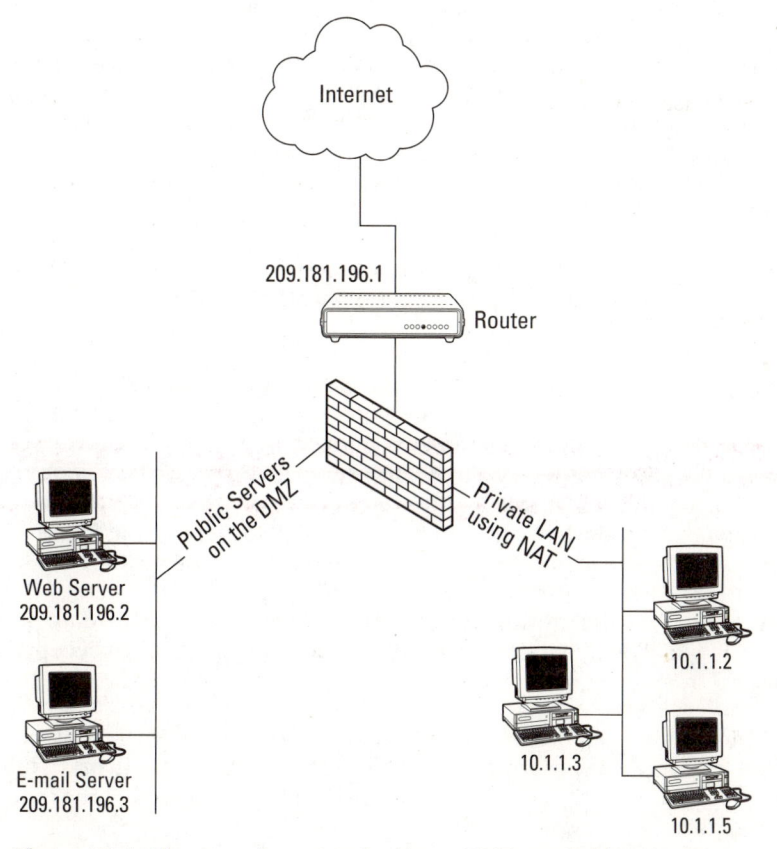

Figure 17-1: Diagram of a network using a DMZ to provide access to public servers

Firewall filtering methods

The basic function of the firewall is to determine what inbound traffic is legitimate and what is not. Four primary methods are used to make these judgments:

1. Packet filters
2. Application-Layer Gateway
3. Circuit-level firewall
4. Stateful inspection

Packet filters

The basic form of controlling access to the network is the process known as packet filtering. Packet filtering is both a tool and a technique that is a basic building block of network security. In the context of a TCP/IP network, a firewall using packet-filter techniques watches each individual IP packet and decodes the header information of all in-bound and out-bound traffic. The firewall then blocks the packet from passing through, or allows the packet to pass based upon the contents of the source address, destination address, source port, and/or destination port. For example, Figure 17-2 illustrates how a packet-filtering firewall can be programmed to deny inbound traffic access to the LAN based on well-known IP port numbers.

In this example, many well-known port numbers such as 21 (FTP), 80 (HTTP), and others are explicitly blocked, while ports 25 (SMTP) and 110 (POP3) are open to allow access to an e-mail server.

Packet-filtering firewalls examine packets at the Network Layer and are application independent, which enables them to deliver good performance and scalability. However, packet filters do not understand the context of any given communication, which makes them easier for hackers to compromise. It isn't terribly difficult to encapsulate a data packet making it "fit" the acceptable rules of a packet-filter firewall. For example, if a weakness exists on the e-mail server depicted in Figure 17-2 that enables someone to execute a program on the e-mail server, a clever hacker can encapsulate an execute command in a standard IP packet and send it to the firewall on port 25. Because the firewall doesn't bother to look at what the data packet wants to "do," it will allow the data because it has been received on an acceptable port number: 25.

A packet-filtering device can be the first line of defense in the network. It blocks inbound packets of specific types from ever reaching the protected network. This is known as ingress filtering. Although not a robust firewall, it can reduce the load on the proxy or application firewall.

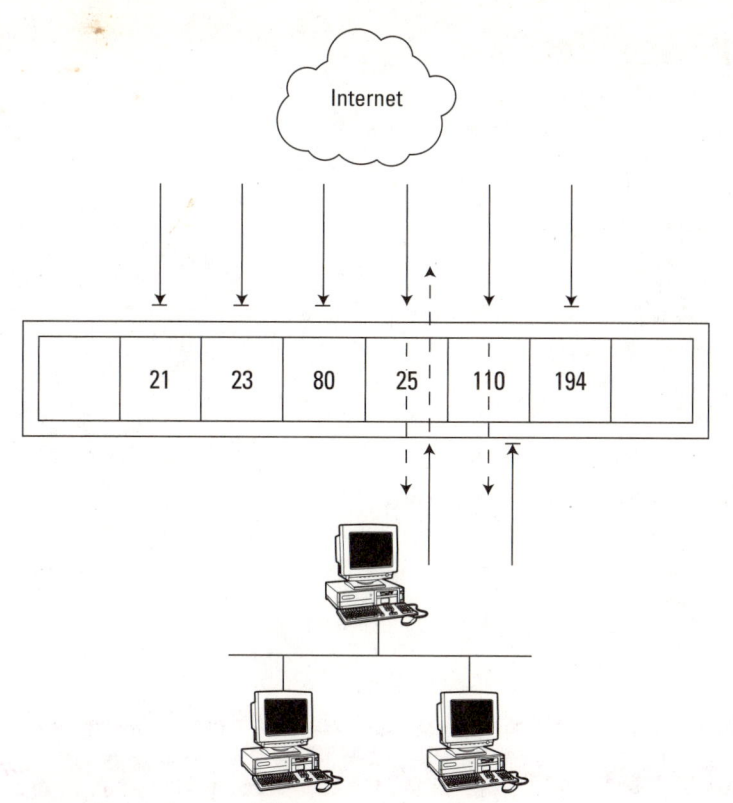

Figure 17-2: Blocking LAN access by filtering IP traffic based on port number

Application-Layer Gateways

Application gateways improve on the packet-filter security by examining all application layers, bringing context information into the decision process. Application-level firewalls operate at the Application Layer of the protocol stack. An application-level firewall runs a proxy server application acting as an intermediary between two systems. Consequently, application-level firewalls are sometimes referred to as *proxy server firewalls*. A device on the LAN sends a request to the server running on the application-level firewall to connect to an external service such as FTP or HTTP. The proxy server evaluates the request and decides to permit or deny the request based on a set of rules that apply to the individual network service. Proxy servers understand the protocol of the service they are evaluating. Thus, only packets that comply with the protocol for the requested service are allowed. From the outside world, the same holds true. In the previous example, if a data packet is sent through an open port, 25 for example, but does not contain Simple Mail Transport Protocol (SMTP) data, the packet is denied. This type of firewall technology boasts additional benefits as well. Because the application protocol is known, detailed audit records, session information, user authentication, URL filtering, and caching can all be performed with ease. Figure 17-3 illustrates the operation of an application-level firewall.

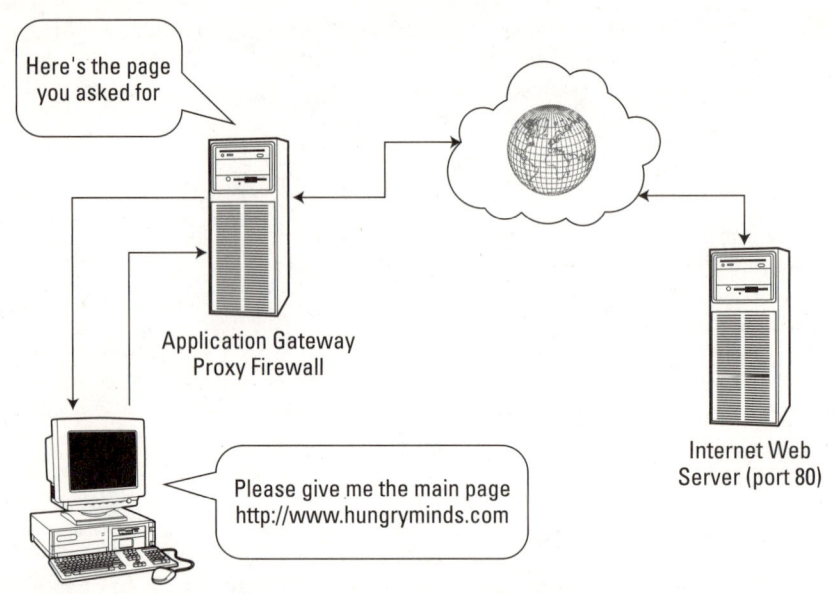

Figure 17-3: Example of an application gateway acting as a proxy to serve a Web page

Arguably, the biggest drawback of the application gateways is that each workstation behind the firewall must be configured to be aware of the firewall and must have client software that is designed to communicate with the proxy software on the firewall.

Circuit-level firewalls

A circuit-level firewall is a second-generation firewall that validates TCP and UDP sessions before opening a connection. After a handshake has taken place, it passes everything through until the session is ended. Circuit-level firewalls operate at the Session Layer of the OSI model and the Transport Layer of the TCP/IP model. Operating at the Transport Layer means a circuit-level firewall actually establishes a virtual circuit between the client and the host on a session-by-session basis. This is the basic process used by Virtual Private Networking, or VPN.

To validate and create a session, the circuit-level firewall examines each connection setup to ensure it follows a legitimate handshake for the Transport Layer being used, typically TCP. No data is transported until the handshake is complete. The firewall maintains a table of valid connections, which includes session state and sequencing information. When a connection is terminated, its table entry is removed and the virtual circuit between the two peers is closed.

Circuit-level firewalls permit access through the firewall with a minimum amount of scrutiny by building a limited form of connection state:

- Handshake
- Established
- Closing

Only those packets that are associated with an established connection are allowed through the firewall. When a connection establishment request is received, the circuit-level firewall checks its rule base to determine whether or not the connection should be allowed. If it is allowed, all network packets associated with that connection are routed through the firewall with no further security checks. This method provides very fast service and a minimal amount of state checking.

A circuit-level firewall maintains two connections per session, one between client and firewall and one between firewall and server. As a result, all outgoing packets appear to have originated from the firewall in a manner analogous to packet-filtering firewalls with NAT. Unlike a packet-filtering firewall, direct contact between the trusted internal network and the untrusted external network is prevented because packets are not shuffled between network interfaces at the IP Layer of the protocol stack.

A circuit-level gateway does have one inherent security risk: After a connection has been established by a circuit-level firewall, any application can run across the connection, because the circuit-level firewall is operating at the Transport Layer of the TCP/IP stack. It cannot examine the application-level content of the packets it is relaying between the trusted network and the untrusted network. An unscrupulous inside user could subvert the firewall and connect to an unsecured Telnet session, multi-user game, or streaming video movie. A hacker on the outside could inject malicious packets into the stream because the circuit-level firewall is blindly relaying packets back and forth across established connections. The hacker could then launch attacks against an internal server that might not be as well secured as the firewall.

Stateful inspection

Stateful inspection overcomes the limitations of previous approaches by providing full application-layer awareness without an intermediary proxy. With stateful inspection, packets are intercepted at the Network Layer where state-related information is extracted. The firewall keeps a state-table of connections whereby it monitors the state of a TCP connection and allows traffic accordingly. Because of this state monitoring, filtering decisions are based not only on administrator-defined rules (as in packet filtering) but also on context that has been established by prior packets that have passed through the firewall. As an added security measure against port scanning, stateful inspection firewalls close off ports until connection to the specific port is requested.

Comparing firewall technologies

No "perfect" firewall solution for every network exists. Security needs differ greatly from network to network and depend highly on what information is located on the network, who needs access to the network, whether the network is connected to the Internet, and other individual concerns. In order to select the best firewall, it is important to understand the methods we just looked at to compare the various options to meet the needs of the situation. Table 17-1 provides a quick summary of the various firewall technologies with the pros and cons of each method.

Table 17-1
Firewall Filtering Method Comparison

Filter Technology	Advantage	Disadvantage
Packet-filter	Application independent High performance Scalable	Low security No application information
Application-Layer Gateways	Good security Application aware	Lower performance Limited application support
Circuit-level firewalls	Very high performance Scalable	High potential for abuse
Stateful inspection	Good Security Medium-high performance Takes less processing power than application-level analysis	Usually available only on enterprise class firewalls (expensive) Unable to apply different rules to different applications

Identifying the Purpose, Benefits, and Characteristics of Using a Proxy

A proxy server provides numerous advantages for connecting a local area network to the Internet. Acting as an Application-Layer Gateway, the proxy provides a strong defense from the outside world. Performing the duties of a firewall, however, is just one benefit of a proxy server.

The proxy can also provide caching services to increase performance, logging services to track Internet use, tools to maximize the use of precious bandwidth, and content filtering to help keep unwanted data off the local network. The proxy can also utilize multiple connection types to easily provide redundancy and automatic failover in the event of a primary line failure. Although configuring and maintaining a proxy can be more difficult than other connectivity solutions, many of these services are available only through the proxy. One service that is well suited for the proxy is protocol routing. For example, an IPX-only based LAN cannot connect directly to the Internet, because the Internet uses only IP. A proxy server placed on the LAN can have one NIC connected to the local network talking IPX and another NIC connected to the Internet talking TCP/IP. In this situation, the proxy is "speaking" two different languages and acts as an interpreter for the local network. Even though the LAN devices don't "speak" the TCP/IP protocol, they can have full access to the Internet by way of the proxy.

Proxy servers can inspect all traffic (in and out) over an Internet connection and determine if anything should be denied transmission, reception, or access. Because this filtering cuts both ways, a proxy server can keep users out of particular Web sites (by monitoring for specific URLs) or to restrict unauthorized access to the internal network by authenticating users. The primary configuration task for a proxy server system is the creation of access policies used to filter Internet traffic. Few decisions can be more politically charged within an enterprise than who is allowed to do what on the Internet, and many privacy-related issues go with such decisions. The proxy server must provide adequate ways to

- ✦ Incorporate the rules for filtering
- ✦ Organize and document those rules

Proxy servers can be dedicated hardware devices with multiple NICs and built-in remote-management tools, or simple software that operates on a standard PC or MAC. Proxies can run under Windows, MAC O/S, Linux, UNIX, and many other operating systems. Proxy's can offer a limited scope of services, such as only HTTP (Web) access, or a full range of application support. One of the most popular Windows-based proxy servers is Wingate, available at www.wingate.com. For Linux systems, the Squid project is one of the more popular and can be found at www.squid-cache.org. In addition, numerous free and shareware proxies are available for all platforms, and they are easily located on the Internet. For dedicated hardware solutions, some of the leading products are manufactured by 3Com (www.3com.com) and Nokia (www.nokia.com).

The proxy server acts as a go-between for users on the LAN. Network users tell the proxy what information they want and it is the proxy's job to go fetch that data. Therefore, the most effective proxy server has two physical connections: one to the local network and another to the Internet (or other external network). You can have a single physical connection to both networks by bonding multiple IP addresses to one NIC, but this situation can weaken the firewall protection of the proxy. Likewise, because the proxy is providing access to unsecured networks, physical access to the proxy should be restricted as necessary to ensure proper security as defined by the corporate policies.

When dial-up access to the Internet is used, the proxy can be connected to the LAN with one NIC and to the Internet via a modem (see Figure 17-4). This then provides Internet access to all users on the LAN with a single modem, phone line, and

Internet access account. The actual connection to the public network could very well be a dedicated connection as well, but because multiple dial-up connections can be costly, the proxy is extremely well suited for networks that must rely on analog connections.

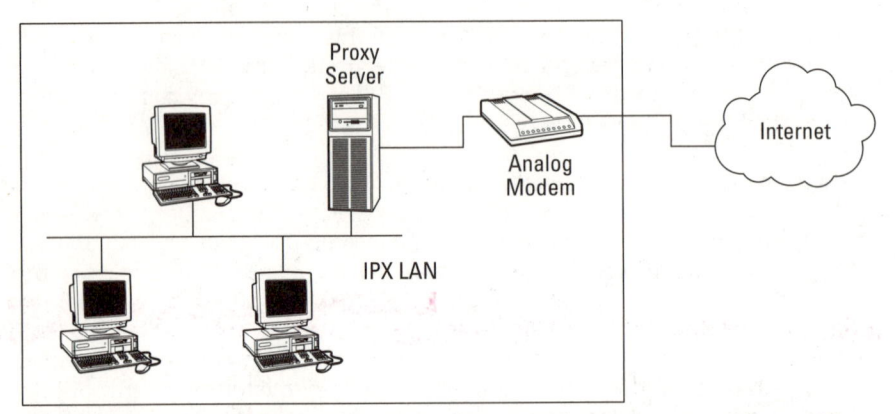

Figure 17-4: Using a proxy server to provide LAN wide Internet access to an IPX based network with a single modem

When access to the Internet is critical, a proxy can provide an easy, automated failover solution. For example, referring to Figure 17-4, assume that a second NIC is connected to a router that provides an always-on digital connection to the Internet. If this primary line fails, the proxy senses the line failure and initiates a dial-up connection using the modem. Because all the LAN users are configured to talk to the proxy for Internet services, no changes are necessary when the backup line is used. Other than the change in performance, the entire failover process is transparent to the LAN users.

A popular feature of many proxy servers is the capability to cache common information. Within any group of people performing tasks of similar interest, such as an office environment, it makes sense that people generally visit the same Web site at least some of the time. Using caching, the proxy can exploit this situation to increase Internet service to the end user. Consider the following scenario: When the first person requests a specific Web site, the proxy connects to that site across the Internet and fetches the text and graphics for the main page. This data is then stored in RAM or on disk (depending on the proxy's cache method). When the next person asks for this same site, the proxy sends the data to the client from its cache, eliminating the need, and the time delay, of going out to revisit the same site. Even if the second (and subsequent) requests are made by the same person, traffic to the Internet is greatly reduced by serving data from the local cache. Special http tags can inform a proxy cache that certain information is dynamic (changes often), and, therefore, the proxy sends the non-dynamic data to the local user and fetches only the new data from the Web site. Internet performance is greatly increased as more information is served from the cache and bandwidth costs can be minimized to save money. Many proxy servers also offer a "pre-cache" option so network administrators can define specific

Web sites to be cached even if no one has asked for it yet, and schedule a refresh of the cached content on a regular basis.

Bastion server

An additional step to protect a network from attack is to put a heavily fortified bastion server behind the firewall. Having a bastion server means that all access to the network from the Internet is required to go through the bastion server. By concentrating all access in a single server, or a small group of servers, it's much easier to protect the entire intranet.

The bastion server does not provide network services itself. When it receives a request from the Internet for a network service, the server passes the request to the appropriate LAN server. Subsequently, it takes the response and passes it back to the Internet.

Proxy server applications can also run on bastion servers. When someone on the LAN wants to get at an Internet resource, they first contact the proxy server on the bastion server, and the bastion server then relays the request to the Internet server. The Internet server sends the information to the proxy server on the bastion server, which in turn passes the information back to the user on the LAN. If a proxy is used in conjunction with the bastion server, you must run both services on the same box or configure the proxy behind the bastion server.

Several means are taken to ensure that the bastion server is as secure as possible — and also to make sure that if the server is hacked in to, LAN security won't be compromised.

To make the bastion server secure, it is stripped of all but the most basic services. A typical network server provides login, file, print, and other services, including access to additional servers. On a bastion server, those services have been prohibited. Because no user accounts exist, it's difficult for someone to break in using passwords. Because such few services are available, even if someone did break in, they wouldn't be able to do much.

For even more security, bastion servers can be put on a private subnet (often referred to as a perimeter network), further isolating the server so that if someone breaks in to it, they can get access to only that subnet, not to the rest of the LAN. A filtering router reviews packets coming from the private subnet, making sure that only authorized incoming requests pass through to the LAN. Figure 17-5 shows how the bastion server would be connected to a LAN on a separate subnet with a proxy server.

Even more security measures can protect the server and LAN, sending alerts to network administrators if someone is trying to break in. The bastion server can log all access to it and keep a secure backup of that log on a physically separate machine connected by the serial port so no one can gain access to the log remotely. System administrators can examine the log for signs of break-ins. Even more powerful are monitoring programs that watch the log and sound an alarm if it detects someone has been trying to break in to the server. Auditing software can also constantly check whether the server software has been altered in any way — a possible sign that an intruder has successfully attacked it and taken control of its resources.

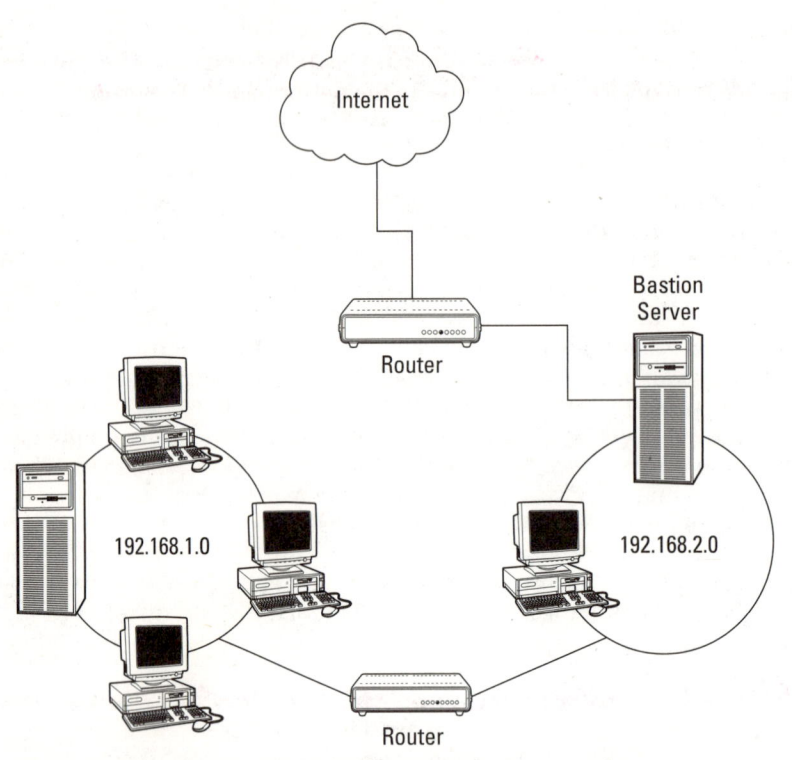

Figure 17-5: Using a bastion server on a separate LAN subnet

Predicting the Impact of a Particular Security Implementation on Network Functionality

A fine line exists between network performance and functionality, and keeping things secured. If one objective had to be met over the other, security would have to be the obvious answer. However, in the real world, network users (and most management people) expect that LAN performance should always be slightly faster than it actually is while taking for granted that the network is secured. The truth is, however, that even simple security measures can adversely affect network performance. As a trained network professional, you should understand which security items can impact network performance so that you can make intelligent decisions when tradeoffs are necessary.

Whenever a security measure is initiated, performance is going to be affected. The more comprehensive a firewall is, the longer it takes to perform its function. Additionally, monitoring logs increase the overhead of the firewall or other security device. All firewall products, including proxies and bastion servers, should offer a detailed logging system. These logs can maintain simple, summary information, or they can record the specifics of every transaction that occurred through the device. These are important tools to identify possible security breaches and must be reviewed on a regular basis (daily, in most cases). The amount of logging configured on the security device directly impacts the performance. The proper balance between network performance and activity monitoring varies depending on needs.

NAT performance overhead

When a device, a router for example, is performing NAT, it has to track a potentially large amount of data. For every outbound request received, the router has to make an entry in its tables and assign a unique (and unassigned) port to the request. Next, it modifies the physical data packet to replace the sending device's IP address with the NAT address. Finally, it sends the packet on to the next hop. When the router receives a corresponding reply, it must scan its NAT tables to match the incoming data with the appropriate request and update the table to reflect the completed transaction. It should be obvious that these processes affect network performance.

The actual amount of degradation that NAT imposes is directly related to the number of active connections and the quality of the NAT product used. Software-based NAT products generally add more overhead than dedicated NAT hardware solutions. One exception to this might be if a PC is dedicated primarily to doing NAT. For the most part, however, a firewall dedicated to protecting the network that incorporates NAT imposes the smallest performance hit.

Proxy/Application Gateways

Proxy/Application Gateway servers also add overhead to normal network traffic due to the amount of tracking necessary. Similar to the NAT tracking tables, the proxy must also maintain lists of MAC addresses that have requested a particular service and keep this information updated throughout the connection processes. The exact performance hit any given proxy imposes is again related directly to the type and quality of the product chosen and the number of services required of the server.

Because the proxy server can be configured to examine the content of all transmissions, it is well suited for filtering out "inappropriate" words or restricting access to "inappropriate" Internet sites. Such filtering can be performed on specific protocol traffic (such as POP3/SMTP for e-mail or HTTP for Web) or it can look at every data packet that passes through. In addition, the proxy may perform virus scanning or scanning for potentially dangerous scripts. All these options have a direct impact on network performance. The exact hit varies greatly from network to network and must be reviewed on a case-by-case basis. Corporate policy dictates how many security services a proxy must provide, which dictates how much overhead the server adds. When tuning a proxy server for performance, a few basic items should be kept in mind:

- Use the fastest NIC possible. Many name-brand network cards use proprietary ASIC (Application-Specific Integrated Circuit) to increase the number of data packets the NIC can handle. In addition, "server class" NICs normally support special buffering techniques to increase NIC performance.

- Keep the proxy on a dedicated switched port when used on Ethernet LANs. As Chapter 3 covers, switches provide better network performance by creating dedicated collision domains between two devices. Therefore, a switch can minimize any potential bottlenecks caused by LAN collisions.

- Use multiple NICs to connect to the private LAN. If network traffic is high, especially traffic destined to the proxy, adding multiple paths to the proxy server can minimize congestions at the hardware level.

- Run the proxy software on a server-class computer. Multiple processors, lots of fast RAM, fast data buses, and other hardware components found in server-class computers help the proxy software do its job with the least amount of degradation imposed by hardware. Like most applications, the proxy software attempts to maximize performance by using physical RAM as much as possible. Adding RAM to the proxy server reduces the process overhead for the most part. Additionally, when hard drive space is needed for memory paging or caching, the server-class (usually SCSI) disk sub-system always out performs systems found in normal desktop computers.

- Set the minimum number of filters and rules as possible. It is always better to err on the side of implementing more security policies than fewer, but you should perform a careful analysis of what security measures are actually needed. Additionally, you should perform a regular review of what security rules are in place, to ensure that the appropriate amount of security is being performed.

- Implement Web caching whenever possible. Web caching should be a mandatory feature when selecting a proxy server. Caching is likely the single, biggest performance boost the server can offer, especially when low-bandwidth Internet connections are used.

- Use the appropriate amount of access speed. Many businesses choose an Internet access method based mostly on monthly cost. It should be clear, however, that analog dial-up connections offer lower performance than a dedicated digital line. You should complete a careful examination of all available options and take into account the total number of people who will access the Internet services. Additionally, any long-term contracts should contain clauses that enable the business to move to newer technologies if something comes available before the end of the existing agreement. For example, you don't want to be locked into a 5-year contract on a $1000.00 monthly T1 line only to find that your provider begins to offer a comparable-speed DSL line for $250.00 per month half-way through the T1 contract.

Preparing for other performance issues

All the security products explained in this chapter have an average packets-per-second rating. Most of the manufacturers publish this figure so the consumer can gauge the average performance of the particular solution. This figure, however, is just a basic measurement and varies greatly under different conditions. When preparing for any WAN implementation, especially Internet access, you must optimize normal LAN performance first. A WAN connection that implements any security device usually adds a noticeable impact on LAN performance. Many of the issues outlined in the previous coverage of proxy servers also apply to general performance issues with firewalls and security policies. The amount of security required for a given network should be defined and reviewed on a regular basis to ensure that overall performance is not hindered by needless security measures. Using quality products and broadband connections greatly reduces the perceivable impact of the added security measures. Lastly, a good, clear, and concise acceptable use policy needs to be established and accepted by all people who use the services being implemented.

Summary

Above all other duties, a network engineer is in charge of securing the data on the LAN. Attacks can come from inside or outside the network. This chapter looked at how firewalls can help keep the bad guys on the outside.

Although the purpose of the firewall is singular — preventing unauthorized access to the network, firewalls can take a number of different approaches. Most processes deal with filtering data packets for acceptable parameters. Protocol filters accept data only for specific types of services, such as HTTP (Web) or SMTP (e-mail). Other filter types go further by examining the actual content of the data to determine its validity.

A common technique used to hide the addresses of the inside network from the outside world is network address translation, or NAT. NAT converts all outbound IP addresses to a single, public Internet address, making an attack against a device behind the firewall more difficult. NAT also reduces the number of necessary public IP addresses needed for an organization to connect multiple devices to the Internet.

One popular security device is the *proxy,* also known as an Application Gateway. Proxy servers act on behalf of the network devices to fetch the requested information from the Internet. Because proxies work at the application level, they can perform a wide variety of services, such as filtering data for "inappropriate" content, scanning for viruses, or restricting access to specific sites based on user, time of day, or physical address of the requesting PC. Proxies are also capable of caching content, which can greatly increase the performance of accessing Web data.

For the exam, remember these key points from this chapter:

- ✦ The firewall is the primary line of defense between the LAN and the outside world. Although firewalls can provide a reasonable amount of security, nothing is 100 percent effective against every possible attack.
- ✦ Firewalls are very effective for keeping unauthorized users out of the LAN, but most security threats exist on the *inside* of the firewall.
- ✦ Firewalls can be either dedicated hardware devices, software running on a standard computer, or part of a router.
- ✦ Network address translation hides the IP addressing scheme of the internal network, making it more difficult for outsiders to gain access to the LAN.
- ✦ IP spoofing is a primary tool used by hackers. Spoofing is a method by which a hacker constructs a harmful data packet using a valid IP address from the LAN, making it appear that the packet was generated originally from the network.
- ✦ A Demilitarized Zone, or DMZ, port on the firewall enables a network to have publicly available servers, such as Web or e-mail servers, connected to the firewall, yet still available to the outside world.
- ✦ The basic form of controlling access to the network is the process known as packet filtering. Data packets can be filtered and either allowed or disallowed, based on the TCP port they attempt to use or the protocol they use.
- ✦ Application Gateways, or proxies, improve on the packet-filter security by examining all application layers, bringing context information into the decision process. Application-level firewalls operate at the Application Layer of the protocol stack.
- ✦ A circuit-level firewall is a second-generation firewall that validates TCP and UDP sessions before opening a connection. After a handshake has taken place, it passes everything through until the session is ended.
- ✦ Stateful inspection provides full application-layer awareness without an intermediary proxy. With stateful inspection, packets are intercepted at the Network Layer where state-related information is extracted.
- ✦ Any security measure that is implemented has a negative effect on overall performance. This effect ranges from unacceptable to unnoticeable depending on the technology used and security levels required. Before installing any WAN product, you should examine and fine tune the LAN performance first.

✦ ✦ ✦

STUDY GUIDE

Assessment Questions

1. A properly configured firewall guarantees protection from the Internet.

    A. True

    B. False

2. Before installing a firewall, this step should be completed:

    A. Install TCP/IP on all network devices.

    B. Change everyone's password.

    C. Create a corporate security policy.

    D. Un-install TCP/IP on all network devices.

3. Which of the following items should be defined in a security policy? (Select all that apply.)

    A. Identify what groups of people require access to the Internet.

    B. Identify the addressing scheme used on the local network.

    C. Describe the nature of the data contained on the network.

    D. Define what security items the firewall logs will contain.

4. Overall, what is the purpose of the firewall?

    A. To provide safe Internet access to multiple users

    B. To allow outside people to access a corporate Web server securely

    C. To enforce an access control policy between two networks

    D. To route network users to the Internet via a Virtual Private Network (VPN) tunnel

5. What type of threat is a firewall useless against? (Select all that apply.)

    A. Internal attacks by disgruntled employees

    B. Trojan horses planted by unsuspecting employees

    C. Network passwords given out to contractors

    D. Denial-of-Service attacks

6. Which network device(s) are good choices for providing firewall services?

    A. Routers

    B. Bridges

    C. A desktop Macintosh computer

    D. A File and Print server

7. Software-based firewalls are capable of protecting only the PC they are installed on.

    A. True

    B. False

8. From a security standpoint, what is the primary benefit of network address translation (NAT)?

    A. Only one public address is used, thereby saving money.

    B. IP addresses outside the normal range of 0-255 can be used.

    C. People on the outside of the firewall see only this single IP address coming from the LAN.

    D. NAT translates all LAN IP addresses to a single IP address that is normally not routable, such as 127.0.0.1, so would-be hackers can route dangerous data packets back into the LAN.

9. A fundamental process used by hackers to gain access to a protected system is to substitute a LAN IP address into a hijacked data packet. What is this process known as?

    A. Network address translation

    B. RIP

    C. Denial of Service

    D. IP spoofing

10. What is a Demilitarized Zone used for?

    A. Trapping potential hackers

    B. Placing public servers on a protected network

    C. Placing servers behind a firewall that allows connections via VPN

    D. Placing servers behind a firewall that allows connections via modem dial-up

11. Packet filters can be defined to allow or disallow access based on which of the following?

   A. Source address, destination address, source port, and/or destination port

   B. A User Authenticate name and password

   C. The NetBIOS computer name

   D. Physical location of the outside connection

12. Packet-filtering firewalls work in which of the following situations?

   A. Only on dedicated firewall devices

   B. At the Data Layer and are application dependent

   C. At the Physical Layer and are application independent

   D. At the Network Layer and are application independent

13. Application gateways improve on the packet-filter security by doing which of the following?

   A. Offering more platforms to operate on

   B. Bringing context information into the decision process

   C. Working at the Network Layer and being application independent

   D. Working at the Network Layer and being application dependent

14. What common feature can proxy servers perform that other firewalls do not?

   A. Provide Web-based administration

   B. Provide detailed access logs

   C. Provide daily summary logs

   D. Provide Web page caching

15. What is a primary drawback to using an Application Gateway server?

   A. It can require client software to be functional.

   B. It must be configured for multiple protocols to be useful.

   C. It requires a bastion server to provide Internet access.

   D. It can only be configured to use NAT.

16. How do circuit-level firewalls operate?

   A. By pre-validating the connections, and then passing all data through untouched

   B. Validating each packet between predetermined end-points

   C. At the Application Level only

   D. Primarily for UDP connections

17. Circuit-level firewalls usually offer the highest level of stateful inspection and best performance.

    A. True

    B. False

18. Because Application Gateways/Proxy servers are able to examine every data packet, they are useful for:

    A. Detecting network errors

    B. Making intelligent routing decisions within the LAN

    C. Translating between protocols, such as Ethernet and Token Ring

    D. Restricting users from accessing specific Web sites or services

19. When designing a new Internet connection, what is one of the first steps to ensure maximum performance?

    A. Use multiple NICs.

    B. Define the security policy.

    C. Eliminate any existing performance issues on the LAN.

    D. Purchase the fastest WAN connection possible.

20. When fine-tuning the Internet connection, keeping in mind proper security needs, which of these items need to be observed?

    A. Set the minimum number of filters and rules as possible.

    B. Minimize Web caching whenever possible.

    C. Run the proxy software on a server-class computer.

    D. Use the fastest NIC possible.

Scenarios

1. Your company has discovered that the purchasing department can save more than 6 percent when placing orders via the Internet. Also, many customers have asked for account information via the Web, so you have been placed in charge of connecting the corporate LAN to the Internet. Upper management has stressed that internal data must be secured at all costs. Your department has already taken all appropriate steps to secure the data from internal threats and disasters. Describe at least one design that meets all these objectives.

2. As a consultant, you have been asked to provide a security proposal for a new customer. The customer maintains all their confidential business data on a mainframe computer that is already isolated from the primary LAN. The Human Resources manager is afraid that some employees may access inappropriate Internet sites and, therefore, would like the capability to control access of all Internet users. Describe what type of security system might best suit this company's needs.

Lab Exercises

Lab 17-1 Examining the Effects of a Firewall

The objective for this hands-on lab exercise is to see how a firewall can prevent access to a network from the Internet. This exercise requires an active Internet connection and a personal firewall program. If you don't have a personal firewall, you can download evaluation copies of Norton Personal Firewall (www.symantec.com), McAfee Firewall (www.mcafee.com), Tiny Software Firewall (www.tinysoftware.com), ZoneAlarm (www.zonealarm.com), or many other similar products. This lab uses the free, non-commercial version of ZoneAlarm. (ZoneAlarm is free for individual and not-for-profit charitable entity use excluding governmental entities and educational institutions). You need a second computer attached to the Internet to complete all aspects of this lab.

1. Gibson Research Corporation has developed several tools for testing the security of any Internet connection. Before installing the firewall software, visit Gibson Research on the Web at www.grc.com. Navigate the front Web page to the section entitled "Shields Up!!"

   The Shields-Up program is a Web-based application that attempts to communicate with your computer using known service protocols and well-known ports. None of these tests are invasive. They are intended solely to identify what ports on your computer are publicly available.

2. Run the "Test My Shields" test and note the results.

3. Run the "Test my Ports" test and note the results.

   Although your results will vary depending on your computer's configuration, more than likely these tests will reveal that some potential security threats exist. Windows, Macintosh, and (some releases of) Linux have server software applications that run by default when the Internet services are installed. If your results indicate that your computer is accessible by means of an internal server process that you are unaware of, you may want to make further reviews of your results.

4. Install (or activate) your personal firewall software. Follow the manufacturer's recommended installation process.

5. Configure the personal firewall software for maximum protection using the manufacturer's recommended settings.

6. Re-run the Shields-Up and Port Probe tests from Gibson Research and compare the results. The firewall software may pop up a message box or use another warning method to alert you to the probes. Affirm these alerts until the probes have completed.

444 Chapter 17 ✦ Study Guide

Answers to Chapter Questions

Chapter Pre-Test

1. The primary purpose of a firewall is to allow or disallow access between the LAN and the Internet based on a security policy.

2. The three types of firewalls are listed here:
   - A dedicated hardware device
   - A router with traffic filtering/firewall capabilities built in
   - A software-based system normally running on a PC or MAC

3. Firewalls can't protect against attacks that don't pass through it, nor can they protect the data against internal threats.

4. A security policy defines what items and what groups of people need protecting.

5. The firewall log files provide an administrator with powerful tools in determining potential security threats.

6. Beyond security, the proxy is used as a "middle man" between the LAN and the Internet so that LAN devices do not need direct access to the Internet in order to receive Internet services.

7. NAT hides the actual IP addresses of the internal network, making it more difficult to break in to from the outside. In addition, because all connections are assigned a single IP address, costs for public IP addresses are greatly reduced.

8. Personal firewalls are a good solution for protecting a single computer. They do not offer protection for any other devices on the LAN, however.

9. Application gateways improve on the packet-filter security by examining all application layers, bringing context information into the decision process.

10. All quality firewall devices have an average "packets-per-second" rating. Most of the manufacturers publish this figure so the consumer can gauge the average performance of the particular solution.

Assessment Questions

1. B. False. The only way to guarantee total security is to not connect to the Internet at all.

2. C. Until the items to be protected are clearly identified, there is no use in installing a firewall.

3. A and C.

4. C. Although various firewall devices might offer additional services, the primary function of the firewall is to enforce an access control policy between two networks.

5. A, B, and C. Firewalls can protect the LAN only against attacks that pass through the firewall.

6. A and C. Routers, dedicated firewall devices, and software running on computers can all act as firewalls.

7. B. False. Although *personal firewalls* protect only the PC they are installed on, many excellent software-based firewall products protect an entire LAN.

8. C. Although NAT does reduce the dependency of multiple public IP addresses, the primary security aspect of NAT is to hide the addressing scheme used on the internal network.

9. D. IP spoofing is the process of constructing a phony IP data packet that contains an IP address that matches the internal network in order to "trick" the firewall into allowing the packet because it appears to originate from the LAN.

10. B. When public servers, such as Web or e-mail servers, are required on a LAN, the safest way to install these are on dedicated DMZ ports on the firewall.

11. A. Packet filtering is based on one or more of the source address, destination address, source port, and/or destination port.

12. D. Packet-filtering firewalls work at the Network Layer and are application independent.

13. B. Because the Application Gateway/Proxy server works at the Application Layer, this security device brings context information into the decision process

14. D. Although the Application Gateway/Proxy server can provide these other items, the one thing they do that the others don't is Web page caching.

15. A. Some proprietary proxy software requires corresponding client software. Others require at least a minimum configuration of identifying the address of the proxy server in order to utilize it.

16. A. Circuit-level firewalls do the entire authentication before any actual data is passed. After the sender is validated, all further data passes through without further examination.

17. B. Although circuit-level firewalls generally offer great performance, they do not perform any authentication based on the protocol's state.

18. D. Because the Application Gateway/Proxy server can examine all packets coming in or going out, they are capable of preventing specific users from accessing specific sites or services.

19. C. Before attempting to fine-tune the WAN connections, you should resolve all possible performance issues of the LAN.

20. A, C, and D. Although other items specific to each network should be addressed, these three items usually offer the best advantages to maximize WAN performance without sacrificing the effectiveness of the security.

Scenarios

1. Because management has mandated that internal information must be secured "at all costs," the only option would be to not connect the main LAN to the Internet at all. You can create a separate network so that the purchasing agents can place their orders separately from the primary network. In addition, you can install dedicated Web servers on this subnet to provide account information to customers. Because the actual customer data will reside on the "non-connected" portion only, the Web-based data will have to be updated manually. Another option might be to use a proxy and bastion server on a separate subnet, although you still cannot provide a "total guarantee" of securing the data.

2. Because no sensitive data exists for you to worry about, just about any firewall product could be deployed safely on this network. However, only the Application Gateway/Proxy server would be able to filter Internet access based on user name, data content, and requested location.

CHAPTER 18

Network Configuration Settings

EXAM OBJECTIVES

- ✦ Differentiate between the following network protocols in terms of routing, addressing schemes, interoperability, and naming conventions:
  - TCP/IP
  - IPX/SPX
  - NetBEUI
  - AppleTalk
- ✦ Explain the issues that must be considered when multiple protocols are running at the same time.

PRE-TEST QUESTIONS

1. What is a nonroutable network communication protocol?
2. What is the primary advantage to using a routable network communication protocol?
3. What does TCP/IP use for network communication?
4. Is NetBIOS a transport protocol?
5. At what time is a computer name defined?
6. What is name resolution?
7. What does IPSEC enable clients to add to data packets?
8. Are NetBIOS names the same as computer names?
9. What is an FQDN?
10. What is a DNS zone?

✦ Answers to these questions can be found at the end of this chapter. ✦

Configuring a network can be a daunting task and the choices you make when setting a network's configuration, the results are often worth the effort. By carefully considering the needs of the organization, the capabilities of the hardware and software on the network, and the purpose of the network, the choices are easily made.

Properly configuring the protocols used on a network boosts its success more than almost anything else. Sure, you must have working hardware and properly installed software — all of which must be compatible — but unless these elements can communicate, no network. Specific configurations of hardware, software, and protocols are what (on a logical level) make a network a network.

This chapter details the various network protocols and the considerations that must be made to properly configure them.

Network Protocols

The world has many countries, and each country has its own common language that is for communications. In much the same way, communications on a network must also use a common "language" for communication to take place. The language of a network is called a protocol. However, a protocol is much more than just a common language. It also defines the rules that two communicating devices must use to ensure successful communication. Protocol rules govern the format of the messages sent back and forth and often even the values placed in the fields of the message elements.

As you read in this chapter, protocols have many and varied characteristics. Starting with the most impactive characteristic: protocols are divided into two different categories — routable and nonroutable.

Nonroutable protocols

Nonroutable protocols are network communication protocols that cannot pass through network routers because they don't have network addressing built into their data packets. Instead, they rely on network broadcasts for communication. Before the explosive growth in the Internet, nonroutable protocols were popular for workgroup environments.

Two major advantages of nonroutable protocols are simplicity of configuration and ease of installation. If there were such a thing as a plug-and-play protocol, the nonroutable protocol would be one.

The primary disadvantage of nonroutable protocols (other than their inability to pass through network routers), is their lack of scalability. Nonroutable protocols like NetBEUI (which is built upon the NetBIOS protocol) rely on broadcast messages to communicate between nodes. Because a router does not pass along broadcast messages, this limits nonroutable protocols to a single network segment, which is in turn limited to a maximum (on an Ethernet network) of 1024 hosts. Although it seems confining, this limit serves the purpose of attempting to avoid network congestion.

The following are examples of nonroutable protocols:

- **DLC (Data Link Control):** Hewlett-Packard developed this protocol for communicating with network print devices.
- **LAT (Local Area Transport):** Digital Equipment Corporation (DEC) developed this protocol, primarily for use with Digital UNIX, VMS, and VAX systems.
- **NetBEUI (Network Basic Input/Output System Extended User Interface):** IBM and Microsoft jointly developed this protocol; it was used with early versions of both OS/2 and Windows NT. NetBEUI is an optional protocol for Windowsd NT 4 and Windows 2000. NetBEUI uses an upper-layer protocol called Server Message Blocks (SMB) to communicate on the network.

Routable

Routable protocools use a form of network addressing able to pass through routers. Network addressing is a task assigned to Layer 3, the Network Layer of the 7-layer OSI model. The primary advantage of a routable protocol is network management. Using routable protocols, a network engineer can segment the network into smaller areas — which reduces the amount of network overhead required for communications. The following are examples of routable protocols that you should be familiar with for the exam:

AppleTalk

AppleTalk was developed by Apple Corporation and is proprietary to Apple and MacIntosh Networks. AppleTalk networks have the following characteristics:

- Network segments are called zones.
- Areas can be configured to communicate with specified zones, and are given priorities according to their network numbers.
- When a client is attempting to communicate with a client in a different zone, the client sends data to its local AppleTalk server — which in turn sends the data to a router configured to communicate with multiple zones.

Although used exclusively for Apple-based networks, other vendors can communicate with Apple networks for collaboration through the use of network services. For example: Microsoft uses Services for Macintosh on Windows NT and Windows 2000 networks to enable the two clients the ability to share information and store it in a universal format, which can be accessed by both clients.

IPX/SPX

IPX/SPX (Internet Packet Exchange/ Sequence Packet Exchange) is Novell's proprietary routable network protocol. IPX/SPX was developed in the late 1980s and quickly became the standard for small, multi-location networks. IPX/SPX has a low network overhead, and can easily be segmented by using network numbers. Similar to AppleTalk routing, when a client is attempting to communicate with a client using a similar network address, the client sends the data to a router, which is configured to communicate with multiple networks.

Microsoft began using its own version of IPX/SPX with Windows NT 3.5. The Microsoft version of IPX/SPX is called NWLink (NetWare Link). NWLink, when used with other Micosoft services, such as Client Services for NetWare (CSNW) and Gateway Services for NetWare (GSNW), enables Microsoft clients access to resources on NetWare servers. A Microsoft client is a computer running a Microsoft operating system and is also running networking client software from Microsoft. Client for Microsoft Networks is an example of a Microsoft client application. Without the use of the additional services of CSNW or GSNW, Microsoft and NetWare clients are restricted to only those client/server applications based on NetBIOS. NetBIOS is discussed in detail later in this chapter.

XNS

Xerox developed Xerox Networking System (XNS) with the development of Ethernet. Using a network numbering system similar to IPX/SPX, clients were able to be segmented on different networks to reduce the network overhead for local communication. XNS was proprietary to Xerox and was not accepted as a standard for network communication.

TCP/IP

TCP/IP (Transmission Control Protocol/Internet Protocol) is a protocol *suite*, not a single protocol (as many would have us believe). The addressing of a TCP/IP packet is what makes it a routable protocol. TCP/IP uses a unique 32-bit address for network communication. This address is a binary representation of three distinct parts: a network portion, subnet portion, and a host portion.

Because of its scalability, TCP/IP is the most commonly used routable protocol. TCP/IP is not proprietary to any single vendor; it is based on standards called *requests for comments* (RFCs), which are issued and managed by the Internet Engineering Task Force (IETF).

> **Tip** You can find information about the IETF and RFCs at www.ietf.org.

A client using TCP/IP performs a small mathematical computation to determine if the destination address (receiver) is on the same network segment as the source (sender). If the addresses are not on the same network segment, the network packet is sent to a default gateway, which routes it to the entry point of the destination network.

Cross-Reference: TCP/IP addressing is covered in detail in Chapter 4.

Network communication

Client names can be either NetBIOS names or hostnames. NetBIOS names are typically used in a Microsoft Network Environment. When a user accesses My Network Places in the most recent Windows versions (or Network Neighborhood in Windows 9x), the user is requesting a NetBIOS name resolution. Before looking at NetBIOS resolution, it is crucial to understand what NetBIOS is and is not.

NetBIOS revealed

Contrary to what you may have heard from self-styled networking experts, *NetBIOS is not a transport protocol* because it does not operate at the Transport layer in the OSI networking model.

NetBIOS is however, a Session-layer *transport* — a somewhat lesser creature. The difference between a transport and a transport *protocol* is that a transport protocol can send a data packet to the network by using a specific form of addressing within the packet. A Session-layer *transport* can only use the established names and pass these names to the transport protocol — at the Transport layer of the network Thus two layers — the Session layer and the Transport layer — work together. The following example shows how.

A user on a network double-clicks a computer through My Network Places. When do so, one of the layers of the 7-layer model is filled in; the layer filled is the Session-layer. The Session-layer data is filled with the name of the computer that the user is trying to contact. The name is passed to the transport layer, where a protocol capable of delivering the packet is selected.

NetBIOS names have the following characteristics:

- Maximum of 15 characters
- Limited to alphanumeric characters
- Must be unique throughout the entire network

Tip: COMPUTER NAMES (NetBIOS NAMES). A *computer name* is user-defined during installation of the network software. A NetBIOS name is defined by the computer name in addition to the service code. The service code used in a NetBIOS Name is represented in hexadecimal notation. The service code is added to the computer name only when using the transport protocol of TCP/IP — and before that can happen, you must enable the NetBT (*NetBIOS over TCP/IP*) protocol.

The following are the most common NetBIOS names on a Microsoft network.

[00h] Workstation Service

[03h] Messenger Service

[20h] Server Service

[1bh] Domain Controller Service

[1eh] Domain Name service (Do not confuse this as DNS, this is simply the NetBIOS name of the domain.)

Example: When a user on Workstation1 tries to connect to Server2, the user connects the workstation service of Workstation1 to the server service of Server2. A computer connects to a different computer on the network using a different service. When a user is requesting a resource or a service the workstation service is used, and when a server is supplying a resource, it uses the server service. NetBIOS indicates which service is being used within a given network packet.

Clients communicate on a network by using one of three identifiers: Names, IP addresses, or MAC Addresses. Recall that all computers on a network have a name specified during the networking software configuration. two types of names that a client can have: NetBIOS Name and Hostname. NetBIOS Names must be unique throughout the entire network, and Hostnames must be unique to their Internet Domain Name. IP addresses are also assigned during the software installation and must be unique throughout the entire network. MAC addresses are hardware defined and must be unique on the local area network as they are not routable. Network Interface Cards (NICs) have a 12-digit hexadecimal address preset by the manufacturer. Because the MAC addresses do not pass through routers, they have to be unique only the local segment.

Each level of communication must have a way of getting information to and from the next level. The process of obtaining this information is called *resolution*. When a user on the network browses the network and clicks on a name of a different computer (Host or NetBIOS), the name has to be resolved to an IP address. Names can be resolved by several methods: network broadcast, name cache, or a name server. When the name is resolved to an IP address, the IP address must be resolved to a MAC address. MAC addresses can be resolved by: network broadcasts or server-based resolution.

Installation and Configuration of Protocols

Every network uses a particular language for communication — and some networks use more than one protocol. Before any protocols can be used, however, they must be installed and configured. The steps needed for installation and configuration of protocols is a simple process, and varies just slightly between operating systems. The specific installation and configuration processes for the three main protocols (NetBEUI, TCP/IP, and IPX/SPX-NWLINK) depend on which Microsoft operating system is in use (Windows 98, Windows NT, or Windows 2000).

NetBEUI installation and configuration

The biggest advantage of using NetBEUI for a network protocol is the ease of installation. If there existed such a thing as a plug and play protocol, NetBEUI would have to be one. To install NetBEUI on one of the Windows operating systems, follow the steps detailed in Labs 18-1 through 18-3.

Lab 18-1 Installing NetBEUI on a Windows 98 System

To install NetBEUI on a Windows 98 system, follow these steps:

1. Access Network Properties (see Figure 18-1) by opening the Control Panel from the Start and Settings menus. Open the Network icon, or right click Network Neighborhood, or ALT and double click Network Neighborhood).

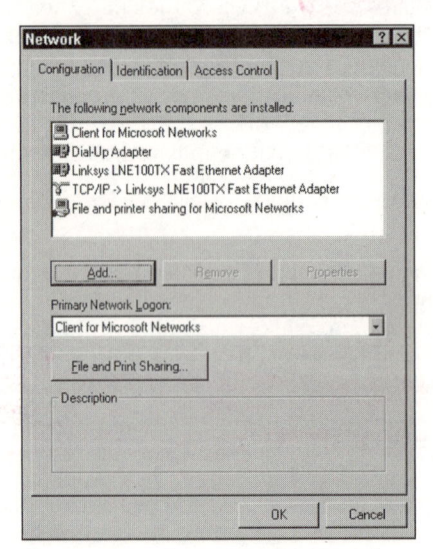

Figure 18-1: The Network Properties window on a Windows 98 system.

2. Select the Add button.

Chapter 18 ✦ **Network Configuration Settings** 455

3. Select Protocol from the Select Network Component Type dialog box and click Add, as shown in Figure 18-2. You may notice a slight delay while the system builds a driver information base for the protocols avaialble on your system.

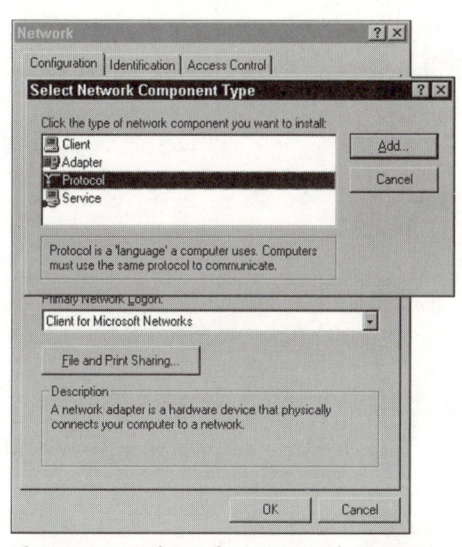

Figure 18-2: The Select Network Component Type dialog box from a Windows 98 Network Properties window.

4. Select Microsoft from the Manufacturers list (left pane) on the Select Network Protocol box, as shown in Figure 18-3.

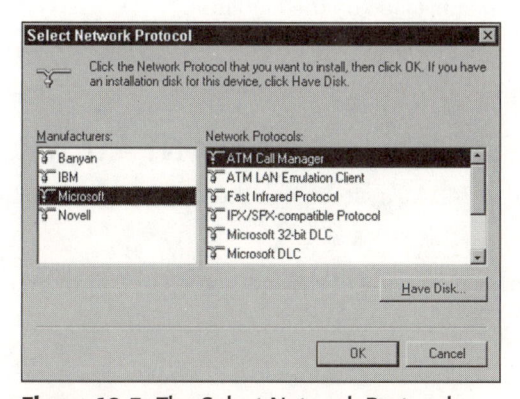

Figure 18-3: The Select Network Protocol dialog box on a Windows 98 system.

5. Select NetBEUI from the Network Protocols list (right pane) and click OK. This returns you to the Network Properties window that lists NetBEUI in the installed network components list, as shown in Figure 18-4.

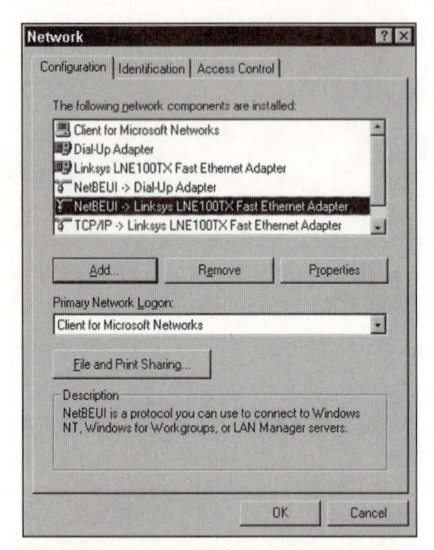

Figure 18-4: A Windows 98 Network Properties window with NetBEUI installed.

6. Select OK. You see a DOS window or two flash on the screen and then the system asks you to restart the computer.

> **Note** When using Win98, the operating system may prompt you for the location of the distribution files if they are not installed on the hard disk.

7. Restart the computer.

Lab 18-2 Installing NetBEUI on a Windows NT 4.0 System

To install NetBEUI on a Windows NT 4.0 system, use these steps (refer to Lab 18-1 for examples):

1. Access Network Properties using one of the methods listed in the Windows 98 process.
2. Select the Protocols tab.
3. Select Add.
4. Select NetBEUI.
5. Specify the location of the distribution files.

6. Select Close.

7. Reboot.

> **Note:** Windows NT also prompts you for the location of the distribution files, but you can avoid this step by specifying the distribution location when selecting the protocol to install.

Lab 18-3 Installing NetBEUI on a Windows 2000 System

To install NetBEUI on a Windows 2000 system, use these steps:

1. Access Network Properties by accessing the Control Panel from My Computer or the Start I Settings menus and opening the Network icon or right click My Network Places and choosing Properties.
2. Select the Properties of the Local Area Connection that will be using NetBEUI.
3. Select Install.
4. Select Protocol.
5. Select NetBEUI.
6. Click Finished. (Guess what — no reboot necessary!)

The configuration of NetBEUI is the same regardless of the operating system being used. One simple reason is that NetBEUI actually has no configuration procedure. The word according to Microsoft that your first and only step in troubleshooting NetBEUI is to *reinstall* NetBEUI.

IPX/SPX-NWLINK installation and configuration

IPX/SPX-NWLINK are mentioned in the same breath because some operating systems use IPX/SPX and others (meaning the Windows operating systems) use NWLINK. For simplicity, both are referenced as NWLINK (even though they work essentially the same and the only difference between them is their manufacturers). Installation and configuration of NWLINK is quite simple, requiring only a few additional entries above NetBEUI. As with NetBEUI, NWLINK installation can vary by operating system.

Two primary differences between installing NetBEUI and NWLINK. You are required to enter two additional settings for NWLINK communication: a Network Number, and a NetWare Login Server. The NetWare Login Server configuration is dependent on the version of NetWare running on the network. If the network is running NetWare Version 3.x and following, or NetWare 4.X running Bindery emulation, you must specify a preferred server. If the network is running NetWare version 4.X and utilizing NetWare Directory Services, you specify the Naming Context, and Tree. The Naming Context and Tree is similar to specifying a DNS (Domain Name System) Domain and Subdomain.

The processes used to install IPX/SPX-NWLINK on Windows 98, Windows NT, and Windows 2000 are detailed in Labs 18-4 through 18-6.

Lab 18-4 Installing NWLINK on a Windows 98 System

To install IPX/SPX-NWLINK on a Windows 98 system, follow these steps (refer to Lab 18-1 and Figures 18-1 through 18-4 for examples of the elements referenced):

1. Access Network Properties using one of the methods listed for Windows 98 in the "NetBEUI installation and configuration" section.
2. Select Add.
3. Select the Protocols Tab.
4. Choose Microsoft from the Manufacturer list on the left.
5. Select IPX/SPX Compatible Transport from the list on the right.
6. Specify the path to the installation files.
7. Specify the Network Number.
8. Specify the NetWare Login Server.
9. Select Close.
10. Reboot.

Lab 18-5 Installing NWLINK on a Windows NT 4 System

To install IPX/SPX-NWLINK on a Windows NT 4 system, follow these steps (refer to Lab 18-1 and Figures 18-1 through 18-4 for examples of the elements referenced):

1. Access Network Properties using one of the methods listed for Windows 98 in the "NetBEUI installation and configuration" section.
2. Select Add.
3. Select the Protocols Tab.
4. Choose Microsoft from the Manufacturer list on the left.
5. Select NWLINK from the list on the right.
6. Specify the path to the installation files.
7. Specify the Network Number.
8. Specify the NetWare Login Server.
9. Select Close.
10. Reboot.

Installing NWLINK on a Windows 2000 System

To install IPX/SPX-NWLINK on a Windows 2000 system, follow these steps:

1. Access Network Properties.
2. Select the NIC you want to use for NWLINK.
3. Select Install.
4. Select Protocol.
5. Select NWLINK.
6. Specify the path to the installation files.
7. Specify the Network Number.
8. Specify the NetWare Login Server.

Troubleshooting the NWLINK Installation

Although troubleshooting NWLINK is a slightly more complicated process than troubleshooting NetBEUI, it entails only three general steps:

1. Ensure that the NIC is working properly and that no faulty cables.
2. Ensure that the correct frame type is being used:
   - NetWare 3.x and 4.x, when running bindery emulation, use 802.3
   - NetWare 4.x, when running NDS, uses 802.2.
3. Ensure that the correct Network Number is being used.

It is possible to configure NWLINK to use multiple frame types. By default, auto frame type detection is selected. When NWLINK is configured for auto frame type detection, only one frame type can be detected. To have multiple frame types, you must configure the frame type detection as manual. For those of you that enjoy a more difficult approach to client protocol configuration, you can also edit the registry key and add the packet value type for the appropriate frame type.

Installation and configuration of TCP/IP

TCP/IP is considered to be the most complex network protocol. TCP/IP is easy to install; however, to configure TCP/IP to work correctly requires a deep level of understanding of IP addressing. Regardless of the operating system, two ways to configure TCP/IP. TCP/IP can be configured manually at the client workstation, or it can be configured automatically from a DHCP Server. few differences in the manual configuration of TCP/IP between the different clients.

When configuring TCP/IP manually, two parameters are required for network communication between clients: the IP address and a Subnet Mask.

> **Note:** Contrary to what is written in many books, a client *does not* need a gateway address configured in the IP properties to communicate on the network. The gateway parameter is only required when a client is communicating with clients on other network segments through a router.

Optional client configuration options that can be manually entered or enabled through DHCP, including:

- **NetBIOS Name Server (WINS):** Specified on the WINS tab in the TCP/IP properties page. When a WINS server is specified, the client registers with the WINS server, and use the WINS server for NetBIOS name resolution. WINS server configuration is covered later in this chapter.
- **Domain Name System (DNS):** DNS is specified on the DNS tab in the TCP/IP properties page. Depending on the server running DNS, the client can register with the DNS server, just as with the WINS server. The client uses the DNS server for Hostname resolution. DNS server and hostname resolution is covered later in this chapter.

Installing TCP/IP

To install TCP/IP on the various Windows operating systems, follow the steps detailed in Labs 18-6 through 18-8.

Lab 18-6 Installing TCP/IP on a Windows 98 System

To install TCP/IP on a Windows 98 system, following these steps (refer to Lab 18-1 and Figures 18-1 through 18-4 for examples of the elements and choices):

1. Access Network Properties.
2. Select Add.
3. Select Protocol then click Add.
4. Choose Microsoft from the list on the left.
5. Choose TCP/IP from the list on the right.
6. Specify the Path.
7. Select either "Obtain an IP AddressAutomatically" or "Specify an IP Address" as a configuration.
8. Reboot.

Lab 18-7 Installing TCP/IP on a Windows NT 4.0 System

To install TCP/IP on a Windows NT 4 system, follow these steps (refer to Lab 18-1 and its accompanying illustrations for examples of the elements and choices):

1. Access Network Properties.
2. Protocols Tab.
3. Select Add.
4. Select TCP/IP.
5. Specify the Installation Path.
6. Select either "Obtain an IP AddressAutomatically" or "Specify an IP Address" as a configuration.
7. Reboot.

Lab 18-8 Installing TCP/IP on a Windows 2000 System

To install TCP/IP on a Windows 200 system, follow these steps:

1. Access Network Properties.
2. Select the NIC that you wish to install TCP/IP on
3. Select Install.
4. Select Protocol.
5. Select Microsoft.
6. Select TCP/IP.
7. Specify the path to the installation files.
8. Choose DHCP or manual configuration.
9. Select Finish.

Windows 2000 TCP/IP Security Considerations

It is important to note that Windows 2000 has additional IP configuration options. When specifying DNS configuration parameters, a client can specify whether to update DNS server information or let DHCP perform the update. In addition to the DNS configuration, IP Security (IPSec) is a new feature of Windows 2000. IPSec enables the client to add encryption to every data packet placed on the network.

You can choose one of three configurations options for IPSec:

+ **Client Respond**: This setting specifies that a client uses IPSec when communicating with a server that requests IPSec. This enables a client to communicate with other clients not using IPSec.

+ **Server Request**: This settings specifies the client requests that all communication use IPSec. When a connection is made to another client that does use IPSec, communication is still enableed.

+ **Server Required**: This setting specifies that all communication uses IPSec. If a requesting client does not use IPSec, communication is denied.

NetBIOS-to-HOST-name resolution

One simple rule that enables you to understand when to use NetBIOS names and when to use `HOST` names. Any network application used only by Microsoft networking clients uses NetBIOS names. Any application that can be used by any networking client, regardless of vendor specification, uses `HOST` names.

NetBIOS names are not the same as computer names. A computer name is specified during the client software installation. The NetBIOS name is used after the installation of TCP/IP. The NetBIOS name uses the computer name along with a *service indicator* — a 2-digit number (in hexadecimal notation) that specifies the service being used for communication.

Using NetBIOS names on a network simplifies the process of connecting a user accont to network resources. Users are not required to remember long IP addresses to make a connection to a resource. NetBIOS names enable users to browse the network by going through Network Neighborhood or through My Network Places. Although the user is not cognizant of what happens when a network resource is requested by name, the system is doing a lot of work behind the scenes to make connection-by-name possible. This magic is called *resolution*. Resolution happens in many different ways, but the order is the same for all NetBIOS.

NetBIOS resolution happens in the following order:

1. **NetBIOS name cache**. When a NetBIOS name has been resolved, the resolved name is placed in the NetBIOS name cache. The NBCache is first checked for name resolution. To manage the cache, an administrator can use the utility NBTSTAT.

2. **WINS Server**. If a name is not resolved through the cache, the WINS server is queried. WINS traffic is a directed data packet and therefore is routable.

Windows Internet Naming Service (WINS) Server

Microsoft's NetBIOS Name Server is called WINS. WINS is a service that runs on a Windows NT or Windows 2000 Server. It is a dynamic service that enables clients to register NetBIOS names at startup, and request name resolution. The following is an example of the WINS process.

1. Workstation A (WA) is configured with TCP/IP and has a WINS server address specified in the properties of TCP/IP. When WA boots up, it sends to the WINS server (WS) a request to register the NetBIOS name that has been configured on the property pages of the network identification.

2. WS checks the database of NetBIOS names and determine whether the requested name is in use. If the name is in use, WA receives a *duplicate name exists on the network* error message. If the name is not in use, WA is successfully registered with the NetBIOS name that was requested.

3. The network is configured with more than 1000 NetBIOS clients that register with WS, and this provides the network with a centralized database of NetBIOS names. This enables any client on the network to request a NetBIOS name resolution from WS.

4. WA browses the network to access a shared resource on Workstation T (WT). WA sends to WS a request for resolution of the name WT.

5. WS receives the request and searches the database for an entry for WT. If an entry exists, WS send to WA the IP address that maps to the entry for WT in the NetBIOS database. If no entry in the NetBIOS database for WT, WS sends a name resolution failed message to WA. When a user receives *the specified name cannot be found on the network*, it might have been a failed resolution request.

Domain Name System

The Domain Name System (DNS) is one of the least understood naming structures in TCP/IP. Often it has been compared to the difficulty of Abstract Mathematics. Actually DNS is a simple naming system that becomes complex when the foundation is learned. The first thing to remember about DNS, and perhaps the most important, is that DNS is a hierarchical naming system. What this means to Network Administrators is that hostnames can be duplicated on the network as long as the names are unique within the domain. If the previous statement seems confusing, not to worry, it only means the foundation of DNS has not been learned, which is something easily fixed.

At the heart of DNS is the `root` directory, denoted modestly with a single period (.) but containing entries for all top-level domains. A Top Level Domain is the end part of a Web address. For example, www.nexusworldwide.com is the Web address for the company for which I work. The end of the name is .com, and the top level domain. The following is a list of the most common top level domains: .com., .edu, .org., gov., .mil, .net, and a few others.

A DNS server reads Web addresses in reverse order. A more accurate name for a Web address is a fully qualified domain name (FQDN). An FQDN is more specific; the name is read right to left and narrows the focus down to a specific host. An FQDN can be further subdivided as shown here:

`Hostname.Domainname.Top-leveldomain.Rootdomain`

Remember that the `root` domain is referenced as a single period at the end of the FQDN. In the earlier example, `www.nexusworldwide.com` can be written as follows:

`www` = hostname

`nexusworldwide` = domain name

`com` = top-level domain

Because DNS is hierarchical, hostnames can match other hostnames, as long as they don't exactly match the hostname of the FQDN.

It would be possible to also have www.nexusworldwide.net, because the FQDNs do not fully match.

DNS is subdivided into *zones* — areas of contiguous name space. In effect, that means all FQDNs in the same zone must have the same two ending names. Thus `server1.nexusworldwide.com`, `server2.nexusworldwide.com`, and `aussie.Australia.nexusworldwide.com` would all be contained in the same zone — even if they represented offices on three continents — because each ends with `.nexusworldwide.com`.

`www.nexusworldwide.com` and `www.australia.nexusworldwide.com` would be different hosts because of the hierarchical structure of DNS. The rule to remember is that if the names are not *exactly* the same, then the names do not conflict on the network. The following two names, for example, would not conflict:

`aussie.Australia.nexusworldwide.com`

`www.australia.nexusworldwide.com`

A DNS zone used to resolve hostnames to IP addresses is called a forward lookup zone. Sometimes a must take an IP address and resolve it to a hostname, you can do so by using a reverse lookup zone. One of the many reasons to use a reverse lookup zone is for the security of websites. The reverse lookup ascertains that the IP addresses which are connecting resolve back to hostnames authorized.

Dynamic Host Configuration Protocol (DHCP)

How long would it take a team of 10,000 administrators to assign an individual IP address to 16,000,000 different machines on a network? Fortunately, a question that should not have to be answered, because DHCP enables administrators the ability to assign IP addresses automatically at client startup. In addition to automatically assigning IP addresses, DHCP can also be configured to provide clients with the addresses of routers, WINS servers, time servers, DNS servers, and many other options.

DHCP uses a form of BOOTP, which is the BOOTPASS protocol. BOOTP passes a request for boot-up information to a server via a network broadcast. Because routers do not typically pass broadcasts, special network services are required to enable DHCP to work in a routed network.

Labeled incorrectly, like many other network services, DHCP is not as difficult as many books would have you believe. The process of installing and configuring DHCP is quite simple, and only a few requirements. First, there has to be a server running the DHCP server service. The server running the DHCP can be any of the following:

- Windows NT
- Windows 2000
- Windows .NET
- Novell 3.X/4.X/5.X
- Apple Server
- Linux running network services
- Unix (any flavor) with DHCP Daemon enabled

Once a server running the DHCP service, a scope must be created. A scope is a range of IP addresses valid for a specific subnet of a network. When the scope is created, the scope must then be activated. After the scope has been activated, client requests for IP addresses can be answered by the DHCP server.

DHCP is one of the most widely used network services available. Nearly all dial-up connections to the Internet are based on DHCP, and large corporate networks rely heavily on DHCP to reduce network administrative overhead. It is most common to see a DHCP environment use private IP addressing to meet internal needs. Private IP addresses encompass only the following address ranges:

- 10.0.0.0 – 10.255.255.255
- 172.16.0.0 – 172.31.255.255
- 192.168.0.0 – 192.168.255.255

These address ranges are considered private because they are not routable through the Internet. The addresses can be routed all over the world and back, but it is not possible to route the private address schemes through Internet routers.

The DHCP process is a set of four steps that can be remembered in the acronym DORA (Discover – Offer – Request – Acknowledgement).

When a DHCP client boots, it requests an IP address from the **ANY** DHCP server by sending a DHCP Discover packet. The packet is sent to all hosts connected to a subnet. All DHCP servers receive the packet and reply with a DHCP Offer packet. The offer packet contains an IP address being offered to the client.

The DHCP client then accepts the first DHCP Offer packet it receives from the DHCP servers. When it receives the first Offer packet, the client responds with a DHCP Request packet. The Request packet is sent to all hosts on network as a broadcast, and every DHCP server that offered the client receives the Request packet. All servers that did not send the requested IP address withdraws the offer.

Once the server that sent out the offer that was accepted receives a request packet back from the client, the server responds with a DHCP Acknowledgement packet (ACK). The ACK packet contains additional client configuration parameters. Additional services like WINS and DNS are specified as DHCP Options.

Once the client receives the DHCP ACK packet, the client then begins using IP.

The Options given out by the DHCP server can reduce network configuration overhead, but if assigned incorrectly, the options can actually make the network traffic worse on a network. It is simple to configure a DHCP server to assign the address of a WINS server, but if the additional option of node type is not assigned, the client does not use WINS. For WINS to work properly, a NetBIOS node type has to be assigned to the client.

All DHCP Options are referenced by three-digit numbers. The following options are most common in DHCP environments:

- 003 = Router
- 006 = DNS server
- 015 = Domain name
- 044 = WINS server, or NetBIOS name server
- 046 = Node-type

Of these four options 046 specifies how the client is to ask for NetBIOS name resolution. The node types available are as follows:

- 0X1 = B-node (broadcast) = A client can only use broadcasts.
- 0X2 = P-node (peer) = A client can only use the WINS server for resolution.

0X4 = M-node (mixed) = A client uses `Bcast` first and then uses WINS.

0X8 = H-node (Hybrid) = A client uses WINS first and then uses `Bcast`.

> **Note** 0X8 (H-node) is the node type that must specified when using a WINS server.

When a client successfully receives an address from a DHCP server, the client is given a *lease* — a period of time that the client is permitted to use the address. For example, the default lease time for a DCHP server running Windows NT is 3 days; the default lease time for a server running Windows 2000 is 8 days.

DHCP clients try to renew the lease at every reboot, and at the halfway point of the lease, whichever comes first. If the client is unable to renew at the halfway point, the client tries again at @@bf 7/8 of the lease time. If the client is unsuccessful at this point, the client starts the DHCP process over again by broadcasting to the network. In the event a DHCP server cannot be contacted, the client continues to use the address until lease expiration. At the lease expiration point, the client ceases to use the IP address.

Some clients do not have normal leases. For example, a special client called a *reserved client* can have an indefinite lease. The reservations that identify reserved clients are based on MAC addresses.

Addresses can also be excluded from the scope. If a scope is defined to have 200 available addresses, but 10 addresses in the middle are used for printers, the addresses for the printers can be excluded from the scope. Once the printer addresses are excluded, the DHCP server does not use them.

> **Note** Exclusions are processed before reservations, and therefore it is not possible to exclude and reserve the same IP address.

Once a client has an address, the user of the client account may need to view address information (or manually renew the lease) to obtain new options from the server. The client operating system dictates how this manual process is done.

Windows 98 clients use the command `winipcfg`. When the `winipcfg` command is run, a graphical window is presented. From within the window, a client can choose to view additional information about the lease. The additional information includes the lease options as well as the time and expiration of the lease. The client also has the option to renew the lease or release the lease.

Windows NT/2000 clients use the command *ipconfig. When the* command is run it displays the current IP configuration of the IP address, the subnet mask and the default gateway.

You have three switches to use with ipconfig. The three primary switches are /all, /release, and /renew.

`ipconfig /all` displays all the IP address configuration data the client received from the server. This includes the lease time, the DHCP Server Address, WINS Server Address, DNS Server Address, and other DHCP option information.

`ipconfig /release` releases the current lease the client has from the DHCP Server. After running `ipconfig /release`, the client can't use IP to communicate on the network.

`ipconfig /renew` manually renews the client lease with the DHCP server. Running `Ipconfig /renew` also enables the client to receive updates of DHCP options.

Summary

Routable protocols are capable of being transmitted outside the local network and across the internetwork to remote networks. Although it may seem obvious, a routable protocol can be routed. On the other hand, nonroutable protocols (which on the Network+ exam is primarily NetBEUI) cannot be routed. Networking protocols are interoperable and can be installed together on a single network. However, a proprietary form of a protocol may need to be used, such as NWLINK, which is Microsoft's version of the IPX/SPX protocol client.

On a local network and out on the Internet, logical computer names must be resolved to their numerical (IP address or MAC address) equivalents. A number of different services can be used for this task, including WINS and DNS.

✦ ✦ ✦

STUDY GUIDE

Assessment Questions

1. In what situation would you use nonroutable protocols? (Choose all that apply)

    A. Large segmented networks

    B. Small segmented networks

    C. Workgroup environments

    D. Single-segment networks with 2000 clients

2. In what situation would you use routable protocols? (Choose all that apply)

    A. Large segmented networks

    B. Small segmented networks

    C. Workgroup environments

    D. Single-segment networks with 2000 clients

3. TCP/IP is: (choose all that apply)

    A. Proprietary

    B. Nonproprietary

    C. Routable

    D. Nonroutable

4. TCP/IP uses _____ for network communication.

    A. NetBIOS name

    B. Hostname

    C. A unique 32-bit address

    D. An FQDN

5. IPSec adds _____ to every data packet placed on the network.

   A. Encryption

   B. Parity bit

   C. A unique 32-bit address

   D. Resolution

6. A DNS server reads Web addresses in what order?

   A. Forward

   B. Reverse

7. Identify the zone for the following addresses: `www.nexusworldwide.net`, `www.australia.nexusworldwide.net`, and `www.stmaarten.nexusworldwide.net`?

   A. `www.nexusworldwide.net`

   B. `.net`

   C. `nexusworldwide`

   D. `nexusworldwide.net`

8. At what point is a computer name specified?

   A. At startup

   B. After the installation of TCP/IP

   C. After installation of IPSec

   D. After installation of client software

9. WINS enables clients to: (choose all that apply)

   A. Request name resolution

   B. Pass requests for boot-up information

   C. Create a hierarchical naming system

   D. Register NetBIOS names at startup

10. DHCP provides clients with: (choose all that apply)

    A. IP addresses

    B. WINS server addresses

    C. Router addresses

    D. DNS server addresses

Answers to Chapter Questions

Chapter Pre-test

1. A nonroutable network communication protocol is a protocol unable to pass through a router because they do not have network addressing built into their data packet and instead must rely upon network broadcasts for communication.

2. The primary advantage to using a routable network communication protocol is first and foremost that it is routable. But it is reduces the overhead for network management because it enables network administrators to break the network down into more manageable network segments.

3. TCP/IP uses a 32-bit address for network communications. This address is a binary representation of three address parts consisting of a network portion, a subnet portion, and a host portion.

4. NetBIOS is not a transport protocol but rather works with a transport protocol to get a data packet to the network. NetBIOS uses names and passes these names to the transport protocol.

5. A computer name is defined at installation of client software.

6. Name resolution is the process of resolving a Host or NetBIOS name to an IP address by one of several methods: network broadcast, name cache, or by using a name server. The IP address must then be resolved to a MAC address by one or two methods: network broadcasts or server-based resolution.

7. IPSec enables clients to add encryption to data packets for increased security.

8. NetBIOS names are NOT the same as computer names. The NetBIOS name is a hexadecimal code added to a computer name when using the transport protocol TCP/IP and you have enabled NetBT, which is NetBIOS over TCP/IP.

9. FQDN is the acronym for Fully Qualified Domain Name. This is another name for a Web address.

10. A DNS zone is an area of contiguous name space used in the Domain Naming System (DNS). A *zone* is identified by two FQDNs that have the same two ending names (such as `nexusworldwide.com`).

Assessment Questions

1. C. Nonroutable protocols are best suited for nonsegmented networks with fewer than 1024 clients. Nonroutable protocols cannot be passed through routers.

2. A, B, D. Routable protocols were developed with segmented networks in mind as they can pass through routers. Routable protocols are suitable for both large and small segmented networks and can also be used in nonsegmented networks. A network with over 1024 clients would require a routable protocol because a nonroutable protocol is based on broadcast communications (which would create too much network traffic on a network of that size or larger).

3. B, C. TCP/IP is a nonproprietary protocol with is completely routable. TCP/IP is based on RFC standards available for all vendors to use. TCP/IP is used on the largest routable network, the Internet.

4. C. TCP/IP uses a unique 32-bit address in a binary representation of three address parts consisting of a network portion, a subnet portion, and a host portion.

5. A. To enhance security, IPSec adds encryption to every data packet placed on the network.

6. B. A DNS server reads Web addresses in reverse order, right to left. It begins with the `root` domain portion of the address, to the top-level domain portion, to the domain name, to the hostname.

7. D. A DNS zone is the area of contiguous name space — a portion of the FQDN shared with other domains on the network.

8. D. A computer name is specified after the installation of the client software.

9. A, D. WINs enables clients to request name resolution and to register NetBIOS names at startup. WINS is a dynamic service that runs on Windows NT or Windows 2000 server.

10. A, B, C, D. DHCP automatically assigns IP addresses to clients at startup. DHCP also provides clients with WINS server addresses, router addresses, DNS server addresses, timer server addresses, and many other options.

Operation

PART IV

In This Part

Chapter 19
TCP/IP Troubleshooting Utilities

Chapter 20
Small/Home Office Network Troubleshooting

Chapter 21
Remote Connectivity Troubleshooting

Chapter 22
Client/Server Network Configuration

Chapter 23
Wiring

Chapter 24
Network Troubleshooting

CHAPTER 19

TCP/IP Troubleshooting Utilities

EXAM OBJECTIVES

✦ Given a troubleshooting scenario, select the appropriate TCP/IP utility from among the following:

- Tracert
- Ping
- Arp
- Netstat
- Nbtstat
- Ipconfig/Ifconfig
- Winipcfg
- Nslookup

✦ Given output from a diagnostic utility, identify the utility and interpret the output

CHAPTER PRE-TEST

1. What TCP/IP utility can you use to test connectivity to a host?
2. What is the proper syntax for using the Ping utility?
3. What TCP/IP utility would you use to see the route a packet takes to its destination?
4. What switch displays a list of switches for the Arp utility?
5. What switch of the `arp` command would you use to display current Arp entries?
6. What TCP/IP utility displays statistics and current TCP/IP connections?
7. What would you find under the Proto column of the output of the Netstat utility?
8. What TCP/IP utility would you use to display the current TCP/IP configuration on a computer running the Windows NT operating system?
9. Ifconfig is used on what operating system?
10. What TCP/IP utility would you use to display the current TCP/IP configuration on a Windows 95/98 system?

✦ Answers to these questions can be found at the end fo the chapter. ✦

Chapter 19 ✦ TCP/IP Troubleshooting Utilities

TCP/IP is by far the most widely used protocol on today's networks. The Network+ exam tests you on the basic concepts and functions of the standard TCP/IP utilities that come with the Microsoft Windows operating system family. You can use these utilities to verify TCP/IP configuration and connectivity. The following TCP/IP utilities are on the exam:

- ✦ Ping
- ✦ Tracert
- ✦ Arp
- ✦ Netstat
- ✦ Nbtstat
- ✦ Ipconfig/Ifconfig
- ✦ Winipcfg
- ✦ Nslookup

Using TCP/IP Utilities

When you are using TCP/IP as the protocol on your network, it is important to be able to troubleshoot this network when problems arise (such as no response from a device on the network) or network traffic slows down. You need to use these utilities to figure out what the problem is before you can implement a solution to fix the problem. The following section covers how to use network troubleshooting utilities to identify and correct problems on your TCP/IP network.

Using the Ping utility

You can use the `ping` command to test connectivity to a host. The Ping utility is one of the most popular TCP/IP utilities that can be found on Microsoft Windows operating systems. In most cases, Ping is executed at a command prompt, but there have been some third-party GUI implementations. You use the `ping` command to find if you can reach a host and if a host is responding. If a Ping test is successful, you get a response from the remote device; if the Ping test fails, you receive a timed out response. The syntax for using the Ping utility is as follows:

    ping <IP address> or <hostname>

Ping uses the ICMP (Internet Control Message Protocol) protocol. When you `ping` any device on your network that has an IP address, the ICMP protocol that is part of that host's TCP/IP stack responds to the request. The response looks something similar to this:

```
ping 205.134.123.12

pinging 205.134.123.12 with 32 bytes of data:

Reply from 205.134.123.12: bytes =32 time<107ms TTL=110
Reply from 205.134.123.12: bytes =32 time<104ms TTL=110
Reply from 205.134.123.12: bytes =32 time<102ms TTL=110
Reply from 205.134.123.12: bytes =32 time<102ms TTL=110

Ping statistics for 205.134.123.12:
Packets: Sent = 4, Received = 4, Lost = 0 (0% loss),
Approximate round trip times in milli-seconds:
Minimum = 102ms, Maximum = 107ms, Average = 103ms
```

Ping sends four packets of 32 bytes by default. We know that this particular station is reachable on the network because we received a reply from the destination station's IP address (205.134.123.12). On the other hand, if this station were not reachable, we would receive the following response:

```
ping 205.134.123.12

pinging 205.134.123.12 with 32 bytes of data:

Request timed out.
Request timed out.
Request timed out.
Request timed out.

Ping statistics for 205.134.123.12:
Packets: Sent = 4, Received = 0, Lost = 4 (100% loss),
Approximate round trip times in milli-seconds:
Minimum = 0ms, Maximum = 0ms, Average = 0ms
```

Ping also includes switches that you can use to specify parameters for the Ping request. To view the different switches, you can use you can type `ping -?` at the command prompt. Table 19-1 lists and describes the switches available for Microsoft Windows 95/98 and NT/2000 Ping utility.

Table 19-1
Windows Ping Utility Switches

Switch	Function
-?	Displays a list of switches that can be used with the Ping utility.
-t	`pings` the specified host until stopped. To see statistics and continue, type Ctrl+Break; to stop, type Ctrl+C.
-a	Resolves addresses to hostnames

Switch	Function
-n count	Number of echo requests to send. The count number of echo requests to send specifies the number of times.
-l size	Sends buffer size
-f	Sets Don't Fragment flag in packet
-I TTL	Time to Live
-v TOS	Type Of Service
-r count	Records route for count hops
-s count	Timestamp for count hops
-j host-list	Loose source route along host-list
-k host-list	Strict source route along host-list
-w timeout	Timeout in milliseconds to wait for each reply

Exam Tip

The exam focuses on the `-a`, `-n count`, `-t` and `-r count` switches. You do not need to memorize every switch.

In the Real World

If you want to `ping` your local TCP/IP interface, you can type `ping 127.0.0.1` or `ping localhost`. Both of these addresses represent the local interface.

Using the Tracert utility

Use the Tracert utility to see the route a packet takes to its destination. Tracert is most used to diagnose problems with routing. The TCP/IP Tracert utility shows you every router interface a TCP/IP packet passes through to its destination. To use Tracert on Microsoft Windows systems, type `tracert <DNS name>` or `<IP address>` at the command prompt. You can use the DNS name or IP address of the host for which you want to find the route. For example, if you want to trace the route a packet takes from your computer to the server that hosts the Comptia Web page, type `tracert www.comptia.org` or `tracert 216.119.103.72`, which is the IP address associated with comptia.org. Whichever one you use, the output of the trace looks something like this:

```
tracert www.comptia.org

Tracing route to www.comptia.org [216.119.103.72]
over a maximum of 30 hops:

  1    25 ms    25 ms    25 ms  24.158.12.1
```

```
  2    27 ms    24 ms    29 ms  10.1.64.129
  3    24 ms    27 ms    23 ms  10.0.184.253
  4    27 ms    28 ms    27 ms  10.0.184.249
  5    25 ms    26 ms    29 ms  10.0.184.245
  6    33 ms    29 ms    32 ms  c1-pos7-0.bflony1.home.net
[24.7.74.25]
  7    36 ms    39 ms    36 ms  c1-pos1-0.hrfrct1.home.net
[24.7.65.253]
  8    37 ms    42 ms    41 ms  c1-pos2-0.cmbrma1.home.net
[24.7.69.25]
  9    39 ms    40 ms    38 ms  home-gw.cb1ma.ip.att.net
[192.205.32.57]
 10    41 ms    38 ms    41 ms  gbr4-p30.cb1ma.ip.att.net
[12.123.40.182]
 11    56 ms    55 ms    54 ms  gbr4-p40.cgcil.ip.att.net
[12.122.2.49]
 12    53 ms    54 ms    53 ms  gbr3-p60.cgcil.ip.att.net
[12.122.1.125]
 13    57 ms    58 ms    60 ms  gbr4-p30.sl9mo.ip.att.net
[12.122.2.206]
 14    72 ms    70 ms    74 ms  gbr1-p70.kszmo.ip.att.net
[12.122.2.41]
 15    70 ms    68 ms    73 ms  gbr2-p60.kszmo.ip.att.net
[12.122.1.94]
 16    75 ms    71 ms    70 ms  gbr4-p20.dlstx.ip.att.net
[12.122.2.113]
 17    90 ms    91 ms    89 ms  gbr2-p30.phmaz.ip.att.net
[12.122.2.106]
 18    90 ms    92 ms    93 ms  gar1-p370.phmaz.ip.att.net
[12.123.142.25]
 19    92 ms    95 ms    92 ms  12.127.141.26
 20    93 ms    94 ms    95 ms  216.119.107.2
 21    97 ms    95 ms    92 ms  www.comptia.org
[216.119.103.72]

Trace complete.
```

In the Real World The Tracert command can identify bottlenecks on your network. Because Tracert maps the route a packet takes to a specific destination, the Tracert output can pinpoint the exact source of the problem.

The first column of output specifies the hop number. The next three columns are the round trip times in milliseconds for three attempts to reach the next router. The fourth column shows the host name and IP address of the responding system. If you are using the Tracert command to troubleshoot a network problem such as a downed server, instead of showing a number in the second column, it displays an asterisk (*), which means the attempt timed out. Table 19-2 lists options for the Tracert utility.

Table 19-2
Windows Tracert Utility Switches

Switch	Function
-?	Displays a list of switches that can be used with the Tracert utility
-d	Does not resolve addresses to hostnames
-h maximum-hops	Maximum number of hops to search for target
-j host-list	Loose source route along host-list
-w timeout	Waits timeout milliseconds for each reply

Using the Arp utility

Every machine that runs a TCP/IP stack has an ARP cache. An ARP cache is a table listing of

- IP addresses
- Associated hardware address (MAC address)

You can use Arp in Microsoft Windows systems to view and configure the local workstation's Arp table. Arp entries in this table can be static or dynamic. A dynamic entry is created when the TCP/IP stack makes an Arp request to a device's IP address on the local segment. The information is added to the Arp table when the MAC address of the requested IP address is found. These entries have a maximum time to live (TTL) in the cache (represented in seconds). When the time to live has expired for an entry, it is removed from the cache.

The Arp utility makes *static* entries. To start the Arp utility, from the command prompt type: `arp`. When you enter `arp` by itself, the `arp` command lists the switches you must use to use the Arp utility. Table 19-3 lists the most popular Arp switches you can use.

Table 19-3
Arp Utility Switches

Switch	Function
-?	Displays a list of switches that can be used with the Arp utility
-a	Displays current Arp entries by interrogating the current protocol data. If inet_addr is specified, the IP and Physical addresses for only the specified computer are displayed. If more than one network interface uses Arp, entries for each Arp table are displayed.
-g	Same as -a
-N if_addr	Specifies an internet address
-d	Deletes the host specified by inet_addr
-s	Adds the host and associates the Internet address inet_addr with the physical address eth_addr. The physical address is given as 6 hexadecimal bytes separated by hyphens. The entry is permanent.

To display the current Arp entries, type `arp -a` at the command prompt. The output should look something similar to this:

```
Interface: 24.155.12.94 on Interface 0x2000002
Internet Address      Physical Address      Type
24.156.16.1           00-00-77-94-0f-de     dynamic
24.156.16.4           00-a0-b3-c5-45-de     dynamic
24.215.16.23          00-08-bf-cc-c7-00     dynamic
```

Tip: The `-g` switch accomplishes the same output as the `-a` switch

Exam Tip: Remember that the command `arp -a` displays the current Arp entries.

This output shows you which MAC address is assigned to which IP address.

You can also delete entries from the Arp table by waiting for the dynamic entries to time out, or you can use the `-d` switch for the static entries. To delete a static entry, type

```
ARP -d <ip address>
```

This command deletes the entry from the Arp table in memory.

Using the Netstat utility

Netstat.

Use the Netstat utility to display statistics and current TCP/IP connections. To display the current statistics and TCP/IP connections, type `netstat` at the command prompt. Using `netstat` without any options shows all TCP/IP connections similar to the following:

```
Proto   Local Address       Foreign Address       State
TCP     Hostname:1010       203.145.160.5:80      ESTABLISHED
TCP     Hostname:1023       25.123.12.6:Pop3      ESTABLISHED
TCP     Hostname:2345       167.126.13.2:25:70    ESTABLISHED
TCP     Hostname:2512       209.72.62.24:22       TIME_WAIT
```

The preceding table has these columns:

- The Proto column displays the protocol being used (in this case, TCP).
- The Local Address column lists the source addresses and source port.
- The Foreign Address column displays
   - The address of the destination system
   - The destination port
- The State column displays the status of each connection.

    This column displays ESTABLISHED after a connection between your system and the destination computer is established

The Netstat utility also has switches you can use to tell Netstat what to display. Table 19-4 lists the Netstat switches you can use.

Table 19-4
The Netstat Utility Switches

Switch	Function
-a	Displays all connections and listening ports
-e	Displays Ethernet statistics. This switch may be combined with the -s option.
-n	Displays addresses and port numbers in numerical form
-p proto	Shows connections for the protocol specified by proto; proto may be TCP or UDP. If used with the -s option to display per-protocol statistics, proto may be TCP, UDP, or IP.
-r	Displays the routing table

Continued

Table 19-4 (continued)

Switch	Function
-s	Displays per-protocol statistics. By default, statistics are shown for TCP, UDP, and IP; the -p option can specify a subset of the default.
Interval	Redisplays selected statistics, pausing interval seconds between each display. Press CTRL+C to stop redisplaying statistics. If omitted, Netstat prints the current configuration information once.

Using the Nbtstat utility

Use the Nbtstat utility to check the NetBIOS status of systems and the IP addresses associated with those systems. You use the Nbtstat utility for three purposes:

- To resolve NetBIOS names
- To track NetBIOS over TCP/IP statistics
- To display the incoming and outgoing details of NetBIOS over TCP/IP connections

Just typing `nbtstat` at the command prompt displays a basic description of Nbtstat and its associated switches. You can use these switches to configure the display of information about NetBIOS over TCP/IP hosts. Table 19-5 lists the Nbtstat switches you can use. Notice that some of the switches are case sensitive.

Table 19-5
Nbtstat Utility Switches

Switch	Function
-a	Lists the remote machine's name table given its name
-A	Lists the remote machine's name table given its IP address
-c	Lists the remote name cache including the IP addresses
-n	Lists local NetBIOS names
-r	Lists names resolved by broadcast and via WINS
-R	Purges and reloads the remote cache name table
-S	Lists sessions table with the destination IP addresses
-s	Lists sessions table converting destination IP addresses to host names via the hosts file

Exam Tip Remember what Nbtstat is used for. Don't bother memorizing its switches.

Using the Ipconfig/Ifconfig utilities

Use the Ipconfig utility for Microsoft Windows NT/2000 systems. Typing `ipconfig` at the command line displays your current TCP/IP configuration. It displays:

- Current IP address, subnet mask, and default gateway
- Identification of the DHCP server (if the system is a DHCP)
- How long the IP address will be used by the client

Refer to Table 19-6 for the list of switches you can use with the Ipconfig utility. Additional switches exist, but these switches are the important ones for the Network+ exam.

Table 19-6
Ipconfig Utility Switches

Switch	Function
-?	Displays a list of switches that can be used with the Ipconfig utility
/all	Displays all adapters and their setting, including DHCP server and lease information, DNS and WINS servers, type of network card and its MAC address, and the standard IP address, gateway, and subnet mask information
/release	Releases the current IP address information assigned by the DHCP server
/renew	Requests new IP address information from the DHCP server. This command is used on client PCs to renew a dynamic IP address.

The Ifconfig utility is the standard utility used to display the current TCP/IP configuration on a UNIX/Linux system. Without any switches, `ifconfig` lists the primary network adapters with their descriptions, MAC addresses, and IP addresses to network cards. Table 19-7 lists switches associated with the Ifconfig utility.

Table 19-7
Ifconfig Utility Switches

Switch	Function
-a	Displays the configuration for all network cards
-eth0 down	Disables the Ethernet 0 interface
-eth0 up	Enables the Ethernet 0 interface
-eth0 <IP address> <subnet mask>	Assigns an IP address that you supply to the Ethernet 0 interface and subnet mask you supply

Using the Winipcfg utility

Winipcfg.

Use the Winipcfg utility to view TCP/IP address information on Microsoft Windows 95/98 operating systems. To run the Winipcfg utility, follow these steps:

1. Choose Start ➪ Run.
2. Type `winipcfg` in the Open box.
3. Click OK. The Winipcfg utility displays the same information as the Ipconfig utility, although it is a Windows GUI utility, as shown in Figure 19-1, not a command line utility.

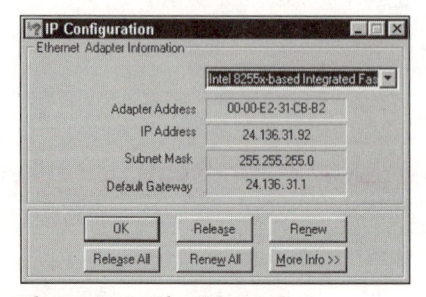

Figure 19-1: The Microsoft Windows 95/98 Winipcfg utility

The Winipcfg window displays these attributes of the selected network device:

✦ Hardware address
✦ IP address

✦ Subnet mask

✦ Default gateway

You can use the drop-down box to see and select the different network devices on your system. Using the Renew and Release buttons, you can renew or release the current network assigned configuration. To view a more detailed representation of the current TCP/IP settings, click the More Info>> button (see Figure 19-2).

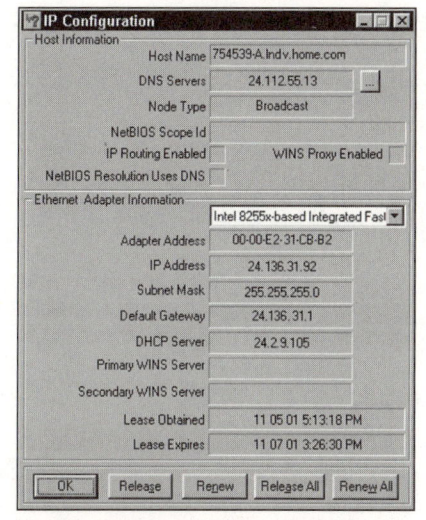

Figure 19-2: Displaying more info of the current TCP/IP settings with the Winipcfg utility

Using the Nslookup utility

Nslookup stands for *Name Server Lookup*. It's a command-line-based utility on UNIX, Linux, and Windows NT/2000 operating systems. Nslookup enables you to query a DNS server for a hostname/IP address. For example, to find a workstation's IP address on your network, at the command prompt type, nslookup <host name>. The host name is the identification name of the workstation you are querying. Nslookup goes to your DNS server and brings back the IP address of the workstation. Your DNS servers are listed in your network settings; Nslookup searches them in order. You can also use the workstation's IP address with Nslookup to return the workstation's host name. The output of querying a workstation with the host name "Workstation1" looks similar to the following:

```
nslookup Workstation1

Server: ln1st5
Address: 192.156.19.2

Non-authoritative answer:
Name: Workstation1
Address: 192.156.19.34
Aliases: Workstation1
```

With the Nslookup utility, you can also specify a DNS server to use. To specify a DNS server to use, follow these steps:

1. Type `nslookup` at the command prompt and press enter.
2. Type `server <server IP address>` to specify a different DNS server.
3. Enter the host you are trying to resolve. Nslookup executes and the output should look similar to the following if you are using the DNS server 10.1.10.1:

   ```
   nslookup
   
   >server 10.1.10.1
   
   Default server: 10.1.10.1
   Address: 10.1.10.1#53
   
   >www.hungryminds.com
   
   Server: 10.1.10.1
   Address: 10.1.10.1#53
   www.hungryminds.com canonical name = hungryminds.com.
   Name: hungryminds.com
   Address: 168.215.86.100
   
   > exit
   ```

Exam Tip You don't see many questions on the Network+ exam about Nslookup. For the exam, remember that Nslookup is a utility that enables you to query a DNS server for a hostname/IP address.

Summary

In this chapter, the different TCP/IP utilities were introduced. You have learned what each utility is used for and which operating system each is associated with. Here are the key points to remember for the Network+ exam:

- ✦ Ping is a command that tests connectivity with another device on the network.
- ✦ Tracert is a command that reports the route a packet takes to its destination. It is most used to diagnose problems.

- Arp resides on Microsoft Windows 95/98 and Windows NT/2000 operating systems and is used to view and configure the local workstation's Arp table. Arp entries in this table can be static or dynamic. The -a switch displays current Arp entries and the -d switch deletes static entries.
- Netstat displays statistics and current TCP/IP connections. Using Netstat without any switches shows all TCP/IP connections.
- Nbtstat checks the NetBIOS status of systems and the IP addresses associated with those systems.
- Ipconfig is a Windows NT/2000 utility used to display the current TCP/IP configuration.
- Ifconfig is a UNIX/Linux utility used to display the current TCP/IP configuration.
- Winipcfg is a Windows 95/98 utility used to display the current TCP/IP configuration.
- Nslookup is a command-line-based utility on UNIX/Linux and Windows NT/2000 operating systems that finds the IP address or host name of a computer on a DNS server.

✦ ✦ ✦

STUDY GUIDE

The Study Guide section provides you with the opportunity to test your knowledge about the Network+ exam objectives that are covered in this chapter. The Assessment Questions provide practice for the real exam, and the Scenarios provide practice with real situations. If you get any questions wrong, use the answers to determine the part of the chapter that you should review before continuing.

Assessment Questions

1. To resolve an IP address to a hostname, what switch would you use with the `ping` command?

    A. `-a`

    B. `-f`

    C. `-t`

    D. `-l`

2. What switch can you use with the `ping` command to determine the type of service?

    A. `-a`

    B. `-v`

    C. `-t`

    D. `-s`

3. Ping sends how many packets out by default?

    A. 2

    B. 4

    C. 6

    D. 8

4. What is the default packet size that Ping sends out?

    A. 8 bytes

    B. 32 bytes

    C. 64K

    D. 128MB

5. What protocol does the Ping utility use?

    A. ICMP

    B. RIP

    C. SPX

    D. IPX

6. What response does the `ping` command generate if the destination station is not reachable?

    A. ESTABLISHED

    B. Unreachable

    C. Request timed out

    D. Unreachable

7. To list the switches used by the Ping utility, what would you type at the command prompt?

    A. `-h`

    B. `-?`

    C. `-info`

    D. `-u`

8. What TCP/IP utility would you use to diagnose problems with routing?

    A. Ping

    B. Nbtstat

    C. Tracert

    D. Netstat

9. What does the first column of the Tracert utility output specify?

    A. Number of hops

    B. The host name

    C. The IP address

    D. Round trip times

10. What switch would you use with the Tracert utility to tell Tracert not to resolve addresses to hostnames?

    A. `-?`

    B. `-w`

    C. `-h`

    D. `-d`

11. What utility uses a table listing of IP addresses and associated MAC addresses?

    A. Ping

    B. Tracert

    C. Arp

    D. Netstat

12. What switch would you use with the `arp` command to delete a static entry?

    A. -r

    B. -d

    C. -g

    D. -n

13. What switch would you use with the `arp` command to display the current Arp entries?

    A. -a

    B. -b

    C. -n

    D. -d

14. What command would you type and execute at the command prompt to display the current statistics and TCP/IP connections on your system?

    A. `tracert`

    B. `ping`

    C. `netstat`

    D. `arp`

15. What switch would you use with the `netstat` command to display all connections and listening ports?

    A. -a

    B. -e

    C. -n

    D. -p

16. What switch would you use with the `nbtstat` command to list local NetBIOS names?

    A. `-A`

    B. `-n`

    C. `-N`

    D. `-a`

17. Ipconfig is used on what operating system?

    A. UNIX

    B. Windows NT

    C. Novell

    D. Linux

18. What switch would you use with the Ipconfig utility to release the current IP address information?

    A. `/unbind`

    B. `/release`

    C. `/unlock`

    D. `/disconnect`

19. Which of the following Ifconfig switches would you use to disable the Ethernet 0 interface?

    A. `-a`

    B. `-eth0 down`

    C. `-eth0 up`

    D. `-eth0`

20. Which of the following Ifconfig switches would you use to display the configuration for all network cards when using the Ifconfig utility?

    A. `-a`

    B. `-eth0 down`

    C. `-eth0 up`

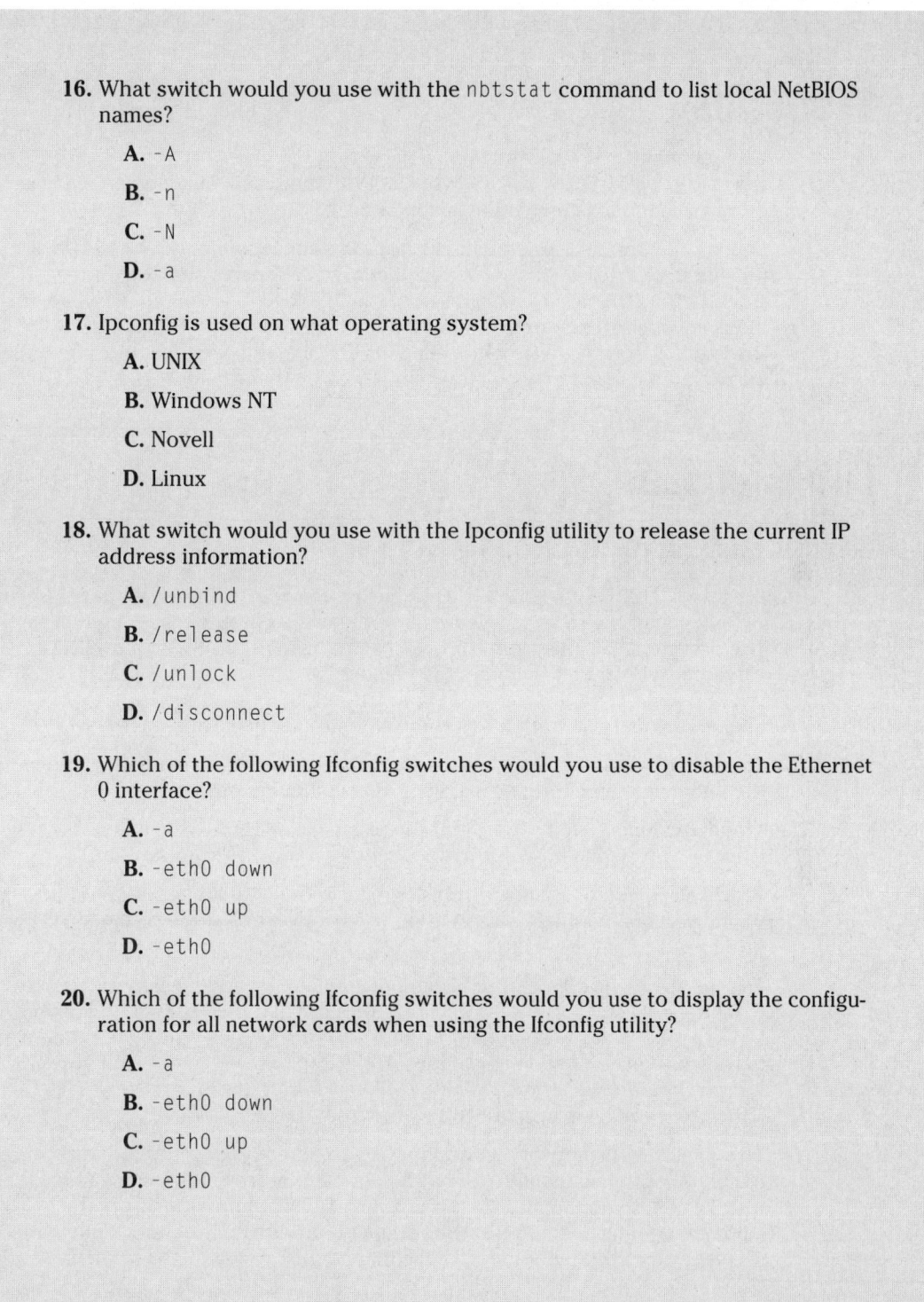

    D. `-eth0`

Scenarios

1. You are unable to connect to a mail server on your network. The IP address of the mail server is 102.12.23.45. What TCP/IP utility can you use to quickly see if the mail server's connection is still active?

2. You are the new network administrator for a small company. The network you are in charge of consists of one Windows NT server and 10 Windows NT workstations that are all assigned a static IP address. Unfortunately, the previous network administrator did not keep a current list of the names of the workstations on the network. What TCP/IP utility can you use to retrieve the workstations' host names by querying them by their IP address?

Lab Exercises

Lab 19-1 Using the `Ipconfig` Utility

The objective of this hands-on lab is to gain experience in using the Windows NT/2000 Ipconfig utility to view, release, and renew the current TCP/IP configuration of your system. For this exercise you need to be in front of a Windows NT or 2000 operating system that is connected to a network.

1. Log on to your workstation by typing in your user name and password.

2. Access a command prompt by choosing Start ▷ Run and then typing `cmd` in the Run dialog box. Click OK to bring up a command prompt.

3. To run Ipconfig, type `ipconfig` at the prompt, and then press Enter. Ipconfig responds by displaying the current IP configuration on your system.

4. To see all current IP configurations (similar to the More Info button on the Windows 95/98 Winipcfg utility), type `ipconfig /all` at the command prompt, and then press Enter.

5. To release the current IP address and disconnect your system from the network, type `ipconfig /release` at the prompt, and then press Enter. If you type `ipconfig` at the command prompt and press Enter, `ipconfig` still displays your current IP configuration settings but you will notice that your IP address, Subnet mask, and Default Gateway entries are now reading 0.0.0.0. You workstation has been disconnected from the network.

6. To connect to the network without having to reboot your system, at the command prompt type `ipconfig /renew`, and then press Enter. Issuing this command enables your adapter to request new TCP/IP information from the DHCP server. By typing `ipconfig` at the command prompt and pressing Enter, you see your new IP configuration. The workstation is re-connected to the network.

Lab 19-2 Using the Ping Command to Check Connectivity with a Web Server

The objective of this hands-on lab is to gain experience using the TCP/IP Ping utility to check connectivity with a Web server. For this exercise you need to be in front of a Windows 9x, Me, or Windows NT/2000/XP operating system that is connected to the Internet.

1. If you are using a Windows NT/2000/XP operating system, access a command prompt by choosing Start ⇨ Run, and then typing cmd in the Run dialog box. Click OK to bring up a command prompt. If you are using a Windows 9x/Me operating system, access a command prompt by choosing Start ⇨ Programs ⇨ MS-DOS Prompt.

2. At the command line, type ping <URL of web page> (such as www.comptia.org) and press Enter.

3. The output of this command should look similar to the following:

    ```
    C:\>ping www.comptia.org

    Pinging www.comptia.org [216.119.103.72] with 32 bytes of
    data:

    Reply from 216.119.103.72: bytes=32 time=94ms TTL=110
    Reply from 216.119.103.72: bytes=32 time=95ms TTL=110
    Reply from 216.119.103.72: bytes=32 time=94ms TTL=110
    Reply from 216.119.103.72: bytes=32 time=92ms TTL=110

    Ping statistics for 216.119.103.72:
        Packets: Sent = 4, Received = 4, Lost = 0 (0% loss),
    Approximate round trip times in milli-seconds:
        Minimum = 92ms, Maximum =  95ms, Average =  93ms
    ```

4. If you receive a reply similar to this output, you have successfully tested to see that the Web server that hosts the CompTIA Web page is active. If it is not active, you receive a Request time out reply.

5. Close the command prompt by typing exit and pressing Enter.

Lab 19-3 Using the Ping –a Command to Resolve an IP Address to a Host Name

The objective in this hands-on lab is to gain experience in using the TCP/IP Ping utility to resolve an IP address to a host name. For this exercise you need to be in front of a Windows 9x, Me, or Windows NT/2000/XP operating system that is connected to the Internet.

1. If you are using a Windows NT/2000/XP operating system, access a command prompt by choosing Start ➪ Run and typing cmd in the Run dialog box. Click OK to bring up a command prompt. If you are using a Windows 9x/Me operating system, access a command prompt by choosing Start ➪ Programs ➪ MS-DOS Prompt.

2. At the command line type ping -a 64.58.76.178, and then press Enter.

3. The output of this command should look similar to the following:

```
C:\>ping -a 64.58.76.178

Pinging www9.dcx.yahoo.com [64.58.76.178] with 32 bytes of
data:

Reply from 64.58.76.178: bytes=32 time=42ms TTL=244
Reply from 64.58.76.178: bytes=32 time=41ms TTL=244
Reply from 64.58.76.178: bytes=32 time=46ms TTL=244
Reply from 64.58.76.178: bytes=32 time=43ms TTL=244

Ping statistics for 64.58.76.178:
    Packets: Sent = 4, Received = 4, Lost = 0 (0% loss),
Approximate round trip times in milli-seconds:
    Minimum = 41ms, Maximum =  46ms, Average =  43ms
```

4. If you receive a reply similar to this output, you have successfully resolved an IP address to a host name, in this case www9.dcx.yahoo.com. In this lab we used the IP address of www.yahoo.com. When you use the -a switch with the Ping utility, the Ping utility resolves the host name from where the IP address originated.

5. Close the command prompt by typing exit and pressing Enter.

Answers to Chapter Questions

Chapter Pre-Test

1. Use the ping command to test connectivity to a host.
2. The proper syntax for using the Ping utility is ping <IP address> or <host name>.
3. Use the Tracert utility to see the route a packet takes to its destination.
4. To display a list of switches for the Arp utility, type arp -? at the command line.
5. To display current Arp entries with the arp command, use the -a switch.
6. The Netstat utility displays statistics and current TCP/IP connections.

7. The proto column of the output of the Netstat utility identifies the protocol being used.

8. To display the current TCP/IP configuration on a computer running Windows NT, use the Ipconfig utility.

9. Ifconfig displays the current TCP/IP configuration on a UNIX system.

10. Use the Winipcfg utility to display the current TCP/IP configuration on a Windows 95/98 system.

Assessment Questions

1. A. To resolve an IP address to a hostname, use the `-a` switch with the `ping` command. The syntax is `ping -a <IP address>`. (For review see the "Using the Ping utility" section.)

2. B. To determine the type of service, use the `-v` switch with the `ping` command. (For review see the "Using the Ping utility" section.)

3. B. By default, Ping sends out four packets of 32 bytes of data. (For review see the "Using the Ping utility" section.)

4. B. The default packet size that Ping sends out is 32 bytes. (For review see the "Using the Ping utility" section.)

5. A. Ping uses the ICMP protocol. (For review see the "Using the Ping utility" section.)

6. C. If the destination station is not reachable, the response from the `ping` command is "Request timed out." (For review see the "Using the Ping utility" section.)

7. B. Use the `-?` switch to list the switches available with the `ping` command. (For review see the "Using the Ping utility" section.)

8. C. By using the Tracert utility, you can identify a problem between your station and the packets destination. Tracert displays all paths that the packet travels. If one of the paths is down, Tracert can identify which one is down. (For review see the "Using the Tracert utility" section.)

9. A. The first column of the output of the Tracert utility specifies the number of hops. 30 hops is the default, but you can specify a different value by using the `-h` switch. (For review see the "Using the Tracert utility" section.)

10. D. The `-d` switch, when used with the Tracert utility, tells Tracert not to resolve addresses to hostnames. (For review see the "Using the Tracert utility" section.)

11. C. The Arp utility uses a table called an Arp cache that lists the current IP addresses and associated MAC addresses. (For review see the "Using the Arp utility" section.)

12. B. Using the `-d` switch with the `arp` command, you can delete static entries from the Arp table. The syntax is `arp -d <IP address>`. (For review see the "Using the Arp utility" section.)

13. A. Using the `-a` switch with the `arp` command displays the current Arp entries. The `-g` switch displays the same results. (For review see the "Using the Arp utility" section.)

14. C. Use the Netstat utility to display the current statistics and TCP/IP connections on your system. (For review see the "Using the Netstat utility" section.)

15. A. Using the `-a` switch with the `netstat` utility displays all connections and listening ports. (For review see the "Using the Netstat utility" section.)

16. B. Using the `-n` switch with the `nbtstat` command outputs a list of local NetBIOS names. (For review see the "Using the Nbtstat utility" section.)

17. B. Ipconfig is used on Windows NT/2000 operating systems. (For review see the "Using the Ipconfig/Ifconfig utilities" section.)

18. B. Using the `/release` switch with `ipconfig` releases the current IP address information. (For review see the "Using the Ipconfig/Ifconfig utilities" section.)

19. B. Using the `-eth0 down` switch with the `ifconfig` command disables the Ethernet 0 interface. (For review see the "Using the Ipconfig/Ifconfig utilities" section.)

20. A. To display the configuration of all networks cards when using the `ifconfig` utility, use the `-a` switch. (For review see the "Using the Ipconfig/Ifconfig utilities" section.)

Scenarios

1. One of the quickest ways to check whether a workstation or server is reachable on your network is to use the `Ping` command. In this case, you know the IP address of the mail server (102.12.23.45). You can `ping` this IP address by typing `ping 102.12.23.45` at the command prompt. If the returned response of the `ping` command returns a reply that the mail server is still active on the network, then some other issue is probably why your workstation cannot connect to the mail server. If the `ping` command returns a `Request timed out` reply, you have to investigate further as to why the mail server is not connected to the network.

2. To query workstation names via an IP address, the TCP/IP utility to use is the Nslookup utility. Nslookup is available on UNIX/Linux and Windows NT/2000 operating systems. To query a workstation's host name by the workstation's IP address, the syntax is `nslookup <IP address>`. When this command is executed, Nslookup retrieves the host name associated with that particular IP address. You can also use Nslookup to query a workstations IP address via the workstation's host name.

Small/Home Office Network Troubleshooting

CHAPTER 20

EXAM OBJECTIVES

- Understand the various remote access methods commonly used to connect dispersed users.
- Understand the PPP and SLIP line protocols and the role they play in remote communications.
- Identify the characteristics of POTS and troubleshooting dial-up connection problems
- Identify the characteristics of *xDSL* and troubleshooting connection problems
- Identify the characteristics of Digital Cable and troubleshooting connection problems
- Identify the characteristics of Home satellite and troubleshooting connection problems
- Identify the characteristics of SOHO Wireless and troubleshooting connection problems

CHAPTER PRE-TEST

1. What type of remote access mimics the connection of a standard LAN connection?
2. What type of remote access provides secure encrypted communications?
3. What two line protocols are commonly used for dial-up TCP/IP connections?
4. What makes SLIP undesirable as an Internet Access line protocol?
5. *What does POTS stand for?*
6. What is a Point-of-Presences?
7. What is accomplished by modulation?
8. What simple change might solve dial-up problems when using an internal PCI modem?
9. To determine the available speed for a DSL connection, how should distance be measured?
10. What inherent characteristic of cable access can negatively affect Internet performance?

✦ Answers to these questions can be found at the end fo the chapter. ✦

Chapter 20 ✦ Small/Home Office Network Troubleshooting

Many new acronyms have made their way into mainstream vocabulary in recent years, among them, SOHO, which stands for *Small Office/Home Office*. With the expanding availably of high-speed, low cost Internet access, the Small Office/Home Office concept is expanding dramatically. The foremost mantra of many new business plans is lean overhead. Although the flashy, buckets-of-money attitude of so many "dot-coms" permeated the new business market not long ago, truly sustainable business models all focus in on keeping expenses low.

Two items that have become common methods of reducing expenses are inexpensive, high-speed communications, and moving workers to home offices, or small group offices, whenever possible. Many employees who don't have to be in the main office prefer the flexibility of working from home and the business saves valuable and expensive office real estate. Not everyone can successfully work from home, but many can. Additionally, many "groups" or departments of people can be located in less-expensive office space, again reducing a business's expenses.

The keys to successfully working from home, or a small office, is often the access to high-speed and reliable communications to both the Internet and possibly back to the main office. Many jobs functions utilize Internet services, and often direct connections to the corporate LAN. Dial-up speed to the Internet may be acceptable in some cases, but analog connections to the LAN are usually unacceptable. As we've seen, Virtual Private Networks, or VPNs, can solve both of these problems and in many cases do it at a reasonable monthly cost.

The traditional method of accessing dedicated, high-speed Internet access is via T-Carrier (T1) lines. The installation costs alone, usually between $3,000.00 to $5,000.00 range, often prohibited this option. Even if the up-front costs were justifiable, monthly fees normally average $1,000.00 of more, which puts these lines out of the reach of most small businesses. Even the lesser-priced frame-relay technology can average well over $500.00 a month, again, often too expensive for most SOHO situations.

New technologies that surged forward in the late 1990s — specifically digital cable and Digital Subscriber Line (DSL) services — started to deliver on the promise of inexpensive, high-speed access. Early in the new millennium, satellite and other wireless methods play increasingly important roles as well. These options have made the SOHO office not only financially feasible, but market-competitive. They have also introduced new challenges for network administrators. In years past, the network hardware and its users were usually confined to the same building — so physically troubleshooting a user's computer was rarely a problem. Although small offices may still have this luxury, physical troubleshooting it is not as for companies who have many users connecting from home offices. Home-office users might be blocks, cities, counties, states, or continents away. New techniques and approaches must be deployed; more end-user technical training is often required as well.

One large mistake that network administrators make (and seem to repeat often) is not realizing that this new breed of end-user does not pose the same security threat as before. Although it used to be prudent to lock an operating system down tight on the LAN, this same practice can cause tremendous loss of productivity if the end-user has to ship a laptop back to the home office simply to replace a failed modem or network card. Network administrators must enable appropriate local administrative privileges to SOHO workers for these situations — and, in effect, redesign network security to accommodate these part-time LAN users.

Although remote access has become a vital and expected extension of the corporate LAN, providing the proper service is often still difficult. End-users, accustomed to faster and faster connection speeds, naturally expect similar results when calling in from home or on the road. Software licensing issues must also be reviewed carefully; many accepted standards have changed in response to the explosion of dial-up connectivity.

Network administrators currently have many available ways to provide remote connectivity to users outside the corporate LAN:

- **Remote node:** Enables the remote location to attach to the LAN as if the telephone line was merely an extension of the network cable. When users connect using remote node, they are prompted to log in to the network, and they gain access to network drives just as if they were stationed at their office PC.

- **Remote control:** This method uses both a remote (home) PC and a locally connected (or *host*) PC — usually the user's corporate-office computer or a dedicated PC in the office — that is always left on so it can be controlled remotely. All the actual processing occurs on the host PC back at the office. Screen displays, keystrokes, and mouse actions are the only sent between the two computers.

- **Terminal services:** Using serial communications, a dedicated terminal server provides multithreaded processing to remote clients. Terminal Services enables an administrator to configure specific "sessions" for each user or group of users. The remote client then accesses the Terminal Server much like a remote control client except that the server can being "controlled" by multiple users at the same time. Windows2000 Server and XP offer Terminal Services as part of the operating system. Other add-on products such as Citrix provide advanced Terminal Service functionality and services for other operating systems.

- **SSH (Secure SHell)** is a program for logging in to and executing commands on a remote machine. It provides secure encrypted communications between two untrusted hosts over an insecure network. X11 connections and arbitrary TCP/IP ports can also be forwarded over the secure channel. When SSH connects and logs in to a specified computer, the user must prove his/her identity to the remote machine which is transmitted across the connection using one of three forms of data encryption. This process makes SSH impervious to Internet eavesdroppers who might otherwise steal account information.

✦ **Virtual private networks (VPNs):** Although VPN technology is not really an access method, the technology is often used in conjunction with remote access. As powerful and inexpensive as the Internet has become, companies have looked for ways of using the Internet for remote connections. Virtual private networks, or VPNs, promise to deliver simplified remote access without the expenses associated with traditional methods. Using the Internet as a transport medium, VPN hardware and software products establish a secured pipe between two computers using data encryption.

Because no official standards define VPN technology at this time, the data-encryption function is proprietary to the solutions being implemented. Most solutions are based on the public-key encryption methods; the encryption is done by software at the PC level while other solutions use special hardware at each end to provide the data encryption. When authentication is established, the remote PC can transfer data to and from the LAN safely and securely. Standards for VPNs are still being established, but many vendors currently offer useable proprietary products.

This chapter examines the various connection options and protocols — along with the unique troubleshooting requirements they bring.

Remote-access protocols (line protocols)

Before looking into the connection methods available for remote access, the different methods of transporting data across wide-area links are worth a look. Because most wide-area data is transported across normal telephone lines, remote access protocols (sometimes called line protocols) encapsulate the LAN protocol packets. When this line protocol reaches the LAN, the line protocol packet is stripped away and the network protocol packet is sent onto the network.

Point-to-Point Protocol

A data-link protocol (Layer 2 of the OSI Model) provides reliable access over serial lines. The Point-to-Point Protocol (PPP) is designed for simple links that transport packets between two hosts. The links provide full-duplex, simultaneous, bi-directional operation, and deliver packets in order; In addition, PPP provides a common solution to connect a variety of hosts, bridges, and routers. In fact, it has become the de-facto standard for dial-up and other serial connections. PPP can encapsulate multiple Network-layer protocols, such as IPX and AppleTalk that provides a easy method of connecting remote users to a corporate LAN of mixed protocols. The PPP protocol was designed to be easy to configure so generally the standard defaults handle all common configurations. By this, I mean, the protocol's self-configuration is implemented through a negotiation mechanism where each end of the link describes to the other its capabilities and requirements. To establish communications over a point-to-point link, each end must first send Link Control Protocol (LCP) packets to configure and test the data link. After the link is established, the peer may be authenticated. Next, PPP must send Network Control Protocol (NCP) packets to choose and configure one or more Network-layer protocols (such as

TCP/IP or IPX). When each of the chosen Network-layer protocols has been configured, datagrams (a packet of information with associated delivery information) from each Network-layer protocol can be exchanged. The link remains configured for communications until explicit commands close the link down, or some external event, such as an inactivity timer expiring occurs. The PPP protocol also can automatically reestablish a failed connection.

Serial Line IP

Serial Line IP (SLIP) is an older Data Link-layer protocol for dial-up access to TCP/IP networks. SLIP is commonly used to gain access to the Internet, and it can also provide dial-up access between two LANs. SLIP transmits IP packets over any serial link (dial-up or private lines) and simply defines a sequence of characters that frame IP packets. SLIP does not provide addressing, packet type identification, error detection/correction, or compression mechanisms. Because the protocol does so little, it is usually easy to implement. SLIP is commonly used on dedicated serial links and sometimes for dial-up purposes and is normally used with line speeds between 1200bps and 19.2Kbps. It is useful for enabling mixes of hosts and routers to communicate with one another (host-host, host-router, and router-router are all common SLIP network configurations). Three major drawbacks to SLIP (that PPP overcomes) are as follows:

- Lack of addressing
- Packet type identification
- Error detection/correction

With SLIP, both computers in the link must know each other's IP addresses for routing purposes. This causes problems when making Internet connections because most ISPs dole out dynamic IP addresses upon connection rather than static addresses.

Without an identifier field for packet types, SLIP can only transmit a single Network-layer protocol. So (for example), in a configuration with two DEC computers that both run TCP/IP and DECnet, don't expect TCP/IP and DECnet to share one serial line while they use SLIP — they can't

Because the SLIP protocol does not provide error detection/correction, other higher-level protocols on the end devices govern requests for the retransmission of bad data. This can add quite a bit of unnecessary overhead to the remote connection.

Characteristics of the Plain Old Telephone System (POTS)

The *plain old telephone system*, or (as it's lovingly dubbed) POTS, is by far the most common method of connecting widely dispersed computers to the Internet — or, for that matter, to a private LAN. The primary reason for this situation is simply the wide availability of POTS. It exists in some form throughout the world, whether in large metropolitan areas or the most remote areas of many third-world countries. Even where local service is not available, cellular technology is quickly filling the gap.

Other than a standard modem, practically no special hardware is necessary for most computers to utilize the POTS system. Nearly all operating systems support dial-up services — and until people become accustomed to faster speeds, analog performance is generally acceptable. Further, most of the world's public telephone networks have been upgraded from their original all-analog systems to a digital backbone and electronic switching — which results in a more reliable analog dial-up service that offers better performance than ever before. New data-compression technologies for analog access are pushing this performance to new heights.

Unfortunately however, not all POTS lines have made the move to a digital backbone. By and large, the infamous *last mile* — the portion of cable from the home or office to the telephone company's central office (CO) — is still analog, which has prevented the delivery of true high-speed digital access at reasonable prices to many SOHO users. Nonetheless, POTS services are still widely used and will be for years to come. Table 20-1 shows some advantages and disadvantages of the POTS system.

Table 20-1
Comparing Advantages and Disadvantages of POTS

Advantages	*Disadvantages*
Wide availability. Nearly any location you want to access a host from has a standard telephone jack nearby.	The user must rely on a public telephone infrastructure of uneven quality; potential dial-up restrictions may apply.
Calls are often free for the end-user, either through a local number or a toll-free number paid for by the company.	If local service is unavailable, long distance calling can quickly add up, making prolonged remote access expensive.
Supported by most operating systems, hardware, and software applications.	Call signal can be problematic. POTS was designed for voice-quality services and sometimes underperforms as a medium for data transmission.
Acceptable speeds when applications and hardware use data compression and other bandwidth-saving technologies.	Speeds higher than 53 Kbps are simply not possible in the U.S. Although current modems can reach 56Kbps transmission speeds, the FCC limits analog communications to a maximum speed of 53Kbps. And even at 53Kbps, the modulation/demodulation process incurs a performance penalty: converting a computer's digital signals to analog for transmission over the phone line (and back to digital on the receiving end) takes time.

POTS is the mainstay access method for nearly all Internet service providers. Large national and International providers such as EarthLink or Sprint, and proprietary services that also provide Internet access such as America On-Line and MSN, contract through local telephone companies to offer local access numbers. These local services are called a Point-of-Presences, or POP. (Not to be confused with the Post Office Protocol –POP- used in e-mail technology). Having a POP in a given area provides local (usually toll-free) telephone numbers to users; region. These local calls are then switched at the telephone company to a long distance carrier to bring the data to the provider. Many of the larger companies will offer more than one telephone number in any one POP to avoid busy signals when lots of users dial-in at the same time.

How Modems Communicate

To transfer data across a POTS line, computers use modems. The term *modem* comes from combining *mod*ulator and *dem*odulator. The modulation process converts digital computer signals (high and low, or logic 1 and 0 states) to analog audio-frequency (AF) tones. Digital highs are converted to a tone having a certain constant pitch; digital lows are converted to a tone having a different constant pitch. These states alternate so rapidly that, if you listen to the output of a computer modem, it sounds like a hiss or roar. The demodulation process converts the audio tones back into digital signals that a computer can understand directly.

The International Telecommunication Union (ITU), an international organization based in Geneva, Switzerland, defines standards for modem use. In addition to many governments, ITU counts as members some leading private-sector companies such as 3Com, Conexant Systems, Lucent Technologies, and Motorola.

Handshaking, compression, and speed negotiation

When two modems start a connection, they exchange a number of signals known as *handshaking*. During the handshake process, the two modems establish a number of settings including whether data will be compressed and how and the maximum speed with which the two devices can reliably communicate.

Data compression is key to faster transmission speeds. Although the physical number of bits that can be sent across a wire at any given time is fairly fixed, by using compression, fewer bits must be transmitted to accomplish the task. Two common compression protocols commonly used are MNP-5, which has a compression ratio of 2:1, and v.42*bis*, which has a 4:1 compression ratio. MNP-5, however, produces a great deal of overhead in its compression, so it actually adds to the time required for transmitting pre-compressed files (.ZIP files, for example). V.42*bis* can sense whether compression is unnecessary, so can speed up transfer of pre-compressed files as well. If V.42*bis* is unavailable, it is best to disable MNP-5 data compression when transferring pre-compressed files.

Most modern modems can transmit data at a variety of speeds. When the receiving modem picks up the phone line, the two devices attempt to communicate at the fastest speeds available. If communications are not established after a short period of time, the modems slow the transfer rates and try again. This process will continue until the minimum speeds of the modems are exhausted, or until the two devices successfully negotiate a reliable rate. Among other problems, noisy telephone lines can cause this negotiated speed to be less than the actual capability of the devices. Likewise, a 56K modem connecting to a 33.3K modem will never reach transmission speeds faster than 33.3Kbps.

Flow control

Although the base communication speed is pre-negotiated, often one modem can send data much faster than the other can receive. *Flow control* is a feature that enables the receiving modem to tell the other to pause while it catches up. Flow control exists as software, as operating-system commands (such as `XON/XOFF`), or as hardware (for example, RTS/CTS).

With software flow control, when a modem must tell the other to pause, it sends a certain character, usually Control-S. When it is ready to resume, it sends a different character, such as Control-Q. Software flow control's only advantage is that it can use a serial cable with only three wires. Because software flow control regulates transmissions by sending certain characters, line noise could generate the character commanding a pause, thus hanging the transfer until the proper character (such as Control-Q) is sent. Also, binary files must never be sent using software flow control, as binary files can contain the control characters. Hardware, or RTS/CTS, flow control uses wires in the modem cable or, in the case of internal modems, hardware in the modem. This is faster and much more reliable than software flow control.

UARTS and data buffering

UARTs, or Universal Asynchronous Receiver/Transmitters, are the method by which computers send information to a serial device, such as a modem. A UART is an integrated circuit that converts parallel input into serial output. The CPU communicates with the serial device by writing in the UART's registers. UARTs have FIFO (First-In, First-Out) buffers through which this communication occurs — the first data to enter the buffer is also the first to leave. Without the FIFO, information would be scrambled when sent by a modem. 16550 UARTs are the current standard and are necessary for high-speed communications under Windows or for DOS applications running in a Windows shell.

Error correction

Error correction is the method by which modems verify that the information sent to them has been undamaged during the transfer. Error-correcting modems break up information into small packets, called frames. The sending modem attaches a checksum to each of these frames. The receiving modem checks whether the checksum matches the information sent. If not, the entire frame is resent. Though error correction may slow down data transfer on noisy lines, it does provide greater reliability. As with data compression protocols, for an error correction protocol to be used, it must be supported by both modems in the connection.

The V.92 Standards

In July 2000, the ITU agreed on three important new standards for voiceband modems. Building on the success of the current V.90 recommendation for modems at data rates up to 56kbit/s, important enhancements have now been agreed in new recommendation ITU-T V.92. The enhancements are as follows:

- An increase of more than 40% in the maximum data rate towards the network to a new maximum of 48k on the best connections;
- Significantly quicker start-up times on recognized connections (15 seconds on average compared to 30 seconds under current standards)
- The ability to put the modem 'on-hold' when the network indicates that an incoming call is waiting.
- New procedures for facilitating modem and connection faultfinding.
- New data-compression techniques.

The new data-compression recommendation is based on the LZJH compression algorithm developed by US-based Hughes Network Systems and offers an improvement in compression of more than 25% beyond the existing V.42*bis*, and a data-compression ratio in the region of 6:1 for a typical Web-browsing connection. As a result, data throughput rates exceeds 300K compared with typical values of 150@nd200K today — significantly reducing download times and speeding up Web browsing. These rates are still slower than those available from other broadband technologies, but they have an advantage: They don't need any special installation on the part of the network provider or expensive equipment for users. As dial-up services move forward, the V.92 standard will continue to play an important role.

Troubleshooting POTS

Although POTS, and dial-up technologies are pretty reliable and operate with minimum trouble, a number of that can go wrong. Having a structured approach to troubleshooting these items will become invaluable over time. The three most common problem areas with dial-up systems are as follows:

- **Physical items:** The modem or the phone lines.
- **Software problems:** Drivers or software conflicts
- **Account information:** Incorrect login name or password

The first step in assuring trouble-free connections is to make sure the modem is installed properly in the first place. When installing a modem it is imperative to install it with the correct modem driver. If at all possible, visit the modem manufacturer's Web site to see whether a new software release is available. If not, use the drivers that were shipped with the modem rather than operating system compatible drivers. How your modem is installed will affect its performance. Follow instructions on the correct installation procedure from the modem's manual. The connect speed between the modem and computer must be at least double the desired speed for the modem to run at. For best results, the port speed in the modem properties should be set to 115200.

Assuming the modem is properly installed, a number of steps to take to identify connection problems. The first step is to verify that the modem being dialed into is available and answering. Dial the number in question using a standard telephone. If the phone number is correct, a modem on the other end should answer the call. If this works, the receiving modem will answer and emit a number of high-pitched tones in an attempt to perform the handshake process described above.

The next troubleshooting step is to verify that the local modem is responding. The exact process varies depending on the operating system you are using, and what modem software you have available. The process involves sending specific commands to the modem and checking the response. This can be accomplished by using any serial communication software that can send and receive keyboard commands to the modem port. For Windows 9*x* and newer systems, the HyperTerminal program can be used. For many other operating systems that provide redirection to COM ports, these tests can be performed at the command line.

Start the communications application and make a connection to the modem's COM port and enter the following commands:

- `AT <enter>`. The AT stands for *ATtention*. When the AT command is issued, the modem should reply with an "OK" signal.
- `ATM1L3X0DT12345 <enter>`. This command first sends the AT (Attention) to signal the modem that it is about to receive information. The M1 command is a universal command to turn the modem's speaker on if it is off. The L3 is the command to raise the modem's speaker volume to the maximum level. The X0 is the command that signals the modem to run the command without waiting for a dial tone (this is useful if modem and voice calls use the same phone line), and the DT12345 command instructs the modem to dial the digits "12345".
- `ATH0 <enter>`. This command simply tells the modem to hang up the connection

If the modem does not respond with a dial tone or positive communication, there may be something physically wrong with either the modem or the COM port. If possible, try to configure the modem to use a different COM port, or try replacing the modem with a known good one.

Troubleshooting an established connection

For situations where the connection is established, but the speeds are unacceptably slow, or frequent line drops occur for no apparent reason, good reason to suspect interference on the line. Line noise imperceptible for voice quality calls can cause havoc for data transmissions. special line testers available to monitor line interference but these tools are normally too costly for average use. Most of the time a call to the local telephone company is necessary. The phone company is responsible to maintain the quality of the line from their central office to your building. If excessive noise originates on that part of the line, the phone company can use special filters to clean it up. Sometimes, however, the source of the noise is internal, from the DMARK area where the telephone company terminates all telephone lines in the building. It is generally up to the building owner to extend these lines to their required area(s). For residential areas, the consumer may pay a small monthly fee to the phone company to maintain this portion of the lines. Line filters can also be installed on the inside wiring to reduce interference.

It is worthy to note, that many nonrecurring situations can cause intermittent connection problems. During times of inclement weather such as electrical storms, heavy winds, and extreme hot or cold temperatures, these conditions can be sources for temporary connection problems with POTS services.

PCI-specific modem problems

The majority of internal modems sold today are PCI cards as opposed to the older ISA (industry standard architecture). The PCI bus enables IRQ sharing, solving many conflict problems that would arise with older ISA devices. In the original PC design, two COM (communication) ports were defined by an I/O address and interrupt. COM1 and COM 3 used IRQ4 while COM2 and COM 4 used IRQ3. In the standard ISA architecture, a conflict would arise if COM1 and COM3 or COM2 and COM4 were in use at the same time.

PCI modems are provided with a driver or 'enumerator' that provides the bridge between the newer PCI bus and the traditional COM port assignments: the driver enables the system to recognize the modem as a traditional COM port with non-standard IRQ assignment.

Most PCI modems use software-based configuration thereby requiring an operating system-specific driver. It is not uncommon for Plug-and-Play operating systems to misidentify the modem and install the wrong driver. In addition, many Windows modems get a generic software driver (that often fails to work properly) if you don't identify your modem exactly while installing it.

Putting the modem in a different PCI slot may solve some PCI modem installation problems. Depending on your system design and BIOS, a conflict may prevent proper modem operation in some, but not all, of your PCI expansion slots. In addition, some vendors have motherboard BIOS updates that address PCI issues - check for updated BIOS for your system.

Other PCI devices may produce conflicts, including some that result in intermittent problems including disconnections. The [PCI] video controller and driver are commonly the cause of this. Some graphics drivers may continuously write data to the PCI based video graphics controller even if the controller is not ready. This may cause clicks and pops in audio (sound-card conflict), display anomalies (unintended artifacts on your screen), and possibly modem disconnections or connectivity problems. Intel identified this problem in 1998, with a recommendation that graphics board vendors address it with a driver modification. Check for video adapter upgrades for your system if you are experiencing these problems.

xDSL and Troubleshooting Connections

The future for computer communication across wide areas, especially access to the Internet, lays in digital broadband technologies. The term broadband simply defines a type of data transmission in which a single wire can carry several channels at once. Cable TV, for example, uses broadband transmission. In contrast, baseband transmission used by most LAN protocols, enables only one signal at a time.

The leading broadband technology in many areas is the Digital Subscriber Line, or DSL. DSL offers affordable high-speed access using existing copper telephone lines with connections up to 35 times faster than dial-up modems. DSL is a proven technology that has been in use in the core telephone network for over a decade. Unlike standard dial-up modems, broadband service is "always on". No connection delays to the remote site, no busy signals, and most importantly, no dropped connections. DSL enables multiple users to connect at the same time which can increase productivity and network flexibility in the office and at home. Telecommuters can gain quick access to the company LAN to conduct business as if they were sitting in their office. xDSL, like many up and coming broadband solutions, carries with it a much lower cost to implement than traditional Frame-relay or "T" carrier solutions.

DSL is copper telephone technology that describes the transportation mechanism between the end-user and the Digital Subscriber Line Access Multiplexer (DSLAM). This is shown in figure 20-1. The DSLAM separates the voice-frequency signals from the high-speed data traffic and routes the DSL traffic between the customer's router, or network interface card, commonly referred to a the Customer Premise Equipment (CPE) and the network service provider's network. The network service provider can route the traffic to the Internet, or to a private LAN also connected to the ATM backbone. The most difficult part of designing a DSL network is getting the co-location rights at the local telephone company. In the USA, the Federal Communications Commission (FCC) has ruled that the baby Bell's must provide a small percentage of their rack space to qualified competitive carriers but the process of actually doing so is rather difficult at best. Many large companies have taken the steps to co-locate DSLAMs in major metropolitan areas but clearly the bulk of DSL service is provided by the Local Exchange Carriers (LECs) themselves.

Although the method of data delivery is the same across all DSL types, DSL is offered in many different "flavors" depending on need, distance, and target marketSince there are multiple types, you may often see the technology described as xDSL where the x indicates the form of DSL service being used. Among these various types, the most common methods are Symmetric (SDSL), Asymmetric (ADSL), Adaptive Rate (aRDSL) and ISDN DSL (IDSL). Table 20-2 shows the differences between these DSL types.

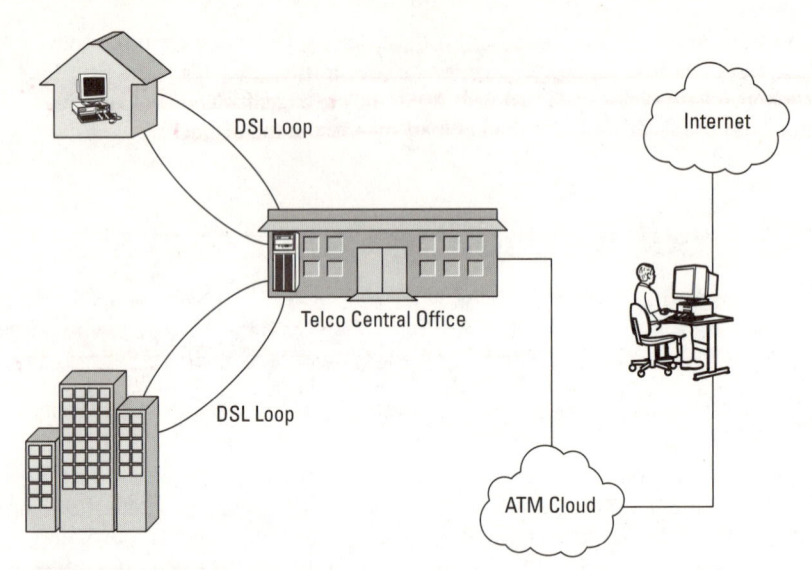

Figure 20-1: DSL describes the Loop between the end-user and the DSLAM located at the CO.

Table 20-2
Differences between DSL delivery types

DSL Type	Features and Benefits
SDSL (Symmetric Digital Subscriber Line):	SDSL is a symmetric service - the upstream speed is the same as the downstream speed. SDSL can deliver high-speed data communications up to 1.54 Mbps. This service is delivered via a single copper pair and is ideal for business applications that would have otherwise been served by an expensive T1. SDSL is normally targeted at the businesses customer and usually offers higher Service Level Agreements (SLA) to guarantee a minimum level of connection "up-time".
ADSL (Asymmetric Digital Subscriber Line)	ADSL is an asymmetric service, which means the downstream speeds are faster than the upstream speeds. This service is ideal for 1 to 5 users with high-speed data needs. It is an excellent solution for home Web users who would like to conduct quick, efficient Web surfing, e-mail, Internet research, large file downloads, video streaming, audio streaming, and 3-D image posting.

DSL Type	Features and Benefits
aRDSL (Adaptive Rate Digital Subscriber Line)	As with ADSL, aRDSL offers faster download speeds than upload speeds, but the actual speed will vary depending on the current load at the ISP. Such a DSL is usually proprietary and offered only by the local telephone companies in the United States.
IDSL (ISDN Digital Subscriber Line)	IDSL is a symmetric service that can deliver high-speed data communication up to 144 Kbps. IDSL is an ideal high-speed service alternative for users living or working outside the metropolitan periphery, beyond the reach of traditional SDSL and ADSL services. In many non-urban areas, the distance between a telephone company's central office and a user's business or home can be substantial. IDSL's strongest asset is its ability to reach up to 36,000 feet for the telephone central office. This is twice the distance of SDSL.

In general, the biggest drawback to xDSL technology is the distance limitations. Distance limits vary by service type (SDSL, ADSL, and IDSL). The nearer a customer is to the telephone company central office (the 'CO'), the more DSL options they have. The appropriate measure of distance is the length of cable between the customer and the central office. The physical length in cable feet is always longer than the distance measured as the crow flies and may not follow logical driving directions. Many older neighborhoods may have telephone lines that run the distance of a single street, and loop back some distance down the road. In cases like this, one side of the street may easily get DSL service while the other side is beyond the distance limits.

New technologies that can extend the range of DSL are coming onto the market and could alleviate the primary impediment to offering high-speed service to smaller markets. Many consumers and businesses typically are located farther than three miles from the phone company's central switching facility, which renders DSL service ineffective. These new technologies range from additional phone company equipment to better data compression methods and promise to add up to 9 additional miles onto the reach of DSL services.

One big advantage of DSL over other broadband technologies is the fact that for those locations within range, the copper telephone lines are already in place. By employing DSL to carry both voice and data on a single copper pair, the must install a new data jack inside the customer premises is eliminated. Almost all homes and businesses are equipped with internal copper wiring over which telephone service is distributed to wall jacks throughout the premises. In the US these employ the ubiquitous RJ-11 modular jack system, proven to be inexpensive and simple to use. Work areas in homes and businesses tend to be naturally co-located with existing wall jacks for voice service. By using DSL over the inside premises wiring, access to high speed data service is no further away than an existing wall jack. No new wiring or wall jack installation is generally required. By taking full advantage of DSL's inherent line sharing capabilities, the truck rolls associated with connecting a dedicated copper loop and with installing a new wall jack are removed. Recent advances in DSL customer premises equipment have further enhanced the carriers' ability to offer user-installable CPE, often resulting in a rapid expansion the customer base.

Traditionally, each DSL installation has involved the use of a line "splitter," which is a passive filter circuit designed to separate the lower frequencies of voiceband traffic from the higher frequencies of DSL traffic. The splitter eliminates crosstalk and interference by preventing high-frequency DSL noise from affecting voice line quality, and by preventing telephone ringing voltages and on-hook/off-hook transitions from affecting the DSL service. In most cases the splitter is installed at the network interface device located just outside the customer premises. Because this part of the installation is external, less coordination between the carrier and customer is required, and the customer need not be present during a technician's visit.

As an alternative to the external splitter approach, many carriers have begun replacing the external splitter with multiple user-installable "microfilters." In this approach, one microfilter plugs into each wall jack where existing telephony equipment (telephones, fax machines, analog modems) are in use. The jack to be used for the high-speed data connection is left without a filter. Microfilters are small plastic-cased devices, typically with one male and one female RJ-11 connector.

A microfilter passes the lower voiceband frequencies to telephones and thus does not affect standard telephone operation. Connecting the DSL router to any unfiltered wall jack enables the equipment to pick up broadband data traffic from the higher frequency spectrum; a high-pass filter within the DSL router ensures that voiceband frequencies do not interfere with its operation. One or more microfilters installed in the customer premises are electrically equivalent to the single splitter used in traditional DSL installations, and neither the existing voice service nor the DSL service is adversely affected. Because even non-technical customers can easily install microfilters, another barrier to DSL service deployment is eliminated.

As wonderful as DSL is for those who qualify, remember that DSL is a copper service. DSL does not work across fiber optic lines and therefore may not be available in new developments where the telephone company has replaced old copper lines with fiber.

Troubleshooting xDSL

Unlike POTS products, xDSL solutions, like all broadband technologies, are generally a yes/no proposition. When access is disrupted, the problem is normally not on the user side. Before calling the DSL provider however, a number of quick troubleshooting items should be performed.

- ✦ Is the DSL router powered on? The DSL router must be operational to route LAN traffic to the service provider. Because the DSL service tends to be so reliable, people often forget to check the DSL router after a power failure.

- Are all the appropriate LEDs lit? The LED indicators will vary from DSL router to DSL router, but most of them will have a WAN and LAN link light. The WAN LED should always be on. This indicates that the DSL router is *trained* up to the DSLAM. If this LED is off or blinking, then the fault is likely in the DSL loop between the CPE and the DSLAM. This could include the inside building wiring or any portion of the telephone line between the building and the CO.

- Is the router physically connected to the LAN properly? The DSL router will have an Ethernet port that connects it to the LAN. If the link light on the DSL router and/or the hub or switch on the LAN is not lit, the problem most likely is a bad patch cable, or port. Try replacing the patch cable with a known good cable, or move the patch cable to a different port on the hub/switch. If the hub/switch link still doesn't light up, try connecting a computer directly to the DSL router. If the computer can access the remote network (or Internet) this way, then the connectivity problem is within the LAN, likely within the hub/switch.

- Using the PING utility try systematically pinging through the remote links. Start by pinging the inside (Ethernet) port on the DSL router. Next ping the outside (WAN) port of the router. Then try to ping the default gateway of the router (which should be the ISP) and finally try pinging an IP address on the Internet. The point at which the pings fail will indicate where the problem is. If the default gateway is reachable, then the problem lies at the service provider, if the gateway is not reachable then the connectivity is likely failing at the DSLAM.

- At this point, a phone call to the LEC and/or service provider is usually necessary. Before any other troubleshooting is performed, the logical path between the CPE and the service provider's router should be rebuilt. Most of the time this process will correct the problem. Although rare, it is sometimes necessary to have the telephone company test the physical phone lines between the CO and the end-user's building.

Digital Cable and Troubleshooting Connection

As stated before, the biggest obstacle to digital, high-speed data communications has been the wire connection entering the building. The break-up of AT&T in the United States left this "last-mile" to the local phone company who were not obligated to share that access. Running new cables into an existing home or office is usually far too expensive to justify.

The obvious solution for many residential customers is the cable TV system. In the past decade the costs for running cables to homes in large numbers had already been expended. This provided a natural pipeline into these locations that bypassed the need for cooperation by the telephone companies. However, the cable TV technology was designed to be a broadcast medium, for the most part, one direction from the cable office out to the residence. Therefore, as demand for Internet access grew, the cable companies again undertook the costly process of overhauling their delivery systems by installing fiber-optic lines and two-way data-transmission capabilities. This is a time consuming and expensive undertaking. As of the 4th quarter of 2001, an estimated 44 million homes in the U.S. and Canada, nearly 40% of those nations' households, equipped for service. Thousands of homes are being upgraded every day, but it will take some time before the U.S. and Canada are completely wired for cable broadband access. Deployment of digital cable in other parts of the world is moving at a much slower pace and greatly depends on the region.

In March of 1998, the ITU approved the Data Over Cable Service Interface Specification, or DOCSIS, standard developed by CableLabs. This specification defines the interface standards for cable modems and supporting equipment. DOCSIS specifies downstream traffic transfer rates between 27 and 36 Mbps over a radio frequency (RF) path in the 50 MHz to 750+ MHz range, and upstream traffic transfer rates between 320 Kbps and 10 Mbps over a RF path between 5 and 42 MHz.

A major difference between cable and DSL lies in the basic nature of the cable system itself. Data travels over cable on a shared loop, therefore individuals see transfer rates drop as more users gain access. This is not only an important notation from a performance standpoint, but from a security stand point as well. As depicted in figure 20-2, it is easy to understand these inherent problems.

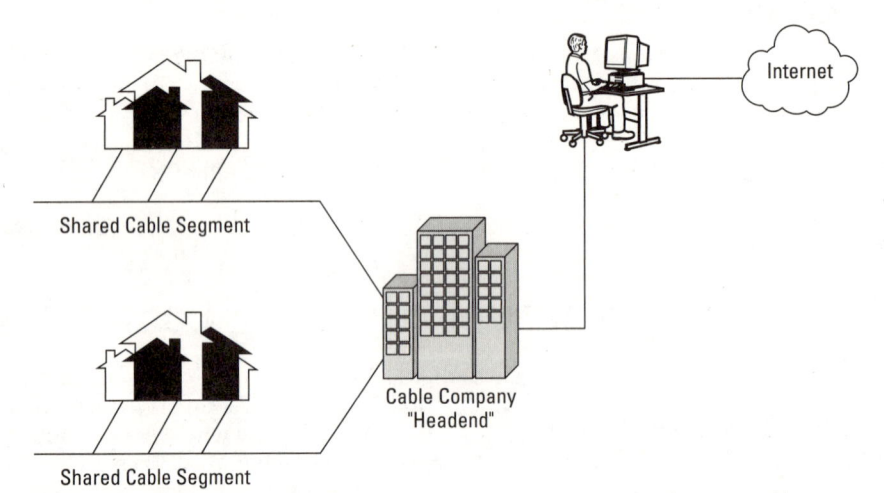

Figure 20-2: The cable access system uses a shared pipeline that can affect performance and security.

Cable companies received the right-of-way to install the original cable by neighborhood "grid". Basically, all houses within the boarders of the same city streets share a single cable segment. Some of these segments only host a few users; others can connect two or three dozen users. The bandwidth for each cable segment is shared among all devices on that segment. Therefore much like the Ethernet protocol used on local-area networks, the more devices trying to transmit and receive data on these segments, the less actual throughput each device receives. The performance is not limited to the number of users, as much as the amount of data transmission used. For example, on a single cable segment, there might only be 6 homes connected, but one of those homes is hosting a data-intensive Internet gaming server and consumes 90% of the available bandwidth. Although most cable providers prohibit such a use, it is not difficult to hide servers behind proxy devices or other routers.

More important for the network administrator is the security issues involved with this shared medium, especially if these connections are to transmit corporate information between the SOHO and main offices. With operating systems such as Microsoft Windows, File and Print sharing services are commonly enabled so a single printer can be shared among 2 or more computers. Additionally, one computer within the SOHO network maybe used as a shared storage device to enhance backup procedures. With these types of shared services running on the local LAN, especially in a peer-to-peer network, the shared devices become available to other people connected to the shared cable segment. Whenever cable access is deployed, dedicated firewalls must be used between the cable routers and the local PC/LAN. In addition, it is highly recommended that all locally shared data folders and printers be configured to require user and password protection.

Cable modem subscribers are typically charged for service on their cable bill, rather than paying the Service Provider directly, but the cable company and ISP have distinct responsibilities. The local cable company is responsible for installing the cable modem and managing the quality of service over the local cable network. At the cable company's main network office, commonly called the "headend", the user is connected to the cable ISP's national backbone. It, in turn, is plugged into the Internet. The ISP actually provides the Internet connectivity, while the cable company provides basic technical support.

Cable access is usually farther reaching than xDSL solutions, but most of the potential subscriber base is residential. Both wired technologies are major advances over analog dial-up services they differ in many aspects. Table 20-3 outlines the basic differences between cable and DSL broadband technologies:

Table 20-3
Differences between Cable and DSL Technologies

	CABLE	xDSL
Target market:	Because cable companies traditionally targeted the residential user for TV, the vast majority of cable installations are in homes rather than offices. Installing cable in commercially zoned areas may be rather expensive and offset the savings of this technology.	xDSL uses existing telephone wire to deliver data and therefore has the potential to offer services equally to residential users and businesses.
Speed:	Cable service is almost always asymmetrical but usually offers much faster download speeds than xDSL. Access speeds are not determined by distances from the headend but might be significantly reduced based on the number of users and types of activities being done on any given cable segment.	The actual speed of xDSL is highly dependant on the distance between the end-user and the telephone company's Central Office. xDSL speeds typically range from 128k to 2mb but the faster speeds are only available to users within a few hundred feet of the CO
Price:	On average, monthly access rates run from $29.95 to $49.95 depending on other packages the user subscribes to. Installation costs are generally free or under $50.00 and users can purchase competitively priced DOCSIS certified routers.	North American rates for DSL vary from $19.95 to over $300.00 depending mostly on speed. Installation costs on dedicated lines can run as much as $500.00 but line shared products installed by the end-user are usually free or under $50.00. Most DSL providers require the purchase of a specific router to match the DSLAM equipment (which generally makes them more costly than cable routers).
Security:	Cable technology relies on at least one common shared segment making the use of a firewall a necessity. Although Internet sniffing is common, people on the same cable segment do not need special equipment to "see" data transmitted between the Internet and other users on their segment.	xDSL is a private line technology meaning that the line between the end-user and the ISP is dedicated to just their traffic. This is inherently more secure than cable although once connected to the Internet, a reliable firewall still must be deployed. No shared segment on xDSL so unlike cable, the service provider can establish secured, private connections.

	CABLE	**xDSL**
Reliability:	Industry standards have been set for hardware and transmission specifications making this technology highly reliable. The primary downfall might be the level of technical support available by some cable companies. When problems do not involve the physical line (which is most of the time) the end-user may be referred to a service provider in another state or local for troubleshooting. Most cable providers do not offer SLA (Service Level Agreements)	As with cable, xDSL is a highly reliable technology with well established standards. Most DSL providers are local and can thereby offer local support for both the physical connections and the access portion. Because the "last mile" is still controlled but the local Telco however, it may be necessary to involve them for some repairs. Many DSL providers offer a business-class service and do have Service Level Agreements (SLAs) for these customers.
Expandability:	Most cable companies require additional fees for adding computers to the cable connection. Although proxy methods you can use to attach more than one PC, the legal requirements prohibit this. Typically, cable companies do not enable Internet servers, such as Web or e-mail servers to be used on the cable connection. Some companies offer business class services that do enable these but for a significantly increased cost.	DSL is generally sold as a fixed bandwidth service and does not place limits on the number of devices connected to the line, in fact many DSL routers are equipped with small Ethernet hubs to directly connect multiple computers to the service. Whether an Internet server is enabled on any given DSL line is up to the service provider. Most providers allow servers to use symmetrical lines but prohibit them from using asymmetrical lines.

Troubleshooting cable access

Much like xDSL, cable access is usually working or it is not. When troubleshooting cable access problems, the same items with the cable router should be followed as with the xDSL router. Make sure the unit is powered on, that all the appropriate lights are on, and all physically cables are properly connected between the computer and the cable router. Recycling the cable router is always a good first step as well.

Because most cable installations are single-device connections, some additional problems and troubleshooting steps pertain to cable:

If the computer does not work at all when connected to the cable router, first check that your basic network settings for your operating system are correctly configured and then check the IP address that has been allocated. (The IP address for Windows 95/98 can be found by running the program "WINIPCFG". For Windows NT/2000/XP run IPCONFIG from a command prompt, and for Unix/Linux, run the program IFCONFIG from the command line). When you have obtained the computer's assigned IP address compare it to the following possibilities:

1. If your IP address is absent or 0.0.0.0, then the network interface is not operational. Possible causes for this are as follows:

    - The Ethernet card (or USB driver) is not working.
    - Required drivers are not installed. Check documentation for the card.
    - You do not have a working Ethernet/USB connection between your PC and the cable router. Check cable and plugs and verify that Ethernet link lights are at both ends.

2. If your IP address is in the range 169.254.*xxx.xxx*, then this indicates that the DHCP client in your computer failed to contact a DHCP server on the network, and Automatic Private IP Addressing (APIPA) is enabled. The computer has automatically been assigned a private IP address that has no access to the public Internet. Possible causes for this are as follows:

    - The computer booted up faster than the cable router did, and the cable router was not ready for service by the time the computer sent out its DHCP request. Make sure the cable router has finished its start-up sequence before booting the computer, or leave the cable router powered on continuously.
    - The Ethernet/USB connection between your computer and the cable router is not working. Check all cable and plugs connections and verify that the Ethernet link lights are lit at both ends. Replace the patch cable with a known good cable and reboot the computer
    - Your computer may have multiple network interfaces and it is sending DHCP requests out on an interface other than the one connected to the cable router.

3. If your IP address is in the range 192.168.100.xxx, then this usually indicates that you have a working connection to your cable router, and the cable router is working, but it is not in contact with the cable network. Cable routers have an internal DHCP server that has issued the 192.168.100.xxx IP Address. At this point a call to the cable company is usually necessary.

Router diagnostics

The DOCSIS standard provides a Web based diagnostic utility built into the cable router. Although a number of products currently available can help diagnose router problems, the following information is intended for generic DOCSIS 2.0-compliant devices

Note Always consult your specific cable router's documentation to check for differences.

Connect to the Web based diagnostic page with your browser using the address: `http://192.168.100.1` (or `http://149.112.50.65/` for older 3Com Tailfin routers)

The downstream figures displayed are only meaningful if the modem is shown as locked onto a downstream frequency (typically 403,000,000, 402,750,000, or 331,000,000 Hz). If, instead, the words `In Progress` are shown beside the frequency, then a downstream frequency has not yet been locked onto. This condition is the equivalent of a flashing Receive light. In such a case, signal strength and signal-to-noise ratio (SNR) values are meaningless, and might refer to some random cable-TV channel being scanned. If `In Progress` persists, then perhaps the downstream signal on the CATV coaxial cable is too weak for the cable modem to detect.

The downstream power level should lie in the range –15 to +15 dBmV. A value of –15 or worse is unacceptable, and indicates a poor downstream signal path. A technician tweaking the CATV levels could aim for a value close to the optimal 0 dBmV, but a good cable modem should be able to work within the broader range of –15 to +15 dBmV, provided the downstream signal-to-noise ratio remains good enough. A reading of 0 dBmV might indicate that the cable modem does not support downstream power measurement, or that it is disabled.

The downstream signal-to-noise ratio (SNR) must be 23.5 dB or higher, and should ideally be 30 dB or higher. The lower the SNR, the more noise is present, and the poorer the performance — the router must keep requesting retransmissions of packets with uncorrectable errors. No sudden cut-off point indicates when the router stops working; performance just degrades as the SNR gets worse. Provided the downstream SNR is at an acceptable level, attaining a precise downstream signal level within the acceptable range does not matter.

The upstream figures displayed will only be meaningful if the modem is shown as Ranged on an upstream frequency. If, instead, it says `'n progress'`or `Down`, then an upstream channel has not yet been locked onto: This condition is the equivalent of a flashing Send light.

The upstream signal level should be in the range +8 to +58 dBmV. Commands from the UBR set it so the signal strength received by the UBR from the router reaches an acceptable level. The lower this figure is, the better the upstream path to the UBR is. A value within the range +25 to +55 dBmV is within spec, and figures in the forties are the most common.

A value at +58 dBmV indicates a poor upstream signal path: some cable modems cannot transmit any more strongly than 58 dBmV, and one cannot tell how far this is following the figure that the UBR would must see a strong enough signal at its end to maintain satisfactory performance. So, if the cable modem goes offline and the upstream signal strength is at +58dBmV, then a poor upstream path is a likely contributor to the problem. On the other hand, an upstream signal strength of +58 dBmV without any other symptoms need not be an immediate cause of alarm — just monitor the situation and keep a record of what you find.

The external cable infrastructure is affected by weather conditions, so you may expect signal levels to vary according to the weather, particularly extreme hot or cold temperatures.

If any of the earlier parameters fail to lie within acceptable limits, you should ask your local cable operator to send a technician to adjust (in the streetside cabinet) the signal levels on your CATV feed or return path.

Characteristics and problems of satellite Internet

When DSL and cable access are not available, satellite access to the Internet (or *satellite Internet* for short) may be worth considering. This technology still has a long way to go to reach the levels of reliability of other broadband services, but for rural Internet user who really wants broadband access, Satellite may offer the only choice. Satellite Internet does not use telephone lines or cable systems, but instead uses a satellite dish for data communications. Some older technologies require that you have an Internet Service Provider for uploads, but newer satellite services provide two-way communications via the satellite link. With these, upload speed is about 128kbps with an average of 500 kbps download speeds which makes satellite systems about 10 times faster than a normal dial-up modem. Two-way satellite Internet consists of:

- ✦ Approximately a two-foot by three-foot dish
- ✦ Two modems (uplink and downlink)
- ✦ Coaxial cables between dish and modem
- ✦ An unobstructed view to the south (the satellites orbit over the equator)

Two-way satellite Internet uses IP multicasting technology, which means that a single satellite can serve 5,000 communication channels simultaneously. IP multicasting sends data to many points at the same time by sending the data in compressed format. Compression reduces the size of the data and the bandwidth requirements. Normal land-based systems have bandwidth limitations that prevent multicasting of this magnitude.

The downlink of older one-way satellite systems works as with the two-way technology except the satellite transmits the data to your computer via the same dish that would enable you to receive a Pay-Per-View television program.

Troubleshooting satellite access

As with satellite TV, trees and heavy rains can affect reception of Internet signals. Initial setup and configuration of the satellite system can be problematic (although most problems and solutions are pretty well documented). Professional installation services may not be available in all regions — so (before you commit to this technology) a call to the prospective service's help desk would be prudent. This will provide a reasonable expectation of the timeliness and quality of assistance you are likely to receive as a customer. The standards for Satellite access are still rather vague and are not truly cross platform at this time. As the technology matures, standards and specifications will make installation and troubleshooting much easier.

Most of the common problems with satellite systems are due to the placement and alignment of the dish. When the reflector is pointed directly at the satellite, the adapter receives a strong signal. If the reflector is not positioned properly, the signal may be weak with errors resulting during data transfers. This signal quality will be worse on cloudy, windy, or rainy days.

To properly position the reflector, three adjustments must be made (and maintained) on the antenna. Specific processes for making these adjustments vary from one manufacturer to another; refer to the owner's guide for complete details. In general, the three critical positions of the dish are

- Polarization (rotation of the antenna)
- Elevation (pointing up or down)
- Azimuth (pointing side to side)

Fine alignments are made with the help of proprietary software. Performing this procedure can be a one or a two-person task, depending on how far the PC is from the antenna. If the antenna is close enough for the person aiming the antenna to hear the computer speaker, you can use the tones generated by the PC as a reference. Otherwise it is best to have a second person watch the computer monitor as it displays the signal strength meter information. If two people are performing the procedure, one person can view the computer monitor and provide feedback to the person aiming the antenna as to how well the signal is being received. Remember that the target for this alignment is 22,300 miles away. The key to success is to make small adjustments, never more that 1/8-inch, and to wait a few seconds between adjustments to give the system time to lock on to the satellite signal.

SOHO Wireless

Two competing wireless technologies for the home use have emerged as opponents (somewhat like to the VCR technology standards that pitted VHS against Betamax in the early days of home video recorders). Many technology companies have chosen sides and support the 11mbps IEEE 802.11B Wi-Fi (Wireless Fidelity) wireless standard while a growing number of companies, such as IBM, Proxim and Cayman

Systems, are now straddling the fence and backing both 801.22B and the 1.6 mbps HomeRF (Home Radio Frequency) developed by Proxim. Also on the horizon is the 802.11a that operates in the 5.4GHz range with transfer speeds of 54mbps. Although 802.11a products should begin to proliferate throughout 2002 and beyond, the prices for these devices will likely limit them to the business market for quite some time.

HomeRF was originally designed for home consumers. "Certified HomeRF" products are generally simpler, more secure, more reliable, and more affordable than Wi-Fi products. HomeRF has quality-of-service support for streaming media, and is the only wireless LAN (so far) to integrate voice. In fact, HomeRF has a chance to become the worldwide standard for cordless phones. It is a 2.4GHz extension of the European standard for digitally enhanced cordless telephony, with added data capability and features such as call waiting, caller ID, forwarding to individual handsets, distinctive ringing, and 911 emergency calling.

HomeRF uses a frequency-hopping technique to deliver speeds of up to 1.6 Mbps over distances of up to 150 ft - too short a range for most business applications, but suitable for the home market that it was specifically developed for. In HomeRF, all devices make use of a "shared secret" network ID (NWID) without which compliant devices will not be permitted to communicate on the HomeRF LAN. From a corporate security perspective however, network administrators don't must worry. A connection that links a HomeRF LAN to the corporate network is no different from a connection that uses an Ethernet card and DSL or cable. All the home gateway sees is an IP connection, so the security mechanisms already in place at the enterprise will still apply.

Although slower, HomeRF is considered generally less expensive to build and maintain and is easier for end-users to install. Companies that support HomeRF are currently petitioning the Federal Communications Commission to increase the amount of channels that companies can use which would boost HomeRF technology to speeds of 10 mbps

If the Home/Personal Wireless market isn't crowed enough yet, also the Bluetooth standard. Conceived initially by Ericsson, before being adopted by a myriad of other companies, Bluetooth is a standard for a small, cheap radio chip to be plugged into computers, printers, mobile phones, and so on. A Bluetooth chip is designed to transmit data to a receiving Bluetooth chip, which will then give the information received to the computer, printer, phone, and so on. The projected low cost of a Bluetooth chip, about $5.00US, and its low power consumption, means you could litcrally place a Bluetooth chip just about anywhere.

The intended use of Bluetooth is to provide short-range connections between mobile devices and possibly the Internet via bridging devices to different networks (wired and wireless) that provide Internet capability. HomeRF and Wi-Fi are wireless technologies optimized for the home environment. Their primary use is to provide data networking and dial tones between devices such as PC's, cordless phones,

Web Tablets, and a broadband cable or DSL router. Although these technologies share the same frequency spectrum, they do not interfere when operating in the same space. In general, Bluetooth devices will be useful, and fully supported in a HomeRF or Wi-Fi network.

Troubleshooting wireless access

Because definable standards differ between the available wireless technologies, no cut and dried troubleshooting tools that will fit every situation. For the most part, access problems with all wireless technologies are similar to wired technologies. Proper configuration of network hardware and software, including but not limited to TCP/IP settings, should be reviewed thoroughly. Access Points (discussed in detail in chapter 3) should be examined to be sure all link lights are active and interconnect cables are securely seated.

The obvious potential problems with wireless are distance limitations and signal interference. If devices cannot locate each other, or if connections drop at random times, carefully examine the distance between each device and between the devices and the access points. If multiple access points are used, make sure they are located within the manufacture's distance limits.

Most wireless technologies will operate properly between walls, ceilings, and floors. However, many electrical wires, lights, motorized fans, telephone lines, and other items stored in the hollows of walls, ceilings, and floors. Any of these can interfere with the spectrum waves and cause connection drops and other problems. Moving the devices around, and repositioning access points can often clear up these problems. Other household devices including some kitchen appliances, wireless telephones, remote control devices, and children's toys can also be culprits. When looking into unexplainable RF problems, apply a systematic approach by eliminating these devices (even temporarily) one at a time and test the connections. Don't over look the wealth of knowledge available from other people's experiences. The Internet is full of Special Interest Groups (SIGs) dedicated specifically to these new wireless products.

Summary

Small and home offices are increasingly important in the business world. Modern, high-speed communications can make these remote locations perform like mere extensions of the corporate LAN. Although current high-speed technologies are still relatively new (and not yet widely available in all areas), consider them when possible — and plan for them as (at least) a future upgrade.

Even with all the advances in high-speed technologies, the Plain Old Telephone System will remain a major access method for years, if not decades, to come. POTS services are widely available worldwide, inexpensive, and offer reasonable speeds for Internet browsing. POTS can also connect to the corporate network but normally require additional services, such as remote control, terminal services, or Secure Shell to provide useable performance.

Analog modems follow a predefined series of steps to make optimal connections. Collectively these steps are called the "handshake" and consist of a number of negotiations before communications begin. When troubleshooting dial-up connections, a direct connection to the modem (using AT commands) can greatly assist in identifying what portion of the process is failing.

The two leading digital technologies are *xDSL* and Cable. DSL is highly distance sensitive. Customers closer to the telephone company's Central Office will have more DSL options. DSL can be provided in symmetrical (same speed up and down) or asymmetrical (faster download than upload speeds). XDSL is a point-to-point technology where each loop is private between the end-user and the service provider.

Cable does not suffer from the distance limitations of xDSL but since most installed cable nodes are residential, the service is geared more to end-users than businesses. Although this isn't normally a problem, cable companies rarely offer guaranteed service level agreements. Cable access is asymmetric and the connection is shared among all users on a city block.

Satellite communications is relatively new but holds the promise of eliminating all location barriers for digital service. A small satellite dish serves to receive Internet (and potential private) data transmissions. Initial installs for satellite access required a separate dial-up ISP service for sending data, but current protocols enable two-way transmission via the satellite link.

Home wirelesses LANs are proliferating due to advances in two major protocols, 802.11b and HomeRF, which are both supported by most major manufacturers. Although 802.11b products are more widely available at this time, HomeRF products are catching up in number and generally cost less for comparable products. 802.11b (Wi-Fi) offer speeds up to 11mbs where HomeRF is currently set at 1.6mb. Because most wireless LANs have less than 5 computers, these speeds are generally acceptable.

For the exam, remember these key points from this chapter:

- Understand the difference between remote access, remote control, terminal services, and Secure Shell.
- Understand the characteristics of the PPP and SLIP line protocols and the differences between them.
- Know the advantages and disadvantages of using POTS for data communications.

✦ Understand the various types of xDSL service (asymmetric ADSL, symmetric SDSL, Rate-Adaptive RADSL, and ISDN IDSL) and how distance plays a role in determining available speeds and services.

✦ Know how cable access differs from telephone line systems and be able to identify the advantages and disadvantage of cable access

✦ Know the basic configuration requirements (dish placement) for satellite service and know that some services require a separate dial-up ISP account to upload data.

✦ Be prepared to explain the major differences between Wi-Fi (802.11b) and HomeRF technologies.

✦ Understand the basic troubleshooting techniques for all remote access services starting with a systematic approach to checking physical layer problems (check power, cables, and link lights) Use known good components when appropriate as part of the troubleshooting process.

✦ Be able to describe the security ramifications of using dedicated services both for the end-user and the corporate LAN.

✦ ✦ ✦

STUDY GUIDE

Assessment Questions

1. Terminal Services use remote node techniques for optimum performance

    A. True

    B. False

2. Which statement best describes a VPN:

    A. Very private network — A LAN with no outside connections

    B. Very private network — A LAN with secured private line remote access

    C. Virtual Private Network — Enables remote users to access private LANs securely across unsecured public networks, such as the Internet

    D. Virtual Private Network — Enables remote users to access private LANs securely by limiting remote access to only secured, private lines

3. Which of these are features of the Point-to-point protocol?

    A. Designed to ease the routing of e-mail messages

    B. Is self healing so data is automatically routed around problem links

    C. Provides a common solution to connect a variety of hosts, bridges, and routers

    D. Can automatically reestablish a failed connection

4. Which of these are benefits that the PPP offers that SLIP does not?

    A. Supports multiple protocols

    B. Can automatically reestablish a failed connection

    C. Provides error detection and correction

    D. Requires predefined IP addressing

5. What is the maximum speed that can be obtained between two modems over a standard POTS connection?

    A. 56K

    B. 53K

    C. 19,000 baud

    D. 33.3K

6. What does the modulation process do?

    A. Converts digital computer signals (high and low, or logic 1 and 0 states) to analog audio-frequency (AF) tones.

    B. Converts analog computer signals (high and low, or logic 1 and 0 states) to digital audio-frequency (AF) tones.

    C. Encapsulates analog data into digital form so information can be transmitted across POTS lines.

    D. Encapsulates digital data into analog form so information can be transmitted across POTS lines.

7. What group is responsible for defining standards for modem technologies?

    A. The Institute of Electrical and Electronic Engineers (IEEE)

    B. The International Telecommunication Union (ITU)

    C. The International Modems Standards Committee (IMSC)

    D. The Federal Communications Commission (FCC)

8. What is the purpose of Flow Control?

    A. Regulates the maximum connection speed of the modem.

    B. Enables ISPs to limit bandwidth of end-users.

    C. Monitors modem traffic for error detection and correction.

    D. Enables one modem to suspend data transmission from a faster modem so it can catch up.

9. What does the new v.92 modem standard propose to increase dial-up speeds?

    A. The use of digital modems on both ends to eliminate the performance hit of the modulation process

    B. Better error correction to limit data retransmissions

    C. A new data-compression recommendation

    D. The ability to put the modem 'on-hold' when the network indicates that an incoming call is waiting

10. What is a common cause of problems with PCI based modems, especially under 32-bit Windows operating systems?

    A. The Plug-and-Play operating system misidentified the modem and installed the wrong driver

    B. The IRQ of the modem conflicts with another device

    C. The I/O range defined on the card conflicts with another device

    D. The external cable exceeds maximum length recommendations

11. Digital Subscriber Line technology

    A. Requires fiber optic lines

    B. Requires copper lines

    C. Has a maximum distance of 6 miles

    D. Is a technology that runs across existing Cable TV coax lines

12. Asymmetric DSL provides:

    A. The same speed up and down

    B. Faster upload speeds than download

    C. Faster download speeds than uploads

    D. Farther distance coverage than symmetrical DSL

13. xDSL Service can share an existing telephone line providing both high-speed data and voice service on the same wire.

    A. True

    B. False

14. What additional equipment was necessary before cable companies could begin providing Internet access?

    A. DSLAMS in the telephone company's Central Office

    B. Repeaters at each city block headend

    C. Second cable lines concurrent with existing lines to provide a path for return data transmission

    D. Fiber-optic lines and two-way data-transmission capabilities

15. What specification defines the interface standards for cable modems and supporting equipment?

    A. 802.11b

    B. DOCWIZ

    C. DOCSIS

    D. HomeRF

16. With Automatic Private IP Addressing (APIPA) is enabled, an IP address of 169.254.100.10 would indicate:

    A. A normal condition. The cable router has assigned a dynamic IP address

    B. A normal condition. The cable router has assigned a static IP address

    C. An error condition. The cable router assigned an addresses that already exists on the Internet or other cable customer

    D. An error condition. The DHCP client in your computer failed to contact a DHCP server on the network

17. If your computer receives an IP address of 192.168.100.10, what can be done to aid in diagnosing connectivity problems?

    A. Pinging the router's default gateway and record the transfer times

    B. Run a tracert to the routers gateway to see where the last hop is

    C. View diagnostic information on the cable router with a Web browser at http://192.168.100.1

    D. Connect to the serial management port, reboot the router and watch for error messages

18. What technology does Satellite services provide to increase performance generally not feasible on land based systems?

    A. FIFO Data buffering

    B. Data compression for secure one-to-one communications

    C. IP multicasting that sends data to many points at the same time by compressing the data

    D. Real-time error detection and correction

19. What is the cause of most communication problems with satellite systems?

    A. Poor uploads speeds by the dial-up ISP connection

    B. Placement and alignment of the dish

    C. Incorrectly installed software drivers

    D. Faulty cables between the dish and computer

20. HomeRF has maximum transfer speeds and distances of:

    A. 11Mb at a maximum of 300ft

    B. 2Mb at a maximum of 600ft

    C. 1.6Mb at a maximum of roughly 150ft

    D. 54Mb at a maximum of roughly 150ft

Scenarios

1. For the past 3 months, your home DSL connection has not exhibited any connection problems. Suddenly you are unable to reach the Internet or the corporate LAN. The link lights on the router appear to indicate proper connections. After recycling the router, all link lights indicate proper operation but no connections can be established. Using the PING utility, tests to the routers gateway fail, as do tests to the inside Ethernet port on the router. The computer is configured for dynamic IP addressing which the DSL router supplies. Checking your computer's IP information, the IP address is 0.0.0.0. What would be the most logical problem?

2. Because neither cable nor *x*DSL is available in your rural neighborhood, you have opted to install a satellite dish for Internet access. Most of the time the Internet service delivers acceptable performance but speeds are beginning to slow down noticeably. On windy days access is often intermittent. What is the likely cause of these problems?

Answers to Chapter Questions

Chapter Pre-test

1. Remote Node: Enables the remote location to attach to the LAN as if the telephone line were merely an extension of the network cable.

2. SSH (Secure SHell) is a program for logging in to and executing commands on a remote machine. It provides secure encrypted communications between two untrusted hosts over an insecure network

3. The Point-to-Point Protocol and the Serial Line IP (SLIP) protocol

4. Both computers in the link must know each other's IP addresses for routing purposes. This causes problems when making Internet connections because most ISPs dole out dynamic IP addresses upon connection rather than permanent static addresses.

5. The *plain old telephone system* is often refereed to as POTS.

6. Large national and International providers such as EarthLink or Sprint, and proprietary services that also provide Internet access such as America On-Line and MSN, contract through local telephone companies to offer local access numbers. These local services are called a Point-of-Presences, or POP

7. The modulation process involves the conversion of the digital computer signals (high and low, or logic 1 and 0 states) to analog audio-frequency (AF) tones. Digital highs are converted to a tone having a certain constant pitch; digital lows are converted to a tone having a different constant pitch.

8. Putting the modem in a different PCI slot may solve some PCI modem installation problems. Depending on your system design and BIOS, a conflict may prevent proper modem operation in some, but not all, of your PCI expansion slots

9. The appropriate measure of distance is the length of cable between the customer and the central office. The physical length in cable feet is always longer than the distance measured as the crow flies and may not follow logical driving directions.

10. The bandwidth for each cable segment is shared among all devices on that segment. Therefore (as with the Ethernet protocol used on local-area networks), the more devices trying to transmit and receive data on these segments, the less actual throughput each device receives.

Assessment Questions

1. B. False. Terminal Services create multiple "remote control" type sessions on a single server that provides reasonable performance and better user administration.

2. C. Virtual Private Network — Enables remote users to access private LANs securely across unsecured public networks, such as the Internet.

3. C and D

4. A, B, and C

5. D. Over all-analog lines, the POTS system can reliably transmit data at 33.3bps. To achieve faster rates, one side of the connection must be digital.

6. A. The modulation process involves the conversion of the digital computer signals (high and low, or logic 1 and 0 states) to analog audio-frequency (AF) tones.

7. B. The standards for modem use are defined by the International Telecommunication Union, or ITU.

8. D. Flow control enables the receiving modem to tell the other to pause while it catches up. Flow control exists as either software, or XON/XOFF, flow control, or hardware (RTS/CTS) flow control.

9. C. The new data compression recommendation is based on the LZJH compression algorithm developed by US-based Hughes Network Systems and gives an improvement in compression of more than 25% beyond the existing V.42*bis*, and a data compression ratio in the region of 6:1 for a typical Web-browsing connection.

10. A. Most PCI modems use software-based configuration; thus they require a driver specific to the operating system in use. Plug-and-Play operating systems have been known to misidentify the modem and install the wrong driver.

11. B. DSL is copper telephone technology that describes the transportation mechanism between the end-user and the Digital Subscriber Line Access Multiplexer (DSLAM).

12. C. ADSL is an asymmetric service, which means its downstream speeds are faster than its upstream speeds. This service is ideal for small numbers of users (1 to 5) who have high-speed data needs.

13. A. True: A microfilter can be installed to pass lower voice-band frequencies to telephones and thus not affect standard telephone operation. Connecting the DSL router to any unfiltered wall jack enables the equipment to pick up broadband data traffic from the higher frequency spectrum.

14. D. As demand for Internet access grew, cable companies undertook the process of overhauling their delivery systems by installing fiber-optic lines and two-way data-transmission capabilities.

15. C. In March 1998, the ITU approved the Data Over Cable Service Interface Specification (DOCSIS) standard developed by CableLabs.

16. If your IP address is in the range 169.254.xxx.xxx, then the DHCP client in your computer failed to contact a DHCP server on the network, and Automatic Private IP Addressing (APIPA) is enabled.

17. A. The DOCSIS standard provides a Web based diagnostic utility built into the cable router. These diagnostic pages are available with a Web browser locally at http://192.168.100.1 (or http://149.112.50.65/ for older 3Com Tailfin routers).

18. C. Two-way satellite Internet uses IP multicasting technology. IP multicasting sends data to many points at the same time by sending the data in compressed format. Compression reduces the size of the data and the bandwidth requirements

19. B. When the reflector is pointed directly at the satellite, the adapter receives a strong signal. If the reflector is not positioned properly, the signal may be weak, resulting in errors during data transfers.

20. C. HomeRF uses a frequency-hopping technique to deliver speeds of up to 1.6 Mbps over distances of up to 150 feet.

Scenarios

1. Because `ping` tests to the inside port of the router fail, and the router's link lights indicate that WAN connectivity is functional, the next logical troubleshooting step is to look at the physical connection between the computer and the router. The first step is to replace the path cable with a known good cable. If that fails, the problem is likely in the network card itself.

2. Most common problems with satellite systems are due to the placement and alignment of the dish. When the reflector is pointed directly at the satellite, the adapter receives a strong signal. If the reflector is not positioned properly, the signal may be weak — resulting in errors during data transfers. Fine adjustments are probably necessary to correct the performance. Remember, too, that signal quality is worse on cloudy, windy, or rainy days.

Remote Connectivity Troubleshooting

CHAPTER 21

EXAM OBJECTIVE

- Given a troubleshooting scenario involving a remote-connectivity problem (such as authentication failure, protocol configuration, or physical connectivity) identify the cause of the problem.

CHAPTER PRE-TEST

1. You can verify the status of a remote access server in _____.
2. For the remote clients to successfully connect to a remote access server, _____ at client and server sides must match.
3. The default number of PPTP and L2TP ports for a VPN server is _____.
4. You can check the connectivity between a VPN client and server by using the _____ command.
5. If a VPN server is a part of an Active Directory domain, it must be added to the _____ group to enable clients to connect to the server.
6. The type of the RAS and IAS servers group is _____.
7. _____ and _____ are two commonly used routing protocols.

✦ Answers to these questions can be found at the end of the chapter. ✦

In today's global business scenario, remote-connectivity solutions are the lifelines of many major organizations. Remote connections allow employees to be mobile, yet have access to essential data. Employees can, at all times, access their corporate networks securely without having to worry about time or place. All they need is a remote connectivity solution configured on their corporate network. But have you ever wondered what happens to business activities if such remote connections do not work? What if the employee can't connect to the private network? What if the employee can connect but cannot access data? All activities come to a standstill, which nobody can afford in this day and time of competitive markets.

This chapter takes a look at some possible solutions to such problems. You, as an administrator, have some ways to ensure that remote connections operate as smoothly as possible.

The chapter is structured to introduce common problems and identify their possible causes in remote-connectivity scenarios. Then the possible solutions take center stage. Finally, a list of available diagnostic tools offers help with identifying and solving problems that may emerge with remote connections.

Troubleshooting RAS

After you configure a RAS server so remote clients can connect to your network, multiple problems still can occur. This is true even if you, as a conscientious administrator, configure the RAS server to the best of your knowledge and devote massive effort to full planning and attention. This section looks at some common problems with RAS — and their possible solutions.

Tip The most common problems with RAS involve connection failures. As a rule of thumb, that's a good place to start looking for solutions.

Common RAS problems

Most common problems related to RAS fall under one of the following categories.

- Remote-access connection cannot be established
- Resources beyond the RAS server cannot be accessed
- Callback feature doesn't work

The subsequent sections identify the most important aspects of these problems: their usual causes and their probable solutions.

Remote-access connection cannot be established

When a remote client is unable to establish connection with the RAS server, you can look out for multiple sources of this problem. For example, the problem might be due to problems with physical connectivity, service configuration, or security issues. Here's a checklist of common causes and probable solutions:

- **Is the modem is working correctly?** Check to see whether the modem is installed properly. Also check the modem for the connecting cable and its connection to the phone line.

- **Is the Routing and Remote Access service running on the RAS server?** Check the Routing and Remote Access window, which can be accessed from Administrative Tools. To check the server status, click Server Status in the console tree.

- **Is remote access enabled on the RAS server?** If the service is not enabled, you can enable the service in the Routing and Remote Access window. Right-click the server for which you want to enable the service and select Properties. In the General tab, check Remote access server.

- **Are the dial-up, PPTP, or L2TP ports enabled for inbound remote-access connections?** If not, enable these ports. To do so, open the Routing and Remote Access window and follow these steps.

    1. In the console tree, right-click Ports under the RAS server (for which you want to configure the ports) and select Properties.

    2. In the Ports Properties dialog box, click the name of the device you want to configure and then click Configure.

    3. In the Configure Device dialog box, check *Remote access connections (inbound only)* to enable remote access.

- **Are the LAN protocols used by the remote clients also configured on the RAS server?** You can view the properties of a specific RAS server by right-clicking the server's name in the console tree (in the Routing and Remote Access window) and then selecting Properties.

- **Are the authentication and encryption methods used on the server also in place on the client?** The server and the client must use at least one common authentication and encryption method.

- **Is the remote-access permission for the user account is set to *Allow access*?** If not, set it accordingly.

- **Has the user at the remote client supplied the correct credentials — username, password, and domain name?** If the credentials are incorrect, they cannot be validated at the remote-access server and the connection is denied.

- **For connections over IPX, are the RAS network numbers within a range used anywhere else in the IPX network?** If they are, the server gets confused and won't allow a RAS connection to happen.

- **Is the client configured to request its own IPX node number?** If it is, the VPN server should also be configured to *allow* IPX clients to request their own IPX node numbers.

- **Are all dial-up ports on the remote-access server already in use?** If so, what you have is the equivalent of a busy signal. You can check the ports by choosing Routing and Remote Access ⇨ Ports.

- **Is the authentication provider of the remote-access server configured properly?** You can use either Windows 2000 or RADIUS to authenticate the credentials of the remote clients. Ensure that the VPN server and the RADIUS server can communicate.

- **When the Windows 2000 fax service is enabled — and the fax service shares a modem with routing and remote access services, does the modem support adaptive answering?** If the modem does not support adaptive answers, disable fax capabilities on the modem so the remote-access connection can be established.

- **If you are not using MS-CHAP v1, does the user password exceed 14 characters?** If it does, then use a different authentication protocol (such as MS-CHAP v2) or modify the password so it doesn't exceed 14 characters.

Resources beyond the RAS server cannot be accessed

Apart from problems related to establishing a remote connection, remote clients might face a twofold problem: Although they can access the RAS server to which they are connected, they have no access to other resources on the internal network of the RAS server. This problem has several causes and some common solutions:

- **Is IP routing enabled on the RAS server to which IP-based remote clients are connected?** If not, enable IP routing in the IP tab of the Properties window for the server.

- **Is the RAS server configured to allow network access for remote clients that use IPX, AppleTalk, or NetBEUI?** If not, enable the network services for these protocols on the server. You can do so in the IPX, AppleTalk, and NetBEUI tabs of the Properties window for the server. If any of the tabs does not appear in the Properties window, it indicates that the respective protocol is not installed — in which case, install that protocol.

- **Are appropriate settings in place to handle the allocation of IP addresses at the remote-access server?** Two standard possibilities exist:

    - **Remote-access server is configured to use static IP address pool:** Check that the hosts and routers of the intranet can reach the destinations of the address ranges of the static IP address pool. If the routes to the remote access client address ranges are missing, remote access clients are not able to receive traffic from locations on the intranet. In such a case, you must add routes corresponding to the address ranges (as defined by the IP address and subnet mask of the range) to the routers on the intranet — or enable the routing protocol of your routed infrastructure on the remote-access server.

- **Remote-access server is configured to use DHCP:** When the DHCP server is not available, the remote-access server allocates IP addresses by using the Automatic Private IP Addressing (APIPA) — these addresses occupy the range from `169.254.0.1` through `169.254.255.254`. However, using APIPA for IP address allocation works only when the network to which the remote access server is attached is also using APIPA addresses.

> **Note:** If your remote-access server is using APIPA even when the DHCP server is available, make sure the proper adapter is selected; not all adapters can provide correct DHCP-allocated IP addresses. By default, the remote-access server chooses the adapter randomly. If (in the case of more than one adapter) the selected adapter does not have the DHCP server available, you can manually select the adapter. You can do so from the IP tab of the Properties window for the server.

- **Are the TCP/IP packet filters preventing the flow of IP traffic?** If so, check, evaluate, and reconfigure those filters.

Callback feature doesn't work

When the remote access server is configured to implement the callback feature, there might be situations when the remote clients trying to get access to the server and the network, do not get the required access. The callback feature may stop working for any of the following reasons:

- **Is callback appropriately configured on the Dial-In properties of the user account?** You can set the callback configuration options in the Dial-in tab of the Properties window for the user account. In this tab, do the following:
    - Check Verify Caller-ID and type the phone number that the user is using to call.
    - Select the callback option that you want to set for the user.

- **Are Link Control Protocol (LCP) Extensions enabled on the PPP tab on the Properties window of the remote-access server?** If not, enable them.

- **Are the callback numbers too long?** You can reconfigure the callback numbers on the Dial-In properties of the user account.

Troubleshooting VPNs

Customarily, troubleshooting VPNs has several areas of focus: IP connectivity, establishing remote-access and demand-dial connections, ensuring appropriate routing, and implementing IPSec. This section looks at some common problems with VPNs — and the possible solutions to these problems.

Common problems with VPNs

The most common problems that occur with VPNs can be summarized into the following broad categories:

- Cannot establish a connection with the VPN server
- Clients cannot connect to hosts beyond the VPN server

Each of these situations has an identifiable cause and solution; the upcoming sections examine some effective responses.

Cannot establish a connection with the VPN server

If a user can't establish a connection with the VPN server, one of three causes might be to blame: a physical connectivity problem, a misconfigured protocol, or an authentication error. To single out the problem area and choose an appropriate solution, first do some standard checks to verify the connection and configuration parameters. After that, the troubleshooting steps are pretty straightforward:

1. Simple as it may sound, check to see whether Routing and Remote Access is enabled on the VPN server.

   Tip: This step is an example of a classic rule: When you troubleshoot any problem, always start at the beginning. (Troubleshooting is often about common sense.)

2. Verify that the VPN server is enabled for remote access.
   - If the VPN server is a part of a Windows 2000 Active Directory domain, verify that the VPN server is a member of the RAS and IAS servers group and that the group type is set to security.
   - Verify that the VPN server is reachable. You can ping the IP address of the server to do so. If pinging is not successful, packet filtering might be the problem area.

   Note: If the `HOST` name is used instead of the IP address, verify that the `HOST` name is being resolved to the correct IP address. A standard method of doing this is to maintain `HOSTS` and `LMHOSTS` files for all remote users. The LMHOSTS file is a plaintext file that tells your computer where to find another computer on a network. The file resides in the Windows directory, and it lists the computer names (NetBIOS) and IP addresses of machines you access on a regular basis.

   - If you're using IPSec, verify that the PPTP and L2TP ports are configured for inbound remote access.

3. Check the authentication and encryption methods used on the server and on the client. The server and the client must use at least one common authentication and encryption method.

4. Ensure that the VPN server supports the LAN protocols used by the client. These protocols should be enabled for remote access on the server.

5. Make sure that the VPN server supports the tunneling protocol used by the client.

6. Make sure that the remote access permission for the user account is set to Allow access.

7. Ensure that the number of PPTP and L2TP ports is configured correctly for the number of concurrent connections you need.

Tip
The default number of ports for PPTP and L2TP is five each. However, if you want a PPTP-only server, set the number of L2TP ports to zero; if you want an L2TP server, set the number of PPTP ports to zero.

8. Verify that the client is passing an authentic username, password, and domain name to connect to the server.

9. Ensure that the IP address assignment is correct. The client's IP address should be a part of the server's IP address pool. If the server is configured to use a static pool of IP addresses, ensure that enough addresses available.

10. For connections over IPX, if the server is configured with a range of IPX network numbers, ensure that the numbers within the range are not used anywhere else in the IPX network.

    If the client is configured to request its own IPX node number, the VPN server should be configured to *allow* IPX clients to request their own IPX node numbers.

11. If the VPN server uses RADIUS to provide authentication, ensure that the VPN server and the RADIUS server can communicate.

12. Check to make sure the user password does not exceed 14 characters (if you are not using MS-CHAP v1). If it does, then either use a different authentication protocol (such as MS-CHAP v2) or modify the password so it doesn't exceed 14 characters.

13. Check that the ISP that you use does not block VPN usage by filtering either PPTP or L2TP packets. If it does, then the only solution you have is to use a different ISP.

These steps represent a standard response to VPN connectivity problems. Even if your network presents you with more complex problems, take heart: When you identify the cause of a problem, the solution practically announces itself.

Clients cannot connect to hosts beyond the VPN server

After the initial connectivity issues have been settled, VPN clients might still encounter problems in remotely accessing the resources in the private network. The clients might be able to connect to the VPN server, but might not be able to access the resources part of the VPN server's internal network. A look at the possible causes can suggest some standard solutions to such problems:

- **Is the VPN server configured to use a static address pool?** If so, the other resources on the network might not be configured to access the IP addresses in the static address range. Check to see whether the IP addresses in this range are reachable by the hosts on the internal network. If not, then add the range of addresses to the routers in the network to enable communication. You can also enable the routing protocol for the network on the VPN server. If the routes to the remote access VPN client subnets are not configured, VPN clients cannot receive data from hosts on the internal network. Routes for the subnets are configured either by specifying static routing entries or by using a routing protocol, such as Open Shortest Path First (OSPF) or Routing Information Protocol (RIP).

- **Are the LAN protocols on the VPN server configured to allow access to the *entire* network?** Configure the VPN server to allow clients to access the entire network. You can also configure the VPN client to act as a router.

- **Are TCP/IP packet filters implemented?** If so, that's a likely source of trouble. Packet filters can prevent flow of data over TCP/IP.

- **Are port-filtering tools, such as firewalls or proxies installed?** If so, check the security and access settings of the proxies and firewalls. Proxy settings and firewalls can prevent clients from accessing specific hosts if you are trying to connect via PPTP.

Your remote-access VPN should operate smoothly after you apply this checklist.

Windows 2000 utilities for diagnosing remote connectivity

Windows 2000 provides you with some diagnostic utilities that you can use to identify connectivity problems — event logging, tracing, and the Network Monitor utility.

Event Logging

In the Event Logging tab in the VPN server properties dialog, you can select the Log the maximum amount of information option. This enables you to view information regarding events that occur during the attempted connection. You can use this log to identify the problem.

Tracing

You can use tracing to record the function calls during an attempted connection. You should be experienced with routing and remote access to understand the traced information. You can enable tracing by selecting Enable Point-to-Point Protocol (PPP) Logging from the Event Logging tab in the VPN server properties dialog.

Network Monitor

You can use Network Monitor to capture and view the information exchanged during an attempted VPN connection. To understand the information captured by the Network Monitor, first be well versed in PPTP, PPP, and IPSec, as well as other remote-connectivity mechanisms and protocols.

Summary

This chapter examined how to troubleshoot common problems with RAS and VPN connectivity. It described possible problems, their causes, possible solutions, and some troubleshooting tools available with Windows 2000 that can help you diagnose connectivity problems.

✦ ✦ ✦

STUDY GUIDE

This study guide presents assessment questions to test your knowledge of the exam topic area.

Assessment Questions

1. For a remote client to establish a connection to a remote access server, the remote access client and the remote access server must be configured to use at least:

    A. One common authentication method.

    B. Two common authentication methods.

    C. Three common authentication methods.

    D. No authentication method.

2. What is the maximum number of characters that can be used for a user password if the authentication protocol used is MS-CHAP v1?

    A. 10

    B. 12

    C. 13

    D. 14

3. When a remote access server uses APIPA, what is the range of addresses allocated?

    A. 169.254.0.1 to 169.254.255.254

    B. 169.254.0.0 to 169.254.255.255

    C. 169.254.0.0 to 169.254.254.255

    D. 169.254.0.1 to 169.254.254.255

4. One of the possible causes for the callback facility not working is:

    A. LCP extensions are disabled.

    B. IP routing is disabled.

    C. User password exceeds 14 characters.

    D. Network access is not allowed for IPX on the remote-access server.

5. While attempting to connect to a VPN server, you notice that you cannot `ping` the server IP address from the client. What could be the possible problem?

   A. The client IP address is not a part of the static IP address pool assigned by the server.

   B. The server does not support TCP/IP.

   C. TCP/IP packet filtering is implemented on the server.

   D. The server is not configured as a router.

6. A VPN client is configured to request its own IPX node number. What settings should you configure on the VPN server?

   A. Do not allow IPX clients to request their own IPX node numbers.

   B. Allow IPX clients to request their own IPX node numbers.

   C. Specify a fixed range of IPX network numbers to be used.

   D. Disable IPX routing on the server.

7. You have a VPN server configured as a PPTP only server. How many L2TP ports can you configure on this server?

   A. 16,384

   B. 5

   C. 0

   D. As many concurrent connections as you need

8. You notice that a VPN client can connect to the VPN server, but cannot access resources on the server's internal network. What could be the problem? (Select all that apply)

   A. The static IP addresses configured on the server are not routed on the internal network.

   B. The LAN protocols on the VPN server are configured to access only the server computer.

   C. TCP/IP packet filtering is implemented on the server.

   D. Enough IP addresses are not configured in the VPN server's static IP address pool.

9. Which of the following utilities can you use for troubleshooting remote connectivity problems? (Select all that apply)

   A. Event Logging

   B. Tracing

   C. Network Manager

   D. Network Monitor

Answers to Chapter Questions

Chapter Pre-Test

1. You can verify the status of a remote access server in the Routing and Remote Access window.
2. For the remote clients to successfully connect to a remote access server, protocols at client and server sides must match.
3. The default number of PPTP and L2TP ports for a VPN server is **5**.
4. You can check the connectivity between a VPN client and server by using the `ping` command.
5. If a VPN server is a part of an Active Directory domain, it must be added to the RAS and IAS servers group to enable clients to connect to the server.
6. The type of the RAS and IAS servers group is security.
7. Open Shortest Path First (OSPF) and Routing Information Protocol (RIP) are two commonly used routing protocols.

Assessment Questions

1. A. For a remote client to establish a connection to a remote access server, the remote access client and the remote access server must be configured to use at least one authentication method. For more information, refer to the section titled "Remote-access connection cannot be established."
2. D. The number of characters that can be used for a user password should not exceed 14 if the authentication protocol used is MS-CHAP v1. For more information, refer to the section titled "Remote-access connection cannot be established."
3. A. When a remote access server uses APIPA, the range of addresses allocated is from 169.254.0.1 to 169.254.255.254. For more information, refer to the section titled "Resources beyond the RAS server cannot be accessed."
4. A. One of the possible causes for the callback facility not working is that the LCP extensions are disabled at the remote access server. For more information, refer to the section titled "Callback feature doesn't work."
5. C. If you cannot ping a VPN server, it implies that TCP/IP packet filtering is implemented that prevents data flow. For more information, refer to the section titled "Cannot establish a connection with the VPN server."
6. B. If the client is configured to request for its own IPX node number, the VPN server should be configured to allow IPX clients to request for their own IPX node numbers. For more information, refer to the section titled "Cannot establish a connection with the VPN server."

7. C. If you want a PPTP only server, set the number of L2TP ports to zero. For more information, refer to the section titled "Cannot establish a connection with the VPN server."

8. A, B, C. All three are possible causes that prevent a client from accessing hosts beyond the VPN server. For more information, refer to the section titled "Clients cannot connect to hosts beyond the VPN server."

9. A, B, D. All three utilities can be used to diagnose remote connectivity problems. For more information, refer to the section titled "Windows 2000 utilities for diagnosing remote connectivity."

Client/Server Network Configuration

CHAPTER 22

EXAM OBJECTIVES

- Given specific parameters, configure a client to connect to the following servers:
  - UNIX/Linux
  - NetWare
  - Windows
  - Macintosh

CHAPTER PRE-TEST

1. _____ resolves a host name on a Linux/UNIX Server.
2. The default port for the FTP protocol is _____.
3. To transfer files from a Linux/UNIX Server to a Windows machine, you need _____.
4. If print services do not get loaded on one of the network servers after rebooting, what would you do to solve the problem?
5. A _____ is the way in which the NWLink protocol formats the data to be sent over the network.
6. Which utility verifies TCP/IP configuration parameters on a host?
7. Which daemon translates NFS requests into actual requests on the local file system?
8. Which command must be executed to update the list of exported file systems for your Linux machine?

✦ Answers to these questions can be found at the end of the chapter. ✦

The basic purpose of networking is to share resources among computers on a network. Imagine a world of stand-alone computers wherein you have to travel or use postal services to merely transfer files from one computer to another. This situation would be a time-consuming, labor-intensive, inefficient way to share resources — difficult even in imagination. Today, computer networks offer a simpler, faster way to share resources with minimum effort — and the whole process is so fast that the efficiency of your work increases tremendously.

Usually, computer networks have a network server and multiple clients connected to this server. The server makes available a number of services for the clients. These services are called *network services*, which enable computers to share resources. Network operating systems, such as Windows NT Server, Windows 2000 Server, NetWare Server, Linux Server, and Macintosh OS X Server, have most network services integrated in them. However, some network services are now being integrated into desktop operating systems, as well. Some common network services are file services, print services, and message services.

This chapter examines how to configure network services on various network operating systems — and how to connect to these servers to access different network services.

Windows NT/2000

When you install Windows NT or Windows 2000 Server, Setup requests information about the network installation, like whether the computer is on a local area network, dialed into a remote network, or both. In this phase, you are also prompted to specify whether Internet Information Service (IIS) must be installed, which network interface card is needed, which network transport protocol is needed, what additional network services are required, and which workgroup or domain the computer joins.

Windows NT/2000 networking capabilities enable Windows NT to share files, printers, and applications with other networked computers. Fortunately, these features need not be installed separately. In this section, you'll learn how to configure the file and print services at the server side and then set up different clients to access these services.

Configuring file and print services

As previously mentioned, networking capabilities are already installed with Windows NT/2000 Server. Therefore, the only task that needs to be performed is to configure the network components, so the network services are accessible by clients.

Configuring file and print services on Windows NT/2000 Server requires you to configure two major attributes of the network:

- Network adapters
- Network protocols — in particular, these three:
  - TCP/IP
  - NWLink IPX/SPX
  - NetBEUI

Configuring the adapter

Network interface cards can be installed during setup, when hardware is changed, or when drivers are updated. For Windows NT Server, the Adapters tab on the Network dialog box in Control Panel, as shown in Figure 22-1, configures network interface cards and drivers. For Windows 2000 Server, you can configure network interface cards from the Local Area Connection Properties dialog box. To access this dialog box, open Network and Dial-up Connections in Control Panel. Then right-click the Local Area Connection icon and choose Properties. Finally, the Local Area Connection Properties dialog box appears in which you can use the Configure button to configure the adapter.

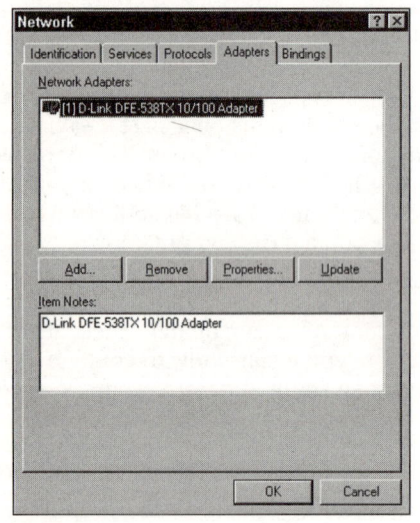

Figure 22-1: The Network dialog box with the Adapters tab active

Using the Adapters tab, you can perform the following functions:

- **Add:** Clicking this button enables you to add a network interface card and its associated driver to your computer.
- **Remove:** Clicking this button enables you to remove the selected network interface card and its driver from the system configuration. As with other Windows NT networking components, when a network interface card is removed, the related software is stored on the computer's hard disk.
- **Properties:** Clicking this button enables you to view and change the settings for a selected adapter card. The Setup dialog box is displayed for the selected network interface card. Using this dialog box, you can configure settings, such as the IRQ level, I/O port address, I/O channel and the transceiver type, for a selected network interface card. The IRQ needs to be set carefully so as to not clash with any other device.

Tip: You need not apply IRQ settings for Plug and Play network adapters.

- **Update:** Clicking this button enables you to update the driver information for the selected network adapter.

Configuring protocols

The Protocols tab in the Network dialog box in the Control Panel installs and configures protocols, as shown in Figure 22-2. For Windows 2000 Server, you can install and configure protocols in the Local Area Connection Properties dialog box using the Install and Properties buttons respectively. You can also remove a protocol by using the Uninstall button in the Local Area Connection Properties dialog box.

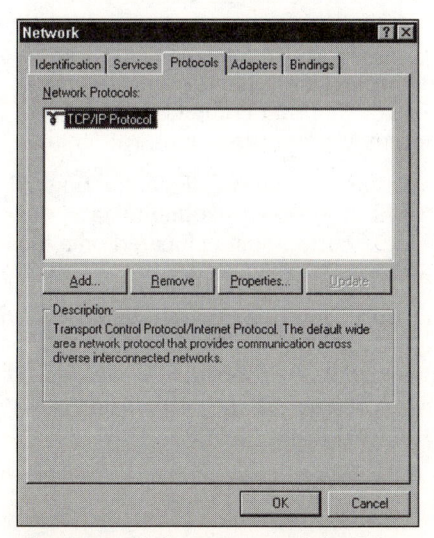

Figure 22-2: The Network dialog box with the Protocols tab active

You can use the Protocols tab to perform the following functions.

- **Add a protocol to the system configuration.** To do so, click the Add button.
- **Remove a selected protocol from the system configuration.** To do so, select the protocol to be removed and then click Remove.
- **View and configure settings for a selected protocol.** To do this, select the protocol to be configured and then click the Properties button.
- **Update a protocol.** To do so, select the protocol to be updated and then click Update.

TCP/IP protocol

TCP/IP core protocols provide a set of standards for how computers based on Windows NT/2000 communicate in a network environment. Configuration of the TCP/IP protocol can be done manually or automatically. For manual TCP/IP configurations, an IP Address, a Subnet Mask, and a Default Gateway need to be assigned. These three parameters need to be configured separately for each network interface card by using TCP/IP. The TCP/IP properties dialog box in the Protocols tab in the Control Panel can be used to enter the TCP/IP configuration parameters, as shown in Figure 22-3.

- **IP address:** This 32-bit address identifies a TCP/IP host. Each computer running TCP/IP requires a unique IP Address; for example, 203.145.205.11. Each IP Address has two parts:
  - **Network ID:** The network ID identifies all hosts on the same physical network.
  - **Host ID:** The host ID identifies a host on the network.
- **Subnet mask:** A *subnet* is a network in a multiple network environment that uses IP Addresses derived from a single network ID. By using subnets, an organization can divide a single large network into multiple physical networks and connect them with routers. A *router* is a device that connects networks of different types, such as those using different architectures and protocols.

  A *subnet mask* blocks part of the IP Address so that TCP/IP can distinguish the network ID from the host ID. When TCP/IP hosts try to communicate, the Subnet Mask determines whether the destination host is located on a local or a remote network. A sample Subnet Mask is 255.255.0.0.
- **Default Gateway:** For communication with a host on another network, an IP Address should be configured for the default gateway. TCP/IP sends packets for remote networks to the default gateway, if no other route is configured on the local host to the destination network. If a default gateway is not configured, communication may be limited to the local network.

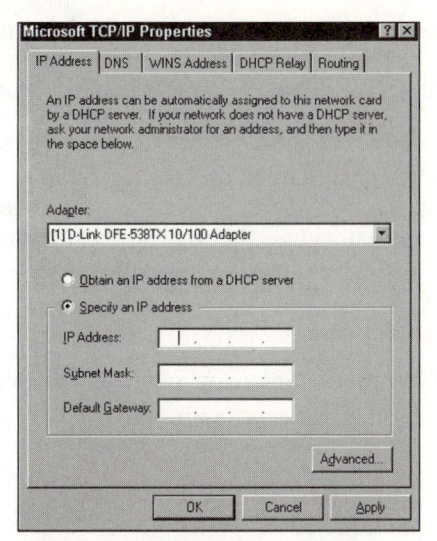

Figure 22-3: The TCP/IP Properties dialog box.

TCP/IP can be configured automatically. The Dynamic Host Configuration Protocol (DHCP) server service, provided by Windows NT Server, performs this task. When a DHCP server is configured on a network, clients that support DHCP can request TCP/IP configuration information (IP Address, Subnet Mask and a Default Gateway) from the DHCP server. Other TCP/IP parameters may also be obtained from the DHCP server, such as DNS and WINS server IP addresses.

The DHCP service can simplify the configuration of TCP/IP. When a DHCP server is available, TCP/IP can be configured automatically through the Obtain an IP Address from a DHCP server option in the IP Address tab in the TCP/IP Properties dialog box. When this radio button is selected, the DHCP client contacts a DHCP server for its configuration information. After receiving this request, the DHCP server assigns an IP Address, Subnet Mask and Default Gateway to the DHCP client.

After TCP/IP has been set up, you can check it by using such Windows NT/2000 utilities as IPCONFIG and PING.

The IPCONFIG utility verifies TCP/IP configuration parameters on a host. This is useful in determining whether the configuration is initialized or if a duplicate IP address has been configured. The command that can check the TCP/IP set is:

```
ipconfig /all
```

If a configuration has been initialized, the IP address, subnet mask, and default gateway is displayed. If a duplicate IP Address has been configured, it appears as configured, but the subnet mask appears as 0.0.0.0. In addition, if DHCP is being used, and the computer can't obtain an IP address, the IP address appears as 0.0.0.0.

After the TCP/IP configuration is verified with the IPCONFIG utility, you can use the Packet Internet Groper (PING) utility to test connectivity. PING is a diagnostic tool that tests TCP/IP configurations and diagnoses connection failures. PING determines whether a particular TCP/IP host is available and is functional. The command is:

```
ping IP_Address
```

If PING is successful, it responds, by default, with the following message four times:

```
Reply from IP_Address
```

You can use the following sequence of steps to check TCP/IP connectivity.

1. Use the IPCONFIG utility to verify that the TCP/IP configuration has been initialized.

    ```
    ipconfig /all
    ```

2. Ping the loopback address to verify that TCP/IP is installed and loaded correctly.

    ```
    ping 127.0.0.1
    ```

3. If pinging the loopback address is successful, ping the IP address of the workstation to verify that it is added correctly and to check for possible duplicate IP addresses.

    ```
    ping <IP_address_of_your_workstation>
    ```

4. If the previous step is successful, ping the IP address of the default gateway to verify that the default gateway is functioning and that the computer can communicate with the local network.

    ```
    ping <IP_address_of_default_gateway>
    ```

5. Ping the IP address of a remote host to verify that the computer can communicate through a router.

    ```
    ping <IP_address_of_remote_host>
    ```

NWLink IPX/SPX protocol

NWLink IPX/SPX Compatible Transport protocol is a 32-bit Microsoft implementation of the IPX/SPX protocol used in NetWare networks. It enables communication between a Windows NT/2000 computer and other machines using IPX/SPX. It supports networking APIs, such as Windows Sockets (Winsock) and NWLink NetBIOS. NWLink also provides NetWare clients to access applications that run on Windows NT/2000 Server, such as Microsoft SQL Server and Microsoft SNA Server.

The configuration of NWLink can be done through the Protocols tab in the Network option of the Control Panel (For Windows NT). For Windows 2000, you can configure NWLink in the Local Area Connection Properties dialog box. Using the NWLink IPX/SPX Properties dialog box, the frame type and the network number for each network interface card on a computer can be specified. In addition, Windows NT/2000 can be set to approach this task in one of two ways:

✦ Automatically detect the frame type

✦ Manually specify a frame type for the network

A frame type is the way in which the NWLink protocol formats the data to be sent over the network. If the computer connects to a NetWare server, the Windows NT/2000-based computer should have the same frame type as the one used by the NetWare server. An incorrect frame type prevents Windows NT/2000-based computers from communicating with NetWare servers. NWLink IPX/SPX Compatible Transport protocol can run on various topologies like Ethernet, Token Ring, and Fiber Distributed Data Interface (FDDI).

As mentioned earlier, you can configure the frame type to be automatically detected on a Windows NT/2000–based computer (provided it has NWLink IPX/SPX Compatible Transport protocol installed on it). If multiple frame types are detected (in addition to the 802.2 frame type), NWLink defaults to the 802.2 Frame Type and the other frame types have to be manually configured by selecting the Manual Frame Type Detection option from the NWLink IPX/SPX Properties dialog box.

Internal Network numbers are entered in an eight digit hexadecimal format, with the default setting being 00000000. Windows NT/2000 uses network numbers to run services such as SQL Server or SNA Server. An internal network number assigns a logical network for NetWare servers. Setting this number enables a NetWare server running on a multinet host to be uniquely identified.

Routing Information Protocol (RIP)—The Routing tab in the NWLink IPX/SPX Properties dialog box, can enable or disable the Routing Information Protocol (RIP). Windows NT/2000 Server can act as an IPX router by using RIP routing over IPX. RIP enables a router to exchange information with neighboring routers.

NetBEUI protocol
The NetBEUI Frame, or NBF, is the implementation of NetBEUI included with Windows NT/2000. On multi-segment networks, Windows NT/2000-based computers running NetBEUI must be connected by bridges instead of routers (A bridge is a device that joins two LANs). This is because NetBEUI is not routable.

Windows NT/2000-based computers provide self-configuration and self-tuning features for the NetBEUI protocol. Apart from this, NetBEUI also provides certain advantages like error protection and small memory overhead. The Windows NT/2000 Setup program automatically configures it during the installation phase.

Windows NT/2000-based computers use NetBEUI for interoperability with older Microsoft network systems, such as LAN Manager and Windows for Workgroups. However, its use causes more broadcast traffic than other protocols because this protocol relies on broadcasts for many of its functions. This includes name registration and discovery.

Accessing file and print services from NetWare clients

Windows NT/2000 Servers are compatible with NetWare so both of them can interoperate. The NetWare compatibility features of Windows NT/2000 Server not only include network protocol support, the NWLink IPX/SPX network protocol, but also a number of special services that help Windows NT/2000 access services on NetWare networks, and NetWare clients to access services on Windows NT/2000 Server. For example, you can enable file and print services at the Windows NT/2000 Server side to be accessed by NetWare clients.

File and print services for NetWare (FPNW) is an add-on service that helps NetWare clients to access Windows NT/2000 file, print, and application services.

FPNW does not require any additional software on the NetWare client. NetWare clients can directly access information on a Windows NT/2000 Server.

Accessing file and print services from Macintosh clients

Windows NT/2000 Server includes a network service called Services for Macintosh that enables Macintosh computers to access files and printers on a Windows NT/20000 computer. When this service is installed and is running, any Macintosh computer with version 6.0.7 or later of the Macintosh operating system and the AppleTalk protocol installed can connect to the Windows NT/2000 Server. The only other requirement is that, if you want to run Services for Macintosh on your Windows NT/2000 Server, you should have also created a Macintosh-accessible volume. Macintosh-accessible volumes can only be created on an NTFS partition.

Services for Macintosh is a network service and must be installed by using the Services tab of the Network icon in Control Panel (For Windows NT). For Windows 2000, you use the Local Area Connection Properties dialog box. When you install Services for Macintosh on Windows NT/2000 Server, the following components are automatically made available on your Windows NT/2000 Server:

- File services for Macintosh
- Print services for Macintosh
- AppleTalk protocol (in the Protocol tab of the Network application in the Control Panel)

Services for Macintosh is compatible with such network architectures as

- ✦ LocalTalk
- ✦ Ethernet
- ✦ Token Ring
- ✦ FDDI

Linux Server

When you install Linux Server, you can select the components you want to install with the operating system. Some of these components include network support, file managers, NFS Server, and SMB (Samba) connectivity. The corresponding packages for the selected components are automatically installed. Thus, most services are installed at the time of installation of the operating system. Also, you can select the services that you want to start on reboot.

You can configure the Linux Server for file and print services to be accessible over Linux/UNIX, NetWare, Windows, or Macintosh network. In this section, you'll see how can you configure the Linux Server for file and print services.

Network File System

The Network File System (NFS) is the means by which Linux/UNIX systems share their file system amongst themselves. NFS was originally developed by Sun Microsystems during the 1980s for UNIX-based systems. Sun Microsystems shared the design and made the protocol a standard, which helped in eliminating any interoperability issues with other operating systems. Linux supports NFS and uses it as the default mode to share directories across other Linux and UNIX systems.

The NFS software is installed automatically when you install Red Hat Linux. For NFS to work, certain NFS services must be running on the NFS server. These services are provided by the following daemons, which must be started for NFS to work.

- ✦ nfsd: This daemon translates NFS requests into actual requests on the local file system. You can use the following command to reconfigure the nfsd service.

    ```
    # killall -HUP rpc.nfsd
    ```

    The killall command kills a process by specifying the process name. The HUP option with the killall command causes most daemons to reread the process configuration files.

- mountd: The `mountd` daemon services the request for mounting and unmounting file systems. After you have modified any of the configuration files for the mountd service, you can use the following command to reconfigure it:

  ```
  # killall -HUP rpc.mountd
  ```

- portmapper: The portmapper service manages the remote procedure calls (RPC) connections, which are used by protocols such as NFS. RPC is a protocol that enables client programs to access the resources on the server. The portmapper service in Linux is called `portmap` (or `rpc.portmap`). You can start the `portmap` daemon from the script present in the `/etc/rc.d/init.d` directory by giving the following command:

  ```
  # /etc/rc.d/init.d/portmap start
  ```

All the preceding services start at boot time, if you configure the `nfs` service to be started at boot time. This can be done with the `ntsysv` utility.

Sometimes, after you change some configuration settings for NFS, you need to stop and start all the services relating to NFS. The `nfs` script under the `/etc/rc.d/init.d` directory can do this. You can start all the NFS services by passing the start option to the nfs script as a parameter.

```
# /etc/rc.d/init.d/nfs start
Starting NFS services:
[  OK  ]
Starting NFS statd:
[  OK  ]
Starting NFS quotas:
[  OK  ]
Starting NFS mountd:
[  OK  ]
Starting NFS daemon:
[  OK  ]
```

By default, all these services are installed with Red Hat Linux and loaded when you boot your system. To check all services to determine whether they're running, you can use the `rpcinfo` command, which is located in the `/usr/sbin` directory. The `-p` option is used with the `rpcinfo` command to check all the RPC programs running on your system. You can also specify the name of a remote machine to find its status.

The following is the complete set of steps that you follow to configure NFS.

1. Ensure that the `portmapper` and `nfsd` services are running on the NFS server.

2. On the NFS server, make the necessary entries in the `/etc/exports` file for the directories that you want to export. Mention the hosts allowed to access the share and state the necessary permissions for each of the hosts.

3. Execute the `/usr/sbin/exportfs -a` command to update the list of exported file systems for your machine.

4. On the NFS client, use the `mount` command to mount the file system of the NFS server, so you can access the directory.

5. If you have to automate the mounting, add the necessary entry in the `/etc/fstab` file.

6. Use the `showmount` command to check the status of the file systems on the server.

Setting up the NFS Server

The NFS server shares its file system with other machines. It specifies the directories that it is willing to export to other machines on the network. Exporting a file system is the same as sharing it. The file systems to be exported along with their permissions and features are specified in the `/etc/exports` file.

You can directly edit the exports file and enter the directories that you want to export. The general structure of the exports file is as follows:

`/directory_to_export host1(permissions) host2(permissions)`

where

- *directory_to_export* represents the directory to be shared. All the sub directories with in this directory are automatically shared.
- *host1* and *host2* represent the computers that can access the shared directory. These hosts can be specified by their IP addresses or their DNS names.
- *permissions* represents the type(s) of access granted to each host for the shared directory. Four especially important permissions are
  - `rw`: This setting provides read and write access, which is the default permission.
  - `ro`: This setting provides read-only access.
  - `no_root_squash`: This setting acknowledges and trusts the client's root account. Without this option, all the requests from the user ID 0 (root) on the client are mapped to nobody's UID on the server. Unless you have full trust in the client security, you don't give this option.
  - `noaccess`: This setting makes everything following the directory inaccessible to a specified client. This capability is useful when you want to export a directory hierarchy to a client but exclude certain subdirectories. The client's view of a directory flagged with `noaccess` is limited. The option only enables reading of the shared directory and not the subdirectories.

For example, consider the following sample entry in the `/etc/exports` file.

`/home 172.17.55.241(rw)`

The entry just given specifies that you are exporting the /home directory, which can be accessed by host 172.17.55.241. After the client host machine is configured to access the home directory, it has read-write (rw) access for the directory.

After you have set up the /etc/exports file, tell Linux about the list of NFS exported file systems. you can do so by the exportfs command. This command is available under the /usr/sbin directory. The exportfs command maintains the current list of the exported file systems for NFS. It can also check for any error that you may have made in the /etc/exports file. The list is kept in the /var/lib/nfs/xtab file. You can use the exportfs -a command to initialize this list with a list of all exported file systems maintained in the /etc/exports file, as in the following example:

    # /usr/sbin/exportfs -a

Setting up the NFS client

NFS clients are machines that access the file system on the NFS server. As Linux can access only the directories available under the root (/) directory, mount the NFS file system.

The mount command

The mount command can mount an NFS file system. The general structure of the command is:

    mount server_name:/exported_dir /dir_to_mount

In the preceding syntax,

- server_name:/exported_dir is the shared directory on the server, which can be specified by its IP address.
- /dir_to_mount is the directory to be mounted on the local machine.

For example to mount the directory, /home, from the machine, 172.17.55.241, you would give the following command:

    # mount 172.17.55.241:/home /home

The /home directory must exist on the local machine.

The umount command

The umount command detaches a file system from the file hierarchy. An example of the umount command is as follows:

    # umount /home

This command unmounts the /home directory from the root hierarchy.

The /etc/fstab File

The fstab file contains descriptive information about the various file systems that have to be mounted automatically at boot time. In the fstab file, you can also specify the options that you have to pass to the `mount` command. The file is usually only read by programs, and the system administrator must maintain it. Each file system is described on a separate line; either tabs or spaces separate the fields on each line.

All the file systems that you want to mount automatically during reboot can be specified in the fstab file.

Samba

The Samba software suite is a collection of programs that implement the *Server Message Block (SMB) protocol*. The SMB protocol, also called the NetBIOS or LanManager protocol, shares files from a Windows machine with remote systems. The Samba suite implements the SMB protocol, which shares resources with Windows-based machines. You can share a directory under Windows and access it from Linux. You can also share a Linux file system to be accessed from Windows. It shares printers connected to either a Linux or a Windows system.

The Samba suite is made up of the following components:

- `smbd`, which is the Server Message Block daemon that provides file and print services to SMB clients. The `/etc/smb.conf` file is the configuration file for the `smbd` daemon.
- The `nmbd` daemon, which provides NetBIOS name-serving and browsing support.
- The `smbclient` utility, which accesses SMB shares on a Windows machine.
- A Web interface provided by SWAT to manage the Samba server.
- The `testparm` utility, which can test the `smb.conf` file.
- The `testprns` utility, which determines whether a printer name is valid for use in a service provided by `smbd`.
- The `smbstatus` utility, which lists the current connections to the `smbd` server.
- The `nmblookup` utility, which allows NetBIOS name queries from the Linux machine.
- The `smbpasswd` utility, which changes the SMB-encrypted passwords on Samba servers.
- The `smbtar` shell script, which backs up SMB shares on tape drives.
- The `smbmount` utility, which mounts a SMB file system.
- The `smbumount` utility, which unmounts an SMB file system.

- The `/etc/lmhosts` file, which maps IP addresses to NetBIOS names. This file is similar to the `/etc/hosts` file.
- The `/etc/smbpasswd` file, which is the Samba encrypted password file.

Configuring Samba

To configure the Samba server on the Linux server, you can use any of the following methods:

- Edit the `/etc/smb.conf` file, directly using a text editor such as `vi`.
- Use the `netconf` utility, which automatically edits the `smb.conf` file.
- Use SWAT to configure Samba, through a browser from a local or remote machine. This also makes the changes in the smb.conf file.

Tip

It is important that you restart the smbd and nmbd daemons after you change the /etc/smb.conf file. This is necessary for the changes to take effect.

Caution

Make sure that you take a backup of the `smb.conf` file before you make any changes to it. This is applicable, regardless of the method that you choose to edit the file.

In the following sections, we'll explore each of these methods to configure Samba.

The /etc/smb.conf file

The `/etc/smb.conf` file is the configuration file for the Samba suite. It contains runtime configuration information for Samba programs. The `smb.conf` file consists of several sections, and each section has parameters to be configured for definite purposes. Each section in the `smb.conf` file (except the `[global]` section) describes a shared resource (known as a *share*). Besides the shares that you create, three special sections exist: `[global]`, `[homes]`, and `[printers]`. The other sections you create are known as *ordinary sections* or *user-defined sections*. They consist of

- The path of a directory that you want to share
- Access rights to be granted for the share

The different sections are

- `[global]`: The parameters in this section apply to the entire Samba server.
- `[homes]`: This section gives a remote user access to only his/her own HOME directory on the Linux machine.
- `[printers]`: This section shares the printers specified in the `/etc/printcap` file.
- User share section: Each share that you create on the Samba server has its own section.

Edit the `smb.conf` file to specify the details of the directory that you have to share. Here's a sample entry:

```
[temp]
     comment = Temporary storage space
     path = /tmp
     read only = No
     guest ok = Yes
```

The preceding entry indicates that you are creating a share for the /tmp directory. The share name is `temp`. A comment is also given, which appears on the client's browser, such as in the Network Neighborhood window. After you have made the necessary changes in the configuration file, you must test the file for its correctness. To test the internal correctness of the `smb.conf` file, you can use the `testparm` program. Here's a sample output of the `testparm` command:

```
# testparm
Load smb config files from /etc/smb.conf
Processing section "[homes]"
Processing section "[printers]"
Processing section "[temp]"
Loaded services file OK.
Press enter to see a dump of your service definitions
```

The output just shown indicates that the file does not have syntax errors. After this, pressing the Enter key displays a complete list of all the configuration settings of the Samba server. It also displays the `smb.conf` file. If the output of the `testparm` command displays any error, you have to correct the `smb.conf` file.

Note After testing the parameters, restart the Samba daemon services so the server can read the configuration file.

The Samba server consists of two daemons, `smbd` and `nmbd`. The `smbd` daemon provides file and print-sharing services and the `nmbd` daemon provides NetBIOS name server support.

To restart the Samba server, issue the following command from the shell prompt:

```
# /etc/rc.d/init.d/smb restart
Shutting down SMB services:
[  OK  ]
Shutting down NMB services:
[  OK  ]
Starting SMB services:
[  OK  ]
Starting NMB services:
[  OK  ]
```

The other options that you can use with this daemon are `start`, `stop`, and `status`.

The netconf utility

If you don't want to remember the syntax related to the `smb.conf` file, you can use the `netconf` utility to create Samba shares. As `netconf` is a section of the `linuxconf` tool, you can use `linuxconf` also.

You can activate Netconf by typing the `netconf` command at the shell prompt. All the options for configuring the Samba server are available here as edit boxes or check boxes — which simplifies setting up and maintaining the server.

The SWAT utility

Samba Web Administration Tool (SWAT) is a Web-based utility, which configures the `smb.conf` file through a Web browser. In addition, a SWAT configuration page has Help links to all the configurable options in the `smb.conf` file.

By default, access to SWAT is disabled. To enable access, follow the steps given following:

1. Check the `/etc/services` file. It must contain the following line:

   ```
   swat 901/tcp
   ```

   This defines the port on which SWAT should be accessed. This line should not be commented.

2. Edit the `/etc/inetd.conf` file to remove the comment before the following line:

   ```
   swat      stream  tcp     nowait.400      root /usr/sbin/swat swat
   ```

3. Restart the inetd daemon by giving the following command:

   ```
   # killall -HUP inetd
   ```

The preceding steps enable you to access SWAT from the browser. To access SWAT, type the address of the machine followed by the port number (that is, 901) from any Web browser, on either a local or a remote machine. You are then prompted to enter the username and password to access SWAT. You must enter the `root` username and access SWAT.

The SWAT home page contains links to configure the [global], [shares], and [printers] sections of the smb.conf file. The home page also has links to the documentation for various utilities, files, and services that maintain the Samba server. Each link brings you to a page from which you can configure its respective section.

Accessing Samba shares from Windows

After you have successfully configured the Samba server and restarted the necessary services, you are ready for accessing the share. From the Windows platform, open the Network Neighborhood window or Windows Explorer and select the Linux Samba server machine.

You can also access the Samba server from the Start ⇨ Run window by typing two backslashes (\\) followed by the NetBIOS name or the IP address of the server (Example: \\172.17.55.242).

Accessing Samba shares from Linux

Samba clients on Linux machines can access the shares made on Windows or other Linux machines by using the following two methods:

- **The smbclient command:** This command provides you with an FTP-like command line interface that enables you to transfer files from a share on an SMB server.

- **The smbmount command:** Instead of using the `smbclient` command, you can get better access by mounting a Samba share using the `smbmount` command.

Novell NetWare Server

As with other network operating systems, Novell NetWare Server also provides many network services. When you install the Server operating system, you are prompted for most networking products and services. Depending on the options selected, you are presented with screens prompting you for further details for completing the configuration of the networking products or services. In this section, you'll learn how to install and configure some networking products and services on NetWare Server 5.1.

Networking protocols

You can install and configure networking protocols in NetWare 5.1 in one of the following ways:

- IP with IPX compatibility mode
- IP only
- IPX only
- Both IP and IPX

IP with IPX compatibility mode

Installing IP enables your network to share data with other IP networks. When you select to install IP, you must supply the following details:

- **IP Address:** For your server to communicate with the Internet, it must have a unique IP address.
- **Subnet mask:** If your network is divided into several small networks, the subnet mask for the small network in which your server is located must be included.
- **Router (Gateway):** For communication between two different networks (for example, a LAN and the Internet), you must supply the address of the router that connects these different networks.

If you select IP, a passive support for IPX is automatically enabled. Thus, if the server receives IPX requests, the NetWare 5.1 Server processes them. This passive support for IPX, which is enabled automatically, is called compatibility mode.

IP only

When you want your server to support only IP and not IPX, disable the IP and IPX compatibility mode. To do so, remove the `LOAD SCMD` command from the `AutoExec.ncf` file.

IPX only

IPX is the traditional protocol from Novell. If you install only IPX, the requests based on other protocols including IP are ignored.

When you install IPX (only), the existing IPX frame types are detected automatically. Any one of the following conditions can be detected.

- **A single IPX frame type:** If a single IPX frame type is detected, it gets installed.
- **Multiple IPX frame types:** If multiple IPX frame types are detected, you are prompted to select the frame types that you want to install.
- **No IPX frame types:** If no frame type is detected, Ethernet_802.2 is installed by default.

Both IP and IPX

You can install both the protocols when your network client applications require both IPX and IP. In this case, both the protocols are actively supported.

Domain Name Service

Domain name service (DNS) is a network service running on a server that enables the server to maintain a list of simple and readable names that match IP addresses. The DNS service can be installed and configured on a NetWare server. Configuring DNS service requires you to specify the following details.

- **Host computer:** To install DNS on NetWare, specify the simple and readable name of the computer with the NetWare Server operating system installed.
- **Domain name:** Represents the hierarchical name, such as MyOffice.com, which represents the organization of your network.
- **Domain name server:** Represents the IP address of the DNS server that maintains the list containing the IP address and host name of the NetWare server being configured.

To configure your NetWare Server 5.1 to provide DNS services, log in to the NetWare server from a Windows workstation after you install the NetWare Server. Then run `SYS:PUBLIC\DNSDHCP\SETUP.EXE` and follow the onscreen prompts to supply the required details.

NetWare FTP services

FTP services enable the transfer of files between FTP clients. You can install FTP services either during the installation of NetWare 5.1 or after you've installed the Server. During installation of the NetWare Server, select Custom in the Installation Options screen. Then, in the Components screen, check the NetWare FTP Server option and follow the onscreen prompts to complete the installation.

You can also install FTP services after NetWare Server is installed. Follow these steps:

1. Access the server top by typing `STARTX` at server console.
2. Select Novell ➪ Install ➪ Add and specify the location of FTP files.

    FTP files are located in the `Products\FTP` directory on the NetWare 5.1 operating server directory.

3. Follow the on-screen prompts to complete the installation.

After the installation is complete, configure FTP services by defining the configuration parameters in the configuration file. The default configuration file is `SYS:/ETC/FTPSERV.CFG`. Some configuration parameters that you can set are.

- Maximum number of FTP sessions that can run concurrently.
- Maximum duration for which the session can remain open.

- The default name space for all users.
- Whether anonymous users can access FTP server.
- The home directory for the anonymous user.

Accessing NetWare services from Windows

Gateway Services for NetWare (GSNW) enables a Window NT/2000 Server to act as a gateway to NetWare resources. GSNW enables Windows NT/2000 Servers to access NetWare file and print resources directly.

To configure GSNW to act as a gateway to NetWare resources, follow these steps:

1. On NetWare Server, create a group called NTGATEWAY.

2. Using the Netadmin utility, create a user account on the NetWare server for the gateway, and add the gateway user account to the NTGATEWAY group.

3. On Windows NT/2000 Server, install GSNW. For Windows NT, you can do so from the Services tab of the Network icon in Control Panel.

    For Windows 2000, you can use the Local Area Connection Properties dialog box to install GSNW.

4. When the installation is complete, restart the computer so that the changes take effect. A GSNW icon gets added in the Control Panel.

5. Double-click the GSNW icon in the Control Panel. The Gateway Service for NetWare dialog box is displayed. Select the preferred server from Select Preferred Server and then click the Gateway button.

6. The Configure Gateway dialog box is displayed. Click Enable Gateway check box. In the Gateway account box, enter the name of the account you created on the NetWare server. Enter the password and retype the password for the account to confirm.

Tip The account used to log in to the NT/2000 Server while configuring GSNW must also be a part of the NetWare server's NTGATEWAY group.

7. Create a share for a resource on the NetWare server by clicking Add. The New Share dialog box is displayed.

8. Enter the Share Name, the Network Path to the share and assign a drive letter to the share. Other Windows NT machines can access the share even if they do not have NetWare client software loaded. Then click OK to complete the process.

The users on the network can now access the NetWare server's resources through the Windows NT/2000 server. You can assign permissions to the share like any other resource on Windows NT/2000.

MAC OS X Server

In addition to the traditional services, such as file services, print services, and security provided by other server software, MAC OS X Server software provides many more services. MAC OS X Server has a native support for the Apache Web server, which is the World's most popular Web server software.

File services provided by MAC OS X Server are more enhanced. Apple File Protocols are included in the native code of the server software resulting in higher speed. Apple File Protocols can run over either AppleTalk or TCP/IP.

QuickTime Streaming Server is another service included in MAC OS X Server. This is an effective service for streaming video over the Web. In this section, you'll learn how to install and configure Mac OS X services.

Installing and configuring Macintosh services

After you install Mac OS X Server and restart the computer, the Mac OS X Server Setup Assistant screen appears. Follow the onscreen prompts that this Setup Assistant presents to you. The general steps follow this sequence:

1. **Introduction:** A welcome screen is displayed. Click the right arrow to go the next step.

2. **Set Keyboard Type:** Select one of the keyboard types and click the right arrow to continue.

3. **Administrator Password:** Enter the Administrator password and click the right arrow to continue.

4. **Select Network Services:** Select the network services that you want to start with server reboot. The next screens that appear depend on the service(s) selected. For this case, select all the services (Apache Web server, QuickTime Streaming server, and Apple file services). Then click the right arrow to continue.

5. **Ethernet Port Planning:** All the Ethernet ports along with the communication option, the protocol(s) (AppleTalk or/and TCP/IP) are listed. Select the communication option for each port and click the right arrow to continue.

6. **Host name & Default Router:** The host name and router information is required for communication using TCP/IP. You can select either to configure automatically, in which case you must have a BootP server, or configure manually. Then click the right arrow to go to the next step.

7. **AppleTalk Computer Name:** Specify the AppleTalk name for your server and proceed to the next step.

8. **AppleTalk Seed Router:** Specify whether the server is the seed router for the network.

9. **AppleTalk Zones:** Specify AppleTalk zones and proceed to the next step. Although creating AppleTalk zones is optional, it can helps you organize a large network.
10. **AppleTalk Home Zone:** Select one of the AppleTalk zones as the home zone and proceed to the next step.
11. **Built-in Ethernet Port:** Specify the IP address and subnet mask for each port on your machine. Proceed to the next step.
12. **NetInfo:** Select whether there exist a NetInfo server on the network. NetInfo provides a central database for your network's resources and users. Then, move to the next screen.
13. **Domain Name Server:** Specify the details for the DNS on the network and proceed to the next screen.
14. **Remote Login:** Specify whether remote login is enabled and go to the next step.
15. **Geographic Location:** Select geographical location corresponding to your location and move to the next step.
16. **Network Time Synchronization:** Select whether the network time synchronization is enabled.
17. **Date & Time:** Specify your local date and time and move to the next step.
18. **Select Web Server Name:** Specify the Internet name for your Apache Web site and proceed to the next screen.
19. **Select QuickTime Movies Folder:** Specify the folder where your QuickTime movies should be stored and move to the next screen.
20. **Create User Accounts:** Create user names. For each user you create, specify the user name, login name, and password.
21. **Automatic Login:** Specify whether automatic login is enabled. Then, move to the next screen.

After you follow the preceding onscreen prompts, the Review Settings screen is displayed, which summarizes the configuration settings for the server. If you are satisfied with the settings, click the Go Ahead button. The final screen is a Conclusion screen. Click Restart for the settings to take effect.

Accessing Macintosh services from Windows

Windows users can access Mac services if the Mac server has File Sharing turned on and if both Mac and Windows have AppleTalk installed. The Mac server must also be running AppleShare server software. Windows clients can also access Mac resources by using third party utilities, such as PC MACLAN, AFP (Apple Share), and Idem.

Summary

This chapter briefed you on how to configure most commonly used network services on different network operating systems. You learned the standard configuration procedures on the following network operating systems.

- **Windows NT/2000 Server:** Configuring file and print services requires you to configure the network adapter and network services.

- **Linux Server:** The NFS services enable Linux/UNIX systems to share their file systems amongst themselves. To share resources with Windows-based machines, you can configure your Linux server for the Samba service.

- **Novell NetWare Server:** When you install network protocols, you can select either to install IP or IPX or IP and IPX both or IP and IPX with compatibility mode. You can also configure your NetWare server to act as DNS server or FTP server.

- **Mac OS X Server:** In addition to the traditional services, Mac OS X Server has built-in services such as Apache Web Server and QuickTime Streaming Server that you can configure to start with the server reboot.

✦ ✦ ✦

STUDY GUIDE

This guide provides a set of assessment questions to help you put your knowledge to test.

Assessment Questions

1. Which of the following specifications need to be provided when configuring TCP/IP manually? (Select all that apply.)

    A. IP address

    B. Subnet mask

    C. Default gateway

    D. DHCP server

2. Which of the following services enable you to configure TCP/IP automatically?

    A. DHCP

    B. FTP

    C. DNS

    D. NDS

3. Which of the following utilities check to see whether TCP/IP has been configured? (Select all that apply.)

    A. `IPCONFIG`

    B. `PING`

    C. `RSH`

    D. `FINGER`

4. Which of the following protocols is configured automatically during the Windows NT/2000 Server setup?

    A. TCP/IP

    B. IPX/SPX

    C. NetBEUI

    D. AppleTalk

5. Which of the following services enable Windows NT/2000 Server to access the NetWare file and print resources directly?

   A. Gateway Services for NetWare

   B. NetStart

   C. FTP services for NetWare

   D. RCP

6. Which of the following services are provided automatically when you install Services for Macintosh? (Select all that apply.)

   A. File services

   B. Print services

   C. FTP services

   D. Telnet services

7. Which of the following daemons manage RPC connections?

   A. nfsd

   B. mountd

   C. portmapper

   D. lockd

8. Which of the following utilities lists the current connections to the smbd server?

   A. smbstatus

   B. testparm

   C. smbtar

   D. nmblookup

9. Which of the following utilities configures the smb.conf file through a Web browser?

   A. File Editor

   B. Samba Admin

   C. NetConf

   D. SWAT

10. Suppose you've selected to install only IPX on NetWare Server and no frame types are detected. In this case, which of the frame type is installed by default?

   A. Ethernet_802.0

   B. Ethernet_802.1

   C. Ethernet_802.2

   D. Ethernet_802.3

Answers to Chapter Questions

Chapter Pre-Test

1. DNS resolves host names on a Linux/UNIX server.
2. The default port for the FTP protocol is 21.
3. To transfer files from a LINUX/UNIX Server to a Windows machine, you need FTP.
4. If print services do not get loaded on one of the network servers after rebooting, you should look at server log files to trace the source of problem.
5. A frame type is the way in which the NWLink protocol formats the data to be sent over the network.
6. The IPCONFIG utility verifies TCP/IP configuration parameters on a host.
7. The `nfsd` daemon translates NFS requests into actual requests on the local file system.
8. You must execute the `/usr/sbin/exportfs -a` command to update the list of exported file systems for your machine (Linux Server).

Assessment Questions

1. A, B, and C. When configuring TCP/IP manually, you should specify the IP address, subnet mask, and default gateway.
2. A. The DHCP service enables you to configure TCP/IP automatically.
3. A and B. The IPCONFIG and PING utilities check if TCP/IP has been configured.
4. C. The NetBEUI protocol is configured automatically during the Windows NT/2000 Server setup.
5. A. The Gateway services for NetWare (GSNW) service enables Windows NT/2000 Server to access the NetWare file and print resources directly.
6. A and B. File and print services are provided automatically when you install Services for Macintosh.
7. C. The `portmapper` daemon manages RPC connections.
8. A. The `smbstatus` utility lists the current connections to the smbd server.
9. D. The SWAT utility configures the `smb.conf` file through a Web browser.
10. C. If you've selected to install only IPX on NetWare Server and no frame types are detected, Ethernet_802.2 frame type is installed by default.

CHAPTER 23

Wiring

EXAM OBJECTIVES

- Given a wiring task, select the appropriate tool
- Given a network scenario interpret visual indicators (e.g., link lights, collision lights, and so on) to determine the nature of the problem

CHAPTER PRE-TEST

1. What type of cable is typically used for token ring?
2. What two cable types are common for Ethernet?
3. What organization has set the standards for most data cabling?
4. What is the minimum Category of UTP wire for 10BaseT?
5. What is one condition where coax is preferred over UTP wire?
6. What is the terminator jack for twisted-pair cable called?
7. When is a crossover cable necessary?
8. What information does a basic media tester provide?
9. What tool is usually necessary when working with patch panels?
10. What is a basic tool for fiber-optic cabling that helps in determining if breaks are in the glass cable?

✦ Answers to these questions can be found at the end of the chapter. ✦

Although wireless networks are gaining in popularity and function, it will still be many years before all wired networks disappear. The physical layer of our systems is ultimately responsible for the delivery of data so the wires and cables play major roles in the LAN. It is critically important for all network engineers and administrators to understand how to create cables properly and how to use the proper tools when cable issues are involved.

Types and Characteristics of Common Network Cables

As LANs and telecommunications began to proliferate, the industry originally responded to the cable needs by supplying separate standards to reflect implementation of industry applications, including the following:

- Quad or 100-ohm unshielded twisted pair (UTP) for telephone/voice
- Shielded twisted pair (STP) for token ring at 150 ohm
- RG58 coax for Ethernet
- RG62 coax for ARCNet and IBM 3270 systems

As the number of LAN installations grew, additional standards were needed to address compatibility and performance issues between suppliers of different equipment. The existing standards weren't adequate. This made installation and maintenance of multiple and incompatible wiring systems difficult for installers and engineers. These serious limitations regarding system operation, adaptability, and maintenance brought about a need for common cabling system requirements. IBM's technical interface specification GA27-3773-1 (standard spec) was the first hierarchy of data communication cabling. To address industry-wide standards, the Electronic Industries Alliance/Telecommunications Industry Association (EIA/TIA) pioneered the EIA/TIA-568A standard for category cabling.

Twisted-pair cable

EIA/TIA standards are designed to be generic and flexible, so that they both

- Support future equipment and service changes.
- Enable successful use of multiple vendor equipment.

The EIA/TIA wiring systems are based on the star topology that may also support several different variations of direct connections, such as

- Ring
- Bus
- Loop

The category rating system was developed by TIA as a response to the industry's request for higher data rate specifications on applications over *unshielded twisted pair* (UTP) and *shielded twisted pair* (STP).

Twisted-pair cables are so called because the primary cable is comprised of smaller wire "pairs" that are twisted together to reduce outside interference. The pairs of wires in UTP cables are colored so that you can identify the same wire at each end. Furthermore, they are usually color coded by pair so that the pairs can also be identified from end to end. Typical Category 5 UTP cables contain 4 pairs made up of a solid color and the same solid color striped onto a white background. Figure 23-1 presents a simple visualization of what a twisted-pair wire looks like.

Figure 23-1: Twisted-pair cable ready for a terminator. In this graphic, the wires have been untwisted at the ends so that they will fit in the channels of the termination plug.

The EIA/TIA category rating system applies only to 100-ohm UTP and STP wiring systems. EIA/TIA-568A also enables

- 150-ohm STP (also called type 1)
- 62.5/125um multi-mode optical fiber

The recommended *minimum* requirement for residential and light commercial installations is 4 pair 100-ohm UTP Category 3 cabling. This standard provides adequate flexibility. For most installations, however, Category 3 and 4 simply don't offer the quality and extensibility of the Category 5 specification. Pair counts have also been consolidated with 4 pair for "desktop" and 25 pair for "backbone" cabling leading the way. Table 23-1 outlines the different categories of cabling as defined in the TIA standards:

Table 23-1
Cable Category Standards

Cable Definition	Use and specification
Category 1	Meets the minimum requirements for analog voice or Plain Old Telephone Service (POTS). 100-ohm UTP cable is preferred for most uses and required for all multi-line applications.
Category 2	Defined as the IBM Type 3 cabling system. IBM Type 3 components were designed as a higher-grade 100-ohm UTP system capable of operating 1 Mbps Token Ring, 5250 and 3270 applications over shortened distances.
Category 3	16 MHz 100-ohm UTP supporting applications up to 10 Mbps. Applications may range from voice to 10BaseT data.
Category 4	20 MHz 100-ohm UTP supporting applications up to 16 Mbps. Applications may range from voice to 16 Mbps token ring.
Category 5	100 MHz, 100-ohm UTP supports applications up to 100 Mbps. Applications may range from voice to TP-PMD (Twisted Pair-Physical Medium Dependent), a standard currently under development by the ANSI X3T9.5 working group that will enable Fiber Distributed Data Interface (FDDI) data to run over UTP cabling at 100 Mbps.)

Network cabling is classified into two main types, backbone and work area.

The backbone cabling system provides interconnections between telecommunications closets, equipment rooms, and entrance facilities. This system includes the backbone cables, intermediate and main cross-connects, terminations, and patch cords used to cross-connect to other backbone systems. The backbone also extends between buildings in a campus environment.

The work area cabling extends from the data wall outlet to the work area components. Work area wiring is designed to be relatively simple to interconnect. This makes moves, adds, and changes easily managed. Work area components are generally classified as the following:

- **Station Equipment:** Computers, data terminals, telephones, and so on
- **Patch Cables:** Modular cords, PC adapter cables, fiber jumpers, and so on
- **Other Adapters:** Other adapters external to the data telecommunications outlet

Table 23-2 outlines the maximum length limitations for patch cables used between the backbone and work area devices. These requirements apply only to wire and cable used for patch cords and cross-connect jumpers:

Table 23-2
Patch Cable Maximum Lengths

Used for	Maximum Length Limits
Main cross-connect	20 meters (66 feet)
Intermediate cross-connect	20 meters (66 feet)
Telecommunications closet	6 meters (20 feet)
Wall to device, or device to device	3 meters (10 feet)

A few guidelines secure reliable network performance:

- Terminate horizontal cables with connecting hardware of the same category or higher.
- Use cables as patch cords and cross-connect jumpers of the same performance category or higher as the horizontal cables they connect.
- UTP cabling systems aren't Category 3, 4, or 5 compliant unless all components of the system satisfy their respective category requirements.

Coax cable

Coaxial cable, often referred to as "coax," was invented in 1929 and first used commercially in 1941. This cable is called "coaxial" because it includes one physical wire (usually copper) that carries the signal surrounded by another concentric physical wire, both running along the same axis. The outer channel serves as a ground and both wires are covered with a layer of insulation, as shown in Figure 23-2. Many coax cables can be placed in a single outer sheathing and, with repeaters, carry information for a great distance.

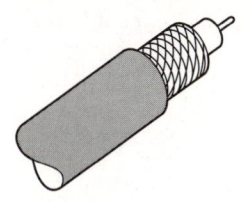

Figure 23-2: An example of a coax cable segment ready for a terminator. The outside insulation is peeled back first, followed by the inner mesh cable to expose the core wire. BNC ends can be either crimped or twisted over the exposed wires.

Cable TV companies use coaxial cable as the signal transport between the community antenna and the end user homes and businesses. Telephone companies sometimes use coaxial cable from their central office to the telephone poles near users, and for many years, coax was widely installed for Ethernet and other types of local area networks.

Because coax is much more resilient to outside interference than twisted-pair cable is, coax is still very useful in areas with high levels of electrical signals or where long distances need to be connected. Coax, however, can't transport Ethernet data any faster than 10 Mbps, which is often less desirable in modern networks.

Coax is normally used on bus topologies (refer to Chapter 1 for more information) and uses BNC connectors. Several physical media are specified in the IEEE 802.3 standard for Ethernet local area networks dealing with coax cable including the following:

- **10Base2:** Thin coaxial cable with a maximum segment length of 185 meters or 606 feet
- **10Base5:** Thick coaxial cable with a maximum segment length of 500 meters or 1,640 feet
- **10Base36:** Broadband coaxial cable carrying multiple baseband channels for a maximum length of 3,600 meters or 11,811 feet

The "10" in the media type designation refers to the transmission speed of 10 Mbps. The "Base" refers to baseband signaling, which means that only Ethernet signals are carried on the medium. The "2," "5," and "36" refer to the coaxial cable segment length (the 185-meter length has been rounded up to "2" for 200).

Using a Wire Crimper

Every network engineer needs a tool kit, and one of the first tools should be a wire crimper. The wire crimper connects the ends on the cables. Faulty cabling causes a high percentage of lost connection problems on a LAN, and many of these problems are related to poorly connected ends. Although inexpensive crimpers (less than

$25.00) are available, an engineer should purchase a higher quality tool to minimize the number of poorly connected ends. Crimpers come in many different styles. A typical crimping tool is shown in Figure 23-3.

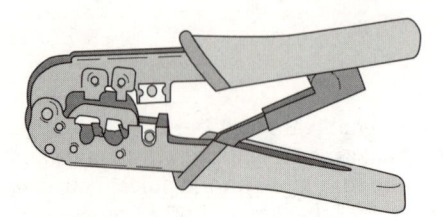

Figure 23-3: Example of an RJ-45 wire crimper used with twisted-pair cables

Some crimpers are designed for a single type of cable and/or cable end, such as RJ-45 for UTP LAN cable, or RJ-11 for telephone cable. Other crimpers are adjustable, or use removable dies to adapt to the different end sizes. Additionally, coax ends require a totally different crimper than twisted-pair cables.

Terminating twisted-pair cables

The cable connectors and jacks that are most used with UTP cables are RJ-45. The RJ simply means *Registered Jack;* 45 specifies the pin numbering scheme. The connector is attached to the cable and the jack is the device that the connector plugs into, whether it is in the wall, the network interface card in the computer, or the hub. The first step in preparing the wire is to strip one inch of the insulation off the end of the twisted-pair cable. Care must be taken to ensure that the inner wire pairs aren't cut. Professionals and other people who terminate large numbers of twisted-pair cables normally purchase a special wire-stripping tool that precisely cuts through the insulation portion. For occasional connecting, a sharp knife and reasonable care should do the job nicely.

The IEEE specification for twisted-pair Ethernet cabling requires that two twisted pairs be used and that one pair be connected to pins 1 and 2, and that the second pair be connected to pins 3 and 6. Pins 4 and 5 are skipped and are connected to one of the remaining twisted pairs. When terminating CAT5 UTP cable, it is important that the natural twist of each pair be carried through as close as possible to the point of termination. EIA/TIA standard 568B requires no more than ½ inch be left untwisted for Category 5. More than ½ inch of untwisted cable affects performance at high bit rates.

The wire color-coding becomes important here. According to the EIA/TIA-568B RJ-45 wiring scheme, the individual wires are arranged, from left to right, in this manner:

1. White/Orange
2. Orange

3. White/Green

4. Blue

5. White/Blue

6. Green

7. White/Brown

8. Brown

Now the wires forming the pairs are gathered together and trimmed so that they can be inserted into the RJ-45 plug. Figure 23-4 illustrates this process.

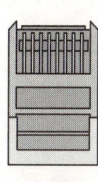

Figure 23-4: Trimmed and paired UTP wire ready for insertion into the RJ-45 plug

To complete the job, follow these steps:

1. Hold the modular plug with the tab down.
2. Make sure the wires are still arranged in the sequence described in the preceding list.
3. Carefully slide the cable into the RJ-45 plug.

   The wires should each slide into a separate channel in the end of the plug. You must work all wires to the very end of the connector or a proper connection may not be made. Figure 23-5 shows how the wires should appear when properly inserted into the RJ-45 plug.

4. After the wires are firmly seated in the plug, and you visually verify that the ends of the wires are snug against the top of the plug, slide the plug into the larger hole of the crimping tool and crimp the connector onto the end of the cable.

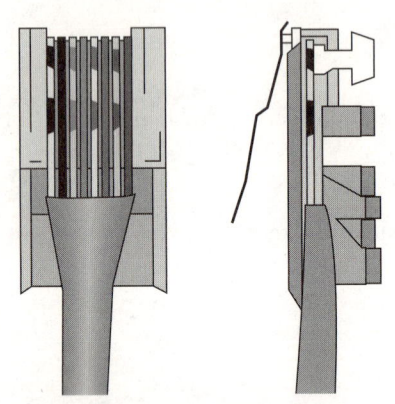

Figure 23-5: This is how the wire pairs should look when properly inserted into the RJ-45 plug.

Crossover cables

When connecting two Ethernet devices, for example to hubs, or two computers without a hub in the middle, a special twisted-pair cable, known as a *crossover cable,* is needed. The cable is called a crossover because the transmit and receive pairs are "crossed over" on one end. The procedures for making a crossover cable are exactly the same as for a normal cable, except that on one end the wire pairs are ordered like this:

1. White/Green
2. Green
3. White/Orange
4. Blue
5. White/Blue
6. Orange
7. White/Brown
8. Brown

Figure 23-6 shows this pattern.

Figure 23-6: This is how the wire pairs should look when making a crossover cable.

Using a Media Tester/Certifier

A vast majority of network problems can be traced down to faulty cabling. If we take that to heart, it only makes sense that we want to be absolutely certain our wiring is in good shape before moving on. It is possible to connect two devices, make a connection, and assume the cable is fine. In reality, the cable might be fine for basic communications but will break down under a heavier load. Oftentimes, cables are run throughout a building during the construction phase and could cost thousands of dollars to replace after the walls and ceilings are in place. Regardless of the reason, it is always in your best interest to use a quality media tester to make sure the wire structure is sound. Installers and maintainers of in-house wiring must use up-to-date cable testers to provide performance testing, cable certification, and continuous support for an installed wire plant. Certification testing

- Confirms that each station cable used on the network is meeting the high signal metrics that govern the wiring side of the LAN.
- Provides a historical benchmark of how cabling is performing at the time of install for later reference.

Certification is a requirement for many warranty programs and should be a requirement for wiring installations of any size.

A basic media tester, like the device shown in Figure 23-7, verifies that

- All the wire pairs are in the proper order
- Contacts on both ends are good

For patch cables and short runs, this is a minimum requirement test.

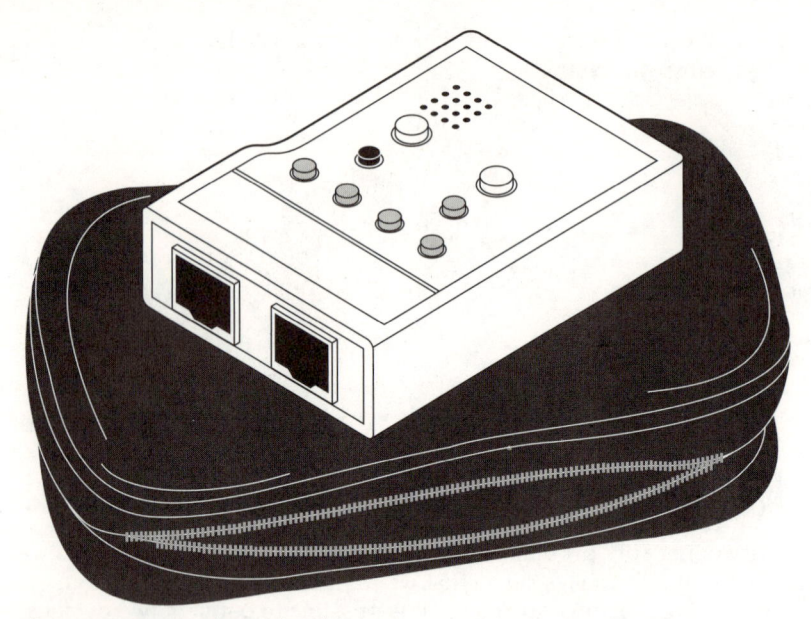

Figure 23-7: A basic patch cable tester

Although each device operates somewhat differently, the basic function is to transmit data packets on one end of the cable and test that the same data is received at the other end. If the data received at the other end does not match the data sent, the tester gives an audio or LED warning. Some of the higher-priced testers identify which wire, or wire pair, is causing the problem.

Because both ends of the cable must be inserted into this type of tester, it isn't a practical device for longer, more complicated wiring jobs. When distances prohibit the use of this simple tester, a two-piece device is necessary. Figure 23-8 shows an example of such a device.

To use a remote device like this, connect one end of the cable to the main unit and insert the other cable end into the remote. Like the basic tester, this unit then sends data packets across the cable and tests for drops or errors. Many of these devices support multiple cable types, such as UTP, STP, coax, and possibly fiber.

Although both of these devices test the continuity of the wire pairs, only higher-end devices can measure overall transmission speeds and provide acceptable industry standard certification. The number and types of tests they perform categorize these cable testers/certifiers. Level I testers measure performance of Category 3 cables only and are considered obsolete for today's environments. These testers shouldn't be used for testing modern wiring.

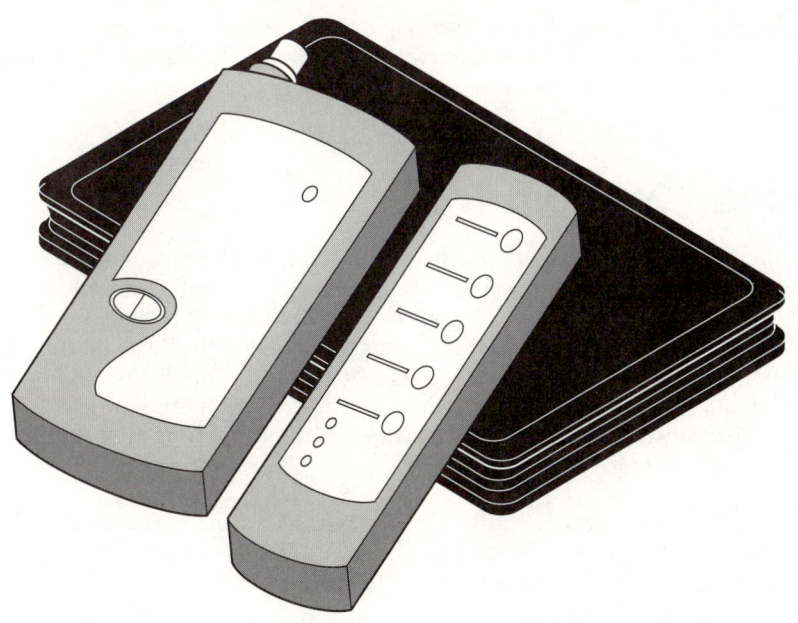

Figure 23-8: A cable tester with a separate remote for longer distances

The first Level II testers performed a limited set of critical tests, including wire map (showing end-to-end physical arrangement of pairs and indicating shorts and opens on the wire), length, attenuation (signal strength loss), and NEXT (Near End Crosstalk). NEXT is a critical measure of how the individual pairs affect each other under the common insulation. Original Cat 5 wiring and testing was designed to support Ethernet and Fast Ethernet, along with 155 Mbps ATM. If properly installed, a large percentage of this early Cat 5 cabling also supports Gigabit Ethernet. However, any legacy Category 5 wiring being considered for such use must be recertified with one of the latest cable testers that measure performance at gigabit speeds.

Enhanced Category 5 wiring has become the most installed cable for new installations. Designed specifically with Gigabit Ethernet in mind, Cat 5E cable is tested with the same 100 MHz sweep as Cat 5, but with tighter specifications on the existing tests and with other metrics added, including delay, ELFEXT (Equal-Level Far End Crosstalk) and return loss. Delay skew testing compares the differences in propagation delay among individual pairs in a cable. ELFEXT is a calculated value based on the difference between a wiring run's far-end crosstalk and its attenuation. This new testing method is referred to as Level IIE and many of these testers sweep beyond the required 100 MHz bandwidth to the 155 MHz range so as to verify an even better margin of performance. Level IIE cable testers should be employed in any new wiring project.

> **In the Real World** — Most distributors are very open to providing a tester for evaluation. Do not pass up this opportunity, because the purchase of a cable tester and accessories can add up to several thousands of dollars.

Using a Punch Down Tool

Size and end-user needs usually dictate how a network is cabled, but almost all networks are improved by following a structured cabling approach. Generally stated, the structured approach starts by using surface jacks or wall faceplates in areas where network devices are needed. These jacks are wired with the cable running back to a main wire closet (sometimes called a homerun) normally located on the same floor. If multiple closets are used, then they in turn are interconnected to the backbone of the network. Within each wiring closet the homeruns are terminated at one or more patch panels.

The patch panel has connectors on the back for the cable runs to the stations. Each of those connectors is wired to an RJ-45 on the front. The RJ-45 connections provide a spot to plug in patch cables to interconnect to hubs, switches, and/or routers.

On many patch panels, the back has Type 110-style connectors color-coded to match the color of the cable pairs. (Type 110 connectors were made popular by AT&T and have generally captured the Category 5 market.) The color-coding goes from pair one to four. For ETI/TIA standards, the 568A-style panels automatically maps the pairs to the correct pins on the RJ45 to make a 568A connection, and likewise the 568B-style panel maps to the pins on the RJ45 to make a 568B connection. When using a 568A or 568B patch panel, it is essential that that style matches the style of every wall plate installed.

The ports on the patch panel are labeled so you know which room the cable runs go to. Most cabling is wired straight through from end to end. That means that pair 1 at the station is connected to pair 1 at the hub, pair 2 is connected to pair 2, and so forth. Sometimes, you may find it necessary to cross-wire some of the pairs between the hubs and workstations, for example to connect a cable modem or directly connect two hubs. With a patch panel, all this cross wiring is done in the patch cable. If you have to make any changes, like moving a station or hub, you just move the patch cable with it, instead of having to reterminate the cable run.

In order to connect the cable wires to the wall jacks, faceplates, and the back of the patch cable, a special tool, known as a punch down, is required. Figure 23-9 shows a punch down tool.

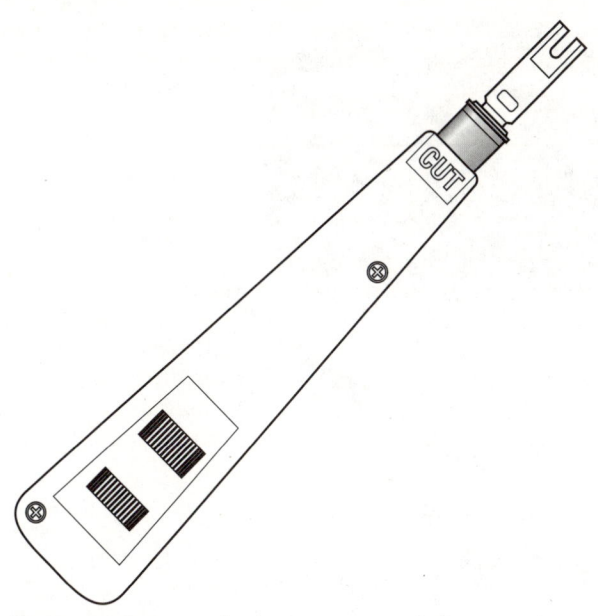

Figure 23-9: A standard type 110 punch down tool

To terminate the cable at the faceplate or punch panel, follow these steps:

1. Remove approximately one inch of the outer insulation from the cable.
2. Untwist the wire pairs.
3. Match the color of the pair to the color of the connector post.
4. Using the tool, "punch" down the wire pair around the post. When you have used sufficient force to secure the connection, the punch down tool makes a slight clicking motion.

Using a Tone Generator

You use the tone generator and inductive probe together to identify one specific wire pair from the others. Figure 23-10 shows a sample of this device. You attach the tone generator (toner) to one end of a vacant pair that must be traced to find the location of a fault, or to identify the opposite end so it can be terminated. The probe is then used to "pick up" the tone, tracing the tone signal either along the wire or at the other end. For this test, the assumption is that a media tester has already been used to verify continuity, polarity, and lack of shorts.

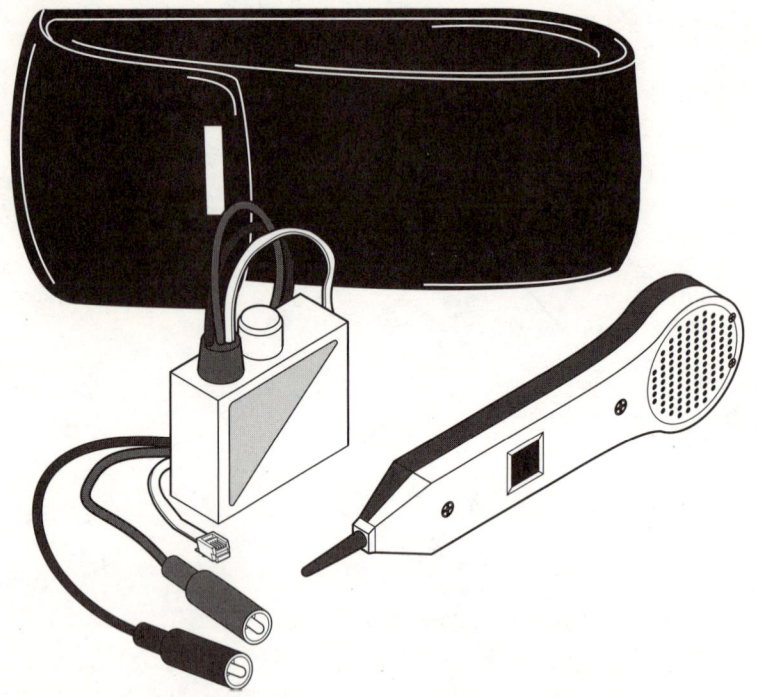

Figure 23-10: A tone generator and probe (sometimes called a "Fox-and-Hound") are indispensable items when doing large cabling jobs.

When pulling many cables from many locations back to the central wire closet, it is next to impossible to identify which end run belongs to any specific wall jack. Therefore, the Tone Generator and probe is an indispensable tool. The following steps, often referred to as "toning out a system," outline how to use these tools:

1. Connect the toner to the leads at the wall jack.
2. Take the probe to the distribution device or telecommunications closet. When you hold the probe near the wire attached to the toner, the tone will be quite strong. (Some lesser volume may be picked up on adjacent leads or pairs, but this is normal.)

   You can verify the proper wire connected to the toner by touching the tip of the probe across the leads. At this point, assuming the continuity tests showed no faults, you would normally punch the leads down.
3. In commercial applications, an earth ground point is available in the telecommunications closet. Test for shorts to ground by attaching one lead of a continuity tester to that ground and running the other lead down the clips of the punch down block. In this manner, the test for shorts to ground can be made after the leads are terminated.

Using Optical Testers

Optical network equipment accepts pulses of light from fiber cabling, converts the pulses to electrical signals for processing, and changes the signals back to light for transmission. Optical devices operate in point-to-point or ring topologies. Point-to-point means that light pulses either get from box A to box B or they don't. No backup exists in the event of a cable cut. Ring technologies offer a bit more redundancy: In the event of a cable cut, a ring can wrap around itself.

When installing and testing fiber cable, you need to make a number of considerations. Handle fiber-optic connectors and cables with care.

+ You shouldn't bend cables too tightly, especially near the connectors, because sharp bends can break the fibers.
+ Dropping the connectors can damage the optical face.
+ Pulling too hard on the connectors themselves may break the fiber in the backshell of the connector.

   If you have any question about the condition of the connectors, you should clean and test them.

Arguably, the most common problem encountered in fiber installations is incorrect optic connections. A fiber-optic link consists of two fibers transmitting in opposite directions to provide full-duplex communications. It isn't uncommon for the transmit and receive fibers to be switched resulting in a transmitter-to-transmitter and receiver-to-receiver connection. A visual tracer makes it easy to verify the proper connections quickly. A visual tracer produces an intense light beam that shines down the cable to visually trace the fiber to the far end.

You can use just about any light source, such as a small flashlight, to examine point-to-point connections, but the device must be capable of shining the light beam down the fiber cable steadily. A special visual tracer tool, as shown in Figure 23-11, enables the engineer to trace fibers up to 2½ miles. You can also use the tracer to check continuity and to find broken fibers in cables. Another recommended use is to check continuity of every fiber in multifiber cables before installation to ensure that all fibers are okay. Installing a cable with bad fibers can be an expensive proposition.

A more powerful tool, the *visual fault locator* (VFL), uses a high-power visible laser coupled to a fiber connector. The VFL uses red lasers with enough power to actually show breaks in the cable through the jacket of the fiber. You can also use it to optimize splices and splice type connectors for verification of proper termination.

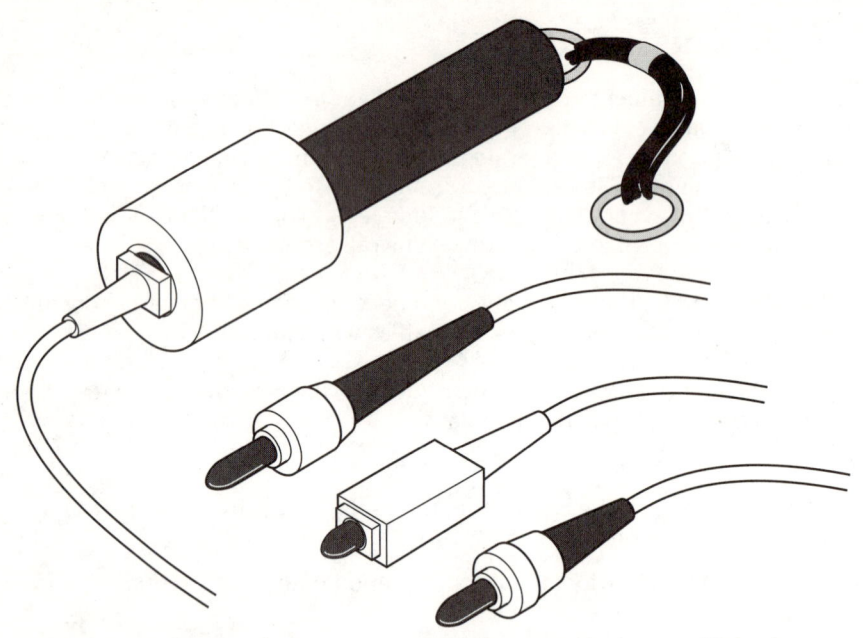

Figure 23-11: The Visual tracer is a small device to send a beam of light down a fiber-optic cable to visually inspect proper connections.

Fiber-optic networks are always specified to operate over a range of loss, typically called the *system margin*. Either too much loss or too little loss can be a problem. Both of these conditions cause high bit error rates in digital systems or poor signal performance in analog systems.

- If the loss is too high, the signal will be low at the receiver, causing a poor signal-to-noise condition.
- If the loss is too low, the power level at the receiver will be too high, causing receiver saturation.

You should perform testing on the complete cable plant, including all individual jumper or trunk cables, and take the appropriate action:

- If the end-to-end (transmitter to receiver) loss measurement for a given fiber is within the network margin specification, record the data for future reference.
- If the loss is too low, note that that fiber probably needs an inline attenuator to reduce receiver power to acceptable levels.
- If the loss is too high, retest each link of the complete cable run to find the bad link.

Possible causes of high end-to-end link loss are

- ✦ Bad connectors
- ✦ Bad splice bushings in patch panels
- ✦ Cables bent too tightly around corners
- ✦ Broken fibers in cables.

You can test the network quickly and easily with a *fiber-optic power meter.* The network transmitter is set to transmit a bit stream of known duty cycle. The power meter is set for calibration on the proper wavelength and the reading units set on watts. To test the received power, the most critical element in the network, merely disconnect the fiber-optic cable connector at the receiver, attach the power meter, and measure the power. If the receiver power is low, disconnecting the source jumper cable at the first available connector and measuring the power with the fiber cable at that point should measure the transmitter power. Alternatively, you can disconnect the cable at the transmitter and replace it with a known good test jumper to measure the coupled power. If you measure the output through a short network jumper cable (less than 30 feet), you don't need to compensate for jumper loss. For longer jumpers, some compensation may be necessary.

If receiver power is low, but transmitter power is high, something is wrong with the cables. You must test them at every connection to isolate the bad cable(s) and/or connectors. You can do this test from either end:

1. Starting from the transmitter or receiver end, follow the network cables to every patch panel.
2. Disconnect the connector and measure the power at each point.

    By making measurements in dB, it is easy to calculate the power loss through the cable at each point by subtracting successive readings.

3. When you find a suspect cable (by noting a larger than expected loss in the cable link) test the suspect cable by the appropriate method described previously.

    - If a cable has attenuation that is higher than specifications, but still transmits light, examine the connectors under a microscope to determine if they have been damaged.
    - If the connectors look good, the best solution may be to replace the cable or switch to a spare.
    - If a visual fault locator is available, you can use it to visually locate breaks in the fiber and find broken connectors.

Given a Wiring Task, Select the Appropriate Tool

Few networks contain a single type of cable throughout. Many networks have grown over the years in segments and had portions migrated from coax to twisted pair. Others have replaced slower coax backbones with fiber optics. Networks with a mix of CAT 3 and CAT 5 cables aren't unusual, either. Most often, fiber cables are contracted out to professional cablers, not installed by casual network engineers or administrators. However, most network administrators often perform such tasks as short runs, temporary runs, and patch cable replacements. Like any profession, to properly perform the required duties, network personnel need to have the proper tools and know how to use them. When reviewing any cable project, you must examine

- Current situation
- Needed results
- Future needs
- Compatibility with existing hardware

Review the following scenarios to test your ability to identify the appropriate tool required.

1. Steven works in the advertising department using a Windows NT workstation attached. The network protocol is TCP/IP running on an all CAT5 100 Mbps Ethernet topology. One morning Steven calls the help desk to report that he cannot log on to the network, although he successfully connected the previous day. Before beginning the troubleshooting process, a check of the problem history log shows that Steven has experienced this problem intermittently before, but no specific problem has been deduced.

   A visual inspection of Steven's computer shows that a link light is on the workstation's NIC. The troubleshooting process begins by following a systematic approach of the most likely problems. The first step is to replace the patch cable from the workstation to the wall jack with a known good patch cable and try logging in again. The login still fails, so the original cable is replaced. The next step is to check the connections in the wiring closet. A laptop computer connected to the same port that Steven's workstation uses successfully connects and logs on to the network. A close examination of the patch panel reveals that two of the twisted-pair wires on the port connecting Steven's wall jack to the hub are loose.

   Given this information, what cable tool is needed to fix the problem?

2. Given the same scenario, assume the wires on the patch panel are good and the known good patch cable solves the login problem. The solution is to make a new patch cable that connects the PC to the wall jack.

   Given this information, what cable tool is needed to fix the problem?

Important Definitions

Cabling is a special niche in the networking field that often becomes a carrier all its own. Although a Network Engineer may not perform many cabling tasks, understanding the nuances of the cable systems is extremely valuable. To properly understand basic cable technologies, it is important to understand some of the common terms used by professional cablers, as presented in the following list.

- **Attenuation:** Attenuation is a measure of the decrease in signal strength along the length of a transmission line. Ensuring low signal attenuation is critical because digital signal processing technology cannot compensate for too much signal attenuation.

- **Attenuation to Crosstalk Ratio (ACR):** A critical consideration in determining the capability of an unshielded twisted-pair (UTP) or screened twisted-pair (ScTP) cabling system is the difference between attenuation and Near End Crosstalk (NEXT). This difference is known as the attenuation to crosstalk ratio (ACR). Positive ACR means that transmitted signal strength is stronger than that of Near End Crosstalk. ACR helps to define a signal bandwidth (200 MHz for Category 6) where signal-to-noise ratios are sufficient to support certain applications. It is interesting to note that digital signal processing (DSP) technology can perform crosstalk cancellation, enabling some applications to expand useable bandwidth up to and beyond the point at which ACR equals zero. Even so, the maximum frequency for which positive ACR is ensured provides a benchmark to assess the useable bandwidth of twisted-pair (balanced) cabling systems.

- **Near End Crosstalk (NEXT) and Equal Level Far End Crosstalk (ELFEXT):** Pair-to-pair Near End Crosstalk (NEXT) requirements quantify undesired signal coupling from adjacent pairs that is received at the same end of the cabling as the transmit end of the disturbing pairs. Standards groups now realize that the sophisticated nature of full-duplex transmission also requires that the crosstalk at the far-end of the cabling be specified. Pair-to-pair Far End Crosstalk (FEXT) quantifies undesired signal coupling at the receive end of the disturbing pairs. ELFEXT is calculated by subtracting attenuation from the far-end crosstalk loss. Poor ELFEXT levels can result in increased bit error rates and/or undeliverable signal packets.

- **Return Loss:** Return loss is a measure of the signal reflections occurring along a transmission line and is related to impedance mismatches that are present throughout a cabling channel. Because emerging applications such as Gigabit Ethernet rely on a full-duplex transmission-encoding scheme (transmit and receive signals are superimposed over the same conductor pair), they are sensitive to errors that may result from marginal return loss performance.

- **Propagation delay & delay skew:** Propagation delay is equivalent to the amount of time that passes between when a signal is transmitted and when it is received at the other end of a cabling channel. The effect is akin to the delay in time between when lightning strikes and thunder is heard—except that electrical signals travel much faster than sound. Delay skew is the difference between the pair with the least delay and the pair with the most delay. Transmission errors that are associated with excessive delay and delay skew include increased jitter and bit error rates.

- **Balance:** Twisted-pair transmission relies on signal symmetry or "balance" between the two conductors in a pair. Maintaining proper balance ensures that cabling systems and components don't emit unwanted electromagnetic radiation and aren't susceptible to electrical noise. Although these parameters aren't industry requirements, the recommendation is that the balance performance of cabling components be ensured through measurements of longitudinal conversion loss (LCL) and longitudinal conversion transfer loss (LCTL).

- **Transfer Impedance**: Shield effectiveness directly affects the capability of shielded twisted-pair cable and connecting hardware to maximize immunity from outside noise sources and minimize radiated emissions. Transfer impedance is a measure of shield effectiveness; lower transfer impedance values correlate to better shield effectiveness.

- **Bandwidth (fiber):** Bandwidth describes the frequency carrying capabilities of a transmission system and is a function of fiber type, distance, and transmitter characteristics. Bandwidth margin maximizes a system's capability to support advanced applications.

Summary

Faulty cables cause a proportionally large number of network problems. Although dedicated cable installers usually perform large cable jobs, all network administrators and engineers should have a firm understanding of basic cable issues and the tools necessary to terminate and/or replace problem cables.

Before you can master the use of cable tools, you must understand how cables work, what types to use under various conditions, and how to terminate them. Besides hardware tools, a collection of "known good" cables are indispensable.

Ethernet networks represent the bulk of modern LANs. The IEEE 802.3 standard for Ethernet local area networks dealing with coax cable specifies several physical media, including 10Base2 (thin coaxial cable), 10Base5 (thick coaxial cable), 10Base36 (broadband coaxial cable), 10BaseT (unshielded twisted pair in a star topology running a maximum of 10 Mbps), 100BaseT (unshielded twisted pair in a star topology running a maximum of 100 Mbps), and Fast or Gigabit Ethernet (unshielded twisted pair or fiber optics in a ring or star topology running a maximum of 1,000 Mbps).

The IEEE Specification for twisted-pair Ethernet cabling requires that two twisted pairs be used and that one pair be connected to pins 1 and 2, and that the second pair be connected to pins 3 and 6. Pins 4 and 5 are skipped and are connected to one of the remaining twisted pairs. When terminating CAT5 UTP cable, it is important that the natural twist of each pair be carried through as close as possible to the point of termination. EIA/TIA standard 568B requires no more than ½ inch be left untwisted for Category 5.

For the exam, remember these key points from this chapter:

- Unshielded twisted pair (UTP) is the most common cable type used today.
- UTP cable is classified by "categories." CAT 5 is the minimum standard for most networks and required for data transfer rates faster than 10 Mbps.
- Use wire crimpers to securely attach termination ends on coax and twisted-pair cables. Coax cables can use twist-on ends that don't require crimpers.
- Twisted-pair wires must be matched in the proper order on both ends in order to transfer data across the wire properly. Twists must be maintained within ½ inch of the end of the cable.
- Use punch down tools to connect twisted-pair wire ends to wall jacks and patch panels.
- Use patch panels commonly in central wiring closets to help organize the maze of computer wires on the network. The face of the patch panel has RJ-45 jacks so patch cables can be matched between the exact wall jack and the hub/switch.
- Cable Certification, as done with special testing equipment, is a requirement for many warranty programs and should be a requirement for wiring installations of any size.
- Use the tone generator and inductive probe together to identify one specific wire pair from the others. Attach the tone generator (toner) to one end of a vacant pair so the inductive probe can identify the opposite end.
- Handle fiber-optic connectors and cables with care. Do not bend cables too tightly, especially near the connectors, because sharp bends can break the fibers.
- The most common problem encountered in fiber installations is incorrect optic connections: transmit is connected to transmit and receive to receive.
- Although you can use about any light source to examine point-to-point fiber connections, only a special visual tracer tool enables the cable engineer to trace fibers up to 2½ miles.

STUDY GUIDE

Assessment Questions

1. Shielded twisted-pair cable is most often used for token ring.

    A. True

    B. False

2. What is/are the primary benefit(s) of the EIA/TIA standards?

    A. Provides category class for coax cable

    B. Provides generic and flexible standards to support future equipment and enable successful use of multiple vendor equipment

    C. Provides Category class for twisted-pair cable

    D. Defines common procedures for installing and testing cable

3. What topology is the EIA/TIA wiring systems based on?

    A. Bus only

    B. Bus or star only

    C. Star but may support several different variations of direct connections, such as ring, bus, and loop

    D. Loop or star only

4. How many wire pairs are contained in typical CAT 5 cable?

    A. 1

    B. 2

    C. 3

    D. 4

5. Which cable category transmits data at 16 MHz on 100-ohm UTP and supports applications up to 10 Mbps?

    A. Category 1

    B. Category 2

    C. Category 3

    D. Category 5

6. Which statement best defines the term "backbone"?

　　A. The main cable segment between the desktop and a wall jack

　　B. The interconnection between telecommunication closets, equipment rooms, and entrance facilities

　　C. The interconnection between patch panels and network hubs or switches

　　D. Coax cable that interconnects two or more local area networks

7. What is the recommended maximum length for patch cables used between a wall jack and a network device, or device-to-device?

　　A. 20 meters (66 feet)

　　B. 3 meters (10 feet)

　　C. 6 meters (20 feet)

　　D. Does not matter

8. Under which condition might coax cable be a good choice?

　　A. When sharp corners are unavoidable

　　B. When cables must be run though concrete walls

　　C. In areas where existing telephone cables cannot carry data signals

　　D. In areas with high levels of electrical signals or where long distances need to be connected

9. What is the maximum distance and speed of 10Base2?

　　A. 10 meters, 2 Mbps

　　B. 185 feet, 10 Mbps

　　C. 200 feet, 100 Mbps

　　D. 2 meters, 10 Mbps

10. What is the name given to the plastic terminating "plugs" used on twisted-pair cables?

　　A. RJ-45

　　B. RJ-11

　　C. UTP-45

　　D. TP-11

11. How many wire pairs are used to transmit data on a CAT-5 cable?

　　A. 4 pairs

　　B. 2 pairs

　　C. 2 pairs for 10 Mbps, 4 pairs for 100+ Mbps

　　D. 6 pairs

12. What is different about a crossover cable compared to a straight-through cable?

    A. The transmit and receive wires are switched on one end.

    B. The transmit and receive wires are switched on both ends.

    C. The transmit and signaling wires are switched on one end.

    D. The transmit and signaling wires are switched on both ends.

13. What is a minimum requirement test for patch cables and short runs?

    A. Using "known-good" cables

    B. Using twist-on ends because they are generally more secure

    C. Checking connectivity directly between two devices first

    D. Using a cable tester to verify that all wire pairs are in the proper order and that the contacts on both ends are good

14. Which statement best describes a Level I cable tester?

    A. It provides basic testing of Category 3, 4, and 5 UTP.

    B. It is outdated for UTP but still valuable for STP and coax.

    C. It measures performance of Category 3 cables only and is considered obsolete for today's environments.

    D. It measures performance of Category 5 cables only, so it shouldn't be used unless Category 3 is the only cable type you deal with.

15. ELFEXT (Equal-Level Far End Crosstalk) is a calculated value based on the difference between which of the following?

    A. The cable's length and bit rate

    B. A wiring run's far-end crosstalk and its attenuation

    C. A wiring run's far-end crosstalk and its overall length

    D. A wiring run's far-end crosstalk and its bit rate

16. What is normally used in a wiring closet to terminate the homeruns from the wall jacks?

    A. Surface mounts

    B. RJ-45 Terminators

    C. Patch panels

    D. The central switch or hub

17. What tool is needed to connect twisted-pair wires to surface mount jacks and faceplates?

    A. Crimper

    B. Punch down

    C. Pliers

    D. Cable tester

18. A tone generator is useful for what?

    A. Detecting network errors

    B. Making intelligent routing decisions within the LAN

    C. Identifying one specific wire pair from the others across long distances

    D. Verifying continuity, polarity, and lack of shorts

19. When working with fiber-optic cables, what two actions can cause serious problems?

    A. Bending the cable too tightly, especially near the connectors

    B. Shining strong ultraviolet lights down the center

    C. Twisting the cable between the thumb and forefinger

    D. Dropping the connectors

20. What are possible causes of high end-to-end link loss when using fiber-optic cables?

    A. Bad connectors

    B. Bad splice bushings in patch panels

    C. Cables bent too tightly around corners

    D. Broken fibers in cables

Scenarios

1. Your company has determined that the ROI (return on investment) to move to Gigabit Ethernet is within an acceptable range. As the network administrator, you have been asked to provide a list of items that need upgrading or replacing in order to accomplish this move. All the hardware has been checked but the big question is whether the existing cable needs to be replaced or not. The whole building was rerun with CAT 5 cable 36 months prior. What recommendation would you make regarding the need to upgrade, or not, the current wire system?

Labs

Lab 23-1 Making a Patch Cable

The objective for this hands-on lab is to see how a patch cable is created. Most of the time you are better off purchasing ready-made patch cables, but times occur when building your own is either necessary or expedient. Even if you're fortunate enough to always have pre-built patch cables available, knowing how to correctly add RJ-45 plugs onto Cat 5 cable is an invaluable skill.

In order to complete this lab, you need the following items:

- ✦ 3 to 10 feet of Category 5 cable
- ✦ (2) RJ-45 ends (you may want to have a few extras handy)
- ✦ RJ-45 Crimper (If you don't have one of these yet, they are generally available at most electronic stores or by mail order on the Internet.)
- ✦ Small wire cutters or sturdy scissors
- ✦ A cable tester or a live network using UTP cabling (A basic hub and a computer accomplish the same results.)

Follow these steps to add the RJ-45 ends to your cable:

1. Using standard wire strippers or a sharp knife, carefully strip one inch of outer insulation off the end of the Cat 5 cable.

2. Untwist and straighten the pairs and arrange them in the following sequence, from top to bottom: (Figure 23-6 shows this pattern.)

    - White/Orange
    - Orange
    - White/Green
    - Blue
    - White/Blue
    - Green
    - White/Brown
    - Brown

3. Using a small wire cutter, cut the wires straight across ½ inch from the jacket.

4. Hold the RJ-45 end with the tab down. Make sure the wires are still arranged in the sequence described in Step 2, and carefully slide the cable into the modular plug. The wires should each slide into a separate channel in the end of the plug. Work all wires to the very end of the connector.

5. Slide the plug into the proper hole of your crimping tool and crimp the connector onto the end of the cable.

6. Repeat this procedure on the opposite end of the cable.

Visually check that your cable ends appear to be seated properly and the RJ-45 plug is securely attached. Using a cable tester, check the cable for continuity. If you don't have a cable tester available, try connecting a computer or other network device up to the LAN (or simply to a test hub) and check the device for connectivity. If the device can communicate on the LAN, the cable is good.

If the cable fails, cut the RJ-45 plug off one end and start the process over for that one end. If the cable still fails, try replacing the RJ-45 plug on the other end of the cable.

After you have a good cable, you may want to mark it with a permanent marker and use it in the future as your "known good" patch cable!

Lab 23-2 Making a Crossover Cable

The objective for this hands-on lab is to create a known-good crossover cable. The process is nearly identical to LAB 23-1, except for the order in which the cable pairs are used on one end of the wire.

1. Attach an RJ45 plug on one end of the patch cable by following Steps 1 through 5 in LAB 23-1.

2. Prepare the other end of the cable by untwisting and straightening the wire pairs. From top to bottom, arrange the wires on this end according to the following sequence. (Figure 23-6 shows this pattern.)

    - White/Green
    - Green
    - White/Orange
    - Blue
    - White/Blue
    - Orange
    - White/Brown
    - Brown

3. Complete Steps 3 through 5 from LAB 23-1.

Many cable testers identify properly constructed crossover cables, but if yours does not, or if you don't have a cable tester, you can also use this cable to directly connect two computers, NIC to NIC. If you can successfully ping the NIC on either computer, your crossover cable is good. You may want to mark this cable and add it to your tool kit as a "known good" crossover cable.

Answers to Chapter Questions

Chapter Pre-Test

1. Although many IBM standards have been used for token ring networks, shielded twisted-pair is currently the cable of choice.
2. All modern implementations of Ethernet use either RG58 coax or unshielded twisted pair.
3. The Electronic Industries Alliance/Telecommunications Industry Association (EIA/TIA) sets the standards for most data cabling.
4. A 10BaseT network requires at minimum cable standard of CAT 3. CAT 5 is required for 100BaseT.
5. Coax is very useful in areas with high levels of electrical signals or where long distances need to be connected.
6. RJ45 is the terminator jack for twisted-pair cable.
7. A crossover cable is necessary when connecting two Ethernet devices, for example to hubs, or two computers without a hub in the middle.
8. A basic media tester verifies that all wire pairs are in the proper order and that the contacts on both ends are good.
9. The loose wires of the twisted-pair cable are connected to color-coded blocks in the rear of the patch panels with corresponding RJ45 jacks in the front. In order to connect the rear wires, a punch down tool is necessary.
10. Shining a light down the end of a fiber-optic cable assists in determining if breaks are in the glass. A good tool designed to provide this light is the visual tracer.

Assessment Questions

1. A. True. Modern token ring networks use shielded twisted-pair cables.
2. B. EIA/TIA standards are generic and flexible to support future equipment and enable successful use of multiple vendor equipment.
3. C. The EIA/TIA wiring systems are based on the star topology that may also support several different variations of direct connections, such as ring, bus, and loop.
4. D. Typical CAT5 UTP cables contain 4 pairs.
5. C. Category 3.
6. B. The backbone cabling system provides interconnections between telecommunications closets, equipment rooms, and entrance facilities.
7. B. 3 meters (10 feet).

8. D. Coax is much more resilient to outside interference, making it very useful in areas with high levels of electrical signals or where long distances need to be connected.

9. B. 185 feet, 10 Mbps: The "10" in the media type designation refers to the transmission speed of 10 Mbps. The "Base" refers to baseband signaling, which means that only Ethernet signals are carried on the medium. The "2" refers to the coaxial cable segment length. (The 185-meter length has been rounded up to "2" for 200.)

10. A. RJ-45. The RJ simply means Registered Jack, and 45 specifies the pin numbering scheme.

11. B. 2 pairs: The IEEE Specification requires that two twisted pairs be used and that one pair be connected to pins 1 and 2 and that the second pair be connected to pins 3 and 6.

12. A. The cable is called a crossover because the transmit and receive pairs are "crossed over" on one end.

13. D. Use a cable tester to verify that all wire pairs are in the proper order and that the contacts on both ends are good.

14. C. Level I testers measured performance of Category 3 cables only and are considered obsolete for today's environments.

15. B. ELFEXT is a calculated value based on the difference between a wiring run's far-end crosstalk and its attenuation

16. C. A patch panel.

17. B. A punch down.

18. C. Identify one specific wire pair from the others across long distances.

19. A and D. Cables shouldn't be bent too tightly, especially near the connectors, and dropping the connectors can damage the optical face

20. A, B, C, and D. All of these items are possible causes of high end-to-end link loss when using fiber-optic cables

Scenarios

1. Enhanced Category 5 wiring has become the most installed cable for new installations. Designed specifically with Gigabit Ethernet in mind, Cat 5E cable is tested with the same 100-MHz sweep as Cat 5, but with tighter specifications on the existing tests and with other metrics added, including delay, ELFEXT (Equal-Level Far End Crosstalk) and return loss. However, original Cat 5 wiring supported Ethernet and Fast Ethernet, along with 155 Mbps ATM. If properly installed, a large percentage of this early Cat 5 cabling also supports Gigabit Ethernet. Therefore, the existing cable system should be adequate, but should be recertified with one of the latest cable testers that measure performance at gigabit speeds.

Network Troubleshooting

CHAPTER 24

EXAM OBJECTIVES

✦ Given a network problem scenario, select an appropriate course of action based on a general troubleshooting strategy. This strategy includes the following steps

- Establish the symptoms
- Identify the affected area
- Establish what has changed
- Select the most probable cause
- Implement a solution
- Test the result
- Recognize the potential effects of the solution
- Document the solution

✦ Given a troubleshooting scenario involving a network with a particular physical topology (for example, Bus, Star/Hierarchical, Mesh, Ring, or Wireless) and including a network diagram, identify the network area affected and the cause of the problem.

✦ Given a network-troubleshooting scenario involving a client-connectivity problem (for example, incorrect protocol/client software/authentication configuration, or insufficient rights/permission), identify the cause of the problem.

✦ Given a network-troubleshooting scenario involving a wiring-and-infrastructure problem, identify the cause of the problem (for example, bad media, interference, network hardware).

CHAPTER PRE-TEST

1. What command can be used to test network connectivity from one computer to another?
2. What is the benefit of using a structured, step-by-step approach to network troubleshooting?
3. Why would network encryption prevent a client from authenticating itself to the network?
4. What should always be installed on either end of a coaxial Bus network?
5. How can the duplex setting of a network card affect network connectivity?
6. When you finish fixing a network problem, what should be the last step in the troubleshooting process?
7. If the Ring is broken on a Token Ring network, what happens?
8. How can EMI affect network connectivity?
9. What should be the first thing to examine when troubleshooting a network problem?
10. What type of problems can affect physical cabling?

✦ Answers to these questions can be found at the end of the chapter. ✦

Network troubleshooting can often be a frustrating and tedious experience — in fact, nerve-wracking if your entire network is down and users can't perform their work. Network problems can originate from a number of places, including client hardware, software, network settings, cabling, protocols, security settings, and network-device failure. This chapter introduces a structured approach for dealing with network issues. This approach enables you to tackle the problem, starting from the initial stage of diagnosing symptoms, and then narrowing down the cause, implementing a solution, and documenting the entire process. This chapter also details some aspects of network troubleshooting in greater detail — such as cabling, network topology issues, and client connectivity.

Network Troubleshooting

When presented with a problem related to networking communications, use a structured approach. This enables you to systematically narrow down the source of your problem in the most efficient manner. With most networking problem scenarios, you can follow this strategy to aid you in finding the root cause:

1. **Establish the symptoms.**

   Initially, you examine the symptoms affecting your network. You should not overreact at the sight of the first symptom, but do some quick tests to discover the real impact of the problem. Jumping to the conclusion that a certain symptom *must be* the culprit can send your inquiry down a mistaken path, wasting valuable troubleshooting time.

   When examining a network problem that has its initial symptoms on a client machine, you should check other clients to see whether they are also experiencing the same problem. Doing so quickly moves you away from the client, and onto the server or networking equipment as the source of the problem.

2. **Identify the affected area.**

   To properly troubleshoot your network problem, you must narrow down the area of the network being affected. This could be only one client, a section or subnet of your network, or even the entire network itself.

   By starting from an affected client and moving upwards from there towards the central networking equipment, you can more easily discover the scope of your problem. A client computer may not be able to connect because its network card is malfunctioning. A server may be the central source of the problem if it fails to automatically address any clients that enter the network. On a large scale, you may have a central router that has been misconfigured or is malfunctioning.

   You may find that the problem has nothing to do with your network at all, and could be further upstream at your Internet service provider, or the Internet itself.

3. **Establish what has changed.**

    Some common problems involve a recent change to networking software or hardware, or the reconfiguration of a network device. When investigating a network problem, you should examine in the days and weeks before whether any aspect of the network has been changed.

    This could be something as simple and innocent as swapping out a hub or switch with a different brand of equipment, or making a small change to the duplex setting of a network card. If you are diligent in documenting your system, you can build a library of records that describe the kinds of changes made to the network. (This measure doesn't prevent users from making undocumented changes on their own, but it's a step in the right direction.)

    Network settings must also be checked carefully. For example, an incorrect IP address or subnet mask setting on a new network device can cause problems across the entire network.

    Knowing what has changed recently can give you clues as to the source of your current problem.

4. **Select the most probable cause.**

    By utilizing diagnostic utilities, and narrowing down the problem to software or hardware, or the location of the device causing the disruption, you should be able to select the most probable cause.

    To test your theory, try to recreate the problem on another (preferably isolated) workstation or device. By recreating the problem, you can verify that what you believe to be the root cause of the problem is correct.

5. **Implement a solution.**

    After narrowing down your problem to the original cause, you must now implement a solution to fix it. This may involve fixing or swapping out hardware, such as a bad network cable, network card, or a hub or switch, and fixing the configuration of software.

    Caution: Make it a rule to be aware of exactly which parts of the network your solution affects — and test the system thoroughly (as explained in Step 6) before you implement your solution. Doing so helps to ensure that the problem is fixed and that the solution has not inadvertently caused another part of the system to malfunction.

6. **Test the result.**

    After implementing a solution to your problem, you should run a number of tests to ensure that the problem is fixed and that none of your previous symptoms still exist. It is also a good chance to test that your solution has not caused problems for other aspects of the network.

    Test connectivity from a client machine to as many other devices as possible, including other computers, network hubs, switches, and routers, external Internet sites, and other networks within your company's LAN or WAN.

7. **Recognize the potential effects of the solution.**

   By changing something on your network or client computers to fix a problem, you may inadvertently cause another part of the network to fail. Before implementing a solution, you should examine your network to see whether this solution will cause another aspect of your network problems. If possible, test your solution in a lab environment. Even if lab facilities are not available, you should be aware of how your solution will affect your network — both now and in the future.

8. **Document the solution.**

   This is one of the most important — yet overlooked — stages of the troubleshooting process. By documenting your problems and their solutions, you create a special database of knowledge that you can use in the future to help you troubleshoot similar problems. Documentation can greatly reduce the time it takes to find a solution; often you don't have to repeat the entire troubleshooting process you went through before.

   You should try to categorize each problem and separate your database of issues, so they can be searched more easily when time is an issue. Write down the specifics of each case, including the exact symptoms and error messages encountered. Describe each step of the troubleshooting process, showing what you tested and what steps were taken to narrow down the cause of the problem.

   Finally, document the *final* solution of your problem. Record any special hardware or software settings that were changed, so you can compare them in the future and make sure you deploy exactly the solution you have worked out.

In the Real World

In a real network failure, time constraints may make the full sequence of eight steps more difficult to complete. Steps 1 through 4, however, should not be skipped; they represent the area in which you can save the most time by properly narrowing down the cause of the problem.

Troubleshooting by Network Topology

The type of networking topology you use for your network can create unique communications issues particular to that design. For example, some problems can be encountered on a Ring network but not a Bus or wireless network. Being aware of the strengths and weaknesses of your particular topology can help you when you are troubleshooting network communication problems.

Ring

For a network using a Ring topology, the integrity of the ring must be maintained at all times for the network to work properly. The most common version of a Ring network is the *Token Ring*, in which data packets can enter the network only if the sending station has the use of a specialized packet called a *token*. The token moves constantly around the ring from device to device, giving each device a turn to communicate with the network. Thus, only one device can communicate on the network at any one time, preventing collisions among network packets(a problem prevalent on Ethernet-based networks). Networking issues on a Ring network will originate from two main areas, the physical cabling, and the devices on the network. Any issue that causes a break in the Ring can bring down the entire network. This is because the token must stop at the break in the network — so it can't traverse the Ring.

Star

A Star network topology is the most commonly used topology in today's networks. Smaller networks can take advantage of the relative ease of setup and the lower costs associated with a Star topology, because all that is needed is a number of network workstations, servers, and devices connected to a main central hub.

Larger networks usually use a fiber-based backbone, connecting multiple distribution closets that contain large hubs and switches connected to the network workstations and devices.

In a Star topology, the main points of failure include the physical cabling, and the hubs, switches, and other network devices that connect everything together. Unlike a Ring network, a disconnected workstation will not cause the entire network to fail, because each workstation has its own separate connection to the main hub.

Mesh

In a Mesh network topology, each device is connected to every other device on the network. Because of these multiple links and built-in redundancy, a cable break or device disconnection will not interrupt the network. Most problems on a Mesh network tend to be more serious, with entire sections of the Mesh network being disabled.

Bus

A Bus network topology is most commonly used in coaxial Ethernet networks. The most common types of networking problems on Bus networks are a result of improper physical cabling installation and lack of proper termination.

To work properly, each end of a Bus network must be terminated with a connector containing a graded resistor. If the cable is not terminated, the network signal may bounce back onto the wiring causing many network packet collisions and disruption.

If you remove a computer from a Bus network, you must ensure that the cable is properly terminated, or, if it is in the middle of the Bus, a special barrel connector should be used to connect the two free coaxial cables together.

Wireless

A wireless network provides a different setting for troubleshooting network problems. With the absence of any physical cabling, we must look to the software and protocols that make up a wireless network to aid in troubleshooting connectivity problems.

Protocols

Two main protocols are used in wireless products: 802.11 and Bluetooth. Unfortunately, these two competing standards do not communicate with each other. For example, if you have an existing 802.11 protocol network, and you wish to add a network device utilizing the Bluetooth protocol, it can't connect to the network.

Interference

Most wireless networks operate within the 2.4Ghz frequency. Unfortunately, this waveband of communications is shared by other common household devices, such as cordless phones and microwave ovens. If you use a 2.4Ghz phone, it may interfere with your wireless communications if you are using them at the same time. To help alleviate this trouble, you may want to use a cordless phone system that uses lower frequencies, such as 900Mhz.

Encryption and Authentication

To ensure maximum security when using wireless communications, encryption and authentications methods should be utilized. If your network is unprotected, an unauthorized user can connect to your network simply by using a regular wireless network card. By encrypting communications or forcing authentication, you greatly reduce the change of unauthorized access to your network.

When troubleshooting connectivity problems on a wireless network, ensure that you are using the proper encryption key to access the network. If you are using authentication, a valid username and password must be used.

Exam Tip For the exam, be prepared for troubleshooting scenarios based on particular network topologies. Know how each topology works, and you should be able to easily spot the problem.

Troubleshooting Client Connectivity

Connecting a client to a network can fail for a multiple number of reasons, from local hardware and software settings, to larger scale network device problems. When troubleshooting client connectivity, you must narrow down the problem step by step, going from the simplest problems to the more complex. This will enable you to make your troubleshooting more efficient and lower the time it takes to arrive at a solution to the problem.

Troubleshooting basics

When troubleshooting a client connectivity problem, you should begin with the simplest first, before moving on to the more complex issues. On a client computer, this means checking the most obvious things, such as making sure the network cable is properly plugged in. More often than not, the most likely cause of the problem is among the simplest items that usually get overlooked. Other items to examine include checking to make sure the network cable is plugged into a wall jack or hub, the basic network settings on the client, and the settings of the network card itself.

To examine the problem in the most efficient manner, you should look at all aspects of the client system before moving on up the chain to other issues such as networking and server problems. Why waste a lot of your time and resources checking all the servers and network equipment for problems, if the cause of the issue is simply an incorrect network-software setting on the client? This can also be quickly judged by checking to see whether other workstations are having similar problems. If not, it is most likely that the problem is with the one client machine only. If you encounter similar problems on your other network workstations and devices, then you know that you have a more serious global network problem.

Diagnostic utilities

To aid in troubleshooting client network connectivity issues, you can utilize several network utilities. For example, on TCP/IP networks, you can use the `ping` command to see whether you can contact another machine on the network. If you can see other machines on the network, then you can try the same command from another machine to see whether it can contact the client computer experiencing the problem. With this simple command, you can quickly find out what machines on the network you can or cannot see. If you cannot contact anything on the network at all, you will know the problem must be with your own client computer.

Hardware problems

Some common hardware problems that can be examined on the client computer are the physical cabling, the network card of the client, and the network device that it connects to.

For network cabling, the most obvious item to examine first is to check whether it is plugged in properly to the network card of the client computer and the wall jack or hub that connects it to the network. Examine the cable for any kinks or damage to the cable itself or connectors. It is always a good practice to replace the network cable with another known working one to eliminate that as the source of the problem.

Next, check the network card of your client machine. Do any lights appear when the network cable is connected? Most network cards have lights that indicate network activity, and duplex and speed settings. If you get no link light, then you have no network connection at all. This situation is most likely caused by a disconnected or damaged cable between the client computer and the central hub. The network card could also be incorrectly configured or faulty. Examine its hardware settings such as IRQ, DMA channel, to ensure that they do not conflict with any other devices on your system. If you have a spare network card, try replacing it to see whether that affects connectivity at all. If the replacement works, then you may have a faulty network card.

If you cannot find any problems with the client hardware, such as cabling and the network card, you should check the hub or switch port that the machine is connected to. Try switching the network cable to another open port on the device. If the network link becomes active, then you may have a faulty port on the network device. You may also need to check the port settings, such as duplex setting and speed. If the port setting is different from that of the client network card, then the client can't connect properly.

Software

If all the hardware you have examined seems to be in working order, then you should next check the software settings of the client computer. A number of different settings can cause a failure in connectivity if set to a wrong value.

Protocols

Your network card should be configured with the protocols used on your network. If your network uses only NetWare IPX/SPX, and you have your network card configured to use TCP/IP, you can't access the network, because no device or machine on the network can understand the protocol you are using to transfer your network information.

On networks that use multiple protocols, you must ensure that those protocols are bound to your network adapters, so your network can understand all communications taking place on it.

Network settings

Depending on the protocol you are using, you must examine your network settings to make sure that your network address and any other settings are configured properly for your network.

For example, if you are using a TCP/IP network, you must ensure that your network IP address and subnet mask are correct for that particular network, and it does not conflict with any other device. Two devices cannot use the same network address, or else only one or neither of the devices can communicate properly on the network.

Some network services such as Dynamic Host Configuration Protocol (DHCP), enable the client to be assigned an IP address automatically as they connect to the network. If these network settings are not configured properly, of if the DHCP server is not working, the client can't obtain an address to communicate with the network.

Speed and duplex setting

Most modern networks run at 10Mbps to 100Mbps on the client side, while the network backbone that connects them all may run at even higher speeds (such as 1000Mbps). Depending on the type of network card or hubs and switches, they may only support one speed. Some network cards and devices can run at multiple speeds, and can autodetect the speed of the network and adjust its settings accordingly. Ensure that your network and network devices are configured to use the same speed.

Similarly, the duplex settings of your network devices should also be examined. Network communications can either run in full or half duplex. Full duplex communications means that network messages can be simultaneously sent and received, while half duplex means that you can only transmit or receive at any one time. If your network is running full duplex, but your network card is only set for half duplex, you may find that your communications may be extremely slow and inconsistent. You should always ensure that the duplex settings for all devices are set the same.

Security and authentication

Sometimes security and authentication mechanisms can inadvertently interfere with network communications. Many highly secure networks use special encrypted communications, in which you can only access network resources if your client computer is installed with the proper encryption key.

Some networks are designed to allow only certain software network addresses — even certain hard-coded MAC addresses on network cards — to communicate with the network. This security measure is intended to ensure that only authorized users can access the network.

Exam Tip For the exam, be aware of the variety of ways that will cause client connectivity problems. Be sure to narrow down the root cause of problem when faced with a troubleshooting scenario.

Wiring and Infrastructure Troubleshooting

Cabling

Problems that affect the physical cabling of a network include improper installation, termination, electromagnetic interference (EMI), attenuation and cabling length, and simple disconnection.

Installation problems

Some problems can originate from the initial cable installation. This can include anything from bad cables to improper wiring and terminations. Having a professional cable installer run your network cable is a good idea, as they will test each cable with a cable tester to ensure that it works properly. If you are making your own network cables, test each one before using them. It is more common for an amateur cable maker to cross wires or improperly terminate the ends with a connector.

EMI

Electromagnetic interference is caused by an electrical device that creates an electromagentic field in a radio frequency spectrum. This may cause signal disruption to other electrical systems, including computers, networking equipment, and cabling. Some types of cabling are more susceptible to electromagnetic interference than others. If you are using shielded twisted pair wiring, your network will be less susceptible to interference because of the shielding on the cabling. If your network is located within an industrial environment, you should examine how close certain high EMI equipment is to the network cabling, especially if it is unshielded.

Cabling length and attenuation

Certain types of cabling have maximum and minimum length standards that must be adhered to. If the cable you are using is too long, the signal's attenuation may cause a disruption. Attenuation is the opposite of amplification; the farther a signal goes along a wire, the weaker it gets. This maximum cabling length can be increased with the use of special repeaters, which will boost the signal at regular intervals along the cabling. Table 24-1 summarizes the maximum lengths of different types of cabling.

Table 24-1
Cabling Minimum and Maximum Lengths

Type of Cabling	Minimum Length	Maximum Length
10BASET Twisted Pair (UTP,STP)	2.5 meters	100 meters
10BASE2 Thinnet Coaxial	0.5 meters	185 meters
10BASE5 Thicknet Coaxial	2.5 meters	500 meters

Cabling

The most typical problems with the physical cabling on a network involve the terminations of the ends of the cable; if the connectors on the ends of your cables are not clamped down properly, they contact the wires and can cause a short circuit. This is common for network administrators who make their own cables, but it can also happen even with professional installers. To fix this, you may have to reclamp the connector again, or cut off the end and terminate with a new connector. You should test the cable with a special cable tester to ensure that all the connections are in place.

Exam Tip For the exam, be aware of the length limitations of certain types of cabling that can lead to network problems.

Hubs / switches / routers

The network devices that connect workstations and servers together on the network can be hubs, switches or routers. Each device contains a number of ports you can use to connect a large number of workstations and servers together on a network. A hub is a simple unintelligent central breakout point for devices. Devices such as switches and routers perform the same function, but contain a level of intelligence to help separate and route traffic between different networks. These devices are often a major cause of failure on a network, because if a hub loses power or is faulty, it will disrupt communications for all devices connected to that hub.

Sometimes only a single port will become faulty, causing the device on that port to lose connectivity. In some cases, the faulty port will create a broadcast storm of network packets, which floods the network with data causing a network-wide slowdown or complete disruption.

When troubleshooting network problems, be sure to examine the network equipment themselves, to ensure that a hardware related problem is not the cause of the communications issues.

If you encounter problems with a broadcast storm due to a faulty device or network port, you should turn off each of your hubs in turn, which will help you narrow down which device on which hub is causing the disruption.

Troubleshooting Resources

Several different types of troubleshooting resources can help troubleshoot specific problems with hardware and software. These resources usually contain the most up-to-date information on specific known issues that the hardware or software has with certain operating systems or devices. Each resource will provide different levels of support. Such resources are as follows:

- Previous Documentation
- Hardware or Software Manual
- Software or Hardware ReadMe File
- Hardware or Software Installation Media
- Manufacturers Web Site
- Telephone Technical Support
- E-mail Support
- Warranty Support

Previous Documentation

As previously discussed in this chapter, it is important to document the solution to any hardware-, software-, or network-related problem. This information is a troubleshooting resource when future problems arise on your network. If you encounter a problem on your network that you have already dealt with, your documentation gives you a head start toward a solution. You can save a lot of troubleshooting time by going back to the documentation and performing the same procedures to fix it.

Customarily, troubleshooting documentation is collected by the network administrator, whether that person is yourself or by the previous network technician. If you inherit old documentation from a previous technician, go through it — compare it with the current network setup and correct it to reflect any new changes.

Hardware or software manual

Most hardware and software will come with a manual. Most manuals have a troubleshooting section at the end of the book for common problems. Some manuals will list special codes and error message in the appendices, which can be compared to the error message or code that the software or a device will display if an error occurs.

Manuals will only contain a list of common problems and their resolution current at the time the manuals were printed. Any new issues discovered since the printing of the manuals, will not be included, although they may sometimes be included separately as errata pages or a ReadMe file on the hardware or software's CD-ROM.

Software or hardware ReadMe file

A ReadMe file usually will contain information that did not make it into the manual. ReadMe files are plain text files that can be found on the installation media of the hardware or software. A ReadMe file will usually contain the latest installation information, default setting, tips, and default settings pertaining to the hardware or software. If you are having trouble with the installation of a specific device or piece of software, always check with the ReadMe file of the specific device or software before you try any of the other troubleshooting resources.

Hardware or software installation media

Most software applications and hardware drivers will come on a CD-ROM. The CD-ROM that comes with your software or hardware may contain important documentation regarding troubleshooting issues. As previously mentioned, the ReadMe file will be located on the installation media but besides the ReadMe file, the CD-ROM may contain special hardware or software diagnostic tools specific to the product.

Just like a manual, the CD-ROM will only contain troubleshooting resources at the time the CD-ROM was created. For the most current information, you should check the vendor's product Web site.

Manufacturer's Web site

The manufacture'rs Web site is the best place to look for current technical support for your product. A manufacturer's Web site will contain up-to-date troubleshooting information and issue resolutions that have been discovered since the initial release of the product. The manufacturer's product software patches and updated drivers are also available for download.

Many manufacturers' Web sites will provide a searchable knowledge base. A searchable knowledge base is a database of any issue that has happened in the past and its resolution. Most searchable knowledge base's can be searched by keyword, by product, or by date.

Telephone technical support

Most people prefer telephone technical support. It is always nice to talk to a real person about software or hardware related problems in hope that they can tell you how to correct a problem right over the phone. Most manufacturers will supply a technical support phone number located in the manual that came with the hardware or software. Most, but not all, technical support phone numbers are toll free support numbers. Most telephone technical support representatives can help you with basic first level technical support.

If the telephone technical support representative is unable to provide a solution to your problem during your conversation, the issue is usually escalated to a second level support technician. At this time, you may be given a technical support case number that the manufacturer's telephone technical support team can use to look up on the progress of the solution for your problem when you call back for an update on the situation.

The down side of using telephone technical support is their popularity and the telephone technical support lines are often busy and you must remain in a calling queue until it is your turn to talk to a technical support representative or you are passed on to an electronic voice that helps you direct your call to the correct department by pressing #1, #2, #3 and so on, which can be quite frustrating. An option to telephone technical support is e-mail technical support.

E-mail support

Most manufacturers offer support for their product through e-mail, with which you can send a message to a technician detailing your problem. E-mail support is good to use on non-critical issues that can wait a few days before a resolution is needed.

The technical support e-mail address can usually be found in the manual that came with the product you are having trouble with. Do not expect a reply back right away, as the mail queues for these types of services are usually long.

Warranty support

You should be entitled to the highest priority support available when a manufacturer's particular product is still under warranty if a problem arises. Depending on the level of your warranty, you should have at least coverage for one year, and preferably at least three years. Warranty support can be mainly conducted in three different ways:

- Telephone/E-mail warranty support
- Return/Replace product
- Maintenance contracts
- Software upgrades

Telephone/E-mail warranty support

With telephone and e-mail warranty support, the same rules apply as previously mentioned for telephone support and e-mail support but some manufacturers will require you to pay a fee to acquire technical support if the product is not under warranty. Most products will come with a one year warranty, which includes one year of technical support.

Return/replace product

If a particular product such as a hub or a router is not functioning correctly and you have or the manufacturer has concluded that the product in question is defective and cannot be fixed and must be mailed in to the manufacture for support, a warranty will cover the shipping and the manufacturer's repair work. If the manufacturer cannot fix the product in question, the manufacturer will mail you out a new working product as long as it is still under warranty.

This method has its advantages and disadvantages. An advantage of this method is that you will not have to pay for any shipping or work done to the product in question because it is covered under warranty. A disadvantage of this method is that if the product in question is a hub or a router and you have to mail it in to the manufacturer or you have to wait for the manufacturer to send you out a replacement part, either way that part will be missing from the network and can cause downtime on the network while you wait for the fixed or replaced part to arrive in the mail.

Maintenance contracts

Maintenance contracts are sometimes offered for sale along with the product that offers a certain amount of support coverage for a varied period of time. Most maintenance contracts will cover support problems during normal business hours with a guarantee of a technician on-site within 24 hours from when the support call was received. A higher price maintenance contract may cover the product all the time, 24 hours 7 days a week with a guarantee of having a technician on-site within 2 to 4 hours. Such support is useful if (for example) if it is covering a network server.

Some companies will hire a network implementation company to install a network from the ground up. The network implementation company will provide and install the necessary servers, network cable, and network devices. Maintenance contracts are usually provided by the network implementation company to have a technician on-site if a problem with a server or a network device occurs. If the problem was with a network device, a technician would bring the exact same make and model of the device having the problem and have it replaced within a 24 hour time period. Maintenance contracts are excellent to have for extra support on your network. Unfortunately, most maintenance contracts are expensive and are rarely renewed after the initial contract has expired.

Software upgrades

Some software vendors will offer support contracts and offer free upgrades to a product when one is released. For example, you might have a network monitoring application Version 2.0 that just had a major release to Version 2.1. Newer versions of software usually contain many bug fixes and functionality improvements. Some software vendors will include a year's worth of free upgrades that, once you have registered your current version of the product, will be sent to you automatically. If the software you have purchased does not include free software upgrades for a certain period of time, some software manufacturers will offer a software maintenance agreement for a fee that will offer upgrades and even technical support for a certain amount of time depending on the agreement. If the software you have purchased does not offer upgrades or a maintenance agreement, you may have to purchase the upgrade, which could be expensive, depending on the product.

Summary

The chapter emphasized a structured approach to network troubleshooting. By using a step-by-step approach, you will be able to solve a network problem quickly and efficiently. This chapter also discussed the problems associated with certain kinds of network topologies. Physical cabling and network devices as it pertains to network problems were discussed, and a section on client connectivity explained what to check when dealing with client network issues. For the exam, keep these key points in mind:

- Structured network troubleshooting approach:
    1. Establish the symptoms
    2. Identify the affected area
    3. Establish what has changed

4. Select the most probably cause
5. Implement a solution
6. Test the result
7. Recognize the potential effects of the solution
8. Document the solution

- Problems associated with network topologies: Ring, Bus, Star, Mesh, wireless
- Client troubleshooting: hardware, software, cabling, protocols, authentication
- Wiring problems: installation, EMI, attenuation, network device ports, cable lengths

This chapter also discussed where to find troubleshooting resources that can help you fix problems on your network. These resources included

- Previous Documentation
- Hardware or Software Manual
- Software or Hardware ReadMe File
- Hardware or Software Installation Media
- Manufacturer's Web Site
- Telephone Technical Support
- E-mail Support
- Warranty Support

✦ ✦ ✦

STUDY GUIDE

The Study Guide section provides you with the opportunity to test your knowledge about the Network+ exam objectives covered in this chapter. The Assessment Questions provide practice for the real exam, and the Scenarios provide practice with real situations. If you get any questions wrong, use the answers to determine the part of the chapter that you should review before continuing.

Assessment Questions

1. Using a structured approach, you have just established the symptoms of the problem. What would you do next?

    A. Establish what has changed

    B. Identify the cause

    C. Identify the affected area

    D. Document the solution

2. Which of the following is the main point of failure on a Star topology — one that will bring the network to a halt?

    A. Physical cabling

    B. Hubs

    C. Monitor

    D. Floppy drive

3. What is one advantage of using a Mesh topology?

    A. Each device is connected to every other device on the network, creating redundancy.

    B. Each device has it's own IP address creating redundancy.

    C. Less cable is used on a Mesh topology.

    D. Mesh topologies only use coaxial cable.

4. What is one type of networking problem common to Bus networks?

    A. The more terminators used, the slower the network becomes.

    B. Lack of proper termination.

    C. Terminating a cable after a workstation has been removed.

    D. Using the wrong NIC card.

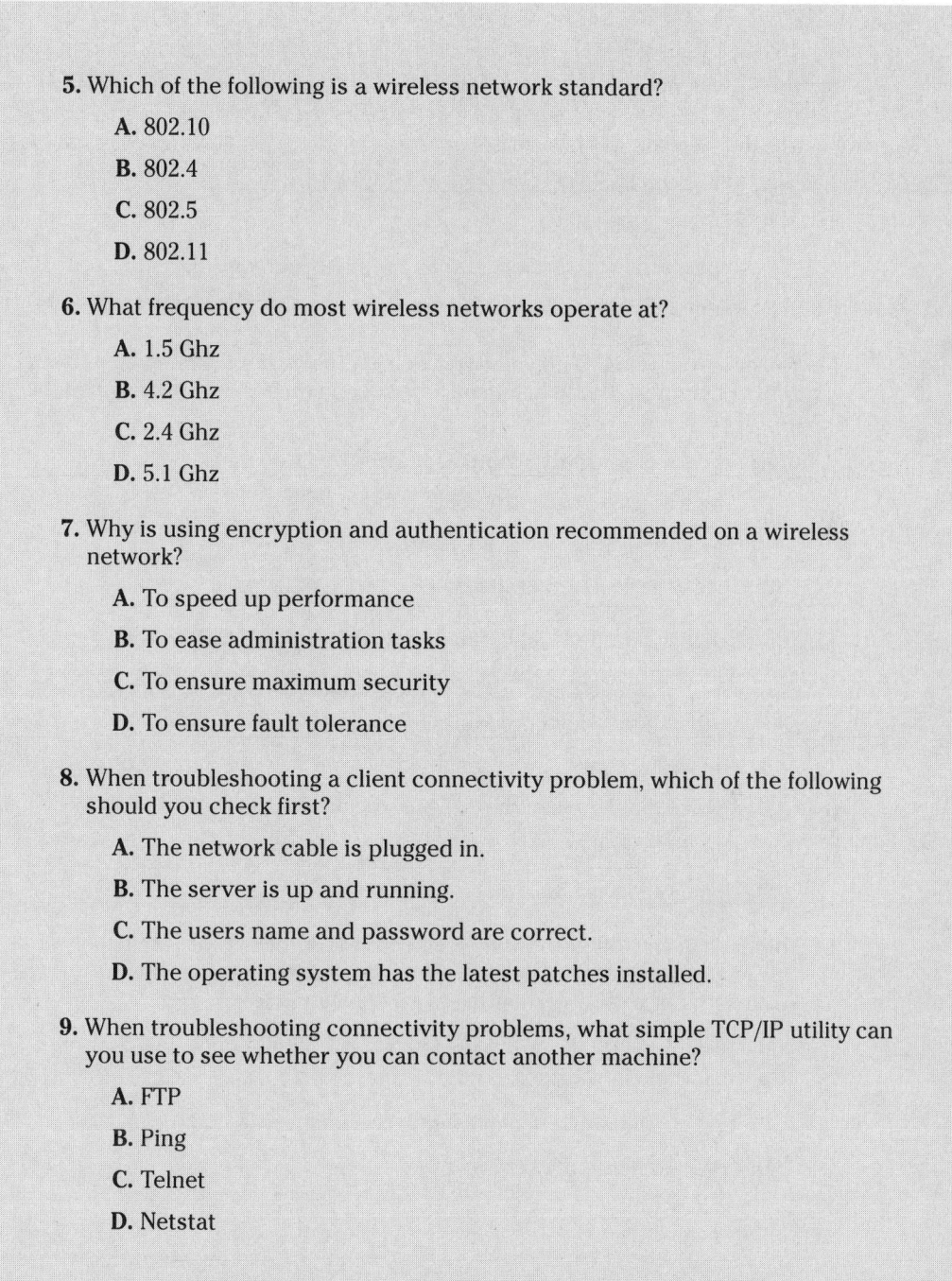

5. Which of the following is a wireless network standard?

   A. 802.10

   B. 802.4

   C. 802.5

   D. 802.11

6. What frequency do most wireless networks operate at?

   A. 1.5 Ghz

   B. 4.2 Ghz

   C. 2.4 Ghz

   D. 5.1 Ghz

7. Why is using encryption and authentication recommended on a wireless network?

   A. To speed up performance

   B. To ease administration tasks

   C. To ensure maximum security

   D. To ensure fault tolerance

8. When troubleshooting a client connectivity problem, which of the following should you check first?

   A. The network cable is plugged in.

   B. The server is up and running.

   C. The users name and password are correct.

   D. The operating system has the latest patches installed.

9. When troubleshooting connectivity problems, what simple TCP/IP utility can you use to see whether you can contact another machine?

   A. FTP

   B. Ping

   C. Telnet

   D. Netstat

10. You are troubleshooting a client's computer that cannot access the network. You suspect the cable might be bad. What is the simplest check to see whether the cable is bad?

    A. Check the link lights on the network card.

    B. Ping the loop back address.

    C. Replace the network cable with a known good one.

    D. Reinstall the network card drivers.

11. You are attempting to download a file from the Internet when you notice no network connectivity. What visual check can you perform to diagnose the problem?

    A. Replace the network cable with a known good one.

    B. Check to see whether the CPU can is working.

    C. Check the NIC card for link light activity.

    D. Check to see whether the power cord is plugged in.

12. You have just installed a new NIC into a client's workstation. You have installed the NIC drivers but the NIC does not function properly. You also notice that your modem is not functioning correctly but it was fine before the NIC was installed. What could be the problem?

    A. The wrong drivers were installed.

    B. IRQ conflict between the NIC and the modem.

    C. The NIC is defective.

    D. You should uninstall the modem.

13. You have been troubleshooting connectivity problems with a client's workstation. You cannot find anything wrong with the client's workstation. What is the next troubleshooting step you should take?

    A. Check the hub or switch the client's workstation is connected to.

    B. Reboot the server.

    C. Replace the network cable with known good one.

    D. Try to telnet to the server.

14. You are troubleshooting a connectivity problem on a client's workstation. You have examined all the hardware and everything seems to be in proper working order, including hubs and switches. What should you check next?

    A. Check software settings

    B. Check NIC link lights

    C. Check PS/2 cable

    D. Check user's network account

15. You have just installed the TCP/IP protocol on a client's workstation that will be connecting to a network running IPX/SPX. When configured, the workstation can't connect to the network. What would be the problem?

    A. The NIC is bad.

    B. The wrong protocol is being used.

    C. The cable is bad.

    D. The users password is being typed in wrong.

16. You have just configured a client's workstation to log on to the network. You assigned 192.123.23.2 as the IP address and 255.0.0.0 as the subnet mask. When restarted, the workstation cannot connect to the network. What could be the problem?

    A. The IP address is invalid.

    B. The network is running the wrong protocol.

    C. The wrong subnet mask was configured.

    D. The NIC is bad.

17. What is the maximum cable length of a 10BASE5 cable segment?

    A. 200 meters

    B. 300 meters

    C. 400 meters

    D. 500 meters

18. What is the maximum cable length of a 10BASE2 cable segment?

    A. 100 meters

    B. 125 meters

    C. 185 meters

    D. 200 meters

19. What is the maximum cable length of a 10BASET cable segment?

    A. 100 meters

    B. 185 meters

    C. 200 meters

    D. 500 meters

20. A user brings to your attention that the network cards lights are blinking. What would you tell the user?

    A. It indicates that drivers need to be installed for the network card.

    B. It indicates a network error.

    C. It indicates network activity.

    D. It indicates a problem with the network card.

Scenarios

1. On a coaxial Bus network within a manufacturing facility, a portion of the network has lost connectivity. Earlier in the day, many workstations were moved to a new location. What are some likely causes of the networking problems?

2. A salesman with a laptop has just traveled to your main office from one of the remote sales offices. All your networks, local and remote, use a wireless system for laptop computers. When he starts up his laptop, he finds that he can't connect to the network. What are some likely causes of the problem?

Answers to Chapter Questions

Chapter Pre-Test

1. The most common command to test network connectivity is to use the ping command. The ping command sends a packet to the specified destination, which then sends back an acknowledgement if it is on the network.

2. By using a structured approach, you can narrow down the source of a problem more quickly and efficiently by going through several steps that begin looking at the simplest to the more complex.

3. If the client is not using the same encryption key for its transmissions, it can't transmit on the network.

4. Each end of the coaxial Bus network must be terminated to enable the network to work.

5. The network can be set for full or half duplex operations. If the network is set for a different duplex setting, you may experience slower and erratic service

6. The last step in finishing the fixing of a network problem is to document the solution. By documenting the solution, you create a special database of knowledge that you can use in the future to help you troubleshoot similar problems.

7. When the Ring is broken on a token Ring network (such as a cable breaks or a workstation goes down), the entire network will go down because the token can't traverse the Ring; the break in the Ring will halt the packet.

8. EMI can affect network connectivity by causing signal disruption to the media and devices on the network.

9. The first step in troubleshooting a network problem is to establish the symptoms. You should not overreact on the sight of the first symptom. It is recommended you do some quick tests to discover the real impact of the problem.

10. Physical cabling can be affected by EMI, attenuation, and over extending the maximum cable lengths.

Assessment Questions

1. C. Identifying the affected area narrows down the part of the network being affected, such as one workstation or even a hub. For review, see the "Network Troubleshooting" section.

2. B. With a Star topology, all devices radiate from a central hub. If the hub fails, the entire network will be disabled. For review, see the "Network Troubleshooting" section.

3. A. With a Mesh topology, each device is connected to every other device on the network. With these multiple connections, a Mesh topology is fault tolerant. For review, see the "Network Troubleshooting" section.

4. B. Without the proper termination, the network signal will bounce back onto the wiring causing network packet collisions. For review, see the "Network Troubleshooting" section.

5. D. The 802.11 is a standard for wireless technologies; the other is called Bluetooth. These two different standards do not communicate with each other. For review, see the "Network Troubleshooting" section.

6. C. Most wireless networks operate at the 2.4 GHz frequency. The problem with this frequency is that it can also be shared by common household devices, such as cordless phones. For review, see the "Network Troubleshooting" section.

7. C. To help protect your wireless network, encryption and authentication methods should be implemented. Third-party users can connect to your wireless network if it is unprotected. Encrypting communications or forcing authentication can greatly reduce the risk of unauthorized users gaining access to your network. For review, see the "Network Troubleshooting" section.

8. A. It is always best to check the simplest first. When you have checked and established that the network cable is plugged in, you can move on to more advanced troubleshooting techniques. For review, see the "Troubleshooting Client Connectivity" section.

9. B. The `ping` command is a simple TCP/IP utility you can use to check to see whether a device on your network is reachable. If the other device is reachable, the `ping` request will receive a reply. If not, the `ping` request times out. For review, see the "Troubleshooting Client Connectivity" section.

10. C. The simplest thing you can do when you suspect the cable might be bad is to replace it with a known good one. If the known good cable fails, then you can rule out that the cable is bad and you can move on to more advanced troubleshooting techniques. For review, see the "Troubleshooting Client Connectivity" section.

11. C. A good way to check for network activity is to visually examine link-light activity on the NIC card. The lights usually flash to indicate network data being sent and received from the cards. For review, see the "Hardware problems" section.

12. B. There would be an IRQ conflict if the modem was working fine before the NIC was installed and then not functioning after the NIC was installed. Devices cannot share the same IRQ. To correct this problem, you would have to assign the NIC to a different available IRQ. For review, see the "Hardware problems" section.

13. A. If everything checks out okay for the workstation and the workstation still cannot connect to the network, check the hub or switch the workstation is connected to. If the hub or switch is faulty, the workstation will not connect to the network. For review, see the "Hardware problems" section.

14. A. If the workstation is configured with the wrong software setting (for example, an incorrect IP address), incorrectly entered subnet masks, or the wrong protocol (even if it's among the protocols that the network uses), then the workstation can't communicate on the network. For review, see the "Network settings" section.

15. B. Because the network is running the IPX/SPX protocol, you will have to install the same protocol on the workstation that will be connecting to that network. For review, see the "Protocols" section.

16. C. The IP address being used is a class C address. The default subnet mask for a class C address is 255.255.255.0. 255.0.0.0 is the subnet mask for a class A IP address. For review, see the "Protocols" section.

17. D. The maximum cable length of a 10BASE5 cable segment is 500 Meters. For review, see the "Wiring and Infrastructure Troubleshooting" section.

18. C. The maximum cable length of a 10BASE2 cable segment is 185 Meters. For review, see the "Wiring and Infrastructure Troubleshooting" section.

19. A. The maximum cable length of a 10BASET cable segment is 100 Meters. For review, see the "Wiring and Infrastructure Troubleshooting" section.

20. C. You would tell the user that the network activity light flashes to signal that packets are being sent and received from the network card. For review, see the "Hardware problems" section.

Scenarios

1. Because a number of workstations have been moved earlier in the day, it is most likely that some part of the Bus network cabling has been disturbed or reconnected improperly. You should examine how each of the workstations have been reconnected by ensuring that there is no break in the Bus cabling, and the right connectors are being used. Another consideration for a Bus network is the terminations, which must be present at the ends of the network segment. Examine the last workstation on the Bus and ensure that it has a proper terminator installed.

2. Different offices may have separate methods of authentication, encryption, and protocols. Check the client's wireless card setting; make sure that the right protocol is being used for your network. Also, your authentication and encryption systems may be totally different. Check the encryption key; compare it with the one you are using for your office (or install one if encryption is not enabled on the client's wireless network card).

What's on the CD-ROM

APPENDIX A

This appendix provides you with information on the contents of the CD-ROM that accompanies this book.

- The following programs are included on this CD:
- Network+ Bible Certification Test Engine
- Freeware version of Acrobat Reader
- Evaluation version of Network Instrument's Observer
- Freeware version of WildPacket's IP Subnet Calculator

Also included is an electronic, searchable version of the book that you can view with Adobe Acrobat Reader.

System Requirements

Make sure that your computer meets the minimum system requirements listed in this section. If your computer doesn't match up to most of these requirements, you may have a problem using the contents of the CD.

For Microsoft Windows 9x/ME or Windows NT/2000/XP

- PC with a Pentium processor running at 120 MHz or faster
- At least 32 MB of RAM
- At least 20 MB of free hard drive space
- Ethernet network interface card (NIC) or modem with a speed of at least 28,800 bps. (For Internet access if needed)
- A CD-ROM drive — double-speed (2x) or faster

Using the CD with Microsoft Windows

To install the items from the CD to your hard drive, follow these steps:

1. Insert the CD into your computer's CD-ROM drive.
2. A window will appear with the following options: Install, Explore, eBook, Links and Exit.

   Install: Gives you the option to install the supplied software and/or the author-created samples on the CD-ROM.

   Explore: Allows you to view the contents of the CD-ROM in its directory structure.

   eBook: Allows you to view an electronic version of the book.

   Exit: Closes the autorun window.

If you do not have autorun enabled or if the autorun window does not appear, follow the steps below to access the CD.

1. Click Start ⇨ Run.
2. When the Run dialog box appears, choose Browse, locate your CD-ROM drive, and double-click your CD-ROM drive to view the contents of the CD-ROM.
3. Double-click the folder of the software that you want to install. For Adobe Acrobat choose the rp500enu.exe program and for the Test engine choose the HMI_Test_Engine.EXE program.
4. Click OK.
5. In the Run dialog box, you should see the path of the software that you want to install. Click the OK button.

For further installation instructions, please consult the README file for the program.

The CD-ROM contains the Network+ Bible Certification Test Engine and the electronic version of the book in Adobe PDF format. The next section is a summary of the contents of the CD-ROM.

Microsoft Windows applications

Every program on the CD-ROM is located in the folder name associated with the name of the software. The following applications that install under Microsoft Windows are on the CD-ROM.

Shareware programs are fully functional, trial versions of copyrighted programs. If you like particular programs, register with their authors for a nominal fee and receive licenses, enhanced versions, and technical support. *Freeware programs* are copyrighted games, applications, and utilities that are free for personal use. Unlike shareware, these programs do not require a fee or provide technical support. *GNU software* is governed by its own license, which is included inside the folder of the GNU product. See the GNU license for more details.

Trial, demo, or *evaluation versions* are usually limited either by time or functionality (such as being unable to save projects). Some trial versions are very sensitive to system date changes. If you alter your computer's date, the programs will "time out" and will no longer be functional.

eBookversion of the Network+ Certification Bible

The complete (and searchable) text of this book is on the CD-ROM in Adobe's Portable Document Format (PDF), readable with the Adobe Acrobat Reader (also included). For more information on Adobe Acrobat Reader, go to `www.adobe.com`.

Network+ Bible Certification test engine

The Network+ Bible Certification test engine will help you test your knowledge of all the objectives covered in this book. The test engine has 300 sample test questions that mimic the real Network+ exam. Also included are detailed explanations of the correct answers.

IP Subnet Calculator

Generates a list of possible subnets and the range of the IP addressing. Choose the number of required hosts or subnets and print it for review on paper.

Observer

This is a great analyzer for small and medium sized networks. It's recommended for use with a packet sniffer.

Troubleshooting

If you have difficulty installing or using the CD-ROM programs, try the following solutions:

- ✦ Turn off any anti-virus software that you may have running. Installers sometimes mimic virus activity and can make your computer incorrectly believe that it is being infected by a virus. (Be sure to turn the anti-virus software back on later.)
- ✦ Close all running programs. The more programs you're running, the less memory is available to other programs. Installers also typically update files and programs; if you keep other programs running, installation may not work properly.

If you still have trouble with the CD, please call the Hungry Minds Customer Service phone number at (800) 762-2974. Outside the United States, call (317) 572-3994 or email at techsupdum@wiley.com. Hungry Minds will provide technical support only for installation and other general quality control items; for technical support on the applications themselves, consult the program's vendor or author.

✦ ✦ ✦

Exam Objectives

APPENDIX B

This appendix provides a table listing the exam objectives for the Network+ Certification Exam. The table is an exhaustive cross-reference chart that links every exam objective to the corresponding chapter in this book.

Table B-1
Network+ Certification

Exam Objective	Chapter
Domain 1.0 - Media and Topologies	
1.1 Recognize the following logical or physical network topologies given a schematic diagram or description – **3%** • Star/hierarchical • bus • mesh • ring • wireless	1
1.2 Specify the main features of 802.2 (LLC), 802.3 (Ethernet), 802.5 (token ring), 802.11b (wireless) and FDDI networking technologies, including – **3%** • Speed • Access • Method • Topology • Media	1
1.3 Specify the characteristics (e.g., speed, length, topology, cable type, etc.) of the following – **3%** • 802.3 (Ethernet) standards • 10BASE-T • 100BASE-TX • 10BASE2 • 10BASE5 • 100BASE-FX • Gigabit Ethernet	2
1.4 Recognize the following media connectors and/or describe their uses – **3%** • RJ-11 • RJ-45 • AUI • BNC • ST • SC	2

Exam Objective	Chapter
Domain 1.0 - Media and Topologies	
1.5 Choose the appropriate media type and connectors to add a client to an existing network. – **3%**	2
1.6 Identify the purpose, features, and functions of the following network components – **5%** • Hubs • Switches • Bridges • Routers • Gateways • CSU/DSU • Network Interface Cards/ISDN adapters/system area network cards • Wireless access points • Modems	3
Domain 2.0 – Protocols and Standards – 25%	
2.1 Given an example identify a MAC address – **1%**	4
2.2 Identify the seven layers of the OSI model and their functions – **2%**	5
2.3 Differentiate between the following network protocols in terms of routing, addressing schemes, interoperability, and naming conventions – **2%** • TCP/IP • IPX/SPX • NetBEUI • AppleTalk	6
2.4 Identify the OSI layers at which the following network components operate – **2%** • Hubs • Switches • Bridges • Routers • Network Interface Cards	5

Continued

Table B-1 *(continued)*

Exam Objective	Chapter
Domain 2.0 – Protocols and Standards – 25%	
2.5 Define the purpose, function and/or use of the following protocols within TCP/IP – **2%** • IP • TCP • UDP • FTP • TFTP • SMTP • HTTP • HTTPS • POP3/IMAP4 • TELNET • ICMP • ARP • NTP	6
2.6 Define the function of TCP/UDP ports. Identify well-known ports. – **2%**	7
2.7 Identify the purpose of the following network services (e.g. DHCP/bootp, DNS, NAT/ICS, WINS, and SNMP) –**2%**	8
2.8 Identify IP addresses (Ipv4, Ipv6) and their default subnet masks. – **2%**	8
2.9 Identify the purpose of subnetting and default gateways. – **2%**	8
2.10 Identify the differences between public vs. private networks – **2%**	9

Exam Objective	Chapter
Domain 2.0 – Protocols and Standards – 25%	
2.11 Identify the basic characteristics (e.g., speed, capacity, media) of the following WAN technologies – **2%** • Packet switching vs. circuit switching • ISDN • FDDI • ATM • Frame Relay • Sonet/SDH • T1/E1 • T3/E3 • Ocx	10
2.12 Define the function of the following remote access protocols and services – **2%** • RAS • PPP • PPTP • ICA	10, 11
2.13 Identify the following security protocols and describe their purpose and function – **2%** • IPsec • L2TP • SSL • Kerberos	11

Continued

Table B-1 *(continued)*

Exam Objective	Chapter
Domain 3.0 Network Implementation – 23%	
3.1 Identify the basic capabilities (i.e. client support, interoperability, authentication, file and print services, application support, and security) of the following server operating systems – **3%** • UNIX/Linux • Netware • Windows • Macintosh	12
3.2 Identify the basic capabilities, (i.e., client connectivity, local security mechanisms, and authentication) of thefollowing clients – **2%**	12
3.3 Identify the main characteristics of VLANs – **2%**	13
3.4 Identify the main characteristics of network attached storage – **2%**	14
3.5 Identify the purpose and characteristics of fault tolerance – **2%**	15
3.6 Identify the purpose and characteristics of disaster recovery – **2%**	15
3.7 Given a remote connectivity scenario (e.g., IP, IPX, dial-up, PPPoE, authentication, physical connectivity etc.), configure the connection. – **2%**	16
3.8 Identify the purpose, benefits and characteristics of using a firewall. – **2%**	17
3.9 Identify the purpose, benefits and characteristics of using a proxy. – **2%**	17
3.10 Given a scenario, predict the impact of a particular security implementation on network functionality (e.g.blocking port numbers, encryption, etc.). – **2%**	17
3.11 Given a network configuration, select the appropriate NIC and network configuration settings (DHCP, DNS, WINS, protocols, NETBIOS/host name, etc.). – **2%**	18
Domain 4.0 Network Support – 32%	
4.1 Given a troubleshooting scenario, select the appropriate TCP/IP utility from among the following – **3%** • Tracert • Ping • Arp • Netstat • Nbstat • Ipconfig/Ifconfig • Winipcfg • Nslookup	19

Exam Objective	Chapter
Domain 4.0 Network Support – 32%	
4.2 Given a troubleshooting scenario involving a small office/home office network failure (e.g., xDSL, cable, home satellite, wireless, POTS), identify the cause of the failure. – **2%**	20
4.3 Given a troubleshooting scenario involving a remote connectivity problem (e.g., authentication failure, protocol configuration, physical connectivity) identify the cause of the problem. – **2%**	21
4.4 Given specific parameters, configure a client to connect to the following servers – **2%** • UNIX/Linux • Netware • Windows • Macintosh	22
4.5 Given a wiring task, select the appropriate tool (e.g., wire crimper, media tester/certifier, punch down tool, tone generator, optical tester, etc.). – **2%**	23
4.6 Given a network scenario interpret visual indicators (e.g., link lights, collision lights, etc.) to determine the nature of the problem. – **2%**	23
4.7 Given output from a diagnostic utility (e.g. tracert, ping, ipconfig, etc.), identify the utility and interpret the output. – **2%**	19
4.8 Given a scenario, predict the impact of modifying, adding, or removing network services (e.g., DHCP, DNS, WINS, etc.) on network resources and users. **2%**	23
4.9 Given a network problem scenario, select an appropriate course of action based on a general troubleshooting strategy. This strategy includes the following steps – **4%** 1. Establish the symptoms 2. Identify the affected area 3. Establish what has changed 4. Select the most probable cause 5. Implement a solution 6. Test the result 7. Recognize the potential effects of the solution 8. Document the solution	24

Continued

Table B-1 *(continued)*

Exam Objective	Chapter
Domain 4.0 Network Support – 32%	
4.10 Given a troubleshooting scenario involving a network with a particular physical topology (i.e., bus, star/hierarchical, mesh, ring, and wireless) and including a network diagram, identify the network area effected andthe cause of the problem. **– 3%**	24
4.11 Given a network troubleshooting scenario involving a client connectivity problem (e.g., incorrect protocol/client software/ authentication configuration, or insufficient rights/permission), identify the cause of the problem. **– 5%**	24
4.12 Given a network troubleshooting scenario involving a wiring/infrastructure problem, identify the cause of the problem (e.g., bad media, interference, network hardware). **– 3%**	24

♦ ♦ ♦

Practice Exam

APPENDIX C

This sixty-five-question Network+ sample exam tests your knowledge on all the Network+ test objectives that are fully covered in this book. By using this exam, which is similar to the real one, you can identify any weak areas that you need to review. At the end of the sample exam, you will find the correct answers, along with explanations and the chapter where the topic is covered.

Exam Questions

1. You have just been hired by a local accounting company to support five users networked via a Star topology. During the course of the day one of the users' computers breaks down. What will happen to the remaining systems in the topology with this one system being down?

    A. All systems on the network will shut down.

    B. The remaining systems on this network will continue to function, but will not be able to access information from the computer that has broken down.

    C. The remaining systems on the network will continue to function but will not be able to access the network.

    D. The remaining systems on this network will continue to function, and will be able to access information from the computer that has broken down.

2. Which of the following is an advantage of a Star Topology?

    A. Easy to install and troubleshoot.

    B. Requires more cable then a Mesh topology.

    C. If only the hub goes down, all the computers on the network will still be able to communicate.

    D. Using a 5 hub with a Star network will increase the speed of the network.

3. Which of the following network topologies uses the most amount of cable?

    A. Star

    B. Mesh

    C. Ring

    D. Bus

4. Which of the following is the IEEE 802 standard for Token Ring?

    A. 802.3

    B. 802.4

    C. 802.5

    D. 802.2

5. The 802.11 standard is for which type of network technology?

   A. Token Ring

   B. Wireless

   C. Bus

   D. Ethernet

6. You are the network technician for a local company. You boss would like to create a separate network in a spare office just for the graphics department. Your boss would like to use cable that can reach at least 200 meters just in case they expand the room in the fall and that each cable can transmit data at a maximum of 10 Mbps. Which of the following cable types would you use for this job?

   A. 10Base5

   B. 10Base2

   C. 10BaseT

   D. 10Base-F

7. Which of the following cable types is knows as Thicknet?

   A. 10Base2

   B. 10BaseT

   C. 10Base5

   D. 10Base-F

8. Which of the following cable type uses fiber-optic technology?

   A. 10BaseT

   B. 10Base-F

   C. 10Base5

   D. 10Base2

9. Which of the following are things you should consider when deciding on a network cable? (choose the best two answers)

   A. Transmission speed

   B. Distance

   C. Color

   D. Manufacturer

10. From the following, which connector uses eight-wires and is very commonly used to connect computers to a local area network?

    A. RJ-11

    B. AUI

    C. BNC

    D. RJ-45

11. In order for your computer system to access the network. What device must be installed on the computer system?

    A. Hub

    B. Network Card

    C. BNC connector

    D. Sound Card

12. Which of the following is the central device used to connect devices in a Star Topology?

    A. Router

    B. Network Card

    C. Hub

    D. Bridge

13. Which type of routing uses special routing protocols that enable routers to exchange data with each other?

    A. Static routing

    B. RIP routing

    C. Dynamic routing

    D. UTP routing

14. Which of the following is the maximum transfer speed of a wireless access point with a range of 100 feet?

    A. 11 Mbps

    B. 5.5 Mbps

    C. 100 Mbps

    D. 2 Mbpss

15. Which of the following consists of a 12 digit hexadecimal address?

   A. IP address

   B. MAC address

   C. Web site address

   D. Cable address

16. What does the acronym PDU stand for?

   A. Protocol Digital Units

   B. Private Data Units

   C. Public Digital Units

   D. Protocol Data Units

17. Which of the following is the 5th layer of the OSI model?

   A. Data Link

   B. Network

   C. Session

   D. Transport

18. Which of the following is an action that the Presentation layer performs?

   A. Reformats data for transmission to and from the network.

   B. Breaks data into pieces when transmitting data and reassembles the pieces when receiving at the destination.

   C. Routes data beyond a LAN by converting IP addresses to physical addresses

   D. Packages data for transmission to and from the Physical layer.

19. How many layers are associated with the OSI model?

   A. 5

   B. 6

   C. 7

   D. 8

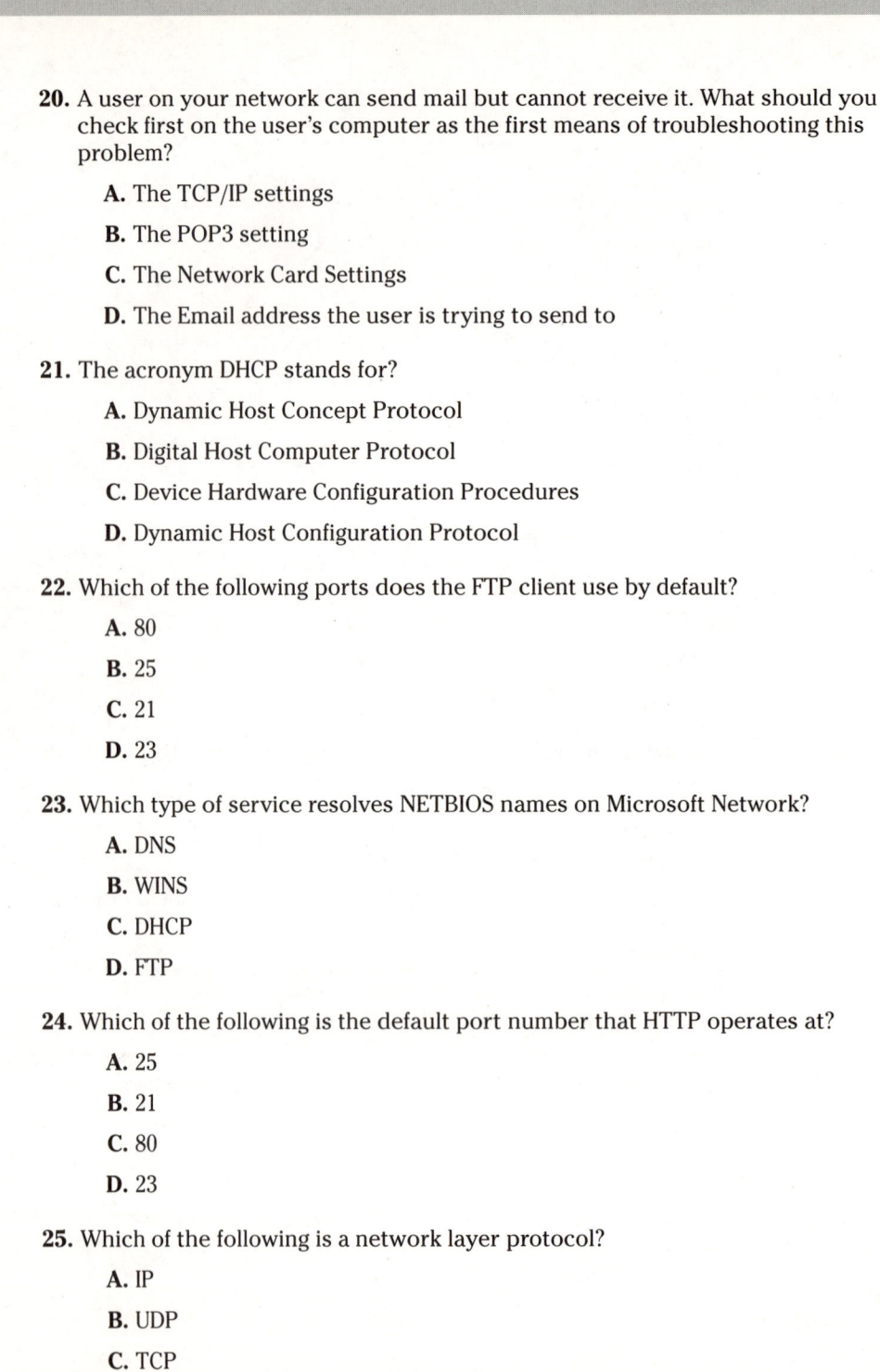

20. A user on your network can send mail but cannot receive it. What should you check first on the user's computer as the first means of troubleshooting this problem?

    A. The TCP/IP settings

    B. The POP3 setting

    C. The Network Card Settings

    D. The Email address the user is trying to send to

21. The acronym DHCP stands for?

    A. Dynamic Host Concept Protocol

    B. Digital Host Computer Protocol

    C. Device Hardware Configuration Procedures

    D. Dynamic Host Configuration Protocol

22. Which of the following ports does the FTP client use by default?

    A. 80

    B. 25

    C. 21

    D. 23

23. Which type of service resolves NETBIOS names on Microsoft Network?

    A. DNS

    B. WINS

    C. DHCP

    D. FTP

24. Which of the following is the default port number that HTTP operates at?

    A. 25

    B. 21

    C. 80

    D. 23

25. Which of the following is a network layer protocol?

    A. IP

    B. UDP

    C. TCP

    D. FTP

26. Which of the following servers would you use to assign IP addresses automatically?

    A. WINS server

    B. DNS server

    C. DHCP Sever

    D. Web Server

27. What would be the simplest name for a network that is accessible to everyone?

    A. Home network

    B. Public network

    C. Private network

    D. Ethernet Network

28. What type of network is used to be restricted to a group of users?

    A. Public Network

    B. Private Network

    C. Home Network

    D. Ethernet Network

29. What type of network was developed to combine the advantages of public and private networks?

    A. Application Network

    B. Open Source Network

    C. Multi-layer Network

    D. Virtual Private Network

30. What does the acronym ATM stand for?

    A. Automatic Translation Module

    B. Asynchronous Transfer Mode

    C. Automatic Transfer Mode

    D. Asynchronous Translation Module

31. Which of the following is the correct definition of Multiplexing?

    A. The transmission of data in single pieces simultaneously along different channels.

    B. The transmission of multiple data pieces are sent separately along different data channels.

    C. The transmission of data in multiple pieces simultaneously along the same channel.

    D. Data that has been transmitted in half-duplex mode.

32. Which of the following is LAN-only non-routable protocol?

    A. TCP/IP

    B. IPX/SPX

    C. FTP

    D. NetBEUI

33. Which part of an operating system is responsible for facilitating communications between the user and the operating system?

    A. Memory

    B. Shell or GUI interface

    C. Multitasking

    D. Data output

34. Which of the following is NOT a characteristic of a network operating system?

    A. Enabling access to a local system resource

    B. Proving access to remote printers

    C. Maintaining system security and user credentials

    D. Granting access to remote applications and resources

35. A peer-to-peer networking model is most often used for what types of purposes?

    A. A central server is used to provide applications to a number of client systems

    B. A common protocol is need to facilitate communications between a server and client machine

    C. When a small group of systems is networked together with no central server

    D. When there is a strong need for a central security database to authenticate users to resources on the network

36. Which of the following is NOT an example of a network operating system?

    A. Unix/Linux

    B. Novell Netware

    C. Windows NT/2000

    D. MS-DOS

37. Which of the following is the most common network protocol used in Apple Macintosh environments?

    A. SPX

    B. Appletalk

    C. IPX

    D. NetBEUI

38. Which of the following factors in a multiple LAN network is a good reason to switch to using VLAN's?

    A. Too many different IP addresses in use

    B. High level of network broadcast traffic

    C. Cannot connect to a WAN

    D. Only a maximum of three LAN's can be networked together

39. How many VLAN's should be implemented on a company's network, that is structured into three departments, sales, marketing, and development?

    A. No VLAN's are needed

    B. One

    C. Six

    D. Three

40. Assigning VLAN's to different ports on a hub or switch is an example of what type of VLAN?

    A. Port-based VLAN

    B. MAC-address-based VLAN

    C. This is not an example of creating a VLAN

    D. Protocol-based VLAN

41. Which of the following is a description of a SAN (Storage Area Network)?

    A. A network that is used a backup to a regular LAN

    B. A tape array that can hold up to fifty tapes

    C. Connecting all storage devices onto a single network

    D. A collection of RAID disk arrays

42. Which disk communications technology is most widely used for high-speed storage requirements such as RAID systems?

    A. SCSI

    B. IDE

    C. SAN

    D. USB

43. What is the purpose of a SCSI terminator?

    A. Allows faster communications on an 8-bit SCSI bus

    B. Stops the cable signal from reflecting off the end of the cable back onto the bus

    C. Repeats the cable signal so that SCSI cable length limitations can be overrun

    D. Used to connect a Wide SCSI bus to a Narrow SCSI bus

44. As backup administrator, you are required to choose the tape technology that will best backup your large 100GB database system. Which of the following would be most appropriate for your purposes?

    A. Reel-to-reel tape

    B. Travan

    C. DAT

    D. DLT

45. After implementing a regular backup plan, which of the following is the most important step in maintaining the integrity of your data?

    A. Keeping a backup log

    B. Labeling your tapes properly

    C. Testing your backups by doing regular test restores

    D. Regularly performing full backups

46. RAID 1 is an example of what type of disk redundancy technology?

   A. Disk mirroring

   B. Disk duplexing

   C. RAID controller duplexing

   D. Disk striping

47. Which power fault tolerance technology will allow you to run your system on batteries until you can safely shut the system down?

   A. Power bar

   B. Power conditioner

   C. Redundant power supplies

   D. UPS

48. Which of the following is a disadvantage of using software RAID instead of hardware RAID?

   A. The boot drive must be on its own non-RAID partition

   B. The need for additional, expensive hardware

   C. Less CPU-intensive than hardware solutions

   D. It is already included with the operating system

49. You have been asked to implement a RAID 5 system on your server. What is the minimum number of hard drives that you will need to implement RAID 5?

   A. Two

   B. Three

   C. Five

   D. Four

50. A user from the sales department requires remote access to the network, as they are traveling a majority of the time. What of the following remote access solutions would be most appropriate in regards to cost, ease of accessibility and security?

   A. Dial-Up RAS connection directly to a server

   B. VPN over a general Internet dial-up connection

   C. A private ISDN line directly to the network

   D. Wireless connection

51. Which of the following is the most common client protocol for dial-up RAS connections?

    A. SLIP

    B. RAS

    C. PPP

    D. NetBEUI

52. For security purposes, what can be used to authenticate users who dial-in to a Windows-based RAS server?

    A. Encrypted PPP protocol

    B. Login and password

    C. NetBEUI

    D. Windows NT/2000 account

53. Your company wants to install a web server that will be available through the Internet to the outside world. Users on the inside will also need to be able to communicate with the server. Which of the following devices will be most appropriate to protect unauthorized intrusion to the inside network from the Web Server?

    A. Firewall

    B. Proxy

    C. Router

    D. VPN

54. What of the following are characteristics of a proxy server?

    A. Provide caching and NAT capabilities

    B. Protect the inside network from outside intrusion

    C. Allow multiple LAN's to coexist simultaneously

    D. Allow for Internet connection redundancy

55. Which of the following is NOT an example of a routable protocol?

    A. IPX/SPX

    B. TCP/IP

    C. NetBEUI

    D. Appletalk

56. Clients on a Windows network need to resolve NetBEUI host names with TCP/IP addresses. What service needs to be installed on the network to perform this function?

    A. DNS server

    B. WINS server

    C. Proxy server

    D. Hosts server

57. A user is having trouble connecting to a computer by its name, however, it can be contacted using its IP address. You suspect that the DNS server may not be working. What TCP/IP utility can be used to determine if the DNS server is resolving addresses?

    A. `ipconfig`

    B. `nbtstat`

    C. `ping`

    D. `nslookup`

58. Users are complaining that they cannot connect to a remote file server. When you check other servers at the remote site, they seem to be fine. What utility can be used to check to see if the remote server is on the network?

    A. `ifconfig`

    B. `nbtstat`

    C. `nslookup`

    D. `ping`

59. A user is trying to dial-in to their Internet ISP. The modem dials, connects to the network, but the user fails to authenticate to the network. What is the most likely cause of the problem?

    A. The modem is malfunctioning

    B. The user is using the wrong protocol

    C. The login or password is incorrect

    D. There is a problem with the phone line

60. A remote user is using a dial-up VPN to try and connect to the internal company network. When the VPN is initiated, it is unable to contact the remote site. The username and password seem to be correct, and there doesn't seem to be anything wrong with the connection. What is the most likely cause of the problem?

   A. The user forgot to enable encryption

   B. The login and password are incorrect

   C. There is a problem with the phone line

   D. There is a problem with the user's modem

61. In order to automatically allocate IP addresses to clients as they enter the network, which service needs to be enabled on the network?

   A. DNS

   B. DHCP

   C. WINS

   D. VPN

62. A new computer cannot access a Class C TCP/IP network. It has just been configured with a Class C IP address with a default subnet mask of 255.255.0.0. What is the most likely cause of the problem?

   A. The IP address is incorrect

   B. The subnet mask is incorrect

   C. A Class C network must use DHCP

   D. The IP address should have been a Class B address

63. What is the main characteristic of a crossover cable?

   A. A crossover cable can support a minimum speed of 100Mbps

   B. A crossover cable is used to connect a modem to a phone jack

   C. The transmit and receive wires are reversed

   D. A crossover cable can only be used to connect to PC's together

64. A new coaxial-based Ethernet network is being installed. What network topology will be used during installation?

   A. Star

   B. Ring

   C. Mesh

   D. Bus

65. A new network has been installed adjacent to your current company building, and Ethernet cables have been run to the new location. When you begin testing network activity, you find that communications are very slow, and in some places, non-existent. What is the most likely cause of the problem?

   A. The cable length exceeds the attenuation limitations of Ethernet

   B. The cables were installed improperly

   C. Not all of the cables were terminated

   D. There is too much EMI interference

Answers to Sample Exam

1. B. With a star topology, all devices are connected by a central hub. If one device on the network breaks down, it will not affect the one device and will not take down the whole network. For review, see Chapter 1.

2. A. An advantage of a Star topology is that it is very easy to install since each device connects to a central hub to communicate with each other which means it does not use a lot of cable as some of the other topologies. Each device is independent from the other devices on the network that makes it much easier to troubleshoot network issues. For review, see Chapter 1.

3. B. A Mesh topology uses the most amount of cable then any other topology. A Mesh topology has a path that exists from each station to every other station in the network. Due to this added fault tolerance, a mesh topology can be rather expensive. For review, see Chapter 1.

4. C. The IEEE 802.5 standard is for Token Ring. The 802.3 standard is for CSMA/CD, the 802.4 standard is for Token Bus, and the 802.6 standard is for Logical Link Control. For review, see Chapter 1.

5. B. The 802.11 standard is for Wireless network technology. Today there is the 802.11a and 802.11b standards, which specifies higher wireless speeds. For review, see Chapter 1.

6. B. A 10base2 cable segment can transmit data at a maximum rate of 10 Mbps, and has a maximum cable length of 200 meters. For review, see Chapter 2.

7. C. 10Base5 network cable is also known as Thicknet. Thicknet cable uses Vampire taps which makes the connection with the inner conductor. Due to the thickness, thicknet cable can be hard to work with. For review, see Chapter 2.

8. B. 10Base-F cable uses fiber-optic technology. Fiber-optic cable transmits light rather then electricity. With this feature Fiber-optic cable is immune to EMI and RFI. For review, see Chapter 2.

9. A and B. When considering network cable, you should always make sure that the cable is fast enough for your network especially in large establishments where many users access the network. The cable's maximum distance must be considered so each cable segment will not be maxed out and develop attenuation. For review, see Chapter 2.

10. D. An RJ-45 connector is an eight-wire connector that look similar to a phone connector but a little larger. RJ-11 connectors use six wires and primarily used to connect telephone equipment. AUI (Attachment Unit Interface) AUI specifies a coaxial cable connected to a transceiver that plugs into a 15-pin socket on the network interface card (NIC). A BNC connector that is used with coaxial cables such as the RG-58 A/U cable used with 10BASE-2 Ethernet. For review, see Chapter 2.

11. B. You system must have a network card installed and configured before your system can access the network. For review, see Chapter 3.

12. C. A hub is the central device used to connect devices in a Star Topology. For review, see Chapter 3.

13. B. With RIP routing, a RIP protocol is uses which the routing tables of all routers are sent to the other routers on the network every 30 seconds. RIP sends the entire routing table at each update interval. For review, see Chapter 3.

14. A. The maximum transfer speed of a wireless access point with a range of 100 feet is 11 Mbps. For review, see Chapter 3.

15. B. A MAC address consists of a 12 digit hexadecimal address. For review, see Chapter 4.

16. D. The acronym PDU stands for Protocol Data Units. PDU is basically another term for a packet that are passed between layers of the OSI networking model. For review, see Chapter 5.

17. C. The Session layer is the 5th layer of the OSI model. The Data Link layer is the 2nd layer, the Network layer is the 3rd layer, and the Transport layer is the 4th layer of the OSI model. For review, see Chapter 5.

18. A. An action the Presentation layer performs is reformatting data for transmission to and from the network. For review, see Chapter 5.

19. C. There are seven layers associated with the OSI model. The seven being: Physical, Data Link, Network, Transport, Session, Presentation and Application. For review, see Chapter 5.

20. B. Since you are able to send email but not receive it, it is a good idea to check the POP3 incoming email settings. POP3 is responsible for contacting the mail server. The user must specify a POP3 mail server during the email account setup process. POP3 is mail delivery only; POP3 does not send mail. For review, see Chapter 6.

21. D. DHCP stands for Dynamic Host Configuration Protocol. For review, see Chapter 6.

22. C. The default port number for FTP is 21. Port 80 is the default port number for HTTP, port 25 is the default port for SMTP, and port 23 is for Telnet. For review, see Chapter 6.

23. B. WINS (Windows Internet Naming Service) is used to resolve NETBIOS names on Microsoft Networks. For review, see Chapter 6.

24. C. The default port number for HTTP is 80. Port 25 is the default port number for SMTP, port 21 is the default port number for FTP and port 23 is the default port number Telnet. For review, see Chapter 6.

25. A. IP is a network layer protocol. UDP is a transport layer protocol, TCP is a transport layer protocol, and FTP is an application layer protocol. For review, see Chapter 6.

26. C. A DHCP server assigns network IP address to clients on the network at start-up. For review, see Chapter 8.

27. B. A public network is a network that is accessible to everyone. The Internet is good example of a public network. For review, see Chapter 9.

28. B. Private networks are usually organization specific or are restricted to a group of users. A Local Area Network is a good example of a private network. For review, see Chapter 9.

29. D. A Virtual Private Network (VPN) is a network that uses a combination of existing dedicated internal networks and the Internet to securely communicate information. A VPN is used to carries private data over a public network. For review, see Chapter 9.

30. B. The acronym ATM stands for Asynchronous Transfer Mode that uses dedicated hardware-switching technology. For review, see Chapter 10.

31. C. Multiplexing is the transmission of data in multiple pieces simultaneously along the same channel. For review, see Chapter 11.

32. D. NetBEUI is a basic non-routable protocol recommended for small networks that do not use a router. For review, see Chapter 11.

33. B. To allow the user to communicate with the operating system, some sort of user interface needs to exist so commands and data can be entered into the system. This interface is typically either text or GUI-based. For review, see Chapter 12.

34. A. There is no need for an operating system to be networked to allow access to local files. Network operating systems are typically used for access to remote files and printers on other systems. For review, see Chapter 12.

35. C. Peer-to-peer networks are typically used for smaller groups of networked computers which do not need a central server to provide access and security to network resources. For review, see Chapter 12.

36. D. MS-DOS, one of the earliest operating systems, is not, on its own, a network operating system such as Windows NT/2000, Novell Netware, or Unix. For review, see Chapter 12.

37. B. The most common network protocol used in Apple Macintosh environments is Appletalk. For review, see Chapter 12.

38. B. With multiple LAN's, the broadcast traffic from each LAN is sent to workstations on all LAN's, causing a lot of network bandwidth bottlenecks. A VLAN can restrict network broadcasts to its own LAN. For review, see Chapter 13.

39. D. To keep network traffic separated between the different groups, you should create three different VLAN's, one for each department. For review, see Chapter 13.

40. A. Assigning VLAN's to different ports on a hub or switch is an example of a port-based VLAN. For review, see Chapter 13.

41. C. A SAN (Storage Area Network) is a network of storage devices, such as tape drives, disk arrays, and CD storage. For review, see Chapter 14.

42. A. SCSI technology is used for high-speed storage requirements, as IDE, or DVD drives are too slow for RAID implementations. SAN is a storage area network, and is not a disk communications technology. For review, see Chapter 14.

43. B. The SCSI terminator stops the cable signal from reflecting off the end of the cable back onto the network, which can cause communications disruption. For review, see Chapter 14.

44. D. DLT technology offers tape capacities of up to 70GB of compressed data. For review, see Chapter 14.

45. C. You must test your backups on a routine basis by performing regular restores of random files. You will never know if your backups or tape hardware is working properly if you do not test them by restoring a file. For review, see Chapter 15.

46. A. RAID 1 is an example of disk mirroring, where the contents of one disk drive are mirrored onto an identical drive. If the primary drive fails, the secondary mirrored drive will take over. For review, see Chapter 15.

47. D. A UPS (Uninterruptible Power Supply) can run the system on batteries in the event of a power failure, to allow you time to properly shutdown the system. For review, see Chapter 15.

48. A. A software RAID solution cannot be used on the boot partition of a system, so a separate boot partition must be created. Unfortunately, this boot partition will not be protected with redundancy in case of failure. For review, see Chapter 15.

49. B. In order to implement a RAID 5 system, which is defined as striping with parity, you will need a minimum of three drives. Any RAID system over RAID 3 needs a minimum of three drives to maintain parity information. For review, see Chapter 15.

50. B. Using a VPN solution is typically the most cost effect and secure, as the user can use any dial-up Internet connection, no matter their location, and open a secure, encrypted channel directly the company's network. For review, see Chapter 16.

51. C. The most commonly used protocol today for RAS connections is PPP. SLIP protocol is an older protocol mostly used in Unix environments. For review, see Chapter 16.

52. D. When dialing in to a Windows-based RAS server, you can use the Windows NT/2000 account system to authenticate clients. For review, see Chapter 16.

53. A. A firewall will sit between the inside and outside networks, and provide a separate LAN called a DMZ (Demilitarized Zone), where the web server will be available to both networks. This way if the web server is compromised by an intruder, they will not be able to access the inside network. For review, see Chapter 17.

54. A. A proxy server allows multiple internal network clients to access the Internet appearing as one IP address. It also provides caching capabilities, to store frequently used data. For review, see Chapter 17.

55. C. NetBEUI is an optional, non-routable protocol used in Windows networks to communicate internally. For review, see Chapter 18.

56. B. The WINS (Windows Internet Naming Service) server is used to resolve NetBEUI host names to IP addresses. The WINS server keeps a table of these names and IP addresses, which the client can query when a name resolution is needed. For review, see Chapter 18.

57. D. To check the ability of the DNS to resolve host names, you can use the command line utility, `nslookup`, (name server lookup), to query the DNS for the IP address of a host name. For review, see Chapter 19.

58. D. To see if a server is alive and on the network, you can use the `ping` command line utility to see if the remote computer answers your `ping` request. For review, see Chapter 19.

59. C. The modem connects to the remote network without any problems, so there is no issue with the modem, protocol, or telephone line. It is most likely that the user's login or password is incorrect. For review, see Chapter 20.

60. A. If the VPN is using encryption, you need to ensure that you also have the same encryption and encryption key configured on your client software. For review, see Chapter 21.

61. B. A DHCP (Dynamic Host Configuration Protocol) server is used to automatically allocate IP addresses to client systems. For review, see Chapter 22.

62. B. The subnet mask indicated is a default Class B subnet mask, it should be 255.255.255.0. For review, see Chapter 22.

63. C. A crossover cable is used to connect two network devices or computers together. The ports on a hub automatically reverse the transmit and receive wires, so to reverse this, the crossover cable must be used. For review, see Chapter 23.

64. D. The bus network topology is most commonly used with a coaxial based Ethernet network. For review, see Chapter 24.

65. A. It is most likely that the cables between the two locations are too long. If they exceed the maximum length, the network signal will degrade. For review, see Chapter 24.

Glossary

APPENDIX D

10Base2 A type of network cable, 10Base2 Ethernet cable runs at 10 Mbps and has a maximum segment length of 185 meters. 10Base2 Ethernet cable runs on coaxial cable, also called Thinnet.

10BaseT A type of network cable, 10BaseT Ethernet networks run at 10 megabits/sec (Mbps) and have a maximum segment length of 100 meters. 10BaseT Ethernet cabling uses UTP and STP cabling.

100BaseT A type of network cable also referred to as Fast Ethernet, 100BaseT runs at 1000 Mbps and the maximum segment length is 100 meters.

1000BaseT A type of network cable also referred to as Gigabit Ethernet, 1000BaseT runs at 1 Gbps and the maximum segment length is 100 meters.

Active Detection A method of intruder detection that scans the network for possible break-ins.

antivirus Software that protects your system from computer viruses and malicious code.

Application Layer The seventh layer of the OSI model, the Application Layer handles communications between how applications access the network and describes application functionality.

application log A Windows NT log file, viewable in Even Viewer, that can keep track of events for network services and applications.

AUI Attachment Unit Interface (AUI) is typically used on Thicknet-based network cards. A transceiver on the AUI connects a Thicknet-based network cable with a 15-pin connector.

bandwidth The amount of data that can be sent across a network medium in a certain period of time.

baseband A network technology that uses single-carrier frequency. Baseband is used for short-distance transmissions. With baseband technology, the complete bandwidth of the medium is used. In contrast, a broadband transmission can support several signals on the same medium, not just one.

baseline A snapshot of the system that is created by Performance Monitor under normal operating conditions. A baseline is used to measure future abnormalities.

BIOS (Basic Input-Output System) A set of instructions performed at system startup that is stored in ROM on the system board.

bottleneck Areas on a network that can slow a computer's performance by creating a queue where processes or functions must wait to be processed or executed.

BNC connector (British Naval Connector) These types of connectors are used to connect and terminate 10Base2 coaxial network cables.

boot sector virus A computer virus that overrides a computer system's boot sector, therefore making it appear as if there is no pointer to your operating system. When a boot sector virus infects your system, you see a "Missing Operating System" or "Hard Disk not Found" error message on your screen.

bridge A device on a network that logically separates one network into segments. A bridge enables two segments to appear to be one network to higher layer protocols.

British Naval Connector See BNC Connector.

broadband A network transmission method in which the transmission medium is divided so that multiple signals can travel across the same medium simultaneously.

browser Used to view WWW pages by using the Hypertext Transfer Protocol (HTTP).

cable A network's physical transmission medium that has one or many conductors or wires protected by a plastic jacket.

CD-R Compact Disk-Recordable drives are used to create and record audio and data CDs.

central processing unit See CPU.

client/server A type of network in which all application resources are stored on a server. Each workstation accesses these resources by requesting the information from the server.

Appendix D ✦ **Glossary**

CMOS See Complementary Metal Oxide Semiconductor.

coaxial cable A type of network cable that is used in Ethernet networks. Coaxial cabling consists of a center wire surrounded by insulation and then a grounded shield of braided wire. The shield minimizes electrical and radio frequency interference.

cold site A site, such as an empty spare office, that a company has available to be used in the event of a disaster at a central network site. The cold site will need to be populated with equipment that the company provides and installs.

Complementary Metal Oxide Semiconductor (CMOS) A chip on a motherboard that stores the BIOS for the PC. When the power is off, the CMOS keeps its information by being powered by a battery.

crossover cable A modified network cable that has its transmit and receive pins reversed on one end. A crossover cable, which is also called a rollover cable, can connect two servers through a network port or connect two hubs that don't have uplink ports.

DAT (digital audio tape) A type of magnetic tape that uses a helical scan to record data.

Data-Link Layer The second layer of the OSI model, the Data-Link Layer defines the logical topology of a network. This layer is also responsible for the method of media access.

default gateway The main router or network device that is used when a network computer is sending information to outside of the current network.

DHCP (Dynamic Host Configuration Protocol) server A server that assigns a network IP address to a client when it connects to the network. With this configuration, each client workstation does not need to be set up with a static IP address. When the client computer starts, it sends a request to the DHCP server to assign it an IP address.

differential backup Backs up data that has changed since the last full backup.

Digital Audio Tape See DAT.

Digital Linear Tape See DLT.

disk duplexing Similar to disk mirroring, except disk duplexing consists of two controllers and two hard drives. (See also disk mirroring.)

disk mirroring Also known as Raid 1, disk mirroring consists of one controller and two hard drives. An exact replica of data from the primary drive exists on the mirrored drive. If the main drive fail, the mirrored drive can immediately take over, so the system can continue to run until the drive is replaced. Mirroring theoretically provides greater read speeds but slower write speeds, because it writes the data to two drives instead of one.

disk striping The most basic implementation of RAID. Known as RAID 0, disk striping is a technique in which data is spread evenly across a number of physical drives to create a large, logical volume. Although this increases performance, there is no redundancy in the case of a disk failure.

DLT (Digital Linear Tape) A type of backup tape that offers greater capacity and speeds than other types of backup tape technologies, enabling much faster backup times and greatly increasing the amount of data that can be stored on one tape.

DNS (Domain Name Service) server Keeps a database of tables that translates Internet domain names to their respective IP addresses.

download The process of transferring a file or files from one computer to another.

downtime Time wasted as a result of a malfunctioning device, computer, or network.

Dynamic Link Library (DLL) Executable Windows code that Windows programmers use so they don't have to write commonly used routines into each program.

electrostatic discharge (ESD) A discharge of static electricity when two dissimilar static electrical charges are brought together. This discharge can damage sensitive computer components, so they must be protected by using special precautions.

Ethernet The most popular network technology in use today. Ethernet is defined by the Institute for Electrical and Electronic Engineers (IEEE) as IEEE standard 802.3. It uses CSMA/CD (Carrier Sense Multiple Access/Collision Detection) to determine how network traffic flows within a network by enabling multiple devices to transmit at the same time. If more than one packet is being transmitted, this creates a collision; one of the packets must wait a period of time before being retransmitted.

event logs Log files containing events such as security and application events.

expansion slot A slot located on the computer's bus. These slots are used to plug in expansion cards to expand the functionality of the computer.

fail over In a mirrored system, when one of the disk drives crashes, the system will fail over to the mirrored drive until the original drive is replaced. The mirrored drive is an exact replica of the main drive, enabling the system to function normally until the failed drive can be replaced.

Father-Son A backup media rotation method that uses a combination of full and differential or incremental backups for a two-week schedule.

fiber-optic cable A very reliable high-speed network cable that uses light to transfer data through glass fibers.

file and print server A server that provides file and print services to clients. Client files are stored on the server. Print services enable clients to send a request to a printer, which is then queued by the print server for delivery to the final destination printer.

File Transfer Protocol See FTP.

firewall Software that helps prevent unauthorized traffic between two networks by examining the IP packets that travel on both networks and ensuring they are from authorized sources.

FTP (File Transfer Protocol) A protocol that uploads or downloads files from an FTP server to or from a client computer.

full backup A backup method that backs up all of the data on a system. Other methods such as incremental or differential backups back up only certain files, depending on the last time they were backed up.

full-duplex A communication technology that enables data to travel in both directions simultaneously.

gateway server Acts as a link between different types of networks, using a combination of hardware and software.

Grandfather A type of backup method that allows for the retention of daily, weekly, and monthly backup tapes for disaster recovery purposes.

Grandfather-Father-Son A type of backup method. Daily backups are the Son, the last full backup of the week is the Father, and the last full backup of the month is the Grandfather.

hacker A person who illegally tries to discover or destroy sensitive information by breaking into networks from a remote system.

half-duplex A type of communication technology that enables data to travel in only one direction at a time.

host adapter A SCSI technology that facilitates communications between the systems bus and the devices on the SCSI bus.

hot site An off-site location that offers full backup computing resources in the event of a physical disaster that disables the central site.

hot spare Used in RAID systems for failed drive recovery. A hot spare is used when a drive fails in any of the arrays. The hot spare will automatically replace the failed drive, without the need to stop or restart a system.

hot swap The capability to pull out and insert devices into a RAID system. After the new device has been inserted, the RAID system will continue to operate with no interruptions.

HTML See Hypertext Markup Language.

HTTP See Hypertext Transfer Protocol.

hub A central device that connects several computers and network devices on a network.

Hypertext Markup Language (HTML) The language used to format the text and graphics that will be displayed in a Web browser. HTML defines how data will be displayed.

Hypertext Transfer Protocol (HTTP) The most common network protocol used for communication between a Web server and a Web browser.

Institute of Electrical and Electronics Engineers, Inc. (IEEE) The international organization responsible for setting standards and guidelines for various electrical and electronic technologies.

incremental backup Backs up data that has changed since the last full or incremental backup.

Internet A large number of individual networks interconnected to create a great global network. These individual networks are interconnected through the use of public telephone lines, cable lines, and satellites.

Internet Service Provider See ISP.

ISP (Internet Service Provider) A company that provides users and companies with access to the Internet, usually for a fee.

LAN (Local Area Network) Created when two or more computers in a limited geographic area are linked so that each computer or device can exchange and share information.

link light Found on a NIC or a hub, a link light is a small light-emitting diode (LED) that is usually green to indicate a successful connection. Sometimes the link light will display a yellow light to indicate no connection.

local area network See LAN.

log file A file that keeps a list of all errors and notices and, usually, the date and time they occurred, as well as any other pertinent information.

mail server A type of server that stores e-mail. Clients connect to the mail server by supplying their mail account information, which enables them to send and receive e-mail.

NetWare A network operating system created by Novell. Versions include 3.x, 4.x, 5.x, and 6.

network analyzer Sometimes called a sniffer; used to monitor and collect information about network data flow.

network interface card (NIC) The physical device that connects computers and other network equipment to the transmission media.

Network Layer The third layer of the OSI model, the network layer is responsible for logical addressing and for translating logical names into physical addresses. This layer controls the routing of data from source to destination and the building and dismantling of packets.

network media The physical media, such as cables, that link computers in a network.

network operating system (NOS) The software (such as Windows NT) that runs on a network server and offers file, print, and other services to clients.

NOS See network operating system.

off-site storage The method of storing backup media in a physically distant location. This will protect the company's data in the event of a disaster, such as a fire or flood in the main building. Off-site storage also improves the company's ability to resume operations.

operating system See OS.

optical media A storage medium from which data is read and to which it is written by lasers. Optical disks can store much more data, up to 6 gigabytes, than most portable magnetic media. Optical media is based on interpreting the reflections of laser light off the surface of the media.

OS (operating system) The software on a computer that basically is a set of computer instructions whose purpose is to define input and output device connections. The OS also provides instructions for the CPU to retrieve and display data.

packet A basic division of data sent over a network.

partition A section of storage area on a computer's hard disk that is like a physically separate hard drive with a unique name. A drive can have one or many partitions, depending on the intended use. This enables different operating systems to be installed on the same hard drive, because they are installed on their own separate partitions.

patch Software that is created for existing programs or operating systems to fix discovered problems.

patch panel The central wiring point for multiple devices to connect to the network.

Physical Layer The first layer of the OSI model, the Physical Layer controls the functional interface.

physical media See network media.

plug-and-play A standard created by Intel that enables components to be automatically configured when added to the computer.

POST (Power On Self Test) Tests that are built into the system BIOS that are performed at system startup.

Power On Self Test See POST.

power spike Occurs when the power level rises above normal and drops back to normal for less than a second.

power surge Occurs when the power level rises above normal and does not drop back down to normal after a few seconds.

Presentation Layer The sixth layer of the OSI model, this layer formats data (graphic-command and character-set conversion). The Presentation Layer is also responsible for data compression and data encryption and for data stream redirections.

protocol A set of rules that determines how computers or devices communicate and exchange data on the network.

proxy server A server that forwards network requests on behalf of another client or server. A proxy server is typically configured to facilitate Internet Web server requests between a client and a Web server.

RAID (Redundant Array of Independent [or Inexpensive] Disks) Used to provide fault tolerance using a configuration of multiple hard disks. Different RAID levels describe the amount and type of fault tolerance provided.

remote notification A method of notifying an offsite network technician if a problem occurs on the network.

Redundant Array of Independent (or Inexpensive) Disks See RAID.

RJ-45 connector A cable connector used for connecting and disconnecting circuits. RJ-45 connectors use an eight-wire (four-pair) system.

router A device used to connect two networks of different topologies. A router enables packets to be transmitted and received between the two networks. A router also determines the best path for data packets from source to destination.

SCSI (Small Computer System Interface) Hardware technology that enables you to connect up to seven internal or external devices.

Session Layer The fifth layer of the OSI model, this layer is responsible for how two systems establish, use, and end a communication link. The Session Layer also defines security authentication and network-naming functions that are required for applications, and it establishes, maintains, and breaks down dialogs between two stations.

Small Computer System Interface See SCSI.

SNMP (Simple Network Management Protocol) A management protocol that sends information about the health of the network to network-management consoles.

Son A backup method strategy. The Son backup method involves performing a full backup everyday.

surge protector Any device that helps protect a computer from spikes and surges in the power line.

tape drives The main device used to hold magnetic tapes to enable the computer to read and write to it.

TCP/IP (Transmission Control Protocol/Internet Protocol) The most widely used network protocol in the world and the protocol the Internet is based upon.

terminator A device that prevents a signal from bouncing off the end of a network cable. If the signal is retransmitted onto the network cabling, it will disrupt other communications being transmitted at the same time.

topology Refers to the actual shape of your local area network. Several types of network topologies exist, such as the bus, star, ring, and mesh, all with their advantages and disadvantages.

Transport Layer The fourth layer of the OSI model, this layer is responsible for checking that the data packet created in the Session Layer was received without errors.

UPS (uninterruptible power supply) A device that supplies battery power to servers in the event of a power failure.

virus A self-replicating and usually malicious code that, after it is executed, can perform harmful actions on your local computer. Viruses can originate from a variety of sources, including the Internet, e-mail, and disk media. The virus code is activated and installed on a local computer when an infected file is executed.

Windows NT A network operating system developed by Microsoft.

WINS (Windows Internet Naming Service) server A Windows NT server that runs WINS. It enables clients to resolve Windows NetBIOS names to standard Internet domain naming conventions.

✦ ✦ ✦

Index

NUMBERS

8-bit SCSI bus size, 337
10Base identifiers, 30
10Base2 standard, 31, 667
10Base5 standard, 31
10BaseF standard, 32
10BaseT standard
 described, 31–32, 667
 shielded twisted-pair cable, 32
 unshielded twisted-pair cable, 32
16-bit SCSI bus size, 337
100BaseT, 667
802 standards, 112–113
802.11 protocol, wireless networks, 615
802.11b (Wireless) standard, 33
802.3z standard, 33
1000BaseT, 667

A

A record, DNS, 170
AALs (ATM adaptation layers), 210
access permissions, NetWare, 274–275
ACK packets, DHCP, 466
ACR (Attenuation to Crosstalk Ration), wiring term, 597
Active Detection, 667
Active Directory, Windows 2000, 295–297
active hubs, 42–43
Adaptive Rate DSL. See aRDSL
Add Printer Wizard, Windows NT/2000, 293
Add User Accounts Wizard, Windows NT/2000, 293
Add/Remove Programs Wizard, Windows NT/2000, 293
Address Resolution Protocol. See ARP
ADMIN account, Novell NetWare 4.x, 263, 273
administration accounts, NetWare, 263, 273
Administrative Wizard, Windows NT/2000, 293
Administrator account, Windows NT/2000, 263
administrators, NOS duties, 263
ADSL (Asymmetric Digital Subscriber Line), 210, 511–513
advanced file attributes, NDS, 268
AFP (Apple Share) utility, Windows clients, 572
agents, SNMP, 174–175
AH (Authentication Header) protocol, IPSec, 240
AIX, UNIX version, 280
analog carrier services, 202
analog modems, 55–56
ANDing, 132
ANSI DS standard, digital carrier services, 202–203
antennas, WAP (Wireless Access Point) placement, 54–55
antivirus, 667
API (application programming interface), operating system element, 260

AppleTalk protocol, 134, 297, 450
appliances, firewall, 423
application gateways, firewalls, 427–428
Application Layer
 application gateways, 427–428
 defined, 667
 OSI model, 104–105
 proxy servers, 430–434
 TCP/IP model, 125
application log, 667
application programming interface. See API, operating system element
application protocols
 Application-Layer, 125–131
 defined, 125
 IPX/SPX, 133–134
 Network-Layer, 132–133
 OSI model, 114–115
 TCP/IP, 125
 Transport-Layer, 131
Application Specific Integrated Circuit. See ASIC chips
application-based firewalls, private networks, 191–192
Application-Layer protocols
 DHCP, 126
 DNS, 126
 FTP, 126
 HTTP (Hypertext Transfer Protocol), 127
 HTTPS (Hypertext Transfer Protocol Secure), 127
 IMAP4, 128
 NNTP, 129–130
 POP3, 128
 Secure IMAP4, 128
 Secure POP3, 128
 SMTP, 128–129
 SNMP, 130
 TELNET, 129
 TFTP, 126–127
 WINS, 127
aRDSL (Adaptive Rate DSL), 511–513
ARP (Address Resolution Protocol)
 MAC address resolution, 76–78
 Network-Layer, 132
 Windows NT/2000, 288
Arp utility, TCP/IP troubleshooting, 481–482
array, RAID element, 367
ASIC (Application Specific Integrated Circuit) chips, 42
asymmetric, 210
Asymmetric Digital Subscriber Line. See ADSL
Asynchronous Transfer Mode. See ATM
asynchronous transmission, OSI model Data Link layer, 109
asynchronously, 206

Index ✦ A–C

ATM (Asynchronous Transfer Mode)
    AALs, 210
    WANs, 208–209
    Windows 2000, 295
ATM adaptation layers. *See* AALs
attenuation, 34, 597, 619
Attenuation to Crosstalk Ration. *See* ACR, wiring term
audit policy, 294
auditing, RAS security, 387
AUI (Attachment Unit Interface) connectors, 34, 667
authentication
    CHAP, 386–387
    client connectivity, 618
    defined, 229
    encrypted, 386–387
    Kerberos, 241–244
    MS-CHAPv1, 387
    MS-CHAPv2, 387
    PAP, 387
    public networks, 187–188
    RAS security, 386
    signed data, 234
    SPAP, 387
    wireless networks, 615
Authentication Header protocol. *See* AH protocol, IPSec

B

B (bearer) channels, ISDN, 212
backbone cabling, 581
backup domain controller. *See* BDC, Windows NT/2000
backups
    copy, 360
    cost considerations, 362
    differential, 360
    disk clustering, 362
    full, 359
    incremental, 360
    off-site storage, 361
    process evaluation, 362
    restore speeds, 362
    restoring from, 361
    scheduling, 360–361
    SSP, 362
    testing, 362
    types, 359–360
balance, wiring term, 598
bandwidth, 667
bandwidth (fiber), wiring term, 598
BAP (Bandwidth Allocation Protocol), 384
base-2 numbering system, IP addressing, 81
baseband, 30, 668
baseline, 668
Basic Input-Output System. *See* BIOS
Basic Rate Interface adapter. *See* BRI ISDN adapter
bastion servers, 433–434
Bayonet Neill Concelman. *See* BNC connector

Bayonet Nut Connector. *See* BNC connector
BBS (Bulletin Board System), NNTP, 129–130
BDC (backup domain controller), Windows NT/2000, 291–292
bearer channels (B channels), ISDN, 51
binary notation, IP addressing, 81–82
BIOS (Basic Input-Output System), 668
B-ISDN (Broadband ISDN), ISDN service level, 213
bit bucket, 132
biz (business), root level domain, 169
BlackICE, personal firewall, 424
Bluetooth protocol, wireless networks, 525, 615
Bluetooth Special Interest Group, WPAN technology, 33
BNC connector (British Naval Connector), 35, 583, 668
BNC connector (Bayonet Neill Concelman), 35
BNC connector (Bayonet Nut Connector), 35
boot sector virus, 668
BOOTP (Bootstrap Protocol), 168
bottlenecks
    defined, 668
    multiple LANs, 311–312
BRI (Basic Rate Interface) ISDN adapter, 51–52, 212–213
bridges
    Collision Domain, 13
    defined, 46–47, 668
    OSI model Data Link layer, 114
    OSI model Physical layer, 114
British Naval Connector. *See* BNC connector
broadband, 668
Broadband ISDN. *See* B-ISDN, ISDN service level
broadcast domain, 46
broadcast storm
    described, 45
    Ethernet protocol, 14
broadcasts
    defined, 132
    Ethernet protocol, 14
    VLANs, 311
browser, 668
Bulletin Board System. *See* BBS, NNTP
bus topology
    advantages/disadvantages, 5–6
    coax cable, 583
    IEEE 802.3 standard, 29
    troubleshooting, 614
buses, SCSI, 337

C

cable access systems
    development history, 515–517
    DOCISI, 516
    versus DSL, 518–519
    router diagnostics, 521–522
    security concerns, 517
    troubleshooting, 519–522
cable category standards, 581
cable modems, 209

Index ✦ C

cable testers, 588–589
cables
    category standards, 581
    coax, 582–583
    color coding, 584–586
    color coding crossover, 586
    cost considerations, 34
    crosstalk issues, 34
    definitions, 597–598, 668
    distance issues, 34
    fiber-optic, 32
    inductive probe tool, 591–592
    installation logistics factor, 34
    network use, 581
    NIC supported types, 41
    optical tester tool, 593–595
    patch length restrictions, 581
    plenum-rated, 31
    punch down tool, 590–591
    shielded twisted-pair, 32
    shielding considerations, 34
    testers, 587–589
    tone generator tool, 591–592
    tool selection, 596
    transmission speed factors, 34
    twisted pair, 579–582
    unshielded twisted-pair, 32
    visual fault locator tool, 593
    wire crimper, 583–587
    wiring closet, 590
cabling
    connector problems, 619
    electromagnetic interference, 619
    installation problems, 618–619
    length restrictions, 619
    SCSI, 337
    terms, 597–598
cache
    ARP, 78
    proxy servers, 432
Caldera OpenLinux, 280
carrier, 29
Carrier Sense, Ethernet, 30
Carrier Sense Multiple Access with Collision Avoidance. *See* CSMA/CA
Carrier Sense Multiple Access with Collision Detection. *See* CSMA/CD
carrier services
    analog, 202
    defined, 201
    digital, 202–203
    DS (digital signal levels), 202–203
    E-carrier levels, 203
    T-carrier levels, 202–203
CAs (Certificate Authorities), 188, 235–238
CD
    install items to Microsoft Windows, 636
    IP Subnet Calculator, 637
    Network+ Bible Certification test engine, 637
    Network+ Certification Bible, ebook version, 637
    Observer, 637
    system requirements, 635
    troubleshooting, 637–638
CD-R, 668
CDs, network storage media, 331
CertCo, certificate-based technology, 127–128
Certificate Authorities. *See* CAs
certificate publishers, 238–239
certificates
    described, 236–238
    HTTPS, 127–128
    public networks, 188
    Secure POP3, 128
Channel Service Unit/Data Service Unit. *See* CSU/DSU
channels, ISDN, 212
CHAP (Challenge Handshake Authentication Protocol)
    RAS, 386–387
    VPNs, 194
checksum, OSI model Transport layer error checking, 106–107
choke packets, dynamic window flow control, 107
CIDR (Classless Interdomain Routing), IP addressing, 86
CIFS (Common Internet File System), Windows NT/2000, 288
ciphers, versus codes, 230–231
ciphertext, 230
circuit switching
    described, 205–206
    versus packet switching, 207–208
circuit-level firewalls, 428–429
classes, IP addressing, 83–86
Classless Interdomain Routing. *See* CIDR, IP addressing
client connectivity
    authentication, 618
    checking basics, 616
    diagnostic utilities, 616
    duplex settings, 618
    hardware problems, 616–617
    network settings, 617
    security, 618
    software problems, 617–618
    speed settings, 618
    troubleshooting protocols, 617
client ports, TCD/UDP, 142
client/server
    defined, 668
    operating systems, 261
clients
    accessing NAS device, 345
    DHCP lease periods, 467
    Macintosh, 300
    NetWare non-support, 265, 299
    RAS connection methods, 383, 385
    reserved, 467
    UNIX/Linux, 300
    WAP, 54
    Windows, 298–299

clustering
  defined, 52
  parallel processing, 342
CMOS (Complementary Metal Oxide Semiconductor), 669
CNAME (canonical name) record, 170
coaxial (coax) cable
  AUI, 34
  BNC connector, 35
  bus topology, 5–6
  defined, 582–283, 669
  star topology, 6–7
  T-carrier systems, 202
codes, versus ciphers, 230–231
cold site, 669
collision detection, Ethernet devices, 13–14
collision domain
  Ethernet devices, 13
  hubs, 43
  switches, 44–46
collisions, Ethernet, 30
color coding
  crossover cables, 586
  twisted-pair cables, 584–585
com (commercial), root level domain, 169
COM (communication) ports, modem connections, 55–56
commands
  ARP, 78
  PING, 132
  SNMP, 175–176
  UNIX/Linux, 285
Common Internet File System protocol. *See* CIFS, Windows NT/2000
communication protocols
  Ethernet, 10–11
  Ethernet 802.2, 11
  Ethernet 802.3, 12
  FDDI, 17–18
  IEEE 802.11b (Wireless), 16–17
  IEEE 802.5, 14–15
community strings, SNMP, 176
compatibility, Windows NT/2000, 290
Complementary Metal Oxide Semiconductor. *See* CMOS
compression
  LZJH, 508
  modem communications, 506–507
computer names, NetBIOS conventions, 452–453
concentrator (hubs)
  described, 42–44
  OSI model Physical layer, 114
  troubleshooting, 620
configurations, VLANs, 316–319
connectionless services, LLC layer, 111
connections
  DSL troubleshooting, 514–515
  modem troubleshooting, 508–511
  modem types, 55–56
  POTS, 504–506
  three-way handshake, 131

connectivity, wireless networks, 615
connectors
  AUI, 34
  BNC, 35, 583, 668
  coax cable, 583
  NIC supported types, 41
  RJ-11, 34
  RJ-45, 32, 34
ConsoleOne, NetWare 5.x, 267
container objects, NDS, 269–270
Control Panel
  creating a dial-up connection, 401–404
  remote client protocol installation, 390–391
  RRAS configuration, 391–401
conversions
  binary to decimal, 83
  CIDR to standard notation, 86–87
  decimal to binary, 82–83
  hex and decimal, 73–75
  standard notation to CIDR, 86
copy backups, 360
Corel Linux, 280–281
CPE (Customer Premise Equipment), DSL networks, 511
CRCs (cyclic redundancy checks), OSI model Transport layer, 105–107
crossover cables
  color coding, 586
  defined, 669
  multiple hubs, 44
cross-platform file sharing, NAS, 344
crosstalk, 32
cryptography, 187, 231–234
CSMA/CA (Carrier Sense Multiple Access with Collision Avoidance), 16
CSMA/CD (Carrier Sense Multiple Access with Collision Detection)
  described, 13
  Ethernet access method, 29–30
CSU/DSU (Channel Service Unit/Data Service Unit), 50–51
Customer Premise Equipment. *See* CPE, DSL networks
customization, UNIX/Linux, 278
cut-through data transport, 46
cyclic redundancy checks (CRCs), OSI model Transport layer, 105–106

D

D (data) channels, ISDN, 212
daemons, NFS, 559–560
DAS (direct-attached storage)
  described, 342
  media, 342
  network problems, 342–343
DAT (digital audio tape), 333, 669
data buffering, modem communications, 507
data channel (D channel), ISDN, 51
data communication cabling, 579
Data Encryption Algorithm. *See* DEA, DES encryption

Data Link Control. *See* DLC
Data Link Layer
    ATM protocol, 209
    OSI model, 110–113
Data Over Cable Service Interface Specification. *See* DOCSIS
data shredding, NetWare 6.x, 268
data storage
    basic requirements, 329–330
    DAS, 342–343
    NAS, 343–347
    network storage media, 330–334
    parallel processing, 341–342
    server-attached storage, 342
    SAN, 347–349
    storage controller interfaces, 334–341
data transport, switches, 45–46
datagrams
    PDUs, 101–103
    UDP, 131
Data-Link Layer
    defined, 669
    devices, 49–50
DDNS (Dynamic Domain Name Server), Windows 2000, 295
DDS (Digital Data Storage) tape media, 333
DEA (Data Encryption Algorithm), DES encryption, 234
Debian GNU/Linux, 281
decryption, 187, 230
default gateway
    defined, 669
    Windows NT/2000 configuration, 554
default route, 49
Demilitarized Zone. *See* DMZ, firewalls
demo versions, 637
demultiplexer, 204
DES encryption, 234
device IDs, MAC address, 79
DEX-Intel-Xerox standard. *See* DIX standard, Ethernet development history
DHCP (Dynamic Host Configuration Protocol)
    ACK packets, 466
    described, 465, 669
    DORA, 466
    environment options, 466
    IP address ranges, 167–168, 465–466
    lease periods, 167–168, 467
    node types, 466–467
    reserved clients, 467
    RFC 1542, 126
    scope, 465, 467
    supported server types, 465
    TCP/IP configuration, 555
    Windows 2000, 295
DHCP Relay Agent, ports, 126
diagnostic utilities, client connectivity, 616
dial-up connections
    configuration settings, 404–407
    New Connection Wizard, 401–404
dial-up networking, RAS configuration, 401–407

differential backup, 360, 669
Diffie-Hellman encryption, 234
digit, 10Base identifier, 30
digital audio tape. *See* DAT
digital carrier services, 202–203
digital certificates, 236–238
Digital Data Storage. *See* DDS tape media
Digital Linear Tape. *See* DLT
digital signal. *See* DS levels
digital signatures
    defined, 188
    signed data, 234
Digital Subscriber Line. *See* DSL
Digital Subscriber Line Access Multiplexer. *See* DSLAM
digital verification, public networks, 187–188
direct-attached storage. *See* DAS
Discover/Offer/Request/Acknowledgement. *See* DORA, DHCP
Disk Administrator, Windows NT/2000, 294
disk clustering, backups, 362
disk duplexing
    defined, 669
    RAID 1, 369–370
disk mirroring, 670
disk striping
    defined, 670
    RAID method, 368–369
disks, RAID element, 367
DIX (DEX-Intel-Xerox) standard, Ethernet development history, 29
DLC (Data Link Control)
    nonroutable protocol, 450
    Windows NT/2000, 288
DLL (Dynamic Link Library), 670
DLT (Digital Linear Tape)
    defined, 670
    tape media, 334
DMA channels, NIC requirements, 41
DMZ (Demilitarized Zone), firewalls, 425
DNAS, NAS implementation, 347
DNS (Domain Name Service)
    described, 463–464, 670
    network service, 168–170
    Novell NetWare Server, 569
    Port 53, 151
    TCP/IP client configuration, 460
    upper-layer protocol, 126
DOCSIS (Data Over Cable Service Interface Specification), 516
documentation, troubleshooting resource, 621
domain controllers
    Windows 2000, 297
    Windows NT/2000, 291–292
domain groups, Windows NT/2000, 292–293
Domain Name Service. *See* DNS
domains
    forest, 296
    root level, 168–169
    Windows NT/2000, 291–292

DORA (Discover/Offer/Request/Acknowledgement), DHCP, 466
download, 670
downtime, 670
drives, adding SCSI, 338
DS (digital signal) levels, 202–203
DSL (Digital Subscriber Line)
    advantages, 513–514
    aRDSL, 511–513
    ASDL, 511–513
    versus cable access systems, 518–519
    cable length considerations, 513
    CPE, 511
    described, 210
    development history, 511
    drawbacks, 513
    DSLAM, 210, 511
    ISDN DSL (IDSL), 511–513
    line splitters, 514
    microfilters, 514
    SDSL, 511–513
    troubleshooting xDSL, 514–515
DSLAM (Digital Subscriber Line Access Multiplexer), 210, 511
dumb terminals, UNIX/Linux, 279
duplex settings, client connectivity, 618
DVDs
    versus CDs, 331–332
    formats, 332
    network storage media, 331–332
Dynamic Host Configuration Protocol. *See* DHCP
Dynamic Link Library. *See* DLL
dynamic routing, 48–49
dynamic window, flow control, 107

E

EAP (Extensible Authentication Protocol), 384
ebook version, *Network+ Certification Bible*, CD, 637
E-carrier levels, digital carrier services, 203
e-commerce
    authentication, 229
    encryption/decryption, 230–235
    non-repudiation, 230
    PKI, 235–239
    private networks, 189–194
    public networks, 187–188
    secure data concept, 230
    VPNs, 194
edu (education), root level domain, 169
EIA/TIA (Electronic Industries Association/Telecommunications Industry Association)
    shielded twisted pair cable, 32
    twisted-pair cables, 579–582
    unshielded twisted-pair cable, 32
EIA/TIA-568A standard for category cabling, 579
EIA/TIA-568B standard, cable color coding, 584–585
EIDE (Enhanced Integrated Data environment) controller, 335
8-bit SCSI bus size, 337

802 standards, 112–113
802.11 protocol, wireless networks, 615
802.11b (Wireless) standard, 16–17, 33, 523
802.15 standard, 33
802.3 standard, 29, 583
802.3z standard, 33
802.5 standard, 14–15
electromagnetic interference. *See* EMI, troubleshooting cables
electrostatic discharge. *See* ESD
ELFEXT (Equal Level Far End Crosstalk), wiring term, 597
e-mail
    POP3, 128
    product technical support, 622–623
EMI (electromagnetic interference), troubleshooting cables, 619
Encapsulating Security Payload protocol. *See* ESP protocol, IPSec
encrypted authentication, RAS security, 386–387
encryption
    ciphers versus codes, 230–231
    DEA, 234
    defined, 187, 230
    DES, 234
    Diffie-Hellman, 234
    digital certificates, 236–238
    Kerberos, 241–244
    key cryptography, 231–234
    key escrows, 234
    public networks, 187
    public-key cryptography, 231–234
    RSA (Rivest-Shamir-Adleman), 234
    Secure IMAP4, 128
    secure-key cryptography, 231
    session key, 234
    signed data, 234
    sockets, 235
    wireless networks, 615
endpoint 235
Enhanced Integrated Data environment. *See* EIDE controller
EPROM (electronic PROM), MAC address, 73
Equal Level Far End Crosstalk. *See* ELFEXT, wiring term
error checking, OSI model Transport layer, 105–107
error correction, modem communications, 507
error identification, switches, 45
ESD (electrostatic discharge), 670
ESP (Encapsulating Security Payload) protocol, IPSec, 240
Ethernet 802.2 protocol, development history, 11
Ethernet 802.3 protocol, development history, 12
Ethernet networks
    10Base identifiers, 30–32
    802.2 standard, 11
    802.3 standard, 12, 29
    access methods, 29–30
    AUI, 34
    broadcast form, 14
    broadcast storms, 14
    bus topology, 5–6

Index ✦ E–F

cabling considerations, 33–34
carrier detection, 29–30
Carrier Sense, 29–30
Collision Detect, 30
Collision Domain, 13
CSMA/CD, 13, 29–30
defined, 670
development history, 10–11, 29
frame (packet) data transmission, 12–12
NIC speed mixing, 42
RJ-45 connector, 34
evaluations version, 637
Event Logging, remote connectivity diagnostics, 543
event logs, 670
Event Viewer, Windows NT/2000, 294
exams
    objectives, 640–646
    sample, 648–666
expansion slot, 670
exponent notation, IP addressing, 81
extended file attributes, NetWare, 274–275
Extensible Authentication Protocol. *See* EAP
external modems, serial port connection, 55–56
extranet VPN, 408

F

Fail-over
    defined, 670–671
    fault tolerance, 364
    proxy servers, 432
Fast SCSI, 340
Fast Token Ring networks, 15
Father-Son, 671
fault tolerance
    defined, 362
    fail-over, 364
    hardware, 364–365
    latency, 363–364
    load balancing, 363
    MTBF, 364
    network, 365
    power, 366
    software, 364
    surge suppressors, 366
    UPS, 366
FDDI (Fiber Distributed Data Interface) protocol, 17–18, 211
FDDI-II (Fiber Distributed Data Interface II), 211
FDM (Frequency Division Multiplexing), 205
Fiber Channel storage controller interface, 340–341
fiber-optic cables
    defined, 671
    Ethernet media, 29
    FDDI, 211
    star topology, 6–7
    T-carrier systems, 202
    testing, 593–595
Fiber-optic Ethernet, 10BaseF standard, 32

file and print server, 671
file attributes, NetWare, 274–275
file servers, limitations as storage, 342–343
file services
    Linux server configuration, 559–563
    NFS client configuration, 562
    NFS server configuration, 561–562
    Windows NT/2000 configuration, 551–558
file systems
    NetWare, 270–272
    NTFS, 287
    UNIX/Linux, 284
File Transfer Protocol. *See* FTP
files, cross-platform sharing, 344
filters
    application gateways, 427–428
    circuit-level firewalls, 428–429
    firewall methods, 426–429
    inherited fights, 274
    packet, 426–427
    RAS, 387
    routers, 48
    stateful inspection, 429
firewalls
    application gateways, 427–428
    application-based, 191–192
    circuit-level, 428–429
    dedicated hardware devices, 423
    defined, 422, 671
    DMZ, 425
    filter method comparisons, 430
    IP spoofing, 424
    NAT box, 171, 424
    packet filters, 426–427
    packet-filtering, 190–191
    personal, 424
    port 80 (HTTP) blocking, 153
    private networks, 189–192
    proxy server, 427–428
    purpose of, 421–422
    routers, 423
    shortcomings, 422–433
    software-based, 424
    stateful inspection, 429
    system security, 153–154
floppy disks, network storage media, 330
flow control
    modems, 507
    OSI model Transport layer communications, 107
forest, 296
formats
    DVD, 332
    tape media, 333
Fox and Hound tool, 591–592
FPNW (file and print services for NetWare), 558
FQDN (Fully Qualified Domain Name), 127
fractional T-1 carrier, 211

frame relay, 211–212
frames
    Ethernet data transmission method, 12–13
    PDUs, 101–103
freeware programs, 637
Frequency Division Multiplexing. *See* FDM
FTP (File Transfer Protocol)
    defined, 126, 671
    Ports 20, 21, 151
FTP Services
    IntranetWare utility, 266
    Novell NetWare Server, 569–570
full backup, 360, 671
full Mesh topology, 8
full-duplex, 671
Fully Qualified Domain Name. *See* FQDN

G

GA27-3773-1 (standard spec), IBM technical interface, 579
gateway server, 671
Gateway Services for NetWare. *See* GSNW
gateways
    application, 427–428
    described, 50
    Windows NT/2000 configuration, 554
Generic Routing Encapsulation. *See* GRE, VPN
Gigabit Ethernet, 802.3z standard, 33
global white pages database. *See* X.500 Directory Service standard
gov (government), root level domain, 169
Grandfather, 671
Grandfather-Father-Son, 671
graphical user interface. *See* GUI
GRE (Generic Routing Encapsulation), VPN, 407
Group Management Wizard, Windows NT/2000, 293
groups
    network sharing, 262–263
    UNIX/Linux accounts, 282
    Windows NT/2000, 292–293
GSNW (Gateway Services for NetWare), 570
guaranteed flow control, OSI model Transport layer, 107
GUI (graphical user interface)
    operating system element, 260
    UNIX/Linux, 279
    Windows NT/2000, 289–290

H

hackers
    defined, 671
    IP spoofing, 424
    malicious, 259
    port scanner issues, 153
half-duplex, 671
handshaking, modem communications, 506–507
hard drives, network storage media, 331
hardware
    client connectivity, 616–617
    fault tolerance, 364–365
    manual, 621
    RAID, 370
    RAS, 389
    Windows 2000 VPN, 409–410
hash, 230
HD-ROM (high-density read-only memory) storage media, 335
headers
    PDUs, 101
    start-of-frame, 15
Hewlett Packard
    HP Open View, 130
    HP-UX, 280
hexadecimal notation, MAC address, 73–75
high-density read-only memory. *See* HD-ROM storage media
home networks, ICS, 172–174
HomeRF (Home Radio Frequency), wireless connections, 525
hop, 49
host adapter, 672
host (node) ID, IP addressing, 83–84
hosts
    defined, 73
    IP address identification, 87–90
    MAC address, 73–80
    NetBIOS name resolution, 462
    RAS intermediary security, 387
    VPN server connection troubleshooting, 542–543
hot site, 672
hot spare, 672
hot swap, 56, 672
Hotmail, POP3 support, 128
HP-UX, UNIX version, 280
HTML (Hypertext Markup Language), 672
HTTP (Hypertext Transfer Protocol)
    defined, 127, 672
    Port 80, 151
HTTPS (HyperText Transfer Protocol Secure), 127–128
hubs
    described, 42–44
    OSI model Physical layer, 114
    troubleshooting, 620
Hughes Network Systems, LZJH compression, 508
Hypertext Markup Language. *See* HTML
Hypertext Transfer Protocol. *See* HTTP
HyperText Transfer Protocol Secure. *See* HTTPS

I

IANA (Internet Assigned Number Authority), well-known ports, 142–151
IBM
    AIX, 280
    compatibility issues, 348
    Token Ring networks, 9–10, 14–16
ICA (Independent Computing Architecture) protocol, 214–215
ICMP (Internet Control Message Protocol), 132, 284
ICS (Internet Connection Sharing), 172–174
IDE (Integrated Data environment controller), 334–336
Idem utility, Windows clients, 572
IDs, SCSI, 338

Index ✦ I

IEEE (Institute of Electrical and Electronics Engineers, Inc.)
    10Base identifiers, 30–32
    10Base2 standard, 31
    10Base5 standard, 31
    10BaseF standard, 32
    10BaseT standard, 31–32
    802 standards, 112–113
    802.11 protocol, 615
    802.11b (Wireless) standard, 16–17, 33, 523
    802.15 standard, 33
    802.3 standard, 29, 583
    802.3z standard, 33
    802.5 standard, 14–15
    defined, 672
    Ethernet protocols, 11–12
    Gigabit Ethernet, 33
    MAC address manufacturer codes, 78–79
    OSI model Data Link layer, 112–113
    POSIX (Portable Operating System Interface), 279
IETF (Internet Engineering Task Force)
    IPSec development, 240
    RFC 1542 (DHCP standards), 126
    RFCs (requests for comments), 451
Ifconfig utility, TCP/IP troubleshooting, 485–486
iFolder, NetWare 6.x, 268
IGMP (Internet Group Management Protocol), 132–133
IKE (Internet key-exchange system), IPSec, 240–241
IMAP4 (Internet Message Access Protocol Version4), 128
incremental backups, 360, 672
Independent Computing Architecture protocol.
        See ICA protocol
inductive probe tool, 591–592
info (information), root level domain, 169
infrared light, WPAN technology, 33
infrastructure, troubleshooting, 618–620
inherited rights filter, NetWare, 274
Install New Modem Wizard, Windows NT/2000, 293
installation
    cabling problems, 618–619
    CD items, 636
installation media, troubleshooting resource, 621–622
Institute of Electrical and Electronics Engineers, Inc. *See* IEEE
Integrated Data environment. *See* IDE
Integrated Services Digital Network. *See* ISDN
internal modems, COM port connections, 55–56
internal protocols, TCP/IP model, 125
International Standards Organization. *See* ISO
International Telecommunication Union. *See* ITU
Internet
    defined, 672
    PKI, 235–239
    POTS connection method, 504–506
    root level domains, 168–169
    WAN example, 201
Internet Assigned Number Authority. *See* IANA,
        well-known ports
Internet Connection Sharing. *See* ICS
Internet Control Message Protocol. *See* ICMP
Internet Engineering Task Force. *See* IETF
Internet Group Management Protocol. *See* IGMP
Internet Layer, TCP/IP model, 125
Internet mail systems, protocols, 128–129
Internet Message Access Protocol Version4. *See* IMAP4
Internet Protocol. *See* IP
Internet Protocol Security. *See* IPSec
Internet Service Providers. *See* ISP
Internet services integration, NetWare 5.x, 267
internetwork, 109, 201
Internetwork Packet Exchange protocol. *See* IPX protocol
Internetwork Packet Exchange/Sequence Packet Exchange.
        See IPX/SPX
intranets, private networks, 189, 408
I/O addresses, NIC requirements, 41
I/O overlapping, RAID benefit, 367
IP (Internet Protocol), 132
IP addresses
    cable modem security issues, 209
    DHCP ranges, 465–466
    NAT, 171–172
    ports, 131
    private networks, 189
    Windows NT/2000 configuration, 554
IP addressing
    binary notation, 81–82
    binary to decimal conversion, 83
    CIDR to standard notation conversion, 86–87
    classes, 83–86
    Classless Interdomain Routing (CIDR), 86
    decimal to binary conversion, 82–83
    described, 80–81
    host calculations, 88–89
    host (node) ID, 83–84
    host identification, 87–90
    loopback, 83
    network ID, 83–84
    network mask, 84–85
    powers of 2, 81
    router determinations, 90
    standard notation, 86
    standard notation to CIDR conversion, 86
    subnet address identification, 89–90
    subnet calculations, 88
    subnet masks, 85–86
    subnetting, 84–86
IP Security. *See* IPSec
IP spoofing, 424
IP Subnet Calculator, CD, 637
Ipconfig utility
    TCP/IP troubleshooting, 485–486
    TCP/IP verification, 555–556
IP/IPX router, RAS, 388–389
IPSec (Internet Protocol Security)
    Network Layer, 239–241
    RAS, 384
    VPN, 194, 408
    Windows 2000 configurations, 461–462

Index ✦ I–L

IPX (Internetwork Packet Exchange) protocol
   described, 133
   NetWare protocol, 272–273
IPX/SPX (Internetwork Packet Exchange/Sequence Packet Exchange)
   installation/configuration, 457–459
   internal protocols, 133–134
   routable protocol, 451
   Windows NT/2000 configuration, 556–557
IRIX, UNIX version, 280
IRQs, NIC requirements, 41
ISAKMP/Oakley protocol, 240
iSCSI, 341
ISDN (Integrated Services Digital Network)
   adapters, 51–52
   B-ISDN level, 213
   BRI level, 212–213
   PRI level, 213
   RAS connection method, 383, 385
   WAN technology, 212–213
ISDN DSL (IDSL), 511–513
ISDN terminal adapter, 51–52
ISO (International Standards Organization)
   IEEE 802.3 standard, 29
   OSI model development, 101
isochronous transmission, OSI model Data Link layer, 109
ISP (Internet Service Provider)
   defined, 672
   PPP, 216–217
   T-1 and T-3 transmission rates, 203
ITU (International Telecommunication Union)
   DOCSIS, 516
   modem standards, 506
   V.92 standards, 508

J

jumpers, modem port connections, 56

K

Kerberos, 241–244, 295
key cryptography, 231–234
key escrows, 234

L

L2F (Layer 2 Forwarding), VPN, 407
L2TP (Layer 2 Tunneling Protocol)
   RAS, 384
   security uses, 244–245
   VPN, 194, 408
L2TP Network Server. *See* LNS protocol
LAC (L2TP Access Concentrator) protocol, 244
LAN (local area network)
   10Base identifiers, 30–32
   bus topology, 5–6
   communication protocols, 10–12
   defined, 5, 672
   Fast Token Ring, 15
   FDDI protocol, 17–18
   IEEE 802.11b (Wireless) standard, 16–17
   Mesh topology, 7–9
   problems with multiple, 311–312
   ring topology, 9–10
   RJ-45 connector, 34
   star topology, 6–7
LAT (Local Area Transport), nonroutable protocol, 450
latency, fault tolerance, 363–364
Layer 2 Forwarding. *See* L2F, VPN
Layer 2 Tunneling Protocol. *See* L2TP
layers
   AALs (ATM adaptation layers), 210
   Application, 104–105
   Data Link, 110–113
   hierarchical OSI model, 103–104
   Network, 109–110
   OSI model, 103–114
   peer, 103
   Physical, 113–114
   Presentation, 105
   Session, 105
   TCP/IP model, 125
   Transport, 105–109
LDAP
   Port 389, 152
   Windows 2000, 295
leaf objects, NDS, 269–270
letter, 10Base identifier, 30
levels
   DS, 202–203
   E-carrier, 203
   ISDN, 212–213
   T-carrier, 202–204
License Wizard, Windows NT/2000, 293
line splitters, DSL connections, 514
link light, 673
Linux
   administration, 282–283
   AIX version, 280
   Caldera OpenLinux, 280
   clients, 300
   commands, 285
   Corel Linux, 280–281
   customization, 278
   Debian GNU/Linux, 281
   development history, 277–278
   dumb terminals, 279
   file systems, 284
   GUI, 279
   HP-UX version, 280
   IRIX version, 280
   LinuxPPC, 281
   Mandrake Linux, 281
   modular architecture, 278
   multitasking, 278
   multiuser capability, 278

performance, 278
permissions, 282–283
POSIX compliance, 279
printing, 283
protocols, 284
Red Hat Linux, 281
root (superuser) account, 263, 282
shell interface, 279
Slackware, 281
software support, 278
Solaris version, 280
stability, 278
SuSE, 281
TCP/IP support, 279
TurboLinux, 281
users/groups accounts, 282
utilities, 285
Yellow Dog Linux, 281
Linux servers
NFS, 559–563
proxy, 431
Samba configuration, 564
LinuxPPC, 281
LLC (logical link control) sublayer, OSI model Data Link layer, 110–112
LNS (L2TP Network Server) protocol, 244
load balancing, fault tolerance, 363
Local Area Network. *See* LAN
Local Area Transport. *See* LAT, nonroutable protocol
local groups, Windows NT/2000, 292–293
local IP address, 49
LocalTalk networks, bus topology, 5–6
log file, 673
logical link control. *See* LLC sublayer, OSI model Data Link layer
logical volumes, NetWare file system, 271–272
lookup tables, routers, 48–49
loopback addressing, 83
LZJH compression, modem communications, 508

M

MAC (Media Access Control) address
    ARP resolution 76–78
    Data Link layer, 112
    device IDs, 79
    EPROM, 73
    hexadecimal notation, 73–75
    IEEE manufacturer codes, 78–79
    name resolution, 76–78
    PROM, 73
    RARP resolution, 76–77
    Windows 98 configuration, 79–80
    Windows 2000 configuration, 79–80
Mac OS X, development history, 298
MAC OS X Server
    accessing from Windows, 572
    configuration, 571–572
Mac-address-based VLANs, 314

Macintosh
    AppleTalk, 134, 297, 450
    clients, 300
    file/print services access methods, 558–559
    MAC OS X Server, 571–572
    TokenTalk, 297
mail server, 673
mail transfers, MX record, 170
mail-drop services, protocols, 128–129
mainframes, network storage media, 334
maintenance contracts, troubleshooting resource, 623–624
malicious hackers, disaster type, 359
Management Information Base. *See* MIB format
Managing File and Folder Access Wizard, Windows NT/2000, 293
Mandrake Linux, 281
manufacturer's Web site, troubleshooting resource, 622
mapped drives, 294
MAU (multistation access unit), 14–15
MD5 (Message Digest 5) standard, CHAP, 386–387
mean time between failures. *See* MTBF, fault tolerance
Media Access Control address. *See* MAC address
media tester/certifier, using, 587–690
Mesh topology
    advantages/disadvantages, 7–9
    troubleshooting, 614
Message Digest 5. *See* MD5 standard, CHAP
MIB (Management Information Base) format
    SNMP commands, 175–176
    SNMP Management Consoles, 130
microfilters, DSL connections, 514
Microsoft Challenge Handshake Authentication Protocol V1. *See* MS-CHAPv1 protocol, RAS authentication
Microsoft Challenge Handshake Authentication Protocol V2. *See* MS-CHAPv2 protocol, RAS authentication
Microsoft Outlook Express, NNTP client, 130
Microsoft Point-to-Point Encryption. *See* MMPE
Microsoft RAS Protocol, 385
Microsoft SNMP Server, 130
Microsoft Windows
    install items from CD, 636
    ports, 152
Microsoft Windows 9x/ME, system requirements, 635
miniport drivers, RAS, 388
MMPE (Microsoft Point-to-Point Encryption), VPN, 408
MNP-5, compression protocol, 506
models, NAS, 346
modems
    cable, 209
    compression, 506–507
    configuration settings, 56–57
    data buffering, 507
    data modulation, 203
    error correction, 507
    flow control, 507
    handshaking, 506–507

Continued

modems *(continued)*
    versus ISDN terminal adapter, 51–52
    LZJH compression, 508
    MNP-5 compression protocol, 506
    PCI troubleshooting, 510–511
    proxy server connections, 431–432
    RAS connection method, 383, 385
    RTC/CTS flow control, 107
    serial-port connections, 55–56
    speed negotiation, 506–507
    speed ratings, 57
    troubleshooting, 508–511
    UARTs, 507
    USB, 56
    v.42bis compression protocol, 506
    V.92 standards, 508
modular architecture, UNIX/Linux, 278
modulation, 203
MS-CHAPv1 protocol, RAS authentication, 387
MS-CHAPv2 protocol, RAS authentication, 387
MTBF (mean time between failures), fault tolerance, 364
multicast, 132
multiple Lans, problems, 311–312
multiplexer, 204
multiplexing
    defined, 204–205
    OSI model Transport layer, 108
multiprocessor kernel, NetWare, 265
multi-protocol routing, RAS support, 384
multistation access unit. *See* MAU
multitasking
    UNIX/Linux, 278
    Windows NT/2000, 289
multiusers
    UNIX/Linux, 278
    Windows NT/2000, 289
MX record, mail transfers, 170

N

name resolution
    MAC address, 76–78
    OSI model Transport layer, 108
namespaces, NetWare, 272
NAS (network-attached storage)
    adding to network, 345
    described, 343–344
    DNAS, 347
    management, 347
    model, 346
    network benefits, 344–345
    operation, 345
    RAID, 346
    TB, 345
    technologies, 346
NAS head, 346
NAT (network address translation)
    firewalls 424
    network services, 171–172

    performance overhead, 435
    private networks, 189
natural disasters, disaster type, 359
Nbstat utility, TCP/IP troubleshooting, 484–485
NCP (NetWare Core Protocol), 133
NDAP protocol, UNIX/Linux, 284
NDIS (Network Driver Interface Specification), RAS, 388
NDS (Novell Directory Services), 267–270
Near End Crosstalk. *See* NEXT, wiring term
net (network), root level domain, 169
NetBEUI (Network Basic Input/Output System Extended User Interface)
    installation/configuration, 454–457
    legacy protocol, 288
    nonroutable protocol, 49, 450
    Windows 98 configuration, 454–456
    Windows 2000 configuration, 457
    Windows NT 4.0 configuration, 456–457
    Windows NT/2000 configuration, 557–558
NetBIOS (Network Basic Input/Output System)
    HOST name resolution, 462
    naming conventions, 452–453
    OSI model Session layer, 105
    Port 139, 152
    RAS gateway, 388
    service indicators, 462
    Session Layer transport, 452
    Windows NT/2000, 288
NetBIOS clients, WINS server configuration, 127
NetBIOS Datagrams (Port 138), 152
Netstat utility, TCP/IP troubleshooting, 483–484
NetWare
    access permissions, 274–275
    ADMIN account, 273
    administration accounts, 273
    client non-support, 299
    defined, 673
    development history, 265–268
    extended file attributes, 274–275
    file system, 270–272
    inherited rights filter, 274
    multiprocessor kernel, 265
    namespaces, 272
    NDS, 267–270
    NLMs, 265
    PCI Hot Plug support, 265
    protocols, 272–273
    SMP, 265
    SUPERVISOR account, 273
    SYS volume, 270–271
    utilities, 275–277
    versions, 265–268
NetWare 3.x
    development history, 266
    SUPERVISOR account, 263
NetWare 4.x
    ADMIN account, 263
    development history, 266

Index ✦ N

NetWare 5.x, development, 267
NetWare 6.x, development, 268
NetWare Administrator, NDS, 268
NetWare clients, file/print services access methods, 558
NetWare Core Protocol. *See* NCP
NetWare IPX/IP Gateway, IntranetWare utility, 266
NetWare Link IPX/SPX compatible protocol. *See* NWLink
NetWare Loadable Modules. *See* NLMs
NetWare Multiprotocol Router w/WAN Extensions, IntranetWare utility, 266
NetWare Web Server, IntranetWare utility, 267
network address translation. *See* NAT
network analyzer, 673
Network Basic Input/Output System. *See* NetBIOS
Network Basic Input/Output System Extended User Interface. *See* NetBEUI
network cabling, types, 581
Network Client Administrator Wizard, Windows NT/2000, 293
Network Driver Interface Specification. *See* NDIS, RAS
network fault tolerance, 365
Network File System. *See* NFS
network ID, IP addressing, 83–84
Network Information System protocol. *See* NIS protocol, UNIX/Linux
network interface card. *See* NIC
Network layer
    defined, 673
    devices, 49–50
    OSI model, 109–110
    stateful inspection, 429
    TCP/IP model, 125
Network Management System. *See* NMS
network mask, IP addressing, 84–85
network media, 673
Network Monitor, remote connectivity diagnostics, 544
Network Neighborhood, Windows NT/2000, 294
Network News Transfer Protocol. *See* NNTP
network numbers, AppleTalk protocol, 134
network operating system. *See* NOS
network protocols, OSI model, 114–115
network services
    BOOTP, 168
    DHCP, 167–168
    DNS, 168–170
    NAT/ICS, 171–174
    OSI model Application layer, 105
    SNMP, 174–176
    WINS, 170–171
network settings, client connectivity, 617
network storage media
    CDs, 331
    DVDs, 331–332
    floppy disks, 330
    hard drives, 331
    mainframes, 334
    tape media, 332–334
network topologies, 5–10
network troubleshooting, procedures, 611–613

Network+ Bible Certification test engine, CD, 637
Network+ Certification Bible, ebook version on CD, 637
network-attached storage. *See* NAS
Network-Layer protocols
    ARP, 132
    ICMP, 132
    IGMP, 132–133
    IP, 132
networks
    backups, 360–362
    cabling considerations, 33–34
    DAS problems, 342–343
    fault tolerance, 362–366
    ICS, 172–174
    NAS benefits, 344–345
    system area, 372
New Connection Wizard, 401–404
newsgroups
    described, 129
    NNTP, 129–130
NEXT (Near End Crosstalk), wiring term, 597
NFS (Network File System)
    daemons, 559–560
    Linux server file/print services, 559–563
NFS clients, file/print sharing configuration, 562
NFS server, file/print sharing configuration, 561–562
NIC (network interface card)
    defined, 41–42, 673
    OSI model Physical layer, 114
    Windows NT/2000 configuration, 552–553
NIS (Network Information System) protocol, UNIX/Linux, 284
NLMs (NetWare Loadable Modules), 265
NMS (Network Management System), 174–176
NNTP (Network News Transfer Protocol), 129–130
node (host) ID, IP addressing, 83–84
non-repudiation, 230
nonroutable protocols, 449–450
NOS (network operating system)
    defined, 259, 673
    administrator user duties, 263
    client/server, 259, 261
    directory schema, 264
    IntranetWare, 266–267
    Mac OS X, 298
    Macintosh, 297–298
    NetWare 3.x, 266
    NetWare 4.x, 266
    NetWare 5.x, 267
    NetWare 6.x, 268
    Novell NetWare, 262, 265–277
    peer-to-peer, 259, 261
    protocols, 264
    TCP/IP protocol, 264
    UNIX/Linux, 262, 277–285
    UNIX/Linux clients, 300
    user/group sharing, 262–263

Continued

NOS (network operating system) *(continued)*
    Windows clients, 298–299
    Windows NT/2000, 262, 286–297
    Windows XP, 287
    X.500 Directory Service standard, 264
Novell Directory Services. *See* NDS
Novell Internet Printing, NetWare 6.x, 268
Novell NetWare. *See* NetWare
Novell NetWare Server
    accessing from Windows, 570
    DNS, 569
    FTP services, 569–570
    GSNW, 570
    networking protocols, 567–568
Nslookup utility, TCP/IP troubleshooting, 487–488
NTFS (NT File System), Windows 2000, 287, 295
NTP (Port 123), 152
NWLink (NetWare Link IPX/SPX compatible protocol)
    installation/configuration, 457–459
    Windows NT/2000 configuration, 288, 556–557

O

objectives, exam, 640–646
objects, 268–270
Observer, CD, 637
octets, 80
off-site storage
    backup advantages, 361
    defined, 673
100BaseT, 667
1000BaseT, 667
Open Shortest Path First protocol. *See* OSPF protocol
open standards, versus proprietary, 348
Open System Interconnection Reference Model.
        See OSI model
operating system. *See* OS
optic connections, testing, 593–595
optical media, 673
optical testers, using, 593–595
org (organization), root level domain, 169
OS (operating system)
    application service management, 260
    defined, 674
OSI model (Open System Interconnection Reference Model)
    Application layer, 104–105
    Data Link layer, 110–113
    described, 101–103
    International Standards Organization (ISO)
        development, 101
    layers, 103–114
    Network layer, 109–110
    PDUs, 101–103
    peer layer, 103
    Physical layer, 113–114
    Presentation layer, 105
    protocols, 114–115, 125–133
    Session layer, 105
    Transport layer, 105–109
OSPF (Open Shortest Path First) protocol, 48–49

P

packet filters, firewalls, 426–427
packet fragmentation, IP, 132
Packet Internet Grouper (PING) command, ICMP, 132
packet switching
    versus circuit switching, 207–208
    described, 206–207
packet-filtering firewalls, private networks, 190–191
packet-level interfaces, RAS, 388
packets
    ACK, 466
    choke, 107
    defined, 190, 674
    Ethernet data transmission method, 12–13
    packet-filtering firewalls, 190–191
    PDUs, 101–103
    PPTP filtering, 387
    sequencing, 108
    TTL, 132
PAP (Password Authentication Protocol), 387
parallel processing, data storage, 341–342
parity bits, OSI model Transport layer error checking, 106
parity data, RAID, 368
partial Mesh topology, 8
partition, 674
passive hubs, 42–43
Password Authentication Protocol. *See* PAP
passwords
    PAP, 387
    secure-key cryptography, 231
    SPAP, 387
patch, 674
patch panel
    defined, 674
    uses, 590
PC MACLAN utility, Windows clients, 572
PCI (Peripheral Component Interconnect)
    Hot Plug, NetWare support, 265
    modems, troubleshooting, 510–511
    NICs, 41
PDC (primary domain controller), Windows NT/2000, 291–292
PDUs (protocol data units), OSI model, 101–103
peer layer, 103
peer-to-peer operating systems, 261
performance
    security overhead, 435–437
    UNIX/Linux advantages, 278
Performance Monitor, Windows NT/2000, 294
Peripheral Component Interconnect. *See* PCI
permissions
    NetWare, 274–275
    UNIX/Linux, 282–283

personal firewalls, 424
personal operating space. *See* POS
physical circuits, versus virtual circuits, 205
Physical Layer
    defined, 674
    OSI model, 113–114
physical media, 674
physical volumes, NetWare file system, 271–272
Ping utility
    connectivity testing, 556
    TCP/IP troubleshooting, 477–479
PKI (public-key infrastructure)
    CAs (certificate authorities), 235–238
    certificate publishers, 238–239
    digital certificates, 236–238
    key administration, 235
    key publishing, 235
    key utilization, 235
places, 73
plain old telephone system. *See* POTS
plenum-rated cables, Teflon Belden 89880, 31
plenums 31
Plug-and-Play technology
    defined, 674
    modems, 55–56
    NIC support, 41
    Windows 2000, 295
point-to-LAN remote-access connection, 383, 385
Point-to-Point Protocol. *See* PPP
Point-to-Point Tunneling Protocol. *See* PPTP
POP3 (Post Office Protocol), 128
POP/IMAP (Ports 110, 143), 152
port 23 (Telnet), 151
port 25 (SMTP), 152
port 53 (DNS), 151
port 80 (HTTP), 151
port 123 (NTP), 152
port 137 (WINS), 152
port 138 (NetBIOS Datagrams), 152
port 139 (NetBIOS Session), 152
port 389 (LDAP), 152
port scanners, system audit, 153
Portable Operating System Interface. *See* POSIX, UNIX/Linux compliance
port-based VLANs, 314
ports
    DHCP Relay Agent, 126
    DNS (Port 53), 151
    firewalls, 153–154
    FTP (Ports 20, 21), 151
    HTTP (Port 80), 151
    IP address, 131
    LDAP (Port 389), 152
    Microsoft Windows, 152
    NetBIOS Datagrams (Port 138), 152
    NetBIOS Session (Port 139), 152
    NTP (Port 123), 152
    POP/IMAP (Ports 110, 143), 152
    Private/Dynamic, 142–143
    Registered, 142–143
    securing methods, 152–154
    serial, 55–56
    service/application updates, 154
    shutting down unused, 152–153
    SMTP (Port 25), 152
    system audit, 153
    TCP/UDP, 141–151
    Telnet (Port 23), 151
    up-link, 44
    well-known, 142–151
    WINS, 127, 152
ports 20 and 21 (FTP), 151
ports 110 and 143 (POP/IMAP), 152
POS (personal operating space), 33
POSIX (Portable Operating System Interface), UNIX/Linux compliance, 279
POST (Power On Self Test), 674
Post Office Protocol version 3. *See* POP3
POTS (plain old telephone system)
    advantages/disadvantages, 505–506
    analog signals, 202
    described, 504–506
    troubleshooting, 508–511
power conditioners, fault tolerance, 366
power fault tolerance, 366
Power On Self Test. *See* POST
power spike, 674
power surge, 674
powers of 2, IP addressing, 81
PPP (Point-to-Point Protocol)
    RAS connection method, 216–217, 385
    SOHO, 503–504
PPTP (Point-to-Point Tunneling Protocol)
    RAS connection method, 217, 383, 385, 387
    VPN, 194, 408
PPTP filtering, RAS, 387
Presentation Layer
    defined, 674
    OSI model, 105
PRI (Primary Rate Interface) ISDN adapter, 51, 213
primary domain controller. *See* PDC, Windows NT/2000
print services
    Linux server configuration, 559–563
    NFS client configuration, 562
    NFS server configuration, 561–562
    Windows NT/2000 configuration, 551–558
printing, UNIX/Linux, 283
privacy. *See also* security
    authentication, 229
    defined, 229
    encryption/decryption, 230–235
    non-repudiation, 230
    PKI, 235–239
    secure data concept, 230
    signed data, 234

private networks
  advantages/disadvantages, 192–193
  application-based firewalls, 191–192
  defined, 189
  firewalls, 189–192
  packet-filtering firewalls, 190–191
  versus public networks, 193
  virtual, 194
private virtual circuit. *See* PVC, frame relay
Private/Dynamic ports, 142–143
private-key cryptography, public networks, 187
products, return/replace, 623
PROM (Programmable Read Only Memory), MAC address, 73
Propagation delay & delay skew, wiring term, 597–598
protocol data units. *See* PDUs, OSI model
protocol-based VLANs, 315
protocols
  802 standards, 11, 112–113
  802.11 protocol, wireless networks, 615
  802.11b (Wireless), 16–17, 33
  802.15, 33
  802.2, 11
  802.3, 12, 29
  802.3z standard, 33
  802.5, 14–15
  AH, 240
  AppleTalk, 134, 297, 450
  application, 125–134
  Application-Layer, 125–131
  ARP, 76–78, 132, 288
  ATM, 208–209
  BAP, 384
  BOOTP, 168
  CHAP, 194, 386–387
  CIFS, 288
  client connectivity, 617
  compression, 506
  CSMA/CA, 13, 16
  CSMA/CD 29–30
  defined, 10, 674
  DHCP, 126, 167–168, 465–468
  DIX, 29
  DLC, 288, 450
  DNS, 126
  EAP, 384
  ESP, 240
  Ethernet, 10–11
  FTP, 126
  GRE, 407
  HTTP (Hypertext Transfer Protocol), 127
  HTTPS (Hypertext Transfer Protocol Secure), 127–128
  ICA, 214–215
  ICMP, 132, 284
  IGMP, 132–133
  IMAP4, 128
  Internet mail systems, 128–129
  IP, 132
  IPSec, 194, 239–241, 384, 408
  IPX, 133, 272–273
  IPX/SPX, 133–134, 451, 556–557
  ISAKMP/Oakley, 240
  Kerberos, 241–244
  L2F, 407
  L2TP, 194, 244–245, 384, 408
  LAC, 244
  LAT, 450
  LNS, 244
  Microsoft RAS Protocol, 386
  MMPE, 408
  MNP-5, 506
  MS-CHAPv1, 387
  MS-CHAPv2, 387
  NAS use, 346
  NCP, 133
  NDAP, 284
  NetBEUI, 49, 288, 450, 557–558
  NetBIOS, 105, 288, 452–453
  NetWare, 272–273
  Network-Layer, 132–133
  NIS, 284
  NNTP, 129–130
  nonroutable, 49, 449–450
  NOS, 264
  NWLink (NetWare Link IPX/SPX compatible protocol), 288, 556–557
  OSI model, 114–115, 125–133
  OSPF, 48–49
  PAP, 387
  POP3, 128
  PPP, 216–217, 385, 503–504
  PPTP, 194, 217, 383, 385, 408
  RADIUS, 384
  RARP, 76–77
  RAS, 390–391
  RAS supported types, 384
  remote access, 214–218
  RIP, 48–49, 288, 388
  routable, 450–451
  RPCs, 105
  SAP, 134
  Secure IMAP4, 128
  Secure POP3, 128
  Services for Macintosh, 288
  SLIP, 216–218, 385, 504
  SMB, 563–567
  SMTP, 128–129
  SNA, 49
  SNMP, 130–131, 174–176
  SOHO, 503–504
  SPAP, 387
  SPX, 133, 272–273
  SPXII, 133
  SSL, 245–247
  TCP, 126, 131

Index ✦ P–R

TCP/IP, 125, 264, 288, 451, 554–556
TELNET, 129
TFTP, 126–127
TokenTalk, 297
Transport-Layer, 131
TSL Handshake, 247
TSL Record, 247
UDP, 131, 284
UNIX/Linux, 284
v.42bis, 506
VPN, 407–408
Windows NT/2000, 287–289
WINS, 127, 288
wireless networks, 615
XNS, 451
proxy servers
    bastion server, 433–434
    cache capabilities, 432
    dedicated hardware devices, 431
    described, 430–433, 675
    fail over, 432
    filtering rules, 431
    firewalls, 427–428
    modem connection methods, 431–432
    traffic inspection methods, 431
Proxy/Application Gateway servers, security overhead, 435–436
PSTN (Public Switched Telephone Network)
    analog signals, 202
    RAS connection method, 385
public address, 49
public key infrastructure. *See* PKI
public networks
    advantages/disadvantages, 188
    defined, 187
    versus private networks, 193
Public Switched Telephone Network. *See* PSTN
public-key cryptography, 187, 231–234
punch down tool, using, 590–591
PVC (private virtual circuit), frame relay, 211
PVC Belden 9880, plenum-rated cable, 31

R

RADIUS (Remote Authentication Dial-In User Service), 384
RAID (Redundant Array of Independent [or Inexpensive] Disks)
    described, 366–367, 675
    development history, 370
    disk duplexing, 369–370
    disk mirroring, 370
    hardware versus software, 370
    I/O overlapping, 367
    parity, 368
    striping, 368–369
    types, 370–372
RARP (Reverse Address Resolution Protocol), MAC address, 76–77
RAS (Remote Access Service)
    auditing, 387
    callback doesn't work, 540
    callback support, 387
    CHAP, 386–387
    client connection methods, 383, 385
    components, 388
    connection cannot be established, 538–539
    described, 383
    dial-in utility, 383
    dial-out capability, 383
    dial-up networking configuration, 401–407
    hardware requirements, 389
    IP/IPX router, 388–389
    Microsoft RAS Protocol, 386
    mimiport drivers, 388
    MS-CHAPv1 protocol, 387
    MS-CHAPv2 protocol, 387
    multi-protocol routing, 384
    NDIS, 388
    NetBIOS gateway, 388
    packet-level interfaces, 388
    PAP, 387
    PPP, 385
    PPTP filtering, 387
    remote client types, 384
    remote-client protocol installation, 390–391
    resources beyond RAS server cannot be accessed, 539–540
    RRAS MMC, 394–401
    security, 384–387
    SLIP, 385
    SPAP, 387
    supported protocols, 384
    troubleshooting, 537–540
    VPN server configuration, 409–411
    WAN connectivity, 384–385
    Windows NT/2000, 21, 294
    Windows 2000 server RRAS configuration settings, 391–401
RDMA (Remote Direct Memory Access), SAN network cards, 52
Read Only community string, SNMP, 176
read operation, NMS, 175–176
ReadMe files, troubleshooting resource, 621
Read-Write community string, SNMP, 176
Ready To Send/Clear To Send. *See* RTC/CTS, OSI model Transport layer
Red Hat Linux, 281
redundant, RAID element, 367
Redundant Array of Independent (or Inexpensive) Disks. *See* RAID
Registered ports, 142–143
remote access, 383
Remote Access Microsoft Management Console. *See* RRAS MMC

remote access protocols
    ICA, 214–215
    PPP, 216–217
    PPTP, 217
    SLIP, 216–218
Remote Access Service. *See* RAS
Remote Authentication Dial-In User Service. *See* RADIUS
remote clients
    RAS protocol installation, 390–391
    RAS types, 384
    WAN connectivity, 384–385
remote connectivity
    RAS, 383–407, 537–540
    SOHO connection methods, 502
    VPN, 407–411
    Windows 2000 utilities, 543–544
remote controls, SOHO connections, 502
Remote Direct Memory Access. *See* RDMA,
        SAN network cards
remote nodes, SOHO connections, 502
remote notification, 675
remote procedure calls. *See* RPCs, 105
remote-access servers, 383
remote-access VPN, 408
repeaters, OSI model Physical layer, 114
replicas, NDS, 268
requests for comments. *See* RFCs, OSI model Session layer
resolution
    FQDN, 127
    NetBIOS clients, 127
    NetBIOS-to-HOST-name, 462
resources, troubleshooting, 620–624
Return Loss, wiring term, 597
Reverse Address Resolution Protocol. *See* RARP,
        MAC address
reverse engineering, Linux development history, 277
RFCs (requests for comments), RFC 1542 (DHCP
        standards), 126
ring topology
    advantages/disadvantages, 9–10
    troubleshooting, 613–614
RIP (Routing Information Protocol)
    dynamic routing, 48–49
    IP/IPX router, 388
    Windows NT/2000, 288
Rivest-Shamir-Adleman encryption. *See* RSA encryption
RJ-11 (Registered Jack-11) connectors, 34
RJ-45 (Registered Jack-45) connectors
    10BaseT standard, 32
    defined, 34, 675
roaming, WAP, 54
root (superuser) account, UNIX/Linux, 263, 282
root level domains, 168–169
root object, NDS, 269–270
routable protocols, 450–451
routers
    bridges, 49–50
    cable access system troubleshooting, 521–522
    Collision Domain, 13
    defined, 48, 675
    firewall capabilities, 423
    IP address determinations, 90
    IP/IPX, 388–389
    network components, 48–50
    OSI model Network layer, 114
    private networks, 189
    RFC 1542 (DHCP standards), 126
    switches, 49–50
    troubleshooting, 620
Routing and Remote Access Server Setup Wizard, 392–394
Routing Information Protocol. *See* RIP
RPCs (remote procedure calls), OSI model Session layer, 105
RRAS (Routing and Remote Access)
    enabling, 391–401
    Routing and Remote Access Server Setup Wizard, 392–394
    RRAS MMC, 394–401
    Windows 2000 server configuration settings, 391–401
    Windows 2000 startup, 389–390
RRAS MMC (Remote Access Microsoft Management
        Console), 394–401
RSA (Rivest-Shamir-Adleman) encryption, 234
RTC/CTS (Ready To Send/Clear To Send), OSI model
        Transport layer, 107

S

SAM (Security Accounts Manager), Windows NT/2000, 291
Samba
    accessing from Windows, 567
    configuration file settings, 564–566
    netconf utility, 566
    SMB protocol configuration, 563–567
    suite components, 563
    SWAT utility, 566
Samba Web Administration Tool. *See* SWAT
SAN (Storage Area Network)
    benefits, 348
    dangers, 349
    described, 347
    lack of standardization, 348
    proprietary technologies, 348
SAN (system-area network), 52, 372
SAN NICs (system-area network cards), 52–53
SAP (Service Advertising Protocol), 134
satellite Internet systems, 522–523
scanners, port, 153
schema, 268
scope, DHCP, 465, 467
SCSI (Small Computer System Interface)
    buses, 337
    cabling, 337
    compare technologies, 339–340
    defined, 336, 675
    drives adding, 338
    Fast SCSI, 340
    IDs, 338
    iSCSI, 341

Index ✦ S   695

standards, 339–340
terminators, 337
transfer rates, 338–339
Ultra SCSI, 340
SDH (synchronous digital hierarchy) standard, 213
SDSL (Symmetric DSL), 511–513
secret-key cryptography, Kerberos, 241–242
Secure IMAP4 protocol, 128
Secure POP3 protocol, 128
Secure SHell. *See* SSH, SOHO connections
Secure Sockets Layer. *See* SSL protocol
secure-key cryptography, 231
security. *See also* privacy
    application-based firewalls, 191–192
    cable access systems, 517
    cable modem issues, 209
    ciphers versus codes, 230–231
    client connectivity, 618
    community strings, 176
    encryption/decryption, 230–235
    firewalls, 153–154, 189–192, 421–430
    Internet mail systems, 128–129
    key cryptography, 231–234
    key escrows, 234
    NAT performance overhead, 435
    packet-filtering firewalls, 190–191
    performance issues, 435–437
    PKI, 235–239
    policy guidelines, 421
    port methods, 152–154
    proxy servers, 430–434
    Proxy/Application Gateway servers, 435–436
    public networks, 187–188
    RAS, 384, 386–387
    routers, 48
    service/application updates, 154
    shutting down unused ports, 152–153
    signed data, 234
    TCP/IP, 461–462
    UNIX/Linux permissions, 282–283
    VPNs, 194
    Windows NT/2000, 292–293
    WINS port issues, 127
Security Accounts Manager. *See* SAM, Windows NT/2000
security hosts, RAS, 387
security policy, guidelines, 421
security protocols
    AH, 240
    ESP, 240
    IKE, 240–241
    IPSec, 239–241
    ISAKMP/Oakley protocol, 240
    Kerberos, 241–244
    L2TP, 244–245
    LAC, 244
    LNS, 244
    SSL, 245–247

    TSL Handshake, 247
    TSL Record, 247
segment length, 10Base identifier, 30
segment type, 10Base identifier, 30
segmenting, 132
Sequenced Packet Exchange. *See* SPX protocol
sequencing, OSI model Transport layer, 108
Serial Line Internet Protocol. *See* SLIP
serial ports, modem connections, 55–56
Server Manager, Windows NT/2000, 294
Server Message Block. *See* SMB protocol, Samba configuration
server ports, TCP/UDP, 142
server-attached storage, bottlenecks, 342
Service Advertising Protocol. *See* SAP
service indicators, NetBIOS, 462
Services for Macintosh, 288, 558
Session Layer
    circuit-level firewalls, 428–429
    defined, 675
    NetBIOS protocol, 452
    OSI model, 105
shareware programs, 637
shell interface, UNIX/Linux, 279
shielded twisted pair cable. *See* STP cables
Shiva Password Authentication Protocol. *See* SPAP
Silicon Graphics, Inc., IRIX, 280
Simple Mail Transport Protocol. *See* SMTP
Simple Network Management Protocol. *See* SNMP
single cable (coax)
    bus topology, 5–6
    star topology, 6–7
single seat administration, NDS, 268
16-bit SCSI bus size, 337
Slackware, Linux version, 281
SLIP (Serial Line Internet Protocol), 218
    RAS connection method, 385
    SOHO, 504
Small Computer System Interface. *See* SCSI
Small Office/Home Office. *See* SOHO
SMB (Server Message Block) protocol, Samba configuration, 563–567
SMP (symmetric multiprocessing), 265
SMTP (Simple Mail Transport Protocol)
    Application-Layer, 128–129
    Port 25, 152
SNA (Systems Network Architecture) protocol, nonroutable, 49
SNMP (Simple Network Management Protocol)
    Application-Layer, 130–131
    commands, 175–176
    components, 174–175
    defined, 675
    MIB, 175
    thresholds, 176
SNMP Agent, 130
SNMP Management Console, 130
SNMP Server, 130

sockets, 235
software
    client connectivity, 617–618
    fault tolerance, 364
    firewalls, 424
    manual, troubleshooting, 621
    RAID, 370
    UNIX/Linux support issues, 278
SOHO (Small Office/Home Office)
    cable access systems, 515–522
    development history, 501–502
    DSL troubleshooting, 514–515
    Internet connection methods, 501
    POTS, 504–511
    PPP, 503–504
    remote access protocols, 503–504
    remote connectivity methods, 502
    remote controls, 502
    remote nodes, 502
    satellite Internet systems, 522–533
    SLIP protocol, 504
    SSH, 502
    terminal services, 502
    VPNs, 503
    wireless technologies, 523–525
Solaris, UNIX version, 280
solutions, troubleshooting, 612–613
Son, 675
SONET standard, 213
Sonic Systems, 423
SonicWall SOHO, firewall appliance, 423
source route bridging, 47
SPAP (Shiva Password Authentication Protocol), 387
speed negotiations, modem communications, 506–507
speed settings, client connectivity, 618
spoofed mail, public network concerns, 187
SPX (Sequence Packet Exchange) protocol
    described, 133
    NetWare protocol, 272–273
SPXII protocol, 133
Squid project, Linux proxy server, 431
SSH (Secure SHell), SOHO connections, 502
SSL (Secure Sockets Layer) protocol, 245–247
SSP (storage service provider), backups, 362
standard notation, subnet masks, 86
star topology
    advantages/disadvantages, 6–7
    EIA/TIA wiring systems, 580
    hub requirements, 42–43
    IEEE 802.3 standard, 29
    troubleshooting, 614
start-of-frame header, Token Ring networks, 15
stateful inspection, firewalls, 429
static routing, 48
static window, flow control, 107
Storage Area Network. *See* SAN

storage controller interfaces
    Fiber Channel, 340–341
    IDE, 334–336
    SCSI, 336–340
storage. *See* data storage
storage service provider. *See* SSP, backups
store-and-forward data transport, 45
STP (shielded twisted pair) cables, 32, 580
strings, community, 176
striping, RAID method, 368–369
subchannels, FDM, 205
subnet masks
    host identification, 87–90
    IP addressing, 84–86
    Windows NT/2000 configuration, 554
superuser (root) account, UNIX/Linux, 282
SUPERVISOR account, NetWare 3.x, 263, 273
surge protector, 675
surge suppressors, fault tolerance, 366
SuSE, Linux version, 281
SWAT (Samba Web Administration Tool), 566
switches, 44–46
    Collision Domain, 13
    OSI model Data Link layer, 114
    OSI model Physical layer, 114
    SAN, 348
    troubleshooting, 620
switching hub, 44–46
Symantec Desktop Firewall, 424
Symmetric DSL. *See* SDSL
symmetric multiprocessing. *See* SMP
synchronization, OSI model Transport layer, 109
synchronous digital hierarchy. *See* SDH standard
synchronous transmission, OSI model Data Link layer, 109
Synchronous Transport Modules, SDH, 213–214
SYS volume, NetWare, 270–271
system audits, ports, 153
system margin, fiber optic system range of loss, 493
System Policy Editor, Windows NT/2000, 294
system requirements, CD, 635–638
system-area network. *See* SAN
system-area network cards. *See* SAN NICs
Systems Network Architecture protocol. *See* SNA protocol, nonroutable

T

T1 line, 50–51
tape drives, 675
tape media, network storage media, 332–334
TB (terabytes), 345
T-carrier levels, digital carrier services, 202–204
TCP (Transmission Control Protocol)
    described, 131
    DNS communications, 126
TCP/IP (Transmission Control Protocol/Internet Protocol)
    Arp utility, 481–482
    default gateway, 554

Index ✦ T

defined, 675
DNS, 463–464
DNS configuration, 460
Ifconfig utility, 485–486
installation/configuration, 459–462
IP address, 554
Ipconfig utility, 485–486, 555–556
layers, 125
Nbstat utility, 484–485
NetBIOS Name Server (WINS) client configuration, 460
Netstat utility, 483–484
NOS, 264
Nslookup utility, 487–488
Ping utility, 477–479, 556
routable protocol, 451
security considerations, 461–462
subnet masks, 554
Tracert utility, 479–481
UNIX/Linux support, 279
Windows NT/2000, 288, 554–556
Winipcfg utility, 486–487
WINS, 463
TCP/UDP (Transmission Control Protocol/User Datagram Protocol) ports
clients, 142
described, 141
server, 142
TCP/IP applications, 142
well-known, 142–151
TDM (Time Division Multiplexing), 205
Teflon Belden 89880, plenum-rated cable, 31
telephone lines
client to RAS server connection method, 383, 385
ISDN service, 51–52
RJ-11 connector, 34
RJ-45 connector, 34
telephone technical support, troubleshooting resource, 622
Telnet application, versus TELNET protocol, 129
TELNET (terminal emulation) protocol
described, 129
Port 23, 151
10Base identifiers, 30
10Base2 standard, 31, 667
10Base5 standard, 31
10BaseF standard 32
10BaseT standard
described, 31–32, 667
shielded twisted-pair cable, 32
unshielded twisted-pair cable, 32
terabytes. See TB
terminal services, SOHO connections, 502
terminating, twisted-pair cables, 584–586
terminator
defined, 676
SCSI, 337
twisted pair cables, 580
TFTP (Trivial File Transfer Protocol), 126–127

Thicknet (thick coaxial cable)
10Base5 standard, 31
BNC, 35
Ethernet media, 29
Thickwire, 10Base5 standard, 31
thin clients, ICA, 214–215
Thinnet (thin coaxial cable)
10Base2 standard, 31
BNC, 31, 35
Ethernet media, 29
three-way handshake, TCP, 131
thresholds, SNMP, 176
tickets, Kerberos, 243
Time Division Multiplexing. See TDM
timers, token-holding, 15
Time-To-Live. See TTL, packets
Token Ring networks
advantages/disadvantages, 9–10
versus Ethernet, 15
IEEE 802.5 protocol, 14–15
MAU, 14–15
Primary ring, 211
Secondary ring, 211
source route bridging, 47
start-of-frame header, 15
token-holding timers, 15
tokens, 14–15
troubleshooting, 613–614
token-holding timers, Token Ring networks, 15
tokens
defined, 14–15
FDDI, 17–18
TokenTalk, 297
tone generator tool, 591–592
tools
cable tester, 588–589
inductive probe, 591–592
media tester/certifier, 587–589
optical testers, 593–595
punch down, 590–591
tone generator, 591–592
visual fault locator, 593
Visual tracer, 594
wire crimper, 583–587
wiring task selection, 596
topology
defined, 676
troubleshooting, 613–615
Tracert utility, TCP/IP troubleshooting, 479–481
tracking, remote connectivity diagnostics, 543
transfer impedance, wiring term, 598
transfer rates, SCSI, 338–339
translations, CSU/DSU, 50–51
Transmission Control Protocol. See TCP
Transmission Control Protocol/Internet Protocol. See TCP/IP
Transmission Control Protocol/User Datagram Protocol. See TCP/UDP ports

transmit On/transmit Off. *See* XON/XOFF, OSI model Transport layer
transparent bridging, 47
Transport Layer
    circuit-level firewalls, 428–429
    defined, 676
    OSI model, 105–109
    TCP/IP model, 125
transport mode, IPSec, 240
transport protocols, OSI model, 114–115
Transport-Layer protocols
    TCP, 131
    UDP, 131
transports, Session Layer, 452
Trap community string, SNMP, 176
trap operation, SNMP, 175–176
Travan tape drives, 333
traversal operations, NMS, 175–176
tree model, NDS, 269–270
trial versions, 637
Trivial File Transfer Protocol. *See* TFTP
troubleshooting
    bus topology, 614
    cable access connections, 519–522
    cable connectors, 619
    cabling, 618–619
    CD, 637–638
    client connectivity, 615–618
    DSL connections, 514–515
    hubs, 620
    implementing solutions, 612
    infrastructure, 618–620
    Mesh topology, 614
    network topologies, 613–615
    NWLINK installation, 459
    POTS, 508–511
    procedures for networks, 611–613
    RAS callback doesn't work, 540
    RAS connection cannot be established, 538–539
    resources, 620–524
    resources beyond RAS server cannot be accessed, 539–540
    ring topology, 613–614
    routers, 620
    satellite Internet systems, 523
    star topology, 614
    switches, 620
    TCP/IP utilities, 475–488
    Token Ring topology, 613–614
    VPN server connections, 541–543
    wireless access, 525
    wireless networks, 615
    wiring, 583–595, 618–620
trust relationships
    Windows 2000, 297
    Windows NT/2000, 292
TSL Handshake protocol, 247
TSL Record protocol, 247

TTL (Time-To-Live), packets, 132
tunneling mode, IPSec, 240
tunnels
    advantages, 408–409
    cannot establish connection with VPN server, 541–542
    defined, 194, 407
    hardware requirements, 409–410
    host/server connection troubleshooting, 542–543
    PPTP protocol, 217
    protocols, 407–408
    SOHO connections, 503
    troubleshooting, 540–543
    types, 408
    Windows 2000 server configuration, 409–411
TurboLinux, 281
twisted-pair cables
    10BaseT standard, 31–32
    EIA/TIA standards, 579–582
    Ethernet media, 29
    POTS, 202
    star topology, 6–7
    T-carrier systems, 202
    terminating, 584–586

U

UARTs (Universal Asynchronous Receivers/Transmitters), 507
UDP (User Datagram Protocol)
    DNS communications, 126
    Transport-Layer, 131
    UNIX/Linux, 284
Ultra SCSI, 340
unicast, 132
uninterruptible power supply. *See* UPS
United States Postal Service, certificate-based technology, 127–128
Universal Asynchronous Receivers/Transmitters. *See* UARTs
Universal Serial Bus. *See* USB, modem connection
UNIX/Linux
    administration, 282–283
    AIX version, 280
    Caldera OpenLinux, 280
    clients, 300
    commands, 285
    Corel Linux, 280–281
    customization, 278
    Debian GNU/Linux, 281
    development history, 277–278
    dumb terminals, 279
    file systems, 284
    GUI, 279
    HP-UX version, 280
    IRIX version, 280
    LinuxPPC, 281
    Mandrake Linux, 281
    modular architecture, 278
    multitasking, 278
    multiuser capability, 278

Index ✦ U–V

performance, 278
permissions, 282–283
POSIX compliance, 279
printing, 283
protocols, 284
Red Hat Linux, 281
root (superuser) account, 263, 282
shell interface, 279
Slackware, 281
software support, 278
Solaris version, 280
stability, 278
SuSE, 281
TCP/IP support, 279
TurboLinux, 281
users/groups accounts, 282
utilities, 285
Yellow Dog Linux, 281
unshielded twisted pair. *See* UTP cables
up-link port, hubs, 44
upper-layer protocols. *See* Application-Layer protocols
UPS (uninterruptible power supply)
    defined, 676
    fault tolerance, 366
USB (Universal Serial Bus), modem connection, 56
User Datagram Protocol. *See* UDP
user error, disaster type, 359
User Manager for Domains, Windows NT/2000, 294
user-request protocols
    DHCP, 126
    DNS, 126
    FTP, 126
    HTTP (Hypertext Transfer Protocol), 127
    HTTPS (Hypertext Transfer Protocol Secure), 127
    IMAP4, 128
    NNTP, 129–130
    POP3, 128
    Secure IMAP4, 128
    Secure POP3, 128
    SMTP, 128–129
    SNMP, 130
    TELNET, 129
    TFTP, 126–127
    WINS, 127
users
    network administrator duties, 263
    network sharing, 262–263
    UNIX/Linux accounts, 282
utilities
    AFP (Apple Share), 572
    Arp, 481–482
    Idem, 572
    Ifconfig, 485–486
    Ipconfig, 485–486, 555–556
    Nbstat, 484–485
    netconf, 566
    Netstat, 483–484

NetWare, 275–277
Nslookup, 487–488
PC MACLAN, 572
Ping, 477–479, 556
port scanner, 153
SWAT, 566
Tracert, 479–481
UNIX/Linux, 285
Windows 2000 remote connectivity, 543–544
Windows NT/2000, 293–294
Winipcfg, 486–487
UTP (unshielded twisted pair) cables
    10BaseT standard, 32
    described, 580
    crosstalk susceptibility, 32

V

v.42bis, compression protocol, 506
V.92 standards, modem communications, 508
VeriSign
    certificate-based technology, 127–128
    digital certificates, 236–238
versions, Windows 2000, 296
VFL (visual fault locator) tool, 593
virtual circuits, 205
Virtual Private Network. *See* VPN
virus, 676
Visual tracer tool, 594
VLANs (virtual local area networks)
    benefits, 312–313
    configuration examples, 316–319
    diagram, 313
    Implicit versus Explicit, 315
    Mac-address-based, 314
    multiple LANs problems, 311–312
    port-based, 314
    protocol-based, 315
    reasons to use, 311–313
    switches, 44–45
    workgroups, 313
volumes, NetWare file system, 270–272
VPN (Virtual Private Network)
    advantages, 408–409
    cannot establish connection with VPN server, 541–542
    defined, 194, 407
    hardware requirements, 409–410
    host/server connection troubleshooting, 542–543
    PPTP protocol, 217
    protocols, 407–408
    SOHO connections, 503
    troubleshooting, 540–543
    types, 408
    Windows 2000 server configuration, 409–411
VPN servers
    configuration settings, 410–411
    connection troubleshooting, 541–543

W

WAN connectivity, RAS methods, 384–385
WAN link, RAS connection method, 383, 385
WANs (wide area networks)
- AALs, 210
- ADSL, 210
- analog carrier services, 202
- ATM protocol, 208–209
- cable modems, 209
- circuit switching, 205–208
- data carrier services, 201–203
- defined, 311
- digital carrier services, 202–203
- DS levels, 202–203
- DSL, 210
- E-carrier levels, 203
- FDDI, 211
- FDDI-II, 211
- frame relay, 211–212
- ICA, 214–215
- Internet as example, 201
- internetwork, 109, 201
- ISDN, 212–213
- modulation, 203
- multiplexing, 204–205
- packet switching, 205–208
- PPP, 216–217
- PPTP protocol, 217
- RAS, 217
- remote access protocols, 214–218
- routers, 48
- SDH standard, 213
- SLIP, 218
- SONET standard, 213
- Synchronous Transport Modules, 213–214
- T-carrier levels, 202–204

WAP (Wireless Access Point), 53–55
warranty support, troubleshooting resource, 623–624
Web sites
- 3Com, 431
- Adobe Acrobat Reader, 637
- BlackICE firewall, 424
- CompTIA, 168
- IANA, 142
- IETF
- Nokia, 431
- Sonic Systems, 423
- Squid project, 431
- Symantec Desktop Firewall, 424
- Wingate, 431
- ZoneAlarm, 424

Webcams, QoS issues, 207
well-known ports, IANA, 142–151
wide area networks. *See* WANs
Wi-Fi standard, 523
window flow control, OSI model Transport layer, 107
window size, TCP, 131

Windows 9.x, RAS support, 383
Windows 95, client operating system, 298–299
Windows 98
- client operating system, 299
- DHCP client command, 467
- ICS, 172–174
- IPX/SPX configuration, 458
- MAC address display, 79–80
- NetBEUI installation/configuration, 454–456
- NWLINK configuration, 458
- TCP/IP configuration, 460

Windows 2000
- Active Directory, 295–297
- ATM, 295
- DDNS, 295
- development history, 295
- DHCP, 295
- domain controllers, 297
- Event Logging, 543
- ICS, 172–174
- IPSec configurations, 461–462
- IPX/SPX configuration, 459
- Kerberos, 243–244, 295
- LDAP, 295
- MAC address display, 79–80
- NetBEUI configuration, 457
- Network Monitor, 544
- NTFS, 295
- NWLINK configuration, 459
- Plug-and-Play, 295
- remote connectivity utilities, 543–544
- RRAS, 389–390
- TCP/IP configuration, 461
- tracing, 543
- trust relationships, 297
- versions, 296

Windows 2000 Advanced Server, 296
Windows 2000 Datacenter Server, 296
Windows 2000 Professional, 296
Windows 2000 Server, 296
- dial-up networking configuration, 401–407
- enabling RRAS, 391–400
- RAS startup, 389–390
- RRAS configuration, 391–401
- VPN configuration, 409–411

Windows clients, 298–299
Windows Explorer, Windows NT/2000, 294
Windows Internet Naming Service. *See* WINS
Windows Me (Millennium Edition)
- client operating system, 299
- ICS, 172–174

Windows NT
- defined, 676
- POSIX compliant, 279

Windows NT/2000
- adapter configuration, 552–553
- Add Printer Wizard, 293

Add User Accounts Wizard, 293
Add/Remove Programs Wizard, 293
administration, 290–293
Administrative Wizard, 293
Administrator account, 263
BDC, 291–292
compatibility, 290
default gateway, 554
DHCP client command, 467–468
Disk Administrator, 294
domain controllers, 291–292
domain groups, 292–293
domains, 291–292
Event Viewer, 294
file/print services configuration, 551–558
Group Management Wizard, 293
GUI, 289–290
Install New Modem Wizard, 293
IP address settings, 554
Ipconfig utility, 555–556
IPX/SPX protocol configuration, 556–557
License Wizard, 293
local groups, 292–293
Managing File and Folder Access Wizard, 293
Microsoft technology integration, 290
multitasking, 289
multiuser, 289
NetBEUI protocol configuration, 557–558
Network Client Administrator Wizard, 293
Network Neighborhood, 294
NTFS file system, 287
NWLink protocol configuration, 556–557
PDC, 291
Performance Monitor, 294
Ping utility, 556
protocol configuration, 553–558
protocol support, 290
protocols, 287–289
RAS, 217, 294, 383
release hierarchy, 286
SAM, 291
security, 292–293
Server Manager, 294
Services for Macintosh, 558
subnet masks, 554
System Policy Editor, 294
system requirements, 635
TCP/IP protocol configuration, 554–556
trust relationships, 292
User Manager for Domains, 294
utilities, 293–294
Windows Explorer, 294
Windows NT 3.x, development history, 289
Windows NT 4.0
    development history, 289
    IPX/SPX configuration, 458
    NetBEUI configuration, 456–457
    NWLINK configuration, 458
    TCP/IP configuration, 461
    versions, 290
Windows NT Server, 290
Windows NT Workstation, 290
Windows operating systems, release hierarchy, 286
Windows XP
    described, 287
    system requirements, 635
Wingate, proxy server, 431
Winipcfg utility, TCP/IP troubleshooting, 486–487
WINS (Windows Internet Naming Service)
    Application-Layer protocol, 127
    described, 463, 676
    network service, 170–171
    Port 137, 152
    Windows NT/2000, 288
WINS server, 463
wire crimper, using, 583–587
wireless access point device, wireless LAN, 17
Wireless Access Point. *See* WAP
wireless connections
    Bluetooth standard, 525
    development history, 523–525
    HomeRF, 525
    troubleshooting, 525
wireless LAN
    802.11g standard, 17
    CSMA/CA, 16
    wireless access point device, 17
Wireless Local Area Networks. *See* WLANS, 802.11b standard
wireless networks
    Mesh topology, 7–9
    troubleshooting, 615
Wireless Personal Area Networks. *See* WPANs
Wireless (IEEE 802.11b) standard, 16–17
wiring
    category standards, 581
    coax, 582–583
    color coding, 584–586
    color coding crossover, 586
    cost considerations, 34
    crosstalk issues, 34
    definitions, 597–598
    distance issues, 34
    fiber-optic, 32
    inductive probe tool, 591–592
    installation logistics factor, 34
    network use, 581
    NIC (network adapter card) supported types, 41
    optical tester tool, 593–595
    patch length restrictions, 581
    plenum-rated, 31
    punch down tool, 590–591
    shielded twisted-pair, 32
    shielding considerations, 34
    testers, 587–589

tool selection, 596
tone generator tool, 591–592
transmission speed factors, 34
troubleshooting, 618–620
twisted pair, 579–582
unshielded twisted-pair, 32
visual fault locator tool, 593
wire crimper, 583–587
wiring closet, 590
wiring closet, 590
wizards
New Connection, 401–404
Routing and Remote Access Server Setup, 392–394
Windows NT/2000, 293
WLANS (Wireless Local Area Networks), 802.11b standard, 33
work area cabling, networks, 581
workgroups, VLANs, 313
workstation, 290
WPANs (Wireless Personal Area Networks), 33
write operation, NMS, 175–176

X

X.25 technology
    RAS, 383, 385
    frame relay development history, 211
X.500 Directory Service standard, 264
xDSL. *See* DSL
XNS (Xerox Networking System), routable protocol, 451
XON/XOFF (transmit On/transmit OFF), OSI model Transport layer, 107

Y

Yellow Dog Linux, 281

Z

Z.E.N.works (Zero Effort Networks), NetWare 5.x, 267
ZoneAlarm, personal firewall, 424
zones, AppleTalk protocol, 134

Hungry Minds, Inc.
End-User License Agreement

READ THIS. You should carefully read these terms and conditions before opening the software packet(s) included with this book ("Book"). This is a license agreement ("Agreement") between you and Hungry Minds, Inc. ("HMI"). By opening the accompanying software packet(s), you acknowledge that you have read and accept the following terms and conditions. If you do not agree and do not want to be bound by such terms and conditions, promptly return the Book and the unopened software packet(s) to the place you obtained them for a full refund.

1. **License Grant.** HMI grants to you (either an individual or entity) a nonexclusive license to use one copy of the enclosed software program(s) (collectively, the "Software") solely for your own personal or business purposes on a single computer (whether a standard computer or a workstation component of a multi-user network). The Software is in use on a computer when it is loaded into temporary memory (RAM) or installed into permanent memory (hard disk, CD-ROM, or other storage device). HMI reserves all rights not expressly granted herein.

2. **Ownership.** HMI is the owner of all right, title, and interest, including copyright, in and to the compilation of the Software recorded on the disk(s) or CD-ROM ("Software Media"). Copyright to the individual programs recorded on the Software Media is owned by the author or other authorized copyright owner of each program. Ownership of the Software and all proprietary rights relating thereto remain with HMI and its licensers.

3. **Restrictions On Use and Transfer.**

    (a) You may only (i) make one copy of the Software for backup or archival purposes, or (ii) transfer the Software to a single hard disk, provided that you keep the original for backup or archival purposes. You may not (i) rent or lease the Software, (ii) copy or reproduce the Software through a LAN or other network system or through any computer subscriber system or bulletin-board system, or (iii) modify, adapt, or create derivative works based on the Software.

    (b) You may not reverse engineer, decompile, or disassemble the Software. You may transfer the Software and user documentation on a permanent basis, provided that the transferee agrees to accept the terms and conditions of this Agreement and you retain no copies. If the Software is an update or has been updated, any transfer must include the most recent update and all prior versions.

4. **Restrictions on Use of Individual Programs.** You must follow the individual requirements and restrictions detailed for each individual program in Appendix A of this Book. These limitations are also contained in the individual license agreements recorded on the Software Media. These limitations may include a requirement that after using the program for a specified period of time, the user must pay a registration fee or discontinue use. By opening the Software packet(s), you will be agreeing to abide by the licenses and restrictions for these individual programs that are detailed in Appendix A and on the Software Media. None of the material on this Software Media or listed in this Book may ever be redistributed, in original or modified form, for commercial purposes.

5. Limited Warranty.

(a) HMI warrants that the Software and Software Media are free from defects in materials and workmanship under normal use for a period of sixty (60) days from the date of purchase of this Book. If HMI receives notification within the warranty period of defects in materials or workmanship, HMI will replace the defective Software Media.

(b) **HMI AND THE AUTHOR OF THE BOOK DISCLAIM ALL OTHER WARRANTIES, EXPRESS OR IMPLIED, INCLUDING WITHOUT LIMITATION IMPLIED WARRANTIES OF MERCHANTABILITY AND FITNESS FOR A PARTICULAR PURPOSE, WITH RESPECT TO THE SOFTWARE, THE PROGRAMS, THE SOURCE CODE CONTAINED THEREIN, AND/OR THE TECHNIQUES DESCRIBED IN THIS BOOK. HMI DOES NOT WARRANT THAT THE FUNCTIONS CONTAINED IN THE SOFTWARE WILL MEET YOUR REQUIREMENTS OR THAT THE OPERATION OF THE SOFTWARE WILL BE ERROR FREE.**

(c) This limited warranty gives you specific legal rights, and you may have other rights that vary from jurisdiction to jurisdiction.

6. Remedies.

(a) HMI's entire liability and your exclusive remedy for defects in materials and workmanship shall be limited to replacement of the Software Media, which may be returned to HMI with a copy of your receipt at the following address: Software Media Fulfillment Department, Attn.: *Network+ Certification Bible*, Hungry Minds, Inc., 10475 Crosspoint Blvd., Indianapolis, IN 46256, or call 1-800-762-2974. Please allow four to six weeks for delivery. This Limited Warranty is void if failure of the Software Media has resulted from accident, abuse, or misapplication. Any replacement Software Media will be warranted for the remainder of the original warranty period or thirty (30) days, whichever is longer.

(b) In no event shall HMI or the author be liable for any damages whatsoever (including without limitation damages for loss of business profits, business interruption, loss of business information, or any other pecuniary loss) arising from the use of or inability to use the Book or the Software, even if HMI has been advised of the possibility of such damages.

(c) Because some jurisdictions do not allow the exclusion or limitation of liability for consequential or incidental damages, the above limitation or exclusion may not apply to you.

7. U.S. Government Restricted Rights. Use, duplication, or disclosure of the Software for or on behalf of the United States of America, its agencies and/or instrumentalities (the "U.S. Government") is subject to restrictions as stated in paragraph (c)(1)(ii) of the Rights in Technical Data and Computer Software clause of DFARS 252.227-7013, or subparagraphs (c) (1) and (2) of the Commercial Computer Software - Restricted Rights clause at FAR 52.227-19, and in similar clauses in the NASA FAR supplement, as applicable.

8. General. This Agreement constitutes the entire understanding of the parties and revokes and supersedes all prior agreements, oral or written, between them and may not be modified or amended except in a writing signed by both parties hereto that specifically refers to this Agreement. This Agreement shall take precedence over any other documents that may be in conflict herewith. If any one or more provisions contained in this Agreement are held by any court or tribunal to be invalid, illegal, or otherwise unenforceable, each and every other provision shall remain in full force and effect.